Diversity and Society

Sixth Edition

This book is dedicated to my mother, Alice T. Healey. May she rest in peace.

—Joe

To Shari, Catherine, Jennifer, and JT with deep gratitude for your unwavering love and companionship. To the undergraduates reading this book: Be open and curious, be critically skeptical, work hard, and have faith. You are our hope for the future.

—Andi

Diversity and Society

Race, Ethnicity, and Gender

Sixth Edition

Joseph F. Healey

Christopher Newport University

Andi Stepnick

Belmont University

Los Angeles | London | New Delhi
Singapore | Washington DC | Melbourne

FOR INFORMATION:

SAGE Publications, Inc.
2455 Teller Road
Thousand Oaks, California 91320
E-mail: order@sagepub.com

SAGE Publications Ltd.
1 Oliver's Yard
55 City Road
London EC1Y 1SP
United Kingdom

SAGE Publications India Pvt. Ltd.
B 1/I 1 Mohan Cooperative Industrial Area
Mathura Road, New Delhi 110 044
India

SAGE Publications Asia-Pacific Pte. Ltd.
18 Cross Street #10-10/11/12
China Square Central
Singapore 048423

Acquisitions Editor: Jeff Lasser
Editorial Assistant: Tiara Beatty
Production Editor: Andrew Olson
Copy Editor: Erin Livingston
Typesetter: C&M Digitals (P) Ltd.
Proofreader: Laura Webb
Indexer: Maria Sosnowski
Cover Designer: Candice Harman
Marketing Manager: Will Walter

Printed in the United States of America

ISBN: 978-1-5063-8905-9

This book is printed on acid-free paper.

Certified Chain of Custody
Promoting Sustainable Forestry
www.sfiprogram.org
SFI-01268

SUSTAINABLE FORESTRY INITIATIVE

SFI label applies to text stock

19 20 21 22 23 10 9 8 7 6 5 4 3 2 1

CONTENTS

Preface   **xvii**

Acknowledgments   **xxiv**

PART 1 • AN INTRODUCTION TO THE STUDY OF MINORITY GROUPS IN THE UNITED STATES   **1**

Chapter 1 • Diversity in the United States: Questions and Concepts   3

Chapter 2 • Assimilation and Pluralism: From Immigrants to White Ethnics   49

PART 2 • THE EVOLUTION OF DOMINANT–MINORITY RELATIONS IN THE UNITED STATES   **101**

Chapter 3 • The Development of Dominant–Minority Group Relations in Preindustrial America: The Origins of Slavery   103

Chapter 4 • Industrialization and Dominant–Minority Relations: From Slavery to Segregation and the Coming of Postindustrial Society   139

PART 3 • UNDERSTANDING DOMINANT–MINORITY RELATIONS IN THE UNITED STATES TODAY   **183**

Chapter 5 • African Americans: From Segregation to Modern Institutional Discrimination and Modern Racism   185

Chapter 6 • Native Americans: From Conquest to Tribal Survival in a Postindustrial Society   249

Chapter 7 • Hispanic Americans: Colonization, Immigration, and Ethnic Enclaves   295

Chapter 8 • Asian Americans: Model Minorities?   347

PART 4 • CHALLENGES FOR THE PRESENT AND THE FUTURE   **397**

Chapter 9 • New Americans, Assimilation, and Old Challenges   399

Chapter 10 • Minority Groups and U.S. Society: Themes, Patterns, and the Future   451

References   **465**

Glossary   **515**

Index   **521**

About the Authors   **541**

DETAILED CONTENTS

Preface	xvii
Acknowledgments	xxiv

PART 1 • AN INTRODUCTION TO THE STUDY OF MINORITY GROUPS IN THE UNITED STATES — 1

Chapter 1 • Diversity in the United States: Questions and Concepts — 3

Minority Groups: Trends and Questions	6
Increasing Diversity	6
What's in a Name?	7
• Questions for Reflection	9
Questions About the Future, Sociology, and the Plan of This Book	10
What Is a Minority Group?	10
• Questions for Reflection	14
Patterns of Inequality	14
Theoretical Perspectives	14
Minority Group Status and Stratification	18
Visible Distinguishing Traits: Race and Gender	19
Race	19
Gender	25
• Questions for Reflection	29
Key Concepts in Dominant–Minority Relations	29
• Applying Concepts	30
Prejudice	31
• Questions for Reflection	34
• Applying Concepts	35
Discrimination	39
Ideological Racism	39
Institutional Discrimination	40
A Global Perspective	41
• Focus on Contemporary Issues: Immigration and Globalization	41
Conclusion	44
Main Points	44

Review Questions   45
Group Discussion   46
   • Answers to Applying Concepts   46
Internet Learning Resources   46
Notes   47

Chapter 2 • Assimilation and Pluralism: From Immigrants to White Ethnics   **49**

Assimilation   51
   Types of Assimilation   51
   The Traditional Perspective on Assimilation: Theories and Concepts   52
   • Questions for Reflection   57
Pluralism   57
   Types of Pluralism   58
   • Questions for Reflection   59
   • Focus on Contemporary Issues: Language and Assimilation   59
Other Group Relationships   61
From Immigrants to White Ethnics   62
   Industrialization and Immigration   64
   European Origins and Conditions of Entry   65
   Chains of Immigration   71
   The Campaign against Immigration: Prejudice, Racism, and Discrimination   72
   • Questions for Reflection   76
Patterns of Assimilation   76
   The Importance of Generations   76
   Ethnic Succession   79
   Continuing Industrialization and Structural Mobility   83
   • Questions for Reflection   83
Variations in Assimilation   84
   Degree of Similarity   84
   Religion   84
   Social Class   85
   Gender   86
   Sojourners   88
   • Questions for Reflection   88
The Descendants of the Immigrants Today   88
   Geographical Distribution   88
   Integration and Equality   90
   The Evolution of White Ethnicity   91
   The Twilight of White Ethnicity?   92
   • Questions for Reflection   94
Contemporary Immigrants: Does the Traditional Perspective Apply?   94
   • Questions for Reflection   95

Implications for Examining Dominant–Minority Relations | 95
   • Comparative Focus: Immigration and Ireland | 96
   • Questions for Reflection | 97
Main Points | 98
   • Applying Concepts | 98
Review Questions | 99
   • Answers to Applying Concepts | 100
Group Discussion | 100
Internet Learning Resources | 100
Note | 100

PART 2 • EVOLUTION OF DOMINANT–MINORITY RELATIONS IN THE UNITED STATES | **101**

Chapter 3 • The Development of Dominant–Minority Group Relations in Preindustrial America: The Origins of Slavery | **103**

The Origins of Slavery in America | 104
   The Labor Supply Problem | 107
   The Contact Situation | 107
   The Creation of Slavery in the United States | 111
   • Questions for Reflection | 112
Paternalistic Relations | 112
   Chattel Slavery | 112
   • Questions for Reflection | 115
The Dimensions of Minority Group Status | 115
   Power, Inequality, and Institutional Discrimination | 115
   • Questions for Reflection | 122
   • Focus on Contemporary Issues: Slavery and Indentured Servitude Today | 122
The Creation of Minority Status for Native Americans and Mexican Americans | 123
   Native Americans | 123
   • Applying Concepts | 124
   • Answers to Applying Concepts | 125
   • Questions for Reflection | 127
   • Comparative Focus: Hawaii | 128
   Mexican Americans | 129
   • Questions for Reflection | 132
Comparing Minority Groups | 132
   • Comparative Focus: Mexico, Canada, and the United States | 133
   • Questions for Reflection | 135
Main Points | 135
Review Questions | 136

Group Discussion   136

Internet Learning Resources   136

Notes   137

Chapter 4 • Industrialization and Dominant–Minority Relations: From Slavery to Segregation and the Coming of Postindustrial Society   139

Industrialization and the Shift from Paternalistic to Rigid Competitive Group Relations   142

The Impact of Industrialization on the Racial Stratification of African Americans: From Slavery to Segregation   143

Reconstruction (1865 to the 1880s)   143

De Jure Segregation   144

• Comparative Focus: Jim Crow Segregation and South African Apartheid   147

• Questions for Reflection   148

• Questions for Reflection   149

The Great Migration (Early 1900s to 1970s)   150

Life in the North   150

Competition with White Ethnic Groups   150

The Origins of Black Protest   152

The Dimensions of Minority Group Status   153

Acculturation and Integration   153

Gender and Race   153

• Questions for Reflection   154

Industrialization, the Shift to Postindustrial Society, and Dominant–Minority Relations: General Trends   155

Urbanization   155

Occupational Specialization   155

Bureaucracy and Rationality   156

Growth of White-Collar Jobs and the Service Sector   156

The Growing Importance of Education   158

A Dual Labor Market   159

Globalization   159

Postindustrial Society and the Shift from Rigid to Fluid Competitive Relationships   160

• Questions for Reflection   161

Gender Inequality in a Globalizing, Postindustrial World   162

• Questions for Reflection   162

Jobs and Income   163

• Comparative Focus: Women's Status in Global Perspective   165

• Questions for Reflection   167

Modern Institutional Discrimination   167

The Continuing Power of the Past   167

Affirmative Action   170

- Questions for Reflection   173
- Focus on Contemporary Issues: Hate Crimes   173
- Questions for Reflection   178

Social Change and Minority Group Activism   178

Main Points   178

Review Questions   179

Group Discussion   180
- Applying Concepts   180
- Answers to Applying Concepts   182

Internet Learning Resources   182

Note   182

PART 3 • UNDERSTANDING DOMINANT–MINORITY RELATIONS IN THE UNITED STATES TODAY $\quad$ **183**

Chapter 5 • African Americans: From Segregation to Modern Institutional Discrimination and Modern Racism $\quad$ **185**

The End of De Jure Segregation   188
Wartime Developments   189
The Civil Rights Movement   189
- Questions for Reflection   194

Developments outside the South   194
De Facto Segregation   194
Urban Unrest   195
The Black Power Movement   196

Protest, Power, and Pluralism   198
The Black Power Movement in Perspective   198
Gender and Black Protest   199
- Questions for Reflection   200

Black–White Relations Since the 1960s: Issues and Trends   201
- Comparative Focus: Race in Another America   201
- Questions for Reflection   202
Continuing Separation   203
The Criminal Justice System and African Americans   208
Increasing Class Inequality   212
Modern Institutional Discrimination   215
The Family Institution and the Culture of Poverty   218
Mixed Race and New Racial Identities   221
- Questions for Reflection   223

Prejudice and Modern Racism   223

Assimilation and Pluralism   227
Acculturation   227

Secondary Structural Assimilation 228

Primary Structural Assimilation 238

• Questions for Reflection 240

• Focus on Contemporary Issues: Does the Election of
President Obama Mean That America Is Post-Racial? 240

Is the Glass Half-Empty or Half-Full? 242

Main Points 244

• Applying Concepts 245

Review Questions 245

• Answers to Applying Concepts 246

Internet Learning Resources 247

Note 247

Chapter 6 • Native Americans: From Conquest to Tribal Survival in a Postindustrial Society

249

Size of the Group 251

Native American Cultures 253

Agriculture, Views on Nature, and Land Ownership 254

Gender and Social Structure 255

• Questions for Reflection 256

Relations with the Federal Government after the 1890s 256

Reservation Life 257

The Indian Reorganization Act (IRA) 259

The Termination Policy 260

Relocation and Urbanization 261

Self-Determination 262

Protest and Resistance 263

Early Efforts 263

Red Power 264

• Focus on Contemporary Issues: Were Native Americans the Victims
of Genocide? 265

Protest and Preservation of Native American Cultures 268

• Questions for Reflection 269

Contemporary Native American–White Relations 270

Natural Resources 270

Attracting Industry to the Reservation 270

• Comparative Focus: Australian Aborigines and
Native Americans 271

• Questions for Reflection 273

Broken Treaties 275

Gaming and Other Development Possibilities 275

Prejudice and Discrimination 277

• Questions for Reflection 279

Assimilation and Pluralism 279

Acculturation 279

Secondary Structural Assimilation 281

Primary Structural Assimilation 286

• Questions for Reflection 287

Comparing Minority Groups 287

Progress and Challenges 288

Main Points 290

• Applying Concepts 291

Review Questions 291

• Answers to Applying Concepts 292

Internet Learning Resources 293

Notes 294

Chapter 7 • Hispanic Americans: Colonization, Immigration, and Ethnic Enclaves **295**

Mexican Americans 300

Cultural Patterns 300

Immigration 301

• Questions for Reflection 310

Developments in the United States 310

Mexican Americans and Other Minority Groups 315

• Questions for Reflection 316

Puerto Ricans 316

Migration (Push and Pull) and Employment 316

Transitions 318

Puerto Ricans and Other Minority Groups 319

• Questions for Reflection 320

Cuban Americans 320

Immigration (Push and Pull) 320

Regional Concentrations 321

Socioeconomic Characteristics 322

Cuban Americans and Other Minority Groups 325

• Questions for Reflection 325

Prejudice and Discrimination 325

Assimilation and Pluralism 326

Acculturation 327

Secondary Structural Assimilation 328

• Comparative Focus: Immigration around the World
versus the United States 332

• Questions for Reflection 333

Primary Structural Assimilation 339

- Questions for Reflection — 340

Assimilation and Hispanic Americans — 341
- Focus on Contemporary Issues: Hispanic Americans and the Evolution of the American Racial Order — 341

Main Points — 344
- Applying Concepts — 344

Review Questions — 345
- Answers to Applying Concepts — 346

Internet Learning Resources — 346

Chapter 8 • Asian Americans: Model Minorities? — 347

Origins and Cultures — 351
- Questions for Reflection — 353

Contact Situations and the Development of the Chinese American and Japanese American Communities — 353
Chinese Americans — 353
Japanese Americans — 358
- Questions for Reflection — 363
- Comparative Focus: Japan's "Invisible" Minority — 364
- Questions for Reflection — 366

Comparing Minority Groups — 366
- Questions for Reflection — 366

Contemporary Immigration from Asia — 367
- Questions for Reflection — 369

Prejudice and Discrimination — 370

Assimilation and Pluralism — 373
Acculturation — 373
Secondary Structural Assimilation — 375
Primary Structural Assimilation — 386
- Focus on Contemporary Issues: How Successful Are Asian Americans? At What Price? — 387

Comparing Minority Groups: Explaining Asian American Success — 389
Asian Americans and White Ethnics — 389
Asian Americans and Colonized Racial Minority Groups — 390

Main Points — 392
- Applying Concepts — 393

Review Questions — 394
- Answers to Applying Concepts — 395

Points to Consider — 395

Internet Learning Resources — 396

Note — 396

PART 4 • CHALLENGES FOR THE PRESENT AND THE FUTURE

PART 4 • CHALLENGES FOR THE PRESENT AND THE FUTURE   **397**

Chapter 9 • New Americans, Assimilation, and Old Challenges   **399**

Current Immigration	401
• Questions for Reflection	403
New Hispanic Groups: Immigrants from the Dominican Republic, El Salvador, and Colombia	403
Three Case Studies	405
Non-Hispanic Immigrants from the Caribbean	407
Two Case Studies	408
Contemporary Immigration from Asia	409
Four Case Studies	410
Middle Eastern and Arab Americans	413
• Focus on Contemporary Issues: Detroit's Arab American Community	416
9/11 and Arab Americans	418
Immigrants from Africa	420
Modes of Incorporation	421
Immigrants and the Primary Labor Market	421
Immigrants and the Secondary Labor Market	421
Immigrants and Ethnic Enclaves	422
Summary	422
• Questions for Reflection	422
• Comparative Focus: The Roma: Europe's "True Minority"	423
• Questions for Reflection	424
Immigration: Issues and Controversies	424
The Attitudes of Americans	424
The Immigrants	427
• Questions for Reflection	428
Costs and Benefits	428
DREAMers	433
• Questions for Reflection	434
• Focus on Contemporary Issues: Birthright Citizenship	435
Is Contemporary Assimilation Segmented?	436
The Case for Segmented Assimilation	437
The Case for Traditional Assimilation Theory	441
Summary	443
• Questions for Reflection	444
Recent Immigration in Historical and Global Context	444
New Immigrants and Old Issues	445
Main Points	446
• Applying Concepts	447

Review Questions   448

    • Answers to Applying Concepts   448

Internet Learning Resources   449

Chapter 10 • Minority Groups and U.S. Society: Themes, Patterns, and the Future   **451**

The Importance of Subsistence Technology   451

The Importance of the Contact Situation, Group Competition, and Power   453

The Importance of Intersectionality   456

Assimilation and Pluralism   457

Minority Group Progress and the Ideology of American Individualism   461

A Final Word   462

Summary   463

Note   464

References   **465**

Glossary   **515**

Index   **521**

About the Authors   **541**

PREFACE

Of the challenges confronting the United States today, those relating to diversity continue to be among the most urgent and the most daunting. Discrimination and the rejection of "others" are part of our national heritage. Along with equality, freedom, and justice, prejudice, racism, and sexism are some of our oldest values. Every part of our society, and virtually every item on the national agenda—welfare and health care reform, policing, crime and punishment, family, education, defense, foreign policy, and terrorism—have some connection with dominant–minority relations.

This textbook contributes to our ongoing national discussion by presenting information, raising questions, and deeply examining relevant issues. Our intent is to help you increase your knowledge, improve your understanding of the issues, and clarify your thinking about social inequalities related to race, ethnicity, gender, and class. We've written for undergraduate students—sociology majors and nonmajors alike. We make few assumptions about students' knowledge of history or sociological concepts, and we try to present the material in a way that you will find accessible and relevant.

For example, we use a unified set of themes and concepts throughout the text. Our analysis is consistent and continuous, even as we examine multiple sociological perspectives and different points of view. We introduce most of the conceptual framework in the first four chapters. Then, we apply these concepts and analytical themes to a series of case studies of racial and ethnic minority groups (e.g., African Americans, Native Americans). Finally, we review and summarize our main points and bring our analysis to a conclusion in the last chapter, where we also speculate about the future.

Our analysis is, generally, macro and comparative. That is, we focus on large groups and social structures—such as social institutions and stratification systems—and we systematically compare and contrast the experiences and situations of America's many minority groups over time. The book follows in the tradition of conflict theory, but it is not a comprehensive statement of that tradition. We introduce and apply other perspectives, but we don't attempt to give equal attention to all current sociological paradigms, explain everything, or include all possible analytical points of view. It couldn't be done! Rather, our goals are (a) to present the sociology of minority group relations in a way that you'll find understandable and intellectually challenging and (b) to address the issues (and tell the stories behind the issues) in a way that is highly readable and that demonstrates the power and importance of sociological thinking.

Although the text maintains a unified analytical perspective, we offer a wide variety of perspectives in our online resources. For example, we offer *Current Debates* for Chapters 1 through 9 (available at http://edge.sagepub.com/diversity6e). The debates focus on an issue taken from the chapter but present the views of scholars and analysts from a variety of disciplines and viewpoints. Without detracting from the continuity of the main analysis, these debates reinforce the idea that no one has all the answers (or, for that matter, all the questions), and they can be used to stimulate discussion, bring additional perspectives to the classroom, and suggest topics for further research.

Additionally, every chapter (except the last) presents personal experiences that compellingly and dramatically foreshadow the material that follows. These introductions include the experiences and thoughts of a wide variety of people: immigrants, writers, politicians, racists, slaves, and "regular" people, among others. Also, each chapter (except the last) includes a section called *Focus on Contemporary Issues* that addresses a specific issue in American society that readers will find current and relevant.

In addition to examining diversity across minority groups (e.g., Native Americans and Hispanic Americans), we stress the diversity of experiences within each minority group (e.g., Puerto Ricans and Cubans). We use an intersectional perspective that explores the ways race, ethnicity, social class, and gender influence one another, creating ever-shifting constellations of dominance and subordination. We focus on American minority groups. However, we've included a considerable amount of comparative, cross-national material. For example, the *Comparative Focus* features explore group relations in other societies.

Finally, we stress the ways American minority groups are inseparable from the American experience—from the early days of colonial settlements to tomorrow's headlines. The relative success of our society is due to the contributions of minority groups as well as those of the dominant group. The nature of the minority group experience has changed as society has changed. To understand America's minority groups is to understand some elemental truths about America. To raise the issues of difference and diversity is to ask what it means, and what it has meant, to be an American.

People's feelings about these issues can be intense, and controversy, indifference, and bitterness can overshadow objective analysis and calm reason. We have little hope of resolving our nation's dilemmas until we address them openly and honestly. This book explores topics that involve conflict between groups. That history is tinged with pain. We discuss topics that can be challenging to learn. And, at times, we quote directly from sources that use language that may be offensive or painful to hear. We have included these elements because we cannot understand (or change) the things we do not face.

FEATURES

- Chapters 1–4 provide a broad conceptual and historical overview of minority groups, dominant–minority group relations, and immigration to the United States.

- Chapters 5–8 focus on major U.S. racial and ethnic groups: African Americans, Native Americans, Hispanic Americans, and Asian Americans.

- Chapter 9 focuses on issues of diversity and inequality for "new Americans" from Africa, the Middle East, Latin America, and the Caribbean.

- **Opening Vignettes** foreshadow the chapter content in a personal way to generate student interest.

- **Questions for Reflection** help students analyze the material, identify key points, and recognize areas needing additional study.

- **Applying Concepts** activities provide students opportunities to use key chapter ideas.

- **Comparative Focus** boxes look at group relations outside the United States.

- **Focus on Contemporary Issues** boxes address current and relevant issues (e.g., modern slavery, hate crimes).

- This book uses an **intersectional approach** that offers a more complex view of diversity within the U. S. and within each minority group. In particular, we focus on how race, ethnicity, social class, and gender statuses combine with each other to produce unique experiences and oppressions.

- **Main Points** summarize key ideas from each chapter and **Review Questions** give students a chance to assess their understanding.

- **Group Discussion** questions provide teachers and students with a way to collectively explore ideas and questions.

CHANGES IN THIS EDITION

- Chapter content has been thoroughly updated from more than 500 new sources, allowing students to learn about the latest research. Expanded content emphasizes current events and applicability of concepts and theories to contemporary social problems (e.g., racial bias in the criminal justice system, immigration issues), including international ones. New examples emphasize an intersectional approach and highlight dominance, oppression, and the distribution of power. Additionally, we emphasize historical trajectory and past-in-present discrimination as much as possible. For example, students can't understand what happened in Ferguson, Missouri without understanding the historical context (1992 Los Angeles riots, 1965 Watts Rebellion).

- More than 80 new and updated tables, maps, and figures

- Updates or additions to the *Comparative Focus* features in Chapters 2, 4, 5, 6, 7, and 8

- Updates or additions to the *Focus on Contemporary Issues* features in Chapters 1, 2, 3, 4, 6, 8, and 9

- New or revised *Opening Vignettes* in Chapters 3 and 5

- Revised or expanded *Questions for Reflection, Review Questions,* or *Group Discussion* questions in each chapter

- We've thoroughly revised the text to make it fresher, more relevant, more approachable, and even easier to understand. For example, we've simplified the writing and sentence structure. Additionally, we've taken steps to highlight social actors and processes by using active voice and by making other changes in language. For example, when possible, we use "enslaved people" instead of "slaves" because the former emphasizes that individuals, through the system of slavery, put humans in bondage. The latter is a social status that hides this important reality.

Some of the new and expanded topics in this edition include the following:

Chapter 1

- The changing social construction of race in the U.S. census

Chapter 2

- Theories of Assimilation (e.g., critiques of unidirectional models, intersectional and bidimensional models)

- The Holocaust (e.g., recent research about Americans' decreasing awareness, the role "everyday people" played, and documentation of more than 40,000 sites such as work "camps")

- Anti-Semitism (the relationship between the Old and New Worlds; European pogroms; and recent increases in anti-Semitic groups, attitudes, and hate crimes)

Chapter 3

- The origins of slavery (e.g., indentured servitude, first laws, widespread acceptance, and ideology)

- Modern theories of acculturation (e.g., multi-directional models)

- Regional variations in the system of slavery (e.g., Deep South states and widespread ownership, use, or benefits for whites)

- The experiences of enslaved women (e.g., division of labor, ideologies of "true womanhood")

Chapter 4

- Hate crimes (expanded explanation and examples such as the Tree of Life synagogue shooting as well as data about LGBTQIA and Muslim Americans)

- Social control of African Americans (e.g., sharecropping and Black Codes during de jure segregation)

- Educational inequalities (e.g., racially segregated, underfunded K–12 public schools) and their influence on college preparedness and competitiveness in the workforce

Chapter 5

- The perception of African Americans as "other" (e.g., "Living While Black"—police being called about African Americans doing "everyday things" in "white spaces")

- Rosa Parks and other pioneers of the civil rights movement

- The War on Drugs and inequalities in the criminal justice system (e.g., disparate sentencing)

- Police-related shootings of African Americans

- Increasing white supremacy, including the "Unite the Right" rally in Charlottesville, VA

- Debates about Confederate monuments and confederate-era symbols (including the "battle flag" and its history)

Chapter 6

- Native Americans' views on nature and land ownership

- Native Americans' views on gender (including two-spirit people and gender fluidity) and how gender organized social life

- The 2016 Dakota Access Pipeline protest

- Similarities with Aboriginal people from Australia

Chapter 7

- Changes in immigration patterns (e.g., increases in unaccompanied minors and people from Central America)

- Changes to immigration policy (e.g., ICE, Homeland Security budgets, family separation)

- Hispanic American immigrant women workers

- DREAMers

- Historical information about Cuba and Puerto Rico

- Measuring the effects of Hurricane Maria in Puerto Rico

- Chicanas in El Movimento (Dolores Huerta, Lopez De La Cruz, Maria Luisa Rangel Juanita Valdez)

Chapter 8

- The role of labor unions in the 19th-century Anti-Chinese movement (e.g., Dennis Kearney of the Workingman's Party, Anti-Coolie Act)

- WWII detention centers for Japanese (and other) Americans as well as the demand for meaningful redress and National Day of Remembrance

- Japan's "invisible" minority: The Barakumin
- The model minority myth and its effects

ANCILLARIES

SAGE edge™ (http://edge.sagepub.com/diversity6e)

SAGE edge offers a robust online environment featuring an impressive array of tools and resources for review, study, and further exploration, keeping both students and instructors on the cutting edge of teaching and learning. SAGE edge content is open access and available on demand. Learning and teaching have never been easier!

SAGE edge for Students

SAGE edge for Students provides a personalized approach to help students accomplish their coursework goals in an easy-to-use learning environment.

- Mobile-friendly **eFlashcards** strengthen students' understanding of key terms and concepts.
- Mobile-friendly practice **quizzes** allow for independent assessment by students of their mastery of course material.
- An online **action plan** includes tips and feedback on progress through the course and materials, which allows students to individualize their learning experience.
- **Learning objectives** reinforce the most important material.
- **Internet Activities** encourage students to apply chapter concepts to the "real world" via oral history archives, online art exhibits, YouTube videos, TED Talks, and more.
- Carefully selected chapter-by-chapter **video links** and **multimedia content** enhance classroom-based explorations of key topics.
- The **Current Debates** resource presents two or more opposing statements from scholars and analysts on controversial questions raised in the chapters (Are Indian sports team mascots offensive?).
- **Public sociology assignments** encourage students to go beyond the classroom and engage with people, organizations, and resources in their local communities to learn more about minority groups and issues.
- **For further reading** lists useful books and articles for additional study on minority groups and intergroup relations.
- Exclusive access to full-text **SAGE journal articles** provides students with carefully selected articles designed to support and expand on the concepts presented in each chapter.

SAGE edge for Instructors

SAGE edge for Instructors supports teaching by making it easy to integrate quality content and create a rich learning environment for students.

- **Test banks** provide a diverse range of pre-written options as well as the opportunity to edit any question and/or insert your own personalized questions to effectively assess students' progress and understanding.

- **Sample course syllabi** for semester and quarter courses provide suggested models for structuring your courses.

- Editable, chapter-specific **PowerPoint®** slides offer complete flexibility for creating a multimedia presentation for your course.

- Carefully selected chapter-by-chapter **video links** and **multimedia content** enhance classroom-based explorations of key topics.

- **Chapter outlines** follow the structure of each chapter, providing an essential reference and teaching tool.

- **Tables & Figures from the printed book** are available in an easily downloadable format for use in papers, handouts, and presentations.

- **Photo essay** ideas and suggestions are provided, along with tips for instructors who assign photo essays in their classrooms.

- The **Current Debates** resource presents two or more opposing statements from scholars and analysts on controversial questions raised in the chapters (Are Indian sports team mascots offensive? Should children be raised genderless?).

- **Public sociology assignments** encourage students to go beyond the classroom and engage with people, organizations, and resources in their local communities to learn more about minority groups and issues.

- **Internet Research Projects** refer students to selected public websites or direct them on guided Internet research in order to gather data and apply concepts from the chapter.

- **For further reading** lists useful books and articles for additional study on minority groups and intergroup relations.

- A **common course cartridge** includes all of the instructor resources and assessment material from the student study site, making it easy for instructors to upload and use these materials in learning management systems such as Blackboard, ™Angel, ®Moodle™, Canvas, and Desire2Learn™.

Exclusive access to full-text SAGE journal articles provides instructors with carefully selected articles designed to support and expand on the concepts presented in each chapter.

ACKNOWLEDGMENTS

It has been a great privilege to work on this edition with Andi Stepnick. She has strengthened this text in countless ways and it has been an enormous pleasure to work with a coauthor who brings such unflagging professionalism, scholarship, and attention to detail. I also thank professors Edwin H. Rhyne and Charles S. Green, the teacher–scholars who inspired me as a student, and Eileen O'Brien, who has contributed enormously to the development of this project. Finally, I thank my colleagues, past and present, in the Department of Sociology and Anthropology at Christopher Newport University: Stephanie Byrd, Cheri Chambers, Robert Durel, Marcus Griffin, Mai Lan Gustafsson, Jamie Harris, Kai Heidemann, Michael Lewis, Marion Manton, Lea Pellett, Eduardo Perez, Iris Price, Virginia Purtle, Tracey Rausch, Andria Timmer, Linda Waldron, and Ellen Whiting. They have been unflagging in their support of this project, and I thank them for their academic, logistical, and intellectual assistance.

—Joseph F. Healey

I am grateful to Joe Healey for being such a thoughtful partner and for inspiring me with his passion for sociology and social justice. I owe thanks to many people for their support, wisdom, and humor throughout the years, especially while I was working on this book. I owe special thanks to my sister, Shari, who inspires me with her wisdom, kindness, loyalty, and tenacity. She supports me in ways too numerous to mention and keeps me going. I owe special thanks to Drs. Patricia Y. Martin and Irene Padavic for helping me to become a better sociological thinker, researcher, writer, and teacher. I thank my colleagues at Belmont University, especially Shelby Longard, Erin Pryor, and Ken Spring. Thanks also to Jerry Adams, Catherine Bush, Laura Carpenter, Cynthia Ann Curtis, Rory Dicker, Kris De Welde, Suzanne Feinstein, Jennifer Hackett, Jennifer James, Jen Levine, Wendy Marsh, and Jennifer Thomas. I appreciate the many kinds of support that my parents have given me over the years. My father, Robert J. Stepnick, deserves special attention for listening to countless project updates and for offering encouragement when the going got tough. Lastly, I am grateful for my students, who remind me why I do this work.

—Andi Stepnick

We both thank Jeff Lasser of SAGE for his invaluable assistance in the preparation of this manuscript, and Nathan Davidson, Dave Repetto, Ben Penner, and Steve Rutter, formerly of SAGE, for their help in the development of this project. Also, we thank Tiara Beatty for her editorial assistance.

This text has benefited in innumerable ways from reviewers who offered valuable insights about the subject matter and about the challenges of college teaching. We thank them for their expertise and for their comments, which led to significant improvements in the scholarship and clarity of this textbook. We are responsible for the shortcomings that remain.

SIXTH EDITION REVIEWERS

Cheryl Renee Gooch, Cumberland County College

George Wilson, University of Miami

Walter Kawamoto, American River College

Jessica Crowe, Southern Illinois University, Carbondale

Ahoo Tabatabai, Columbia College

Dayang Hajyrayati Awg Kassim, University of Malaysia, Sarawak

Eric Jorrey, Central Ohio Technical College

Michele Ponting, PACA Adult Learning

FIFTH EDITION REVIEWERS

Ronald Huskin, Del Mar College

Roblyn Rawlins, The College of New Rochelle

Fiona Hennah, Coleg y Cymoedd

Kate D'Arcy, University of Bedfordshire

Wen Wang, California State University, Northridge

Only when lions have historians will hunters cease to be heroes.

—African Proverb

Not everything that is faced can be changed, but nothing can be changed until it is faced.

—James Baldwin

AN INTRODUCTION TO THE STUDY OF MINORITY GROUPS IN THE UNITED STATES

Chapter 1.   Diversity in the United States: Questions and Concepts

Chapter 2.   Assimilation and Pluralism: From Immigrants to White Ethnics

The United States is a nation of groups as well as individuals. These groups vary in many ways, including their size, wealth, education, race, ethnicity, culture, religion, and language. Some groups have been part of American[1] society since colonial days, while others have formed recently.

Questions of unity and diversity are among the most pressing issues facing the United States today. How should these groups relate to one another? Who should be considered American? Should we stress our diversity and preserve the many cultural heritages and languages that currently exist? Should we encourage everyone to adopt Anglo American culture and strive to become more similar? Or should we celebrate our differences? Is it possible to do both?

We begin to address these questions and other related issues in Chapters 1 and 2. Our goal is to help you develop a broader, more informed understanding of the past and present forces that have created and sustained the groups that make up American society. We'll sustain this focus throughout this book.

DIVERSITY IN THE UNITED STATES

Questions and Concepts

Who am I? . . . Where do I fit into American society? . . . For most of my 47 years, I have struggled to find answers to these questions. I am an American of multiracial descent and culture [Native American, African American, Italian American, and Puerto Rican]. In this aspect, I am not very different from many Americans [but] I have always felt an urge to feel and live the intermingling of blood that runs through my veins. American society has a way of forcing multiracial and biracial people to choose one race over the other. I personally feel this pressure every time I have to complete an application form with instructions to check just one box for race category.

—Butch, a 47-year-old man[2]

Actually, I don't feel comfortable being around Asians except for my family . . . I couldn't relate to . . . other Asians [because] they grew up in [wealthier neighborhoods]. I couldn't relate to the whole "I live in a mansion" [attitude]. This summer, I worked in a media company and it was kind of hard to relate to them [other Asians] because we all grew up in a different place . . . the look I would get when I say "Yeah, I'm from [a less affluent neighborhood]" they're like, "Oh, oh" like, "That's unfortunate for your parents, I'm sorry they didn't make it."

—Rebecca, a 19-year-old Macanese-Chinese-
Portuguese woman[3]

Yeah, my people came from all over—Italy, Ireland, Poland, and others too. I don't really know when they got here or why they came and, really, it doesn't matter much to me. I mean, I'm just an American. . . . I'm from everywhere . . . I'm from here!

—Jennifer, a 25-year-old white American woman[4]

What do Butch, Rebecca, and Jennifer have in common? How do they differ? They think about their place in American society in very different ways. All are connected to a multitude of groups and traditions but not all find this fact interesting or important. One feels alienated from the more affluent members of her group, one seeks to embrace his multiple memberships, and one dismisses the issue of ancestry as irrelevant and is comfortable and at ease being "just an American."

Today, the United States is growing more diverse in culture, race, religion, and language. The number of Americans who identify as multiracial or who can connect themselves to different cultural traditions is increasing. Where will this increasing diversity lead us? Will our nation fragment? Could we dissolve into warring enclaves—the fate of more than one modern nation? Or can we find connection and commonality? Could we develop tolerance, respect, or even admiration for one another? Can we overcome the legacies of inequality established in colonial days? Can Americans embrace our nation's increasing diversity and live out our motto, *E Pluribus Unum* (out of many, one)?

This book raises many questions about the past, present, and future of group relationships in America. For example, what historical, social, political, and economic forces shaped those relationships historically and how are they shaping contemporary group relations? How do racial and ethnic groups relate to each other today? What kind of society are we becoming because of immigration? What does it mean to be an American? What kind of society do we want to become and how can we move in that direction?

America is a nation of immigrants and groups. Today, about 13.5% of the U.S. population was born in some other nation. The population of some states is more than one fifth foreign-born (e.g., California is 28% foreign-born), and some cities are more than one third foreign-born (e.g., New York is 37% foreign-born; U.S. Census Bureau, 2017c). Since the infancy of our society, Americans have been arguing, often passionately, about inclusion and exclusion and about unity and diversity. Every member of our society is, in some sense, an immigrant or the descendant of immigrants. Even Native Americans migrated to this continent, albeit thousands of years ago. We are all from somewhere else, with roots in other parts of the world. Some Americans came here in chains; others came on ocean liners, on planes, on busses, and even on foot. Some arrived last week, while others have had family here for centuries. Each wave of newcomers has altered our social landscape. As many have observed, our society is continually under construction and seems permanently unfinished.

Today, America is remaking itself yet again. Large numbers of immigrants are arriving from around the world, and their presence has raised questions about what it means to be an American, who should be granted U.S. citizenship, and how much diversity is best for society. How do immigrants affect America? Are they bringing new energy and revitalizing the economy? Are they draining resources such as school budgets, health care, and jobs? Both? How do they affect African Americans, Native Americans, and other groups? Are they changing what it means to be an American? If so, how?

In 2008, Americans elected Barack Obama to become our nation's first African American president. To some, this victory suggested that the United States has finally become what people often claim it to be: a truly open, "color-blind" society where one succeeds based on merit. In 2016, Donald Trump became our country's 45th president. Some see the rise of racist and xenophobic speech and actions that emerged during our most recent election season as a kind of backlash—not just against Democrats or the political system, but against the diversity initiatives that expanded under the Obama administration.

Even as we debate the implications of immigration, other long-standing issues about belonging, fairness, and justice remain unresolved. Native Americans and African Americans have been a part of this society since its start, but they've existed largely as outsiders—as slaves, servants, laborers, or even enemies—to the mainstream, dominant group. In many ways, they haven't been treated as "true Americans" or full citizens, either by law or custom. The legacies of racism and exclusion continue to affect these groups today and, as you'll see in future chapters, they and other American minority groups continue to suffer from inequality, discrimination, and marginalization.

Even a casual glance at our schools, courts, neighborhoods, churches, or corporate boardrooms—indeed, at any nook or cranny of our society—reveals pervasive patterns of inequality, injustice, and unfairness and different opportunities. So, which is the "real"[5] America: the land of acceptance and opportunity or the one of insularity and inequity?

Some of us feel intensely connected to people with similar backgrounds and identify closely with a specific heritage. Others embrace multiracial or multiethnic identities. Some people feel no particular connection with any group or homeland. Others are unsure where they fit in the social landscape. Group membership, including our race or ethnicity, gender, class, and sexual orientation, shape our experiences and, therefore, how we think about American society, the world, and ourselves. Additionally, group membership shapes the opportunities available to us and to others.

How do we understand these contrasts and divisions? Should we celebrate our diversity or stress the need for similarity? How can we incorporate all groups while avoiding fragmentation and division? What can hold us together as a nation? The U. S. may be at a crossroads concerning these issues. Throughout this book, you'll have an opportunity to reexamine the fundamental questions of citizenship and inclusion in our society. This chapter reviews the basic themes to help you do that effectively.

MINORITY GROUPS: TRENDS AND QUESTIONS

Because our group memberships shape our experiences and worldviews, they also affect the choices we make, including those in the voting booth. People in different groups may view decisions in different ways due to their divergent group histories, experiences, and current situations. Without some knowledge of the many ways someone can be an American, the debates over which direction our society should take are likely to be unmeaningful or even misunderstood.

Increasing Diversity

The choices about our society's future may feel especially urgent because the diversity of American society is increasing dramatically, largely due to high rates of immigration. Since the 1960s, the number of immigrants arriving in America each year has more than tripled and includes groups from around the world.

People's concerns about increasing diversity are compounded by other unresolved issues and grievances. For example, in Part 3, we document continuing gaps in income, poverty rates, and other measures of affluence and equality between minority and dominant groups. In many ways, the problems currently facing African Americans, Native Americans, Hispanic Americans, Asian Americans, and other minority groups are as formidable as they were a generation (or more) ago. Given these realities, how can America better live out its promise of equality for all?

Let's consider the changing makeup of America. Figure 1.1 presents the percentage of the total U.S. population in each of the five largest racial and ethnic groups. First, we'll consider this information at face value and analyze some of its implications. Then, we'll consider (and question) the framing of this information, such as group names and why they matter.

Figure 1.1 shows the groups' relative sizes from 1980 through 2010 (when the government last conducted the census) and it offers the projected relative sizes of each group through 2060. The declining numbers of non-Hispanic whites reflect the increasing diversity in the United States. As recently as 1980, more than 8 out of 10 Americans were non-Hispanic whites, but by the middle of this century, non-Hispanic whites will become a numerical minority. Several states (Texas, California, Hawaii, and New Mexico) already have "majority minority" populations. And for the first time in history, most babies born in the U. S. (50.4%) are members of minority groups (U.S. Census Bureau, 2012b).

Researchers predict that African American and Native American populations will increase in absolute numbers but will remain similar in relative size. However, Hispanic American, Asian American, and Pacific Islander populations will grow dramatically. Asian American and Pacific Islander groups together constituted only 2% of the population in 1980, but that will grow to 10% by midcentury. The most dramatic growth,

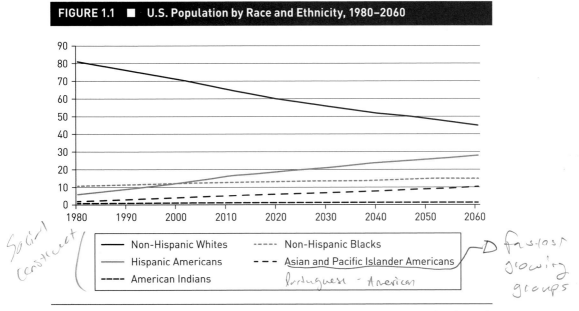

FIGURE 1.1 ■ U.S. Population by Race and Ethnicity, 1980–2060

Legend:
— Non-Hispanic Whites
----- Non-Hispanic Blacks
Hispanic Americans
- - - Asian and Pacific Islander Americans
---- American Indians

[handwritten annotations: "Social construct", "Portuguese - American", "fast/last growing groups"]

Source: U.S. Census Bureau (2017a). National Population Projections. https://www.census.gov/data/tables/2017/demo/popproj/2017-summary-tables.html

Note: Hispanics may be of any race.

however, will be among Hispanic Americans. In 2002, this group surpassed African Americans as the largest minority group. Researchers expect it will be almost 30% of the U. S. population by 2060.

Projections about the future are educated guesses based on documented trends, but they suggest significant change. Our society will grow more diverse racially and culturally, becoming less white and less European—and more like the world as a whole. Some people see these changes as threats to traditional white, middle-class American values and lifestyles. Other people view these demographic changes as part of the ebb and flow of social life. That is, society has changed ever since it began; this is merely another phase in the great American experiment. Which viewpoints are most in line with your own and why?

What's in a Name?

The group names we used in Figure 1.1 are arbitrary, and no group has clear or definite boundaries. We use these terms because they are familiar and consistent with the labels used in census reports, much of the sociological research literature, and other sources of information. Although such group names are convenient, this doesn't mean that they are "real" in any absolute sense or equally useful in all circumstances. These group names have some serious shortcomings. For example, they reflect social conventions whose meanings change over time and location. To underscore the social construction of racial and ethnic groups, we use group names interchangeably (e.g., blacks and African Americans; Hispanic Americans and Latinos). Nevertheless, issues remain.

First, the race/ethnic labels suggest groups are homogeneous. While it's true that people within one group may share some general, superficial physical or cultural traits (e.g., language), they also vary by social class, religion, gender, sexual orientation, and in many other ways. People within the Asian American and Pacific Islander group, for example, represent scores of different national backgrounds (Japanese, Pakistanis, Samoans, Vietnamese), and the categories of Native American or Alaska Native include people from hundreds of different tribal groups. If we consider people's other social statuses such as age and religious affiliation, that diversity becomes even more pronounced. Any two people within one group (e.g., Hispanics) might be quite different from each other in some respects and similar to people from "different" racial/ethnic groups (e.g., whites).

Second, people don't necessarily use these labels when they think about their own identity. In this sense, the labels aren't "real" or important for all the people in these racial/ethnic groups. For example, many whites in the U. S. (like Jennifer, quoted in the chapter opening) think of themselves as "just American." Many Hispanic Americans think of themselves in relation to ethnic origin, such as Mexican or Cuban (see Chapter 7). Or they may identify with a particular region or village in their homeland. For LGBTQIA[6] group members, sexual orientation may be more important to their identity than their race or ethnicity. Thus, the labels don't always reflect the ways people think about themselves, their families, or where they come from. The categories are statistical classifications created by researchers and census takers to help them organize information and clarify their analyses. They don't grow out of or always reflect people's everyday realities.

Third, although the categories in Figure 1.1 are broad, several groups don't neatly fit into them. For example, where should we place Arab Americans and recent immigrants from Africa? These groups are relatively small (about 1 million people each), but there is no clear place for them in the current categories. Should we consider Arab Americans as "Asian," as some argue? Should recent immigrants from Africa be in the same category as African Americans? Should we create a new group for people of Middle Eastern or North African descent? The point is that such classification schemes have somewhat ambiguous boundaries.

Further, we can't neatly categorize people who identify with more than one racial or ethnic group (like Butch, quoted in the chapter opening). The number of "mixed-group" Americans is relatively small today—about 3% of the total population (U.S. Bureau of the Census, 2015a). However, between 2000 and 2016, the number of people who chose more than one racial or ethnic category on the U.S. census increased by 33% (from 2.4% to 3.2% of the total population) (Jones & Bullock, 2012; U.S. Census Bureau, 2017b). This trend is likely to continue increasing rapidly because of the growth in interracial marriage.

To illustrate, Figure 1.2 shows dramatic increases in the percentage of "new" marriages (couples that got married in the year prior to the survey date) and all marriages that unite members of different racial or ethnic groups (Livingston & Brown, 2017). Obviously, the greater the number of mixed racial or ethnic marriages, the greater the number of mixed Americans who will be born of such partnerships. One study estimates that the percentage of Americans who identify with two or more races will more than double between 2014 (when it was 2.5%) and 2060 (when it will be 6.2%; Colby & Ortman, 2015, p. 9).

Finally, we should note that group names are **social constructions**,[7] or ideas and perceptions that people create in specific historical circumstances and that reflect particular power relationships. For example, the group "Native Americans" didn't exist before

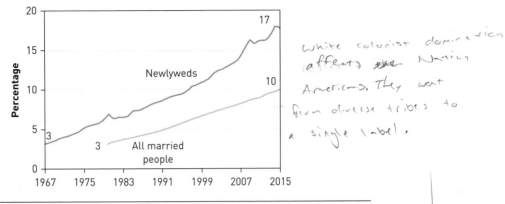

FIGURE 1.2 ■ Interracial and Interethnic Marriages in the United States, 1967–2015

Source: Livingston and Brown (2017).

[Handwritten margin note: White colonist domination affects the Native Americans. They went from diverse tribes to a single label.]

the European exploration and colonization of North America. Before then, hundreds of separate indigenous societies, each with its own language and culture, lived across North America. Native Americans thought of themselves primarily in terms of their tribe and had little awareness of the many other groups spread across the vast expanse of the North American continent. However, European conquerors constructed them as one group: the enemy. Today, many Americans see Native Americans as one group. This reflects their historical defeat and domination by white European colonists, which led to Native Americans' current status as a minority group in a largely white society.

Likewise (although through different processes), African, Hispanic, and Asian Americans came to be seen as separate groups as the result of their unequal interactions with white Americans. These group labels have become real because people *believe* they are real. We use these familiar group labels to facilitate our discussion of complex topics, but they don't reflect some unchangeable truth or reality regarding racial or ethnic groups.

[Handwritten note: Influence ... about race → ... about status]

QUESTIONS FOR REFLECTION

1. If asked about your group membership, which of the groups in Figure 1.1 would you choose, if any? Do you feel that you belong to one group or several? How much does your group membership shape your circle of friends, your experiences, and your worldview? How important is your group membership to your self-identity?

(Continued)

(Continued)

2. Savannah is a white, 27-year-old woman who was raised in Georgia but now lives in South Dakota. She is an Episcopalian, has a degree in computer science, and makes $60,000 a year. She is married to Tom, her college sweetheart. Winona is a 40-year-old woman and a member of the Lakota nation. She was raised in South Dakota but moved to California to pursue her career as a pharmacist. She is married to Robert and they have one child. Although the census would classify Savannah and Winona as belonging to different racial/ethnic groups, they are similar in many ways. In what ways are their similarities more significant than their differences?

3. Over the past 5 to 10 years, what signs of increasing diversity have you seen in your community? What benefits and challenges have come with that increasing diversity?

4. What does it mean to be American? If you asked Americans, a popular answer might be *freedom*. What does that mean to you—freedom to do what? Or freedom from what? How do you think people of other countries or generations might respond?

QUESTIONS ABOUT THE FUTURE, SOCIOLOGY, AND THE PLAN OF THIS BOOK

At our country's inception, the law recognized only white Anglo-Saxon Protestant men of elite classes as full citizens deserving of specific rights (e.g., voting) and opportunities (e.g., education). Most of us would agree that this definition of *American* is far too narrow. Given the changing U.S. population (Figure 1.1), you may wonder who should count as American. What does it mean to be an American? Does diversity threaten societal cohesion? Likewise, what problems might come from narrow definitions of what it means to be an American?

We've raised several complex questions in these first few pages. The answers aren't obvious or easy to come by. There is no guarantee that we, as a society, will be willing or able to resolve all the issues related to intergroup relations. However, the issues won't disappear or resolve themselves if we ignore them. We'll never make progress unless we address the issues honestly and with an accurate base of knowledge and understanding. We hope this book helps you develop thoughtful, informed positions on these issues.

Throughout our inquiry, we'll rely on sociology and other social sciences for concepts, theories, and information to gain a greater understanding of the issues. The first two chapters introduce many of the ideas that will guide our investigation. Part 2 explores how relations between the dominant group and minority groups have evolved over time. Part 3 analyzes the current situation of U.S. racial and ethnic minority groups. Finally, Part 4 explores many of the challenges facing our society (and the world) and offers conclusions from our inquiry.

WHAT IS A MINORITY GROUP?

A common vocabulary will help us understand and discuss the issues with greater clarity. The mathematical connotation of the term **minority group** implies that minority groups are small. However, they can be quite large—even a numerical majority. For example, most sociologists consider women a minority group, although they are a numerical majority of the U.S. population. Whites are a numerical minority in South Africa, accounting for less than 10% of the population (Central Intelligence Agency, 2017). However, they've been the most powerful and affluent group in that nation's history. Despite the end of **apartheid** (a state-sanctioned racial inequality) in South Africa, whites keep their advantage in many ways (e.g., economically, politically). Therefore, sociologists would consider them the dominant group.

Sociologists define minority status in terms of the distribution of resources and power. We use the definition of minority group developed by Wagley and Harris (1958) that emphasizes these characteristics:

1. Minority group members experience a pattern of *disadvantage or inequality*.

2. Minority group members share a *visible trait or characteristic* that differentiates them from other groups.

3. Minority group members are *aware* of their shared status with other group members.

4. Group membership is usually *determined at birth*.

5. Members tend to *form intimate relationships* (close friendships, dating partnerships, and marriages) *within the group*.

Next, we briefly explain these five characteristics. Because inequality and visibility are the most important characteristics of minority groups, we'll examine them in even more detail later in the chapter.

1. **Inequality**. The first and most important defining characteristic of a minority group is its *inequality* (some pattern of disadvantage). The degree of disadvantage varies over time and location and includes such slight irritants as a lack of desks for left-handed students or a policy of racial or religious exclusion at an expensive country club. (Note, however, that you might not agree that the irritant is slight if you're a left-handed student awkwardly taking notes at a right-handed desk or if you're a golf aficionado who happens to be African American or Jewish American.) The most significant inequalities include exploitation, such as slavery and **genocide** (the intentional killing of a group, such as the mass execution of Jews, Slavs, Roma, gays and lesbians, and others under Nazi rule in Germany).

Whatever its scope or severity, whether it affects people's ability to gain jobs, housing, wealth, political power, police protection, health care, or other valued resources, the pattern of disadvantage is the key characteristic of a minority group. Because the group has less of what society values, some people refer to minority groups as *subordinate groups*.

The pattern of disadvantage members of the minority group experience results from the actions of another group that benefits from and tries to sustain the inequality. This advantaged group is the **dominant group**. We use the latter term most frequently because it reflects the patterns of inequality and the lack of power experienced by minority groups. Keep in mind that the inequalities we see today were established in the past, sometimes centuries ago or more. Privilege exists even when the beneficiaries are unaware of it.

2. **Visibility.** The second defining characteristic of a minority group is some *visible trait* or characteristic that sets members apart and that the dominant group holds in low esteem. The trait can be cultural (e.g., language, religion, speech patterns, or dress styles), physical (e.g., skin color, stature, or facial features), or both. Groups defined primarily by their cultural characteristics such as Irish Americans and Jewish Americans are **ethnic minority groups**. Groups defined primarily by their physical characteristics, such as African Americans and Native Americans, are **racial minority groups**. These categories overlap. So-called ethnic groups may also have what some people see as distinguishing physical characteristics (e.g., the stereotypical Irish red hair or "Jewish nose"). Racial groups may also have (or be thought to have) cultural traits that differ from the dominant group (e.g., differences in dialect, religious values, or cuisine).

These distinguishing traits help identify minority group members and separate people into distinct groups. Thus, they help to maintain the patterns of disadvantage. That is, the dominant group has (or at one time had) enough power to create the distinction between groups and thus solidify a higher position for itself. These markers of group membership are crucial. Without visible signs, it would be difficult or impossible to identify who was in which group, and the system of minority group oppression would collapse.

The characteristics marking the boundaries between groups usually aren't significant in and of themselves. They are selected for their visibility and convenience and, objectively, may be trivial and unimportant. For example, scientists now conclude that skin color and other so-called racial traits have little scientific, evolutionary, medical, or biological importance (Gannon, 2016; Yudell, Roberts, DeSalle, & Tishkoff, 2016). For example, darker skin color simply reflects the body's response to sunlight. In areas with greater sunlight (closer to the equator), people's bodies produce melanin, which screens out the sun's ultraviolet rays and protects the skin. Skin color emerged as an important marker of group membership in our society through a complex and lengthy historical process, not because it has any inherent significance. Again, these markers of minority group membership become important because people give them significance (e.g., superiority, inferiority).

3. **Awareness.** A third characteristic of minority groups is that the members are aware of their differentiation from the dominant group and their shared disadvantage. This shared social status can provide a sense of solidarity and serve as the basis for strong intragroup bonds. As noted earlier, minority and dominant groups can experience life differently. Thus, minority group members may have worldviews that are markedly different from those of the dominant group and from other minority groups. For example, public opinion polls often show sizeable group differences about the seriousness and extent of discrimination in America. Figure 1.3 shows persistent and sizeable gaps in the percentage of nationally representative samples of whites and blacks who agree that blacks and whites have equal job opportunities. Given their different group histories, experiences, and locations in the social hierarchy, it may not surprise you that black Americans see more racial inequality than whites. Even after President Obama's election in 2008, the percentage of black Americans who believed equal opportunity exists was about half the rate of white Americans.

Both groups have become more pessimistic about equal opportunity in recent years. A 2016 national poll showed that only 71% of Americans believed black children

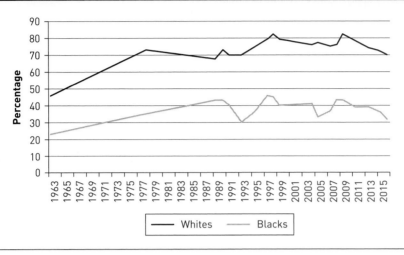

FIGURE 1.3 ■ **Do Black Americans Have the Same Chances as White Americans to Obtain the Same Level of Employment? 1963–2016**

Source: Gallup (2017a).

have the same opportunity as white children to get a good education. This is the lowest percentage on record since Gallup began asking that question in 1962, less than a decade after the Supreme Court voted to desegregate public schools in *Brown v. the Board of Education* (1954). Only 70% believe black Americans have equal opportunities to get housing, which is the lowest rating on this question since 1989 (J. M. Jones, 2016).

4. **Ascription**. A fourth characteristic of minority groups is that, generally, membership is an **ascribed status** given to them, often at birth. The traits that identify minority group membership are typically hard to change. Thus, minority group status is usually involuntary and for life.

5. **Intimate Relationships.** Finally, minority group members tend to form emotionally close bonds with people like themselves, for example, as close friends, dating partners, and legal spouses or cohabitational partners. (Members of the dominant group do this, too.)

Pervasive racial and ethnic segregation of neighborhoods, schools, and other areas of American society influence who one meets or spends time with on a regular basis. In some cases, the dominant group dictates this pattern. For example, many states outlawed interracial marriages until the U.S. Supreme Court declared laws against **miscegenation** unconstitutional in the 1967 case, *Loving v. Virginia* (Bell, 1992).

The Wagley and Harris (1958) multipart definition of a minority group encompasses "traditional" minority groups such as African Americans and Native Americans but we can apply it to other groups. For instance, women as a group fit the first four criteria, and we can analyze their experience with many of the same concepts and ideas that guide our analysis of racial and ethnic minority groups. Similarly, we can apply this concept to Americans who are gay, lesbian, bisexual, or transgender; to Americans with disabilities;

to Americans who are left-handed; and to Americans who are very old, very short, very tall, or very obese. We hope that you gain insights about a wide variety of groups and people by applying ideas from this book.

QUESTIONS FOR REFLECTION

5. Which parts of the definition of a minority group apply to gay and lesbian Americans? Which parts, if any, apply to other groups of interest that are not defined as American minority groups, such as Christians or men? What do your answers suggest about differences between minority and majority groups?

PATTERNS OF INEQUALITY

The most important defining characteristic of minority group status is inequality. As you'll see, minority group membership affects access to jobs, education, wealth, health care, and housing. It is associated with a lower (often much lower) proportional share of goods and services and more limited opportunities for upward mobility.

Stratification is the hierarchical ranking of societal groups that results in the unequal distribution of goods and services. Every human society, except the simplest hunter–gatherer societies, is stratified to some degree. You can visualize these divisions as horizontal layers (or strata) that differ from one another by the amount of resources they command. Economic stratification results in different **social classes**. Many criteria (e.g., education, age, gender, power, parent's social class) may affect a person's social class position and their access to goods and services. Minority group membership is one of these criteria, and it has a powerful impact on the distribution of resources in the U. S. and in other societies.

The next section considers different theories about the nature and dimensions of stratification. Then, we discuss how minority group status relates to stratification.

Theoretical Perspectives

Sociologist (and other social scientists) have been concerned with stratification and inequality since the formation of sociology in the 19th century. We highlight four of the most significant thinkers in this section. An early and important contributor to our understanding of the significance of social inequality was Karl Marx, the noted social philosopher and revolutionary. Half a century later, sociologist Max Weber (pronounced *Mahks Vay-ber*), a central figure in the development of sociology, critiqued and elaborated on Marx's view of inequality. Gerhard Lenski was a modern sociologist whose ideas about the influence of economic and technological development on social stratification are relevant for comparing societies and understanding the evolution of intergroup relations. Finally, we consider another modern sociologist, Patricia Hill Collins, who argues for an intersectional approach to inequality, which views inequalities based on class, race or ethnicity, gender (and so on) as a single, interlocking system of inequality.

FIGURE 1.4   ◪   Class in the United States

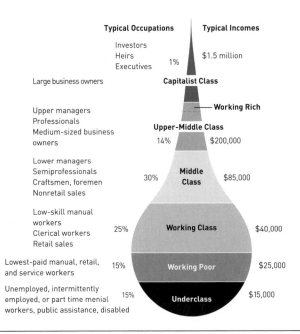

Source: Gilbert, 2011.

Karl Marx

Although best known as the father of modern communism, Karl Marx was also the primary architect of a political, economic, and social philosophy that has played a signifi-cant role in world affairs for more than 170 years. Marxism is a complex theory of history and social change in which inequality is a central concern.

Marx argued that the most important source of inequality in society was the system of economic production. He focused on the **means of production,** or the materials, tools, resources, and social relationships by which a society produces and distributes goods and services. In an agricultural society, the means of production include land, draft animals, and plows. In an industrial society, the means of produc-tion include factories, commercial enterprises, banks, and transportation systems, such as railroads.

In Marx's view, all societies include social classes that struggle over the means of production. In industrial societies, the rise of capitalism created a new, simplified class system with two classes. The **bourgeoisie,** or capitalist class, owns or controls the means of production. It benefits from that arrangement and exploits and oppresses the **proletariat** or working class. Marx called them "two great hostile camps" (Marx & Engels, 1967, p. 1). He believed that class conflict was inevitable and that, ultimately, the working class would revolt against the bourgeoisie and create a society without exploitation, coercion, or inequality. That is, it would create a classless society.

classless society (handwritten margin note)

Property, Prestige, Power (handwritten margin note)

Marx is consistently named one of the most influential thinkers of all time; yet, scholars and others have extensively critiqued or modified his ideas. Nevertheless, modern social science owes a great deal to his insights about inequality, class struggle, social conflict, and group relations, as you'll see in upcoming chapters.

Max Weber

One of Marx's major critics was Max Weber, a German sociologist who did most of his work around the turn of the 20th century. Weber saw Marx's view of inequality as too narrow. Weber argued that inequality included dimensions other than one's relationship to the means of production. Weber expanded on Marx's view of inequality by identifying three separate components of stratification.

First, economic inequality is based on ownership or control of wealth (such as property) and income (money from employment, interest on bank holdings, or other payments). This is like Marx's concept of class, and Weber used the term **class** for this specific form of inequality.

A second dimension of stratification involves differences in **prestige**, or the amount of honor, esteem, or respect that people give us. Different factors influence prestige, including one's class position, family lineage, athletic ability, and physical appearance. Group membership also affects prestige. People typically give less prestige to minority group members than dominant group members.

The third component of stratification is **power**, or the ability to influence others, impact the decision-making process of society, and pursue and protect one's self-interest and achieve one's goals. One source of power is a person's standing in politically active organizations that lobby state and federal legislatures, such as labor unions or interest groups. Some politically active groups have access to great wealth and can it to promote their causes. Other groups may rely more on their size and ability to mobilize large demonstrations to achieve their goals. Political organizations and the people they represent vary in the power that they can mobilize to control political decision making.

Typically, these three dimensions of stratification go together: wealthy, prestigious classes are generally more powerful (more likely to achieve their goals or protect their self-interest) than low-income groups or groups with little prestige. However, power is a separate dimension: even very impoverished groups have sometimes found ways to express their concerns and pursue their goals.

Weber's concept of stratification offers more complexity than Marx's. For example, instead of simply being bourgeoise or proletariat, Weber suggests that people can be elite in some ways but not in others. For example, an aristocratic family that has fallen on hard financial times might belong to the elite in terms of family lineage and prestige but not in terms of wealth. Or a major figure in the illegal drug trade could enjoy substantial wealth but be held in low esteem.

Gerhard Lenski

Societal evolution (handwritten margin note)

Gerhard Lenski is a modern sociologist who expands on Weber's ideas by analyzing stratification in the context of societal evolution, or the **level of development** of a society (Nolan & Lenski, 2004). Lenski argues that the degree of inequality or the criteria affecting a group's position is closely related to **subsistence technology**, or how the society meets people's basic needs for food, water, shelter, and so on. For example, preindustrial agricultural societies rely on human and animal labor to generate the food necessary to sustain life. Inequality in these types of societies centers on control of land and labor because they are the most important means of production for that level of development.

In modern industrial societies, land ownership isn't as crucial as control of financial, manufacturing, and commercial enterprises. Because the control of capital is more important than control of land for those societies, the level of development and the nature of inequality, differs.

The U. S. and other more-industrialized societies have entered another stage of development, so they are often referred to as **postindustrial societies**. In postindustrial societies, developments in new technology, computer-related fields, information processing, and scientific research create economic growth. Additionally, one's economic success is closely related to formal education, specialized knowledge, and familiarity with new technologies (Chirot, 1994, p. 88; see also Bell, 1973).

These changes in subsistence technology, from agriculture to industrialization to an information-based society, alter the stratification system. As the sources of wealth, success, and power change, so do the relationships between minority and dominant groups. For example, the shift to an information-based, high-tech, postindustrial society means that the advantages conferred by higher levels of education are magnified. Groups that have less access to schooling will likely rank low on all dimensions of stratification.

Patricia Hill Collins

Sociologist Patricia Hill Collins (2000) calls for an approach to the study of inequality and group relations that recognizes the multiplicity of systems of inequality and privilege in society. Some stratification systems are based on social class, while others categorize and rank people by their gender, race, ethnicity, sexuality, age, disability, and other criteria. Most people have complex social statuses, some more privileged and some less privileged. For example, consider a heterosexual, college-educated man with a professional job. These social statuses rank high in the United States. But what if he is Latino or bisexual? These latter statuses put him at a disadvantage in a society where whiteness and heterosexuality are more valued.

Collins stresses intersectionality, a view that acknowledges that everyone has multiple group memberships and that these crisscross or intersect to create different experiences for people with varying combinations of statuses. For example, the realities faced by gay, white-collar, Mexican American men are different from those faced by heterosexual, blue-collar Puerto Rican women, although both would be counted as *Hispanic* in Figure 1.1. From this perspective, you can see that no singular, uniform Hispanic American (or African American or Asian American) experience exists. Thus, we need to recognize how gender, class, sexual orientation, and other factors intersect with and reinforce one another.

Collins and other intersectional theorists critique the tendency to see inequality in terms of separate simple dichotomous systems, such as those based on class (blue collar vs. white collar), race (black vs. white), or gender (men vs. women). An intersectional approach involves seeing how these statuses link together to form a "matrix of domination." For example, white Americans aren't a homogenous dominant group. Some group members, such as women or poor whites, are privileged in terms of their race (white) but subordinate in terms of their gender (women) or class (poor). Collins's ideas help us see that who is the oppressed and who is the oppressor changes across social contexts, and people can occupy privileged and subordinated statuses simultaneously.

The separate systems of domination and subordination overlap and reinforce one another. This matrix of domination shapes people's opportunities, experiences, and perceptions. As you'll see in later chapters, race and gender interact with each other and create especially disadvantaged positions for people who rank lower on both dimensions simultaneously (e.g., see Figure 5.5, which shows that black women consistently earn less income than either black men of the same race and white women of the same gender).

Likewise, stereotypes and other elements of prejudice are gendered. For example, some stereotypical traits might be applied to all African Americans (such as laziness), but others are applied only to women (e.g., "uppity") or men (e.g., "thug").

An intersectional approach stresses the multiplicity of systems of inequality and analyzes the connections between them. It sees groups as complex, not uniform. In this book, we'll use an intersectional lens to explore how class and gender influence racial and ethnic minority group experiences. However, you can apply an intersectional approach to other dimensions of power and inequality, including disability, sexual orientation, and religion.

Minority Group Status and Stratification

The theoretical perspectives we've just reviewed raise three important points about the connections between minority group status and stratification. First, minority group status affects access to wealth and income, prestige, and power. In America, minority group status has been and continues to be one of the most important and powerful determinants of one's **life chances**, or opportunities and access to resources such as nutritious food, health care, education, and a job that provides a good income. We explore these complex patterns of inequality in Part 3, but observation of American society reveals that minority groups control proportionately fewer resources and that minority group status and stratification are complexly intertwined. Consider, for example, the life chances of two 18-year-olds. One is white, comes from a wealthy family, was educated in excellent private schools, had the opportunity to travel the world on holiday, and has had the opportunity to network with members of the American elite. The other is a recent immigrant who fled the war in Syria. This one is smart, hardworking, and proficient in English but has a low overall level of education, which makes it hard to find work that pays a living wage. Which person has had and will have greater life chances?

Second, although social class and minority group status are correlated, they are different dimensions of inequality and they vary independently. The degree to which one status affects the other varies by group and across time. Some groups, such as Irish or Italian Americans, have experienced considerable upward **social mobility** (or movement) within the class stratification system although they faced considerable discrimination in the past. Furthermore, as stressed by the intersectional approach, minority groups are internally divided by systems of inequality based on class, status, or power. Some members of a minority group can be successful economically, wield great political power, or enjoy high prestige while the majority of group members experience poverty and powerlessness.

Likewise, members of the same social class vary by ethnicity, race, gender, sexual orientation, religion, age, and other social statuses.

Third, dominant–minority group relationships are created by the struggle to control valued goods and services. Minority group structures (such as slavery) emerge so that the dominant group can control commodities such as land or labor, maintain its position at the top of the stratification system, or eliminate perceived threats to its well-being. Struggles over property, wealth, prestige, and power lie at the heart of every dominant–minority relationship. Marx believed that the ruling class shaped all aspects of society to sustain the economic system that underlies its privileged position. The treatment of minority groups throughout American history provides a good deal of evidence to support Marx's point, as you'll see in upcoming chapters.

VISIBLE DISTINGUISHING TRAITS: RACE AND GENDER

In this section, we focus on the second defining characteristic of minority groups: the visible traits that represent membership. The boundaries between dominant and minority groups have been established along a wide variety of lines, including religion, language, skin color, and sexuality. Let's consider two of the more visible and permanent markers of group membership—race and gender.

Race

Historically, race has been widely misunderstood, but the false ideas and exaggerated importance people have attached to race haven't merely been errors of logic that are subject to debate. At various times and places, ideas about race have resulted in some of the greatest tragedies in human history: immense exploitation and mistreatment, such as slavery and genocide. Myths about race continue today, though in different forms. To decrease the likelihood of further tragedies, it's important to cultivate accurate understandings about race.

Thanks to advances in genetics, biology, and physical anthropology, we know more about what race is and, more importantly, what race isn't. We can't address everything in these first few pages, but we can establish a basic framework and use the latest scientific research to dispel some of the myths.

Race and Human Evolution

Humans first appeared in East Africa more than 160,000 years ago. Our ancient ancestors were hunters and gatherers who slowly wandered away from their ancestral region in search of food and other resources. Over the millennia, our ancestors traveled across the entire globe, first to what is now the Middle East and then to Asia, Europe, Australia, and North and South America (see Figure 1.5) (Gugliotta, 2008; Hirst, 2017).

"Racial" differences evolved during this period of dispersion, as our ancestors adapted to different environments and ecological conditions. For example, consider skin color, the most visible "racial" characteristic. As noted earlier, skin color derives from a pigment

FIGURE 1.5 ■ **The Migration of Anatomically Modern Humans**

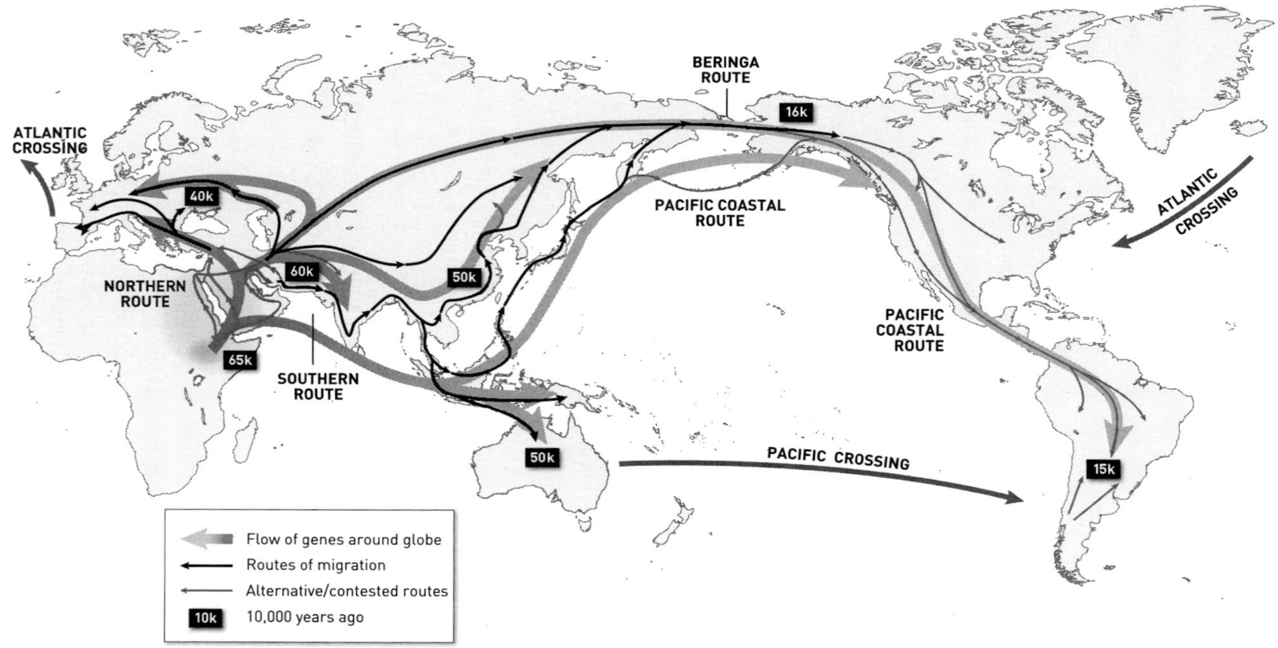

Source: Gugliotta (2008).

called *melanin*. In areas with intense sunlight, at or near the equator, melanin screens out the sun's ultraviolet rays, helping to prevent sunburn and, more significantly, skin cancer. Thus, people from equatorial locations produce higher levels of melanin and have darker skin than people who live farther away from the equator (Jablonski & Chaplin, 2010). This almost certainly means that the first humans were dark skinned and that lighter skin colors are the more recent adaptation reflecting migration away from the equator (see Figure 1.6).

The lower concentration of melanin in people adapted to areas with less intense sunlight may also be a biological adaptation to a particular ecology. Lighter skin maximizes vitamin D synthesis, which is important for the absorption of calcium and protection against health problems such as rickets. That is, the skin color of any group reflects the melanin in their skin that helps them balance the need for vitamin D against the need to protect their skin from ultraviolet rays (Jablonski & Chaplin, 2010).

The period of dispersion and differentiation, depicted in Figure 1.5, began to end about 10,000 years ago, when some of our hunting and gathering ancestors developed a new subsistence technology and established permanent agricultural villages. Over the centuries, some settlements grew into larger societies, kingdoms, and empires that conquered and absorbed neighboring societies, some of which differed culturally, linguistically, and racially from each other. The great agricultural empires of the past—Roman, Egyptian, Chinese, Aztec—united different peoples, reversed the process of dispersion and differentiation, and began a phase of consolidation and merging of human cultures and genes. Over the next 10,000 years following the first settlements, human genes were intermixed and spread around the world, eliminating any "pure" races (if such ever existed).

The differentiation created during the period of global dispersion was swamped by consolidation, a process that was greatly accelerated starting about 500 years ago when European nations began to explore and conquer much of the rest of the world (e.g., India, Africa). This consolidation of groups continues today. For example, we can see it with the increasing numbers of Americans who identify as multiracial. We see similar patterns across the world and throughout recent history.

Race and Western Traditions

Europeans had been long aware of racial variation but, aided by breakthroughs in ship design and navigation, the nations of Western Europe began regularly traveling to Africa, Asia, and eventually North and South America in the 1400s. The contact with the peoples of other continents resulted in greater awareness and curiosity about observable physical differences such as skin color.

European travel required tremendous time and resources. The goal wasn't exploration for the sake of exploration, but to lay claim to valued resources (such as gold) that existed elsewhere. In the process, European nations such as England, France, Spain, and Russia conquered, colonized, and sometimes destroyed the peoples and cultures they encountered. This political and military domination (e.g., English colonization of India, French colonization of West and North Africa) required an *ideology* (belief system) to support it. From the beginning, Europeans linked physical variation with judgments about the relative merits of other races: People from conquering nations thought they were racially and culturally superior to the nations and peoples they conquered.

FIGURE 1.6 ■ Skin Color Variation by Latitude

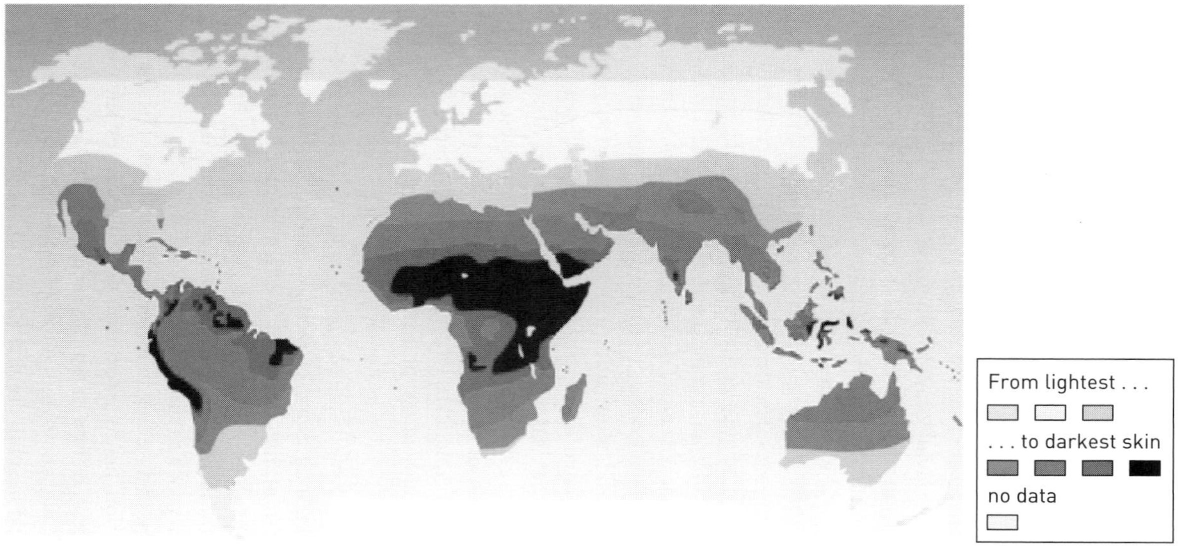

From lightest . . .

. . . to darkest skin

no data

Source: Chapman (2004).

Since then, other countries have justified military conquest, genocide, exploitation, and slavery with similar racist and xenophobic thinking. But, the toxic form of racism that bloomed during the expansion of European power continues to haunt the world today. It was the basis for the concept of race that took root in the United States.

Race and Biology

Europeans primarily used race to denigrate, reject, and exclude nonwhites. However, as the tools of modern science developed, some people tried to apply the principles of scientific research to the concept of race. These investigations focused on constructing typologies or taxonomies to classify every person of every race into a category. Some typologies were quite elaborate, with numerous races and subraces. For example, the "Caucasian" race was often subdivided into Nordics (blond, fair-skinned Northern Europeans), Mediterraneans (dark-haired Southern Europeans), and Alpines (people between those categories, with qualities from both).

One major limitation of these classification systems is that the dividing lines between the so-called racial groups are arbitrary. There is no clear, definite point where, for example, "black" skin color stops and "white" skin color begins. The characteristics used to define race blend imperceptibly into one another. Additionally, one racial trait (skin color) can appear with others (e.g., hair texture) in an infinite variety of ways. A given individual might have a skin color that people associate with one race, the hair texture of a second, the nasal shape of a third, and so forth.

Although people vary in their physical appearance, these differences don't sort themselves out in ways that enable us to divide people into precise groups like species of animals. The differences between the so-called human races aren't at all like the differences between elephants and butterflies. The ambiguous and continuous nature of "racial" characteristics makes it impossible to establish categories that have clear, nonarbitrary boundaries. Even the most elaborate racial typologies can't address the fact that many individuals fit into more than one category while others don't fit into any of them. So, who gets to decide how many groups exist and what racial group people belong to? We'll address that question in future chapters.

Over the past several decades, advances in genetic research have provided new insights into race that negate the validity of such racial typologies and the racial myths associated with them. One significant finding is that genetic variation *within* the traditional racial groups is greater than the variation *between* those groups (American Sociological Association, 2003; Gannon, 2016). That is, any two randomly selected members of the "black" race will probably vary genetically from each other *at least* as much as they do from a randomly selected member of the "white" race. This finding refutes traditional, nonscientific ideas that racial categories accurately reflect groups of homogeneous people. In other words, the traditional American perception of race as based primarily on skin color has no scientific validity.

The Social Construction of Race

Sociologist W. E. B. Du Bois wrote that the "problem of the twentieth century is the problem of the color line" ([1903] 1997, page 45 c.f. Lee & Bean, 2007). You can see the "color line," and how race is socially constructed, by examining changes in U.S. census categories.

The first census, in 1790, used only three racial categories—whites, other free persons, and slaves. The first census after the Civil War ended used white, black, mulatto, and Indian. By 1890, the categories were:

- White

- Black (a person who is more than three fourths black)

- Mulatto (a person who is three eighths to five eighths black)

- Quadroon (*quad* meaning *four*, or one fourth black)

- Octoroons (*octo* meaning *eight*, one eighth or any other amount of "black blood")

- Indian

- Chinese

- Japanese

The Chinese and Japanese categories reflect Asian immigration to the United States. The subcategories of *quadroon* and *octoroon* were an attempt to measure race in more detail, but still along a black–white dichotomy (Blank, Dabady, & Citro, 2004). Identifying the amount of "blackness" was more complicated than it sounded, and the census didn't use those categories again. However, southern states continued efforts to do so by introducing the "one-drop rule." Under this law, a person with any trace of black ancestry, even "one drop" of African blood, was defined as black and subject to the limitations of extreme racial inequality. Thus, it rigidly solidified the black–white color line in law and in custom.

The Census Bureau continues to add ethnic categories as new immigrants come to the United States For now, ethnic categories fall under one of these "racial" categories: white, black/African American, Native American/Alaskan Native, Asian (e.g., Chinese, Japanese, Native Hawaiian), and other. The Census Bureau notes that people of Hispanic origin may be of any race. Therefore, it asks people of Hispanic origin to identify their place of origin such as Cuba, Puerto Rico, or Mexico.

The census has changed in other ways, too. In 1960, the Census Bureau mailed its form to urban residences and for the first time, respondents could choose their racial identity. (In prior decades, the census taker determined each person's race. This change was important for giving people agency to self-identify their race, but it may also have produced more accurate information. That is, given the prejudice and discrimination against nonwhites, people may have been more likely to choose *white* when the census taker was nearby.) The first census to ask about Hispanic origin happened in 1980. The 2000 census was the first to allow people to identify as multiracial by selecting more than one category (Lowenthall, 2014). For example, someone could identify as white and Cuban. Yet, even with these changes, the category *white* has remained remarkably consistent over time.

Despite its scientific limits, the idea of race continues to shape intergroup relations in America and globally. Race, along with gender, is one of the first things people notice about one another. Because race is still a significant way of differentiating people, it remains socially important. In addition to discrimination by out-group members, ideas about race can also shape relations *within* a perceived racial group. For example, people within groups and outside of them may see lighter-skinned African Americans as superior to darker-skinned African Americans; thus, they may treat lighter-skinned people better. Walker (1983) named this *colorism*. Such discrimination reflects the dominant racial hierarchy that prefers lighter skin tone and presumed European facial features and body types (Harris, 2008, p. 54). While an important area of study, we (like other researchers) focus on broadly defined racial groups that affect all group members (see Blank, Dabady, & Citro, 2004, p. 29).

So, how does the idea of race remain relevant? Because of the way they developed, Western concepts of race have social and biological dimensions. Sociologists consider race a social construction whose meaning has been created and sustained not by science but by historical, social, economic, and political processes (see Omi & Winant, 1986; Smedley, 2007). For example, in Chapter 3, we'll analyze the role of race in the creation of American slavery and you'll see that the physical differences between blacks and whites became important *as a result* of that system of inequality. The elites of colonial society needed to justify their unequal treatment of Africans and seized on the visible differences in skin color, elevated it to a matter of supreme importance, and used it to justify the enslavement of blacks. That is, the importance of race was socially constructed as the result of a particular historical conflict, and it remains important not because of objective realities, but because of the widespread, shared social perception that it is important.

Gender

You've seen that minority groups can be internally differentiated by social class and other factors. Gender is another source of differentiation. Like race, **gender** has visible and socially meaningful components that make it convenient for categorizing people and organizing society. Historically, people have used visible biological characteristics such as genitalia to assign people into two sexes, female or male. (Almost 2% the U.S. population are intersex, having biological characteristics from more than one sex category [see Fausto-Sterling, 1993].)

Americans primarily recognize two gender statuses: boy/man and girl/woman. Babies are given a gender based on their sex. For example, when a fetal ultrasound for sex shows a penis, people declare, "It's a boy!" As you'll learn, gender is also a social construct. These ideas about what is masculine or feminine influence **gender norms**, or societal expectations about proper behavior, attitudes, and personality traits. Gender norms vary across time and from one society to another.

Sociologists and other social scientists have documented the close relationship between gender and inequality. Typically, men (as a group) possess more property, prestige, and power than women. Figure 1.7 provides some perspective on the global variation in gender inequality. The map shows the Gender Gap Index, a statistic that measures the amount of inequality between women and men based on variables such as education, labor market participation, reproductive health (e.g., maternal mortality rate), and political representation. As you can see, gender equality is generally highest in the more-industrialized nations of North America and Western Europe and lowest in Africa (e.g., Niger, Mali, Democratic Republic of Congo, Côte d'Ivoire, Liberia, Sierra Leone, Gambia, Mauritania, Benin) and the Middle East (e.g., Yemen, Afghanistan, Saudi Arabia, Egypt, Syria, Iran).

FIGURE 1.7 ■ Gender Inequality Worldwide

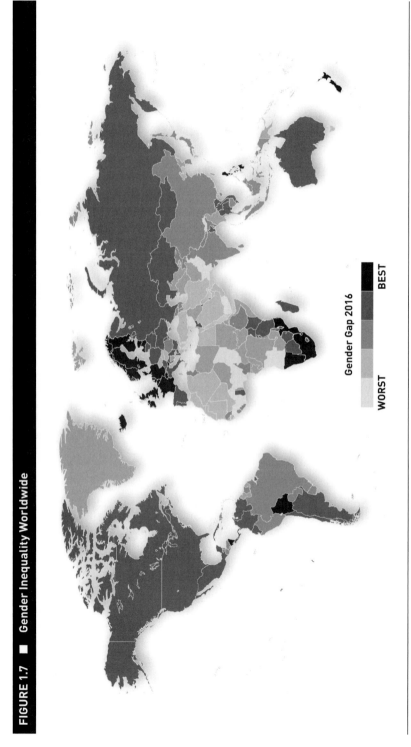

Source: Florida (2012). From "The Geography of Women's Economic Opportunities" by Richard Florida. The Atlantic Cities. January 11, 2012. Map by Zara Matheson of the Martin Prosperity Institute. Reprinted with permission.

Although Western European and North American societies rank relatively high on gender equality, gender discrimination continues to be a major issue in many of them. For example, a consistent—and large—gender income gap exists in many of them, and women are decidedly underrepresented in the most lucrative and powerful occupations (see Figure 4.4). While many societies have made progress, gender inequality appears likely to continue for generations.

Part of the problem is that all societies, including Western European and North American ones, have strong histories of **patriarchy**, or systems of dominance by men. As with racial and class stratification, dominant groups have greater resources. In patriarchal societies, men (as a group) have more control over the economy and more access to leadership roles in business, politics, education, and other institutions. Parallel to forms of racism that sought to justify and maintain racial inequality, **sexism** is an ideology that justifies and maintains gender inequality. For example, people in some societies view women as "delicate," "too emotional," and physically weak for the demands of "manly" occupations. (In the U. S. and other societies, these ideas about gender were also racialized, applying only to white women. The same men who placed white women "on a pedestal" didn't hesitate to send enslaved women into the fields to perform the most difficult, physically demanding tasks.)

Even in the most progressive societies, women possess many characteristics of a minority group, especially a pattern of disadvantage based on group membership marked by visible characteristics. We consider women to be a distinct minority group. However, in keeping with our intersectional approach, we'll address women's and men's experiences *within* each racial or ethnic minority group, as well. As stressed in the intersectional approach, the experience of racial or ethnic minority group membership varies by gender (and class, etc.). Likewise, the way gender is experienced isn't the same for every racial or ethnic (or other) group. Therefore, some African American women may share common interests and experiences with white women and different interests and experiences compared to African American men. In other cases, those constellations of interests and experiences would probably change.

Those in power generally write about history from their own standpoint—ignoring, forgetting, or trivializing minority group experiences. For instance, slave owners for much of the history of slavery. Laws against education kept slaves illiterate, leaving few mechanisms for recording their thoughts or experiences. A more accurate picture of slavery has emerged only since the mid-20th century, when scholars started to reconstruct the experiences of enslaved Africans from nonwritten documentation (such as oral traditions, including folklore and songs) and from physical artifacts (such as quilts, pottery, and religious objects; e.g., see Fennell, 2013; Levine, 1977).

Despite these advances, the experiences of women minorities are much less well known and documented than men's. One important trend in contemporary scholarship is to correct this skewed focus by systematically incorporating gender as a vital factor for understanding minority group experiences (Baca Zinn & Thornton Dill, 1994; Espiritu, 1996).

The Social Construction of Gender

Social scientists see race as a social construction created under certain historical circumstances (e.g., slavery) when it was needed to justify the unequal treatment of nonwhite groups. What about gender? Have socially created ideas enabled and rationalized men's higher status and their easier access to power, prestige, and property? Figure 1.7 shows that every nation has some degree of gender inequality—though it varies a lot. Does that inequality result from popular ideas about gender? For example, are boys and men naturally more aggressive, competitive and independent, and girls and women naturally more cooperative, helpful, and fragile? Where do these ideas come from? If gender isn't a social construction, why do ideas about what girls/women and boy/men are like vary across time (e.g., 1400, 1776, 2019) and place (e.g., China, Afghanistan, Sweden)? Why do ideas about what they should and shouldn't do vary? And why does gender inequality vary? Many people look to the role of biology when explaining such variation. Yet, if people's biology (e.g., chromosomes, hormones) is fairly constant across time and location, wouldn't gender be as well? Let's dig a bit deeper.

First, the traits people commonly see as typical for women or men aren't disconnected, separate categories. Every person has them, to some degree. To the extent that gender differences exist at all, they are manifested not in absolutes but in averages, tendencies, and probabilities. Many people consider aggressiveness a masculine characteristic, but some women are more aggressive than some men. As with race, research shows that there is more variation *within* categories (e.g., all women, all men) than between them—a finding that seriously undermines the view that gender differences are biological (Basow, as cited in Rosenblum & Travis, 2002).

Second, gender as a social construction is illustrated by the fact that what people think is "appropriate" behavior for women and men varies over time and from society to society. The behavior people expected from a woman in Victorian England isn't the same as those for women in 21st-century America. Likewise, the gender norms for men in 500 CE China are different from those in Puritan America. This variability makes it difficult to argue that the differences between the genders are hardwired in the genetic code; if they were, these variations wouldn't exist.

Third, the relationship between subsistence technology and gender inequality illustrates the social nature of gender norms. As noted previously, humans evolved in East Africa and relied on hunting and gathering to meet their basic needs. Our distant ancestors lived in small, nomadic bands that relied on cooperation and sharing for survival. Societies at this level of development typically divided adult labor by gender (often men hunting, women gathering). Because everyone's work was crucial to survival, gender inequality was minimal (Dyble et al., 2015). Women's subordination seems to have emerged with settled agricultural communities, the first of which appeared about 10,000 years ago in what is now the Middle East. People in preindustrial farming communities didn't roam, and people could accumulate (and store) wealth (see Dyble et al., 2015). Survival in these societies required the combined labor of many people; thus, large families were valued. Women became consigned to domestic duties, especially having and raising children. Because the infant mortality rate in these societies was high (approximately 50% or more), women spent much of their lives confined to their homes, pregnant or nursing, far removed from the possibility of participating in other extra-domestic life, such as contending for community leadership roles.

Industrialization and urbanization, linked processes that began in the mid-1700s in Great Britain, changed the cost–benefit ratios of childbearing. As people moved to cities, the expense of having children rose, and work increasingly required education and literacy—both possible for women and men. Thus, gender inequality probably reached its peak in preindustrial agrarian societies and declined as societies industrialized. As women increasingly participated in life outside of their homes, they gathered additional resources (e.g., income, networks) that put them on more level footing with men. Thus, it's probably not surprising that the push for gender equality is associated with industrial societies and that gender equality is highest in industrial and postindustrial societies (see Figure 1.7).

Researchers continue to explore the links between biology and gender (e.g., see Hopcroft, 2009; Huber, 2007; Udry, 2000). However, at its core, gender is primarily social, not biological (Booth, Granger, Mazur, & Kivligham, 2006, pp. 167–191; see also Ridgeway, 2011, pp. 18–23). Gender, like race, is a social construction, especially when people treat the supposed differences between men and women as categorical, natural, and fixed and then use those ideas to deny opportunity and equality to women.

QUESTIONS FOR REFLECTION

6. In what ways do gender and race exist apart from people's perceptions of them? How are these constructs similar? Different?

KEY CONCEPTS IN DOMINANT–MINORITY RELATIONS

When people discuss issues such as dominant–minority group relations, the discussion often turns to matters of prejudice and discrimination. This section introduces and defines four concepts to help you understand dominant–minority relations in the United States.

This book addresses how individuals from different groups interact and how groups interact with each other. Thus, we need to distinguish between what is true for individuals (the more psychological level of analysis) and what is true for groups or society (the sociological level of analysis). Additionally, it's helpful to connect these levels of analysis.

At the individual level, what people *think* and *feel* about other groups may differ from how they *behave* toward members of another group. A person might express negative feelings about other groups in private but deal fairly with group members in face-to-face interactions. Groups and entire societies may display similar inconsistencies. A society may express support for equality in its official documents (e.g., laws) while simultaneously treating minority groups in unfair, destructive ways. For example, contrast the commitment to equality stated in the Declaration of Independence ("All men are created equal") and the actual treatment of enslaved Africans, Anglo American women, and Native Americans at that time.

At the individual level, social scientists refer to the thinking/feeling part of this dichotomy as *prejudice* and the doing part as *discrimination*. At the group level, the term **ideological racism** describes the thinking/feeling dimension and **institutional discrimination** describes the doing dimension. Table 1.1 depicts the differences among these four concepts.

TABLE 1.1 ■ Four Concepts in Dominant–Minority Relations		
	Level of Analysis	
Dimension	**Individual**	**Group or Societal**
Thinking/feeling	Prejudice	Ideological racism
Doing	Discrimination	Institutional discrimination

Applying Concepts

We list real and hypothetical events below. Identify which are examples of cognitive prejudice, affective prejudice, individual discrimination, ideological racism, or institutional discrimination, and briefly explain your reasoning. Some incidents may include elements that reflect more than one concept.

	Incident	Concept	Explanation
1	After learning that a Hispanic family is purchasing the house next door, Mrs. James, a white American, says, "Well, at least they're not black."		
2	Three friends put bacon on the door of a mosque. They spray-paint "Muslims not wanted," too.		
3	The U.S. Secret Service settles a class-action lawsuit with black agents for repeatedly passing them over for promotions.		
4	Tom Smith, the CEO of Smith's Bank, didn't hire Judy Washington as the head of his human resources department. He worries that she might focus too much on family issues. Although he thinks she seems like a "tough broad," he fears she might get "too emotional" in decision making and in carrying out difficult tasks like firing people.		
5	A task force investigation finds that the city police disproportionately focused on African Americans. African Americans make up about one third of the city's population but were 72% of all investigative street stops. Further, 74% of the 404 people shot by the police between 2008 and 2015 were black.		
6	Professor Jones is talking with Professor Jimenez and says, "I just can't stand it anymore. Students today are so lazy. They won't read for class. They don't seem to care about their homework. They don't want to listen in class—they just want to text all day. It's disgusting."		

See the Answers to Applying Concepts section toward the end of the chapter.

Prejudice

Prejudice is the tendency of an individual to think about some groups in negative ways, to attach negative emotions to those groups, and to prejudge individuals based on their group memberships. Individual prejudice has two aspects: **cognitive prejudice**, or the thinking aspect, and **affective prejudice**, or the feeling part. A prejudiced person thinks about other groups in terms of **stereotypes** (cognitive prejudice), generalizations that they think are true for all group members. Examples of familiar stereotypes include notions such as "women are emotional," "Jews are stingy," "blacks are lazy," and "the Irish are drunks." A prejudiced person also experiences negative emotional responses to other groups (affective prejudice), including contempt, disgust, arrogance, and hatred.

People vary in their levels of prejudice, and levels of prejudice vary in the same person from one time to another and from one group to another. We can say that people are prejudiced to the extent that they use stereotypes in their thinking about other groups or have negative emotional reactions to other groups.

The two dimensions of prejudice are highly correlated with each other; however, they are distinct and separate aspects of prejudice and can vary independently. One person may think entirely in stereotypes but feel no particular negative emotional response to any group. Another person may feel a strong aversion toward a group but be unable to articulate a clear or detailed stereotype of that group.

Individual prejudice, like all aspects of society, evolves and changes. Historically, Americans' prejudice was strongly felt, overtly expressed, and laced with detailed stereotypes. Overt forms declined after the civil rights era of the 1950s and 1960s but didn't disappear; however, vast numbers of Americans came to view them as problematic. In modern societies that emphasize mutual respect and tolerance, people tend to express prejudice in subtle, indirect ways. Prejudice might manifest in language that functions as a kind of code (for instance, when people associate "welfare cheats" or criminality with certain minority groups). We'll explore modern forms of prejudice later, but we need to be clear that you should not mistake the general decline of blatant prejudice against minority groups in modern society for its disappearance. As you'll see, many of the traditional forms have reasserted themselves in recent years.

Causes of Prejudice

Prejudice is a complex phenomenon with multiple causes and manifestations. In this section, we'll take a macrosociological approach and examine theories about prejudice that are related to culture, social structure, and group relationships.

Group Competition and the Origins of Prejudice Every form of prejudice—even the most ancient—started at some specific point in history. If we go back far enough in time, we can find a moment that predates antiblack prejudice, anti-Semitism, negative stereotypes about Native Americans or Hispanic Americans, or antipathy against Asian Americans. What sorts of conditions create prejudice?

The single most important factor in the origin of prejudice is competition between groups. Prejudice originates in the heat of that competition and is used to justify and rationalize the privileged status of the winning group. If we go back far enough, we can find an instance when one group successfully dominates, takes resources from, or eliminates a perceived threat by another group. The successful group becomes the dominant group, and the other becomes the minority group.

Why is group competition associated with the emergence of prejudice? Typically, prejudice doesn't cause group competition; it results from it. Prejudice functions to mobilize emotional energy for conflict, justify rejection and attack, and rationalize the structures of domination that result from the competition, such as slavery or segregation. Groups react to the competition and threat presented by other groups with hostility and by stereotyping those groups. Prejudice emerges from the resulting high levels of emotion, which can persist for years (even centuries) after the end of the original conflict.

Research shows a relationship between prejudice and competition in many settings and situations from labor strikes to international war to social psychology labs. In future chapters, you'll learn about the role of prejudice during the creation of slavery in America, as a reaction to periods of high immigration, and as an accompaniment to many forms of group competition. To illustrate our point about group competition and prejudice, we'll examine a classic experiment—The Robber's Cave—conducted in the 1950s at a summer camp for 11- and 12-year-old boys.

Social psychologist Muzafer Sherif divided the campers into two groups: the Rattlers and the Eagles (Sherif, Harvey, White, Hood, & Sherif, 1961). The groups lived in different cabins, and the staff continually pitted them against each other in a wide range of activities. They set up games, sports, and even housekeeping chores in a competitive way so that winners would earn individual and group prizes. As the competition intensified, the boys in each group developed and expressed negative feelings (prejudice) against the other group. Competition and prejudicial feelings grew intense and were expressed in name-calling, taunting, and raids on the other group and in the burning of each other's flags.

In another phase of the experiment, Sherif attempted to reduce the boys' negative feelings for one another by bringing the campers together in various pleasant situations featuring food, movies, and other rewards. The rival groups didn't get along and tensions remained high. Then, Sherif created situations that required the rival groups to work together. For example, the researchers sabotaged some plumbing to create a drinking water "emergency." Camp staff blamed "vandals." Both groups had to work together to fix the problem, intergroup prejudice declined, and eventually, they formed friendships across groups.

In the experiment, as in real group relationships, prejudice arose to mobilize feelings and to justify the rejection and attacks (verbal and physical) against the out-group. When group competition was replaced by cooperation, the levels of prejudice eventually disappeared. This suggests that competition causes prejudice, not the other way around.

However, we must be cautious in generalizing from the Robber's Cave experiment. Researchers conducted the experiment in an artificial environment with young boys (all white) who had no earlier acquaintance with one another and no history of grievances or animosity. Thus, these results may be only partially generalizable to group conflicts in the real world. Nonetheless, Robber's Cave illustrates a fundamental connection between group competition and prejudice that we'll discuss in future chapters. Competition and the desire to protect resources and status, and to defend against threats from other groups—perceived or real—are the primary motivations for the creation of prejudice and structures of inequality that benefit the dominant group.

Culture, Socialization, and the Persistence of Prejudice Prejudice originates in group competition but it can persist in intense ways, long after the episode that sparked it has faded from memory. How does prejudice persist through time?

In his classic analysis of American race relations, *An American Dilemma* (1944/1962), Swedish economist Gunnar Myrdal argued that prejudice is perpetuated over time by a **vicious cycle** (see Figure 1.8). First, during the contact situation, the dominant group uses its power (e.g., guns, iron shackles, the law) to force the minority group into an inferior social position (e.g., slaves). Second, dominant group members create ways of thinking that justify the racial hierarchy. (Prejudice at the individual level and racist ideology at the societal level.) Third, everyday observation of the minority group's inferior status reinforces ideas about the group's inferiority. For example, white Europeans enslaved Africans. Slaves, as the minority group, became (and stayed) impoverished due to their position at the bottom of the racial hierarchy. The widely accepted belief in slaves' inferiority allowed dominant group members to continue their discriminatory treatment. This discrimination reinforced slaves' inferior status, which continued to validate the prejudice and racism and, in turn, justified further discrimination. Over several generations, a stable, internally reinforced system of racial inferiority becomes an integral, seemingly natural, and (at least for the dominant group) accepted part of everyday life.

Culture can be slow to change, and once created, prejudice will be sustained over time just like any set of attitudes, values, and beliefs. Future generations will learn prejudice in the same way and for the same reasons they learn any other aspect of their culture. Thus, prejudice and racism come to us through our cultural heritage as a package of stereotypes, emotions, and other ideas. We learn which groups are "good" and which are "bad" in the same way we learn table manners and religious beliefs (Pettigrew, 1958; Pettigrew, 1971, p. 137; Simpson & Yinger, 1985, pp. 107–108). When prejudice is part of the cultural heritage, individuals learn to think and feel negatively toward other groups as a routine part of **socialization**, even if that socialization doesn't seem overt or intended. Much of the prejudice expressed by Americans—and by the people of other societies—is the typical result of routine socialization in families, communities, and societies that are, to some degree, racist. Given our long history of intense racial and ethnic conflict, it probably isn't surprising that Americans continue to manifest stereotypical ideas about and resentment toward other groups.

FIGURE 1.8 ■ Myrdal's Vicious Cycle

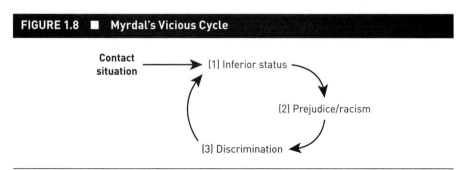

Source: Adapted from Myrdal (1944/1962).

QUESTIONS FOR REFLECTION

7. How are the ideas in this section sociological? How do they differ from more psychological theories of prejudice and discrimination?

The Development of Prejudice in Children Children learn prejudice through socialization. Children become aware of group differences (e.g., black vs. white) at an early age, even as early as six months (Katz, 2003, p. 898). By age three or younger, they recognize the significance and the permanence of racial groups in society and can accurately classify people based on skin color and other cues (Brown, 1995, pp. 121–136; Katz, 1976, p. 126). Once children mentally establish the racial categories, they begin learning the attitudes and stereotypes associated with those groups, and affective and cognitive prejudice begin to grow at an early age.

Children can acquire prejudice even when parents and other caregivers don't teach it overtly or directly. Adults control the socialization process and valuable resources (food, shelter, praise), and children are motivated to seek their approval and conform to their expectations (at least in the early years). Additionally, children face strong pressure to learn and internalize the perceptions of the older generation, and even a casual comment or an overheard remark can establish or reinforce negative beliefs or feelings about members of other groups (Ashmore & DelBoca, 1976). Some people say that racial attitudes are "caught and not taught." That is, children don't need to be directly instructed about presumed minority group characteristics.

Additionally, research shows that children are actively engaged in their learning and that their levels of prejudice reflect their changing intellectual capabilities. Children as young as five to six months old can make some simple distinctions (e.g., by gender or race) between categories of people. The fact that this capability emerges so early in life suggests that it isn't simply a response to adult teaching. "Adults use categories to simplify and make sense of their environment; apparently children do the same" (Brown, 1995, p. 126). Gross, simplistic distinctions between people may help very young children organize and understand the world around them. The need for such primitive categorizations may decline as the child becomes more experienced in life and more sophisticated in their thinking. Doyle and Aboud (1995), for example, found that prejudice was highest for younger children and actually decreased between kindergarten and the third grade. The decline was related to increased awareness of racial similarities (and differences) and diverse perspectives on race (see also Black-Gutman & Hickson, 1996; Bronson & Merryman, 2009; Brown, 1995, pp. 149–159; Cristol & Gimbert, 2008; Powlishta, Serbin, Doyle, & White, 1994; Van Ausdale & Feagin, 2001). Thus, changing levels of prejudice in children may reflect an interaction between children's changing mental capacities and their environment rather than a simple or straightforward learning of racist cultural beliefs or values.

Social Distance Scales

Further evidence for the cultural nature of prejudice is provided by research on the concept of **social distance**, which is related to prejudice but isn't quite the same thing. Social distance is the degree of intimacy that a person is willing to accept in their relations with members of other groups. On this scale, the most intimate relationship would be close kinship, and the most distant relationship would be exclusion from the country. The seven degrees of social distance, as specified by Emory Bogardus (1933), the inventor of the scale, are as follows:

1. To close kinship by marriage

2. To my club as personal chums

3. To my street as neighbors

4. To employment in my occupation

5. To citizenship in my country

6. As visitors only to my country

7. Would exclude from my country

Research using social distance scales demonstrates that Americans rank other groups in similar ways across time and space. The consistency indicates a common frame of reference or set of perceptions, a continuity of vision possible only if perceptions have been standardized by socialization in a common culture.

Applying Concepts

Do you have a sense of social distance from other groups? Has it changed over the past 10 years? Use the seven degrees of social distance to show the level of intimacy you would feel comfortable sharing with members of each of the groups listed below. Also, estimate the degree of social distance you would have felt for each group 10 years ago.

How did you acquire your sense of social distance? Was it from your family or community, or is it based on actual experience with members of these groups? Do you think it was "caught and not taught"? Why has it changed over the past 10 years (if it has)?

Group	Your Social Distance Score Today	Your Social Distance Score 10 Years Ago
White Americans		
Irish		

(Continued)

(Continued)

Group	Your Social Distance Score Today	Your Social Distance Score 10 Years Ago
Russians		
Italians		
Native Americans		
Jews		
Mexicans		
African Americans		
Chinese		
Muslims		

Turn to Table 1.2 to see the group rankings over time.

Table 1.2 presents some results of administrations of the scale to samples of Americans from 1926 to 2011. The groups are listed by the rank order of their scores for 1926. In that year, the sample expressed the least social distance from the English and the most distance from Asian Indians. While the average social distance score for the English was 1.02, indicating virtually no sense of distance, the average score for Asian Indians was 3.91, indicating a distance between "to my street as neighbors" to "to employment in my occupation."

First, as you read Table 1.2, note the stability in the rankings. The actual *scores* (not shown) generally decrease from decade to decade, indicating less social distance and presumably a decline in prejudice over the years. The group rankings, however, tend to be consistently the same. Considering the changes that America experienced between 1926 and 2011 (e.g., the Great Depression; World War II, the Korean War, and the Cold War with the former Soviet Union; the civil rights movement; the resumption of large-scale immigration; the 9/11 attacks), this overall continuity in group rankings is remarkable.

Second, note the order of the ranking: people rank groups with origins in Northern and Western Europe the highest, followed by groups from Southern and Eastern Europe. They rank racial minorities at the bottom. These preferences reflect the relative status of these groups in the U.S. hierarchy of racial and ethnic groups. The rankings also reflect the relative amount of exploitation and prejudice directed at each group over the course of U.S. history.

Finally, note how the relative positions of some groups change with international and domestic relations. For example, rankings for the Japanese and Germans fell at the end of World War II (1946). Comparing 1977 with 1946, Russians fell and Japanese rose, reflecting changing patterns of alliance and enmity in the global system of societies.

TABLE 1.2 ■ Social Distance Scores of Selected Groups (Ranks for Each Year)			
Group	**1926**	**1946**	**1977**	**2011**
English (British)	1	3	2	4
Americans (white)	2	1	1	1
Canadians	3	2	3	3
Irish	5	4	7	5
Germans	7	10	11	8
Russians	13	13	29	20
Italians	14	16	5	2
Poles	15	14	18	14
Native Americans	18	20	10	12
Jews	19	19	15	11
Mexicans	21	24	26	25
Japanese	22	30	25	22
Filipinos	23	23	24	16
African Americans	24	29	17	9
Turks	25	25	28	—
Chinese	26	21	23	17
Koreans	27	27	30	24
Asian Indians	28	28	27	26
Vietnamese	—	—	—	28
Muslims	—	—	—	29
Arabs	—	—	—	30
Mean (all scores)	2.14	2.12	1.93	1.68
Range	2.85	2.57	1.38	1.08

Sources: 1926–1977 (Smith & Dempsey, 1983, p. 588); 2011 (Parrillo & Donoghue, 2013).

Note: Values in the table are ranks for that year. For example, the Irish were ranked fifth of 28 groups in 1926, rose to fourth of 30 in 1946, and so forth. To conserve space, some groups and ranks have been eliminated.

The dramatic rise of African Americans in 2011 may reflect declining levels of overt prejudice in American society, and the low rankings of Muslims and Arabs in 2011 may reflect negative feelings related to the terrorist attacks on September 11, 2001.

Although these patterns of social distance scores support the general point that prejudice is cultural, this body of research has some important limitations. The respondents were college students from a variety of campuses, not representative samples of the population, and the differences in scores between groups are sometimes very small.

Still, the stability of the patterns can't be ignored: the top two or three groups are always Northern European, Poles and Jews are always ranked in the middle third of the groups, and Koreans and Japanese always fall in the bottom third. African Americans and Native Americans were ranked toward the bottom until the most recent rankings.

How do we explain the consistency of group rankings from the 1920s to 2011? The stability strongly suggests that Americans view these groups through the same culturally shaped lens. A sense of social distance, a perception of some groups as higher or better than others, is part of the cultural package of intergroup prejudices we acquire through socialization in America. The social distance patterns illustrate the power of culture to shape individual perceptions and preferences and attest to the fundamentally racist nature of American culture.

Modern Racism: A New Face of Prejudice?

It is clear from national headlines (e.g., the white supremacist rallies in Charlottesville, Virginia in 2017 and Portland, Oregon in 2018) that traditional, blatant prejudice is still very much a part of American society. At the same time, some forms of prejudice are changing and evolving, especially those found in mainstream society and "polite company." Public opinion polls show that, for most Americans, the willingness to express the blunt, overt feelings and ideas of traditional prejudice has declined in recent decades. Some might say that this decline means that individual prejudice is becoming less of a problem in America. However, a growing body of research argues that the apparent decline is misleading and that, for many Americans, prejudice has evolved into a subtler but just as consequential form called **modern racism**, *symbolic racism*, and *color-blind racism*. This new form is a more indirect and complex way of thinking or expressing negative feelings about minority groups or about one's opposition to changes in dominant–minority relations (see Bobo, 1988, 2001; Bobo, Charles, Krysan, & Simmons, 2012; Bonilla-Silva, 2001, 2006; Kinder & Sears, 1981; Kluegel & Smith, 1982; McConahy, 1986; Sears, 1988; for a review, see Quillian, 2006).

People who are prejudiced in these ways typically reject "old-fashioned" blatant prejudice and the traditional view that racial inferiority is innate or biological. They often proclaim their allegiance to the ideals of equality of opportunity and treatment for all. Analysis of their thinking, however, reveals prejudice beneath the surface of these egalitarian sentiments, powerfully influencing their views of racial issues.

Sociologist Eduardo Bonilla-Silva (2006, p. 28), one of the leading researchers in this area, argues that people express the new form of prejudice in seemingly neutral language or objective terms. For example, the modern racist might attribute the underrepresentation of people of color in high-status positions to cultural rather than biological factors ("*they* don't emphasize education enough") or explain continuing residential and school segregation by the "natural" choices people make ("*they* would rather be with their own kind"). This kind of thinking rationalizes the status quo and permits dominant group members to live in segregated neighborhoods and send their children to segregated schools without guilt or hesitation. It obscures the myriad, not-so-subtle social forces that created segregated schools, neighborhoods, and other manifestations of racial inequality in the first place and maintains them in the present (e.g., see Satter, 2009). This framework permits people to ignore the social, political, and economic realities that actually create and sustain racial inequality and, by this **selective perception**, to support a kind of racism without appearing to be a racist. We'll return to the subject of modern racism frequently, especially in Chapter 5.

The Sociology of Individual Prejudice

The sociological approach to prejudice stresses several points. Competition between groups results in prejudice. Prejudicial thinking helps people mobilize feelings and emotional energy for competition and rationalize the creation of minority group status. Then, it becomes a part of the cultural heritage passed on to later generations as part of their taken-for-granted world, where it helps to shape their perceptions and reinforces the group inferiority that created it in the first place. Although it has evolved into a subtler form, prejudice remains an important force in American society and will continue as long as there are patterns of inequality and systems of group privilege and disadvantage that require justification by the dominant group.

Discrimination

Discrimination is the unequal treatment of people based on their group membership. For example, an employer might not hire someone because they are African American (or Puerto Rican, Jewish, Chinese, etc.). If the unequal treatment is based on the individual's group membership (e.g., race/ethnicity, gender, sexual orientation, religion), the act is discriminatory. Just as the cognitive and affective aspects of prejudice can be independent, discrimination and prejudice don't necessarily occur together. Even highly prejudiced individuals may not act on their negative thoughts or feelings. In social settings regulated by strong egalitarian codes or laws (e.g., restaurants and other public facilities), people who are highly bigoted in their private thoughts and feelings may follow the norms in public. However, when people approve of prejudice in social situations, such support can produce discrimination from otherwise unprejudiced individuals. In the southern U. S. during the height of segregation and in South Africa during the period of state-sanctioned racial inequality called *apartheid*, it was usual and customary for whites to treat blacks in discriminatory ways. Regardless of individuals' actual level of prejudice, they faced strong social pressure to conform to the official forms of racial superiority and discrimination.

Ideological Racism

Ideological racism is a belief system asserting that a particular group is inferior; it is the group or societal equivalent of individual prejudice. Members of the dominant group use ideological racism to legitimize or rationalize the unequal status of minority groups. Through the process of socialization, such ideas pass from generation to generation, becoming incorporated into the society's culture. It exists separately from the individuals who inhabit the society (Andersen, 1993, p. 75; See & Wilson, 1988, p. 227). An example of a racist ideology is the elaborate system of beliefs and ideas that attempted to justify slavery in the American South. Whites explained their exploitation of slaves in terms of the supposed innate racial inferiority of blacks and the superiority of whites.

In later chapters, we'll explore the relationship between individual prejudice and racist ideologies at the societal level. For now, we'll make what may be an obvious point: People socialized into societies with strong racist ideologies are likely to internalize those ideas and be highly prejudiced; for example, a high level of personal prejudice existed among whites in the antebellum American South or in other highly racist societies, such as in South Africa under apartheid. Yet, ideological racism and individual prejudice are different phenomena with different causes and different locations in the society. Racism isn't a prerequisite for prejudice and prejudice can exist in the absence of racist ideology.

Institutional Discrimination

Institutional discrimination is the societal equivalent of individual discrimination. It refers to a pattern of unequal treatment, based on group membership, built into the daily operations of society, whether or not it is consciously intended. Public schools, the criminal justice system, and political and economic institutions can operate in ways that put members of some groups at a disadvantage.

Institutional discrimination can be obvious and overt. For many years following the American Civil War, practices such as poll taxes and rigged literacy tests (designed to ensure failure) prevented African Americans in the South from voting. Well into the 1960s, elections and elected offices in the South were restricted to whites only. The purpose of this blatant pattern of institutional discrimination was widely understood by African American and white southerners alike: It existed to disenfranchise the African American community and to keep it politically powerless (Dollard, 1937).

At other times, institutional discrimination may operate subtly and without conscious intent. For example, if schools use biased aptitude tests to determine which students get to take college preparatory courses, and if such tests favor the dominant group, then the outcomes are discriminatory—even if everyone involved sincerely believes that they are merely applying objective criteria in a rational way. If a decision-making process has unequal consequences for dominant and minority groups, institutional discrimination may well be at work.

Although individuals may implement and enforce a particular discriminatory policy, it is better to recognize it as an aspect of the institution as a whole. For example, election officials in the South during segregation didn't (and public school administrators today don't) have to be personally prejudiced to implement discriminatory policies.

However, a major thesis of this book is that racist ideologies and institutional discrimination are created to sustain the stratification system. Widespread institutional discrimination maintains the relative advantage of the dominant group. Members of the dominant group who are socialized into communities with strong racist ideologies and a great deal of institutional discrimination are likely to be personally prejudiced and to routinely engage in acts of individual discrimination. The mutually reinforcing patterns of prejudice, racism, and discrimination on the individual and institutional levels preserve the respective positions of dominant and minority groups over time.

Institutional discrimination is one way that members of a minority group can be denied access to goods and services, opportunities, and rights (such as voting). That is, institutional discrimination helps sustain and reinforce the unequal positions of racial and ethnic groups in the stratification system.

A GLOBAL PERSPECTIVE

In future chapters, we'll discuss additional concepts and theories and apply those ideas to minority groups in the United States. However, it is important to expand our perspective beyond our country. Therefore, we'll also apply our ideas to the histories and experiences of other peoples and places. If the ideas and concepts developed in this book can help us make sense of intergroup relations around the world, we'll have some assurance that they have some general applicability and that the dynamics of intergroup relations in the U. S. aren't unique.

On another level, we must also take into account how economic, social, and political forces beyond our borders shape group relations in the United States. As you'll see, American society can't be understood in isolation because it is part of the global system of societies. Now, more than ever, we must systematically analyze the complex interconnections between the domestic and the international, particularly with respect to immigration issues. The next section explores one connection between the global and the local.

FOCUS ON CONTEMPORARY ISSUES
IMMIGRATION AND GLOBALIZATION

Immigration is a major concern in our society today, and we'll address the issue in the pages to come. Here, we'll point out that immigration is a global phenomenon that affects virtually every nation in the world. About 258 million people—about 3.4% of the world's population—live outside their countries of birth, and the number of migrants has increased steadily over the past several decades (United Nations Department of Economic and Social Affairs, 2018). Figure 1.9 depicts the major population movement from 1990 to 2000 and demonstrates the global nature of immigration. Note that Western Europe is a major destination for immigrants, as is the United States.

What has caused this massive population movement? One very important underlying cause is *globalization*, or the increasing

(Continued)

(Continued)

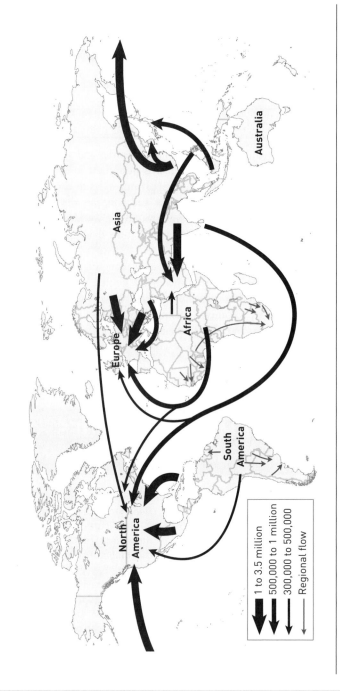

FIGURE 1.9 ■ Major Global Migration Flows, 1990–2000

Source: Adapted from *Stalker's Guide to Migration*, Peter Stalker; and World Map: Global Migration, La Documentation Francaise.

interconnectedness of people, groups, organizations, and nations. This process is complex and multidimensional, but perhaps the most powerful dimension of globalization—especially for understanding contemporary immigration—is economics and the movement of jobs and opportunity from place to place. People flow from areas of lower opportunity to areas with greater opportunity.

To illustrate, consider the southern border of the United States. For the past several decades, there's been an influx of people from Mexico and Central America, and the presence of these newcomers has generated a great deal of emotional and political heat, especially because many of these migrants are undocumented.

Some Americans see these newcomers as threats to traditional American culture and the English language, and others associate them with crime, violence, and drug smuggling. Others see them simply as people trying to survive as best they can, desperate to support themselves and their families. Few, however, see these immigrants as the human consequences of the economic globalization of the world.

What is the connection between globalization and this immigrant stream? The population pressure on the southern border has been in large part a result of the North American Free Trade Agreement (NAFTA), implemented in 1994. NAFTA united the three North American nations in a single trading bloc—economically globalizing the region—and permitted goods and capital (but not people) to move freely between Canada, the U. S., and Mexico.

Among many other consequences, NAFTA opened Mexico to the importation of food products produced at very low cost by the giant agribusinesses of Canada and the United States. This cheap food (corn in particular) destroyed the livelihoods of many rural Mexicans and forced them to leave their villages in search of work. Millions pursued the only survival strategy that seemed at least remotely sensible: migration north. Even the worst job in the U. S. pays many times more than the average Mexican wage.

Even as NAFTA changed the economic landscape of North America, the U. S. became increasingly concerned with the security of its borders (especially after the terrorist attacks of September 11, 2001) and attempted to stem the flow of people, partly by building fences and increasing the size of the Border Patrol. The easier border crossings were quickly sealed, but this didn't stop the pressure from the south. Migrants moved to more difficult and dangerous crossing routes, including the deadly, forbidding Sonoran Desert in southern Arizona, resulting in an untold number of deaths on the border since the mid-1990s. Since then, border immigration has continued to be a concern for Americans. Most recently, President Donald Trump used this concern as one of his major appeals to voters in his 2016 election campaign. Figure 1.10 displays one estimate of recent deaths in southern Arizona, but these are only the bodies that were discovered. Some estimates put the true number at 10 deaths for every recovered corpse, suggesting that that approximately 30,000 (or more) migrants have died in Arizona since the mid-1990s. The relationship between NAFTA and immigration to the U.S. is only one aspect of a complex global relationship. Around the world, significant numbers of people are moving from less-industrialized nations to those with more-industrialized, affluent economies. The wealthy nations of Western Europe, including Germany, Ireland, France, and the Netherlands, are also receiving large numbers of immigrants, and many citizens of these nations are concerned about their jobs, communities, housing, and language—and the integrity of the national cultures changing in response. Many Americans have similar concerns. The world is changing, and contemporary immigration must be understood in terms of changes that affect many nations and, indeed, the entire global system of societies.

(Continued)

(Continued)

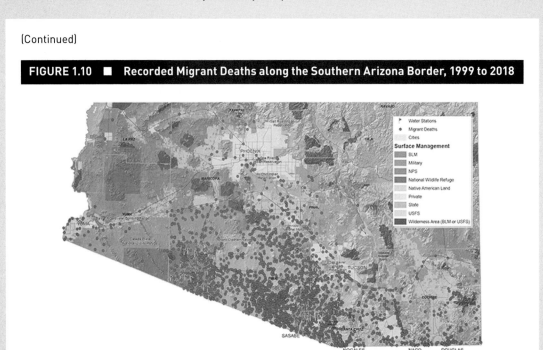

FIGURE 1.10 ■ Recorded Migrant Deaths along the Southern Arizona Border, 1999 to 2018

Source: Humane Borders (2018).

CONCLUSION

This chapter raises many questions. Our goal in writing this book is to teach you how to apply the sociological perspective to the world around you. With the concepts, theories, and body of research developed over the years, we can illuminate and clarify the issues. In many cases, we can identify approaches and ideas that are incorrect and those that hold promise. Sociology can't answer all questions, but it provides important research tools and ideas to help you think with greater depth and nuance about the issues facing our society.

Main Points

- The U. S. faces significant challenges in dominant–minority relationships. Although many historic grievances of minority groups remain unresolved, our society is becoming increasingly diverse, and with that diversity comes costs and benefits.

- The United States is a nation of immigrants, and many different groups and cultures are represented in its population.

- A minority group has five defining characteristics: a pattern of disadvantage, identification by some visible trait, awareness of its minority status, a membership determined at birth, and a tendency to marry within the group.

- A stratification system has three different dimensions (class, prestige, and power), and the nature of inequality in a society varies by its level of development. Minority groups and social class are correlated in complex ways.

- Race is a criterion widely used to identify minority group members. Scientists have largely discredited race as a biological concept. However, as a social category, race powerfully influences the way we think about one another and how we organize society.

- Minority groups are internally differentiated by social class, age, region of residence, and many other variables. Four crucial concepts for analyzing dominant–minority relations are prejudice, discrimination, ideological racism, and institutional discrimination.

Review Questions

1. What is the significance of Figure 1.1? What are some of the limitations and problems with the group names it uses? How are the group names social constructions? Does America's increasing diversity represent a threat, an opportunity, or a bit of both? Should we celebrate group differences, or should we strive for more unity and conformity? What are the advantages and disadvantages of stressing unity and conformity? Explain each answer in detail.

2. Wagley and Harris developed their five-part definition of a minority group with racial and ethnic minorities in mind. What other groups share those five characteristics? Does the definition apply to gays and lesbians? To religious groups such as Mormons or Muslims? To women? What about people who are left-handed or very overweight or very short? Consider all five characteristics.

3. What is a social construction? As social constructions, how are race and gender the same and how do they differ? What does it mean to say, "Gender becomes a social construction—like race—when it is treated as an unchanging, fixed difference and then used to deny opportunity and equality to women"? Consider the changing social constructions of race over time suggested by the Census Bureau categories. What do you make of them? Which categories make sense to you and why? How do those categories reflect particular meanings or ways of thinking at the time?

4. When analyzing dominant–minority relations, why is it important to take a global perspective? What can we learn by looking outside the U. S.? Besides immigration, how does globalization shape dominant–minority relations in America?

5. Explain the terms in Table 1.1. Cite an example of each from your own experiences, those of someone you know, or from current events, then compare them. How does *ideological racism* differ from *prejudice*? How does *institutional discrimination* differ from *individual discrimination*? Why is it important to analyze the societal level in addition to the individual level?

Group Discussion

Discuss two or three of the Review Questions (above) with your classmates. How are your answers similar? How are they different? Did you have any disagreements? How did you resolve them? What was the most important thing you learned from this chapter and from your group discussion?

Answers to Applying Concepts

	Concept	Explanation
1	Cognitive prejudice	Mrs. James seems to be thinking in terms of the traditional stereotype regarding the desirability of African Americans and Hispanics.
2	Discrimination	These hostile behaviors are targeted toward members of the local mosque because of their membership in the group, *Muslims*. The sign on the door is clear; the bacon reflects the rejection of Islamic guidelines against eating pork. It defiles the mosque.
3	Institutional discrimination	In this case, the Secret Service appears to have had a discriminatory policy. This discrimination reflects a broad pattern of treatment, not an individual action.
4	Cognitive prejudice	Mr. Smith uses stereotypical thinking about women as more interested in family issues than work-related ones a human resources director might need to address. Although he sees Ms. Washington as a "tough broad" he puts her in the category of "emotional women."
5	Institutional discrimination	This example comes from an analysis of Chicago policing that suggested a pattern of unequal treatment for blacks there. Institutional discrimination can be overt (e.g., laws requiring segregated schools). At other times, it's subtle. Behaviors that lead to inequality don't have to be intentional to be discriminatory.
6	Affective prejudice	Professor Jones is expressing strong feelings of anger and contempt for students. (She's also stereotyping them as lazy.)

Internet Learning Resources

SAGE edge™ offers teachers and students easy-to-use resources for review, study, and further exploration. See **http://edge.sagepub.com/diversity6e**

Notes

1. When we use *America* or *American*, we are referring to the United States of America and its citizens. We recognize that people living in North and South America are also Americans.

2. Schwartzbaum, S. E., & Thomas, A. J. (2008). *Dimensions of multicultural counseling.* Thousand Oaks, CA: SAGE, p. 92.

3. O'Brien, E. (2008). *The racial middle: Latinos and Asian Americans living beyond the racial divide.* New York: New York University Press, p. 45.

4. Personal communication, June 2009.

5. We sometimes use quotation marks to indicate social constructs or widely held beliefs about what is real or true. For example, "race" or "Caucasian."

6. LGBTQIA stands for lesbian, gay, bisexual, transgender, queer/questioning, intersex, and asexual/ally. We also use LGBT+ at times to include a broader range of people.

7. Boldfaced terms are defined in the glossary at the end of this book.

ASSIMILATION AND PLURALISM

From Immigrants to White Ethnics

We have room for but one flag, the American flag. . . . We have room for but one language and that is the English language, . . . and we have room for but one loyalty and that is a loyalty to the American people.

—Theodore Roosevelt, 26th president of
the United States, 1915

If we lose our language [Ojibwa] . . . I think, something more will be lost. . . . We will lose something personal. . . . We will lose our sense of ourselves and our culture. . . . We will lose beauty—the beauty of the particular, the beauty of the past and the intricacies of a language tailored for our space in the world. That Native American cultures are imperiled is important and not just to Indians. . . . When we lose cultures, we lose American plurality—the productive and lovely discomfort that true difference brings.

—David Treuer (2012, pp. 304–305)

Welcome to America. Now, speak English.

—Bumper sticker, 2017

In the United States, people speak 350 different languages, including more than 150 different Native American languages (U.S. Census Bureau, 2015c). Although most of these languages are spoken by small numbers of people, the sheer number of languages suggest the scope of contemporary American diversity.

Consider the quotations at the beginning of this chapter. What do you think? Does the range of languages and cultures they reflect create confusion and inefficiency in our society? Is there room for only one language, as Roosevelt suggested? Or does diversity enrich society? How much does it matter if a language disappears? Would we, as Treuer suggests, lose our sense of ourselves? Our culture, beauty, and the "productive and lovely discomfort" of difference?

Americans (and the citizens of other nations) must consider such questions as we address issues of inclusion and diversity. Should we encourage groups to retain their unique cultural heritage, including their language, or should we stress conformity? How have we addressed these issues before? To what effect? And how should we approach them in the future?

———————————————

In this chapter, we'll keep looking at the ways that ethnic and racial groups in America can relate to each other. We'll use two key sociological concepts, *assimilation* and *pluralism*, as the foundation of our discussion. In brief, **assimilation** is a process where formerly distinct and separate groups merge socially and come to share a common culture. As a society undergoes assimilation, group differences decrease. **Pluralism** exists when groups maintain their individual identities. In a pluralistic society, groups remain distinct, and their cultural and social differences persist over time.

In some ways, assimilation and pluralism are different processes, but they aren't mutually exclusive. They may occur together in various combinations within a society. Some racial or ethnic groups may assimilate while others maintain (or even increase) their differences. As we'll see in Part 3, virtually every minority group in America has, at any given time, some members who are assimilating and others who are preserving or reviving traditional cultures. Some Native American groups for example, are pluralistic. They live on or near reservations, are strongly connected to their heritage, practice the "old ways" as much as they can, and speak their native languages. Other Native Americans are mostly assimilated into the dominant society: They live in urban areas, speak English only, and know relatively little about their traditional cultures. Assimilation and pluralism are important forces in the everyday lives of Native Americans and most other minority group members.

American sociologists became concerned with these processes, especially assimilation, due to a massive migration from Europe to the United States that occurred between the 1820s and the 1920s. More than 31 million people crossed the Atlantic during this time, and a great deal of energy has been devoted to documenting, describing, and understanding the experiences of these immigrants and their descendants. These efforts have resulted in the development of a rich and complex body of research that seeks to explain how newcomers are incorporated into American society. We'll call this the *traditional* perspective.

This chapter begins with a consideration of the traditional perspective on assimilation and pluralism, and briefly examines other possible group relationships. Then we'll apply concepts and theories of the traditional perspective to European immigrants and their descendants, and we'll develop a model of American assimilation based on those experiences. We'll use this model of American assimilation throughout this book to analyze other minority group experiences.

Since the 1960s, the U. S. has experienced a second mass immigration. These newest immigrants differ in many ways from those who came earlier. Therefore, one important issue is whether the theories, concepts, and models based on the first mass immigration (from the 1820s to the 1920s) apply to this second wave. We'll briefly discuss some of these issues in this chapter and we'll explore them in detail in Part 3. Finally, we'll consider the implications of Chapters 1 and 2 for our exploration of intergroup relations throughout the rest of the book.

ASSIMILATION

We begin with the topic of assimilation because the emphasis in American group relations has historically focused on the goal of assimilation rather than pluralism (Lee, 2009). This section presents some of the most important sociological theories and concepts used to describe and analyze the assimilation of the 19th-century European immigrants into American society.

Types of Assimilation

Assimilation is a general term for a process that can take different forms. One type of assimilation is expressed in the metaphor of the **melting pot**—an idea based on smelting pots once used to melt different metals together to create something new. This type of assimilation occurs when diverse groups come together and create a new, unique society with a common culture. The idea of the melting pot suggests that American culture would change immigrants and, in turn, immigrants would change America (Thernstrom, 2004, p. 48). The popular view of assimilation emphasizes sharing and inclusion, sees assimilation positively, and suggests that American society would continuously be recreated as new immigrants arrived.

Although it is a powerful image, the melting pot metaphor doesn't accurately describe how assimilation occurred for American minority groups (Abrahamson, 1980, pp. 152–154). Some groups—especially racial minority groups—were largely excluded from the melting process, resulting in a melting process with a distinct Anglocentric flavor. As Schlesinger (1992) argues, "For better or worse, the white Anglo-Saxon Protestant tradition was for two centuries—and in crucial respects still is—the dominant influence on American culture and society" (p. 28).

Assimilation in the U. S. is more accurately called **Americanization** or **Anglo conformity** because the leaders of American society, with the support of the public, designed assimilation to maintain "American" ways—for example, the English language and the British-type institutional patterns created during the early years of American society.

President Roosevelt's quote that opened this chapter is a good example of the historic emphasis on Anglo conformity. Today, many Americans agree with Roosevelt. In a recent survey of almost 5,000 people, 72% of respondents—down from 77% when the survey was done in 2001—agreed that "it is essential that immigrants living in the U.S. learn to speak English." Jones (2013) shows that 58% of Hispanic Americans agreed with this statement (compared with 67% of blacks and 77% of whites). The apparent agreement between these groups may reflect different personal experiences and views of the world. For some whites, the response may mix prejudice against non-English speakers with support for Americanization. Hispanics, more likely to be recent immigrants, may have lower rates of agreement based on their direct—possibly challenging—experiences navigating the monolingual (English only) institutions of American society.

Under Anglo conformity, immigrant and minority groups are expected to adapt to Anglo American culture as a precondition of acceptance and access to better jobs, education, and other opportunities. This type of assimilation means that minority groups have had to give up their traditions and adopt Anglo American culture. Certainly, many groups and individuals were (and remain) eager to undergo Anglo conformity, even if it meant losing much or all of their heritage. For others, the emphasis on Americanization created conflict, anxiety, demoralization, and resentment. In Part 3, we consider how different minority groups have experienced and responded to the pressures of Anglo conformity.

The Traditional Perspective on Assimilation: Theories and Concepts

As noted earlier, the traditional perspective on assimilation emerged from research about European immigrants who came to America between the 1820s and the 1920s. Sociologists and other scholars working in this tradition made invaluable contributions, and their thinking is impressively complex and comprehensive. This doesn't mean, however, that they've exhausted the possibilities or answered (or asked) all the questions. Theorists working in the pluralist tradition and contemporary scholars studying the experiences of recent immigrants have questioned many aspects of traditional assimilation theory and have made a number of important contributions of their own.

Robert Park

Robert Park's research provided the foundation for many theories of assimilation. In the 1920s and 1930s, Park was one of a group of scholars who played a major role in establishing sociology as an academic discipline in the United States. Park felt that intergroup relations go through a predictable set of phases that he called a **race relations cycle**. When groups first come into contact (e.g., through immigration, conquest, or by other means), relations are conflictual and competitive. However, the process (*cycle*) eventually moves toward assimilation, or the "interpenetration and fusion" of groups (Park & Burgess, 1924, p. 735).

Park argued further that assimilation is inevitable in a democratic and industrial society. That is, in a political system based on democracy, fairness, and impartial justice, all groups should eventually secure equal treatment under the law. Additionally, in industrial societies, people's abilities and talents—rather than their ethnicity or race—will be the criteria used to judge them. Park believed that as the United States continued to modernize, urbanize, and industrialize, race and ethnicity would gradually lose their importance, allowing the boundaries between groups to eventually dissolve. The result, he thought, would be a more "rational" and unified society (see also Geschwender, 1978, pp. 19–32; Hirschman, 1983).

Social scientists have examined, analyzed, and criticized Park's conclusions for decades. One frequent criticism is that he didn't specify a time frame for the completion of assimilation. Therefore, his idea that assimilation is "inevitable" can't be tested. Until the exact time when assimilation is deemed complete, we won't know whether his theory is wrong or whether we haven't waited long enough. Another criticism of Park's theory is that he doesn't describe the assimilation process in much detail. How would assimilation proceed? How would everyday life change? Which aspects of the group would change first? What do you think about these criticisms?

Milton Gordon

Gordon sought to clarify some of the issues Park left unresolved. He made a major contribution to theories of assimilation in his book, *Assimilation in American Life* (1964). Gordon broke down the overall process of assimilation into seven subprocesses; we'll focus on the first three. Before considering these phases of assimilation, let's consider some new concepts.

Gordon makes a distinction between the cultural and the structural components of society. **Culture** encompasses all aspects of the way of life associated with a group of people. It includes language, religious and other beliefs, customs and rules of etiquette, and the values and ideas people use to organize their lives and interpret their existence. The **social structure**, or structural components of a society, includes networks of social relationships, groups, organizations, stratification systems, communities, and families. The social structure organizes societal labor and connects individuals to one another and to the society.

It's common in sociology to separate the social structure into primary and secondary sectors. The **primary sector** includes interpersonal relationships that are intimate and personal, such as families and groups of friends. Groups in the primary sector are small. The **secondary sector** consists of groups and organizations that are more public, task oriented, and impersonal. Organizations in the secondary sector are often very large and include businesses, factories, schools and colleges, and bureaucracies.

Now we can examine Gordon's earliest stages of assimilation (see Table 2.1).

1. **Acculturation** or **cultural assimilation**. Minority group members learn the dominant group's culture. For groups that immigrate to the United States, acculturation to the dominant Anglo American culture may include changes great and small, including learning English, changing eating habits, adopting new values and norms, and altering the spelling of family names.

2. **Integration** or **structural assimilation**. The minority group enters the society's social structure. Integration typically begins in the secondary sector and gradually moves into the primary sector. That is, before people can form friendships with members of other groups (integration into the primary sector),

TABLE 2.1 ■ Gordon's Stages of Assimilation	
Stage	**Process**
1. Acculturation	The minority group learns the culture of the dominant group, including language and values.
2. Integration (structural assimilation)	
a. At the secondary level	Minority group members enter the public institutions and organizations of the dominant society.
b. At the primary level	Minority group members enter the cliques, clubs, and friendship groups of the dominant society.
3. Intermarriage (marital assimilation)	Minority group members marry members of the dominant group on a large scale.

Source: Adapted from Gordon (1964, p. 71).

they must first become acquaintances. The initial contact between groups often occurs in public institutions such as schools and workplaces (integration into the secondary sector). The greater their integration into the secondary sector, the more equal the minority group will be to the dominant group in income, education, and occupational prestige. According to Gordon, once a group has entered the institutions and public sectors of the society, integration into the primary sector and the other stages of assimilation will follow inevitably (although not necessarily quickly). Measures of integration into the primary sector include the extent to which people have acquaintances, close friends, or neighbors from other groups.

3. **Intermarriage** or **marital assimilation**. When integration into the primary sector becomes substantial, the basis for Gordon's third stage of assimilation is established. People are most likely to select spouses from among their primary relations. Thus, in Gordon's view, primary structural integration typically comes before intermarriage.

Gordon argued that acculturation was a prerequisite for integration. Given the stress on Anglo conformity, a member of an immigrant or minority group wouldn't be able to compete for jobs or other opportunities in the secondary sector of the social structure until he or she had learned the dominant group's culture. Gordon recognized, however, that successful acculturation doesn't automatically ensure that a group will begin the integration phase. The dominant group may still exclude the minority group from its institutions and limit the opportunities available to the minority group. Gordon argued that "acculturation without integration" (or Americanization without equality) is a common situation in America for many minority groups, especially the racial minority groups.

In Gordon's theory, movement from acculturation to integration is the crucial step in the assimilation process. Once integration occurs, the other subprocesses would inevitably occur, although movement through the stages could be very slow. Gordon's idea that assimilation runs a certain course in a particular order echoes Park's ideas about the inevitability of the process.

Recent scholarship calls Gordon's conclusions about American assimilation into question. For example, the individual subprocesses that Gordon saw as occurring in a certain order can happen independently of one another (Yinger, 1985, p. 154). For example, a group may integrate before acculturating. Also, many researchers no longer think of the process of assimilation as necessarily linear or one-way (Greeley, 1974). Groups (or segments thereof) may reverse direction and become less assimilated over time by reviving parts of their traditional culture such as language or by revitalizing ethnic organizations or associations such as the Irish Social Club of Boston.

Ngo (2008), among others, offers critiques of assimilationist models such as Gordon's, suggesting that a one-size-fits-all, unidirectional (stage) approach to acculturation overlooks a number of important issues. Because immigrants differ, it's logical to think that their assimilation process would, too. An intersectional approach can help us understand this critique and the diversity of immigration experiences. For example, how might the immigration and assimilation process be for a 16-year-old, middle-class, heterosexual Catholic girl from Russia moving to Nashville, TN? How would that experience be different for a 40-year-old gay Muslim man from Nigeria? How would age, sexual orientation, religious affiliation, gender, and class shape not only their immigration process, but their lives?

Gans (1997, c.f. Ngo, 2008) observes that many early scholars of assimilation were white men who had little experience with immigrants or speaking foreign languages. Thus, their conceptualization of the assimilation process may reflect their own backgrounds and, perhaps, ethnocentric assumptions that assimilation into the dominant culture is desirable and completely possible. Critics also point out that such models ignore power dynamics, as if assimilation is merely a matter of one's effort and will. Do all immigrants have an equal chance at full assimilation? To what degree should we consider structural and cultural inequities that immigrants face? For example, can people fully assimilate if the host (or dominant) culture doesn't want them there? As we'll see in future chapters, the degree to which minority groups have assimilated into the dominant culture varies. Thus, it may be useful to keep these critiques in mind.

Some scholars suggest that idealizing assimilation models such as Gordon's—for example, by using it as the framework for national immigration policy—is akin to a form of colonization (see Ngo, 2008). They point out, also, that cultures influence one another. Because of such critiques, scholars have developed other models of assimilation. For example, Berry (1980) offers a bidimensional model and argues that we need to consider people's cultural identity and connection to or participation in the host society. When these two factors are taken into account, four possibilities result: (1) assimilation (which he defines as a desire to interact with the new culture and low interest in retaining one's ethnic heritage), (2) separation (immigrants maintain the culture of their heritage and reject the host culture), (3) integration (immigrants keep their cultural heritage but also adopt the receiving culture), and (4) marginalization (immigrants reject their cultural heritage and that of the host nation).

These critiques and others are useful to consider because as social life changes, our theoretical models for understanding them may need to change, too. Nonetheless,

Gordon's model continues to guide our understanding of the assimilation process. For example, research on contemporary immigrants often involves assessing their experiences in Gordon's terms (Alba & Nee, 1997). In fact, Gordon's model provides a major organizational framework for the case study chapters in Part 3.

Human Capital Theory

Why did some European immigrant groups acculturate and integrate more rapidly than others? Although not a theory of assimilation per se, **human capital theory** offers one possible answer to this question. This theory states that *status attainment*, or the level of success an individual achieves in society, is a direct result of educational attainment, personal values and skills, and other individual characteristics and abilities. From this perspective, education is an investment in human capital, similar to an investment a business might make in machinery or new technology. The greater the investment in a person's human capital, the higher the probability of success. Blau and Duncan (1967), in their pioneering statement of status attainment theory, found that even the relative advantage that comes from having a high-status father is largely mediated through education. That is, high levels of affluence and occupational prestige aren't so much due to being born into a privileged status as they are the result of the superior education that affluence makes possible.

Human capital theory answers questions about the differing pace of upward mobility for immigrant groups in terms of the resources and cultural characteristics of the group members, especially their levels of education and familiarity with English. From this perspective, people or groups who fail haven't tried hard enough, haven't made the right kinds of educational investments, or have values or habits that limit their ability to compete with others and move up the social class ladder.

Human capital theory is consistent with traditional American ideals. Both frame success as an individual phenomenon, a reward for hard work, sustained effort, and good character. Both assume that success is equally available to everyone and that the society distributes rewards and opportunities fairly. Both generally see assimilation as a highly desirable, benign process that blends diverse peoples and cultures into a strong, unified society. Thus, people or groups that resist Americanization or question its benefits are seen as threatening or illegitimate.

On one level, human capital theory is an important theory of success and upward mobility, and we'll use it occasionally to analyze the experiences of minority and immigrant groups. However, because human capital theory resonates with American "common sense" views of success and failure, people may use it uncritically, ignoring the flaws in the theory.

We'll offer a final judgment on the validity of human capital theory at the end of this book, but you should be aware of its major limitations. First, human capital theory is an incomplete explanation of the minority group experience because it doesn't take into account all the factors that affect mobility and assimilation. Second, its assumption that American society is equally open and fair to all groups is simply wrong. We'll illustrate this issue and point out other strengths and limitations of this perspective as we move through this book.

QUESTIONS FOR REFLECTION

1. What are the limitations of the melting-pot view of assimilation?

2. Why does Gordon place acculturation as the first step in the process of assimilation? Could one of the other stages occur first? Why or why not?

3. What does human capital theory leave out? In what ways is it consistent with American values?

PLURALISM

Sociological discussions of pluralism often begin with a consideration of Horace Kallen's work. Kallen argued that people shouldn't have to surrender their culture and traditions to become full participants in American society. He rejected the Anglo-conformist, assimilationist model and contended that the existence of separate ethnic groups, even with separate cultures, religions, and languages, was consistent with democracy and other core American values. In Gordon's terms, Kallen believed that integration and equality were possible without extensive acculturation and that American society could be a federation of diverse groups, a mosaic of harmonious and interdependent cultures and peoples (Kallen, 1915a, 1915b; see also Abrahamson, 1980; Gleason, 1980).

Assimilation has been such a powerful theme in U.S. history that in the decades following the publication of Kallen's analysis, support for pluralism was low. In recent decades, however, people's interest in pluralism and ethnic diversity has increased, in part because the assimilation that Park expected (and that many Americans assumed would happen) hasn't occurred. Perhaps we haven't waited long enough, but as the 21st century unfolds, social distinctions among the racial minority groups in America show few signs of disappearing. In fact, some people question whether assimilation is desirable or not. Additionally, white ethnicity hasn't disappeared, although it has weakened and changed form. We review some of these changes at the end of this chapter.

Another reason for the growing interest in pluralism is the increasing diversity of American society (see Figure 1.1). Controversies over issues such as "English only" language policies, bilingual education, and eligibility for government benefits for immigrants are common and often bitter. Many Americans feel that diversity or pluralism has exceeded acceptable limits and that the unity of the nation is at risk.

Finally, developments around the world have stimulated interest in pluralism. Several nation–states have reformed into smaller units based on language, culture, race, and ethnicity. Recent events in India, the Middle East, former Yugoslavia, the former USSR, Canada, and Africa (to mention a few) have provided dramatic and often tragic evidence of how ethnic identities and hostilities can persist for decades (or even centuries) of submergence and suppression in larger national units.

In contemporary debates, discussions of diversity and pluralism are often couched in the language of **multiculturalism**, a general term for programs and ideas that stress mutual respect for all groups and for the multiple heritages that have shaped the United States. Some aspects of multiculturalism are controversial and have evoked strong opposition. In many ways, however, these debates merely echo a recurring argument about the character of American society, a debate we'll revisit throughout this book.

Types of Pluralism

You can distinguish various types of pluralism by using some of the concepts introduced in the discussion of assimilation. **Cultural pluralism** exists when groups haven't acculturated and each maintains its own identity. The groups might speak different languages, practice different religions, and have different value systems. The groups are part of the same society and might live in adjacent areas, but in some ways, they live in different worlds. Many Native Americans are culturally pluralistic and are committed to preserving their traditional culture. The Amish, a religious community sometimes called the *Pennsylvania Dutch*, are a culturally pluralistic group, also. They are committed to a way of life organized around farming, and they maintain a culture and an institutional life that is largely separate from the dominant culture (see Hostetler, 1980; Kephart & Zellner, 1994; Kraybill & Bowman, 2001).

Following Gordon's subprocesses, a second type of pluralism exists when a group has acculturated but not integrated. That is, the group has adopted the Anglo American culture but doesn't have full and equal access to the institutions of the dominant society. In this situation, called **structural pluralism**, cultural differences are minimal, but the groups occupy different locations in the social structure. The groups may speak with the same accent, eat the same food, pursue the same goals, and subscribe to the same values, but they may also maintain separate organizational systems, including different churches, clubs, schools, and neighborhoods. Under structural pluralism, groups practice a common culture but do so in different places and with minimal interaction across group boundaries. An example of structural pluralism occurs on Sunday mornings in the Christian churches of the United States, where local congregations are often identified with specific ethnic groups or races. What happens in the various churches—the rituals, expressions of faith, statements of core values and beliefs—is similar and expresses a common, shared culture. Structurally, however, this common culture is expressed in separate buildings and by separate congregations.

A third type of pluralism reverses the order of Gordon's first two phases: integration without acculturation. This situation is exemplified by a group that has had some material success (e.g., measured by wealth or income) but hasn't become fully Americanized (e.g., become fluent in English or adopted uniquely American values and norms). Some immigrant groups have found niches in American society in which they can survive and occasionally prosper economically without acculturating very much.

Two different situations illustrate this pattern. An **enclave minority group** establishes its own neighborhood and relies on interconnected businesses, usually small in scope, for its economic survival. Some of these businesses serve the group, while others serve the society. The Cuban American community in South Florida and Chinatowns in many larger American cities are two examples of ethnic enclaves.

A similar pattern of adjustment, the **middleman minority group**, also relies on small shops and retail firms, but the businesses are more dispersed throughout a large area rather than concentrated in a specific locale. Some Chinese American communities fit this second pattern, as do Korean American grocery stores and Indian American–owned motels (Portes & Manning, 1986). We discuss these types of minority groups further in Part 3.

The economic success of enclave and middleman minorities is partly due to the strong ties of cooperation and mutual aid within their groups. The ties are based on cultural bonds that would weaken if acculturation took place. In contrast with Gordon's idea that acculturation is a prerequisite to integration, whatever success these groups enjoy is due in part to the fact that they've *not* Americanized. At various times and places, Jewish, Chinese, Japanese, Korean, and Cuban Americans have been enclave or middleman minorities, as we'll see in future chapters (see Bonacich & Modell, 1980; Kitano & Daniels, 2001).

The situation of enclave and middleman minorities—integration without acculturation—can be considered either a type of pluralism (emphasizing the absence of acculturation) or a type of assimilation (emphasizing the relatively high level of economic equality). Keep in mind that assimilation and pluralism are not opposites; they can occur in many combinations. It's best to think of acculturation, integration, and the other stages of assimilation (or pluralism) as independent processes.

QUESTIONS FOR REFLECTION

4. Is America becoming more pluralistic? Explain. What are some of the costs and some of the benefits of increasing pluralism?

5. What are the differences between middleman and enclave minority groups? Do these groups challenge the idea that assimilation moves step-by-step in a certain order?

FOCUS ON CONTEMPORARY ISSUES
LANGUAGE AND ASSIMILATION

The bumper sticker mentioned at the start of the chapter expresses a common sentiment: "Welcome to America. Now, speak English." Many Americans are concerned about the increase in the number of non-English speakers in their communities, and the bumper sticker succinctly—if crudely—expresses the opinion that newcomers should learn English as a condition for acceptance. In Gordon's terms, the slogan expresses support for Anglo conformity, the model that guided the assimilation of immigrants in the past.

(Continued)

(Continued)

The bumper sticker also reflects a common concern: How well can we manage a multilingual society? Americans from all walks of life and political persuasions wonder about the difficulties of everyday communication and the problems created when people speak multiple languages. Also, people wonder if increasing language diversity will weaken social solidarity and the sense of unity that every society requires to function effectively. In 2015, as we noted previously, about 350 different languages were spoken in the U. S., and about 21% of the population spoke a language other than English at home (U.S. Census Bureau, 2015c). Most of these languages, except Spanish, have few speakers. Still, people wonder if this multiplicity of tongues threatens unity and efficiency. What does sociological research reveal about language acculturation for today's immigrants?

For the first great wave of immigrants to America—those who came from Europe between the 1820s and the 1920s—language acculturation happened by generation. The first generation largely lived and died speaking their native language. Their children learned English in school and often served as bilingual go-betweens for their parents and the society. However, they largely failed to pass on their parent's language to their children. The third generation tended to grow up in nonethnic settings and speak English as their first and only language. Thus, by the third (or fourth) generation, English had replaced the old language, especially after immigration from Europe ended in the 1920s and 1930s and few newcomers arrived to keep the old ways alive.

Today, more than 90 years since the end of the first mass wave of immigration, the importance of language isn't lost on immigrants, and language acculturation appears to be following, more or less, a similar generational pattern. Historically, the immigrant generation tends to speak their native language, the second generation tends to be bilingual, and the third generation speaks English only (Taylor, Lopez, Martinez, & Velasco, 2012).

For many Americans, the finding that language acculturation is occurring today as it did in the past will seem counterintuitive. Their everyday experience in their communities tells them that the use of non-English languages (particularly Spanish) is *not* waning over the years but is growing more common.

The persistence of the "old" language reflects the continuing high rate of immigration. Even as the children and grandchildren of immigrants learn English, knowledge of the old language is replenished by newcomers. That is, assimilation and pluralism are occurring simultaneously in America today: The movement of the second and third generations toward speaking English is counterbalanced by continuing immigration. The assimilation of European immigrant groups was sharply reinforced by the cessation of immigration after the 1920s. Language diversity today is sustained by the continuing flow of new immigrants. This is an important difference in the assimilation experience of the two waves and we'll explore it more in future chapters. For now, we can say that immigration today will continue, newcomers will keep the old languages alive, and some people will perceive this linguistic diversity as a problem or even as a threat.

Given these trends, it seems likely that language will remain an important political issue in the years ahead. Although Americans espouse diverse opinions on this topic, one widely supported proposal is to make English the official language of America (as suggested by the bumper sticker slogan). Generally, English-only laws require that the society's official business (including election ballots, court proceedings, public school assemblies, and street signs) be conducted *only* in English.

Some questions come to mind about these laws. First, are they necessary? Would such laws speed up the acquisition of English in the first generation? This seems unlikely, since a large percentage of immigrants arrive with little formal education and low levels of literacy in their native language, as you'll see in future chapters. Furthermore, the laws would have little impact on the second and third generation, since they are already learning English at the "normal," generational pace.

Second, what's behind people's support for these laws besides concern about language diversity? Recall the concept of modern racism (subtle ways of expressing prejudice or disdain for some groups without appearing to be racist). Is support for English-only laws an example of modern racism? Does the English-only movement hide a deeper, more exclusionist agenda? Is it a way of sustaining the dominance of Anglo culture, a manifestation of the ideological racism?

Of course, not all supporters of English-only laws are racist or prejudiced. Our point is that some (and possibly many) of those feelings and ideas are prejudicial. We must carefully sort out the real challenges created by immigration, assimilation, and language diversity from the more hysterical and racist concerns.

OTHER GROUP RELATIONSHIPS

This book concentrates on assimilation and pluralism because they're the most typical forms of group relations in the United States. Two other minority group goals include separatism and revolution (Wirth, 1945). **Separatism** is when the minority group wants to sever political, cultural, and geographic ties with the society. Thus, separatism goes well beyond pluralism. Some Native Americans such as the Lakota have expressed pluralist and separatist goals. Other ethnically based groups, such as Native Hawaiians and the Nation of Islam, have pursued separatism. Outside of the U. S., separatist groups exist in French Canada, Scotland, Chechnya, Cyprus, southern Mexico, and scores of other places, too.

A minority group promoting **revolution** seeks to become the dominant group or create a new social order, sometimes in alliance with members of other groups. Although some American minority groups (e.g., the Black Panthers) have pursued revolution, this goal has been relatively rare in the United States. Revolutionary minority groups are more commonly found where one nation has conquered and controlled another racially or culturally different nation, such as African countries colonized by France and the United Kingdom (e.g., Morocco).

Additionally, the dominant group may pursue goals other than assimilation and pluralism, including forced migration or expulsion, extermination or genocide, and continued subjugation of the minority group. Chinese immigrants were the victims of a policy of expulsion, beginning in the 1880s, when the Chinese Exclusion Act (1882) closed the door on further immigration and concerted efforts were made to encourage Chinese people to leave the United States (see Chapter 8). Native Americans were the victims of expulsion, too. In 1830, the American government forced all tribes living east of the Mississippi to migrate West. This expulsion, along with other harmful policies, led to what some consider genocide (see Chapters 3 and 6).

The most infamous example of genocide is the Holocaust (1941–1945). While many Americans are familiar with Hitler and the Nazi Party, many are unaware that Hitler's political career started in 1919, that a 1933 vote by Germany's Parliament in support of the "Enabling Act" solidified his power, and that an election in 1934 made him Germany's head of state (The National WWII Museum, n.d.).

Survey research done in 2018 suggests that many Americans lack basic facts about the Holocaust. For example, 11% of adults were "unaware" or "not sure" if they knew about the Holocaust; among Millennials 18- to 34-years-old, the rate was 22%. During the Holocaust, at least six million Jews and millions of other minority group members such as the Roma (then called *gypsies*), gay people, and people with disabilities were murdered—though new estimates are higher. However, almost one third (31%) of all respondents put the figure at two million, but among Millennials, the rate was higher (41%). The majority (84%) knew the Holocaust occurred in Germany, but most were unaware about the Holocaust occurring in 16 German-occupied and Axis-occupied countries (Schoen Consulting, 2018), including Belgium, France, Hungary, Italy, Libya, Norway, Poland, Romania, and Russia (Megargee, 2009). More than a third (37%) knew about Poland, where approximately 3.5 million Jews died. However, only 5%–6% of respondents knew about the Holocaust in Estonia, Lithuania, and Latvia (Schoen Consulting, 2018).

Since 1999, more than 400 researchers have documented 42,500 locations where 15–20 million people—most of whom were Jewish—were imprisoned or killed between 1933 to 1945. (Not all deaths were recorded, but these are best estimates based on available data. See Longerich, 2010.) These include 30,000 slave labor camps; 1,150 Jewish ghettos; 980 concentration camps; 1,000 prisoner-of-war camps, among others (Lichtblau, 2013; Megargee, 2009). Almost half of Americans couldn't name one of them (Schoen Consulting, 2018). Perhaps this lack of awareness is reflected in the finding that 25% of the Americans surveyed said that "Jews still talk too much about what happened to them in the Holocaust" (Anti-Defamation League, 2017c).

Contrary to popular belief, research suggests that thousands of "regular people" knew about these facilities in their towns and villages and either worked at them or saw them regularly. Indeed, Gellately (2002) argues that "ordinary people served as the eyes and ears of the police" and acted as informants for anything remotely "suspicious" while Thamer (1986 c.f. Ezard, 2001) argues that tens of thousands of people supported the Holocaust because they didn't want to know what was happening and, therefore, "did not ask any questions." Tragically, many other examples of contemporary genocide exist, including those in Cambodia, Rwanda, Bosnia, and Herzegovina. As of this writing, two of the most recent genocides are happening in Myanmar (formerly called *Burma*) and in Sudan.

Continued subjugation occurs when the dominant group exploits a minority group and seeks to keep them powerless. The system of slavery in the antebellum South is an example. Dominant groups may simultaneously pursue different policies with different minority groups and may change policies over time.

FROM IMMIGRANTS TO WHITE ETHNICS

In this section, we'll explore the experiences of the minority groups that stimulated the development of what we're calling the traditional perspective on assimilation. A massive immigration from Europe began in the 1820s. Over the next century, millions of people made the journey from the Old World to the New. They came from every corner of the European continent: Germany, Greece, Ireland, Italy, Poland, Portugal, Russia, Ukraine, and scores of other nations and provinces. They came as young men and women seeking jobs, as families fleeing religious persecution, as political radicals fleeing the police, as farmers seeking land and a fresh start, and as paupers barely able to scrape together the cost of their passage. They came as immigrants, became minority groups upon their arrival, experienced discrimination and prejudice in all its forms, went through all the varieties and stages of assimilation and pluralism, and eventually merged into the society that had once rejected them so viciously. Figure 2.1 shows the major European sending nations.

These immigrants were a diverse group, and their experiences in America varied along crucial sociological dimensions. For example, native-born (white European) Americans marginalized and rejected some groups (e.g., Italians and other Southern Europeans) as

FIGURE 2.1 ■ Approximate Number of Immigrants to the United States for Selected European Nations, 1820–1920

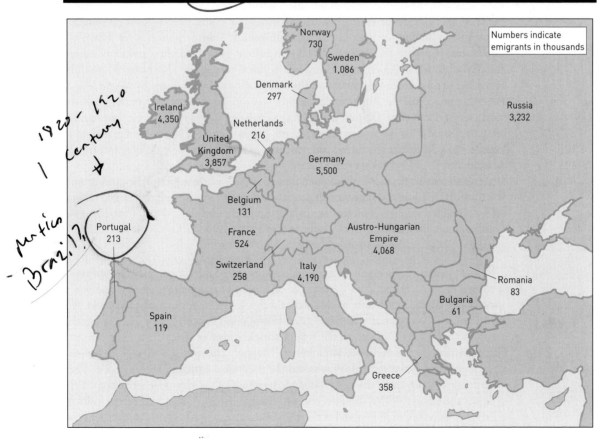

Source: Adapted from Immigration in America.

racially inferior while they viewed others (Irish Catholics and Eastern European Jews) as inferior because of their religions. And, of course, gender shaped the immigration experience—from start to finish—which was decidedly different for women and men.

Social class was another major differentiating factor: Many European immigrants brought few resources and very low human capital. They entered American society at the bottom of the economic ladder and often remained on the lowest occupational and economic rungs for generations. Other groups brought skills or financial resources that led them to a more favorable position and faster rates of upward mobility. All these factors—race, gender, and class—affected their experiences and led to very different outcomes in terms of social location, mobility paths, and acceptance within American society.

This first mass wave of immigrants shaped the United States in many ways. When the immigration started in the 1820s, America was an agricultural nation clustered along the East Coast, not yet 50 years old. The nation was just coming into contact with Mexicans in the Southwest, slavery was flourishing in the South, and conflict with Native Americans was intense and brutal. When this period of intense immigration ended in the 1920s, the U.S. population had increased from fewer than 10 million to more than 100 million. Society had industrialized, stretched from coast to coast, established colonies in the Pacific and the Caribbean, and become a world power.

It was no coincidence that America's industrialization and rise to global prominence occurred simultaneously with European immigration. These changes were intimately interlinked and were the mutual causes and effects of one another. Industrialization fueled the growth of American military and political power, and the industrial machinery of the nation depended heavily on the flow of labor from Europe. By World War I, for example, 25% of the American labor force was foreign-born, and more than half the workforce in New York, Detroit, and Chicago consisted of immigrant men. Immigrants were the majority of the workers in many important sectors of the economy, including coal mining, steel manufacturing, the garment industry, and meatpacking (Martin & Midgley, 1999, p. 15; Steinberg, 1981, p. 36).

In the sections that follow, we explore the experiences of these groups, beginning with the forces that caused them to leave Europe and come to the United States and ending with an assessment of their present status in American society.

Industrialization and Immigration

What forces stimulated this mass movement of people? Like any complex phenomenon, immigration from Europe had a multitude of causes, but underlying the process was a massive and fundamental shift in subsistence technology: the **industrial revolution**. We mentioned the importance of subsistence technology in Chapter 1. Dominant–minority relations are intimately related to the system a society uses to satisfy its basic needs, and those relations change as the economic system changes. The immigrants were pushed out of Europe as industrial technology wrecked the traditional agricultural way of life. They were drawn to America by the jobs created by the spread of the very same technology. Let's consider the impact of this fundamental transformation of social structure and culture. Industrialization began in England in the mid-1700s, spread to other parts of Northern and Western Europe, and then, in the 1800s, to Eastern and Southern Europe. As it rolled across the continent, the industrial revolution replaced people and animal power with machines and new forms of energy (steam, coal, and eventually oil and gas), causing an exponential increase in the productive capacity of society. (See Figure 2.2 for a detailed time line.)

At the dawn of the industrial revolution, most Europeans lived in small, rural villages and survived by traditional farming practices that had changed very little over the centuries. The work of production was **labor-intensive**, done by hand or with the aid of draft animals. Productivity was low, and the tasks of food production and survival required the efforts of virtually the entire family working ceaselessly throughout the year.

Industrialization destroyed this traditional way of life as it introduced new technology, machines, and sources of energy to the tasks of production (e.g., steam engines). The new technology was **capital-intensive** (dependent on machine power). As agriculture modernized, the need for human labor in rural areas decreased. During this time, landowners consolidated farmland into larger and larger tracts for the sake of efficiency, further decreasing the need for human laborers. Yet, as survival in this rapidly changing rural economy became more difficult, the rural population began growing. In response to these challenges, peasants left their home villages and moved to urban areas. Factories were being built in or near the cities, opening up opportunities for employment. The urban population tended to increase faster than the job supply. Thus, many migrants couldn't find work and had to move on; many of them responded to opportunities in the United States. At the same time, the abundance of frontier farmland encouraged people to move westward, contributing to a fairly constant demand for labor in the East Coast areas, places that were easiest for Europeans to reach. As industrialization took hold on both continents, the population movement to European cities and then to North America eventually grew to become one of the largest in human history.

The timing of migration from Europe followed the timing of industrialization. The first waves of immigrants, often called the **Old Immigration**, came from Northern and Western Europe starting in the 1820s. A second wave, the **New Immigration**, began arriving from Southern and Eastern Europe in the 1880s. Figure 2.3 shows the waves and rates of legal immigration up to 2017. Note that the New Immigration was much more voluminous than the Old Immigration, and that the number of immigrants declined drastically after the 1920s. Later, we'll explore the reasons for this decline and discuss the more recent (post-1965) increase in immigration—overwhelmingly from the Americas (mostly Mexico) and Asia—in Chapters 7 and 8.

European Origins and Conditions of Entry

The European immigrants varied from one another in innumerable ways. They followed different pathways into the United States, and their experiences were shaped by their cultural and class characteristics, their countries of origin, and the timing of their arrival. Some groups encountered much more resistance than others, and different groups played different roles in the industrialization and urbanization of America. To discuss these diverse patterns systematically, we distinguish three subgroups of European immigrants: Protestants from Northern and Western Europe, the largely Catholic immigrant laborers from Ireland and from Southern and Eastern Europe, and Jewish immigrants from Eastern Europe. We look at these subgroups in the approximate order of their arrival. In later sections, we'll consider other sociological variables such as social class and gender that further differentiated the experiences of people in these groups.

FIGURE 2.2 ■ Time Line of the Industrial Revolution, 1712–1903

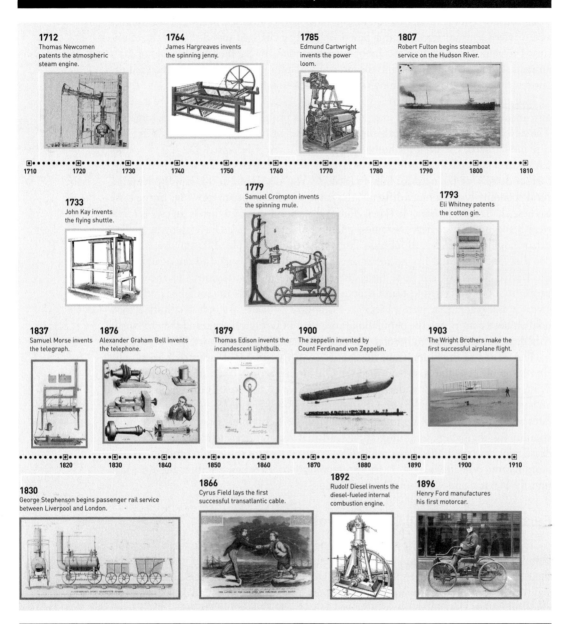

1712
Thomas Newcomen patents the atmospheric steam engine.

1764
James Hargreaves invents the spinning jenny.

1785
Edmund Cartwright invents the power loom.

1807
Robert Fulton begins steamboat service on the Hudson River.

1710 1720 1730 1740 1750 1760 1770 1780 1790 1800 1810

1733
John Kay invents the flying shuttle.

1779
Samuel Crompton invents the spinning mule.

1793
Eli Whitney patents the cotton gin.

1837
Samuel Morse invents the telegraph.

1876
Alexander Graham Bell invents the telephone.

1879
Thomas Edison invents the incandescent lightbulb.

1900
The zeppelin invented by Count Ferdinand von Zeppelin.

1903
The Wright Brothers make the first successful airplane flight.

1820 1830 1840 1850 1860 1870 1880 1890 1900 1910

1830
George Stephenson begins passenger rail service between Liverpool and London.

1866
Cyrus Field lays the first successful transatlantic cable.

1892
Rudolf Diesel invents the diesel-fueled internal combustion engine.

1896
Henry Ford manufactures his first motorcar.

Source: Time line of Industrial Revolution, 1700–1900 is adapted from *Industrial Revolution: Timeline, Facts, and Resources, Research* by B. Sobey, TheFreeResource.com.

FIGURE 2.3   ■   Legal Migration to the United States by Region of Origin, 1820–2016

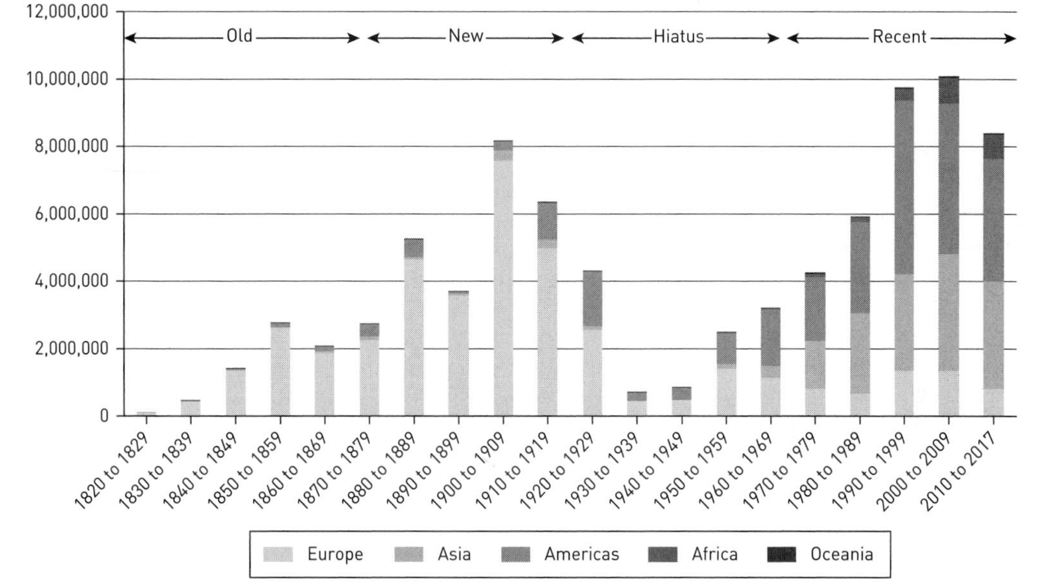

Source: Data from Table 2, Persons Obtaining Legal Permanent Resident Status by Region and Selected Country of Last Residence: Fiscal Years 1820 to 2017. *2017 Yearbook of Immigration Statistics.* U.S. Department of Homeland Security.

Northern and Western Protestant Europeans

Northern and Western European immigrants included Danes (from Denmark), Dutch, English, French, Germans, Norwegians, Swedes, and Welsh. These groups were similar to the dominant group in their racial and religious characteristics. They also shared many American values, including the **Protestant ethic**—which stressed hard work, success, and individualism—and support for the principles of democratic government. These similarities eased their acceptance into a society that was highly intolerant of religious and racial differences. These immigrant groups experienced a lower degree of ethnocentric rejection and racist disparagement than the Irish and immigrants from Southern and Eastern Europe. Northern and Western European immigrants came from nations just as developed as the United States. Thus, these immigrants tended to be more skilled and educated than other immigrant groups, and often brought money and other resources with which to secure a comfortable place for themselves in their new society. Many settled in the sparsely populated Midwest and in other frontier areas, where they farmed the fertile land that became available after the conquest and removal of Native Americans and Mexican Americans (see Chapter 3). By dispersing throughout the midsection of the country, they lowered their visibility and their degree of competition with dominant group members. Two brief case studies, first of Norwegians and then of Germans, outline the experiences of these groups.

Immigrants from Norway Norway had a small population base, and immigration from this Scandinavian nation to America was never large in absolute numbers.

However, "America fever" struck here, as it did elsewhere in Europe, and on a per capita basis, Norway sent more immigrants to America before 1890 than any other European nation except Ireland (Chan, 1990, p. 41).

The first Norwegian immigrants were moderately prosperous farmers searching for cheap land. They found abundant acreage in upper-Midwest states, such as Minnesota and Wisconsin, but the local labor supply was too small to cultivate the available land effectively. Many turned to their homeland for help and used their networks of relatives and friends to recruit a labor force. Thus, chains of communication and migration linking Norway to the Northern Plains were established, supplying immigrants to these areas for decades (Chan, 1990, p. 41). Today, the farms, towns, and cities of the upper Midwest still reflect this Scandinavian heritage.

Immigrants from Germany The stream of immigration from Germany was much larger than that from Norway. In the latter half of the 19th century, at least 25% of the immigrants each year were German (Conzen, 1980, p. 406) and they left their mark on the economy, political structure, and cultural life of their new homeland. In 2015, about 45 million Americans (14.4%) traced their ancestries to Germany—more than to any other country, including England and Ireland (U.S. Census Bureau, 2016a).

The German immigrants who arrived in the early 1800s moved into the newly opened farmland and the rapidly growing cities of the Midwest, as had many Scandinavians. By 1850, Germans had established communities in Milwaukee, St. Louis, and other Midwestern cities (Conzen, 1980, p. 413). Some German immigrants followed the trans-Atlantic route of the cotton trade between Europe and the southern United States and entered through the port of New Orleans, moving from there to the Midwest and Southwest.

German immigrants arriving later in the century were more likely to settle in urban areas, in part because fertile land was less available. Many of these city-bound German immigrants were skilled workers and artisans, and others found work as laborers in the rapidly expanding industrial sector. The influx of German immigrants into the rural and urban economies is reflected in the fact that by 1870, most employed German Americans were involved in skilled labor (37%) or farming (25%; Conzen, 1980, p. 413).

German immigrants took relatively high occupational positions in the U.S. labor force, and their sons and daughters were able to translate that relative affluence into economic mobility. By the dawn of the 20th century, large numbers of second-generation German Americans were finding their way into white-collar and professional careers. Within a few generations, German Americans had achieved parity with national norms in education, income, and occupational prestige.

Assimilation Patterns Assimilation for Norwegian, German, and other Protestant immigrants from Northern and Western Europe was consistent with the traditional model discussed earlier. Although members of these groups felt the sting of rejection, prejudice, and discrimination, their movement from acculturation to integration and equality was relatively smooth, especially when compared with the experiences of racial minority groups. Table 2.3, later in this chapter, illustrates their relative success and high degree of assimilation.

Immigrant Laborers from Ireland and Southern and Eastern Europe

The relative ease of assimilation for Northern and Western Europeans contrasts sharply with the experiences of non-Protestant, less-educated, and less-skilled immigrants. These immigrant laborers came in two waves. The Irish were part of the Old Immigration that began in the 1820s, but the bulk of this group—Bulgarians, Greeks, Hungarians, Italians, Poles, Russians, Serbs, Slovaks, Ukrainians, and scores of other Southern and Eastern European groups—made up the New Immigration that began in the 1880s.

Peasant Origins Most of the immigrants in these nationality groups (like many recent immigrants to America) were peasants or unskilled laborers, with few resources other than their willingness to work. They came from rural, village-oriented cultures in which family and kin took precedence over individual needs or desires. Family life for them tended to be patriarchal and autocratic; that is, men dominated decision making and controlled family resources. Parents expected children to work for the good of the family and forgo their personal desires. Arranged marriages were common. This cultural background was less consistent with the industrializing, capitalistic, individualistic, Protestant, Anglo American culture of the United States and was a major reason that these immigrant laborers experienced a higher level of rejection and discrimination than the immigrants from Northern and Western Europe.

The immigrant laborers were much less likely to enter the rural economy than were the Northern and Western European immigrants. Much of the better frontier land had already been claimed by the time these new immigrant groups arrived, and a large number of them had been permanently soured on farming by the oppressive and exploitative agrarian economies from which they were trying to escape (see Handlin, 2002).

Regional and Occupational Patterns The immigrant laborers of this time settled in the cities of the industrializing Northeast and found work in plants, mills, mines, and factories. They supplied the armies of laborers needed to power the industrial revolution in the U. S., although their view of this process was generally from the bottom looking up. They arrived during the decades when the American industrial and urban infrastructure was being constructed. They built roads, canals, and railroads and the buildings that housed the machinery of industrialization. For example, the first tunnels of the New York City subway system were dug, largely by hand, by laborers from Italy. Other immigrants found work in the coalfields of Pennsylvania and West Virginia and the steel mills of Pittsburgh, and they flocked by the millions to the factories of the Northeast.

Like other low-skill immigrant groups, these newcomers were employed in jobs where strength and stamina were more important than literacy or skilled labor. In fact, as industrialization proceeded through its early phases, the skill level required for employment declined. To keep wages low and take advantage of what seemed like an inexhaustible supply of cheap labor, industrialists and factory owners developed technologies and machines that required few skills and little knowledge of English to operate. As mechanization proceeded, unskilled workers replaced skilled workers. Not infrequently, women and children replaced men because they could be hired for lower wages (Steinberg, 1981, p. 35).

Assimilation Patterns Eventually, as the generations passed, the prejudice, systematic discrimination, and other barriers to upward mobility for the immigrant laborer groups weakened, and their descendants began rising out of the working class. Although the first and second generations of these groups were largely limited to jobs at the unskilled or semiskilled level, the third and later generations rose in the American social class system. As Table 2.3 shows (later in this chapter), the descendants of the immigrant laborers achieved parity with national norms by the latter half of the 20th century.

Eastern European Jewish Immigrants and the Ethnic Enclave

Jewish immigrants from Russia and other parts of Eastern Europe followed a third pathway into American society. These immigrants were a part of the New Immigration and began arriving in the 1880s. Unlike the immigrant laborer groups, who were generally economic refugees and included many young, single men, Eastern European Jews were fleeing religious persecution and arrived as family units intending to settle permanently and become citizens. They settled in the urban areas of the Northeast and Midwest. New York City was the most common destination, and the Lower East Side became the best-known Jewish American neighborhood. By 1920, about 60% of all Jewish Americans lived in the urban areas between Boston and Philadelphia, with almost 50% living in New York City. Another 30% lived in the urban areas of the Midwest, particularly in Chicago (Goren, 1980, p. 581).

Urban Origins In Russia and other parts of Eastern Europe, Jews had been barred from agrarian occupations and had come to make their livelihoods from jobs in the urban economy. For example, almost two thirds of the immigrant Jewish men had been tailors and other skilled laborers in Eastern Europe (Goren, 1980, p. 581). When they immigrated to the U. S., these urban skills and job experiences helped them find work in the rapidly industrializing U.S. economy of the early 20th century.

Other Jewish immigrants joined the urban working class and took manual labor and unskilled jobs in the industrial sector (Morawska, 1990, p. 202). The garment industry in particular became the lifeblood of the Jewish community and provided jobs to about one third of all Eastern European Jews residing in the major cities (Goren, 1980, p. 582). Women and men worked in the garment industry. Jewish women, like the women of more recent immigrant laborer groups, created ways to combine their jobs and their domestic responsibilities. As young girls, they worked in factories and sweatshops, and after marriage, they did the same work at home, sewing precut garments together or doing other piecework such as wrapping cigars or making artificial flowers, often assisted by their children (Amott & Matthaei, 1991, p. 115).

An Enclave Economy Unlike most European immigrant groups, Jewish Americans became heavily involved in commerce. Drawing on their experience in the "old country," many started businesses and small independent enterprises. Jewish neighborhoods were densely populated and provided a ready market for all kinds of services such as bakeries, butcher and candy shops, and other retail enterprises.

Capitalizing on their residential concentration and close proximity, Jewish immigrants created an enclave economy founded upon dense networks of commercial, financial, and social cooperation. The Jewish American enclave survived because of the cohesiveness of the group; the willingness of wives, children, and other relatives to work for little or no monetary compensation; and the commercial savvy of the early immigrants. Also, a large pool of cheap labor and sources of credit and other financial services were available within the community. The Jewish American enclave grew and provided a livelihood for many of the immigrants' children and grandchildren (Portes & Manning, 1986, pp. 51–52). As with other enclave groups that we'll discuss in future chapters, including Chinese Americans and Cuban Americans, Jewish American economic advancement preceded extensive acculturation. That is, they made significant strides toward economic equality before they became fluent in English or were otherwise Americanized.

Americanized Generations One way an enclave immigrant group can improve its position is to develop an educated and acculturated second generation. The Americanized, English-speaking children of these immigrants used their greater familiarity with the dominant society and their language facility to help preserve and expand the family enterprise. Furthermore, as the second generation appeared, the American public school system was expanding, and education through the college level was free or inexpensive in New York City and other cities (Steinberg, 1981, pp. 128–138). There was also a strong push for the second and third generations to enter professions, and as Jewish Americans excelled in school, resistance to and discrimination against them increased. By the 1920s, many elite colleges and universities, such as Dartmouth, had established quotas that limited the number of Jewish students they would admit (Dinnerstein, 1977, p. 228). These quotas weren't abolished until after World War II.

Assimilation Patterns The enclave economy and the Jewish neighborhoods the immigrants established proved to be an effective base from which to integrate into American society. The descendants of the Eastern European Jewish immigrants moved from their ethnic neighborhoods years ago, and their positions in the economy—their pushcarts, stores, and jobs in the garment industry—were taken up by more recent immigrants. When they left the enclave economy, many second- and third-generation Eastern European Jews didn't enter the mainstream occupational structure at the bottom, as the immigrant laborer groups tended to do. They used the resources generated through the hard work, skills, and entrepreneurship of the early generations to gain access to prestigious and advantaged social class positions (Portes & Manning, 1986, p. 53). Today, Jewish Americans, as a group, surpass national averages in levels of education and income (Masci, 2016) and occupational prestige (Sklare, 1971, pp. 60–69; see also Cohen, 1985; Massarik & Chenkin, 1973). The relatively higher status of Russian Americans (shown in Table 2.3) is due, in part, to the fact that many are of Jewish heritage.

Chains of Immigration

Immigrants tend to follow chains established and maintained by group members. Some versions of the traditional assimilation perspective (especially human capital theory) treat immigration and status attainment as purely individual matters. To the contrary, scholars have demonstrated that immigration to the U. S. was in large measure a group (sociological) phenomenon. Immigrant chains stretched across the oceans, held together by the ties of kinship, language, religion, culture, and a sense of connection (Bodnar, 1985; Tilly, 1990).

Here is how chain immigration worked (and, although modified by modern technology, continues to work today): Someone from a village in, for instance, Poland would make it to the United States. This successful immigrant would send word to the home village, perhaps by hiring a letter writer. Along with news and adventure stories, they would send their address. Within months, another immigrant from the village, another relative perhaps, would show up at the address of the original immigrant. After months of experience in the new society, the original immigrant could lend assistance, provide a place to sleep, help with job hunting, and orient the newcomer to the area.

Before long, others would arrive from the village in need of the same sort of introduction to the mysteries of America. The compatriots would typically settle close to one another, in the same building or on the same block. Soon, entire neighborhoods were filled with people from a certain village, province, or region. In these ethnic enclaves, people spoke the old language and observed the old ways. They started businesses, founded churches or synagogues, had families, and began mutual aid societies and other organizations. There was safety in numbers and comfort and security in a familiar, if transplanted, set of traditions and customs.

Immigrants often responded to American society by attempting to recreate as much of their old world as possible within the bustling metropolises of the industrializing Northeast and West Coast. They did so, in part, to avoid the harsher forms of rejection and discrimination and also for solidarity and mutual support. These Little Italys, Little Warsaws, Little Irelands, Greektowns, Chinatowns, and Little Tokyos were safe havens that insulated the immigrants from the dominant American society and helped them to establish bonds with one another, organize group life, pursue their own group interests, and have some control over the pace of their adjustment to American culture. For some groups and in some areas, the ethnic subcommunity was a short-lived phenomenon. For others (such as the Jewish enclave discussed earlier, for example), the neighborhood became the dominant structure of their lives, and the networks continued to function long after the arrival of group members in the United States.

The Campaign against Immigration: Prejudice, Racism, and Discrimination

Today, it may be hard to conceive of the bitterness and intensity of the prejudice that greeted the Irish, Italians, Jews, Poles, and other new immigrant groups (though it parallels anti-immigrant sentiment held by some Americans today toward different immigrants). Even as immigrants became an indispensable part of the workforce, Americans castigated, ridiculed, attacked, and disparaged them. The Irish were the first immigrant laborers to arrive; thus, they were the first to experience this intense prejudice and discrimination. White Americans waged campaigns against them; mobs attacked Irish neighborhoods and burned Roman Catholic churches and convents. Some employers blatantly refused to hire the Irish, often posting signs that read "No Irish Need Apply." Until later arriving groups immigrated and pushed them up, the Irish were mired at the bottom of the job market (Blessing, 1980; Dolan, 2010; Potter, 1973; Shannon, 1964).

Other groups felt the same sting of rejection as they arrived. Italian immigrants were particularly likely to be the victims of violent attacks; one of the most vicious took place in New Orleans in 1891. The city's police chief was assassinated, and rumors of Italian involvement in the murder were rampant. The police arrested hundreds of Italians, and nine were brought to trial. All were acquitted. Yet, anti-Italian sentiment ran so high that a mob lynched 11 Italians while police and city officials did nothing (Higham, 1963; Zecker, 2011).

Anti-Catholicism

Much of the prejudice against the Irish and the new immigrants was expressed as anti-Catholicism. Prior to the mid-19th century, Anglo American society had been almost exclusively Protestant. Catholicism, with its Latin masses, saints, celibate clergy, and cloistered nuns seemed alien, unusual, and threatening to many Americans. The growth of Catholicism in the U. S., especially because it was associated with non-Anglo immigrants, raised fears among Protestants that their religion was threatened or would lose status. This fear was stoked by false rumors that the pope prohibited Protestants from worshipping in Rome (Franco, 2008) and that with increasing numbers of Catholics in the U. S., such prohibitions could make their way to America (Wilensky-Lanford, 2015).

Although Protestant Americans often stereotyped Catholics as a single group, Catholic immigrants differed, primarily by their home country. For example, the Catholicism that people practiced in Ireland differed significantly from the Catholicism practiced in Italy, Poland, and other countries (Inglis, 2007). Therefore, Catholic immigrant groups often established their own parishes, with priests who could speak their native language. These cultural and national differences often separated Catholic groups, despite their common faith (Herberg, 1960).

Anti-Semitism

For two millennia, Christians have chastised and persecuted European Jews as the "killers of Christ" and stereotyped them as materialistic moneylenders and crafty business owners (Dollinger, 2005; Rozenblit, 2010). The stereotype that links Jews and money lending has its origins in the fact that in premodern Europe, the Church forbade Catholics to charge interest for loans (Cuddy, Fiske, & Glick, 2008). Jews were under no such restriction, and they filled the gap within the economy (Berger, 2010; Frankel, 1997; Jaher, 1996; Lansford, 2007).

Because people brought these ideas to the New World, Jewish immigrants faced prejudice and racism (or **anti-Semitism**). For example, in 1654, after being forced to leave Dutch Brazil (then a Portuguese colony), 23 Jews sought asylum in the Dutch colony of New Netherland—now New York (Stuyvesant, 1995). The Dutch government gave them permission to enter. However, the local director general of New Netherland petitioned to have them leave, saying they were a "deceitful race . . . [who should] be not allowed to further infect and trouble this new colony (Jacobson, 1999, p. 171). His petition was rejected, but such anti-Semitic ideas remained.

Anti-Semitic views intensified in the 1880s when large numbers of Jewish immigrants from Russia and Eastern Europe arrived. Their arrival was fueled, in part, by violent anti-Jewish pogroms. The word *pogrom* means "to wreak havoc, to demolish violently"; they resulted in the theft and destruction of Jewish property as well as physical assault, including rape. One of the first happened in 1821, but they became widespread in Russia and Ukraine between 1881–1884. Another wave happened between 1918 and 1920 in Belarus and Poland. Over the years, pogroms resulted in the deaths of tens of thousands of Jews (United States Holocaust Memorial Museum, n.d.). The most well-known pogrom, *Kristallnacht* (*The Night of Broken Glass*), took place in 1938 throughout Germany, Austria, and the Sudetenland (now part of Czechoslovakia). In just two days, these attacks, orchestrated by the Nazi leadership, left a path of destruction: 7,500 Jewish-owned businesses were plundered or destroyed, 267 synagogues were destroyed (usually by being burned down), and Jewish cemeteries were desecrated. Thousands of Jews were terrified, physically attacked, and forced to perform humiliating acts. Approximately 30,000 Jewish men were arrested and sent to concentration camps. After Kristallnacht, the Nazis passed many anti-Jewish laws and required Jews to pay an "atonement tax" of 1 billion Reichsmark (United States Holocaust Memorial Museum, n.d.). In 1938, that would be $401,606,426 (Marcuse, 2018) or $7,108,573,821.07 in 2017, after being adjusted for inflation (Friedman, n.d.).

Unfortunately, anti-Semitism didn't end with the demise of the Nazi regime. Data from a sample of 53,100 people in 100 countries, when applied to the total population in those countries, suggest that more than one billion people worldwide have anti-Semitic beliefs (Anti-Defamation League, 2017a). However, attitudes varied by country and changed over time. After taking the margin of error into account, a follow-up 2015 poll of 10,000 people in 19 of those countries showed increases in anti-Semitism in Italy, The Netherlands, and Romania, while Poland, Russia, and Ukraine showed decreases. In America, such attitudes decreased significantly since the 1960s. However, anti-Semitism has increased in the last few years (Anti-Defamation League, 2017a).

Mass Immigration

Before the mass immigration of Eastern European Jews began in the late 1800s, anti-Semitism in the United States was relatively mild, perhaps because the group was so small. As European immigration continued and the Jewish population in America grew, anti-Semitism increased in intensity and viciousness. Many Americans continued to believe the old stereotypes of Jews as cunning, dishonest merchants (and worse). In the late 19th century, whites began banning Jews from social clubs, summer resorts, businesses such as hotels (R. C. Kennedy, 2001) and other organizations (Anonymous, 1924; Meenes, 1941; Shevitz, 2005). Some posted notices such as, "We prefer not to entertain Hebrews" (Goren, 1980, p. 585) and "Patronage of Jews is Declined" (Bernheimer, 1908, p. 1106). Such language attempted to mask blatant discrimination. It hinted at forms of modern racism to come.

By the 1920s and 1930s, the Ku Klux Klan (KKK) and other extreme racist groups espoused anti-Semitism. Because many of the political radicals and labor leaders of the time were Jewish immigrants, anti-Semitism became fused with a fear of Communism and other anti-capitalist doctrines in America and throughout Europe (Muller, 2010). Anti-Semitism became prominent among American prejudices and some well-known Americans espoused anti-Semitic views. For example, Henry Ford, the founder of Ford Motor Company and one of the most famous men of his time, believed "the Jews" were responsible for WWI and a host of other things. In 1919, he bought a newspaper to communicate his views, most notably in a 91-week series called "The International Jew, the World's Foremost Problem," later published as a book. According to Logsdon (n.d.), it was "the largest and most damaging campaign against Jews ever waged in the United States." Additionally, it had tremendous influence on Hitler and, by extension, the Nazis. Similarly, Father Charles Coughlin, a Catholic priest, reached millions of people through his radio program (Selzer, 1972) and through a newsletter for an organization he started, the National Union for Social Justice (NUSJ). The NUSJ had millions of members who pledged to "restore America to the Americans" (Carpenter, 1998, p. 71; Greene & Newport, 2018). A federal investigation declared him pro-Nazi and guilty of restating enemy propaganda (United States Holocaust Memorial Museum, n.d.).

Anti-Semitism reached a peak before World War II, then decreased before reemerging after the war (Norwood, 2013). Social norms at the time made it easy for people to express anti-Semitic views or to discriminate against Jews. In the 1960s, people began expressing anti-Semitism in subtler forms (Benowitz, 2017; Borstelmann, 2009; Nirenberg, 2014). One notable exception to this is anti-Semitism within many extremist groups, which remains significant, overt, and hostile. In the past few years, the number of such groups has increased, as have anti-Semitic incidents. Though some groups names are recognizable (e.g., Aryan Nations, KKK), others mask the groups' beliefs (e.g., Creativity Movement, Vanguard America, Vinlanders Social Club). Not all groups share the same exact ideology; for example, white nationalists, "skinheads," and KKK-related organizations are slightly different. However, many came together in August 2017 for a "Unite the [Alt] Right" rally, which made their anti-Semitism clear. For example, some shouted "Jews will not replace us" and "blood and soil," the latter is a reference to Nazi ideology (Swaney, 2004).

Some targeting of Jews increases during economic recession and may be related to the stereotypical view of Jewish Americans as extremely prosperous and materialistic, as often depicted in media such as film and television (Cohen, 1982). The type of prejudice that occurs under these conditions is called "envious prejudice" (Cuddy et al., 2008). Today, most Americans don't have anti-Semitic views but research by the Anti-Defamation League (ADL) done in 2016 found that about 34 million Americans do—an increase since 2014 (ADL, 2017b). Similarly, anti-Semitic incidents have increased 57% since 2016, the highest number on record (ADL, 2017a). The ADL documented 1,986 incidents, including assault, harassment, and destruction of property (e.g., desecration of Jewish cemeteries or anti-Semitic messages spray-painted on synagogues). However, most (52%) respondents expressed concern for anti-Semitism, especially attacks on Jewish people (ADL, 2017b).

A Successful Exclusion

The prejudice and racism directed against the immigrants also found expression in organized, widespread efforts to stop the flow of immigration. A variety of anti-immigrant organizations appeared almost as soon as the mass European immigration started in the 1820s. The strength of these campaigns waxed and waned, largely in harmony with the strength of the economy and the size of the job supply. Anti-immigrant sentiment intensified, and the strength of its organized expressions increased during hard times and depressions and tended to soften when the economy improved.

The campaign ultimately triumphed with the passage of the National Origins Act in 1924, which established a quota system limiting the number of immigrants that America would accept each year from each sending nation. This system was openly racist. For example, the quota for European nations was based on the proportional representation of each nationality in America as of 1890. Legislators chose this year because it predated the bulk of the New Immigration and, therefore, gave nearly 70% of the available immigration slots to the nations of Northern and Western Europe, despite the fact that immigration from those areas had largely ended by the 1920s.

Moreover, the National Origins Act banned immigration from Asian nations altogether. At this time, almost all parts of Africa were still the colonial possessions of various European nations and received no separate quotas. (That is, the quota for African immigrants was zero.) The National Origins Act drastically reduced the number of immigrants that would be admitted into the United States each year. Figure 2.2 shows the effectiveness of the numerical restrictions. By the time the Great Depression took hold of the American economy in the 1930s, immigration had dropped to the lowest level in a century. The National Origins Act remained in effect until 1965.

QUESTIONS FOR REFLECTION

6. What forces motivated people to leave Europe and come to North America? How did these motives change from time to time and from place to place?

7. What motivated the forces of resistance and discrimination in the United States? How did the exclusionists triumph? What roles did class play in these processes?

8. Look at the interactive map called "Here's Everyone Who's Immigrated to the U.S. Since 1820" (http://metrocosm.com/animated-immigration-map/). What ideas from the chapter help you understand these changing patterns? Do the changing patterns offer any useful insights for debates about current immigration? How?

PATTERNS OF ASSIMILATION

In this section, we'll explore some of the common patterns of assimilation followed by European immigrants and their descendants, including assimilation by generation, ethnic succession, and structural mobility. Research in the traditional perspective shows that these patterns are consistent with Gordon's model of assimilation.

The Importance of Generations

People today—social scientists, politicians, and ordinary citizens—often do not recognize the time and effort it takes for a group to become completely Americanized. For most European immigrant groups, the process took generations. It was the immigrant's grandchildren or the great-grandchildren (or even great-great-grandchildren) who completed acculturation and integration. Mass immigration from Europe ended in the 1920s. However, the assimilation of some European ethnic groups wasn't completed until late in the 20th century.

Here is a summary of how assimilation proceeded for European immigrants: The first generation, the actual immigrants, settled into ethnic neighborhoods, such as Little Italy in New York City. They made limited movement toward acculturation and integration. They focused their energies on social relationships within their own groups, especially family networks. Many of them—usually men—had to leave their neighborhoods for work and other reasons, and this required some familiarity with the society. The people had to learn some English and taking a job outside the neighborhood is, almost by definition, a form of integration. Nonetheless, this first generation of immigrants primarily lived within a version of the old country, which they had recreated within the new.

The second generation—the immigrants' children—were psychologically or socially marginalized because they were partly ethnic and partly American but not full members of either group. They were born in America but in households and neighborhoods that were ethnic, not American. They learned the old language first and were socialized in the old ways. As they entered childhood, however, they entered the public schools and became socialized into the Anglo American culture.

Often, what they learned at school conflicted with their home lives. For example, old country family values included expectations for children to put family interests before self-interests. Parents arranged marriages, or at least heavily influenced them; marriages were subject to parents' approval. These customs conflicted sharply with American ideas about individualism and romantic love. Cultural differences like these often created painful conflict between the ethnic first generation and their Americanized children.

As the second generation progressed toward adulthood, they tended to move away from the old neighborhoods, often motivated by desires for social mobility. They were much more acculturated than their parents, spoke English fluently, and enjoyed a wider range of opportunities, including occupational choices. Discriminatory policies in education, housing, and the job market sometimes limited them. However, they were upwardly mobile, and in pursuit of their careers, they left behind their ethnic communities and many of their parents' customs.

The third generation—the immigrants' grandchildren—were typically born and raised in nonethnic settings. English was their first (and often only) language, and their beliefs and values were thoroughly American. Family and kinship ties with grandparents and the old neighborhood often remained strong and weekend and holiday visits along with family rituals revolving around the cycles of birth, marriage, and death connected the third generation to the world of their ancestors. However, they were American; their ethnicity was a relatively minor part of this generation's identities and daily life.

The pattern of assimilation by generation progressed as follows:

- The first generation began the process of assimilation and was slightly acculturated and integrated.

- The second generation was very acculturated and highly integrated (at least into the society's secondary sectors).

- The third generation finished the acculturation process and enjoyed high levels of integration at the secondary and the society's primary sectors.

Table 2.2 illustrates Italian American's patterns of structural assimilation. As the generations change, this group's educational and occupational characteristics converge with those of white Anglo-Saxon Protestants (WASPs). For example, the percentage of Italian Americans with some college shows a gap of more than 20 points between the first and second generations and WASPs. However, third- and fourth-generation Italians are virtually identical to WASPs on this measure of integration in the secondary sector of society. Likewise, the other differences between Italians and WASPs shrink from generation to generation.

The first five measures of educational and occupational attainment in Table 2.2 show the generational pattern of integration (or structural assimilation). The sixth measures marital assimilation, or intermarriage. It displays the percentage of men of "unmixed" (100% Italian) heritage who married women outside the Italian community. Note once more the tendency for integration, now at the primary level, to increase across the generations. The huge majority of first-generation men married within their group (only 21.9% married non-Italians). By the third generation, 67.3% of the men were marrying non-Italians.

This model of step-by-step, linear assimilation by generation fits some groups better than others. For example, immigrants from Northern and Western Europe (except for the Irish) were generally more similar, culturally, to the dominant group in the U. S., and they tended to be more educated and skilled. Thus, they were accepted more quickly than other immigrant groups, which helped them complete the assimilation process in three generations or less.

In contrast, immigrants from Ireland and from Southern and Eastern Europe were mostly uneducated, unskilled people who were more likely to join the huge groups of industrial laborers who ran the factories, mines, and mills. These immigrants were more

TABLE 2.2 ■ Some Comparisons between WASPs and Italians

Indicators	WASPS*	Generation		
		First	Second	Third and Fourth
1. Percentage with some college	42.4%	19.0%	19.4%	41.7%
2. Average years of education	12.6	9.0	11.1	13.4
3. Percentage with white-collar jobs	34.7%	20.0%	22.5%	28.8%
4. Percentage with blue-collar jobs	37.9%	65.0%	53.9%	39.0%
5. Average occupational prestige	42.5	34.3	36.8	42.5
6. Percentage of "unmixed" Italian men marrying non-Italian women	N/A	21.9%	51.4%	67.3%

Source: Adapted from Alba (1985, Tab. 5-3, 5-4, 6-2). Data are originally from the NORC General Social Surveys (1975–1980) and the Current Population Survey (1979). Copyright © 1985 Richard D. Alba.

*WASPs weren't separated by generation, and some of the differences between groups may be the result of factors such as age. That is, older WASPs may have levels of education more comparable to first-generation Italian Americans than to those of WASPs as a whole.

likely to remain at the bottom of the American class structure for generations; indeed, they only attained middle-class prosperity in the second half of the 20th century. As mentioned earlier, Eastern European Jews followed a distinctly different pathway to assimilation. Although widespread anti-Semitic attitudes and policies limited them, they formed an enclave that served as a springboard to launch the second and third generations into the society.

It's important to keep generational patterns in mind when examining current immigration to the United States. It's common for people to criticize contemporary newcomers (especially Hispanics) for their slow pace of assimilation. But this process should be considered in the light of the generational time frame for assimilation followed by European immigrants. Modern forms of transportation allow immigration to happen quickly. Assimilation, however, is slow.

Ethnic Succession

A second factor that shaped the assimilation experience is captured in the concept of **ethnic succession**, or the ways European ethnic groups unintentionally affected one another's positions in the society's class structure. The overall pattern was that each European immigrant group tended to be pushed to higher social class levels and more favorable economic situations by the groups that arrived after it. As more experienced groups became upwardly mobile and moved from the neighborhoods that served as their ports of entry, new groups of immigrants replaced them and began the process anew. Some cities in the Northeast served as ethnic neighborhoods—the first haven in the new society—for various successive groups. Some places, such as the Lower East Side of New York City, continue to fill this role today.

This process of ethnic succession can be understood in terms of the second stage of Gordon's model: integration at the secondary level (see Table 2.1), or entry into the public institutions and organizations of the larger society. Three pathways of integration tended to be most important for European immigrants: politics, labor unions, and the church. We'll discuss each in turn, illustrating with the Irish, the first immigrant laborers to arrive in large numbers; but the general patterns apply to all white ethnic groups.

Politics

The Irish tended to follow the Northern and Western Europeans in the job market and social class structure and were, in turn, followed by the wave of new immigrants. In many urban areas of the Northeast, they moved into the neighborhoods and took jobs left behind by German laborers. After a period of acculturation and adjustment, the Irish began creating their own connections to mainstream American society to improve their economic and social positions. They were replaced in their neighborhoods and at the bottom of the occupational structure by Italians, Poles, and other immigrant groups arriving after them.

As the years passed and the Irish gained more experience, they forged more links to society. Specifically, they allied themselves with the Democratic Party and helped construct the political machines that dominated many city governments in the 19th and 20th centuries, including Boston, Philadelphia, and Chicago (Erie & Kogan, 2016). Machine politicians were often corrupt and even criminal, regularly subverting the election process, bribing city and state officials, using city budgets to fill the pockets of the political bosses and their followers, and giving city jobs to people who provided favors and faithful service. Nevertheless, the political machines gave their constituents and loyal followers valuable social services. Machine politicians, such as Boss Tweed of Tammany Hall in New York City, found jobs, provided food and clothing for the destitute, aided victims of fires and other calamities, and intervened in the criminal and civil courts (Golway, 2014; Warren, 2008).

Much of the urban political machines' power resulted from their control of city budgets. The machines' leaders used municipal jobs and city budgets as part of a "spoils" or patronage system that granted rewards to their supporters and allies. A faithful Irish party worker might be rewarded for service with a job in the police department or another city agency. Private businesspeople might be rewarded with lucrative contracts to supply services or perform other city business (Menes, 2001).

The political machines served as engines of economic opportunity and connected Irish Americans to a central and important institution of the dominant society. Using the resources controlled by local governments as a power base, the Irish (and other immigrant groups after them) began integrating into American society (Menes, 2001).

Labor Unions

The labor movement provided another connection among the Irish, other European immigrant groups, and American society. Although virtually all white ethnic groups had a hand in the creation and eventual success of the movement, many of the founders and early leaders were Irish. For example, Terence Powderly, an Irish Catholic, founded one of the first American labor unions. In the early 20th century, about one third of union leaders were Irish and more than 50 national unions had Irish presidents (Bodnar, 1985; Brody, 1980).

As the labor movement grew in strength and acquired legitimacy, its leaders gained status, power, and other resources, and the rank-and-file membership gained job security, increased wages, and better benefits. In short, the labor movement provided another channel through which resources, power, status, and jobs flowed to the white ethnic groups.

Because of how jobs were organized, union work typically required communication and cooperation across ethnic lines. The American workforce at the turn of the 20th century was multiethnic and multilingual. To represent diverse workers' as a single social class, union leaders had to coordinate and mobilize the efforts of many different cultural groups. Thus, labor union leaders became important intermediaries between society and European immigrant groups.

European immigrant women were heavily involved in labor movement and some filled leadership roles, including top positions, such as union president (although usually in women-dominated unions). One of the most important union activists was Mother Jones, an Irish immigrant who worked tirelessly to organize miners:

> Until she was nearly one hundred years old, Mother Jones was where the danger was greatest—crossing militia lines, spending weeks in damp prisons, incurring the wrath of governors, presidents, and coal operators—she helped to organize the United Mine Workers with the only tools she felt she needed: "convictions and a voice." (Forner, 1980, p. 281)

Women workers often faced opposition from men workers and from employers. The major unions weren't only racially discriminatory but also hostile to organizing women. For example, in the early 20th century, companies required women laundry workers in San Francisco to live in dormitories and work from 6 a.m. until midnight. When they applied to the international laundry workers union for a charter, men union members blocked them from joining. The women eventually went on strike and won the right to an eight-hour workday in 1912 (Amott & Matthaei, 1991, p. 117). Women in other protest movements have had to deal with similar opposition from men, as you'll see in future chapters.

Women led some of the labor movement's most significant events. For example, one of its first victories was the Uprising of 20,000 (also known as the *New York Shirtwaist Strike of 1909*). Thousands of mostly Jewish and Italian girls and women (many in their teens) staged a strike opposing the garment industry's abusive working conditions (Kheel Center, 2017). Despite factory owners and machine bosses hiring people to attack the strikers and the local police unlawfully assaulting the participants, the strike managed to last four months. The strikers eventually won union recognition from many employers, a reversal of a wage decrease, and a reduction in the 56- to 59-hour workweek (Goren, 1980, p. 584).

Despite their efforts, European immigrant women were among the most exploited segments of the labor force, often relegated to the lowest-paying jobs in difficult or unsafe working conditions. (Today, we'd call them *sweatshops*.) For example, they were the primary victims of one of the greatest tragedies in U.S. labor history. In 1911, a fire swept through the Triangle Shirtwaist Company, a garment industry shop on the 10th floor of a building in New York City. The fire spread rapidly, fueled by paper and fabric scraps. Because of concerns that workers would take breaks or steal fabric, management locked and guarded the doors (von Drehle, 2004, p. 265). Overcrowding and a lack of exits (including a collapsed fire escape) made escape nearly impossible. Many workers leaped to their deaths to avoid being killed by fire. One hundred forty-six people were killed, 120 of them were young immigrant women, the youngest only 14 years old. The disaster outraged the public, and more than a quarter of a million people attended the victims' funerals. The incident fueled a drive for reform and improvement of work conditions and safety regulations (Amott & Matthaei, 1991, pp. 114–116; see also Kheel Center, 2017; Schoener, 1967).

Religion

Religious institutions provided a third avenue of mobility for the Irish and other white ethnic groups. The Irish were the first large group of Catholic immigrants to come to the U. S. and therefore were in a favorable position to dominate the church's administrative structure. The Catholic priesthood became largely Irish and, as these priests were promoted through the Church hierarchy, they eventually became bishops and cardinals. The Catholic faith was practiced in different ways in different nations. As other Catholic immigrant groups began arriving, conflict within the Irish-dominated church increased. Italian and Polish Catholic immigrants demanded their own parishes in which they could speak their own languages and celebrate their own customs and festivals. Dissatisfaction was so intense that some Polish Catholics broke with Rome and formed a separate Polish National Catholic Church (Lopata, 1976, p. 49).

The other Catholic immigrant groups eventually began supplying priests and other religious functionaries and to occupy Church leadership positions. Although the Irish continued to disproportionately influence the Church, it served as a power base for other white ethnic groups to gain acceptance and become integrated into mainstream American society (McCook, 2011).

Other Pathways

Besides party politics, the union movement, and religion, European immigrant groups forged other not-so-legitimate pathways of upward mobility. One alternative to legitimate success was offered by crime, a pathway that has been used by every ethnic group to some extent. Crime became particularly lucrative and attractive when Prohibition, the attempt to eliminate alcohol use in the U. S., went into effect in the 1920s. The criminalization of liquor didn't lower the demand, and Prohibition created an economic opportunity for those willing to take the risks involved in manufacturing and supplying alcohol to the American public.

Italian Americans headed many of the criminal organizations that took advantage of Prohibition. Criminal leaders and organizations with roots in Sicily, a region with a long history of secret antiestablishment societies, were especially important (Alba, 1985, pp. 62–64). The connection among organized crime, Prohibition, and Italian Americans is well known, but it isn't widely recognized that ethnic succession oper-ated in organized crime as it did in the legitimate opportunity structures. The Irish and Germans had been involved in organized crime for decades before the 1920s. The Italians competed with these established gangsters and with Jewish crime syndicates for control of bootlegging and other criminal enterprises. The patterns of ethnic suc-cession continued after the repeal of Prohibition in 1933, and members of groups newer to urban areas, including African Americans, Jamaicans, and Hispanic Americans, have recently challenged the Italian-dominated criminal families.

You can see ethnic succession in sports, too. Since the beginning of the 20th century, sports have offered a pathway to success and affluence that has attracted millions of young people. Success in many sports requires little in the way of formal credentials, education, or English fluency; historically, sports have been particularly appealing to the young men in minority groups that have few resources or opportunities.

For example, at the turn of the 20th century, the Irish dominated boxing, but box-ers from the Italian American community and other new immigrant groups eventually replaced them. Each successive wave of boxers reflected the concentration of a particular ethnic group at the bottom of the class structure. The succession of minority groups continues today, with boxing now dominated by African American and Latino fighters (Rader, 1983, pp. 87–106). We can see a similar progression, or "layering," of ethnic and racial groups in other sports.

The institutions of American society, whether legitimate or illegal, reflect the relative positions of minority groups at a moment in time. Just a few generations ago, European immigrant groups dominated crime and sports because they were blocked from legiti-mate opportunities. Now, it's racial minority groups, still excluded from the mainstream job market and mired in the urban underclass, that supply disproportionate numbers of people for these alternative opportunity structures.

Continuing Industrialization and Structural Mobility

We've already mentioned that dominant–minority relations typically change with changes in subsistence technology. The history of European immigrant groups throughout the 20th century illustrates this relationship. Industrialization is a continuous process. As it proceeded, the nature of work in America evolved and changed and created opportunities for upward mobility for the white ethnic groups. One important form of upward mobility throughout the 20th century, called **structural mobility**, resulted more from changes in the structure of the economy and the labor market than from any individual effort or desire to get ahead.

Structural mobility is the result of the continuing mechanization and automation of the workplace. As machines replaced people in the workforce, the supply of manual, blue-collar jobs that had provided employment for so many first- and second-generation European immigrant laborers dwindled. At the same time, the supply of white-collar jobs increased, but access to the better jobs depended heavily on educational credentials. For white ethnic groups, a high school education became much more available in the 1930s, and college and university programs expanded rapidly in the late 1940s, spurred in large part by the educational benefits made available to World War II veterans. Each generation of white ethnics, especially those born after 1925, was significantly more educated than the previous generation, and many were able to translate their increased human capital into upward mobility in the mainstream job market (Morawska, 1990, pp. 212–213).

The descendants of European immigrants became upwardly mobile not only because of their individual ambitions and efforts but also because of the changing location of jobs and the progressively greater opportunities for education. Of course, the pace and timing of this upward movement was highly variable from group to group and from place to place. Ethnic succession continued to operate, and the descendants of the most recent European immigrants (Italians and Poles, for example) tended to be the last to benefit from the general upgrading in education and the job market.

Still, structural mobility is key to the eventual successful integration of all ethnic groups. In Table 2.3, you'll see differing levels of educational attainment and income for white ethnic groups. During these same years, racial minority groups, particularly African Americans, were excluded from the dominant group's educational system and from the opportunity to compete for better jobs. We'll discuss these patterns of exclusion more in Parts 2 and 3.

QUESTIONS FOR REFLECTION

9. To understand the process of assimilation, why do we need to consider generation(s)?

10. What were the major institutional pathways through which European immigrants adapted to American society? Can you cite evidence from your home community of similar patterns for immigrant groups today?

VARIATIONS IN ASSIMILATION

In the previous section, we discussed patterns common to European immigrants and their descendants. Now we address some of the sources of variation and diversity in assimilation, a complex process that is never identical for any two groups. Sociologists have paid particular attention to how similarity, religion, social class, and gender shaped the overall assimilation of the descendants of the mass European immigration. They've also investigated the way in which immigrants' reasons for coming to this country have affected the experiences of different groups.

Degree of Similarity

Since the dominant group consisted largely of Protestants with ethnic origins in Northern and Western Europe and especially in England, it isn't surprising to learn that the degree of resistance, prejudice, and discrimination encountered by the different European immigrant groups varied, in part by how much they differed from these dominant groups. The most significant differences included religion, language, cultural values, and, for some groups, physical characteristics (often viewed as "racial"). Thus, Protestant immigrants from Northern and Western Europe experienced less resistance than the English-speaking Catholic Irish, who in turn were accepted more readily than the new immigrants, who were non–English speaking and overwhelmingly non-Protestant.

The preferences of the dominant group correspond roughly to the arrival times of the immigrants. The most similar groups immigrated earliest, and the least similar tended to be the last to arrive. Because of this coincidence, resistance to any one group of immigrants tended to fade as new groups arrived. For example, anti-German prejudice and discrimination never became particularly vicious or widespread (except during the heat of the World Wars) because the Irish began arriving in large numbers at about the same time. Concerns about the German immigrants were swamped by the fear that the Catholic Irish could never be assimilated. Then, as the 19th century drew to a close, immigrants from Southern and Eastern Europe—even more different from the dominant group—began arriving and made concerns about the Irish seem trivial.

Additionally, the New Immigration was far larger than the Old Immigration (see Figure 2.2). Southern and Eastern Europeans arrived in record numbers in the early 20th century. The sheer volume of the immigration raised fears that American cities and institutions would be swamped by hordes of what were seen as racially inferior, unassimilable immigrants, a fear that resonates today in our debates about modern immigrants.

Thus, a preference hierarchy was formed in American culture that privileged Northern and Western Europeans over Southern and Eastern Europeans, and Protestants over Catholics and Jews. These rankings reflect the ease with which the groups assimilated and have made their way into society. As the social distance scores in Table 1.2 showed, this hierarchy of ethnic preference is still a part of American prejudice, although it's much more muted today than during the peak of immigration.

Religion

Gordon and other scholars of American assimilation recognized that religion was a major factor that differentiated the experiences of European immigrant groups.

Protestant, Catholic, and Jewish immigrants lived in different neighborhoods, occupied different niches in the workforce, formed separate groups and networks of affiliation, and chose their marriage partners from different groups.

Sociologist Ruby Jo Kennedy's research (1944) documented the importance of religion for European immigrants and their descendants. Specifically, she studied intermarriage among Catholics, Protestants, and Jews in New Haven, Connecticut, from 1870 to 1940. She found that immigrants generally chose marriage partners from certain ethnic and religious groups. For example, Irish Catholics married other Irish Catholics, Italian Catholics married Italian Catholics, Irish Protestants married Irish Protestants, and so forth for all the ethnic and religious groups that she studied.

However, later generations showed a different pattern: The immigrants' children and grandchildren continued to select marriage partners from groups bounded by religion, but not much by ethnicity. For example, later generations of Irish Catholics continued to marry other Catholics (religion) but were less likely to marry other Irish (ethnicity). As assimilation proceeded, the ethnic group boundaries faded (or "melted"), but religious boundaries didn't. Kennedy (1944, 1952) described this phenomenon as a ***triple melting pot***: a pattern of structural assimilation within each of the three denominations (Catholics, Jews, Protestants).

Will Herberg (1960), another important scholar of American assimilation, also explored the connection between religion and ethnicity. He noted that the pressures of acculturation didn't equally affect all aspects of ethnicity. European immigrants and their descendants were strongly encouraged to learn English. However, they weren't as pressured to change their beliefs, and religion was often the strongest connection between later generations of immigrants and their immigrant ancestors. The American tradition of religious tolerance allowed the European immigrants' descents to preserve this connection to their ethnic heritage without others seeing them as un-American. Therefore, the Protestant, Catholic, and Jewish faiths eventually came to occupy roughly equal degrees of legitimacy in American society.

Thus, for the descendants of the European immigrants, religion became a way to express their ethnicity. For many members of this group, religion and ethnicity were fused, and ethnic traditions and identities came to have a religious expression.

Social Class

Social class is a central feature of social structure, and it isn't surprising that it affected the European immigrant groups in several ways. First, social class combined with religion to shape the social world of the descendants of the European immigrants. Gordon (1964) concluded that United States in the 1960s incorporated four melting pots (one for each of the major ethnic or religious groups and one for black Americans), each internally subdivided by social class. In his view, the most significant structural unit within American society was the **ethclass**, defined by the intersection of the religious, ethnic, and social class boundaries (e.g., working-class Catholic, upper-class Protestant). Thus, people weren't "simply American" but tended to identify with, associate with, and choose their spouses from within their ethclass.

Second, social class affected structural integration. The vast majority of the post-1880s European immigrants were working class. They "entered U.S. society at the bottom of the economic ladder, and . . . stayed close to that level for the next half century;" thus "ethnic history has been essentially working-class history" (Morawska, 1990, p. 215; see also Bodnar, 1985). For generations, many groups of Eastern and Southern European immigrants didn't acculturate to middle-class American culture but to an urban working-class, blue-collar one. Even today, ethnicity for many groups remains interconnected with social class factors.

Gender

Historically, scholars didn't study women's lives. They either didn't consider it important, or they assumed that women's lives were the same as men's lives. At the time, societal norms encouraged women to focus on home and family and discouraged women from interacting with men they didn't know. Women were discouraged from having a public life, which resulted in them having much less access to education, fewer leadership roles in the community, and less outside employment, especially in prestigious or high-paying occupations. Immigrant women may have felt these prohibitions most strongly and they, like others, may have been wary of researchers. This made it harder to gain access to immigrant women for the few researchers who were interested in women's lives. Due to lack of education and interaction in the greater society, immigrant women had fewer opportunities to learn English. So, in cases where access was possible, language barriers could complicate matters. Thus, although a huge body of research about immigration exists, the bulk of it focuses on immigrant men. As with women of virtually all minority groups, researchers documented immigrant women's experiences far less often (Gabaccia, 1991; Weinberg, Gabaccia, Diner, & Seller, 1992). However, the research that has been done shows that immigrant women played multiple roles during immigration and the assimilation process. The roles of wife and mother were central, but they were involved in many other activities.

Generally, male immigrants preceded women, and sent for the women (and children) in their lives only after securing lodging, jobs, and some stability. However, women immigrants' experiences were quite varied, often depending on the economic situation and cultural traditions of their home societies. In some cases, women were prominent among the "first wave" of immigrants who began the process of acculturation and integration. For example, during the latter part of the 19th century, more than 1 million Irish people sought refuge elsewhere, in large part due to the Great Famine, sometimes called the *Great Hunger* or the *Irish Potato Famine*, which killed more than 1 million of them. (See the Comparative Focus section.)

The famine led to changes in rules of land ownership, marriage, and inheritance, which made it hard for single women to marry and to find work (Flannagan, 2015; Jackson 1984). Interestingly, Kennedy (1973, p. 66) notes that more Irish women (55,690) than men (55,215) emigrated between 1871 and 1891; a high percentage of Irish immigrants were young, single women. They came to America seeking opportunities for work. Typically, they worked as domestics, doing cooking, cleaning, and childcare (Maurer, 2017), a role that permitted them to live "respectably" in a family setting. In 1850, about 75% of all employed Irish immigrant women in New York City worked as servants. The second most prevalent form of employment was in textile mills and factories (Blessing, 1980; see also Steinberg, 1981). This pattern continued, and as late as 1920, 81% of employed Irish-born immigrant women worked as domestics.

Due to the economic situation of immigrant families, other immigrant women typically worked outside of their homes, too, though the type and location of the work varied. For example, Italian women rarely worked outside the home because of strong patriarchal norms in Italian culture, including a strong prohibition against contact between women and men they didn't know (Alba, 1985). Thus, Italian women primarily worked from home: taking in laundry or boarders or doing piecework for the garment industry. Those employed outside the home tended to work in single-gender settings among other immigrant women. As a result, Italian women tended to be far less acculturated and integrated than Irish women.

Eastern European Jewish women experienced another pattern of assimilation. Most came with their husbands and children as refugees from religious persecution. Therefore, few were breadwinners. They "worked in small shops with other family members" while others worked in the garment industry (Steinberg, 1981, p. 161).

Generally, social norms dictated that immigrant women, like other working-class women, should quit working after they married, while their husbands were expected to support them and their children. However, many immigrant men couldn't earn enough to support their families, and their wives and children were required by necessity to contribute to the family budget. Immigrant wives sometimes continued to work outside the home, or they found other ways to make money. They took in boarders, did laundry or sewing, tended gardens, and were involved in many other activities that permitted them to contribute to the family income while staying home attending to family responsibilities.

A 1911 report on Southern and Eastern European households found that about half kept lodgers. The income from this activity amounted to about 25% of the husbands' wages. Children contributed to the family income by taking after-school and summer jobs (Morawska, 1990, pp. 211–212). Compared with immigrant men, immigrant women spent much more time at their homes and in their neighborhoods. Thus, they were less likely to learn to read or speak English or otherwise acculturate. However, this made them significantly more influential in preserving the heritage of their groups.

When they sought employment outside the home, they found opportunities in the industrial sector and in clerical and sales work, occupations that quickly became stereotyped as "women's work." Employers saw working women as wanting only to supplement family finances, and they used that assumption to justify lower wages for women. In the late 1800s, "whether in factories, offices, or private homes . . . women's wages were about half of those of men" (Evans, 1980, p. 135). This assumption hurt all immigrant women but single and widowed women the most because they didn't have husbands who could bring in most of the necessary income.

Finally, in addition to their other responsibilities, women were the primary keepers of "old country" traditions. Husbands were often more involved in the society, giving them greater familiarity with Anglo culture and the English language. Women, even when employed, tended to spend more time at home and in the neighborhood. They tended to be more culturally conservative and more resistant to Anglo values and practices than immigrant men. Therefore, immigrant women were more likely to practice traditional foodways and dress, speak to their children in the old language, and observe the time-honored holidays and religious practices. Thus, they performed crucial cultural and socialization functions. This pattern remains among many immigrant groups today in the United States and in Western Europe.

Sojourners

Some versions of the traditional perspective and the taken-for-granted views of many Americans assume that assimilation is desirable and therefore desired by immigrants. However, European immigrant groups varied widely in their interest in Americanization; this attitude greatly shaped their experiences.

Some groups were very committed to Americanization. For example, Eastern European Jews came to America because of religious persecution. They came fearing for their lives. They planned to make America their home because they had no possibility of returning and had nowhere else to go. (Israel wasn't founded until 1948.) They committed to learning English, becoming citizens, and familiarizing themselves with their new society as quickly as possible.

Other immigrants had no intention of becoming American citizens and, therefore, had little interest in becoming Americanized. These **sojourners**, or "birds of passage," intended to return to the old country once they had accumulated enough capital to be successful. Because immigration records aren't very detailed, it's hard to know the exact numbers of immigrants who returned to the old country (see Wyman, 1993), but we know, for example, that a significant percentage of Italian immigrants were sojourners. Although 3.8 million Italians landed in the United States between 1899 and 1924, around 2.1 million departed during that same time (Nelli, 1980, p. 547).

QUESTIONS FOR REFLECTION

11. What are some of the most important variations in the ways European immigrants adjusted to American society?

12. What was the *triple melting pot*, and how did it function?

13. What important gender role differences existed in European immigrant groups? Would you guess that men or women would be more likely to be sojourners? Why?

THE DESCENDANTS OF THE IMMIGRANTS TODAY

Geographical Distribution

Figure 2.4 shows the geographical distribution of 15 racial and ethnic groups across the United States. The map displays the single largest group in each county and offers great detail. However, we'll focus on some of the groups mentioned in this chapter, including Norwegian, German, Irish, and Italian Americans. (The Jewish population is too small to appear on this map. You'll also notice that this map, unlike others in this book, is somewhat old. The most recent census [2010] didn't ask people about their ancestry; therefore, we can't provide a newer snapshot. This is one example of why it's important to collect data—to see how trends change.)

FIGURE 2.4 ■ Ancestry with Largest Population in Each County, 2000

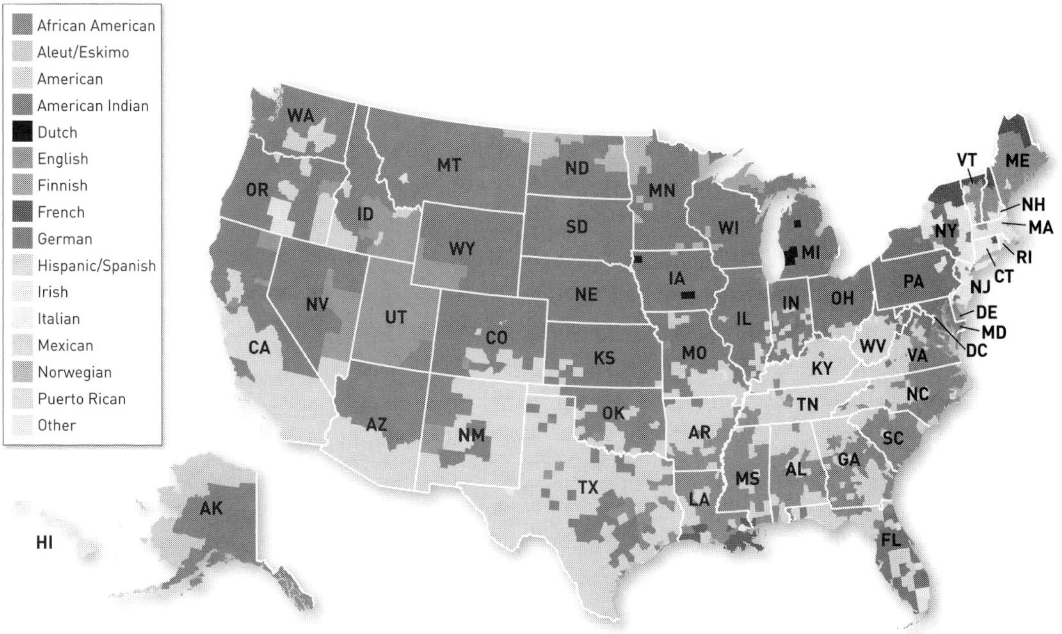

Legend:
- African American
- Aleut/Eskimo
- American
- American Indian
- Dutch
- English
- Finnish
- French
- German
- Hispanic/Spanish
- Irish
- Italian
- Mexican
- Norwegian
- Puerto Rican
- Other

Source: U.S. Census Bureau (2004).

As noted in Figure 2.4, Germans are the single largest ancestry group in America (see the predominance of gray from Pennsylvania to the West Coast). Also note how the map reflects this group's original settlement areas, especially in the Midwest. Norwegian Americans (and Swedish Americans) are numerically dominant in some sections of the upper Midwest (e.g., northwestern Minnesota, northern North Dakota). Irish Americans and Italian Americans are concentrated in their original areas of settlement—the Irish in Massachusetts and the Italians concentrated more around New York City.

Thus, almost a century after the end of mass immigration from Europe, many of the immigrants' descendants haven't gone far from where their ancestors settled. The map also shows that the same point could be made for other groups, including blacks (concentrated in the "black belt" across the states of the old Confederacy), Mexican Americans (concentrated along the southern border from Texas to California), and Native Americans (their concentration in the upper Midwest, eastern Oklahoma, and the Southwest reflects the locations of the reservations where they were forced after the end of the Indian wars).

Given all that has changed in American society over the past century—industrialization, population growth, urbanization, and massive mobility—the stable location of white ethnics (and other ethnic and racial groups) seems remarkable. Why aren't people distributed more randomly across the nation's landscape?

That stability is easier to explain for some groups than others. African Americans, Mexican Americans, and Native Americans were limited in their geographic and social mobility by institutionalized discrimination, racism, and limited resources. We'll examine the power of these constraints in later chapters.

For white ethnics, however, the power of exclusion and rejection waned as the generations passed and immigrants' descendants assimilated and integrated. Their current locations may suggest that the United States is a nation of groups and of individuals. Our group memberships, especially family and kin, exert a powerful influence on our decisions about where to live and work and, despite the transience and mobility of modern American life, can keep people connected to their relatives, the old neighborhood, their ethnic roots, and the sites of their ancestors' struggles.

Integration and Equality

One important point about white ethnic groups (the descendants of the European immigrants) is that they are almost completely assimilated today. Even the groups that were the most despised in earlier years (e.g., the Irish) are now acculturated, integrated, and thoroughly intermarried. Consider Table 2.3, which shows the degree to which nine of the more than 60 white ethnic groups had become integrated as far back as 1990. The groups include the two largest white ethnic groups (German and Irish Americans) and

TABLE 2.3 ■ Median Household Income, Percentage of Families Living in Poverty, and Educational Attainment for Selected White Ethnic Groups, 1990				
	Median Household Income	Percentage of Families Living in Poverty	Percentage Who Completed High School or More	Percentage Who Received an Undergraduate Degree or More
All Americans	$30,056	10%	75.2%	20.3%
Russian	$45,778	3.6%	90.8%	49%
Italian	$36,060	4.9%	77.3%	21%
Polish	$34,763	4.3%	78.5%	23.1%
Ukrainian	$34,474	4%	77.5%	28.3%
Swedish	$33,881	4.5%	87.3%	27.4%
German	$32,730	5.5%	82.7%	22%
Slovak	$32,352	3.8%	78.2%	21.6%
Norwegian	$32,207	5.1%	85.9%	26%
Irish	$31,845	6.5%	79.6%	21.2%

Source: U.S. Census Bureau (2008).

seven others that represent a range of geographic origins and times of immigration (U.S. Census Bureau, 2008).

The table shows that by 1990, all nine of the groups selected were at or above national norms ("All Americans") for all measures of equality. Variation exists among the groups, but all exceeded the national averages for high school and college education and they had dramatically lower poverty rates, usually less than half the national average. All nine groups exceed the national median for household income—some by a considerable margin—Russians, for example, many of whom are also Jewish.

The evidence for assimilation and equality in other areas is persuasive. For example, the distinct ethnic neighborhoods that these groups created in American cities (e.g., Little Italy, Greektown, Little Warsaw) have faded away or been taken over by other groups. Additionally, the rate of intermarriage between members of different white ethnic groups is quite high. For example, data from the 1990 census showed that about 56% of all married whites have spouses with ethnic backgrounds different from their own (Alba, 1995, pp. 13–14).

The Evolution of White Ethnicity

Integration into the American mainstream was neither linear nor continuous for the descendants of European immigrants. Over the generations, white ethnic identity sporadically reasserted itself in many ways; two are especially notable. First, later generations tended to be more interested in their ancestry and ethnicity than earlier generations. Hansen (1952) captured this phenomenon in his **principle of third-generation interest**: "What the second generation tries to forget, the third generation tries to remember" (p. 495). Hansen observed that the immigrants' children tended to minimize or de-emphasize ("forget") their ethnicity to avoid society's prejudice and intolerance and compete on more favorable terms for jobs and other opportunities. As they became adults and started families of their own, the second generation (the immigrants' children) tended to raise their children in nonethnic settings, with English as their first and only language.

By the time the third generation (the immigrants' grandchildren) reached adulthood, American society had become more tolerant of white ethnicity and diversity (especially of New Immigrant groups that arrived last). Unlike earlier generations, the third generation had little to risk and, therefore, tried to reconnect with its grandparents and roots. These descendants wanted to understand the "old ways" and their ethnic heritage and they wanted to incorporate it into their personal identities, giving them a sense of who they were and where they belong.

Ironically, the immigrants' grandchildren couldn't recover much of the richness and detail of their heritage because their parents had tried to forget it. Nonetheless, the desire of the third generation to reconnect with its ancestry and recover its ethnicity shows that assimilation isn't a simple, one-dimensional, or linear process.

In addition to this generational pattern, the strength of white ethnic identity also responded to the changing context of American society, including other groups. For example, in the late 1960s and early 1970s, there was a notable increase in the visibility of and interest in white ethnic heritage, an upsurge sometimes called the **ethnic revival**. The revival manifested itself in many ways. Some people became more interested in their families' genealogical roots, and others increased their participation in ethnic festivals, traditions, and organizations. The "white ethnic vote" became a factor in local, state, and national politics, and appearances at the churches, meeting halls, and neighborhoods associated with white ethnic groups became almost mandatory for candidates for office. People organized demonstrations and festivals celebrating white ethnic heritages, often sporting buttons and bumper stickers proclaiming their ancestry. Politicians, editorialists, and intellectuals endorsed, legitimized, and reinforced the ethnic revival (e.g., see Novak, 1973), which were partly fueled by the desire to reconnect with ancestral roots—although most groups were well beyond their third generations by the 1960s. More likely, ethnic revival was a reaction to the increase in pluralistic sentiment at the time, including the pluralistic, even separatist assertions of other groups. In the 1960s and 1970s, virtually every minority group generated a protest movement (e.g., Black Power, Red Power, Chicanismo) and proclaimed a recommitment to its own heritage and to the authenticity of its own culture and experiences. The visibility of these calls for cultural pluralism helped make it more acceptable for European Americans to express their own ethnic heritage.

The resurgence of white ethnicity also had some political and economic dimensions that relate to issues of inequality and competition for resources. In the 1960s, a white-ethnic urban working class made up mostly of Irish and Southern and Eastern European groups still remained in the neighborhoods of the industrial Northeast and Midwest and they continued to breathe life into the old networks and traditions (see Glazer & Moynihan, 1970; Greeley, 1974). While many Americans were beginning to view cultural pluralism as legitimate, this ethnic working class began feeling threatened by minority groups of color (blacks, Hispanics) who increasingly lived in adjoining neighborhoods, therefore in direct competition with white ethnics for housing, jobs, and other resources.

Many white ethnic working-class people saw racial minority groups as inferior and perceived the advances made by these groups as unfair, unjust, and threatening. Additionally, they reacted to what they saw as special treatment based on race, such as affirmative action. They had problems of their own (e.g., declining number of good, unionized jobs; inadequate schooling) and believed that their problems were being given lower priority and less legitimacy because they were white. The revived sense of ethnicity in the urban working-class neighborhoods was, in large part, a way of resisting racial reform and expressing resentment for the racial minority groups. Thus, the revival of white ethnicity that began in the 1960s was also fueled by competition for resources and opportunities. As you'll see throughout this book, such competition commonly leads to increased prejudice toward people who are perceived as different while simultaneously creating a sense of cohesion among same-group members.

The Twilight of White Ethnicity?[1]

As the conflicts of the 1960s and 1970s faded, white ethnic groups left their old neighborhoods and rose in the class structure. This contributed to the slow demise of white ethnic identity. Today, white ethnic identity has become increasingly nebulous and largely voluntary. Sociologists call this **symbolic ethnicity** or an aspect of self-identity that symbolizes one's roots in the old country but is otherwise insignificant. That is, these descendants of the European immigrants feel vaguely connected to their ancestors, but this doesn't affect their lifestyles, circles of friends and neighbors, job prospects, eating habits, or other everyday routines (Gans, 1979; Lieberson & Waters, 1988). They may express this part of their identities only on occasion; for example, by joining ethnic or religious celebrations such as St. Patrick's Day (Irish Americans) or Columbus Day (Italian Americans). Because many people have ancestors from more than one ethnic group, they may change their sense of group affiliation over time, sometimes emphasizing one group's traditions and sometimes another's (Waters, 1990). In stark contrast to their ancestors, members of racial minority groups, and recent immigrants, the descendants of the European immigrants have choices: They can emphasize their ethnicity, celebrate it occasionally, or ignore it completely. In short, symbolic ethnicity is superficial, voluntary, and changeable.

White ethnic identity may be on the verge of disappearing. For example, based on a series of in-depth interviews with white Americans from various regions of the nation, Gallagher (2001) found a sense of ethnicity so weak that it didn't even rise to the level of "symbolic." His respondents were the products of ancestral lines so thoroughly intermixed and intermarried that any trace of a unique heritage from a particular group was completely lost. They had virtually no knowledge of the experiences of their immigrant ancestors or of the life and cultures of the ethnic communities they had inhabited, and for many, their ethnic ancestries were no more meaningful to them than their states of birth. Their lack of interest in and information about their ethnic heritage was so complete that it led Gallagher (2001) to propose an addendum to Hansen's principle: "What the grandson wished to remember, the great-granddaughter has never been told."

At the same time, as more specific white ethnic identities are disappearing, they're also evolving into new shapes and forms. In the view of many analysts, a new identity is developing that merges the various ethnic identities (e.g., *German American*, *Polish American*) into a single, generalized *European American* identity based on race and a common history of immigration and assimilation. This new identity reinforces the racial lines of separation that run through contemporary society, but it does more than simply mark group boundaries. Embedded in this emerging identity is an understanding, often deeply flawed, of how white immigrant groups succeeded and assimilated in the past and a view, often deeply ideological, of how the racial minority groups and many recent immigrants should behave today. These understandings are encapsulated in "immigrant tales": legends that stress heroic individual effort and grim determination as key ingredients leading to success in the old days. These tales feature impoverished, victimized immigrant ancestors who survived and made a place for themselves and their children by working hard, saving their money, and otherwise exemplifying the virtues of the Protestant ethic and American individualism. They stress the idea that past generations became successful despite the brutal hostility of the dominant group and with no government intervention, and they equate the historical difficulties faced by European immigrants with those suffered by racial minority groups (e.g., slavery, segregation, and attempted genocide). They strongly imply—and sometimes blatantly assert—that the latter groups could succeed in America by simply following the example set by the former (Alba, 1990; Gallagher, 2001).

These accounts mix versions of human capital theory and traditional views of assimilation with prejudice and racism. Without denying or trivializing the resolve and fortitude of European immigrants, equating their experiences and levels of disadvantage with those of African Americans, Native Americans, and Mexican Americans is widely off the mark, as you'll see in future chapters. These views support an attitude of disdain and lack of sympathy for the multiple dilemmas faced today by the racial minority groups and many contemporary immigrants. They permit a subtler expression of prejudice and racism and allow whites to use these highly distorted views of their immigrant ancestors as a rhetorical device to express a host of race-based grievances without appearing racist (Gallagher, 2001).

Alba (1990) concludes as follows:

The thrust of the [emerging] European American identity is to defend the individualistic view of the American system, because it portrays the system as open to those who are willing to work hard and pull themselves out of poverty and discrimination. Recent research suggests that it is precisely this individualism that prevents many whites from sympathizing with the need for African Americans and other minorities to receive affirmative action in order to overcome institutional barriers to their advancement. (p. 317)

What can we conclude? The generations-long journey from immigrant to white ethnics to European American seems to be ending. The separate ethnic identities are merging into a larger sense of whiteness that unites immigrants' descendants with the dominant group and provides a rhetorical device for expressing disdain for other groups, especially African Americans and undocumented immigrants.

QUESTIONS FOR REFLECTION

14. In what ways are the descendants of European immigrants seen as successful?

15. What is Hansen's principle? Why is it significant? What is Gallagher's addendum to this principle? Why is it important?

16. Does white ethnic identity have a future? Why or why not?

CONTEMPORARY IMMIGRANTS: DOES THE TRADITIONAL PERSPECTIVE APPLY?

Does the traditional perspective—based on the experiences of European immigrants and their descendants—apply to more recent immigrants to America? Will contemporary immigrants duplicate the experiences of earlier groups? Will they acculturate before they integrate? Will religion, social class, and race be important forces in their lives? Will they take three generations to assimilate? More than three? Fewer? What will their patterns of intermarriage look like? Will they achieve socioeconomic parity with the dominant group? When? How?

Sociologists (policymakers and the general public) are split in their answers to these questions. Some social scientists believe that the traditional perspective on assimilation doesn't apply and that the experiences of contemporary immigrant groups will differ greatly from those of European immigrants. They believe that assimilation today is fragmented (known as **segmented assimilation**) and will have several different outcomes: Some contemporary immigrant groups will integrate into the middle-class mainstream, but others will be permanently mired in the impoverished, alienated, and marginalized segments of racial and ethnic minority groups. Still others may form close-knit enclaves based on their traditional cultures and become successful in America by resisting the forces of acculturation (Portes & Rumbaut, 2001, p. 45).

In stark contrast, other theorists believe that the traditional perspective on assimilation remains relevant and that contemporary immigrant groups will follow the established pathways of mobility and assimilation. Of course, the process varies by group and location, but even the groups that are the most impoverished and marginalized today will, eventually, move into mainstream society.

We can't say how the debate will be resolved, but we'd note that this debate is reminiscent of the critique of Park's theory of assimilation. In both cases, the argument is partly about time: Even the most impoverished and segmented groups may find their way into the economic mainstream at some time in the future. One's perception of the nature of modern American society creates other related debates. Is American society today growing more tolerant of diversity, more open and equal? If so, this would seem to favor the traditionalist perspective. If not, this trend would clearly favor the segmented-assimilation hypothesis. Although we won't resolve this debate, we'll consider the traditional and segmented views on assimilation as a useful framework to understand the experiences of these groups (see Chapters 5–8).

QUESTIONS FOR REFLECTION

17. What is *segmented assimilation*, and why is this an important concept? How would social class and gender relate to the debate over whether contemporary assimilation is segmented?

IMPLICATIONS FOR EXAMINING DOMINANT–MINORITY RELATIONS

In Chapters 1 and 2, we've introduced many of the concepts and themes that form the foundation of this book. Although the connections between the concepts are complex, we can summarize the key points so far.

First, we discussed the five components of minority group status in Chapter 1. Being in a minority group has much more to do with lack of power and the distribution of resources than with the size of the group. Additionally, we addressed themes of inequality and differentials in status in our discussion of prejudice, racism, and discrimination. To understand minority relations, we must examine some basic realities of human society: inequalities in wealth, prestige, and the distribution of power. To discuss changes in minority group status, we must be prepared to discuss changes in how society does business, makes decisions, and distributes education, income, jobs, health care, and other opportunities.

Second, we've raised questions about how our society should develop. We've discussed assimilation and pluralism, including their variations. For more than a century, social scientists have extensively studied both paths. Additionally, political leaders, decision makers, and citizens have discussed them. Yet, in many ways, Americans seem more divided than ever about which path the country should take. We'll continue to analyze and evaluate both pathways throughout the book.

COMPARATIVE FOCUS
IMMIGRATION AND IRELAND

FIGURE 2.5 ■ Migration into and out of Ireland, 1987–2017

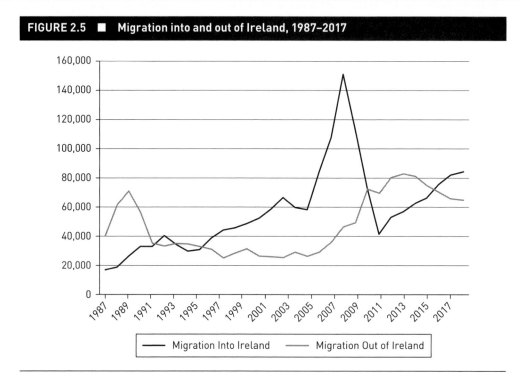

Source: Central Statistics Office [Ireland] (2017).

Just as the U. S. has been a major receiver of immigrants for the past 200 years, Ireland has been a major supplier. Mass migration from Ireland began with the potato famines of the 1840s and continued through the end of the 20th century, motivated by continuing hard times, political unrest, and unemployment. This mass out-migration—combined with the death toll of the famines—cut the 1840 Irish population of over 8 million in half in a few decades. The population today is still only about 4.8 million.

History rarely runs in straight lines. In the 1990s and into the 21st century, after nearly 200 years of supplying immigrants, Ireland (along with other nations of Northern and Western Europe) became a receiver. As Figure 2.5 shows, the number of newcomers entering Ireland soared between 1987 and 2007, and the number of people leaving decreased. Around 2007, the trend reversed: The number of newcomers plummeted, and the historic pattern of out-migration reappeared. Then, in the most recent years, the pattern changed again as migration to Ireland increased and out-migration leveled off and began decreasing.

What explains these patterns? Fortunately, answers are not hard to find. The influx of immigrants starting in the late 1980s was largely a response to rapid economic growth. The Irish economy—the so-called Celtic Tiger—had entered a boom phase, spurred by investments from multinational corporations and the benefits of joining the European Economic Union. Irish nationals who had left to seek work abroad returned home in large numbers, and people from Europe and other parts of the world also began arriving. Ireland also began receiving refugees and people seeking asylum from Africa, the Middle East, and other troubled areas.

The changes from 2007 to about 2012 have an equally obvious cause. The global economy faltered badly in 2007, and the Irish economy followed suit. Banks failed, companies went bankrupt, the housing market collapsed, and jobs disappeared. The Irish returned to their historic role as a supplier of immigrants to other economies around the world. In recent years, the Irish economy recovered from the global Great Recession and migration patterns shifted accordingly. We should also note that recent immigration into Ireland is much more global and shares many characteristics with recent immigrants to the United States (O'Connell, 2016).

These migration patterns have created significant changes in Ireland. For example, the number of Irish of African and Asian descent has increased by a factor of 8 since 1996. (They are, respectively, 1% and 2% of the total population.) Over the centuries, many diverse groups (e.g., Vikings, Spanish, and Anglo-Normans) have become part of Ireland but for the first time, the Irish are considering issues of racial diversity.

QUESTIONS FOR REFLECTION

18. What similarities can you see between immigration to Ireland and immigration to the United States?

19. Do you suppose that immigrants to Ireland will be assimilated in the same way as immigrants to the United States? If you could travel to Ireland, what questions would you ask about the assimilation process?

Main Points

- Assimilation and pluralism are two broad pathways of development for intergroup relations. However, they can appear together in various combinations.

- In the U. S., assimilation hasn't followed the melting pot model (where people from different groups contribute fairly equally to a new culture). Instead, Anglo conformity (or Americanization) has been the dominant model.

- Gordon theorized that assimilation occurs in stages: acculturation, integration at the secondary and primary levels, and intermarriage. He saw integration as the most crucial.

- The experience of assimilation varied by religion, social class, gender, the extent of sojourning, and even physical appearance.

- In Gordon's view, it is common for American minority groups, especially racial minority groups, to become acculturated but not integrated. Once a group has begun to integrate, the other stages should follow.

- Assimilation for European immigrant groups generally followed a three-generation pattern, with the grandchildren of the original immigrants completing the process. Ethnic succession occurred when newly arrived groups of immigrants pushed older groups up the occupational structure.

- There are three variations of pluralism: cultural (or "full") pluralism, structural pluralism, and enclave (or "middleman") minority groups.

Applying Concepts

To practice using Gordon's model of assimilation (see Table 2.1), we've written some questions about immigrant assimilation experiences to consider. Sociologists document social patterns. Yet each of you has a unique family history of one form or another. Therefore, we've provided you with some options based on what's most appropriate for you:

1. If you're a third- or fourth-generation immigrant whose family came from Europe, you may be able to interview your grandparents or great-grandparents about your family's assimilation experiences, which would make this exercise particularly meaningful, interesting, and fun.

2. If your family immigrated from somewhere else and you have older family members that you can interview (e.g., grandparents, great grandparents), ask them about their immigration experience.

3. Interview older people that you know, such as teachers or neighbors.

4. Imagine what answers a third- or fourth-generation immigrant might say based on what you've learned in this chapter.

Next, identify which part of Gordon's model each question below tests. If you think of other questions that would fit, consider them as well. Place the letter of each question in the appropriate row of the box below.

A. What language did you speak at home when you were growing up?

B. What was your total household income last year?

C. (If married/partnered) Does your spouse/partner share your religious faith?

D. (If married/partnered) Does your spouse/partner share your ethnic background?

E. Did your parents have the same ethnic background? How about your grandparents?

F. Did you vote in the most recent presidential election?

G. What percentage of your friends share your ethnic background?

H. What percentage of your friends share your religious faith?

I. What is the highest level of education you have achieved?

J. Has your family name been changed or Americanized? If so, what was the original name and what did it become? How and why did that name change occur?

Stage	Items
Acculturation	
Integration (secondary level)	
Integration (primary level)	
Marital assimilation	

Turn the page to find our answers.

Review Questions

1. Summarize Gordon's model of assimilation. Identify and explain each stage and how the stages are related. Explain Table 2.2 in terms of Gordon's model.

2. "Human capital theory is not so much wrong as it is incomplete." Explain this statement. What does the theory leave out? What are the strengths of the theory? What questionable assumptions does it make?

3. What are the major dimensions along which the experience of assimilation varies? Explain how and why the experience of assimilation can vary.

4. Define *pluralism* and explain how it differs from *assimilation*. Why has interest in pluralism increased? Explain the difference between structural and cultural pluralism and cite examples of each. Describe enclave minority groups in terms of pluralism and in

terms of Gordon's model of assimilation. How have contemporary theorists added to the concept of pluralism?

5. Define and explain *segmented assimilation* and explain how it differs from Gordon's model. What evidence is there that assimilation for recent immigrants isn't segmented? What is the significance of this debate for the future of American society?

For other minority groups (e.g., African Americans)? For the immigrants?

6. Do American theories and understandings of assimilation apply to Ireland? Do you suppose that immigrants to Ireland will assimilate in the same way as immigrants to the United States? If you could travel to Ireland, what questions would you ask about the assimilation process?

Answers to Applying Concepts

Stage	Items
Acculturation	A, J
Integration (secondary level)	B, F, I
Integration (primary level)	G, H
Marital assimilation	C, D, E

Group Discussion

Bring your answers to the Applying Concepts exercise to class. Compare your answers with your classmates' answers. Consider the issues raised in the questions above and in the chapter and develop some ideas about why various groups are where they are relative to each other and to the total population.

Internet Learning Resources

SAGE edge™ offers teachers and students easy-to-use resources for review, study, and further exploration. See **http://edge.sagepub.com/diversity6e**

Note

1. This phrase comes from Alba (1990).

THE EVOLUTION OF DOMINANT–MINORITY RELATIONS IN THE UNITED STATES

Chapter 3. The Development of Dominant–Minority Group Relations in Preindustrial America: The Origins of Slavery

Chapter 4. Industrialization and Dominant–Minority Relations: From Slavery to Segregation and the Coming of Postindustrial Society

The chapters in Part 2 explore several questions: Why do some groups become minorities? How and why do dominant–minority relations change over time? These aren't merely academic questions. Understanding the dynamics that created and sustained prejudice, racism, discrimination, and inequality in the past will help you understand group relations in the present and future. This knowledge is crucial if we, as Americans, live up to our country's democratic ideals. By understanding these dynamics, you can help create social change.

Both chapters in Part 2 feature African Americans as the primary case study. Chapter 3 focuses on the preindustrial United States and the creation of slavery and also considers the experiences of Native Americans and Mexican Americans during the same time. Chapter 4 analyzes how the Industrial Revolution changed group relations. Specifically, it focuses on the shift from slavery to segregation for African Americans and their migration from the South. Throughout the 20th century, industrial technology continued to evolve and shape group relationships in the United States. We'll begin to explore the consequences of these changes in Chapter 4.

In the next two chapters, you'll use the concepts that you learned in Part 1. Additionally, we'll introduce you to some important new concepts and theories.

By the end of Part 2, you'll be familiar with most of the conceptual framework that we'll use in the rest of this book.

A Note on the Morality and the History of Minority Relations in America: Guilt, Blame, Understanding, and Communication

Very often, when people confront issues of inequality, they react on a personal level. Some might feel a sense of guilt about the troubling aspects of America's history. Others might respond with anger about the injustice and unfairness that remains in the United States. Some might feel indifferent toward the events we'll discuss in Chapters 3 and 4. Or they may argue that it's no longer relevant or important. These reactions are common. Yet, the awful things we'll discuss *did* happen, and they were done largely by white Europeans and their descendants. African Americans, Native Americans, Mexican Americans, and other minority groups were victims, and they paid a terrible price for the early growth and success of white American society. No amount of denial can change these facts.

Yet, European Americans don't have a monopoly on greed, bigotry, or viciousness. Some minority group members facilitated this domination and exploitation. For example, the slave trade relied on black African *slavers*, or traffickers. Some Native Americans captured, bought, and sold slaves, including people from other tribes and black Africans when the slave market made it more profitable than keeping them as indentured servants (Pekka, 2008). They helped Europeans establish a white-dominated society in other ways, too. Additionally, some Mexicans cheated other Mexicans out of their land and assisted in the creation of white dominance. Yet, more frequently, minority groups have fought for justice, equality, and liberty—the ideals on which America was founded.

Likewise, dominant group members have worked to end oppression, bigotry, and racial stratification. For example, some white southerners opposed slavery and fought for abolition (Stephens, 1861). Others attempted to stop discrimination toward Native Americans and Mexicans. Some people devoted (and sometimes gave up) their lives for these causes. Therefore, we discourage a good-guy/bad-guy approach to this subject matter.

Guilt, anger, denial, and indifference are common reactions to this material but do little to advance understanding. Additionally, they can inhibit communication between members of diverse groups and prevent us from making the changes necessary to live up to our nation's ideals. The historical background and sociological concepts in these chapters will give you a useful perspective on the intergroup complexities in America's past, which is vitally important for understanding the present.

We'll present the facts as neutrally as possible. As student-scholars, your goals should be to learn the realities of American society and understand and apply relevant sociological concepts and principles to the society around you—not to indulge in elaborate moral denunciations of American society or deny the realities of what happened.

3

THE DEVELOPMENT OF DOMINANT–MINORITY GROUP RELATIONS IN PREINDUSTRIAL AMERICA

The Origins of Slavery

The year was 1781, and the *Zong*, with its cargo of 440 African slaves, had been sailing for months. The overcrowded ship had only 20 crewmembers, which made it difficult to maintain proper sanitation and prevent the spread of disease. Many enslaved people and two crew members died during the journey. Others were sick. Water was running out. The captain believed that the sickest slaves would die. The slaves were insured as property and he knew that the ship's insurance would cover losses due to drowning but not for natural causes. Thus, he ordered the crew to throw 54 slaves overboard, chained together. By the time the *Zong* reached its destination, 232 enslaved people—53% of them—had died.[1]

The slave trade that brought Africans to the New World was a business that involved calculating profit. It was covered by the same insurance companies that backed farmers, bankers, and merchants. To the captain and owners of the *Zong*, the people thrown overboard were merely cargo, entries in a ledger book. Yet, those books often recorded the enslaved person's gender, country of origin, embarkation and disembarkation points, names, and ages (for example, Magee [aged 6], Sarlar [aged 11], Hoodan [aged 8], and Kesongo [aged 6]). These children were just some of 15 million people who were part of the largest forced migration in history (Emory University, 2013).

What led to this businesslike approach to human trafficking? How did the slave trade get linked to the British colonies that, eventually, became the United States? How could a nation that from its earliest days valued liberty and freedom be founded on slavery? Why does the institution of slavery matter today?

From the first settlements in the 1600s until the 19th century, most people relied directly on farming for food, shelter, and other necessities. Land and labor were central concerns. The struggle to control these resources led directly to the creation of minority group status for three groups: African Americans, Native Americans, and Mexican Americans. Why did the colonists create slavery? Why were Africans enslaved more than Native Americans or others? Why did Native Americans lose their land and most of their population by the 1890s? How did the Mexican population in the Southwest become *Mexican American*? How did gender affect minority group members' experiences?

In this chapter, we'll use concepts from Part 1 to answer these questions. We'll also introduce new ideas to help you understand the processes that create minority groups. To illustrate them, we'll analyze the establishment of black slavery in colonial America—arguably the single most significant event in America's early years. Additionally, we'll consider the subordination of Native Americans and Mexican Americans as significant case studies. In Chapter 4, we'll analyze African American experiences through segregation, and in Chapter 5, we'll explore them in the contemporary era. We'll address the development of minority group status for Native Americans and Mexican Americans in Chapters 6 and 7, respectively.

Two broad themes provide the foundation for this chapter and the rest of the book:

1. The type of dominant–minority group relation is primarily a function of societal characteristics, particularly its subsistence technology (i.e., how the society meets its basic needs, including food and shelter). Lenski argues that the subsistence technology affects every other aspect of the social structure. (See Chapter 1.)

2. The contact situation—the conditions under which groups first come together— is the most significant factor in the creation of minority groups. The type of contact situation produces long-lasting consequences for the minority group and the extent of racial or ethnic stratification, the amount of racism and prejudice, the possibilities for assimilation, pluralism, and equality, and virtually every other aspect of the dominant–minority relationship.

THE ORIGINS OF SLAVERY IN AMERICA

By the early 1600s, the Spanish had conquered much of Central and South America, and the influx of gold, silver, and other riches from the New World had made Spain a powerful nation. Following Spain's lead, England sought to establish its presence in the Western Hemisphere, but its efforts at colonization were more modest. By the early 1600s, the English had established only two small colonies: Plymouth, Massachusetts, settled by pious Protestant families, and Jamestown, Virginia, populated primarily by men seeking their fortunes.

By 1619, the Jamestown residents had fought with the local natives and struggled continuously to eke out a living from the land. Starvation, disease, and death were common, and the future of the colony was in doubt.

In August 1619, an English ship arrived with 20–30 Africans. These first blacks in the British American colonies were originally from Angola, which was a colony of Portugal at that time. They were taken from a Spanish slave ship and the ship's captain traded them for provisions (Historic Jamestown, 2018; see also Austin, 2018).

The details of the lives of these first Africans may never be known; nevertheless, this was a landmark event in the formation of what would become the United States. The strained relations between the English settlers and Native Americans, together with these first Africans, raised an issue that has never been fully resolved: How should different groups in our society relate to each other?

In 1619, England and its colonies didn't have a formal system of slavery. However, they depended heavily on **indentured servants**, contract laborers who are obligated to serve a master for a specific number of years. At the end of the indentureship, the servants became free citizens (PBS, 1998d). Although colonists treated these first Africans slaves as commodities, given the established system, they probably became indentured servants (Wolfe & McCartney, 2015).

The system of American slavery evolved gradually. There was little demand for African labor, and by 1624, only 23 black people lived in Virginia (Austin, 2018, p. 5). By midcentury, that number increased to about 300 (Franklin & Moss, 1994, p. 57). In the decades before the development of slavery, some African indentured servants became free citizens. Some became successful farmers and landowners and, like their white neighbors, used African and white indentured servants to supply labor (Smedley, 2007, p. 104). Between 1630 and 1680, a steady influx of about 50,000 indentured servants from the British Isles arrived at the Virginia colonies (Wolfe & McCartney, 2015). After being released from their indentureship, these newly freed citizens tended to strike out on their own, settling on available land. As the arrival of new indentured servants decreased, landowners who relied on them faced a continually uncertain supply of labor. The need for labor lead to changes in laws and customs that made it legal for whites to enslave Africans, including children (Morgan, 1975, p. 154). In 1641, the Massachusetts colony formally recognized slavery and in 1705, the Virginia General Assembly declared,

> All servants imported and brought into the Country . . . who were not Christians in their native Country . . . shall be accounted and be slaves. All Negro, mulatto and Indian slaves within this dominion . . . shall be held to be real estate. If any slave resists his master . . . correcting such slave, and shall happen to be killed in such correction . . . the master shall be free of all punishment . . . as if such accident never happened. (PBS, 1998b)

In the following century, hundreds of laws were passed to further formalize the status of Africans in colonial America (see Wolfe & McCartney, 2015). By the 1750s, slavery had been thoroughly institutionalized in law and in custom and colonists widely accepted the idea that a person could own another person.

FIGURE 3.1 ■ Slave Trade Routes, 1518–1850

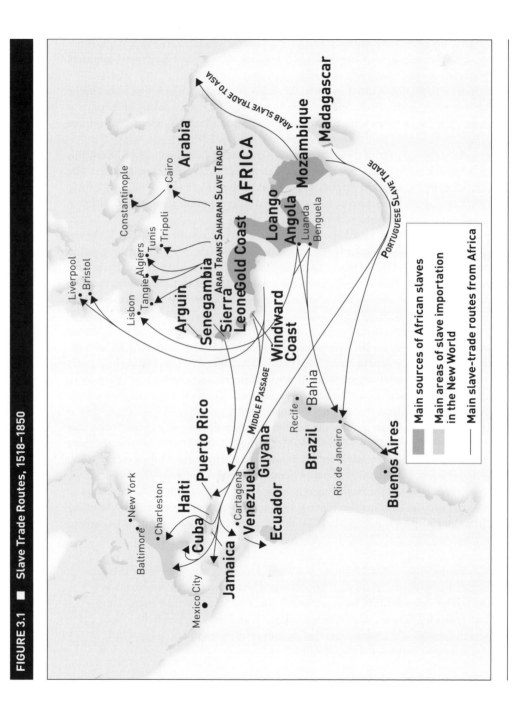

The low demand for indentured servants from Africa suggests that slavery wasn't inevitable. So, what caused it? Why did the colonists deliberately create this repressive system? Instead of going to Africa for slaves, why didn't they enslave Native Americans or the white indentured servants already in the colonies?

The Labor Supply Problem

American colonists saw slavery as a solution to several problems. The business of the colonies was agriculture, and farm work at this time was labor intensive and performed almost entirely by hand. The industrial revolution wouldn't occur for another two centuries, and few labor-saving devices were available to ease the burden of work.

As colonial society developed, a specific form of agricultural production grew. The **plantation system** was based on cultivating and exporting crops such as sugar, tobacco, and rice grown on large tracts of land using a large, cheap labor force. Profit margins were generally small. Planters—individuals who enslaved many people, as opposed to farmers who owned none or few (Kolchin, 1993, p. xiii)—wanted to keep the costs of production as low as possible. If landowners could maintain a large, disciplined, and cheap workforce, they could maximize their profits (Curtin, 1990; Morgan, 1975).

The colonies sometimes exploited the closest tribes of Native Americans for their labor power. However, by the time the plantation system had evolved, local tribal communities had dwindled because of warfare and, especially, disease brought by colonists. Other Indian nations across the continent had enough power to resist enslavement. Additionally, it was relatively easy for Native Americans to escape back to their communities, since they knew the geography. Thus, the colonists failed to solve their labor supply problem by using Native Americans (Lewy, 2004).

The colonists came to see African slaves as the most logical, cost-effective way to solve their vexing shortage of labor. The African slave trade that served the Spanish and Portuguese colonies of South America had been established in the 1500s and could be expanded to fill the needs of the British colonies (see Figure 3.1). The colonists created slavery to cultivate their lands and generate profits, status, and success. Thus, they established the paradox at the core of American society: The construction of a society devoted to individual freedom and liberty in the New World "was made possible only by the revival of an institution of naked tyranny foresworn for centuries in the Old [World]" (Lacy, 1972, p. 22).

The Contact Situation

The conditions under which groups first come into contact determine the immediate situation of the minority group and shape future intergroup relations. In Chapter 1, we discussed the role of group competition in creating prejudice. Below, we develop these ideas by introducing two key theories toward understanding the contact situation.

The Noel Hypothesis

Sociologist Donald Noel (1968) identified three features of the contact situation that, in combination, lead to inequality between groups. The **Noel hypothesis** states, "If two or more groups come together in a contact situation characterized by ethnocentrism, competition, and a differential in power, then some form of racial or ethnic stratification will result" (p. 163). If the contact situation has all three characteristics, some dominant–minority group structure will develop.

Noel's first characteristic, **ethnocentrism**, is the tendency to judge other individuals, groups, or societies by your own cultural standards. Ethnocentrism may be a universal component of human society and some degree of ethnocentrism helps people identify with a particular group, allowing them to create and maintain social cohesion. Without some minimal level of pride in and loyalty to one's own society and cultural traditions, people would have no particular reason to follow the informal norms and laws, honor the sacred symbols, or cooperate with others to accomplish the daily work needed by society (see Sumner, 1906). Yet, ethnocentrism can have negative consequences. When ethnocentrism exists to any degree, people generally sort themselves along group lines based on characteristics that they believe differentiate *us* from *them*. At best, ethnocentrism creates a social boundary line that group members recognize and typically follow. At its worst, it can lead people to view other people and cultures not as *different* but as *inferior*, which can have powerful consequences.

Noel's second factor, **competition**, refers to a struggle over scarce resources. As you saw in Chapter 1, competition between groups often leads to negative feelings (prejudice) and actions (discrimination). In competitive contact situations, the victorious group becomes the dominant group and the losers become the minority group. The competition may be for land, jobs, housing, educational opportunities, labor, political office, or anything else that both groups desire or that one group has and the other group wants.

Competition provides the dominant group with the motivation to establish superiority. The dominant group serves its own interests by ending the competition and by exploiting, controlling, eliminating, or otherwise dominating the minority group.

The third characteristic of the contact situation is a **differential in power** between the groups. Recall from Chapter 1 that power is the ability of a group to achieve its goals despite opposition from other groups. Three factors influence a group's power:

1. **Size**: All things being equal, larger groups tend to be more powerful.

2. **Organization**: Groups that are organized, disciplined, and have good leadership have a better chance of achieving their goals.

3. **Resources**: Resources can include anything from land to information to legitimacy to money. The greater the number and variety of a group's resources, the greater that group's potential ability to dominate other groups.

Thus, a larger, better-organized group with more resources will generally be able to impose its will on smaller, less well-organized groups with fewer resources.

Table 3.1 shows the Noel hypothesis. Note how each factor shapes the contact situation and potentially produces racial or ethnic inequality. If ethnocentrism is present during the contact situation, the groups will recognize their differences and maintain their boundaries. If competition is also present—even if the competition is more perceived than real—the group that eventually dominates will attempt to maximize its share of scarce commodities by controlling or subordinating the group that eventually becomes the minority group. The differential in power allows the dominant group to establish a superior position. Think of it this way:

- Ethnocentrism influences *who* the dominant group dominates.

- A sense of competition provides the dominant group with a reason *why* it should establish a structure of dominance.

- Power is *how* the dominant group imposes its will on the minority group.

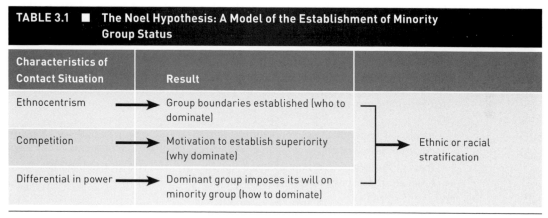

TABLE 3.1 ■ The Noel Hypothesis: A Model of the Establishment of Minority Group Status

Characteristics of Contact Situation	Result	
Ethnocentrism →	Group boundaries established (who to dominate)	
Competition →	Motivation to establish superiority (why dominate)	→ Ethnic or racial stratification
Differential in power →	Dominant group imposes its will on minority group (how to dominate)	

Source: Based on Noel (1968).

We'll use this model to analyze changes in dominant-minority relations over time. Additionally, you can apply the Noel hypothesis to the creation of other types of minority groups.

The Blauner Hypothesis

Sociologist Robert Blauner also analyzed the contact situation. He identified two different initial relationships—colonization and immigration. His analysis is complex and nuanced; we'll summarize his thinking in terms of what we'll call the **Blauner hypothesis**. It states:

> Minority groups created by colonization will experience more intense prejudice, racism, and discrimination than those created by immigration. Furthermore, the disadvantaged status of colonized groups will persist longer and be more difficult to overcome than the disadvantaged status faced by groups created by immigration. (Blauner, 1972, pp. 52–75)

Colonized minority groups, such as African Americans, are forced into minority status by the dominant group's greater military and political power. At the time of contact, the dominant group attacks the colonized group's culture and subjects them to massive inequalities. The dominant group assigns minority group members to positions, such as slaves, from which any form of assimilation is extremely difficult and perhaps even forbidden by the dominant group. Frequently, minority group members are identified by highly visible physical characteristics that help maintain and reinforce the oppressive system. Thus, minority groups created by colonization experience harsher and more persistent rejection and oppression than groups created by immigration.

Immigrant minority groups are, at least to some degree, voluntary participants in the host society. That is, although the decision to immigrate may be motivated by extreme pressures, such as famine or political persecution, immigrant groups may have some control over their destinations and their positions in the host society. Thus, they don't occupy positions that are as markedly inferior as those of colonized groups. They retain enough internal organization and resources to pursue their own self-interests, and they commonly experience easier movement toward equality and more rapid acceptance within the dominant society. The boundaries between dominant and immigrant minority groups aren't so rigidly maintained, especially when the groups are racially similar. In discussing European immigrant groups, for example, Blauner (1972) states that entering American society

> involved a degree of choice and self-direction that was for the most part denied to people of color. Voluntary immigration made it more likely that . . . European . . . ethnic groups would identify with America and see the host culture as a positive opportunity. (p. 56)

Acculturation and integration were significantly more possible for European immigrant groups than for the groups formed under conquest or colonization, as you'll see in future chapters.

Blauner (1972) stresses that the initial differences between colonized and immigrant minority groups have consequences that persist long after first contact. For example, based on measures of equality that reflect integration into the secondary sector of society (i.e., relationships and organizations that are public and impersonal, such as average income, years of education, and unemployment rate), descendants of European immigrants are equal with national norms today (see the second step in Gordon's model of assimilation in Chapter 2). In contrast, descendants of colonized and conquered groups (e.g., African Americans) are, on average, below the national norms on virtually all measures of equality and integration (see Chapters 5–8 for specifics).

Think of Blauner's two types of minority groups as opposite ends of a continuum, with intermediate positions in between. Enclave and middleman minorities hold one such intermediate position. These groups often originate as immigrant groups who bring some resources with them and, thus, have more opportunities than colonized minority groups. However, they're usually racially distinct from Anglo Americans, and certain kinds of opportunities are closed to them.

For example, until World War II, laws expressly forbade Chinese immigrants from obtaining American citizenship. Federal laws restricted the entrance of Chinese immigrants, and state and local laws restricted their opportunities for education, jobs, and housing. For these and other reasons, we can't equate Asian and European immigrant experiences or patterns (Blauner, 1972, p. 55). Because enclave and middleman minority groups combine characteristics of the colonized and the immigrant minority group experience, we can predict that in terms of equality, they'll occupy an intermediate status between the more assimilated white ethnic groups and the colonized racial minorities.

Blauner's typology is an extremely useful conceptual tool for analyzing dominant–minority relations, and we use it extensively. In Part 3, we've arranged the case studies in approximate order from groups created by colonization to those created by immigration. Of course, it's difficult to measure the extent of colonization precisely; thus, the exact order is somewhat arbitrary.

The Creation of Slavery in the United States

Noel's hypothesis helps explain why colonists enslaved black Africans instead of white indentured servants or Native Americans. First, all three groups were the objects of ethnocentric feelings on the part of the elite groups that dominated colonial society. White Europeans perceived black Africans and Native Americans as different for religious and racial reasons. Many white indentured servants were Irish Catholics, criminals, and often the very poor. (Overlap exists between those groups, too.) They also occupied a low social status and the British Protestants who dominated colonial society perceived them as different and inferior.

Second, some type of competition existed between the colonists and all three groups. The competition with Native Americans was direct and focused on controlling land. Competition with indentured servants, white and black, was more indirect. These groups were the labor force that the landowners needed to work on their plantations and to become successful in the New World.

Noel's third variable, differential in power, is the key variable that explains why whites enslaved Africans significantly more than other groups. During the first several decades of colonial history, the balance of power between the colonists and Native Americans often favored Native Americans (Lurie, 1982, pp. 131–133). They outnumbered the colonists by a considerable margin and were highly organized, were familiar with the territory, and had experienced warriors. Indeed, they mounted devastating attacks on the colonists (e.g., 1622 in Virginia) and may have had the ability to eliminate the English population—or come close to it—for some decades after first contact. However, the power differential between the groups shifted over time. As you'll see in Chapter 6, as the colonies grew in population and resources, they began systematically depriving the tribes of resources (e.g., land). This depravation, combined with deaths from European diseases, decimated the Indigenous population.

White indentured servants had the advantage of being preferred over black indentured servants (Noel, 1968, p. 168). Their greater desirability gave them bargaining power to negotiate better treatment and more lenient terms compared to black indentured servants. If the planters had attempted to enslave white indentured servants, this source of labor would have dwindled even more rapidly.

Africans, however, didn't freely choose to enter the British colonies. They became indentured servants by force and coercion. In Blauner's terms, they were a colonized group. Thus, they had no bargaining power. Unlike Native Americans, they had no nearby relatives, no knowledge of the countryside, and no safe havens to which to escape. Table 3.2 summarizes the impact of these three factors on the three potential sources of labor in colonial America.

TABLE 3.2 ■ The Noel Hypothesis Applied to the Origins of Slavery			
Potential Sources of Labor	**Three Causal Factors**		
	Ethnocentrism	Competition	Differential in Power During Contact Period
White indentured servants	Yes	Yes	No
Native Americans	Yes	Yes	No
Black indentured servants	Yes	Yes	Yes

Source: Based on Noel (1968).

QUESTIONS FOR REFLECTION

1. How do the concepts of subsistence technology and contact situation relate to the origins of slavery in colonial America?

2. How do the three concepts in Noel's hypothesis apply to the decision to create slavery?

3. Blauner identifies two types of minority groups. How does this distinction apply to Africans in colonial America?

4. Why were African indentured servants—not white indentured servants or Native Americans—selected as the labor supply for slavery?

PATERNALISTIC RELATIONS

Recall the first theme in this chapter: The nature of intergroup relationships reflects the characteristics of the larger society. The most important and profitable unit of economic production in the colonial South was the plantation, and a small group of wealthy land-owners dominated the region. A society with a small elite class and a plantation-based economy will often develop a form of minority relations called **paternalism** (van den Berghe, 1967; Wilson, 1973).

The key features of paternalism are significant power differentials and inequalities between dominant and minority groups, elaborate and repressive systems of control over the minority group, caste-like barriers between groups, elaborate and highly stylized codes of behavior and communication between groups, and low rates of overt conflict.

Chattel Slavery

As slavery evolved in the colonies, the dominant group shaped the system to fit its needs. To solidify control of enslaved people's labor, the plantation elite designed an elaborate system of laws and customs that gave slave owners legal power over enslaved people. These laws defined slaves as **chattel**, or private property, rather than as human beings. Enslaved people had no civil or political rights and couldn't own property, sign contracts, bring lawsuits, or even testify in court (except against another slave). The law forbid enslaved people to read or write and didn't recognize their marriages. The law gave slave owners the authority to determine almost every aspect of a slave's life, including work schedules and conditions (including types and severity of punishment), living arrangements, and even names (Elkins, 1959/2013; Franklin & Moss, 1994; Genovese, 1974; Jordan, 1968; Stampp, 1956). Additionally, slave owners could separate husbands and wives as well as parents and children.

A Closed System

In colonial America, slavery became synonymous with race. Race, slavery, inferiority, and powerlessness became intertwined in ways that still affect how black and white Americans think about each other (Hacker, 1992). Slavery was a **caste system**, a closed stratification system in which the social class you are born into was permanent. Additionally, slave status was passed on to slaves' children. Whites, no matter what they did, couldn't become slaves.

In a paternalistic system, rigid, strictly enforced codes of etiquette governed the interactions between dominant and minority group members. Whites expected slaves to demonstrate their lower status (e.g., by showing deference and humility toward whites). Plantation and farm work required close and frequent contact between blacks and whites. These rigid behavioral codes made it possible for blacks and whites to work together without threatening the power and status differentials inherent in the system. These status differentials were maintained by social rather than by geographical separation.

Pseudotolerance

The frequent but unequal interactions allowed the whites to maintain an appearance of tolerance, even benevolence, toward enslaved people. Though they ruled with complete authority, slave owners expressed their prejudice and racism as paternalism or positive affection (Wilson, 1973, pp. 52–55). For example, whites might point out that they supplied slaves with clothing and shelter. Or whites might act in ways they deemed good for the enslaved person. (As you'll see in Chapter 6, Indigenous people also experienced paternalism by whites who wanted to "civilize" them.) The system defined slaves as property—yet enslaved people and slave owners were, undeniably, human beings. Research suggests that some enslaved people accepted their status as chattel, and some didn't hate their owners as much as they hated the system of slavery. Slavery was founded, at its heart, on a contradiction. As Parish notes,

> The master learned to treat his slaves both as property and as men and women, the slaves learned to express and affirm their humanity even while they were constrained in much of their lives to accept their status as chattel. (1989, p. 1)

Powerlessness and Resistance

The slaves' powerlessness made it difficult for them to directly challenge the institution of slavery or their position in it. Laws typically permitted slave owners to severely punish or even kill enslaved people for acts of defiance.

Researchers estimate that about 250 slave rebellions happened in America. In 1831, an educated slave and minister, Nat Turner, led the deadliest one in U.S. history. It illustrates the futility of overt challenge and the degree of repression built into the slavery system. As the revolt spread, the state militia engaged the growing slave army in battle. Over several days, more than 100 enslaved people and 57 white people died. The government later executed Nat Turner and at least 21 others for their role in this resistance. White vigilantes killed many more.

This rebellion alarmed white southerners, especially slave owners. Consequently, they tightened the system of control over enslaved people, making it even more repressive (Franklin & Moss, 1994, p. 147). Unfortunately, Nat Turner's attempt to lead enslaved people to freedom resulted in greater oppression by the dominant group.

Other slaves were more successful. Some, especially those in states bordering Northern free states, ran away. The difficulty of escaping and the low chance of reaching the North didn't deter thousands of people from attempting it, some of them repeatedly. Many runaway slaves received help from the underground railroad, an informal network of safe houses supported by African Americans and whites involved in **abolitionism**, the movement to abolish slavery. It operated from 1830 to 1861 and was one of many tactics abolitionists used to fight the system of slavery (National Park Service, n.d.). The best known "conductor" on the underground railroad was Harriet Tubman, a former slave. An important abolitionist (and suffragist), Tubman helped more than 300 people on the path to freedom (PBS, 1998c).

Besides running away and open rebellion, enslaved people resisted slave owners (and, by extension, the system of slavery) in other ways, too; for example, by learning to read and write (which was often forbidden by law or by owners), stealing from their slave owners or destroying owners' property, sabotaging machinery to impede production, or damaging crops. Some enslaved people turned to violence, fighting and sometimes killing their owners. Still others, tragically, injured themselves to reduce their property value. The most desperate committed suicide (PBS, 1998b). Some of these actions may fall more into the category of noncooperation than of deliberate political rebellion (Parish 1989). However, these actions were widespread and demonstrate agency on the part of enslaved people to resist the system that oppressed them.

African American Culture

Most enslaved people were neither docile victims nor unyielding rebels. As the institution of slavery developed, they developed ways to resist and survive their oppression. Most worked to create a life for themselves and their families within the repressive restraints of the plantation system. Enslaved people forged their culture in response to the realities of slavery, much of it manifested in folklore, music, religion, family and kinship structures, and other aspects of daily life (e.g., foodways) (Blassingame, 1972; Genovese, 1974; Gutman, 1976).

QUESTIONS FOR REFLECTION

5. How did the plantation system shape slavery in colonial America?

6. Define *chattel slavery* and *caste system.* How do they apply to the American system of slavery? Would you say the U. S. still has a racial caste system? Explain.

7. How did enslaved people resist their oppression? How did their minority group status affect their ability to be successful? What were the risks associated with resistance?

THE DIMENSIONS OF MINORITY GROUP STATUS

Concepts from Part 1 will help you understand the situation of African Americans under slavery with greater depth.

Power, Inequality, and Institutional Discrimination

The key concepts for understanding the creation of slavery are power, inequality, and institutional discrimination. The plantation elite used its power and resources to relegate black Africans to an inferior status. Institutionalized discrimination implemented and reinforced the system of racial inequality and became a central component of life in the antebellum South. Legal and political institutions developed to benefit whites, particularly slave owners.

Prejudice and Racism

What were the attitudes and feelings of the people involved in the system of slavery? What was the role of personal prejudice? How and why did the ideology of antiblack racism start? As you learned in Chapter 1, individual prejudice and ideological racism are more the *results* of systems of racial inequality than the *causes* of it (Jordan, 1968, p. 80; Smedley, 2007, pp. 100–104). White colonists didn't originally enslave black people because of prejudice or a dislike of blacks. They did it to solve a labor supply problem. However, prejudice and racism were essential to creating blacks' minority group status and to rationalizing and explaining the emerging system of advantage enjoyed by whites (Wilson, 1973, pp. 76–78).

Prejudice and racism provide convenient and convincing justifications for exploitation. They help insulate systems, such as slavery, from questioning and criticism by making them appear reasonable, even desirable. During the early 1800s, the American abolitionist movement heavily attacked the slavery system. The ideology of antiblack racism was strengthened in response (Wilson, 1973, p. 79). The greater the opposition to a system of racial stratification or the greater the magnitude of the exploitation, the greater the need for its beneficiaries to justify, rationalize, and explain it. Thus, the intensity, strength, and popularity of antiblack Southern racism actually peaked almost 200 years after slavery began.

Once created, dominant group prejudice and racism became widespread ways of thinking about the minority group. In the case of colonial slavery, antiblack beliefs and feelings became part of the standard package of knowledge, understanding, and "truths" shared by dominant group members. As the institution of slavery solidified, prejudice and racism were passed from generation to generation. For succeeding generations, antiblack prejudice became just another perspective on the world learned during socialization. To summarize, antiblack prejudice and racism began as part of an attempt to control the labor of black indentured servants, it became embedded in early American culture, and became an integral part of the socialization process for future generations (see Myrdal's "vicious cycle" in Chapter 1).

Figure 3.2 shows these conceptual relationships. Racial inequality arises from the contact situation, as the Noel hypothesis states. As the dominant–minority relationship develops, prejudice and racism arise to rationalize one group's benefit at the expense of another group. Over time, a vicious cycle develops as prejudice and racism reinforce the inequality between groups, which was the cause of the prejudice and racism in the first place. Thus, as Blauner's hypothesis states, the subordination of colonized minority groups is perpetuated over time.

FIGURE 3.2   ■   A Model for the Creation of Prejudice and Racism

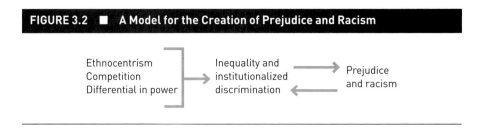

Assimilation

Researchers have done an enormous amount of work to document and understand the American system of slavery, and research on it continues today. Some issues remain unsettled; one of the more controversial and consequential of these concerns the effect of slavery on enslaved people.

Apologists for the system of slavery and some historians of the South writing early in the 20th century accepted the rationalizations stemming from antiblack prejudice. They argued that slavery was beneficial for black Africans. For example, Phillips (1918) said that British American slavery operated as a "school for civilization" that rescued savages from the jungles of Africa and exposed them to Christianity and Western values and norms (which whites assumed to be superior). Some argued that slavery was protected slaves from the evils and exploitation of the factory system in the industrial North. These racist views were most popular more than a century ago, early in the development of social science. These views are largely untenable except by the most racist individuals, particularly as research continue to document the many powerful, advanced civilizations of Africa, including those in Western Africa, where most enslaved people originate.

At the opposite extreme, historian Stanley Elkins (1959/2013) compared s¹ with Nazi concentration camps, which he likened to a "perverted patriarchy" (p. Elkins compared the below-deck areas of slave ships with the cattle cars that took Je. to concentration camps. Elkins pondered the psychological impact of slavery on enslaved people (Rodriguez, 1997, p. 245). He asserted that slavery brainwashed and dehumanized enslaved people, stripping them of their heritage and culture. Elkins asserted that slaves sought to please their owners like people in concentration camps sought to appease Nazis (Rodriguez, 1997, p. 564). Some scholars view this argument as overstated at best and highly problematic at worst, saying that, at the very least, Elkins relied too heavily on plantation owners' views and not enough on evidence about the lived experiences of enslaved people. Recent scholarship has refuted or modified Elkins's ideas. Despite the criticism, the general questions that Elkins asked about the institution of slavery and its impact on enslaved people are useful to consider.

After Elkins's publication, a third perspective regarding the impact of slavery emerged. It argued that enslaved people retained a sense of self and a firm anchor in their African traditions, despite the horror and abuse they suffered under slavery. This view stresses the importance of kinship, religion, and culture in helping enslaved people cope and, at times, even thrive in small ways (see Blassingame, 1972; Genovese, 1974). Alex Haley's (1976) semi-autobiographical family history, *Roots,* poignantly shows this view. The 1977 mini-series, based on the book, was one of the most watched television shows in history. (It was remade in 2016.)

Archeological research supplies evidence that enslaved people actively maintained their culture, sometimes in symbolic ways. For example, archeologists have unearthed blue beads, carved crosses, pottery, and other artifacts throughout the South. Such objects may seem ordinary to the untrained eye; however, they connected people to the spiritual traditions of their ethnic roots. For example, crossed lines carved into pottery or coins may represent how the BaKongo people of Africa thought about the universe (Fennell, 2013; Orser, 1994). The vertical line of the cross represented the separation of earthly and spirit worlds. The horizontal line symbolized the sun's daily movement from East to West. Together, the cross symbolized the cycle of birth and death (Fennell, 2013, p. 6).

Additionally, these objects helped unite enslaved people from diverse cultures. They may not have spoken the same language, but some had similar belief systems (Fennell, 2013, p. 11). Although some slaves converted to Christianity, archeologists and anthropologists believe they were more likely to merge Christian ideas into their original belief systems (Fennell, 2013, p. 13). Under oppressive conditions such as slavery, the cultural components most likely to survive are those similar to those of their oppressors (Davidson, 2004, p. 35). This would explain why images such as the cross survived. It's likely that slave owners interpreted them as evidence that their slaves accepted Christianity. Early researchers viewed such objects similarly—as Christian symbols—and didn't understand the original cultural meanings. Those early perspectives supported the traditional, unidirectional model of acculturation. Newer, more accurate perspectives incorporate this cultural awareness and suggest that acculturation occurs through interaction and goes in both directions (Bornstein 2017; Davidson, 2004).

Researchers continue to study the impact of slavery and Americans continue to debate it. (We can't address every perspective here. See the Current Debates at http://edge.sage pub.com/diversity6e/) However, it's clear that African Americans, in Blauner's (1972) terms, were a "colonized" minority group who were extensively—and coercively—acculturated. Language acculturation began on the slave ships, where people from dozens of different tribal and language groups were shackled together. Though physically linked, language differences hindered their ability to communicate, which lowered the potential for resistance and revolt (Hall, 2009, p. 45; Mannix, 1962).

The plantation elite, their agents, and other colonists couldn't understand their slaves' languages. Thus, they made slaves speak English. This dictate caused African languages to largely die out within a generation or two. However, some African words and language patterns remain. The Gullah Geechee, for example, speak in a way that closely parallels the Creole used in the Bahamas, Barbados, and Belize and reflects several African linguistic traditions as well as English (Gullah Geechee Cultural Heritage Corridor, n.d.).

These rare cultural remnants suggest that acculturation isn't always a one-way process. However, to the extent that culture depends on language and belief systems, Africans under slavery experienced forced, massive acculturation. Although enslaved people developed new cultural forms and social relationships in response to this process (Blauner, 1972, p. 66). Because they were a colonized minority group, enslaved people had little choice but to acculturate—their survival depended on it.

Regional Variations and the System of Slavery

Southern agrarian society developed into a complex social system stratified by race, gender, and class. As Table 3.3 shows, enslaved people made up almost 40% of the southern population in 1860, but that rate varied by geographical location. In Arkansas, about 1 in 4 (26%) people were enslaved; in South Carolina and Mississippi, that rate was more than double (57% and 55% respectively). Note, also, that in South Carolina and Mississippi, enslaved people outnumbered the free population, a reminder that minority groups status is about power, not numbers (Minnesota Population Center, 2016).

In the seven Deep South states where the agricultural economy depended on slave labor (Alabama, Florida, Georgia, Louisiana, Mississippi, South Carolina, and Texas), just under half the population—approximately 2,312,352 people—was enslaved (Minnesota Population Center, 2016; also see Dubrulle, 2016; Hall, 2011). The percentage of families who owned slaves varied by region but generally reflected the pattern described previously. That is, the Deep South states had the highest rates of slave ownership among families. For example, almost half of families in South Carolina (46%) and in Mississippi (49%) owned slaves. The lowest rates of family ownership were in Arkansas (20%), Tennessee (25%), and Virginia (26%).

Contrary to popular belief, it wasn't only the wealthy who owned slaves. In 1850, 1% of the wealthiest families owned more than 100 people each (the "large planters"). However, 25% of southern whites owned slaves, too. Teasing out the patterns further illustrates this class-based social hierarchy. The plantation elite, small in number but wealthy and politically powerful, were at the top of the hierarchy. Most whites in the South were small farmers, and relatively few of them owned slaves. Of those who did, half enslaved between one to four people, and 75% didn't own any (Franklin & Moss, 1994, p. 123; PBS, 1998a; see Table 3.3).

However, to understand the *system* of slavery, we can't limit our discussion to slave owners because that obscures how many other whites people benefitted from slavery. For example, farmers who couldn't afford to own slaves occasionally rented them on an as-needed basis. Likewise, many white women who didn't technically own slaves relied heavily on enslaved people—especially women—to help with labor-intensive "cooking, caring, and cleaning" (Anderson, 2000; see Table 3.4). Coates (2010) explains how far-reaching the system of slavery was:

> Slave labor was as much a part of life in the antebellum South as heat in the summer. . . . Southerners who didn't own slaves could not avoid coming in regular, frequent contact with the institution. They hired out others' slaves for temporary work. They did business with slaveholders, bought from or sold to them. They utilized the products of others' slave labor. They traveled roads and lived behind levees built by slaves. Southerners across the Confederacy, from Texas to Florida to Virginia, civilian and soldier alike, were awash in the institution of slavery.

Gender Relations

The principal line of differentiation in the antebellum South was race. However, each racial group was also stratified by gender. The gender hierarchy was a patriarchal one. White women were subordinate to white men. Black women were subordinate to black men. The degree of gender inequality in slave communities was less than among whites, since slaves had little autonomy and few resources to begin with. African American women were at the bottom of the social system. For black women slaves, the constraints were triple. As White (1985, p. 15) notes, they were "Black in a white society, slave in a free society, women in a society ruled by men."

Racial and gender ideologies of the time idolized Southern white women, especially elites who symbolized feminine ideals of purity, piety, submissiveness, and domesticity (Welter, 1966, p. 152). Enslaved women (and poor white women) did some of the hardest, most physically demanding, and least "feminine" work; for example, in agriculture or domestic work, which required intense physical strength, given that labor-saving products such as electric tillers and washing machines didn't exist. These ideas about femininity and true womanhood couldn't exist simultaneously with the realities of enslavement. If enslaved women could possess feminine virtues, who could justify enslaving them? Their labor was needed; without it, work and profit would decrease (Amott & Matthaei, 1991, p. 146). Prejudice and racism were needed to justify the system of slavery.

Because of their vulnerability and powerlessness, enslaved women were at risk for sexual victimization by men, especially those of the dominant group. As Blassingame (1972) wrote,

> Many white men considered every slave cabin a house of ill-fame. Often through "gifts" but usually by force, white overseers and planters obtained the sexual favors of black women. Generally speaking, the women were literally forced to offer themselves "willingly" and receive a trinket for their compliance rather than a flogging for their refusal. (p. 83)

Gender and Daily Life Everyday life differed for men and women slaves. Although they sometimes worked with the men, especially during harvest time, women typically

TABLE 3.3 ■ Slave Ownership in the South

	Total Population	Total Enslaved People	Free Population	Percentage of Enslaved People	Number of Slaveholders	Total Number of Families	Percentage of Families Owning Slaves
Alabama[*]	964,201	435,080	529,121	45.12%	33,730	96,603	35%
Arkansas[*]	435,450	111,115	324,335	25.52%	11,481	57,244	20%
Florida[*]	140,424	61,745	78,679	43.97%	5,152	15,090	34%
Georgia[*]	1,057,286	462,198	595,088	43.72%	41,084	109,919	37%
Louisiana[*]	708,002	331,726	376,276	46.85%	22,033	74,725	29%
Mississippi[**]	791,305	436,631	354,674	55.18%	30,943	63,015	49%
North Carolina	992,622	331,059	661,563	33.35%	34,658	125,090	28%
South Carolina[*]	703,708	402,406	301,302	57.18%	26,701	58,642	46%
Tennessee	1,109,801	275,719	834,082	24.84%	36,844	149,335	25%
Texas[*]	604,215	182,566	421,649	30.22%	21,878	76,781	28%
Virginia	1,596,318	490,865	1,105,453	30.75%	52,128	201,523	26%
South	9,103,332	3,521,110	5,582,222	38.68%	316,632	1,027,967	32%
Deep South	4,969,141	2,312,352	2,656,789	46.53%	181,521	494,775	37%

Source: Based on Results from the 1860 Census, http://www.civil-war.net/pages/1860_census.html

*Indicates the Deep South states, where agriculture depended heavily on slave labor and where almost half (46.53%) of the population were enslaved people. We calculated the percentage of families owning slaves by taking the number of slave holders (i.e., head of household) and dividing by the number of families.

TABLE 3.4 ■ The Structure of Free Southern Society, 1860		
Group	**Size**	**Notes**
Large planters (1000 or more acres)	< 1% of white families	The wealthiest class who had disproportionate social and political power compared to their size. Most enslaved 50+ people.
Planters (100–1,000 acres)	Approx. 3% of white families	Enslaved 20–49 people. This group also controlled a great deal of wealth in the South; many politicians were from this group.
Small slaveholders	Approx. 20% of white families	Owned < 20 slaves. Most were farmers, a few were merchants.
Non-slaveholding whites	Approx. 75% of white families	This group farmed small plots of land, generally to feed their families. About 1/5 of them didn't own land. Some were day laborers.
Free blacks	3% of all free families	Few free blacks lived in the Deep South; most lived in the upper South (e.g., Maryland). Due to legal and social restrictions, they had limited opportunity for economic advancement. Many were tenant farmers or day laborers.
Slaves	Approximately 3.5 million	Approximately 75% worked on plantations and medium-sized farms. Another 10% did hard physical labor. All were considered "below whites."

Source: Adapted from Goldfield et al. (2002).

worked in gender-segregated groups organized around domestic and farm chores. In addition to working in the fields, they attended the births and cared for the children of both races, cooked and cleaned, wove cloth and sewed clothes, and did the laundry. The women often worked longer hours than the men, doing housework and other chores after the men had gone to bed (Robertson, 1996, p. 21; White, 1985, p. 122).

The group-oriented nature of their tasks gave enslaved women an opportunity to develop relationships with one another. They cooperated in their chores, including caring for their children. Their networks helped them resist the system of slavery, too. For example, enslaved women sometimes induced abortions rather than bring children into bondage. Because they often served as midwives, they could disguise the abortions as miscarriages (White, 1985, pp. 125–126). Enslaved women's networks provided them with mutual help for everyday problems, solace and companionship, and some ability to buffer and resist slave owners' power and oppression (Andersen, 1993, pp. 164–165).

The American system of slavery brutally exploited blacks. However, in some ways, enslaved women were more—and differently—oppressed than enslaved men. Additionally, the racial oppression experienced by enslaved women sharply differentiated their lives from those of white women, the "Southern Belles"—idolized as chaste and virtuous.

QUESTIONS FOR REFLECTION

8. Explain and evaluate this statement: *The key concepts for understanding American slavery are power and inequality, not prejudice or racism.*

9. Were enslaved people acculturated? Were they integrated? Under what conditions? How do acculturation and integration relate to Blauner's distinction between immigrant and colonized minorities?

10. What did enslaved women and white women have in common—that is, how did gender shape their lives? How did race make their lives different? What do your answers suggest about the need for an intersectional approach to understanding the world?

FOCUS ON CONTEMPORARY ISSUES
SLAVERY AND INDENTURED SERVITUDE TODAY

You might think of slavery as a distant piece of history. The idea that a person could be owned by another person and bought and sold like live-stock might seem bizarre, especially in a culture now so devoted to individual happiness. Yet, the institution of slavery exists around the world, including in America and other advanced industrial nations.[2]

Research suggests that 30 million or more people are currently enslaved (International Labour Organization, 2017). Contemporary slavery takes many forms, but all feature dynamics similar to those suggested in the Noel hypothesis: The motivation is a desire for profits, and the populations from which slaves are taken are relatively powerless and lack the resources to defend themselves. Additionally, ethnocentrism plays a role as enslaved people and slave owners are frequently from different cultures or racial or religious groups.

Many modern-day slaves live in their home countries. They're forced into bondage by various means, including debt bondage. In this system, individuals aren't owned outright, but they work for little or no wages until some debt is paid off. However, high interest rates prevent them from paying off their debts. For example, Skinner (2008) reports the case of a man in India working to pay off a debt of $0.62 cents incurred by his great-grandfather in 1958. With interest rates of 100% per year, he is forced to work in a quarry for no pay, three generations after the debt was originally incurred.

Most people forced to do labor are in Southeast Asia, especially India and China. Others are part of an international trafficking system that's aided by globalization, instantaneous communication, and rapid, cheap travel. A large part of this trafficking is connected to commercial sexual enterprises such as prostitution and pornography. Sex trafficking predominately involves children and women. Traffickers find their victims in less-industrialized nations where many people have been displaced from their village communities and are no longer protected by traditional familial, religious, or political institutions. Traffickers trick women into believing that they're being hired for legitimate jobs such as domestic work or childcare in a more-industrialized nation. When workers arrive at their destination, the traffickers take their travel documents and force them into sex work. Traffickers isolate them and keep them powerless by their lack of documents, their illegal status, and their inability to speak the language of the new country. Their situation reflects the same power differentials between enslaved people and slave owners in the American slavery system (e.g., the owners' ability to treat slaves as they pleased).

The United States is a prime destination for victims of sex trafficking and for other workers who are held captive by forms of debt bondage. Some modern slaves provide the unskilled labor that keeps enclaves such as Chinatowns functioning, while others work in agriculture, the seafood industry, landscaping, construction,

and other areas. Many workers enter America legally as guest workers. However, once here, there is little federal or state oversight of their situation. According to one report, these workers are often abused, forced to live and work in horrible conditions, and cheated of their wages by the brokers that brought them into the country (Bauer, 2008).

While similar in many ways to the system of American slavery, modern forms of involuntary servitude are different, too. Modern slaves can be shipped around the world in hours or days instead of traveling for months. Instead of cotton plantations, enslaved people today work in factories and brothels. Like all forms of slavery, however, the modern versions are involuntary, coercive, and maintained by violence and force.

THE CREATION OF MINORITY STATUS FOR NATIVE AMERICANS AND MEXICAN AMERICANS

Two other groups became minorities during the preindustrial period. In this section, we'll review the dynamics of these processes and make some comparisons with African Americans. As you'll see, the Noel and Blauner hypotheses provide some extremely useful insights for understanding these experiences.

Native Americans

As Europeans entered the New World, they encountered hundreds of societies that had lived on this land for thousands of years. Native American societies were highly variable in culture, language, size, and subsistence technology. Some were small, nomadic hunter–gatherer bands, while others had more developed societies in which people lived in settled villages and tended large gardens. Regardless of their characteristics, the relentless advance of white society eventually devastated them all. Contact began in the East and established a pattern of conflict and defeat for Native Americans that continued until the last of the tribes were defeated in the late 1800s. The continual expansion of white society into the West allowed many settlers to fulfill their dreams of economic self-sufficiency, but Native Americans, who lost not only their lives and their land but also much of their traditional way of life, paid an incalculable price.

An important point to recognize is that there is no such thing as *the* American Indian. Rather, there were—and are—hundreds of different Native American tribes or nations, each with its own language, culture, home territory, social structure, and unique history. They share similarities but also have differences. For example, the forest-dwelling tribes of Virginia lived in longhouses and cultivated gardens while the nomadic Plains tribes relied on hunting to satisfy their needs. Because of space constraints, we can't discuss every tribal community. Nonetheless, it's important to be aware of that diversity and to be sensitive to the variety of peoples and histories within the category of *Native American.*

Applying Concepts

The institution of slavery lives on, although its dynamics are different from the system developed in colonial America. Slavery has been outlawed in much of the world, and modern technology has lessened the need for labor-intensive forms of work, at least in more-industrialized nations. However, machines haven't entirely replaced people, and the moral consensus that made slavery illegal hasn't spread everywhere.

How many people are enslaved today? Who are they? Where are they? What work do they do? See if you can answer the following questions about modern slave labor. You may not be able to answer all the questions correctly, but we hope this exercise will pique your curiosity. The Chapter 3 Internet Activity (http://edge.sagepub.com/diversity6e/) will give you an opportunity to learn more about modern slavery, including how it is similar to and different from historic forms.

1. How many people are enslaved today? _____

2. In what form of work are most modern-day slaves involved?

    a. Agricultural labor

    b. Sex work

    c. Other _____

3. Who enslaves the majority of people?

    a. Governments

    b. Private business

    c. Individuals

4. What region of the world has the most slaves? _____

5. What group is the most vulnerable to slavery?

    a. Men

    b. Women

    c. Children

Check the next page to find our answers.

A second crucial point is that many Native American tribes are vastly diminished in size or no longer exist. When Jamestown was established in 1607, millions of Native Americans were living in what would eventually become the United States. By 1890, when the Indian Wars finally ended, fewer than 250,000 Native Americans remained. By the end of the nearly 300-year-long contact situation, Native American populations had declined by as much as 95% (Mann, 2011; Wax, 1971, p. 17; see also McNickle, 1973).

Very little of this population loss was due directly to warfare. Most Native Americans died from diseases brought by the colonists such as measles, influenza, smallpox, cholera, and tuberculosis (Wax, 1971, p. 17; see also Oswalt & Neely, 1996; Snipp, 1989). Others died from starvation as Europeans took over Indigenous hunting grounds and garden plots and slaughtered game, such as the buffalo, to the point of extinction. The result of the contact situation for Native Americans very nearly approached genocide.

Native Americans and the Noel and Blauner Hypotheses

We've already used Noel's hypothesis to analyze why Europeans didn't enslave Indigenous people during the colonial era to the same extent as Africans. Their competition with whites centered on land, not labor, and the Indian nations were often successful in resisting domination (at least temporarily). As American society spread to the West, competition over land continued, and the growing power, superior technology, and greater resource base of the dominant group gradually pushed Native Americans to near extinction.

Answers to Applying Concepts

The answers come from the most recent report by the International Labor Office (ILO) of the United Nations.

1. The ILO estimates 24.9 million people are enslaved in forced labor. That's up from 20 million in 2012.

2. Enslaved people are forced to work in numerous enterprises. The most egregious offenders are in manufacturing (e.g., textile labor), construction, farming, and domestic work (e.g., housekeepers).

3. Individuals and organizations in the private sector enslave the most people—nearly 16 million of them. Another 4.8 million people were enslaved in sexual labor and state authorities enslaved another 4.1 million people in forced labor.

4. Asia and the Pacific have the highest rate of people doing forced labor (4 of every 1,000). The Americas have lowest rate at 1.3 per 1,000 people.

5. Most people enslaved in the private sector labor are girls and women (9.2 million), while 6.8 million are boys and men. Additionally, indigenous people and migrant laborers are at high risk.

Source: International Labour Organization (2017).

Various attempts were made to control the persistent warfare, the most important of which occurred before independence from Great Britain. In 1763, the British Crown ruled that the various tribes were considered "sovereign nations with inalienable rights to their land" (see Lurie, 1982; McNickle, 1973; Wax, 1971). That is, each tribe was to be treated as a nation–state, like France or Russia, and the colonists couldn't simply expropriate tribal lands. Rather, negotiations had to take place, treaties had to be signed by all parties, and tribes had to be compensated for any loss of land.

After the American Revolution, the newborn federal government continued this policy in theory but often ignored it in reality. The principle of sovereignty is important because it established a unique relationship between the federal government and Native Americans. Because white society ignored the policy and regularly broke the treaties, Native Americans have unique legal claims against the federal government.

East of the Mississippi River, the period of open conflict was brought to a close by the Indian Removal Act of 1830, a policy of forced emigration. The law required that all Eastern tribes move west of the Mississippi. Some tribes went without resistance, others fought, and some fled to Canada rather than move to the new territory. Regardless, the Indian Removal Act "solved" the perceived Indian problem in the East. Today, we still see the impact of this law in the relative scarcity of Native Americans in the eastern United States. Most Native Americans live in the western two thirds of the country.

In the West, the grim story of competition for land accompanied by rising hostility and aggression repeated itself. Wars were fought, buffalo were killed, territory was expropriated, atrocities were committed, and the fate of the tribes became increasingly certain. By 1890, the greater power and resources of white society had defeated the Indian nations. All the great warrior chiefs were dead or imprisoned, and almost all Native Americans were living on reservations controlled by federal agencies. The reservations consisted of land set aside by the government during treaty negotiations. Often, these lands weren't the traditional homelands and were hundreds or even thousands of miles from what the tribe considered to be home. Additionally, reservations were usually on undesirable or worthless land.

The 1890s mark a low point in Native American history, a time of great demoralization and sadness. The tribes had to adapt to reservation life and new forms of subordination by the federal government. Although elements of tribal life survived, the tribes were impoverished and generally without resources, which limited their ability to pursue their own interests.

Native Americans, in Blauner's terms, were a colonized minority group who faced high levels of prejudice, racism, and discrimination. Similar to African Americans, they were controlled by paternalistic systems (the reservations) and, in numerous ways, were coercively acculturated. Furthermore, according to Blauner, the negative consequences of colonized minority group status persist long after the contact situation has been resolved. As you'll see in Chapter 6, the experiences of Native Americans after the 1890s provide significant evidence to support Blauner's prediction.

Gender Relations

In the centuries before contact with Europeans, Native American societies distributed resources and power in a variety of ways. Some Native American societies were highly stratified, and many practiced forms of slavery. Others stressed equality, sharing of resources, and respect for the autonomy and dignity of each individual, including women and children (Amott & Matthaei, 1991, p. 33). Native American societies were generally patriarchal and followed a gender-based division of labor, but this didn't mean that women were subordinate. In many tribes, women held positions of great responsibility and controlled the wealth. For example, among the Iroquois (a large and powerful federation of tribes located in the Northeast), women controlled the land and the harvests, arranged marriages, supervised the children, and were responsible for the appointment of tribal leaders and decisions about peace and war (Oswalt & Neely, 1996, pp. 404–405). It wasn't unusual for women to play key roles in religion, politics, warfare, and the economy. Some women became highly respected warriors and chiefs (Amott & Matthaei, 1991, p. 36).

Gender relations were affected in many ways during the prolonged contact period. In some cases, the relative status and power of women rose. For example, the women of the Navajo tribe (located mainly in what is now Arizona and New Mexico) were traditionally responsible for the care of herd animals and livestock. When the Spanish introduced sheep and goats into the region, the importance of this sector of the subsistence economy increased, and women's power and status grew with it.

In other cases, women were affected adversely. The women of the tribes of the Great Plains, for example, suffered a dramatic loss following the contact period. In these tribes, women were primarily responsible for gardening and men typically hunted. When horses were introduced from Europe in the 1500s, the productivity of the men hunters greatly increased. As men's economic importance increased, women lost status and power.

Women in the Cherokee Nation—a large tribe whose original homelands were in the Southeast—similarly lost considerable status and power. Traditionally, Cherokee land was cultivated, controlled, and passed down by the women. Under the pressure to assimilate, the Cherokee abandoned this matrilineal pattern for the European pattern of men's ownership. In doing so, they hoped (futilely, as it turned out) to acculturate and avoid relocation under the Indian Removal Act of 1830 (Evans, 1989, pp. 12–18).

Summary

By the end of the contact period, the surviving Native American tribes were impoverished, powerless, and clearly subordinate to white society and the federal government. Like African Americans, Native Americans were sharply differentiated from the dominant group by race, and, in many cases, the tribes were internally stratified by gender. As was the case with African American slaves, the degree of gender inequality within the tribes was limited by their overall lack of autonomy and resources.

QUESTIONS FOR REFLECTION

11. What was the nature of the competition between British colonists and Native Americans? How did this differ from the competition between Anglos and blacks? What were the consequences of these differences?

12. In Blauner's terms, were Native Americans a colonized minority group? Explain.

13. How did gender relations vary across Indigenous groups? How did gender relations change after contact with white Europeans?

COMPARATIVE FOCUS
HAWAII

The contact situation and the system of group relations that evolved on the island nation of Hawaii provide an instructive contrast with the history of Native Americans. In 1788, while Native Americans and whites continued their centuries-long struggle, white Europeans made first contact with the indigenous people of Hawaii. However, conquest and colonization didn't follow the initial contact. Early relations between the islanders and Europeans were organized around trade and commerce—not agriculture—as was the case in the United States, South Africa, Northern Ireland, and many other places. Thus, the contact situation didn't lead immediately to competition over the control of land or labor.

Indigenous Hawaiian society was highly developed and had sufficient military strength to protect itself from the relatively few Europeans who first came to the islands. Thus, two of the three conditions stated in the Noel hypothesis as necessary for the emergence of a dominant–minority situation—competition and power differences—weren't present at first contact. Anglo dominance didn't emerge until decades later. Contact with Europeans brought other consequences, including smallpox and other diseases to which Native Hawaiians had no immunity. Death rates rose, and the native population fell from about 300,000 in 1788 to less than 60,000 a century later (Kitano & Daniels, 1995, p. 137). As relations between the islanders and Europeans developed, the land was gradually used for commercial agriculture. By the mid-1800s, white planters had established sugar plantations, an extremely labor-intensive enterprise often associated with systems of slavery (Curtin, 1990). By that time, however, there weren't enough Native Hawaiians to fill the demand for labor, and the planters began to recruit abroad, mostly in China, Portugal, Japan, Korea, Puerto Rico, and the Philippines. Thus, the original immigrants of the Asian American groups we discuss in Chapter 8 came first to the Hawaiian Islands, not to the mainland.

The white plantation owners came to dominate the island economy and political structure. Other groups, however, weren't excluded from secondary structural assimilation. Laws didn't ban entire groups from public institutions, and practices such as legally enforced school segregation are nonexistent in Hawaiian history. Americans of Japanese ancestry have been some of the leading Hawaiian politicians. And unlike many Japanese Americans on the mainland, those living in Hawaii weren't incarcerated during World War II. Most other groups have taken advantage of the relative openness of Hawaiian society and have carved out niches for themselves.

In terms of primary structural assimilation, rates of intermarriage among the various groups are much higher in Hawaii than on the mainland, reflecting the openness to intimacy across group lines that has characterized Hawaii since first contact. About 42% of all marriages in Hawaii from 2008 to 2010 were interracial, a much higher rate than for any other state (Wang, 2012, p. 10). In particular, Native Hawaiians have intermarried freely with other groups (Kitano & Daniels, 1995, pp. 138–139).

Although Hawaii has no history of the most blatant and oppressive forms of group discrimination, it's not a racial paradise. Ethnic and racial stratification exist, as do prejudice and discrimination. Native Hawaiians, like Native Americans and other colonized groups, have developed organizations to pursue compensation for lands illegally taken and to resolve other grievances. There have been reports of attacks on whites by Native Hawaiians, including incidents that some call hate crimes (Kasindorf, 2012). However, the traditions of tolerance and acceptance remain strong in the island state.

Mexican Americans

As the U.S. population increased and spread across the continent, contact with Mexicans inevitably occurred. Spanish explorers and settlers had lived in what is now the southwestern United States long before the wave of American settlers broke across this region. For example, Santa Fe, New Mexico, was founded in 1598, nearly a decade before Jamestown. As late as the 1820s, Mexicans and Native Americans were almost the sole residents of the region.

By the early 1800s, four areas of Mexican settlement had developed, roughly corresponding with what would become Texas, California, New Mexico, and Arizona. These areas were sparsely settled, and most Mexicans lived in what was to become New Mexico (Cortes, 1980, p. 701). The region's economy was based on farming and herding. Most people lived in villages and small towns or on ranches and farms. Social and political life was organized around family and the Catholic Church and tended to be dominated by an elite class of wealthy landowners.

Texas

The first effects of America's expansion to the West were felt in Texas early in the 1800s. Mexico was no military match for its neighbor to the north, and the farmland of East Texas was a tempting resource for cotton-growers in the American South. Anglo Americans began to immigrate to Texas in sizable numbers in the 1820s. By 1835, they outnumbered Mexicans 6 to 1. Attempts by the Mexican government to control these immigrants were ineffective and eventually precipitated a successful Anglo American revolution (with some Mexicans joining the Anglos). At this point in time, competition between Anglos and Texans of Mexican descent (called *Tejanos*) was muted by the area's abundance of land and opportunity. Population density was low, fertile land was readily available for all, and the "general tone of the time was that of intercultural cooperation" (Alvarez, 1973, p. 922).

Competition between Anglo-Texans and Tejanos became increasingly intense. When the U. S. annexed Texas in the 1840s, full-scale war broke out, and Mexico was defeated. Under the Treaty of Guadalupe Hidalgo in 1848, Mexico ceded much of its southwestern territory to the United States. In the 1853 Gadsden Purchase, the U. S. acquired the remainder of the territory that now composes the southwestern United States. Because of these treaties, the Mexican population of this region had become, without moving an inch from their villages and farms, a conquered people and a minority group.

Following the war, intergroup relations continued to sour, and the political and legal rights of the Tejano community were often ignored in the Anglo hunger for land. Increasingly impoverished and powerless, the Tejanos had few resources with which to resist the growth of Anglo American domination. They were badly outnumbered and stigmatized by the recent Mexican military defeat. Land that had once been Mexican increasingly came under Anglo control, and widespread violence and lynching by Anglos reinforced the growth of Anglo dominance (Moquin & Van Doren, 1971, p. 253).

California

In California, the Gold Rush of 1849 spurred a massive population movement from the East. Early relations between Anglos and *Californios* (native Mexicans in the state) had been relatively cordial, forming the basis for a multiethnic, bilingual state. The rapid growth of an Anglo majority after statehood in 1850 doomed these efforts, however, and the Californios, like the Tejanos, lost their land and political power.

Laws were passed that encouraged Anglos to settle on land traditionally held by Californios. Mexican American landowners had to prove that their deeds to the land were valid. The Californios protested the seizure of their land but found it difficult to argue their cases in the English-speaking, Anglo-controlled court system. By the mid-1850s, a massive transfer of land took place, moving land into Anglo American hands (Mirandé, 1985, pp. 20–21; see also Pitt, 1970).

Other laws passed in the 1850s made it increasingly difficult for Californios to retain their property and power as Anglo Americans became the dominant group and the majority of the population. Anglo Americans suppressed the area's Mexican heritage and eliminated it from public life and institutions such as schools and local government. For example, in 1855, California repealed a requirement in the state constitution that all laws be published in Spanish and English (Cortes, 1980, p. 706). Anglo Americans used violence, biased laws, discrimination, and other means to exploit and repress Californios, and the new wealth generated by gold mining flowed into Anglo hands.

Arizona and New Mexico

The Anglo immigration into Arizona and New Mexico was less voluminous than that into Texas and California, and both states retained Mexican numerical majorities for a number of decades. In Arizona, most of the Mexican population were immigrants who sought work on farms, ranches, and railroads or in mines. Arizona's economic and political structures quickly came under the control of the Anglo population.

Only in New Mexico did Mexican Americans retain some political power and economic clout, mostly because of the relatively large size of the group and their skill in mobilizing for political activity. New Mexico didn't become a state until 1912, and Mexican Americans continued to play a prominent role in governmental affairs even after statehood (Cortes, 1980, p. 706).

In other words, the contact situation for Mexican Americans was varied by region. Although some areas were affected more rapidly and more completely than others, the ultimate result was the creation of minority group status for Mexican Americans (Acuña, 1999; Alvarez, 1973; Gomez, 2008; McLemore, 1973; McWilliams, 1961; Moore, 1970; Stoddard, 1973).

Mexican Americans and the Noel and Blauner Hypotheses

The causal model we've applied to the origins of slavery and the domination of Native Americans also provides a way of explaining the development of minority group status for Mexican Americans. Ethnocentrism was present during the first contact between Anglo immigrants and Mexicans. Many American migrants to the Southwest brought the prejudices and racism they'd acquired with regard to African Americans and Native Americans. In fact, many of the settlers who moved into Texas came directly from the South in search of new lands for cotton cultivation. They readily transferred their prejudiced views to Mexicans—at least the poorer ones, who they stereotyped as lazy and shiftless (McLemore, 1973, p. 664).

The visibility of group boundaries was heightened and reinforced by physical and religious differences. Mexicans were racially a mixture of Spaniards and Native Americans, and differences in skin color and other physical characteristics provided a convenient marker of group membership. Additionally, the vast majority of Mexicans were Roman Catholic, whereas the vast majority of Anglo Americans were Protestant.

Competition for land began with the first contact between the groups. However, for many years, population density was low in the Southwest, and the competition didn't immediately or always erupt into violent domination and expropriation. Nonetheless, the loss of land and power for Mexicans living in the Southwest was inexorable, although variable in speed.

The power differentials between the groups varied and this partly explains why Anglo domination was established faster in some places. In Texas and California, the subordination of the Mexican American population followed quickly after a rapid influx of Anglos and the military defeat of Mexico. Anglo Americans used their superior numbers and military power to acquire control of the political and economic structures and expropriate the resources of the Mexican American community. In New Mexico, the groups were more evenly matched in size, and Mexican Americans were able to retain a measure of power for decades.

Unlike Native Americans, however, Anglos coveted Mexican labor. On plantations, ranches, and farms and in mining and railroad construction, Mexican Americans became a vital source of inexpensive labor. During times of high demand, Anglos encouraged more workers to emigrate from Mexico. When the demand for workers decreased, Anglos forced these laborers back to Mexico. This pattern of labor flow continues today.

As with African Americans and Native Americans, the contact period with Anglos established a colonized status for Mexican Americans throughout the Southwest. The dominant group suppressed Mexican culture (including language), revoked Mexican property rights, and lowered Mexican Americans' status. In countless ways, they were subjected to coercive acculturation. For example, in 1860, California banned Spanish in public schools and severely restricted bullfighting and other Mexican sports and recreational activities (Moore, 1970, p. 19; Pitt, 1970).

In contrast to African Americans, Mexican Americans were in close proximity to their homeland and maintained close ties with their families and communities. Constant movement across the U.S.–Mexican border kept Mexican heritage, including Spanish language use, alive in the Southwest. Nonetheless, 19th-century Mexican Americans fit Blauner's category of a colonized minority group, and the suppression of Mexican culture was part of the process by which the dominant culture was established.

Anglo American economic interests benefited enormously from the conquest of the Southwest and the colonization of the Mexican people. Growers and other businesspeople came to rely on the cheap labor provided by Mexican Americans and immigrant and day laborers from Mexico. The region grew in affluence and productivity, but Mexican Americans were now outsiders in their own land and didn't share in the prosperity. The Anglo American land grab of the 1800s and the conquest of the indigenous Mexican population are one of the roots shaping Mexican American relations with the dominant U.S. society today.

Gender Relations

Although Indigenous people living in the Southwest had a clear gender-based division of labor, women and men viewed each other, largely, as equals. After the arrival of

Anglo Americans, Mexican society became much more patriarchal. These characteristics tended to persist after their conquest and the creation of the group's minority status.

Most Mexican Americans lived in small villages or on large ranches and farms. Women were the primary caretakers of their families, devoting energies to child rearing and household tasks. As Mexican Americans were reduced to a landless labor force, women along with men suffered the economic devastation that accompanied military conquest by a foreign power. The kinds of jobs available to the men (mining, seasonal farm work, railroad construction) often required them to be away from home for extended periods of time, and women, by default, began to do the economic and other tasks traditionally done by men.

Poverty and economic insecurity severely strained family structures. Cultural understandings about patriarchy became moot when men were absent for long periods of time, which increased Mexican American women's decision-making power. Men's absence compelled women to also work outside of their homes for families to survive economically (Becerra, 1988, p. 149). In some ways, the economics of conquest led to increased power for women and laid the foundation for the increased equality that has emerged over time.

The consequences of contact varied. For example, wealthier Mexican American women had greater power than poor women. Similar to enslaved black women, Mexican American women faced oppression due to the combination of their racial, ethnic, and gender statuses.

QUESTIONS FOR REFLECTION

14. What was the nature of the competition between Anglos and Mexican Americans? How did this compare with the competition between Anglos and Native Americans and between Anglos and black Americans?

15. In Blauner's terms, were Mexican Americans a colonized or immigrant minority group? Why?

16. How were Mexican American gender relations affected by contact with Anglo society?

COMPARING MINORITY GROUPS

Native Americans and enslaved Africans were the victims of the explosive growth of European power in the Western Hemisphere that began with Columbus's voyage in 1492. Europeans needed labor to fuel the plantations of the mid-17th–century American colonies and settled on enslaving people from Africa as the most logical, cost-effective means of resolving their labor supply problems. Black Africans had a commodity the colonists coveted (labor), and the colonists subsequently constructed a system to control and exploit this commodity. To satisfy the demand for land created by the stream of European immigrants to North America, the threat represented by Native Americans had to be eliminated. Once their land was expropriated, Native Americans ceased to be of much concern. The only valuable resource they possessed—their land—was under the control of white society by 1890, and Native Americans were thought to be unsuitable as a source of labor.

Mexico, like the United States, had been colonized by a European power—in this case, Spain. In the early 1800s, the Mexican communities in the Southwest were a series of outpost settlements, remote and difficult to defend. Through warfare and a variety of other aggressive means, Mexican citizens living in this area were conquered and became an exploited minority group.

African Americans, Native Americans, and Mexican Americans, in their separate ways, became involuntary players in the growth and development of European and, later, American economic and political power. None of these groups had much choice in their respective fates; all three were overpowered and relegated to an inferior, subordinate status. Many views of assimilation (such as the "melting pot" metaphor discussed in Chapter 2) have little relevance to these situations. These minority groups had little control over their destinies, their degree of acculturation, or even their survival as a group. These three groups were coercively acculturated in the context of paternalistic relations in an agrarian economy. Meaningful integration (structural assimilation) wasn't a real possibility, especially for African Americans and Native Americans. In Gordon's (1964) terms, we might characterize these situations as "acculturation without integration" or *structural pluralism* (see Chapter 2). Given the grim realities described in this chapter, Gordon's terms seem a little antiseptic, and Blauner's concept of colonized minority groups seems far more descriptive.

COMPARATIVE FOCUS
MEXICO, CANADA, AND THE UNITED STATES

How do the experiences of the Spanish and the French in the Western Hemisphere compare with those of the British in what became the United States? What roles did the contact situation and subsistence technology play?[3]

The Spanish conquered much of what is now Central and South America about a century before Jamestown was founded. In 1521, they defeated the Aztec empire, located in what is now central Mexico. The Aztec empire was large and highly organized. The emperor ruled over scores of subject nations, and the great majority of his subjects were peasants who farmed small plots of land. When the Spanish defeated the Aztecs, they destroyed cities and temples, but not the social structure; instead, they used it for their own benefit. For example, the Aztec empire had financed its central government by collecting taxes and rents from citizens. The Spanish simply grafted their own tax collection system onto this structure and diverted the flow from the Aztec elite classes (which they had, at any rate, destroyed) to themselves (Russell, 1994, pp. 29–30).

The Spanish tendency to absorb rather than destroy operated at many levels. Thus, Aztec peasants became Spanish (and then Mexican) peasants, occupying roughly the same role in the new society as they had in the old, save for paying their rents to different landlords. Additionally,

(Continued)

(Continued)

there was extensive intermarriage between the groups, but, unlike the English in their colonies to the north, the Spanish recognized the resultant racial diversity. They recognized as many as 56 different racial groups, including whites, *mestizos* (mixed European–Indian), and *mulattoes* (mixed European–African) (Russell, 1994, p. 35).

The society that emerged was highly race conscious, and race was highly correlated with social class: The elite classes were white, and the lower classes were nonwhite. However, the large-scale intermarriage and the official recognition of mixed-race peoples established the foundation for a racially mixed society. Today, most of the Mexican population is mestizo, although people of "purer" European ancestry continue to monopolize elite positions.

The French colonized Canada around the same time the English established their colonies farther south. The dominant economic enterprise in the early days wasn't farming but trapping and the fur trade, and the French developed cooperative relations with some tribes to develop this enterprise. They, like the Spanish in Mexico, tended to absorb Native American social structures, and there was also a significant amount of intermarriage, resulting in a mixed-race group, called the *Metís*, who had their own identities and their own settlements along the Canadian frontier (Russell, 1994, p. 39).

Note the profound differences in these three contact situations. The Spanish confronted a large, well-organized social system and found it expeditious to adapt Aztec practices to their own benefit. The French developed an economy that required cooperation with at least some Native American tribes, and they, too, found benefits in adaptation. The tribes the English encountered were much smaller and much less developed than the Aztecs, and there was no reason for the English to adapt to or absorb their social structures. Furthermore, because the business of the English colonies was agriculture (not trapping), the competition at the heart of the contact situation was for land, and Native Americans were seen as rivals for control of that most valuable resource.

Thus, the English tended to exclude Native Americans, keeping them on the outside of their emerging society and building strong boundaries between their own "civilized" world and the "savages" that surrounded them. The Spanish and French colonists adapted their societies to fit with Native Americans, but the English faced no such restraints. They could create their institutions and design their social structure to suit themselves (Russell, 1994, p. 30).

As you've have seen, slavery was one of the institutions based on African labor created in the English colonies. Slavery was also practiced in New Spain (Mexico) and New France (Canada), but the institution evolved in very different ways in those colonies and never assumed the importance that it did in America. Why? As you might suspect, the answer has a lot to do with the contact situation. The Spanish and French attempted large-scale agricultural enterprises that might have created a demand for imported slave labor. In New Spain, however, a supply of Native American peasants was readily available and, although Africans helped shaped modern Mexico racially and socially, demand for black slaves never matched that of the English colonies. Similarly, in Canada, enslaved Africans were sometimes used, but farmers there tended to rely on labor from France for their agricultural needs. The British opted for slave labor from Africa over indentured labor from Europe, and the French made the opposite decision.

Finally, note that many of the modern racial characteristics of these three neighboring societies were foreshadowed in their colonial origins (e.g., the greater concentration of African Americans in the U. S. and the more racially diverse population of Mexico). The differences run much deeper than race alone, of course, and include differences in class structure and relative levels of industrialization and affluence. For our purposes, however, this brief comparison of the origins of dominant–minority relations underscores the importance of the contact situation in shaping group relations for centuries to come.

QUESTIONS FOR REFLECTION

17. What were the key differences in the contact situations in New Spain, New France, and the British colonies? How do the concepts of competition and power apply?

18. What are some contemporary differences between Mexico, the United States, and Canada that might be traced to the contact situation?

Main Points

- Dominant–minority relations are shaped by societal characteristics. In particular, the nature of the subsistence technology affects group relations, culture, family structure, and virtually all aspects of social life. The single most important factor in the development of dominant–minority relations is the contact situation; it produces long-term consequences.

- The Noel hypothesis states that ethnic or racial stratification occurs when a contact situation is characterized by ethnocentrism, competition, and a power differential. American colonists enslaved Africans instead of white indentured servants or Native Americans because only the Africans fit all three conditions. American slavery was a paternalistic system.

- Blauner's hypothesis states that minority groups created by colonization will experience greater, more long-lasting disadvantages than minority groups created by immigration.

- Prejudice and racism are more the results of systems of racial and ethnic inequality than

they are the causes. They serve to rationalize and stabilize these systems.

- The colonists' competition with Native Americans centered on control of the land. Native American tribes were conquered and pressed into a paternalistic relationship with white society. Native Americans became a colonized minority group subjected to forced acculturation.

- Mexican Americans were the third minority group created during the preindustrial era. Mexican Americans competed with white settlers over land and labor. Like Africans and Native Americans, Mexican Americans were a colonized minority group subjected to forced acculturation.

- Conquest and colonization affected men and women differently. Women's roles changed, sometimes becoming less constrained by patriarchal traditions. These changes were always in the context of increasing powerlessness and poverty for the group. Minority women have been doubly oppressed by their gender and their minority group status in comparison to white women and minority men.

Review Questions

1. State and explain the two themes presented at the beginning of the chapter. Apply each to the contact situations between white European colonists and African Americans, Native Americans, and Mexican Americans. Identify and explain the key differences and similarities among the three situations.

2. Explain what a plantation system is and why this system of production is important for understanding the origins of slavery in colonial America. Why are plantation systems usually characterized by (a) paternalism, (b) huge inequalities between groups, (c) repressive systems of control, (d) rigid codes of behavior, and (e) low rates of overt conflict?

3. Explain the Noel and Blauner hypotheses and how they apply to the contact situations covered in this chapter. Explain the following key terms: *ethnocentrism*, *competition*, *power*, *colonized minority group*, and *immigrant minority group*. How did group conflict vary when competition was over land rather than labor?

4. Explain the role of prejudice and racism in the creation of minority group status. Do prejudice and racism help cause minority group status, or are they caused by minority group status? Explain.

5. Compare gender relations in each of the contact situations discussed in this chapter. Why do the relationships vary?

6. What does it mean to say that, under slavery, acculturation for African Americans was coerced? What are the implications for assimilation, inequality, and African American culture, given this type of acculturation?

7. Compare the contact situations of Native Hawaiians and Native Americans. What were the key differences in their contact situations? How are these differences reflected in the groups' current situations?

8. Compare the contact situations in colonial America, Canada, and Mexico. What groups were involved in each situation? What was the nature of the competition, and what were the consequences?

Group Discussion

Go to this book's companion website (http://edge.sagepub.com/diversity6e) and complete the Internet Activity about modern slavery. Bring your answers to class and discuss them with your classmates. Focus on comparing modern and colonial American slavery, especially the roles of ethnocentrism and power, subsistence technology, demand and supply, human rights, and enforcement efforts. What surprised you the most? Based on what you learned, how can you help decrease or end modern slavery?

Internet Learning Resources

SAGE edge™ offers teachers and students easy-to-use resources for review, study, and further exploration. See **http://edge.sagepub.com/diversity6e**

Notes

1. This account is based on Walvin's research. He notes that the number of enslaved people on board and killed was debated when the case came to court. Walvin put the count at 442 enslaved people on board and 132 dead—the court agreed. The Trans-Atlantic Slave Trade Database puts the count at 440 enslaved people, 232 of whom died. Other scholars put the counts higher or lower, but within that range.

2. For a powerful account of how a form of slavery survived the Civil War, see Blackmon (2009).

3. This section is largely based on Russell (1994).

4

INDUSTRIALIZATION AND DOMINANT–MINORITY RELATIONS

From Slavery to Segregation and the Coming of Postindustrial Society

A war sets up in our emotions: one part of our feelings tells us it is good to be in the city, that we have a chance at life here, that we need but turn a corner to become a stranger, that we need no longer bow and dodge at the sight of the Lords of the Land. Another part of our feelings tells us that, in terms of worry and strain, the cost of living in the kitchenettes is too high, that the city heaps too much responsibility on us and gives too little security in return. . . .

The kitchenette, with its filth and foul air, with its one toilet for thirty or more tenants, kills our black babies so fast that in many cities twice as many of them die as white babies. . . .

The kitchenette scatters death so widely among us that our death rate exceeds our birth rate, and if it were not for the trains and autos bringing us daily into the city from the plantations, we black folk who dwell in northern cities would die out entirely over the course of a few years. . . .

The kitchenette throws desperate and unhappy people into an unbearable closeness of association, thereby increasing latent friction, giving birth to never-ending quarrels of recrimination, accusation, and vindic-tiveness, producing warped personalities.

The kitchenette injects pressure and tension into our individual person-alities, making many of us give up the struggle, walk off and leave wives, husbands, and even children behind to shift for themselves. . . .

The kitchenette reaches out with fingers of golden bribes to the officials of the city, persuading them to allow old firetraps to remain standing and occupied long after they should have been torn down.

The kitchenette is the funnel through which our pulverized lives flow to ruin and death on the city pavement, at a profit.

—Richard Wright[1]

Richard Wright (1908–1960), one of the most powerful writers of the 20th century, grew up in the South during the height of the Jim Crow system. He wrote about many of the issues discussed in this chapter. He passionately expresses hatred for segregation and bigotry in his major work, *Native Son* (1940), and his memoir, *Black Boy* (1945). In 1941, Wright helped to produce *Twelve Million Black Voices*, a folk history that uses photos and brief essays to powerfully comment on three centuries of oppression experienced by African Americans.

This excerpt was adapted from "Death on the City Pavement," which expresses Wright's view of the massive African American migration out of the South to the North, beginning in the early 1900s in response to Jim Crow segregation. Like many others, Wright's bittersweet journey involved trading harsh, rural repression for overcrowded urban ghettos. Housing discrimination, overt and covert, confined African American migrants to the least desirable, most overcrowded areas of the city—in many cases, the neighborhoods that had first housed European immigrants. Unscrupulous landlords subdivided buildings into the tiniest possible apartments ("kitchenettes"). African American migrants, as impoverished newcomers, were forced to cope with overpriced, substandard housing as best they could.

One theme that you learned in Chapter 3 was that a society's subsistence technology affects group relations, culture, family structure, and virtually all aspects of social life. Specifically, agrarian technology and the desire to control land and labor profoundly shaped dominant–minority relations in America's formative years. The agrarian era ended in the 1800s. Since then, the United States has experienced two major transformations in subsistence technology; each transformed dominant–minority relations and required the creation of new structures and processes to maintain racial stratification and white privilege. In this chapter, we'll explore a corollary of that Chapter 3 theme: *Dominant–minority group relations change as the subsistence technology changes.*

The Industrial Revolution was the first transformation in subsistence technology; it began in the early 19th century when machine-based technologies began to develop, especially in the North. In the agrarian era, farming and other work was labor intensive, done by hand or with the aid of draft animals. During industrialization, work became capital-intensive (see Chapter 2), and machines replaced people and animals.

The new industrial technology rapidly increased the productivity and efficiency of the American economy and quickly changed every aspect of society, including work, politics, communication, transportation, family life, birth and death rates, education, and, of course, dominant–minority relations. The groups that had become minorities during the agrarian era (e.g., African Americans, Native Americans, and Mexican Americans) faced new possibilities and new dangers. Industrialization also created new minority groups, new forms of exploitation and oppression, and, for some, new opportunities to move up in American's social structure. In this chapter, we'll explore this transformation and its effects on African Americans' status, focusing primarily on the construction of Jim Crow segregation in the South starting in the 1870s. Later, in Part 3, we'll consider the impact of industrialization on other minority groups.

The second transformation in subsistence technology happened in the mid-20th century as America (and other advanced industrial societies) entered the postindustrial era, sometimes called **deindustrialization**. This shift in subsistence technology included two significant changes: (1) a decline in the manufacturing sector of the economy, which resulted in a decrease in the supply of secure, well-paid, blue-collar, manual-labor jobs, and (2) an expansion of the service- and information-based sectors of the economy, which led to an increase in the relative proportion of white-collar and high-tech jobs.

Like the 19th-century industrial revolution, this second transformation profoundly changed every aspect of modern society, including dominant–minority relations. Indeed, as the subsistence technology continues to evolve, every facet of American society—work, family, politics, popular culture—is also transformed. Later in this

TABLE 4.1 ■ Three Subsistence Technologies and the United States		
Technology	**Key Trends and Characteristics**	**Dates**
Agrarian	Labor-intensive agriculture. Control of land and labor are central.	1607 to early 1800s
Industrial	Capital-intensive manufacturing. Machines replace animal and human labor.	Early 1800s to mid-1900s
Postindustrial	The "information society." The economy shifts from manufacturing to a service economy.	Mid-1900s to the present

chapter, we'll examine the 20th-century transformation, focusing on its implications for minority groups. Additionally, we'll examine some new concepts—especially **modern institutional discrimination**—to better understand group relations during this time. Finally, we'll lay the groundwork for the chapter case studies in Part 3, which examine the consequences of postindustrial society for America's minority groups.

Table 4.1 summarizes the characteristics of the three major subsistence technologies that we consider throughout the book. As America moved through these stages, group relations and the nature of racial stratification changed.

INDUSTRIALIZATION AND THE SHIFT FROM PATERNALISTIC TO RIGID COMPETITIVE GROUP RELATIONS

As we noted in Chapter 2, the industrial revolution began in England in the mid-1700s and spread to the rest of Europe, to the United States, and eventually throughout the world. The key innovations accompanying this change in subsistence technology were the application of machine power to production and the harnessing of inanimate sources of energy, such as steam and coal, to fuel machines. As machines replaced humans and animals, work became much more productive, the economy grew, and the volume and variety of the goods produced increased dramatically.

In an industrial economy, the close, paternalistic control of minority groups that existed in agrarian societies became irrelevant. Paternalistic relationships such as slavery exist in societies with labor-intensive technologies and help organize and control a large, involuntary, and geographically immobile labor force. An industrial economy, in contrast, requires a workforce that is geographically and socially mobile, skilled, and literate. Furthermore, with industrialization comes urbanization, and close, paternalistic controls are difficult to maintain in cities.

Thus, as industrialization progresses, agrarian paternalism gives way to **rigid competitive group** relations (see Table 4.2). Under this system, minority group members are freer to compete for jobs and other valued commodities with dominant group members, especially those in the lower class. As competition increases, threatened members of the dominant group become more hostile and attacks on minority groups typically increase.

Paternalistic systems directly dominate and control the minority group and its labor. However, in rigid competitive systems, the threatened segments of the dominant group seek to defend their privilege and minimize or eliminate minority-group competition for jobs, housing, or other valuable goods or services (van den Berghe, 1967; Wilson, 1973).

Paternalistic systems such as slavery required minority group members to participate, although involuntarily. Rigid competitive systems, in contrast, limit the ability of minority group members to participate in the job market, schools, politics, and other areas of social life. In some cases, the dominant group completely eliminates competition from the minority group.

The 1924 National Origins Act is one example of this control (see Chapter 2). The goal of this legislation was to stop European immigration and, by extension, to protect Americans' jobs and wages. In this chapter, we'll consider similar dominant group attempts as America shifted from an agricultural to an industrial economy. Specifically, we will examine efforts to keep African Americans powerless and impoverished—to maintain the system of black–white racial stratification.

THE IMPACT OF INDUSTRIALIZATION ON THE RACIAL STRATIFICATION OF AFRICAN AMERICANS: FROM SLAVERY TO SEGREGATION

Industrial technology began to transform American society in the early 1800s, but its effects weren't felt equally in all regions. Northern states industrialized first, while the plantation system and agricultural production continued to dominate the South. This economic diversity was one of the underlying causes of the regional conflict that led to the Civil War. Because of its more productive technology, the North had more resources and defeated the Confederacy in a bloody war of attrition. When the Civil War ended in April 1865, slavery was abolished and black–white relations in the South entered a new era.

The southern system of race relations that developed after the Civil War was designed, in part, to continue the control of African American labor that had been institutionalized under slavery. Additionally, it was intended to end any political or economic threat from the African American community.

This rigid competitive system became highly elaborate and inflexible, partly because of visible markers of group membership (e.g., skin color) and long history of inferior status and powerlessness of African Americans in the South, and partly because of the particular needs of southern agriculture. In the next section, we'll examine black–white relations from the end of the Civil War through the ascendance of segregation in the South and the mass migration of African Americans to the industrializing cities of the North. It should provide you with greater understanding of how rigid competitive systems operate.

Reconstruction (1865 to the 1880s)

Reconstruction, from 1865 to the 1880s, was a brief respite in the long history of oppression experienced by African Americans. During this time, the Union army occupied southern states, and federal agencies focused on reintegrating former Confederate states into the Union and establishing and enforcing rights for newly freed African Americans. In 1865, the government established the Bureau of Refugees, Freedmen, and Abandoned Lands (also known as the *Freedmen's Bureau*) to provide food, shelter, medical aid, and other necessities to millions of formerly enslaved people. It opened 3,000 schools and colleges and helped newly freed blacks negotiate employment contacts, start businesses, and legalize their marriages. African Americans played a pivotal role, for example, by building and operating more than 500 schools throughout the South (Troost, n.d.; Washington, 2005; Wormser, n.d.-b).

In 1869, Congress passed the Fifteenth Amendment to the Constitution which granted citizens the right to vote regardless of "race, color, or previous condition of servitude."

During the next decade, more than a half million black men in the South registered to vote. (Women didn't gain that right until 1920.) Additionally, more than 1,400 held offices (e.g., state legislatures, Congress) and served as police officers and in other positions from which they had previously been excluded. Though they now had significant political power, African Americans faced great opposition as they pursued new opportunities (Constitutional Rights Foundation, n.d.; Lawson, 2009; Smithsonian National Museum of American History, n.d.-a; also see Foner, 2011).

In 1866, President Andrew Johnson (serving after Lincoln's assassination) vetoed the Freedmen Bureau's funding, saying the costs were too great and that it interfered with states' rights. Though slaves had suffered discrimination for centuries, Johnson believed the aid unfairly advantaged former slaves over whites (especially poor whites). Further, he worried that African Americans would become lazy and reliant on government assistance (National Park Service, 2015b). Congress overrode the veto, but after years of pressure from white southerners, it ended the program in 1872 (Troost, n.d.; Wormser, n.d.-b). The controversial 1876 presidential election led to a shift in policies—in particular, the withdrawal of the federal government from the South.

Reconstruction, over by 1877, was too brief to change two significant legacies of slavery. First, centuries of bondage left black southerners impoverished, largely illiterate and uneducated, and with few resources. When new forms of racial oppression appeared, it was difficult for African Americans to defend their group interests. These developments are consistent with Blauner's hypothesis: Colonized minority groups face greater difficulties in improving their disadvantaged status because they confront greater inequalities and have fewer resources at their disposal.

Second, the heritage of prejudice and racism remained ingrained in southern culture. Though the Fifteenth amendment to the Constitution made African Americans full and equal citizens, white southerners were predisposed by their cultural legacy to continue seeing blacks as they had for centuries and to see racial inequality and the exploitation of African Americans as normal or even desirable. As the federal government withdrew, whites constructed a new oppressive social system based on the assumption of racial inferiority (C. Anderson, 2016).

De Jure Segregation

The system of race relations that replaced slavery was **de jure segregation**, sometimes called the **Jim Crow system**. *De jure* means "by law." Under de jure segregation, the minority group is physically and socially separated from the dominant group and relegated to an inferior social position in all aspects of social life. Neighborhoods, stores, busses, restaurants, theaters, stadiums, parks, and employment were racially segregated. At the height of Jim Crow, courtrooms used different Bibles for black and white witnesses to swear on (Woodward, 1974, p. 118); in Arkansas, it was illegal "for any white prisoner to be handcuffed . . . or tied to a negro prisoner"; and in Birmingham, it was illegal "for a negro and white person to play together or [be] in company with each other in any game of cards or dice, dominoes or checkers." In Mississippi, it was even illegal for anyone to "present for public acceptance . . . arguments . . . in favor of social equality . . . between whites and negroes (Smithsonian National Museum of American History, n.d.-b).

The logic of segregation created a vicious cycle (see Figure 1.8). As the law excluded African Americans from mainstream society, their poverty and powerlessness increased. Their lack of power and resources made it easier for whites to mandate other forms of inequality. African Americans' inequality reinforced racial prejudice and made it easy for whites to justify racial inequality.

The Origins of De Jure Segregation

Although the South lost the Civil War, its class structure and agrarian economy stayed relatively intact. The Noel hypothesis helps explain why the Jim Crow system evolved. It states that (1) people are ethnocentric and identify with particular groups and (2) groups compete for resources. After Reconstruction, most whites were still prejudiced against blacks and the voting power of a large black electorate threatened the political and economic dominance of elite whites. Thus, after federal troops withdrew, whites mobilized their power to construct Jim Crow, control black southerners, and end group competition that threatened the majority group (C. Anderson, 2016).

Control of Black Labor

Though slavery was now illegal, the plantation elite still needed a workforce (C. Anderson, 2016; Blackmon, 2009). Yet the Civil War caused massive economic disruption and physical destruction, leaving the plantation elite short on cash and liquid capital. Moreover, with emancipation, plantation owners were "intellectually bereft" (Blackmon, 2009, p. 26). Slaves had experience and understood the details of cotton production. Now, the elite no longer controlled black labor or knowledge.

Southern legislatures tried to force African Americans into involuntary servitude by passing laws known as the *Black Codes*. For example, most southern states made vagrancy illegal. Vagrancy laws stemmed from stereotypes about blacks being lazy—the same belief that President Johnson held when he vetoed funding for the Freedman's Bureau. Under vagrancy laws, the police could arrest blacks for "not [working] under the protection of a white man" (Blackmon, 2009, p. 53). In Florida, this included "wandering or strolling about or leading an idle, profligate, or immoral course of life." Penalties for breaking these laws included a fine "not exceeding $500," imprisonment for up to a year, or being sold to the highest bidder for as much as twelve months (Dyke & Sparhawk, 1865, p. 29).

The Black Codes provided the foundation for "neo-slavery" (Blackmon, 2009) by allowing states to rent African Americans out as convict labor. This practice was (and is) legal under the Constitution's Thirteenth Amendment, which states that "Neither slavery nor involuntary servitude, *except as a punishment for crime whereof the party shall have been duly convicted*, shall exist within the United States, or any place subject to their jurisdiction" (Library of Congress, 1865; for an argument about the "new Jim Crow," see Alexander, 2012).

Millions of free blacks needing employment now competed with poor white day laborers for work (Blackmon, 2009). With few options, approximately 75% to 80% of former slaves pursued **sharecropping**, a system developed by the plantation elite to solve their labor problem (Boyer, Clark, Hawley, Kett, & Rieser, 2008, p. 369). African Americans wanted contracts to guarantee fair compensation and working conditions and some got them with the help of the Freedmen's Bureau (Schurz, 1865). However, some plantation owners demanded contracts that often mirrored the oppressive conditions of slavery. For example, workers couldn't leave the property without written permission, had to obey all commands, and were expected to act in a servile manner. When rules were broken, whites could impose almost any punishment, including whipping (Bailey, n.d.; Blackmon, 2009, p. 27; Schurz, 1865). Nevertheless, the threat of arrest and imprisonment created by vagrancy laws compelled many black sharecroppers to sign oppressive contracts with plantation owners.

While arrangements varied, generally, former slaves agreed to work for a share of the profit when crops were sold. Landowners provided shelter, food, and clothing on credit and deducted money for land, tool, or water use. Landowners kept the accounts and often cheated workers by inflating costs and claiming that they were still owed money after profits had been split. While the sharecropping system decreased the direct control of landowners, it didn't create much economic mobility for African Americans. In fact, the sharecropping system bound sharecroppers to the land for years (Geschwender, 1978, p. 163; Logan, 2015; Schurz, 1865).

As the South industrialized, white workers protected themselves from competition for these better-paying jobs by excluding black workers from labor unions and by establishing strong antiblack laws and customs. By 1910, more than 50% of African Americans worked in agriculture and 25% worked in domestic jobs (e.g., house cleaning; Geschwender, 1978, p. 169). African Americans' participation rates in some economic sectors dropped lower than during slavery. For example, in 1865, 83% of skilled craftspeople in the South were African Americans. By 1900, only 5% held such positions (Geschwender, 1978, p. 170). The laws and customs of the Jim Crow system drastically limited the options and life opportunities available to black southerners and denied them opportunities such as education, employment, and full political participation. Nevertheless, African Americans continued to push for equality and the lives they wanted (PBS, n.d.).

Political and Civil Rights under Jim Crow

A final force behind the creation of de jure segregation was political. As the 19th century ended, a wave of populism spread across the country in response to changes caused by industrialization. This movement attempted to unite poor whites and blacks in the rural South against the elite classes.

The possibility of losing power frightened the economic elite, who fanned the flames of racial hatred and used an effective divide-and-conquer strategy that split the emerging coalition of poor whites and blacks. By working to deprive African American men of their right to vote, the white elite classes in states throughout the South eliminated the possibility of future threats (Woodward, 1974).

The creation of literacy tests, poll taxes, and property requirements disenfranchised the black community. Whites officially justified literacy tests as promoting a better-informed electorate, but they were rigged to favor white voters. The requirement that voters pay a tax or prove ownership of a certain amount of property could also disenfranchise poor whites, but again, the implementation of these policies was racialized and not systematically enforced for white voters (Constitutional Rights Foundation, n.d.).

These practices were extremely effective. The political power of southern blacks—which became so strong during Reconstruction—was virtually nonexistent by the early 20th century. In Louisiana in 1896, more than 100,000 African American men were registered to vote and constituted the majority of voters in 26 parishes (counties). In 1898, the state adopted a new constitution with strict voting requirements; for example, a person couldn't vote unless their father or grandfather was eligible to vote by January 1, 1867 (i.e., "grandfather clauses")—before the Fourteenth and Fifteenth Amendments (which guaranteed voting rights to black men) had been passed. Thus, such requirements effectively eliminated black men from the electorate. By 1900, only about 5,000 African American men were registered to vote in Louisiana. Other states followed suit, leading to similar declines throughout the South. As a result, black representation at the federal, state, and local levels decreased significantly. By 1905, African American political power-lessness was a reality (Franklin & Moss, 1994, p. 261; Lawson, 2009, p. 14). For example, George H. White of North Carolina left Congress in 1901. He was the last black congressman from the South until the 1970s.

The U.S. Supreme Court legally sanctioned white privilege in *Plessy v. Ferguson* (1896) by ruling that states could require separate facilities for African Americans as long as they were equal to white facilities. People often refer to the principle established by *Plessy v. Ferguson* as "separate but equal" but that statement doesn't reflect reality. Most facilities (e.g., schools, parks) provided for black southerners were vastly inferior to those for whites.

Reinforcing the System

Under de jure segregation, strict rules for racial etiquette emphasizing African Americans' inferior status governed interactions between blacks and whites. For example, African Americans had to act deferentially toward whites, addressing them as "mister" or "ma'am," looking downward, and using the back doors of white-owned homes or businesses. Blacks who ignored these norms risked retaliation such as arrest or physical harm, including lynching. Between 1877 and 1950, officials (e.g., judges, police), secret organizations (e.g., the KKK), and individuals lynched 4,084 African Americans, primarily boys and men (Equal Justice Initiative, 2017; Franklin & Moss, 1994, p. 312).

COMPARATIVE FOCUS
JIM CROW SEGREGATION AND SOUTH AFRICAN APARTHEID

Other nations practiced legalized, state-sponsored racial segregation similar to Jim Crow. One of the most infamous systems was South African apartheid. Though differences between the two systems existed, they shared many similarities.

Most importantly, the dominant group in both countries (whites) constructed these systems to control and exploit the minority group (blacks) and to keep them powerless. Each segregation system shaped most areas of life, including neighborhoods, schools, workplaces, theaters, parks, public buildings, busses, beaches, and water fountains.

Whites benefited from the cheap labor created under both systems. For example, white families of modest means could afford gardeners, cooks,

(Continued)

(Continued)

cleaners, and nannies to make their lives easier. Cheap labor lowered costs in many industries (e.g., farming, construction), which resulted in lower prices for produce, cotton, and other goods. Blacks in both countries were paid much less than whites and experienced much higher rates of poverty.

Blacks in both systems were politically disenfranchised and closely controlled by police. For example, laws governed where blacks could live, who they could marry, the jobs they could hold, and so on. Elaborate customs governed interactions between the races and displayed and reinforced group power differentials. Violence and threats of violence from the police, terrorist groups, and vigilantes reinforced both systems.

Under the leadership of Nelson Mandela, Martin Luther King Jr., and others, people in both countries worked to end racial oppression. They shared a belief in the fundamental dignity and value of all people and they shared common organizational strategies, such as protests

and boycotts. Governments in both countries responded to minority group activism with repressive tactics (e.g., imprisonment).

Legalized segregation in both countries ended only after prolonged, intense conflict. Apartheid ended in the early 1990s after almost 50 years of existence. Some argue that apartheid was more repressive than Jim Crow segregation and more viciously defended by the dominant group. Why? Part of the reason is simple arithmetic. Whites in South Africa were a numerical minority (less than 10% of the population) and felt that their privileged status was under extreme threat from the black numerical majority. White South Africans had a "fortress mentality" and feared that they would be swamped by blacks if they allowed even the slightest lapse in the defense of their racial privilege (Hönke, 2013).

Today, both countries continue to deal with the legacies of racial segregation as racial divisions run deep. Neither has completely resolved its issues of racial fairness, justice, and equality.

QUESTIONS FOR REFLECTION

1. Why did whites in both countries respond so violently to black protest movements? What was at stake, as they saw it?

2. Besides population sizes, what differences can you identify between the two systems? For example, is it important that the Jim Crow system was regional and apartheid was national? What are the implications of this difference?

Increases in Prejudice and Racism

At the start of the 20th century, the United States—not only the South—remained a racist society. As with slavery, whites rationalized the Jim Crow system through stereotypes, ideologies of racial inferiority, and widespread antiblack sentiment. As the system of white racial advantage solidified, prejudice and racism toward blacks increased and created an especially negative brand of racism in the South (Wilson, 1973, p. 101).

FIGURE 4.1   ■   Distribution of the African American Population in the United States, 1790–1990

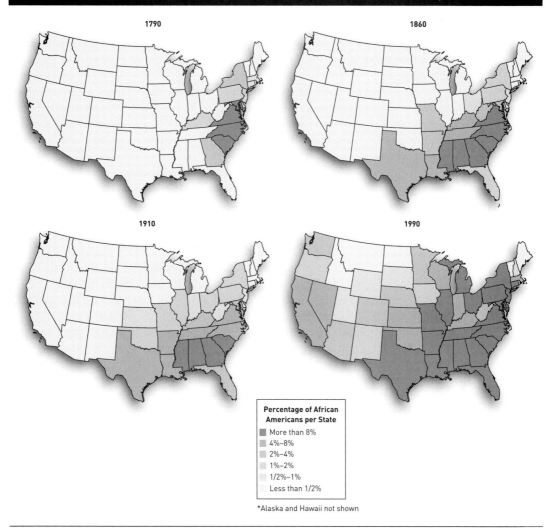

Source: Bureau of the census, U.S. Department of Commerce.

QUESTIONS FOR REFLECTION

3. How did the paternalistic system of race relations become a rigid, competitive one?

4. How does the Noel hypothesis, especially competition and power differentials, apply to the Jim Crow system of segregation?

5. From a sociological perspective, what were the most important features of de jure segregation? Why?

The Great Migration (Early 1900s to 1970s)

African Americans had an option that wasn't available under slavery: freedom of movement. They weren't legally tied to a specific master or plot of land. Slowly at first, African Americans left the South to seek opportunities elsewhere. This massive population movement, called the *Great Migration*, happened in waves similar to European immigration.

In discussing the Great Migration, some people say that African Americans voted against southern segregation with their feet. By the end of 1919, approximately one million blacks had moved away from the South; by 1978, almost six million had left. Their migration increased when hard times hit southern agriculture and it slowed during better times.

As Figure 4.1 shows, the black population was highly concentrated in the South as recently as 1910, a little more than a century ago. By 1990, African Americans had become much more evenly distributed across the nation, settling in the Northeast and the upper Midwest. Since 1990, the distribution of the black population has remained roughly the same, though some African Americans have begun moving back to the South.

Figure 4.2 shows that in addition to movement away from the South, the Great Migration also involved migration from the countryside to the city. A century ago, blacks were overwhelmingly rural; today, more than 90% live in urban areas. Thus, an urban black population living outside of the South is a 20th-century phenomenon.

The significance of this population redistribution is manifold. Most important, perhaps, was the fact that African Americans moved from areas of great resistance to racial equality to areas of lower resistance to social change. In northern cities, for example, it was far easier for black people to register and vote. As their political power increased, African Americans were able to acquire crucial resources for the civil rights movement of the 1950s and 1960s.

Life in the North

What did African American migrants find when they got to the industrializing cities of the North? Life in the North was better for most of them. The growing northern African American communities relished the absence of Jim Crow laws and oppressive racial etiquette, the relative freedom to pursue employment, and the greater opportunities for education. Many aspects of African American culture—literature, poetry, and music—flourished in this new atmosphere of freedom. However, life in the North fell far short of utopia as African Americans faced new forms of oppression and exploitation called *de facto segregation*, which we'll discuss in Chapter 5 (Wilkerson, 2011).

Competition with White Ethnic Groups

It's useful to consider African Americans' migration from the South in terms of intergroup relations. Black southerners began moving to the North as European immigration was ending. By the time substantial numbers of blacks had settled in the North, European immigrants and their descendants had had years, decades, and even generations to establish themselves in job markets, labor unions, political systems,

FIGURE 4.2 ■   Percentage of African Americans Living in Urban Areas, 1890–2010

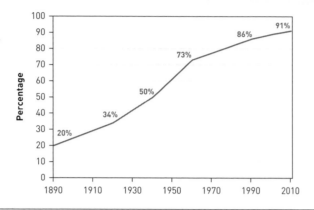

Source: 1890 to 1960 (Geschwender, 1978); 1980 and 1990 (Pollard & O'Hare, 1999); 2000 (U.S. Census Bureau, 2000b); 2010 (U.S. Census Bureau, 2013b).

neighborhoods, and other aspects of social life. Many European ethnic groups had experienced discrimination and rejection, and their hold on economic security and status remained tenuous for much of the 20th century.

Within this context, European immigrants often saw newly arriving black migrants as a threat. Industrialists and factory owners reinforced this belief by using African Americans as cheap labor and strikebreakers. White ethnic groups responded by excluding African Americans from their labor unions and other associations and limiting their impact on the political system. Often, white ethnics successfully maintained segregated neighborhoods and schools (although the legal system didn't sanction blatant de jure segregation).

A sense of competition led to hostile relations between black southern migrants and white ethnic groups, especially those in the lower classes. (Ironically, newly arriving African Americans actually helped white ethnics achieve upward mobility. See the discussion concerning ethnic succession in Chapter 2.) As whites became increasingly concerned about the growing presence of African Americans, they became more accepting of white ethnic groups (e.g., Ukrainians, Slovaks). At the same time, the more educated and skilled descendants of the original immigrants came of age and entered the workforce, further helping these groups rise in the social class structure (Lieberson, 1980).

For more than a century, newly arriving European immigrant groups helped to push earlier groups up the ladder of socioeconomic success. However, blacks got to the cities after European immigration had been curtailed. Thus, no new large groups of immigrants arrived to continue the pattern of ethnic succession for African Americans in the North. Instead, American cities developed concentrations of low-income blacks who were economically vulnerable and politically weak and whose position was further solidified by antiblack prejudice and discrimination (Wilson, 1987, p. 34).

The Origins of Black Protest

As mentioned earlier, African Americans have always resisted their oppression. Under slavery, the inequalities they faced were so great and their resources so meager that their protest was ineffective. With the increased freedom following the abolition of slavery, a national African American leadership developed and spoke out against oppression and founded organizations that eventually helped lead the fight for freedom and equality. Even at its birth, the black protest movement was diverse and incorporated a variety of viewpoints and leaders.

Booker T. Washington was the most prominent African American leader prior to World War I. Born into slavery, Washington became the founder and president of Tuskegee Institute, a college in Alabama dedicated to educating African Americans. His public advice to African Americans in the South was to be patient, to accommodate the Jim Crow system for the time being, to raise their levels of education and job skills, and to take full advantage of whatever opportunities became available. This nonconfrontational stance earned Washington praise and support from the white community and widespread popularity in the nation. However, he worked behind the scenes to end discrimination and implement full racial integration and equality (Franklin & Moss, 1994, pp. 272–274; Hawkins, 1962; Washington, 1965).

Washington's most vocal opponent was W. E. B. Du Bois, an activist and intellectual trained in sociology. (Many view him as the father of American sociology and he conducted important sociological research on the lives of African Americans. See Morris, 2015.) Du Bois was born in the North and educated at some of the leading universities of the day. Among his many other accomplishments, Du Bois was part of a coalition of blacks and white liberals who founded the National Association for the Advancement of Colored People (NAACP) in 1909. Du Bois rejected Washington's accommodationist stance and advocated immediate pursuit of racial equality and a direct assault on de jure segregation (Morris, 2015). Almost from the beginning of its existence, the NAACP filed lawsuits that challenged the legal foundations of Jim Crow segregation (Du Bois, 1961). As you'll learn in Chapter 5, this legal strategy eventually led to the demise of Jim Crow segregation.

Though Washington and Du Bois differed on strategy and tactics, they agreed on the goal of an integrated, racially equal nation. A third leader emerged early in the 20th century and called for a very different approach to the problems of U.S. race relations. Marcus Garvey immigrated to America from Jamaica during World War I. He argued that the white-dominated society was hopelessly racist and would never truly support integration and racial equality. He advocated separatist goals, including a return to Africa. Garvey founded the Universal Negro Improvement Association in 1914 in his native Jamaica and founded the first U.S. branch in 1916. Garvey's organization was very popular for a time in African American communities outside the South, and it helped to establish some of the themes and ideas of black nationalism and pride in African heritage that would become prominent again in the pluralistic 1960s (Essien-Udom, 1962; Garvey, 1969, 1977; Vincent, 1976).

These early leaders and organizations helped lay the foundations for later protest movements, but prior to the mid-20th century, they made few improvements in the situation of African Americans. Jim Crow was a formidable opponent, and African Americans lacked the resources to successfully challenge the status quo until some basic structural features of American society had changed (well into the 20th century).

THE DIMENSIONS OF MINORITY GROUP STATUS

Acculturation and Integration

During this era of southern segregation and African American migration to the North, black–white relations involved a system of structural pluralism combined with great inequality. Excluded from the mainstream but freed from the limitations of slavery, African Americans across the U. S. developed their own communities and organizations such as businesses, schools, churches, social clubs (Wilkerson, 2011). Like European immigrants during the same era, blacks worked to solve their own problems and meet their own needs, even as they pushed for greater equality within the larger society.

During segregation, African Americans with leadership roles in the church, education, and business emerged as a new but small middle class. They helped create a network of black colleges and universities to educate the children of the growing middle class. This critical infrastructure enabled African Americans to develop the resources and leadership that, in the decades ahead, would attack the structures of racial inequality head-on.

Gender and Race

Industrialization and the Great Migration created new possibilities for African Americans; yet, African Americans in both the North and South continued to face exploitation and exclusion. Because of their position within America's racial and gender hierarchies, black women continued to be one of its most vulnerable groups.

A flurry of weddings followed emancipation as African Americans gained the right to marry their chosen partners (Blassingame, 1972; Staples, 1988; Washington, 2005). Also, economic pressures resulting from gender discrimination compelled some black women to marry. For example, landowners often refused to contract with single women or widows for sharecropping or tenancy, leaving women few options for paid labor in the South. They could marry or migrate north (Bloome & Muller, 2015).

With emancipation, the legal control of married black women shifted from slave owners to husbands. Landowners expected women to work under the sharecropping contracts signed by their husbands. Working in the fields while also caring for homes and families meant that black women probably worked more than black men or white women (Jones, 1985). This arrangement was reminiscent of their lives under slavery and many black women chose to leave the labor force to focus on their families and homes. This created significant agricultural labor shortages in some areas (Gutman, 1976; Mann 1989; Staples, 1988).

Former slaves were hardly affluent, however, and as sharecropping and segregation began to change race relations in the South, black women often had to return to the fields or to domestic work to survive. One formerly enslaved woman noted that women "do double duty, a man's share in the field and a woman's part at home" (Evans, 1989, p. 121). During the bleak decades following the end of Reconstruction, southern black families—and black women in particular—lived "close to the bone" (p. 121).

During the Great Migration, African American women's lives paralleled those of European immigrant women. The men often moved first. After they attained some financial stability or when the pain of separation became too great, men sent for the women (Almquist, 1979, p. 434). Additionally, thousands of African American women left on their own to work as domestic servants in the North, often replacing European immigrant women who had moved up the economic ladder (Amott & Matthaei, 1991, p. 168).

In the North, discrimination and racism created constant problems of unemployment for black men, and their families often relied on women's incomes to make ends meet. It was comparatively easy for women to find employment, but only in low-paying, less desirable jobs. In the South and the North, African American women worked outside the home at higher rates than white women. For example, in 1900, 41% of African American women were employed, compared with only 16% of white women (Staples, 1988, p. 307).

In 1890, more than a generation after slavery ended, 85% of African American men and 96% of African American women were employed in two occupational categories: agriculture and domestic/personal service. By 1930, 90% of employed African American women were still working in those areas. The rate for African American men in those jobs dropped to 54% (most of the remaining 46% of men were unskilled workers who would have a hard time finding other employment; Steinberg, 1981, pp. 206–207). Since segregation began, African American women have had consistently higher unemployment rates and lower incomes than African American men and white women (Almquist, 1979, p. 437). These employment differences continue today as you'll see in Chapter 5.

Following emancipation, some issues (such as the right to vote) divided men and women, regardless of race. The abolitionist movement, which was instrumental in ending slavery, supported universal voting rights. However, it largely abandoned that goal to focus on securing the vote for African American men. Ratification of the Fifteenth Amendment in 1870 earned them that right, but the Nineteenth Amendment enfranchising women wouldn't pass until 1920 (Almquist, 1979, pp. 433–434; Evans, 1989, pp. 121–124).

QUESTIONS FOR REFLECTION

6. Why did African Americans migrate to the North in the early 20th century? Did this move improve their situation? Explain.

7. What protest strategies did African Americans develop in the early 20th century? How did the group's overall situation shape these strategies?

8. Did African Americans become more or less acculturated and integrated during the Jim Crow era? Explain.

9. How did gender shape the lives of African Americans during this time?

INDUSTRIALIZATION, THE SHIFT TO POSTINDUSTRIAL SOCIETY, AND DOMINANT–MINORITY RELATIONS: GENERAL TRENDS

The industrialization that began in the 19th century continued to shape dominant–minority relations and the larger society throughout the 20th century. In many ways, our country today bears little resemblance to society then. The population in 2019 is almost 10 times larger than in 1870. American society has urbanized rapidly and new organizational forms (e.g., multinational corporations, bureaucracies) and modern technologies (e.g., computers, the Internet, cell phones) dominate everyday life. Levels of education have risen, and public schools have produced one of the most literate populations and best-trained workforces in the world's history. Minority group statistics generally parallel these broader trends: Populations grew and became more urbanized (even more than the general population), average levels of education increased, and group members participated in a growing range of occupations.

Despite improvements, virtually all U.S. minority groups continue to face racism, discrimination, poverty, and exclusion. As industrialization continued, the mechanisms for maintaining racial stratification also evolved, morphing into forms that are subtle and indirect but as formidable as Jim Crow.

In this section, we'll examine the social processes that began in the industrial era and continue to shape the postindustrial era. We'll show how these processes changed American society and how they affected minority groups in particular. Then, we'll summarize how these changes coincided with a transition from the rigid competitive system of the Jim Crow era to a new type of group relations called *fluid competitive* relations. We'll keep our discussion broad, seeking only to establish a general framework that we can use to understand the impact of industrialization and deindustrialization on group relations in the case studies of Part 3.

Urbanization

We've already noted that urbanization made close, paternalistic controls of minority groups irrelevant. For example, the racial etiquette required during southern de jure segregation, such as African Americans deferring to whites on sidewalks, tended to disappear in crowded urban communities.

Besides weakening dominant group controls, urbanization also created the potential for minority groups to mobilize large numbers of people. As you learned in Chapter 1, the size of a group can be a source of power. However, without the freedom to organize, size means little. Urbanization increased the concentration of people who now had the freedom to organize.

Occupational Specialization

One of the first and most important results of industrialization was increasing occupational specialization. The growing needs of an urbanizing population increased the types of jobs available (e.g., in the production, transportation, and sale of goods and services).

Industrial production also stimulated occupational specialization, since complex manufacturing processes could be done more efficiently when broken into smaller tasks. Since it was easier and more efficient to train workers in simpler, specialized jobs, work was subdivided and assembly lines invented. As a result, the division of labor became increasingly complex and the number of occupations grew.

The complexity of the industrial job structure made it difficult to maintain rigid, caste-like divisions of labor between dominant and minority groups. Rigid competitive forms of group relations, such as Jim Crow segregation, became less viable as the job market changed and diversified. Simple, clear rules about who could do which jobs began to disappear.

As the more repressive systems of control weakened, job opportunities for minority group members increased. However, as the relationship between one's group membership and available positions in the job market became more blurred, conflict between groups increased. For example, as noted earlier, African Americans moving to the North often found themselves in competition for jobs with members of white ethnic groups, labor union members, and others.

Bureaucracy and Rationality

As industrialization continued, corporations came to have workforces numbering in the hundreds of thousands. Gigantic factories commonly employed thousands of workers. Bureaucracies developed to coordinate these huge workforces, and they became the dominant form of organization in the economy and in society.

Bureaucracies are large-scale, impersonal, formal organizations that govern by detailed rules and regulations (i.e., "red tape") that generally apply to everyone. Bureaucracies are "rational" in that they try to accomplish tasks in the most efficient ways. Although they typically don't attain the ideal of rational efficiency, which involves the elimination of favoritism (Perrow, 1986), bureaucracies tend to recruit, reward, and promote employees based on competence and performance (Gerth & Mills, 1946).

Because they stress rationality and objectivity, bureaucracies can counteract the more blatant forms of discrimination (e.g., racism, sexism) and increase the opportunities available to minority group members. Although other social forces often nullify these outcomes (see Blumer, 1965), these antiprejudicial tendencies are much weaker—or don't exist at all—in preindustrial economies.

We can see the impact of rationality and scientific thinking by examining the history of the concept of race. Decades of scientific research show that race doesn't determine intelligence, dependability, competence, or similar characteristics. Today, virtually the entire scientific community rejects old beliefs (see Chapter 1). This research helped undermine traditional prejudice as well as formal systems of privilege based solely on race (e.g., segregated school systems).

Growth of White-Collar Jobs and the Service Sector

Industrialization changed the composition of the labor force. As work became more complex and specialized, the need to coordinate and regulate the production process increased. Thus, bureaucracies and other organizations grew larger still. Within these organizations, white-collar occupations—those that coordinate, manage, and deal with paperwork—increased throughout much of the century. Simultaneously, mechanization and automation reduced the number of manual or blue-collar jobs, and white-collar occupations became the dominant sector of the U.S. job market.

The changing workforce can be illustrated by looking at the proportional representation of three different types of jobs:

1. **Extractive (or primary) occupations** help produce raw materials, such as food and agricultural products, minerals, and timber. Jobs in this sector often involve unskilled manual labor, require little formal education, and are generally low paying.

2. **Manufacturing (or secondary) occupations** transform raw materials into finished products; for example, assembly line jobs that transform steel, rubber, plastic, and other materials into automobiles. Similar to jobs in the extractive sector, these blue-collar jobs involve manual labor but typically require higher skill levels. They offer greater rewards than extractive occupations.

3. **Service (or tertiary) occupations** provide services, not products. As urbanization increased and self-sufficiency decreased, work in this sector grew. Examples of tertiary occupations include teacher, police officer, waiter, nurse, and cabdriver.

Figure 4.3 depicts the course of industrialization and the corresponding changes in the labor market. In 1850, when industrialization was beginning in America, most of the workforce (almost 70%) was in the extractive sector, primarily in agriculture. As industrialization progressed, the manufacturing (or secondary) sector grew, reaching a peak around World War II. Today, in the postindustrial era, the large majority of U.S. jobs are in the service (or tertiary) sector.

As noted earlier, the shift from blue-collar jobs and manufacturing since the 1960s is sometimes called *deindustrialization*, or the shift to a postindustrial subsistence technology. Since the 1960s, the U.S. economy has lost millions of unionized, high-paying factory jobs as companies have moved to other nations where wages are considerably lower. Robots and other automated manufacturing processes led to the elimination of other jobs and will continue to do so (Manyika et al., 2017).

Most job growth in America today is in the service sector and researchers expect that trend to continue (U.S. Bureau of Labor Statistics, 2017a). Service-sector jobs are either low-skilled, low-paying jobs with little security and few (if any) benefits or advancement opportunities (e.g., waiter, cashier) or they are well-compensated technical, professional, or administrative jobs with demanding entry requirements (e.g., physician or nurse).

The changing job market structure sheds light on the sources of wealth and power in America as well as on intergroup competition. Over the past half century, U.S. job growth has been either in areas where educationally deprived minority group members find it difficult to compete or in areas that offer little compensation, upward mobility, or security. As you'll see in Part 3, the economic situation of many contemporary minority groups reflects these fundamental trends.

FIGURE 4.3 ■ The Changing U.S. Workforce: Distribution of Jobs from 1850 to 2010

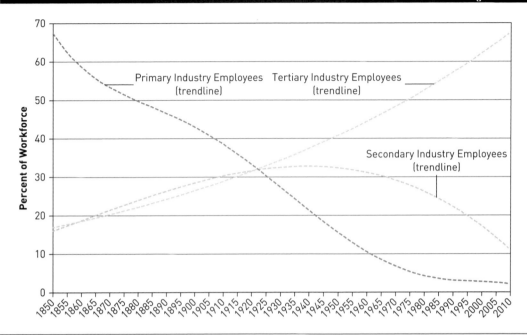

Source: For data for 1840 and 1990, adapted from Lenski, Nolan, & Lenski (1995); for 2000, calculated from U.S. Census Bureau (2005, pp. 385–388); for 2010, calculated from U.S. Census Bureau (2012b, pp. 393–396).

The Growing Importance of Education

Education is increasingly important for employability in the U. S. and in other advanced industrial nations. A high school or, increasingly, college degree has become the minimum entry-level requirement. However, opportunities for high-quality education aren't distributed equally across the U.S. population. Although the average educational levels of minority groups have increased since World War II, some minority groups, especially those created by colonization, have been systematically excluded from education (e.g., African Americans under Jim Crow).

Today, minority children are still much more likely to attend segregated, underfunded, deteriorating public schools (see Orfield & Lee, 2007). Thus, they are more likely to be taught by less-experienced teachers and to be in overcrowded classrooms that limit the attention teachers can give them (Ashkenas, Park, & Pearce, 2017). Additionally, underfunded schools lack educational resources from basic supplies such as paper and updated textbooks to computers and lab or musical equipment that would help prepare students for college. During the 2014–2015 school year, 94% of public school teachers spent their own money buying supplies. Unfortunately, that can't offset resource inequalities (U.S. Department of Education, 2018).

Unequal school funding and resources is compounded by the fact that minority students are much more likely to come from poor families and live in poor, economically segregated neighborhoods with fewer resources, including human and social capital.

For example, their parents are less likely to have college degrees and are less likely to be able to volunteer at schools (Reardon, Robinson-Cimpian, & Weathers, 2014). The resulting achievement gap weakens the country "internationally, economically and morally," according to a report by the Equity and Excellence Commission (2013, p. 39), a federal advisory committee commissioned by Congress.

Educational equity in K–12 public schools means that minority children are less likely to be prepared for college or to attend college (Ashkenas, Park, & Pearce, 2017; Boschma & Brownstein, 2016). Even for those accepted into college, many don't transition to college in the fall after their senior year, a phenomenon known as "summer melt" (Castleman & Page, 2014; Rall, 2016). These and other factors mean that minority students, especially poor ones, are less likely to be competitive in the labor market, exacerbating racial income gaps and resulting in racialized skills and income gaps. Again, it's important to see how present-day inequalities are rooted in racial segregation and discrimination from the past. For example, Carruthers and Wanamaker (2016) argue that such wage inequality today would decrease by 40%–51% if the 1940s public school system had truly been "separate but equal."

A Dual Labor Market

The changing composition of the labor force and increasing importance of educational credentials has split the U.S. labor market into two segments or types of jobs. The **primary labor market** includes jobs usually located in large bureaucratic organizations. These positions offer higher pay, more security, better opportunities for advancement, health and retirement benefits, and other amenities. Entry requirements include college degrees, even when people with fewer years of schooling could competently perform the work.

The **secondary labor market**, sometimes called the *competitive market*, includes low-paying, low-skilled, insecure jobs. Many of these jobs are in the service sector. They don't represent a career, per se, and offer little opportunity for promotion or upward mobility. Typically, they don't offer health or retirement benefits, have high rates of turnover, and are part-time, seasonal, or temporary.

Many American minority groups are concentrated in the secondary job market. Their exclusion from better jobs is perpetuated not so much by direct or overt discrimination as by their lack of access to the educational and other credentials required to enter the primary sector. The differential distribution of educational opportunities in the past and in the present effectively protects workers in the primary sector from competition from minority groups.

Globalization

Over the past century, America became an economic, political, and military world power with interests around the globe. These worldwide ties have created new minority groups through population movement and have changed the status of other minority groups. Immigration to this country has been considerable for the past three decades. The American economy is one of the most productive in the world, and a job, even from the low-paying secondary sector, is the primary goal for millions of newcomers. For other immigrants, this country continues to play its historic role as a refuge from political and religious persecution.

Many of the wars, conflicts, and other disputes in which America has been involved have had consequences for American minority groups. For example, Puerto Ricans and Cuban Americans became U.S. minority groups as the result of processes set in motion during the Spanish–American War of 1898. World War I and World War II created new job opportunities for many minority groups, including African Americans and Mexican Americans. After the Korean War in the early 1950s, international ties were forged between the U. S. and South Korea, and this led to an increase in immigration from that nation. In the 1960s and 1970s, America's military involvement in Southeast Asia led to the arrival of Vietnamese, Cambodians, Hmong, and other immigrant and refugee groups from that region. Recent wars in Iraq and Afghanistan have also produced new communities of immigrants and refugees.

Dominant–minority relations in America have been increasingly played out on an international stage, as the world has become more interconnected by international organizations, such as the United Nations; by ties of trade and commerce; and by modern means of transportation and communication. In a world where most of the population is nonwhite and many nations are composed of peoples of color, the treatment of racial minorities by the U.S. dominant group has come under increased scrutiny. It is difficult to preach principles of fairness, equality, and justice—which America claims as its own—when domestic realities suggest an embarrassing failure to fully implement these standards. Part of the incentive for the U. S. to end blatant systems of discrimination such as de jure segregation came from the desire to maintain a leading position in the world.

POSTINDUSTRIAL SOCIETY AND THE SHIFT FROM RIGID TO FLUID COMPETITIVE RELATIONSHIPS

The coming of postindustrial society brought changes so fundamental and profound that they are often described as a revolution: from an industrial society based on manufacturing to a postindustrial society based on information processing and computer-related or other new technologies. As subsistence technology evolved, so did American dominant–minority relations. The rigid competitive systems (such as Jim Crow) associated with earlier phases of industrialization gave way to **fluid competitive systems** of group relations.

In fluid competitive relations, formal or legal barriers to competition—such as Jim Crow laws or South African apartheid—no longer exist. Geographic and social mobility are greater and the limitations imposed by minority group status are less restrictive and burdensome. Rigid caste systems of stratification, in which group membership determines adult statuses and opportunities (e.g., education, jobs) are replaced by more open class systems, in which the relationships between group membership and wealth, prestige, and power are weaker. Because fluid competitive systems are more open and the position of the minority group is less fixed, the fear of competition from minority groups becomes more widespread in the dominant group, and intergroup conflict increases. Table 4.2 compares the characteristics of the three systems of group relations.

Compared with previous systems, the fluid competitive system is closer to the American ideal of an open, fair system of stratification in which effort and competence are rewarded and race, ethnicity, gender, religion, and other personal characteristics are irrelevant. However, as you'll see in future chapters, these characteristics still affect opportunities for minority group members, even in fluid competitive systems. As the Noel hypothesis suggests, people identify with particular groups and competition for resources plays out along group lines. Consistent with Blauner's hypothesis, minority groups formed by colonization remain at a disadvantage as they pursue opportunities and resources (e.g., education, prestige).

QUESTIONS FOR REFLECTION

10. Why did black–white relations shift from a rigid to a fluid competitive system? What was the role of subsistence technology in the shift?

11. What are the key changes in the shift to postindustrial subsistence technology? What are the implications of these changes for American minority groups?

TABLE 4.2 ■ Characteristics of Three Systems of Group Relations

	Systems of Group Relations		
		Competitive	
	Paternalistic	Rigid	Fluid
Subsistence technology	**Agrarian**	**Industrial**	**Postindustrial**
Stratification	**Caste.** Group determines status.	**Mixed.** Elements of caste and class. Status largely determined by group.	**Variable.** Status strongly affected by group. Inequality varies within groups.
Division of labor	**Simple.** Determined by group.	**More complex.** Job largely determined by group, but some sharing of jobs by different groups.	**Most complex.** Group and job are less related. Complex specialization and great variation within groups.
Contact between groups	**Common**, but statuses unequal.	**Less common**, and mostly unequal.	**More common.** Highest rates of equal-status contact.
Overt intergroup conflict	**Rare**	**More common**	**Most Common**
Power differential	**Maximum.** Minority groups have little ability to pursue self-interests.	**Less.** Minority groups have some ability to pursue self-interests.	**Least.** Minority groups have more ability to pursue self-interests.

Source: Based on Farley (2000, p. 109).

GENDER INEQUALITY IN A GLOBALIZING, POSTINDUSTRIAL WORLD

Deindustrialization and globalization transformed gender relations along with relations among racial and ethnic groups. Around the world, women have been taking on new responsibilities, sometimes forgoing roles as wife and mother and facing new challenges. In the United States, the transition to a postindustrial society has changed gender relations and women's status in several ways.

Women and men are now generally equal in terms of education levels (for example, see Figures 4.4 and 4.5), and the shift to fluid competitive group relations has weakened the barriers to gender equality, along with those to racial equality, although formidable obstacles remain. Other characteristics of modern society have influenced women's changing roles: smaller families, higher divorce rates, and rising numbers of single mothers who must work outside the home to support themselves and their children.

One of the most fundamental changes in U.S. gender relations has been the increasing participation of women in the paid labor force, a change related to both demographic trends (e.g., lower birth rates) and changing aspirations. Women are now employed at almost the same levels as men. In 2016, for example, 70% of unmarried women (vs. about 82% of unmarried men) and about 66% of married women (vs. about 91% of married men) had jobs in the paid labor force. Furthermore, between 1970 and 2009, the workforce participation of married women with children increased from a little less than 40% to over 70% (U.S. Bureau of Labor Statistics, 2017b).

Historically, women worked in a narrow range of women-dominated jobs; for example, as nurses and elementary school teachers. Today, women's professional aspirations and employment patterns have broadened significantly. Figure 4.4 illustrates the changing gender composition within four pairs of careers from 1983–2017. In each field (e.g., dentistry), you'll see an occupation traditionally filled by women (e.g., dental hygienist) and a comparable but higher-status and more lucrative occupation traditionally dominated by men (e.g., dentist). On the left side of the figure, you'll see the percentage of women employed in each job. The four shaded bars show women's changing employment in these jobs in five selected years. While the jobs historically

QUESTIONS FOR REFLECTION

12. Is the glass half-empty or half-full for women today? Consider how the comparison group—for example, women of the past or men of the present—might influence the answer.

13. Consider the advances and restrictions for women described in this section. How might they be influenced by race, class, sexual orientation, or religion? For example, to what degree do men of every class, race, and ethnicity have gender privileges compared to similar women? To what degree can women take advantage of educational and occupational opportunities, regardless of religion, sexual orientation, and other social statuses?

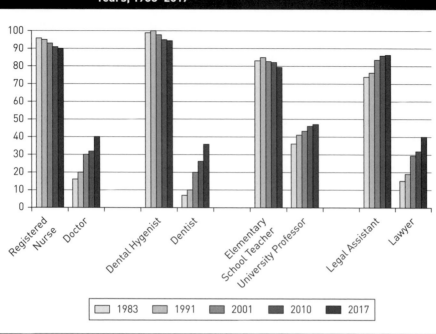

FIGURE 4.4 ■ Percentage of Women in Selected Occupations for Selected Years, 1983–2017

Legend: 1983 | 1991 | 2001 | 2010 | 2017

Sources: For figures for 1983 and 1991 (calculated from U.S. Census Bureau, 1993, pp. 392–393); for 2001 (calculated from U.S. Census Bureau, 2002, pp. 587–588); for 2010 (calculated from U.S. Census Bureau, 2012c, pp. 393–394).

dominated by women remain so, the percentage of women in higher-status occupations has increased dramatically. Despite the fact that women are making inroads, the more lucrative careers remain disproportionately filled by men.

Jobs and Income

As with many other minority groups, the economic status of women has improved over the past few decades but has stopped well short of equality. For example, as displayed in Figure 4.5, there is a persistent, although decreasing, gender gap in income. Note that the chart shows both the median incomes (in 2017 dollars to control for inflation) for men and women (read from the left vertical axis) and the percentage of men's incomes that women earn (read from the right vertical axis). Also note that the graph only includes full-time, year-round workers.

On the average, women workers today earn about 80% of what men earn, up from about 64% in 1955. The relative increase in women's income is due to a variety of factors, including the movement of women into more lucrative careers, as shown in Figure 4.4. Another cause of women's rising income is that some of the occupations in which women are highly concentrated have benefited from deindustrialization and the shift to a service economy. For example, job opportunities in the finance, insurance, and real estate sector of the job market have expanded rapidly since the 1960s. Since a high percentage of workers in this sector are women, this has elevated women's average salaries in general (Farley, 1996, pp. 95–101).

A third reason for the narrowing gender income gap has more to do with men's wages than women's. Before deindustrialization began to transform American society, men monopolized the more desirable, higher-paid, unionized jobs in the manufacturing sector. For much of the 20th century, many blue-collar jobs paid enough to support a comfortable lifestyle (e.g., a home, vacations) with enough left over to save for a rainy day or the kids' college education. However, as we've discussed, deindustrialization resulted in corporations moving jobs outside of the U. S. to locations where labor is cheaper. Other jobs were lost to automation. Many jobs were replaced by low-paying service sector jobs. Figure 4.5 shows the results of these factors. That is, while women's wages increased steadily between the 1950s and 2017, men's wages have remained virtually level since the early 1970s. In other words, the narrowing of the gender wage gap isn't all due to women's progress.

These large-scale, macrolevel forces have tended to raise women's status and narrow the income gap, but they haven't equalized gender relations. Far from it! For example, although women and men generally have equivalent education attainment, women tend to get lower returns on their investment in human capital. Figure 4.6 compares men and women full-time workers in 2016 and shows a wage gap at every level of education. Wages rise as education increases for both women and men, but the wage gap persists. Generally, the wage gap increases as education rises, which may, in part, reflect the fact that wages for workers with lower education (especially less than high school) are so low to begin with.

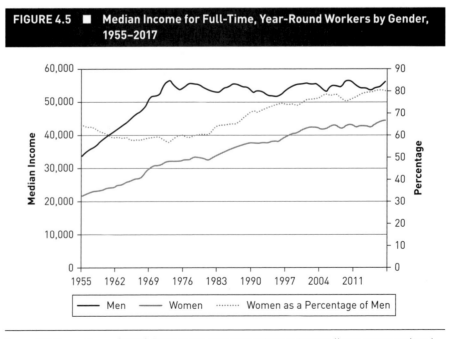

FIGURE 4.5 ■ Median Income for Full-Time, Year-Round Workers by Gender, 1955–2017

Source: U.S. Census Bureau (2018b). "Historical Income Tables" Table P-36 https://www.census.gov/data/tables/time-series/demo/income-poverty/historical-income-people.html.

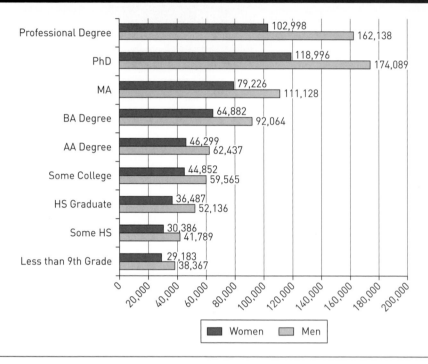

FIGURE 4.6 ■ Average Annual Income for Full-Time, Year-Round Workers Ages 25–64 by Gender and Educational Attainment, 2016

Source: U.S. Census Bureau (2017h).

COMPARATIVE FOCUS

WOMEN'S STATUS IN GLOBAL PERSPECTIVE

On October 9, 2012, in the Swat region of Pakistan, an armed assailant attacked 15-year-old Malala Yousafzai while she was riding a bus to school. Gunmen sought her out and even asked for her by name. They fired several bullets; one hit Malala in the head.

The reason for the attack? Malala wanted an education and was an outspoken advocate for girls' education, blogging under a pseudonym about her experiences as a girl living under Taliban rule. The Taliban sent the gunmen to assassinate her because by speaking out and

going to school, she publicly and repeatedly violated the organization's rules regarding women's proper place.

Malala survived the attack and was transported to the United Kingdom, where she underwent a lengthy and painful recovery (Peer, 2012). Far from being intimidated, she resumed her advocacy for girls' education and was frequently featured by the mass media in Western Europe, America, and around the globe. In recognition of her courage, eloquence, and passion, she was awarded the Nobel Peace Prize in 2014 (sharing

(Continued)

(Continued)

TABLE 4.3 ■ Status of Women in Select Nations, 2018				
	Nation			
Variables	Mali	Pakistan	Chile	Sweden
Percentage of labor force in agriculture	80.00	42.30	9.20	2.00
Mother's mean age at first birth	18.80	23.60	22.00	29.10
Maternal mortality rate (deaths of mothers per 100,000 live births)	587.00	178.00	22.00	4.00
Total fertility rate (average number of children per woman, lifetime)	6.01	2.62	1.80	1.88
Percentage literate				
Men	45.00	70.00	98.00	99.00
Women	22.00	46.00	97.00	99.00

Source: Central Intelligence Agency (2018).

that honor with Kailash Satyarth) and becoming the youngest person to be so recognized.

Why was Malala willing to risk her life? How oppressed are women in Pakistan? How does the status of Pakistani women compare to that of women in other nations?

In Pakistan and around the globe, women are moving out of their traditional and often highly controlled and repressed status. Rates of early marriage and childbirth are falling, and education levels and participation in the paid labor force are rising. Today, almost half (48.5%) of women worldwide are in the paid labor force (vs. 75% of all men), although they still tend to be concentrated in lower-status, less-lucrative, and more-insecure jobs everywhere (Catalyst, 2018; United Nations Department of Economic and Social Affairs, Population Division, 2013).

The women of Pakistan aren't as repressed as women in many other nations, including Saudi Arabia, where women only recently won the right to vote (2015) and the right to drive (2018). Some simple statistics will illustrate the range of possibilities. Table 4.3 provides information on women's status in four nations representing various levels of development, locations, and religious backgrounds.

As we've noted, women's status is partly a function of subsistence technology. Mali is the most agricultural of these four nations (with 80% of its workforce in farming), and the women there have more children earlier in life and are far more likely to die in childbirth. They're also much less educated than the women of other nations and the men of their own nation.

Pakistan is less agricultural than Mali, and women's status is relatively higher, although they're much less likely than men to be educated. Note, also, that the statistics suggest that Pakistani women are still largely focused on producing and maintaining large families.

Women's status generally rises as industrialization and urbanization proceed, as indicated by the profiles of Chile and Sweden. Sweden is more industrialized than Chile, and Swedish women have fewer children (often later in life) and are as educated as men in their nation.

Why does women's status generally improve as societies move away from agricultural subsistence technology? One reason, no doubt, is the changing economies of childbearing: Large families are useful in the labor-intensive economies of agrarian nations, but children become increasingly expensive in modern urban-industrial economies. Also, consistent with Malala's point, more-educated women tend to make different choices about their career and family and about their own life goals.

QUESTIONS FOR REFLECTION

14. What can you infer about the lives of women in Mali from Table 4.3? Would they live in the city or countryside? Would they attend school? What power would they have regarding family, including childbirth? What kinds of activities would they pursue? What dreams would they have for their daughters? For their sons? How might their lives compare with those of women in Sweden or America?

15. How would higher levels of education affect women in developing nations? How would wide-sweeping changes in women's lives affect those societies?

MODERN INSTITUTIONAL DISCRIMINATION

In general, American minority groups continue to lag behind national averages in income, employment, and other measures of equality, despite the greater fluidity of group relations, the end of legal barriers such as Jim Crow, the dramatic declines in overt prejudice (see Chapter 5), and laws designed to ensure that people are treated without regard to race, gender, or ethnicity. After all this change, shouldn't there be more equality and less racial stratification?

As we'll discuss in Chapter 5, many Americans attribute persistent patterns of inequality to minority group members, such as their supposed lack of willpower or motivation to get ahead. In the remaining chapters, however, we argue that the major barriers facing minority groups in postindustrial, post–Jim Crow America are pervasive and subtle but still powerful forms of discrimination that together can be called *modern institutional discrimination*.

As you read in Chapter 1, institutional discrimination is built into the everyday operation of society's social structure. Routine procedures and policies of institutions and organizations put minority group members at a disadvantage. In the Jim Crow era, for example, African Americans were deprived of the right to vote by overt institutional discrimination, which meant they could acquire little political power.

The forms of institutional discrimination that persist today are subtler and more difficult to document than the overt discrimination of the past. Modern institutional discrimination isn't necessarily linked to prejudice held by dominant group members. It can be unintentional and the decision makers who implement it may think they are behaving rationally and in the best interests of their organizations. As you'll see, this kind of discrimination is primarily manifested in the inequalities facing minority groups, not in the intentions or prejudices of dominant group members.

The Continuing Power of the Past

Many forces conspire to maintain racial stratification today. Some stratification is a historical legacy; for example, **past-in-present institutional discrimination** involves practices in the present that have discriminatory consequences because of some pattern of discrimination or exclusion in the past (Feagin & Feagin, 1986, p. 32).

One form of past-in-present discrimination is related to common workplace seniority policies. In these systems, workers who have been on the job longer receive higher incomes, more privileges, and other benefits, such as longer vacations. The "old-timers" often have more job security because official policies state that they should be the last person to be fired or laid off in the event of hard times. Workers and employers alike may think of the seniority-based privileges as rewards for years served, familiarity with the job, and so forth.

Such "last hired, first fired" policies may seem perfectly reasonable, neutral, and fair. However, they can create discriminatory results in the present. That's because women and racial/ethnic minorities were excluded from specific occupations in the past by racist or sexist labor unions, discriminatory employers, or both. As a result, these workers may have fewer years of experience than white men and, therefore, may be the first to go when layoffs are necessary.

Racial differences in home ownership provide a second example of the myriad ways in which the past shapes the present and maintains the moving target of racial stratification. Today, about 72% of non-Hispanic whites own their own homes, and these houses have a median value of $179,000. In contrast, only 44% of non-Hispanic blacks are homeowners, and the median value of their homes is $125,900 (U.S. Census Bureau, 2013a). Homeownership is an important source of family wealth, because home equity can be used to establish credit, to finance businesses and other purchases and investments, and to fund children's education. What is the origin of these huge differences in family wealth?

Part of the answer lies in events that occurred decades ago. As you know, President Franklin D. Roosevelt's administration responded to the Great Depression of the 1930s, in part, by instituting the New Deal: a variety of programs that provided assistance to distressed Americans. What isn't so widely known is that these programs were racially discriminatory and provided few or no benefits to African Americans (Massey, 2007, p. 60; see also Katznelson, 2005; Lieberman, 1998).

The Federal Housing Administration (FHA) administered one of the New Deal programs that offered low-interest mortgages that made home ownership possible for millions of families. However, the FHA policies ignored the effect of racially restrictive covenants (agreements that forbade whites from selling or renting homes to people of color) when they assessed neighborhoods and created maps color-coded by perceived risk level. Neighborhoods with even a small number of African Americans could be redlined (or marked in red) to reflect the view that they were risky for making loans. Banks used the FHA ratings and as a result, African Americans in these neighborhoods couldn't get bank loans, no matter how good their personal finances (Coates, 2014; Rothstein, 2017).

Together, these and other discriminatory practices effectively excluded black Americans from homeownership (Massey, 2007, pp. 60–61; Massey & Denton, 1993, pp. 53–54). Thus, another racial divide was created that, over the generations, has helped countless white families develop wealth and credit but made it impossible for black families to qualify for homeownership, the "great engine of wealth creation" (Massey, 2007, p. 61).

More broadly, racial residential segregation—which is arguably the key factor in preserving racial stratification in the present—provides another illustration of modern institutional discrimination. The overt Jim Crow–era laws and customs that created racially segregated neighborhoods and towns in the past were abolished decades ago. The 1968 Fair Housing Act made housing discrimination illegal—though some city- and statewide laws have eroded that policy. African Americans continue to be concentrated in all or mostly black neighborhoods (see, e.g., Figure 4.7), many of which are also characterized by inadequate services and high levels of poverty and crime.

Audit studies document some of the practices that preserve racial residential segregation in the present. Researchers conducting audit studies use participants who are similar in most ways except the one characteristic that's being tested. In research on racial fairness in housing, for example, testers might have identical education, employment, credit, and finance histories. Researchers will attempt to control as many variables as possible so that the participants' height, age, clothing, and speech may

FIGURE 4.7 ■ Concentration of Whites, Blacks, and Hispanics in Chicago, 2008

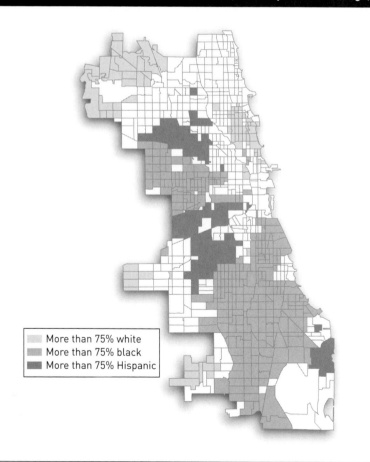

Source: Center for Governmental Studies, Northern Illinois University.

be quite similar, too. Findings show that black testers are steered away from white neighborhoods, required to pay higher down payments or deposits, and charged higher interest rates. Sometimes realtors, owners, or managers tell black testers that the property has already been sold or rented or they may give false or misleading information to discourage black testers from buying or renting the property (see Pager & Shepherd, 2008, for a review).

The result is that blacks are discouraged from breaking the housing color line but not directly, blatantly, or in ways that clearly violate the law. The gatekeepers (e.g., real estate agents, landlords, mortgage bankers) base their behavior not on race per se but on characteristics associated with race—accent, dialect, home address, and so forth—to make decisions about what levels of service and responsiveness to provide to customers.

Audit studies have also documented racial discrimination in the job market (e.g., see Bertrand & Mullainathan, 2004). Other forms of modern institutional discrimination include the use of racially and culturally biased standardized tests in school systems, the pattern of drug arrests that sends disproportionate numbers of black teenage boys and young men to jail and prison (see Chapter 5 for more on this trend), and decisions by businesspeople to move their operations away from center-city neighborhoods. Part of what makes modern institutional discrimination so challenging to document is that race, ethnicity, or gender may not be a conscious or overt part of these decision-making processes. Still, the results are that blacks and other minorities—in the past as in the present—are filtered away from opportunities and resources and racial stratification is maintained, even in the new age of a supposedly color-blind society.

Modern institutional discrimination routinely places black Americans in less desirable statuses in education, residence and home ownership, jobs, the criminal justice system—indeed, across the entire expanse of the socioeconomic system. The result is racial stratification maintained not by monolithic Jim Crow segregation or slavery but by a subtle and indirect system that is the "new configuration of inequality" (Katz & Stern, 2008, p. 100). We'll apply the concept of modern institutional discrimination throughout the case study chapters in Part 3.

Affirmative Action

Modern institutional discrimination is difficult to identify, measure, and eliminate, and some of the most heated disputes in recent group relations have concerned public policy and law in this area. Among the most controversial issues is **affirmative action**, a group of programs that attempt to reduce the effects of past discrimination or increase diversity in the workplace and in schools. In the 1970s and 1980s, the Supreme Court found that programs designed to favor minority employees as a strategy for overcoming past discrimination were constitutional (e.g., *Firefighters Local Union No. 1784 v. Stotts*, 1984; *Sheet Metal Workers v. EEOC*, 1986; *United Steelworkers of America, AFL-CIO-CLC v. Weber*, 1979).

Virtually all these early decisions concerned blatant policies of discrimination, which are becoming increasingly rare as we move farther away from the days of Jim Crow. Even so, the decisions were based on narrow margins (votes of 5 to 4) and featured acrimonious and bitter debates. More recently, the Supreme Court narrowed the grounds on which such past grievances could be redressed (e.g., *Adarand Constructors Inc. v. Pena*, 1995).

A Case of Discrimination?

One affirmative action case said to "change the landscape of civil rights law" of programs in the workplace is *Ricci v. DeStefano* (2009), involving firefighters in New Haven, Connecticut (Liptak, 2009). In 2003, the city administered a test for promotion in the city's fire department. More than 100 people took the combination written and oral test. Blacks passed at half the rate of whites and Hispanics, but only the top 19 scorers would be promoted. Because no African American scored high enough, the city threw out the results because the results suggested bias against African Americans.

This decision reflects the legal concept of *disparate impact*. That is, if a practice has unequal results, federal policy and court precedents tend to assume that the practice is racially biased. The city feared that using these possibly tainted test scores might result in lawsuits by black and other minority firefighters. Instead, a lawsuit was filed by several white and Hispanic firefighters who *had* qualified for promotion, claiming that invalidating the test results amounted to reverse racial discrimination. In 2009, the Supreme Court ruled 5 to 4 in favor of the white and Hispanic plaintiffs.

This case illustrates some of the difficult issues that accompany attempts to address modern institutional discrimination. The issue in *Ricci v. DeStefano* isn't overt Jim Crow discrimination but rather a test that might be discriminatory in its results, although not in its intent. New Haven wanted to avoid racial discrimination. So, how far do employers need to go to ensure racial fairness, especially given years of overt discrimination that has disadvantaged many groups? Should policies and procedures be judged by their outcomes or their intents? What does *fairness* and *equal treatment* mean in a society in which minority groups have only recently won formal equality and still have lower access to quality schooling and jobs in the mainstream economy? Can there be a truly fair, race-neutral policy for employment and promotion in the present when opportunities and resources in the past were allocated on the basis of race for so long? If the problem is color coded, can the solution be color neutral?

Higher Education and Affirmative Action

Colleges and universities have been another prominent battleground for affirmative action programs. Since the 1960s, many institutions of higher education have implemented programs to increase the number of minority students on campus at the undergraduate and graduate levels, sometimes admitting minority students who had lower grade point averages (GPAs) or test scores than those of dominant group students who were turned away. In general, advocates of these programs have justified them in terms of redressing the discriminatory practices of the past or increasing diversity on campus and making the student body a more accurate representation of the surrounding society. To say the least, these programs have been highly controversial and the targets of frequent lawsuits, some of which have found their way to the highest courts in the land.

Recent decisions by the U.S. Supreme Court have limited the application of affirmative action to colleges and universities. In two lawsuits involving the University of Michigan in 2003 (*Grutter v. Bollinger* and *Gratz v. Bollinger*), the Supreme Court held that the university's law school *could* use race as one criterion in deciding admissions but that undergraduate admissions *could not* award an automatic advantage to minority applicants—universities could consider an applicant's race but only in a limited way, as one factor among many.

In more recent cases involving affirmative action in higher education, the Supreme Court further narrowed the ability of universities to consider race in admissions decisions. One case, decided in June 2013, was *Fisher v. University of Texas at Austin*. The University of Texas (UT) had been using a unique admissions system, according to which the top 10% of the student body in each high school in Texas were automatically admitted. Because of the residential segregation in towns and cities across the state, the student body at many high schools is disproportionately black, white, or Hispanic, and the 10% rule guarantees substantial diversity in the UT student body. Some 80% of the students are selected by this method. The remaining 20% are selected using a variety of criteria, including race and ethnicity. It is common for selective institutions such as UT to use many criteria—not only test scores—to diversify their student body.

The case was brought by Amy Fisher, a white student who wasn't admitted to UT. She argued that some of the admitted minority students had lower GPAs and test scores than she did. The university argued that the educational benefit of a diverse student body justified its partial and limited use of race as one admission criterion among many.

The Supreme Court sent the case back to the federal appeals court with instructions to apply a strict standard: Race could be used as an admission criterion only if there were no workable race-neutral alternatives that would result in a diverse student body. The case returned to the Supreme Court in 2016 and, in something of a surprise decision, the decision was made in favor of UT (Liptak, 2016). The decision was a victory for affirmative action but was based on a narrow majority (4 to 3) and the justices made it clear that their endorsement was narrow and specific to this particular case.

In the second recent decision (*Schuette v. BAMN*), decided in April 2014, the Supreme Court upheld an amendment to the state constitution of Michigan that banned the use of race as a factor in admissions and hiring decisions in all state agencies. This decision effectively ended affirmative action in any form in Michigan and in several other states with similar laws. Despite the partial victory for affirmative action in the 2016 *Fisher* decision, it seems that the role of affirmative action in higher education has been severely curtailed.

The Future of Affirmative Action

What lies ahead for affirmative action? On one hand, there is a clear trend in court decisions to narrow the scope and applicability of these programs. Also, there is very little public support for affirmative action, especially for programs that people perceive as providing specific numerical quotas for minority groups in jobs or university admissions. For example, in 2016, a representative sample of Americans was asked in a survey if they supported "preferential hiring and promotion of blacks." Only 18% of white respondents expressed support. Somewhat surprisingly, less than half (41%) of black respondents supported it (National Opinion Research Council, 1972–2016).

On the other hand, although white (and many minority group) Americans object to fixed quotas, people support programs that expand the opportunities available to minority groups, including enhanced job training, education, and recruitment in minority communities (Wilson, 2009, p. 139). Programs of this sort are more consistent with traditional ideologies and value systems that stress individual initiative, personal responsibility, and equality of opportunity.

Many businesses and universities are committed to the broad principles of affirmative action and see the need to address past injustices and the usefulness and desirability of creating diversity in the workplace and classroom. Thus, they are likely to sustain their programs to the extent allowed by court decisions and legislation into the future. Some affirmative action programs, especially those that stress equality of opportunity, may continue in some limited form. However, the Trump administration has signaled that it doesn't support affirmative action. For example, in August 2017, the U.S. Department of Justice announced that it would investigate colleges and universities that it said discriminated against white students in their admissions programs (Savage, 2017).

QUESTIONS FOR REFLECTION

16. What is modern institutional discrimination, and how does it differ from traditional or blatant institutional discrimination? What are some of the common forms of modern institutional discrimination?

17. What is affirmative action? How has it been used to combat modern institutional discrimination?

FOCUS ON CONTEMPORARY ISSUES
HATE CRIMES

The FBI defines a **hate crime** as a "criminal offense against a person or property motivated in whole or in part by an offender's bias against a race, religion, disability, sexual orientation, ethnicity, gender or gender identity" (Farivar, 2017). Assailants often choose their victims randomly. They attack or intimidate people because of their group membership (e.g., women, Jews, transpeople), not because of who they are as individuals. Hate crimes aren't done for profit or gain but are expressions of hatred, disdain, or prejudice. Recent examples include the murder of six people in a Sikh temple in 2012, the killing of nine people in an African Methodist Episcopal Church in 2015, the killing of 49 people at a gay nightclub in 2016, and the killing of 11 people at the Tree of Life Synagogue in Pittsburgh in 2018. Hate crimes may include acts of intimidation and harassment, such as cross burnings or nooses at black churches, swastikas painted on Jewish synagogues or cemeteries, and arson or vandalism of Muslim mosques. Individuals

(Continued)

(Continued)

carry out hate crimes but they learn ideas from others, including groups such as the Ku Klux Klan (KKK) and White Aryan Resistance (WAR). Such groups are thriving, thanks, in part, to the Internet, which allows them to spread their ideas easily and cheaply. Additionally, the Internet allows members to communicate with one another electronically—even internationally— which offers anonymity and a sense of shared purpose (Gerstenfeld, Grant, & Chang, 2003; William & Adler, 2015).

Does the recent increase in hate crimes contradict the notion that blatant prejudice is on the decline, as discussed in Chapter 1? What is the connection between race-based hate crimes and the larger shift toward modern (subtle) racism? What's caused the recent increase in hate crimes and what are the implications?

Extremist groups and race-related hate crimes occurred in the earliest days of America's history (e.g., conflicts with Native Indians, the kidnapping and enslavement of Africans). They have continued, in different forms, ever since. For example, the

KKK formed as a social group for former Confederate soldiers right after the Civil War ended. That group developed into a terrorist organization. The Klan played a significant role in politics at various times and places—not only in the South. During the 1920s, the KKK had millions of members and influenced many U.S. senators, governors, and local politicians (Rothman, 2016).

The Federal Bureau of Investigation (FBI) has been collecting hate crime data since 1996. Unfortunately, not all localities classify or report such incidents in the same way. Additionally, some victims are afraid to report hate crimes to the police. In fact, a recent report by the U.S. Bureau of Justice Statistics suggests that nearly two thirds of hate crimes went unreported. Thus, the number of hate crimes is probably higher than the official rate (Farivar, 2017; for one analysis, see Fears, 2007).

Keep that in mind as you review the data below. Figure 4.8 reports the breakdown of hate crime victims in 2016 and shows that most incidents were motivated by race, ethnicity, or ancestry. In the majority of these racial cases

FIGURE 4.8 ■ Breakdown of 7,509 Single-Bias Hate Crime Incidents Reported in 2016

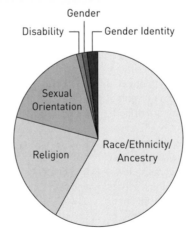

Source: FBI (2018).

(52%), the victims were black Americans. White Americans were 19% of the victims and Hispanics or Latinos were 10%. Most of the religious incidents (52%) involved Jewish victims, and the majority (62%) of the attacks motivated by the sexual orientation of the victims were directed against gay men (FBI, 2017). Although the highest number of hate crimes involves race or ethnicity, when we account for their size in the population, people who are LGBT+ had a higher chance of being targeted. Of hate crimes involving LGBT+ people, the majority were against transpeople of color (Park & Mykhyalyshyn, 2016).

The Southern Poverty Law Center (SPLC) also tracks hate groups and hate crimes. In 2018, it identified 953 active hate groups (SPLC, 2018) that it defines as having "beliefs or practices that attack or malign an entire class of people, typically for their immutable characteristics" (Potok, 2013). These groups include the KKK, various white power groups, and black groups such as the Nation of Islam. The SPLC website maintains a map showing the locations of hate groups (see Figure 4.9). As you'll see, hate groups (and hate crimes) exist throughout the nation.

Figure 4.10 displays the number of hate groups documented by the SPLC since the turn of the century. According to their analysis, the numbers rose dramatically after 2000 because of anger over illegal Hispanic immigration and concerns that the United States was quickly becoming non-Anglo. They attribute the decline after 2012 to a tendency of these groups to move to the Internet rather than conduct on-the-ground activities and the more recent increase to the 2016 Trump presidential campaign, which "flirted heavily with extremist ideas" (SPLC, 2017a).

What causes hate crimes and what kind of people commit them? McDevitt, Levin, and Bennett (2002) assert that more than two thirds of hate crimes are done by small groups of thrill seekers who are looking for excitement rather than looking for a specific person

to hurt. They tend to be young, and many go along with biased group leaders rather than challenging or leaving the group. Thrill seekers tend to seek victims outside of their own communities. Defensive perpetrators are the second most common type; they act because they feel that outsiders are invading their community or threatening resources or status. Defenders tend to act when triggered by something; for example, if they see someone they think doesn't belong in their neighborhood (Gerstenfeld, 2004, pp. 73–75; McDevitt, Levin, & Bennett, 2002; National Institute of Justice, 2008; Pezzella, 2016).

Frustration and fear can fuel hate crimes; for example, if someone believes that a minority group makes unfair progress at their group's expense or if they feel their jobs, incomes, neighborhoods, or society are threatened. Given America's history, one might expect that the white Americans who feel most threatened are toward the bottom of the stratification system: lower-class whites. Though most lower-class white men don't commit hate crimes, evidence suggests men from these classes commit the bulk of hate crimes. They also make up the majority of members in extremist groups (Schafer & Navarro, 2004). For them, attacks on minorities are attempts to preserve their group's position in society.

The connection between social class and hate crimes might reflect some broad structural changes in the economy, especially the shift from an industrial, manufacturing economy to a postindustrial, information-processing economy. This change has meant a decline in the supply of secure, well-paying, blue-collar jobs. Many manufacturing jobs have been lost to other nations with cheaper workforces; others have been lost to automation and mechanization.

The tensions resulting from the decline in desirable employment opportunities for people with lower levels of education have been exacerbated by industry downsizing, increasing inequality in the class structure, and rising

(Continued)

(Continued)

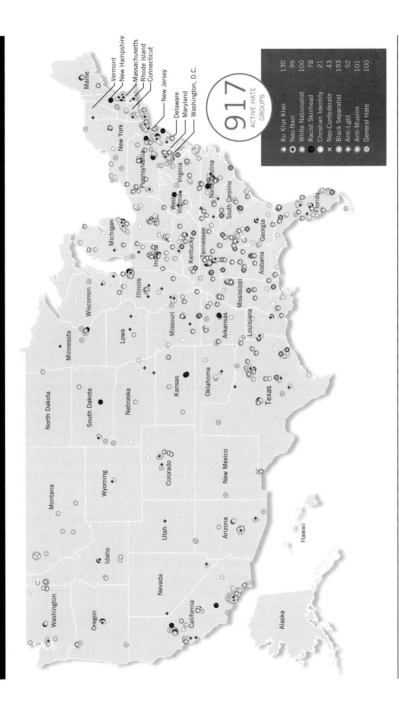

FIGURE 4.9 ■ Location of Hate Groups in the United States, 2018

917 ACTIVE HATE GROUPS

Ku Klux Klan	130
Neo-Nazi	99
White Nationalist	100
Racist Skinhead	78
Christian Identity	21
Neo-Confederate	43
Black Separatist	193
Anti-Lgbt	52
Anti-Muslim	101
General Hate	100

Source: Southern Poverty Law Center (2018).

FIGURE 4.10 ■ Number of Hate Groups, 1999–2017

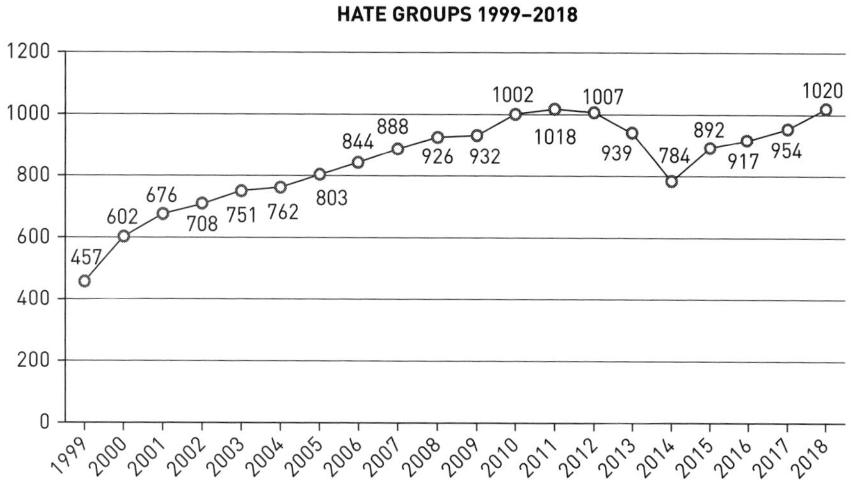

HATE GROUPS 1999–2018

Data points: 457 (1999), 602 (2000), 676 (2001), 708 (2002), 751 (2003), 762 (2004), 803 (2005), 844 (2006), 888 (2007), 926 (2008), 932 (2009), 1002 (2010), 1018 (2011), 1007 (2012), 939 (2013), 784 (2014), 892 (2015), 917 (2016), 954 (2017), 1020 (2018)

Source: Southern Poverty Law Center (2018).

costs of living. These economic forces have squeezed the middle and lower ranges of the dominant group's class system, creating considerable pressure and frustration, some of which may be directed at minority groups, including immigrants.

The idea that many hate crimes involve scapegoating (the practice of redirecting anger and frustration away from actual causes to substitute targets) is also supported by the spontaneous, unplanned, and highly emotional nature of these crimes. Consider how these themes of economic dislocation and scapegoating are illustrated in the 1982 murder of Vincent Chin, a frequently cited example of an American hate crime. Chin, who was Chinese American, was celebrating at a club in Detroit eight days before he was to be married. Two drunken autoworkers who blamed Japanese auto companies for their unemployment confronted him. Making no distinction between Chinese and Japanese (or American and Japanese), the autoworkers attacked and

murdered Chin with a baseball bat. Apparently, any Asian would have served as a scapegoat for their resentment and anger (Levin & McDevitt, 1993, p. 58; see also U.S. Commission on Civil Rights, 1992, pp. 25–26).

Several studies support these ideas. One study found that at the state level, the rate of hate crimes increased as unemployment rose and as the percentage of the population between 15 and 19 years old increased. Also, the rate fell as average wages rose (Medoff, 1999, p. 970; see also Jacobs & Wood, 1999). Another study, based on county-level data gathered in South Carolina, found a correlation between white-on-black hate crimes and economic competition (D'Alessio, Stolzenberg, & Eitle, 2002). Finally, Arab Americans have been victimized by a rash of violent attacks since September 11, 2001 (Ibish, 2003). These patterns are exactly what one would expect if the perpetrators of hate crimes tended to be young men motivated by a sense of threat and economic distress.

(Continued)

QUESTIONS FOR REFLECTION

18. Which theories of prejudice provide the most convincing explanations of hate crimes? Why?

19. How do you understand differing rates of hate crime for different groups (e.g., transpeople, Muslims, whites)? What are some explanations for the regional distribution of hate groups displayed in Figure 4.9?

20. How can an intersectional approach help us better understand hate crimes?

SOCIAL CHANGE AND MINORITY GROUP ACTIVISM

This chapter focused on the continuing industrial revolution and its impact on minority groups in general and black–white relations in particular. Generally, we view changes in group relations as the result of the fundamental transformation of the U.S. economy from agrarian to industrial to postindustrial. However, the changes in the situation of African Americans and other minority groups didn't "just happen" as America modernized. Although broad structural changes in American society created opportunities to pursue favorable change, the realization of these opportunities came from the efforts of the many who gave their time, their voices, their resources, and sometimes their lives in pursuit of racial justice in America. Since World War II, African Americans have often been in the vanguard of protest activity, and we focus on the contemporary situation of this group in the next chapter.

Main Points

- Group relations change as the subsistence technology and the level of development of the society change. As nations industrialize and urbanize, dominant–minority relations change from paternalistic to rigid competitive forms.

- As a postindustrial society emerged, group relations in America shifted from rigid competitive group systems to fluid competitive systems.

- In the South, slavery was replaced by de jure segregation, a system that combined racial separation with great inequality. The Jim Crow system was intended to control the labor of African Americans and eliminate their political power. It was reinforced by coercion and intense racism and prejudice.

- Black southerners responded to segregation, in part, by moving to urban areas outside the South, particularly in the Northeast and Midwest. The African American population enjoyed greater freedom and developed some political and economic resources away from the South, but a large concentration of low-income, relatively powerless African Americans developed in the poor neighborhoods.

- In the early 20th century, protest organizations and leaders developed strategies to combat Jim Crow segregation and improve the status of African Americans. The resources and relative freedom of blacks living outside the South was critically important to the various movements that dramatically changed American race relations, starting in the middle of the 20th century.

- In response to segregation, the African American community developed a separate institutional life centered on family, church, and community. An African American middle class emerged. Combining work with family roles, African American women were employed mostly in agriculture and domestic service during the era of de jure segregation and were one of the most exploited groups.

- Urbanization, specialization, bureaucratization, the changing structure of the occupational sector, the increasing importance of education, and other trends have changed the shape of race relations.

The shifts in subsistence technology created more opportunity and freedom for all minority groups but also increased the intensity of struggle and conflict.

- Paternalistic systems are associated with an agrarian subsistence technology and the desire to control a large, powerless labor force. Under industrialization, group relationships feature more competition for jobs and status and lower levels of contact between groups. As a postindustrial society began to emerge, group relations in America shifted from rigid competitive group systems to fluid competitive systems. Postindustrial subsistence technology is associated with the highest levels of openness and opportunity for minorities, along with continuing power differentials between groups.

- Modern institutional discrimination consists of subtle, indirect, difficult-to-document forms of discrimination that are built into society's daily operation. These forms include past-in-present discrimination and other policies, such as the use of racially biased school aptitude tests and drug laws that are more punitive for minority groups. Affirmative action policies are intended, in part, to combat these forms of discrimination.

Review Questions

1. The opening paragraph of this chapter offers a corollary to two themes from Chapter 3: *Dominant–minority group relations change as the subsistence technology changes.* How does the material in this chapter illustrate the usefulness of that idea?

2. Explain paternalistic and rigid competitive relations and link them to industrialization. How does the shift from slavery to de jure segregation illustrate the dynamics of these two systems?

3. What was the Great Migration to the North? How did it change American race relations?

4. Explain the transition from rigid competitive to fluid competitive relations and explain how this transition is related to the coming of postindustrial society. Explain the roles of urbanization, bureaucracy, the service sector of the job market, and education in this transition.

5. What is modern institutional discrimination? How does it differ from traditional institutional discrimination? Explain the role of affirmative action in combating each.

6. Explain the impact of industrialization and globalization on gender relations. Compare and contrast these changes with the changes that occurred for racial and ethnic minority groups.

7. What efforts have been made on your campus to combat modern institutional discrimination? How effective have these efforts been?

Group Discussion

1. Why did de jure segregation happen? What was at stake? Who gained and who lost? Be sure to discuss class and gender differences in connection with these issues.

2. How was the Jim Crow system sustained across time? What was the role of prejudice and racism? Subsistence technology? Law and custom? How was violence used to enforce the system? What organizations were involved in the creation and persistence of segregation?

3. What does it mean to call this system *rigid competitive*? How did it differ from the paternalistic system of slavery?

4. How did the black community react to segregation? What means of resistance and escape were available? Were they effective? Why or why not?

5. Why did de jure segregation end? What macro-level changes in subsistence technology made segregation untenable? Why?

Applying Concepts

How have the trends discussed in this section affected you and your family? If America hadn't industrialized, where would your family live? What kind of career would your parents and grandparents have had? Would you have had the opportunity for a college education?

You can get some insight on the answers to these questions by researching your family history over the past several generations and completing the table below. You may not have all the information requested, but that might be a good reason to give your parents or grandparents a call! If you don't know your family history and can't get that information, consider asking a friend, neighbor, professor, or someone else you know about their family background.

To complete the table, pick *one* ancestor from each generation, perhaps the one you know the most about. To get you started and provide a comparison, the table is completed for the authors. When you get to the bottom row of the table, fill in the blanks in terms of your desires or plans. Would you rather live in the city, suburbs, or country? What is your ideal job or the career for which you are preparing? What degree are you pursuing?

Healey			
Generations	**Residence**	**Education**	**Occupation**
Great-grandparent	City	Unknown, perhaps as much as six years	Coal miner, board member of labor union
Grandparent	City	High school	City clerk
Parent	City	High school, some college	Agent for the Internal Revenue Service
Healey	Suburbs	PhD	College professor
Stepnick			
Generations	**Residence**	**Education**	**Occupation**
Great-grandparent	Rural	2 years	Road supervisor
Grandparent	Rural	9 years	Coal miner, machinist
Parent	City	DDS	Dentist
Stepnick	City	PhD	College professor
You			
Generations	**Residence**	**Education**	**Occupation**
Great-grandparent			
Grandparent			
Parent			
You			

Answers to Applying Concepts

Based on the trends discussed in this chapter, and as partially illustrated by Healey's and Stepnick's family histories, it's likely that you'll see these trends in the family history that you studied:

1. Movement from rural to urban residence.

2. Decrease in jobs in the primary sector (extractive jobs such as farmer or coal miner) and secondary sector (manufacturing jobs)

3. Increase in service-sector jobs

4. Increase in education

Of course, each family is unique, and it's entirely possible that the family history that you studied won't follow any of these trends. Nonetheless, given the pressures created by these macro-level changes, the bulk of families should conform to most of these tendencies. Did your family follow or buck the trends?

Internet Learning Resources

SAGE edge™ online offers teachers and students easy-to-use resources for review, study, and further exploration. See **http://edge.sagepub.com/diversity6e**

Note

1. From Wright, R. (1941). *Twelve million black voices.* New York, NY: Thunder's Mouth Press.

UNDERSTANDING DOMINANT–MINORITY RELATIONS IN THE UNITED STATES TODAY

Chapter 5. African Americans: From Segregation to Modern Institutional Discrimination and Modern Racism

Chapter 6. Native Americans: From Conquest to Tribal Survival in a Postindustrial Society

Chapter 7. Hispanic Americans: Colonization, Immigration, and Ethnic Enclaves

Chapter 8. Asian Americans: Model Minorities?

In Part 3, we'll emphasize the current situation of American racial and ethnic minority groups and investigate how contemporary intergroup relations developed. We'll explore how minority and dominant groups respond to each other and to a changing society. Additionally, we'll examine how minority groups define and pursue their self-interests in interactions with other groups and within the broader society, including its culture and social institutions.

We'll continue using the themes and ideas from earlier chapters to analyze the current situation of specific minority groups (case studies). For example, we'll continue using the Noel hypothesis to analyze and understand contemporary dominant–minority patterns. Additionally, we've organized Chapters 5–8 to roughly follow the Blauner hypothesis. That is, colonized groups (e.g., African Americans, Native Americans) come before groups created by immigration (e.g., Hispanic Americans, Asian Americans).

The history and present conditions of each minority group are unique; no groups have had the same experiences. To help identify and understand these differences, we use prior concepts together with a common comparative frame of reference. We stress assimilation and pluralism; inequality and power; and prejudice, racism, and discrimination. For ease of comparison, the final sections of Chapters 5–8 use the same headings and subheadings, in the same order.

Much of the conceptual frame of reference that we'll use to analyze the upcoming case studies can be summarized in six themes. You've already learned the first six; you'll learn the last theme in Chapters 5–8.

1. Consistent with the Noel hypothesis, the present conditions of America's minority groups reflect their contact situations, especially the nature of their competition with the dominant group (e.g., competition for land versus competition for labor) and the size of the group power differential at first contact.

2. Consistent with the Blauner hypothesis, minority groups created by colonization experience economic and political inequalities that have lasted longer and been more severe than those experienced by groups created through immigration.

3. Power and economic differentials and barriers to upward mobility are especially pronounced for groups identified by racial or physical characteristics as opposed to cultural or linguistic traits.

4. Consistent with themes in Chapters 3 and 4, dominant–minority relations reflect the economic and political characteristics of the larger society and change as those characteristics change. Changes in the subsistence technology of the larger society are particularly significant. The shift from a manufacturing to a service economy (deindustrialization) is a key factor shaping contemporary dominant-minority relations.

5. We can analyze the development of group relations, historically and in the future, in terms of assimilation (more similarity) and pluralism (more diversity). Group relations in the past (e.g., the degree of assimilation allowed or required of the minority group) mainly reflected the dominant group's needs and wishes. Although the pressure for Americanization is still considerable, more flexibility and variety exist in group relations today.

6. Since World War II, minority groups have gained significantly more control over the direction of group relations. This reflects the decline of traditional prejudice in America as well as minority groups' successful efforts to protest, resist, and change patterns of exclusion and domination. These successes have occurred, in large part, because American minority groups have increased their political and economic resources.

5

AFRICAN AMERICANS

From Segregation to Modern Institutional Discrimination and Modern Racism

When I was out with my oldest daughter, who's [four years old], we were in a shopping mall, in a garage in Los Angeles . . . and there was a lady, who was with her husband. And I could tell they were just really nervous around me. And then we went to an ATM—I had to get some money—and there's another couple and I heard the woman say, "Hurry up, let's go, let's go." Like I was going to rob them, and my daughter was all like, "What happened, dad? What was that all about?" And I have to go into this conversation, "Well honey, sometimes people look at the color of my skin and they think I am a threat to them."

Sometimes if I am walking down a street or something, I am whistling Frozen songs just to prove that . . . "Hey I have kids, I am not a threat to you. I just want to go home to my family." So often people just view this as, "Oh gosh, you're just whining" or "they are just making excuses or pulling out some mythical race card that doesn't exist." This is a real thing.

—Doyin Richards (a blogger who writes
about fathers and fathering)

It's like we are seen as animals. Treated like animals. It's not easy.

—William Jones (high-end retail worker)

[I was] walking home in my beautiful upper-middle-class neighborhood in DC, when the cops start following me—kind of like this cat-and-mouse thing. They are in their car, and you know, every time I move, they move. And we get up to my house and I just stop on the street and say, "What are you doing?" And then they say, "What are you doing?" I say, "I live here." They say, "Prove it." They made me go to my porch, and then when I got there I said, "You know what, I don't have to prove anything." I knew this because I am a law professor. They said, "We are not leaving until you go in the house, because we think you're a burglar." I say, "You're doing this because I am black." They said, "No, we are not, we're black too," and that was true. These were African American officers. Even they were [racially] profiling me, another black man.

—Paul Butler (law professor)

Every day, I live and operate with that feeling of fragility, that feeling that I could be taken out at any time. I am a chokehold away from being Eric Garner.

—Ben Saunders (psychology professor)

These opening narratives describe a common experience for African American men—being seen by others as a threat or an outsider, guilty of something without reason. These perceptions are strikingly similar to the stereotypes about black men under slavery and Jim Crow. Why do they persist? What are the consequences?

Shopkeepers watch black boys and men with special attention; police routinely stop, question, and frisk them; and pedestrians may cross the street when they see a black man approaching. People think black men are bigger than white men of comparable size (Wilson, Hugenberg, & Rule, 2017). They view black boys over the age of 10 as older than they are—by about 4.5 years—and "less innocent" than other children (Goff et al., 2014). At school, black boys are punished more often and more harshly than white boys, even for the same behaviors. Administrators are more likely to suspend and expel black children, even *preschoolers,* compared to white children (U.S. Department of Education Office for Civil Rights, 2014). Even black boys with disabilities are disproportionately restrained at school compared with white boys with disabilities (Lewin, 2012; research about black girls and women reports similar findings).

African Americans are aware of these perceptions, which takes an emotional and physical toll (Butler, 2018; Davis, Vakalahi, & Scales, 2015). Sometimes the price is quite high. The news is filled with cases in which interactions, shaped by presumptions, have escalated quickly and turned violent. One noteworthy example happened in 2012 when George Zimmerman, an occasional participant in a neighborhood watch group, stopped 17-year-old Trayvon Martin as he walked home from the store because he "looked suspicious." The situation escalated, and Zimmerman shot and killed Martin. He was acquitted of homicide in 2013.

The research demonstrates that on many levels, people (especially whites) continue to see African Americans as outsiders, apart from and alien to the (white) American mainstream. Certainly, America has made progress toward racial justice and inclusion. However, as this chapter will show, African Americans still suffer from race-based inequalities that are deeply rooted in the past. Thus, America's struggle for racial equality is far from over.

More than 100 years ago, at the start of the 20th century, African Americans primarily lived in the rural South. Jim Crow stripped away the legal and civil rights that they briefly enjoyed during Reconstruction (1865–1880s). They had limited access to quality education and had few occupational choices. Whites exploited them through the sharecropping system and blocked them from the better-paying industrial jobs in urban areas. Additionally, African Americans had few political rights and few ways to express their concerns and grievances to the larger society or to the world.

Since then, the United States has seen greater equality between the dominant and minority groups, including African Americans. The election of Barack Obama as president of the United States in 2008 and 2012 is, perhaps, the single most significant sign of progress. If we take a "glass half-full" perspective, we see signs of improvement in most areas of social life. For example, African Americans are earning advanced degrees in greater numbers than ever before and are employed in diverse occupations. They've reached the highest levels of society, serving on the Supreme Court and in other important government positions, leading some of the most important corporations (e.g., American Express, Time Warner), and teaching at our most prestigious universities. Some of the best-known, most successful, most respected people in the world are African American: Martin Luther King Jr. (civil rights leader), Maya Angelou (writer), Thurgood Marshall (Supreme Court Justice), Beyoncé (entertainer), Muhammad Ali (athlete/activist), Serena and Venus Williams (athletes/entrepreneurs), Colin Powell (Secretary of State), Shirley Chisolm (congressperson/activist) August Wilson (playwright), Oprah Winfrey (media mogul), Ta-Nehisi Coates (scholar/writer), Michelle Obama (former First Lady/author) and Toni Morrison (Pulitzer prize–winning author), to name a few.

Additionally, African Americans continue to break barriers. For example, in 2012, Ava DuVernay became the first black woman to win the Best Director award at Sundance

Film Festival (Hall & Renee, 2016). In 2015, Misty Copeland became the first African American woman to become the lead dancer for the world-renowned American Ballet Theatre ("Misty Copeland, Top 100," 2016). That same year, Vincent R. Stewart became the first African American director of the U.S. Defense Intelligence Agency, Loretta Lynch became the first black woman to serve as the U.S. attorney general (Chung, 2015), and Michael Curry became the first black presiding bishop of the Episcopal church (Associated Press, 2015). In 2016, Maurice Ashley became the first African American grandmaster nominated to the U.S. Chess Hall of Fame. Simone Biles won four gold medals (and a bronze medal) in women's gymnastics—the first American woman to do so at a single Olympic game (Hall & Renee, 2016). Finally, in 2018, Stacey Abrams became the first African American woman nominated for state governor by a major party.

Compared with 150 years ago, African Americans' lives are much improved. However, social scientists caution against using a few examples, such as those listed above, as evidence of larger societal trends. As you'll see, the journey to racial equality is far from accomplished. A large percentage of African Americans continue to experience exclusion, prejudice, discrimination, and persistent inequalities in education, health care, housing, employment, and other areas of social life. They have fewer resources to fall back on in hard times and weaker connections to the sources of power and privilege. The glittering success stories of the most famous African Americans obscure the significant problems faced by many others.

To understand contemporary black–white relations, you must understand the watershed events of the recent past: the end of de jure segregation, the triumphs (and limitations) of the civil rights movement of the 1950s and 1960s, the urban riots and Black Power movement of the 1960s, and the continuing racial divisions within the United States since the 1970s. Behind these events were powerful pressures of industrialization and modernization: the shift from rigid to fluid competitive group relations, deindustrialization, modern institutional discrimination, changing distributions of power and forms of intergroup competition, the shift from traditional prejudice to modern racism, and ideas about assimilation and pluralism. In general, you'll see that black–white relations changed as a direct result of resistance, protest, and the concerted actions of thousands of people of all races and ethnicities.

THE END OF DE JURE SEGREGATION

As a colonized minority group, African Americans entered the 20th century facing extreme inequality, relative powerlessness, and sharp limitations on their freedom. Their most visible enemy was the system of de jure segregation in the South, the rigid competitive system of group relations that controlled most African Americans' lives.

Why and how did de jure segregation—segregation by law—end? Recall from Chapter 4 that dominant–minority relationships change as the larger society and its subsistence technology change. As America industrialized and urbanized during the 20th century, a series of social, political, economic, and legal processes were set in motion that ultimately destroyed Jim Crow segregation.

The mechanization and modernization of agriculture in the South had a powerful effect on race relations. As machines replaced people, farm work became less labor-intensive and landowners' need for a large, powerless workforce declined (Geschwender, 1978, pp. 175–177). Thus, one of the primary motivations for Jim Crow segregation and the sharecropping system lost importance.

Additionally, the modernization of southern agriculture helped spur African Americans' migration northward and to southern urban areas. Outside the rural South, it was easier for African Americans to vote and to pursue different avenues for improving their lives. The power of the growing African American vote was first felt in the 1930s and was significant enough to make a difference in local, state, and even national elections by the 1940s. In 1948, for example, President Harry Truman recognized that he couldn't be reelected without the support of African American voters. Therefore, the Democratic Party adopted a civil rights plank in the party platform—the first time since Reconstruction that a national political party had taken a stand on race relations (Wilson, 1973, p. 123).

The weight of these changes accumulated slowly. De jure segregation ended as it had begun: gradually and in a series of discrete events. By the mid-20th century, white resistance to racial change was weakening and the power resources of African Americans were increasing. This enhanced freedom and strength fueled many efforts that hastened the demise of Jim Crow segregation. Understanding why Jim Crow segregation ended is essential to understanding modern black–white group relations.

Wartime Developments

One of the first successful applications of the growing stock of black power resources occurred in 1941, as America was mobilizing for war against Germany and Japan. Despite the crisis atmosphere, racial discrimination was common, even in the defense industry. A group of African Americans, led by labor leader A. Philip Randolph, head of the Brotherhood of Sleeping Car Porters, threatened to march on Washington to protest discriminatory treatment (Brown, 2015).

To forestall the march, President Franklin D. Roosevelt signed an executive order banning discrimination in defense-related industries and created a watchdog federal agency, the Fair Employment Practices Commission, to oversee compliance with the new policy (Franklin & Moss, 1994, pp. 436–437; Geschwender, 1978, pp. 199–200). This was significant in two ways. First, a group of African Americans had their grievances heard at the highest level of society and they succeeded in getting what they wanted. Underlying their effectiveness was the rising political and economic power of the African American community outside the South and the need to mobilize everyone for a world war. Second, the federal government made an unprecedented commitment to fair employment rights for African Americans. This alliance between the federal government and African Americans was tentative, but it foreshadowed some of the dynamics of racial change that would occur in the 1950s and 1960s.

The Civil Rights Movement

The **civil rights movement** was a multifaceted campaign to end legalized segregation and ameliorate the massive inequalities experienced by African Americans. The campaign lasted for decades and included courtroom battles, protest marches, education, voter registration drives, boycotts, and other forms of activism. We begin by looking at the movement's successful challenge to legalized racial segregation.

Brown v. Board of Education of Topeka

In 1954, the Supreme Court's ruling on *Brown v. Board of Education of Topeka* delivered the single most powerful blow to de jure segregation. It reversed the *Plessy v. Ferguson* decision of 1896 (see Chapter 4) and ruled that racially separate facilities are inherently unequal and, therefore, unconstitutional. Segregated school systems—and all other forms of legalized racial segregation—would have to end.

The landmark *Brown* decision was the culmination of decades of planning and effort by the National Association for the Advancement of Colored People (NAACP) and individuals such as Thurgood Marshall, the NAACP's chief counsel. (Marshall became a Supreme Court Justice in 1967.) The NAACP's strategy was to dismantle Jim Crow laws by finding instances when an African American's civil rights had been violated, then suing the relevant governmental agency.

The NAACP intended for the impact of these lawsuits to extend far beyond each specific case. The goal was to persuade the courts to declare segregation unconstitutional not only in the specific instance being tried but also in all similar cases. The *Brown* (1954) decision was the ultimate triumph of this strategy. The significance of the Supreme Court's decision was not that Linda Brown—the child in whose name the case was argued—would attend a different school or even that the Topeka, Kansas, school system would be integrated. Instead, the significance was the court's rejection of the *principle* of de jure segregation in the South and, by extension, throughout America.

Southern states responded to *Brown* (1954) by mounting massive resistance campaigns, which allowed Jim Crow laws to remain on the books for years. Most white southerners strongly supported the system of racial privilege and attempted to forestall change through a variety of means, including violence and intimidation. The Ku Klux Klan (KKK), largely dormant since the late 1920s, reappeared, along with other racist terrorist groups such as the White Citizens' Councils. White politicians and other leaders competed with one another to express the most adamant statements of racist resistance (Wilson, 1973, p. 128). One locality, Prince Edward County in central Virginia, chose to close its public schools for five years rather than integrate them. During that time, white children attended private, segregated academies. The county provided no schooling for African American children (Franklin, 1967, p. 644). If they wanted to attend school, they had to travel outside the county, but most black families didn't have the resources to send them.

Nonviolent Direct Action Protest

The principle established by *Brown* (1954) was assimilationist: It ordered the dominant group to open its educational institutions freely and equally to all. Southern states and communities overwhelmingly rejected this principle. Centuries of racist tradition and privilege were at stake and it would take considerable collective effort to overcome southern resistance.

The central force in this struggle was a protest movement that many people trace to Montgomery, Alabama. There, in 1955, Rosa Parks was riding the bus home from work.

The driver ordered her to surrender her seat to a white man. She refused, and the police arrested her for violating a local segregation ordinance. Although Parks didn't plan her civil disobedience that day, it didn't "just happen." She had prepared for it—by engaging in activism for years and by training in nonviolent direct action, including a desegregation workshop at the Highlander Folk School in Tennessee just months before her arrest (Theoharis, 2013).

Her case galvanized the African American community. They organized a city bus boycott led by Reverend Martin Luther King Jr., then a new minister in town. They created carpools, shared taxis, and walked or biked to and from work, school, worship services, and other places—sometimes for miles. The boycott drew attention, sympathy, and resources from people across the world. They stayed off the buses for more than a year until the courts ruled that Alabama's segregated city buses were unconstitutional.

Many lesser-known actions paved the way for Parks and the Montgomery boycotts. For example, from 1905 to 1906, African Americans in Nashville, Tennessee, effectively boycotted the city's streetcars (Cardona, 2015). And in 1953, blacks in Baton Rouge, Louisiana, successfully boycotted the city's busses and created the model for the Montgomery boycott. Courageous individuals forged the path for Parks. For example, in 1946, Irene Morgan, age 27, was riding the bus back to Maryland after visiting her mother in Virginia. When the bus became crowded, the driver asked her to give up her seat; she refused saying that Virginia's law didn't apply to travel across states (Wormser, n.d.-a). A police officer got involved and grabbed Morgan, but she fought back. A court found her guilty. She paid the $100 fine for resisting arrest (equivalent to about $1,300 in 2019) but wouldn't pay the $10 fine for violating segregation laws. The NAACP took her case before the Supreme Court (*Morgan v. Virginia*, 1946). Instead of arguing the case on the grounds of racial inequality, they contended that segregated seating on interstate travel violated the U.S. constitution. The Court agreed, saying such practices were "an undue burden on commerce" (Pilgrim, 2007).

Many southern private bus companies skirted this verdict by passing segregation rules. In 1947, the Congress of Racial Equality organized to fight them. Sixteen men (8 black and 8 white) traveled by bus on a "Journey of Reconciliation." The white men sat in the colored section and black men sat in the white section. Some were arrested and jailed, including Bayard Rustin, who was sentenced to 30 days on a chain gang. Ever the activist, he published a report about his horrific experience, which led to prison reforms. He would go on to become one of the movement's leaders, and the group's action became a model for the Freedom Rides (Stanford University, n.d.).

In 1952, Sarah Louise Keys was traveling across state lines by bus, sitting toward the front. When a new driver boarded, he asked her to move. When she refused, the driver had the other passengers get on a different bus. Local law enforcement arrested, fined, and jailed Keys, and a North Carolina court upheld her conviction. The NAACP took her case before the Supreme Court (*Sarah Keys v. Carolina Coach Company*, 1955). Less than a week before Parks's arrest, it ruled in Keys's favor (Richardson & Luker, 2014, pp. 267–268). The case was heralded as a "symbol of a movement that cannot be held back" (McCabe & Roundtree, 2009, p. 154).

The movement's central strategy was **nonviolent direct action,** which involved confronting de jure segregation head-on, not in the courtroom or the state legislature but where people experienced it (e.g., busses, stores, theaters). The movement adopted principles of nonviolence based on Christian doctrine and the teachings of Mohandas K. Gandhi, Henry David Thoreau, and others. Dr. King (who earned his undergraduate degree in sociology) expressed this philosophy in numerous speeches and publications: People should confront the forces of evil rather than the people who were doing evil (see King., 1958, 1963, 1968). The movement didn't want to defeat or humiliate its enemies; it wanted to gain their support. As King (1958) said, nonviolent action wasn't a method for cowards; it required courage and discipline (pp. 83–84).

The movement used different tactics, including sit-ins at segregated restaurants, protest marches, prayer meetings, and voter registration drives. The police and terrorist groups such as the KKK often responded to these efforts with brutal repression and violence. Protesters were routinely imprisoned and physically attacked not only by white bystanders and by police who used fists and billy clubs but also by police dogs, high-pressure water cannons, and tear gas. The violent resistance sometimes included murder, such as the 1963 bombing of a black church in Birmingham, Alabama, which took the lives of four little girls, and the 1968 assassination of Dr. King. Resistance to racial equality was intense. It would take more than prayers and protests to end de jure segregation, and Congress finally provided the necessary tools to do so (see D'Angelo, 2001; Halberstam, 1998; Killian, 1975; King, 1958, 1963, 1968; Lewis & D'Orso, 1999; Morris, 1984).

Landmark Legislation

The successes of the civil rights movement, combined with changing public opinion and the legal principles established by the Supreme Court, coalesced in the mid-1960s to stimulate the passage of two laws that ended Jim Crow. First, in 1964, President Lyndon B. Johnson urged Congress to pass the Civil Rights Act (CRA). The law banned discrimination based on race, color, gender, religion, or national origin by publicly owned facilities (e.g., city pools), facilities open to the public (e.g., stores, theaters), and programs receiving federal aid (e.g., colleges).

Second was the 1965 Voting Rights Act (VRA), which required that federal, state, and local governments treat all citizens equally in election practices. For example, it banned literacy tests, whites-only primaries, poll taxes, property requirements, and other practices used to prevent African Americans from registering to vote. The VRA gave the franchise back to black southerners for the first time since Reconstruction and laid the groundwork for increasing black political power.

We cannot overstate the significance of these two laws for ending state-sponsored racial discrimination and furthering the nation's commitment to equality and justice. The principles of the CRA are now firmly implanted in American culture and law, and the hypocrisies of the past that granted equal rights only to whites seem like hopelessly outdated relics.

Unlike the CRA, the VRA was specifically designed to remedy discriminatory practices occurring in specific states in the mid-1960s. Congress has renewed the VRA periodically, most recently in 2006, when it was extended with bipartisan support through 2031 (Hagler, 2015). However, in 2010, many states began creating new voting regulations that some argue diluted the progress made by the VRA.

The most significant change to the VRA happened in 2013, when the Supreme Court ruled that parts of it were unconstitutional because they violated the "fundamental principle of equal [state] sovereignty" (see *Shelby County v. Holder*, 2013). The majority opinion also said that such protections were unnecessary because "things have changed dramatically" (Roberts, 2013). Justice Ginsberg (2013), writing for the minority, argued with this interpretation, saying the court's decision was "like throwing away your umbrella in a rainstorm because you are not getting wet." (We'll consider implications of this decision in the section on political power.)

The Successes and Limitations of the Civil Rights Movement

Why did the civil rights movement succeed? A comprehensive list of reasons would be lengthy; so, we'll focus on important causes most consistent with the points we've made about dominant–minority relations throughout this book.

1. *Changing subsistence technology.* The continuing industrialization and urbanization of America—and the South in particular—weakened Jim Crow's rigid competitive system of minority group control and segregation. (See our discussion of the impact of the changing subsistence technology and the end of paternalistic controls in Chapter 4, including Table 4.2.)

2. *An era of prosperity.* Following World War II, America enjoyed a period of prosperity into the 1960s. Consistent with the Noel hypothesis, this was important because it reduced the intensity of intergroup competition, at least outside the South. During prosperous times, resistance to change weakens. If the economic "pie" is expanding, the "slices" that minority groups claim can increase without threatening to reduce anyone else's portions, and prejudice generated by intergroup competition is held in check (see the Robber's Cave experiment in Chapter 1). Thus, these good times muted the dominant group's sense of threat sparked by the civil rights movement.

3. *Increasing resources in the black community.* Some economic prosperity of this era found its way into African American communities and increased their economic and political resources. Networks of independent organizations, owned and operated by African Americans, were created or grew in size and power (e.g., colleges, businesses, churches). This increasingly elaborate infrastructure of the black community included protest organizations such as the NAACP and provided material resources, leadership, and "people power" to lead the fight against discrimination.

4. *Assimilationist goals.* The civil rights movement demanded civil, legal, and political rights for African Americans, but within a framework that emphasized liberty, equality, freedom, and fair treatment. Thus, many whites didn't feel threatened by the movement's philosophy and goals, which they saw as consistent with mainstream American values, especially in contrast to the intense, often violent resistance by southern whites.

5. *Coalitions.* Black southerners had few resources other than their numbers and courage. However, the perceived legitimacy of the movement's goals created opportunities to form alliances with other groups such as white liberals, Jews,

and college students. By mobilizing these groups' resources (e.g., legitimacy, money, political power, labor power), black southerners were in a much stronger position to challenge their opposition.

6. *Mass media*. Widespread sympathetic mass media coverage, particularly television, was crucial to the movement's success. The frequent broadcasts of whites brutally attacking African Americans protesting for equal rights outraged many Americans and reinforced the moral consensus needed to eventually reject traditional racial prejudice and Jim Crow segregation.

The civil rights movement ended de jure segregation, but its confrontational tactics, effective against Jim Crow, were less useful in fighting race-based inequalities such as the unequal distribution of opportunities and resources between whites and blacks (such as jobs, wealth, political power, education, and other valued goods and services). These issues had long been the primary concern of African Americans outside the South and they're what we'll examine next.

QUESTIONS FOR REFLECTION

1. How did broad social changes help end Jim Crow segregation? How did individuals and organizations aid in this process? Which seems most important, and why?

2. How did Supreme Court decisions or other legal changes affect segregation?

3. How do the concepts of *competition* and *power differentials* in the Noel hypothesis apply to the demise of the Jim Crow system of segregation?

4. Explain the important reasons for the success of the civil rights movement. Which seem most significant and why?

DEVELOPMENTS OUTSIDE THE SOUTH

De Facto Segregation

Chapter 4 discussed some of the difficulties that African Americans encountered as they left the rural South, such as frequent discrimination by labor unions, employers, and white ethnic groups. Racial discrimination outside the South was less constant and less overt but still pervasive, especially in housing, education, and employment.

The pattern of racial separation and inequality outside the South during this time is **de facto** ("in fact" or by practice) **segregation.** As opposed to Jim Crow or South African apartheid, no public laws mandated racial separation, but it existed all the same. Consider it as de jure segregation in disguise.

Many people imagine that de facto segregation "just happens" as people choose where to live, work, shop, or worship—perhaps, for example, out of the desire to be with one's "own kind." However, this is not the case. De facto segregation results from intentionally racist decisions and actions by governmental and quasi-governmental agencies, such as real estate boards, school boards, and zoning boards (see Massey & Denton, 1993, pp. 74–114; also see Loewen, 2005). When local and state authorities actively colluded with private citizens behind the scenes, ignored racist practices within their jurisdictions, and "simply refrained from enforcing black social, economic, and political rights so that private discriminatory practices could do their work," that was de facto segregation (Massey, 2007, p. 57). For example, shortly after World War I, the real estate board in Chicago, Illinois, adopted a policy requiring its members, on penalty of "immediate expulsion," to enforce racial residential segregation (Cohen & Taylor, 2000, p. 33; Rothstein, 2014). The city hadn't passed any laws, but the result was the same: Black Americans were treated differently and unequally.

African Americans outside the South faced more poverty, higher unemployment, and lower-quality housing and schools than whites. Yet, there wasn't an obvious equivalent to a Jim Crow system that was creating inequalities and, therefore, there was no obvious system to fight. The triumphs of the civil rights movement in the South had little impact on the lives of blacks living elsewhere. In the 1960s, the African American community outside the South expressed its frustration over the slow pace of change in two main ways: urban unrest and the creation of a new movement that rose to prominence as the civil rights movement began to fade.

Urban Unrest

Full racial equality continued to seem remote to many African Americans living outside the South. In the mid-1960s, the frustration and anger within urban black communities erupted into a series of violent uprisings. The riots began in the summer of 1965 in Watts, a black neighborhood in Los Angeles, California.

Racial violence wasn't a new phenomenon in America. Race riots had existed as early as the Civil War and sometimes included considerable violence. Earlier race riots involved whites attacking African Americans, often invading and destroying black neighborhoods (e.g., see D'Orso, 1996; Ellsworth, 1982; Phillips, 2016). For example, the Memphis massacre of 1866, Thibodaux massacre in 1887, and the Springfield Race Riot of 1908. One of the most significant occurred over two days in 1921, when whites destroyed the Greenwood District of Tulsa, Oklahoma, also known as "Black Wall Street." Hundreds of people died, and many more were injured. Most African Americans' homes were destroyed, as were their churches, businesses, a hospital, and other community buildings—1,200 buildings total (Oklahoma Commission to Study the Tulsa Race Riot of 1921, 2001, p. 12). However, the riots of the 1960s were different.

The urban unrest of the 1960s, in contrast, consisted largely of attacks by African Americans against white-owned businesses operating in black neighborhoods and against the police (almost all white), who they saw as an army of occupation and whose use of excessive force precipitated the riots (Conot, 1967; Mozingo & Jennings, 2015; National Advisory Commission, 1968). For example, the 1965 "Watts Rebellion" occurred after police stopped an African American man, Marquette Frye, on suspicion of drunk driving (Alonso, 1998). The situation quickly escalated. (The police claimed that Frye resisted arrest. Frye said that when his mother tried to stop the police from impounding their vehicle, the police "roughed [her] up" and knocked him unconscious.) During the altercation, a large crowd gathered and quickly grew angry, viewing the situation as another example of excessive force by the police (United Press International, 1986). The riot lasted five days. More than $40,000,000 of property was destroyed, 34 people died, 1,032 people were injured, and almost 4,000 people were arrested (Alonso, 1998; Hinton, 2016, pp. 68–72).

Housing discrimination against blacks (and others) contributed to massive overcrowding in Watts and other minority neighborhoods. Remember from Chapter 4 that approximately 1.6 million African Americans left the South to live elsewhere in the country during the first wave of the Great Migration. Millions more left during the second wave that began in 1940. Between 1940 in 1965, the black population of Los Angeles increased almost 5.5 times (Simpson, 2012).

Like other parts of the country, Los Angeles was racially segregated due to redlining and other housing-related discrimination (e.g., higher rents for minorities). Additionally, real estate covenants barred people of color from renting or buying certain properties. Thus, in 1940, African Americans (and other racial/ethnic minorities) had to live in only 5% of residential Los Angeles, creating significant overcrowding in those parts of the city (Alonso, 1998).

As more African Americans (and Asians and Hispanics) moved into Los Angeles, pressures to find housing increased. Minorities tried moving into other neighborhoods but were subjected to violence or threats of violence (e.g., cross burnings) from whites who wanted to keep them out of "their" neighborhoods. During this time, the Los Angeles suburbs grew as record numbers of white families left the city because people of color were moving in. This phenomenon, called *white flight*, also occurred throughout the country (see Woldoff, 2011).

To address widespread patterns of discrimination, the Rumford Fair Housing Act of 1963 made it illegal for property owners to deny housing to anyone because of race, ethnicity, gender, physical ability, religion, and so on. However, in 1964, Californians approved Proposition 14, which gave property owners the right to "decline to sell, lease or rent such property to such person or persons as he, in his absolute discretion, chooses" (Brilliant, 2010, p. 193). Though the courts ruled Proposition 14 unconstitutional in 1966, "Prop 14" made it harder for people of color (and others) to find housing. Because it contributed to the extreme pressure facing the Watts community, it also contributed to the 1965 riots (Alonso, 1998; Theoharis, 2006, pp. 47–49).

The Black Power Movement

The urban riots of the 1960s were an unmistakable sign that the problems of race relations didn't end with the death of Jim Crow segregation. Outside the South, the problems were different and necessitated different solutions. Even as the civil rights movement was celebrating its victory in the South, a new protest movement was rising in prominence.

The **Black Power movement** was a loose coalition of organizations and individuals that encompassed a variety of ideas and views, many that differed sharply from those of the civil rights movement. Most Black Power advocates rejected the civil rights movement's assimilationist goals, arguing that integration would cause African Americans to become part of the very system that had oppressed, denigrated, and devalued them for centuries. Instead, Black Power groups embraced black nationalism and celebrated black identity, including African heritage, and encouraged racial pride, the latter exemplified by a popular saying of the day, "Black is beautiful!"

Most Black Power supporters believed that white racism and institutional discrimination, buried deep in the core of American culture and society, were the primary causes of racial inequality. They believed that to become truly empowered, blacks would have to liberate themselves and become self-sufficient on their own terms. They created alternate ways to meet their needs, such as urban farms and food co-ops, restaurants and other businesses, medical facilities, media, and schools—all owned and run by African Americans.

The Black Panther Party (for Self-Defense) was one well-known expression of the Black Power movement. In the beginning (1966), it focused on creating armed, open carry street patrols to monitor police and guard against police brutality, which had been frequent. The Panthers argued that every American had the right to own and carry a gun. (Their legal battles began to shift public attitudes about the Second Amendment, which, until that time, was of extremely low importance to most Americans. See More Perfect, 2018.) As they gained national attention, the dominant image of militant blacks with guns became equated with the broader Black Power movement and it frightened many Americans, especially whites who remained largely unaware of the social programs (e.g., education, food security) created by the Panthers and other Black Power organizations to improve the lives of African Americans.

The Nation of Islam

The ideological roots of Black Power were centuries old. In the 1920s, Marcus Garvey popularized many of them. In the 1960s, the Nation of Islam (NOI), sometimes called *black Muslims*, embraced and further developed them. The NOI is one of the best-known and most militant organizations within the Black Power movement. They denounced the hypocrisy, greed, and racism they saw in the larger society and advocated staunch resistance to and racial separation from white America.

The NOI did more than talk. Pursuing the goals of autonomy and self-determination, members opened businesses in African American neighborhoods and tried to deal only with Muslim-owned black companies. Their goal was to create a separate, independent black-owned economy that would support and develop the African American community by supplying jobs and creating capital that would allow them to expand their efforts (Essien-Udom, 1962; Lincoln, 1961; Malcolm X, 1964; Marable, 2011; Wolfenstein, 1993).

The NOI and other Black Power groups distinguished between racial separation and racial segregation. They viewed the former as empowering because, as a group, they'd grow stronger by becoming more autonomous. They saw the latter as a system of inequality controlled by the dominant group, which kept the black community powerless. Thus, the Black Power groups worked to find ways in which African Americans could develop their own resources and deal with the dominant group from a more powerful position, a strategy similar to the ethnic enclaves created by other minority groups (see Chapter 2).

Malcolm X was the best-known representative for the NOI and was one of the most charismatic figures of the 1960s. He powerfully articulated the values and goals of the Black Power movement. Born Malcolm Little, he converted to Islam while in prison. He rejected his "slave name" and adopted *X* to reflect his unknown heritage.

Malcolm X became the group's chief spokesperson and a well-known but threatening figure to many white Americans. After a dispute with Elijah Muhammad, the leader of the NOI, Malcolm X founded his own organization and continued to express and develop the ideas of black nationalism. In 1965, like so many protest leaders of the era, someone assassinated him (Marable, 2011).

Black Power leaders such as Malcolm X advocated autonomy, independence, and a pluralistic direction for the African American protest movement. They saw the black community as a colonized, exploited population that needed liberation from the unyielding racial oppression of white America, not integration into the system that oppressed them. In the 1970s, the group splintered into different factions. One sought greater assimilation into the dominant society. The other seems to have become more radicalized, leading to their classification by some as a hate group (Southern Poverty Law Center, n.d.).

PROTEST, POWER, AND PLURALISM

The Black Power Movement in Perspective

By the end of the 1960s, the riots had ended, and the most militant and dramatic manifestations of the Black Power movement had faded. In many cases, the passion of Black Power activists was countered by the violence of the police and other agencies, such as the FBI. Many of the movement's most powerful spokespeople were dead, in jail, or in exile. America's commitment to racial change wavered and weakened as other concerns, such as the Vietnam War, competed for public attention. In 1968, Richard M. Nixon was elected president and made it clear that his administration wouldn't ally itself with the black protest movement. The federal government's commitment to racial equality decreased. The boiling turmoil of the mid-1960s faded, but the idea of Black Power had become thoroughly entrenched in the African American community.

Some pluralistic themes of Black Power were a reaction to the failed assimilation and integration efforts of the 1950s and 1960s. Widely publicized court decisions had chipped away at racial inequalities (e.g., *Brown v. Board of Education).* The government had passed legislation to foster equality (e.g., CRA, VRA). Presidents, congresspeople, ministers and rabbis, and other leaders had pledged support for racial equality. Yet, for many African Americans, not much had changed. Their parents' and grandparents' problems continued to constrain their lives and many expected that these problems would affect their children's lives, too. The Black Power ideology was a response to America's failure to go beyond the repeal of Jim Crow and fully implement the promises of integration and equality.

Black nationalism, however, was more than simply a reaction to a failed dream. In the context of black–white relations in the 1960s, the Black Power movement served many purposes. First, along with the civil rights movement, it offered new ways of defining what it meant to be black in America and new ways of seeing African Americans. The dominant cultural stereotypes of black Americans emphasized their supposed laziness, irresponsibility, dangerousness, and inferiority. The Black Power movement rejected these ideas, emphasizing, instead, black power, seriousness of purpose, intelligence, beauty, assertiveness, independence, and courage.

Second, Black Power served as a new rallying cry for solidarity and unified action. Following the success of the civil rights movement, Black Power focused attention on America's "unfinished business"—continuing inequalities between blacks and whites.

Finally, Black Power's ideology offered an analysis of the problems of American race relations in the 1960s. The civil rights movement had analyzed race relations in terms of integration, equality of opportunity, and an end to exclusion. After the demise of Jim Crow, that analysis became less relevant. A new language was needed to describe and analyze continuing racial inequality. Black Power argued that the continuing problems of American race relations were structural and institutional, not individual. Therefore, the next steps toward actualizing racial equality and justice would require a fundamental and far-reaching restructuring of society. Ultimately, most white Americans, as the beneficiaries of societal arrangements, didn't support restructuring society. Thus, the necessary energy and commitment had to come from African Americans pursuing their own self-interests.

The nationalistic and pluralistic demands of the Black Power movement evoked a sense of threat and defensiveness in white society. By questioning the value of assimilation and celebrating a separate African heritage equal in legitimacy with white European heritage, the Black Power movement raised questions about the worth and validity of Anglo American values and norms. Many Black Power spokespersons condemned Anglo American values fiercely and openly and implicated them in creating and maintaining a centuries-long system of racial repression. Today, more than 50 years after the successes of the civil rights movement, many people still perceive the demands and critiques from the black community as threatening.

Gender and Black Protest

Paradoxically, the civil rights and Black Power movements accepted many of that era's gender stereotypes (some of which remain); for example, that men are "naturally better" leaders or "more intelligent" than women. As in the larger society (e.g., workplaces, schools, places of worship), men dominated leadership positions and many members viewed women as men's supporters, not equal partners, in the fight for racial equality. For example, when Rosa Parks joined the NAACP in 1943, the local leader, Edgar Nixon, reportedly said, "Women don't need to be nowhere but the kitchen" (Theoharis, 2013, p. 28). However, he asked Parks to become the organization's secretary a "woman's job" that opened the door for her later activism. According to activist Gwendolyn Zoharah Simmons, even getting resources to do their work was challenging. Women "had to fight for resources" like "good typewriters and a good car . . . because the guys would get first dibs on everything" (Simmons, 2011). The women challenged that sexism. For example, the women in the Student Nonviolent Coordinating Committee (SNCC) wrote position papers to protest their relegation to clerical positions and to being called "girls" (Andersen, 1993, p. 284).

Similarly, the NOI emphasized girls' and women's subservience, imposed a strict code of behavior (e.g., rules about clothing), and organized many activities by gender. Given the continuing failures of the civil rights movement, some black women viewed this "patriarchal bargain" with NOI as reasonable, even desirable, if it led to safety, independence, and greater financial stability for themselves and African Americans as a group (McDuffie, 2018; Taylor, 2017).

Thus, the battle against racism and the battle against sexism were separate struggles with separate, often contradictory agendas (Amott & Matthaei, 1991; Theoharis, 2013). Although often denied organizational leadership roles, black women were key participants—many people view them as the backbone of both movements. When the protest movements began, African American women were already heavily involved in communities and used their skills, intellect, creativity, and energy to further the cause of racial equality. Even if relegated to less glamorous but vital organizational work, black women shaped how the movements developed (Evans, 1979; Taylor, 2017).

Fannie Lou Hamer, an African American who became a prominent civil rights movement leader, illustrates the importance of women's activism. Born in 1917 to sharecropper parents, Hamer's life was so circumscribed that until she attended her first rally at the beginning of the civil rights movement, she was unaware that African Americans could—even theoretically—register to vote. The day after the rally, she quickly volunteered to register:

> I guess if I'd had any sense I'd have been a little scared, but what was the point of being scared? The only thing they could do to me was kill me and it seemed like they'd been trying to do that a little bit at a time ever since I could remember. (Amistad Research Center, n.d.)

She devoted herself entirely to the civil rights movement, helping to organize Mississippi's Freedom Summer, for example. Later, she founded the Freedom Party, which successfully challenged the racially segregated Democratic Party and the all-white political structure of the state of Mississippi. Because of her activism, Hamer lost her job, was evicted from her house, and was jailed and beaten on several occasions (Evans, 1979; Hamer, 1967).

Much of the energy that motivated black protest was forged in the depths of segregation and exclusion, a system of oppression that affected all African Americans. However, social class and gender significantly shaped African American's lives. Black women experienced distinct multiple jeopardy created by the interlocking systems of racism and sexism combined with class (particularly within a capitalist economy; Jones, 1949). As you'll see in upcoming sections, those patterns still remain.

QUESTIONS FOR REFLECTION

5. How did de facto segregation differ from de jure segregation? Were the differences cosmetic or substantial? Explain.

6. How and why did the Black Power movement differ from the civil rights movement?

7. To what degree did the Black Power movement succeed in achieving its goals? Explain.

8. What were some of the important gender dimensions of black protest movements?

9. Compare women's experiences under Jim Crow segregation with that of the antebellum South. How did they reflect the larger society?

BLACK–WHITE RELATIONS SINCE THE 1960s: ISSUES AND TRENDS

Black–white relations have changed since the 1960s and the U. S. has taken steps toward reducing racial inequality and increasing integration. Barack Obama's election to the presidency—unimaginable just decades ago—stands as one unmistakable symbol of racial progress. Indeed, it was a breakthrough so stunning that many Americans claimed it meant the U. S. had become post-racial and that race no longer influenced people's lives. As you'll see, that argument doesn't hold up to evidence.

Without denying improvements, Americans must also recognize that progress in many areas has stagnated; basic patterns of black inequality and white dominance persist. Remaining problems are deeply rooted in and inextricably mixed with the structure and operation of society. As in earlier eras, we can't address contemporary racism and racial inequality apart from larger societal changes, especially changes in subsistence technology. Next, we'll examine the continuing racial separation that characterizes much of American society and we'll apply many prior concepts to contemporary black–white relations.

COMPARATIVE FOCUS
RACE IN ANOTHER AMERICA

One of the key characteristics of traditional American antiblack prejudice is a simple two-race view: Everyone belongs to one and only one race; a person is either black or white. At its core, this perspective suggests ideas about black inferiority that were at the heart of the American system of slavery and Jim Crow segregation in the South. Southern states (and a few others) formalized this racial dichotomy in law and in custom in many ways, including the "one-drop rule." If a person had any trace of black ancestry, even "one drop" of "African blood," the law defined them as black and subjected them to all the related consequences of that label.

This dichotomous white/black construction of race contrasts sharply with many other nations. One useful comparison is between Brazil and the United States. Although the two countries' racial histories run parallel in many ways, people in them perceive race very differently.

Most people in Brazil identify with one of about 10 racial categories, including *branco* (white), *moreno* (brown), *moreno claro* (light brown), *claro* (light), *pardo* (mixed race), and *negro* and *preto* (black) (Telles, 2004, p. 82). However, when the government asked people to describe their race in something equivalent to our census, they got 134 categories, including "pinkish white," "burnt yellow," and "cinnamon," among others (Garcia-Navarro, 2015).

Race is more fluid in Brazil. Qualities such as hair texture, eye color, ethnicity, and social class (e.g., education, occupation, income) affect one's race in Brazil (Caldwell, 2008; Flavia et al., 2003). For example, people with higher-class status are considered "whiter"

(Continued)

(Continued)

than those of lower status, regardless of their actual skin color (Bucciferro, 2015; Wade, 1997). Additionally, people may be viewed as "whiter" simply by marrying a lighter-skinned person (Hernandez, 2007).

Past scholarship has likened Brazil to a racial utopia (Freyre, 1946) and Brazil has taken pride in being called a racial democracy. Yet, more expansive constructions of race don't mean that Brazil is egalitarian. Their construction of race connects *whiteness* to wealth, education, and success while associating *blackness* with poverty, lack of refinement, and other negative qualities.

Prejudice, discrimination, and widespread racial inequalities remain a part of Brazilian society. Brazilian sociologist Antonio Risério says, "It's clear that racism exists in the United States. It's clear that racism exists in Brazil. But they are different kinds of racism" (Risério, 2007, p. 17; c.f. Reid, 2014, p. 181). In Brazil, black and multiracial Brazilians have higher illiteracy, unemployment, and poverty rates and are less likely to have access to a university education than white Brazilians (Bourcier, 2012; Gradín, 2007). Additionally, they are more likely than whites to experience police-based violence (Salhani, 2015). Whites dominate the more prestigious and lucrative occupations and the leadership positions in the economy and in politics, while black Brazilians are concentrated at the bottom of the class system, with multiracial people in between (Haan & Thorat,

2012; Marteleto, 2012). In short, Brazilian patterns mirror our own.

Consider these points:

- The foundation for contemporary race relations in Brazil was laid in the distant past—just like America's. The Portuguese, the colonial conquerors of Brazil, were mostly single men. They married women from other racial/ethnic groups and produced multiracial children. European settlers in the American colonies often already had families. For those that didn't, miscegenation laws prevented intermarriage.

- In Brazil, people didn't equate slavery as thoroughly with race as in America, where slavery, blackness, and inferiority were tightly linked in the dominant ideology. However, Brazilians did link "blackness" with inferiority, which contributed to its somewhat fluid construction of race (including the tendency for people to "self-whiten"). Contemporary social inequalities reflect these racial ideologies.

After slavery ended, Brazil didn't go through a period of legalized racial segregation, similar to the Jim Crow system in the American South or apartheid in South Africa. Since groups had always mingled, Brazil had a smoother societal transition after the end of slavery ("Affirming a Divide," 2012).

QUESTIONS FOR REFLECTION

10. Compare the social construction of race in America and Brazil. Why do the differences exist? What's their effect?

11. How does contact situation shape contemporary race relations in these two societies?

Continuing Separation

Just over 50 years ago, a presidential commission charged with investigating black urban unrest warned that America was "moving towards two societies, one black, one white, separate and unequal" (National Advisory Commission, 1968, p. 1). The phrase "moving towards" incorrectly suggests that America was racially unified at one time. Nevertheless, the warning seems prophetic.

African Americans' lives have improved in many ways (e.g., increasing wealth, greater political power) and contemporary race relations have improved. However, inequality and power differentials between blacks and whites continue as the legacy of our past. In many ways, black and white Americans still live in separate worlds, especially when we consider social class and residence. The black urban poor lead lives that barely intersect with the lives of the affluent whites in suburbia.

While Barack Obama's election inspired strong optimism about the future of race relations, the current mood is pessimistic, as national polls over the last two decades show. In 1996, more than half (54%) of the adults surveyed saw racism in America as a "big problem." When Obama took office in 2009, that rate dropped dramatically to 26%. By 2015, people's optimism had faded: 50% of the respondents saw racism as a major problem, a rate that increased to 57% in 2017 (Neal, 2017). While both whites and blacks expressed increasing concern about racism, the rate in 2017 was significantly higher for blacks (81%) than for whites (52%; Neal, 2017).

As full racial equality and integration continue to seem remote, frustration and anger run high among both blacks and whites, though sometimes for different reasons. (See our discussion about the differences in black and white beliefs about race relations in Chapter 1.) Next, we'll explore some signs of the continuing separation between black and white Americans.

Continuing Separation: The Social Construction of Race, Difference, and Danger

Racial segregation still exists in some forms—in neighborhoods, schools, workplaces, and churches, for example. For African Americans, segregation results in higher rates of unemployment, poverty, incarceration, and lower rates of degree completion, home ownership, and voting.

"Living While Black" (LWB) describes a phenomenon that's recently gained national attention because it illustrates continuing race-based exclusion or segregation. LWB occurs when whites feel concern, suspicion, or discomfort about blacks and call the police as a result (Lockhart, 2018b). These reactions suggest that some whites feel, at least to some degree, that African Americans don't belong in particular places, which seems reminiscent of Jim Crow segregation (Billings, 2017).

Whites' apprehension about black people is recognizable; what's new about LWB is that (1) these interactions are typically documented with cell phone cameras and (2) the calls are about black people doing everyday activities in "white spaces" where blacks "are typically absent, not expected, or marginalized when present" (Anderson, 2015, p. 10). In 2018, for example, white people called the police about African Americans eating at restaurants, moving into an apartment, working out, napping in a dorm's common area, cashing a check at the bank, sitting in a coffee shop, barbequing, being at the pool, mowing a lawn in their neighborhood, golfing, delivering newspapers, checking out of an Airbnb rental, and calling someone from their hotel lobby (Lockhart, 2018b; Nash, 2018; Patton & Farley, 2018).

These examples may seem trivial to some people, but Anderson (2015, p. 15) argues that they reflect an attempt by white people to protect what they see as "theirs." That assessment, if true, suggests an underlying sense of tension and competition that's at the root of prejudice and discrimination. Additionally, these examples indicate broader suspicions aimed at black people. For example, 40% of African Americans surveyed in 2017 as part of a national study reported people being afraid of them specifically because of their race. Ideas about men and masculinity magnified people's fear of black men. More than half of black men (57%) reported people being fearful of them (NPR, Robert Wood Johnson Foundation, & Harvard T. H. Chan School of Public Health, 2017a, p. 10). Just 7% of white people and 11% of white men reported people being afraid of them due to their race (NPR et al., 2017c, p. 12). Similarly, a national survey in 2016 by the Pew Research Center found that almost half (47%) of the black respondents thought someone had viewed them with suspicion because of their race at some point over the last year. These and other experiences are marginalizing and result in blacks feeling the need to justify their existence (Lockhart, 2018a) and to carefully navigate predominantly white settings in particular (Anderson, 2018).

Some people might suggest that calling the police simply reflects a desire to stay safe. Others might propose that callers are trying to do good, not harm. We don't have the intimate details of every case; besides, the callers, like most people, probably aren't aware of their biases. We'd offer that these aren't either/or situations (e.g., "they're trying to help" *or* "they're racist") as much as those involving both/and. That is, people want to be safe *and* they've internalized stereotypes of black people that were created hundreds of years ago and that have largely gone unchallenged. It might be helpful to ask, why don't whites call the police about Asian men or white women doing everyday activities? And why are there so many "white settings" to begin with?

Although whites' attitudes about blacks have improved, the LWB phenomenon suggests two kinds of continuing separation between blacks and whites. The first is at the level of abstract thinking and feeling, the other is in the physical world where people go about their daily lives. To create racial equality, we'll have to address both.

Continuing Separation: Protests, Riots, and Activism

One major source of discontent and frustration for African Americans (and others) involves police actions toward them. Several major police-related incidents have sparked violence and riots. One of the most widely publicized examples was incited by the 1991 beating of Rodney King by police officers in Los Angeles. National and international news outlets covered the incident widely, showing video of the police using a Taser and kicking and hitting King with a nightstick, even as he lay on the ground. The video stunned the nation; in only 81 seconds, officers kicked or hit him 56 times (Matiash & Rothman, 2016; Sastry & Bates, 2017).

Four officers were charged with assault with a deadly weapon and use of excessive force. Contrary to most people's expectations, an all-white jury acquitted them of almost all charges. On hearing word of the acquittals, communities in several cities erupted into violence. The worst disturbance occurred in the Watts section of Los Angeles—the same location as the 1965 Watts Rebellion. More than 60 people died and 2,300 were injured. More than 1,100 buildings, valued between $785 million and $1 billion, were destroyed. Police arrested about 12,000 people (Kim & Kim, 1999; Lee, 2015; *Los Angeles Times* Graphics Staff, 2012; Wilkens, 1992).

The 1992 riots illustrate two ingredients that have triggered black collective protest and violence since the 1960s: police behavior and the pervasiveness of recording devices. Today, cell phones and police cameras can supply important visual evidence about these interactions. Yet, focusing closely on the interaction can make it easy to forget the larger social context. For example, in 2009 in Oakland, California, Oscar Grant, a 23-year-old black man, was returning from New Year's Eve celebrations when police got reports of a fight on a subway train.[1] Police detained several people. Something happened, police pushed Grant to the ground, and Officer Johannes Mehserle shot him in the back. Mehserle claimed that Grant was reaching for his waistband—possibly for a gun—when he fired the fatal shot. In fact, Grant was unarmed. Individuals recorded the incident on their phones and official police cameras recorded it, too. The videos quickly went viral (McKinley, 2009). Many people saw Grant's death as intentional and unprovoked, since he appeared to be cooperating. Yet, the court found Mehserle guilty of a lesser charge: involuntary manslaughter (McKinley, 2010). He was sentenced to two years in prison, which many people saw as a mild reprimand. The community—primarily African American but also including whites, Asians, and Hispanics—responded with both peaceful protests and violent rioting (Bulwa, 2010; Egelko, 2009).

The 2014 police shooting of Michael Brown in Ferguson, Missouri, sparked some of America's most significant recent protests. The incident garnered international attention and led to investigations by Amnesty International, governmental agencies, and a host of independent researchers. Findings pointed to racial tensions within the predominately black community that stemmed from persistent discrimination by members of a nearly all-white police (Lowery, Leonnig, & Berman, 2014). The U.S. Department of Justice (2015) noted "a pattern or practice of unlawful conduct."

Community members held a candlelight vigil on the evening of the shooting and several hundred went to the police headquarters, held their hands in the air, and chanted, "Hands up, don't shoot" (Lurie, 2014). On the streets, the interaction between police and citizens escalated quickly. As the crowd grew, the police became concerned about unruly individuals; they responded by bringing in 150 police officers with riot gear. Anger mounted and protestors vandalized vehicles, broke windows, looted stores, and confronted the police (Tribune Wire Reports, 2014). The police used riot gear and other crowd control tactics, to little avail. Missouri Governor Jay Nixon turned the situation over to the Missouri State Highway Patrol, who took a different approach. They arrived without riot gear, vowed not to block the streets, and promised to listen to people's concerns (Hartmann, 2014).

Racial tensions in Ferguson persisted and smaller protests continued for several months. A grand jury heard evidence regarding the criminal liability of the police officer (Darren Wilson) who fired the fatal shot. The governor declared a state of emergency in anticipation of the verdict. When the grand jury didn't indict officer Wilson, peaceful protests (and some angry clashes) resumed, lasting eight days and involving tens of thousands of people in 170 American cities, Canada, England, and elsewhere (Almasy & Yan, 2014a, 2014b). Activists had come to Ferguson from across the country, many on long bus trips that echoed the Freedom Rides of the 1960s. Protestors chanted "Black Lives

Matter," a phrase first used in 2013 after the death of Trayvon Martin to focus attention on antiblack racism, especially "state-sanctioned violence" against blacks (Black Lives Matter Global Network, n.d.).

As in earlier decades, discontent generated a new movement for racial equality: the Black Lives Matter (BLM) Global Network. The movement has adopted some philosophies and tactics from the civil rights and Black Power movements but it's modified and expanded them with a modern, intersectional approach. It seeks racial equality, but unlike earlier movements, it is explicitly against sexism, homophobia, and other forms of prejudice and discrimination. As with prior movements, public opinion about BLM is mixed: 55% of Americans support the movement while 34% oppose it (Neal, 2017).

In some ways, recent unrest mirrors the protests and riots that emerged from the civil rights movement. The protests and mass violence were spontaneous and expressed diffuse but bitter discontent with the racial status quo. They signaled the continuing racial inequality, urban poverty and despair, and the reality of separate communities, unequal and hostile.

Continuing Separation: Envisioning the Past and Future

The shooting of Michael Brown became a conduit for societal discussions about race-related issues. One topic that continues to produce fierce debate concerns Civil War monuments and other Confederate-related objects in public places such as parks, school grounds, and town squares.

Americans who disapprove of their presence say they represent a limited view of southern history that's focused on only one perspective of the Civil War. Without sociohistorical context, like one might find in a museum, these objects symbolically honor the system of slavery and the people who supported it. For many, especially African Americans, the continued presence of these objects, especially in public spaces, suggests formal, continuing approval of antiblack racism and disregard for black Americans (Agiesta, 2015). The mayor of New Orleans articulated these concerns in a speech about the city's removal of its remaining Civil War monuments:

> It immediately begs the questions, why there are no slave ship monuments, no prominent markers on public land to remember the lynchings or the slave blocks; nothing to remember this long chapter of our lives; the pain, the sacrifice, the shame. . . . So for those self-appointed defenders of history and the monuments, they are eerily silent on what amounts to this historical malfeasance, a lie by omission. There is a difference between remembrance of history and reverence of it. (Landrieu, 2017)

Yet, meaning is subjective. Many Americans, especially southern whites, equate Confederate-era objects with "Southern pride." They say this includes love of family, brotherhood, sacrifice in war, individualism, taking a stand, and the importance of honoring one's ancestors. For them, keeping these objects in the public view is an important reminder of those ideals.

Generally, opinions about confederate symbols fall along racial lines. For example, in a 2015 survey, 75% of southern whites called the Confederate flag "a symbol of pride." The same amount of southern African Americans (75%) saw it as "a symbol of racism"

(Agiesta, 2015). These differing views are part of what fueled protests in 2015 after South Carolina decided to remove the Confederate flag from its State House grounds (Rosenblatt & Siemaszko, 2017), a decision hastened by Dylann Roof's killing of nine African Americans at Emanuel African Methodist Episcopal Church in Charleston.

The flag's placement at the capitol goes back to 1961, near the zenith of the civil rights movement. Until the 1940s, people rarely used the flag except in Civil War reenactments, to honor the dead, or in Confederate veterans' parades (Bruzgulis, 2015; Strother, Ogorzalek, & Piston, 2017a, 2017b). However, its meaning changed, and it surged in popularity after the "Dixiecrat revolt" of 1948 when white southerners walked out of the Democratic National Convention to protest the party's civil rights goals and actions.

Whatever its historic meaning, the Confederate battle flag became a symbol of segregation. A "flag fad" broke out across the country (and in military bases abroad), peaking between 1950–1952 when millions of flags in various forms (e.g., pins, cloth) were sold (Coski, 2009, p. 111). Some southern states began incorporating aspects of it into their state flags as visible reminders of their resistance to civil rights (Coski, 2009). These efforts increased with the decision in *Brown v. the Board of Education*. For example, two years after *Brown,* Georgia changed its state flag to highlight the Confederate emblem. A proposal for its change suggested a desire to honor southern tradition, yet it didn't mention the Civil War or Confederate soldiers as part of its motivation. Rather, it said that school integration was "an affront and challenge to [those] traditions" and it vowed "to protect and maintain the segregation of the races in our schools" (Strother et al., 2017b).

Instead of redesigning its state flag, South Carolina started flying the Confederate flag atop its statehouse in 1961, ostensibly to celebrate the Confederate War Centennial but also establishing its segregationist stance. Some 50 odd years later, new civil rights activists would bring the flag down, in the spirit of joy and hope, amidst clamor and resentment, and as part of a continuing struggle between groups.

Nowhere has this contemporary struggle been more shocking than in Charlottesville, Virginia, at a white nationalist (WN) rally in 2017. The gathering was one of the largest of its kind in America in decades. Groups such as the KKK, neo-Nazis, neo-Confederates, the Proud Boys, and various militia came from around the country (Morlin, 2017).

Over the past few years, people have started calling these groups, collectively, the *Alt-Right*—as if they are merely an "alternative" choice. This label is part of a larger effort to become more mainstream. As such, at least one major group has replaced the swastikas on its uniforms and banners with the Odal Rune (ᛟ), a lesser known Nazi symbol (Kovaleski, Turkewitz, Goldstein, & Barry, 2016). Most rally participants proudly displayed symbols of their group membership such as shields emblazoned with Iron or St. Andrew's crosses, white robes and pointed hats, and, for many, confederate flags—in this context, an unmistakable symbol of white supremacy.

They planned to protest the scheduled removal of a Robert E. Lee statue from a local park, but the event was part of a larger mission to "Unite the Right"—specifically, to build a coalition of white Americans who, a century ago, would have felt divided due to ethnic heritage (e.g., Irish, French) or region (e.g., northerners, southerners). One speaker noted this upending of the historical pattern when he rhetorically pitted whites against nonwhites, saying, "We are all White, and that means we are all in the same boat now" (Law, 2017). Participants carried torches and shouted phrases such as "You will not replace us" (sometimes "Jews will not replace us"). On one level, this phrase signifies their resistance to the statue's planned removal. On another, it suggests the participants' sense of being replaced within the nation's changing demographics, what some of them call "white genocide" (Kessler, 2017; Law, 2017). They were met with resistance by locals and activists (including "anti-fascists") from around the country. Most of the protests were peaceful, but violent clashes resulted in three deaths and dozens of injuries, leading the governor to declare a state of emergency (Stolberg & Rosenthal, 2017).

In the context of the Dixiecrat Revolt (1948) and *Brown* (1954), we can view the addition of the Confederate symbols to state flags, city buildings, and public spaces as symbolic resistance to racial equality generally and to federal civil rights laws of the era specifically (Bruzgulis, 2015; Coski, 2009; Strother et al., 2017a, 2017b). Similarly, we can interpret 21st-century battles about race-related objects, such as Confederate monuments, as representative of group struggles to define meaning, history, and identity. Both provide evidence of the continuing separation between black and white Americans.

The Criminal Justice System and African Americans

No area of race relations seems more volatile and controversial than the relationship between the black community and the criminal justice system. There's a long history of considerable mistrust and resentment between the police and minorities, and it's common for African Americans to see the system as stacked against them.

A Biased Criminal Justice System?

The perception of bias isn't without justification. As we've shown, the criminal justice system has a long history of mistreating or abusing African Americans (e.g., the Black Codes, during desegregation). Within this context, it's understandable that African Americans are more likely than whites to view the police and the criminal justice system with suspicion. For example, a 2016 nationally representative poll found that 76% of black respondents felt the American criminal justice system is biased against blacks compared with 45% of whites. Alternatively, Gallup Poll data for 2011–2016 (combined) showed that twice as many whites (58%) have "a great deal or quite a lot" of confidence in the police compared with 29% of blacks (Newport, 2016).

In 2017, results from a comprehensive national study, Discrimination in America (DIA), showed comparable patterns. This study is interesting because researchers conducted five comparable surveys across five major racial/ethnic groups. In addition to asking about general perceptions about group experiences, questions also asked about *personal* experiences of discrimination that respondents felt happened because of their race. In this way, the surveys also assess perceptions of prejudice. Of course, it's difficult to say whether someone's personal experiences of discrimination shape general attitudes about discrimination or the reverse. Nevertheless, the findings are striking. Half (50%) of the African American participants reported personal experiences of discrimination by police because of their race—five times more than whites (10%; NPR et al., 2018, p. 8). More than half (54%) said that African Americans, as a group, "often" experience police discrimination and 29% said it "sometimes" happens (NPR et al., 2017a, p. 34, Q16).

The vast majority of social science research has documented pervasive bias in the criminal justice system, at all levels, against African Americans (and other minorities). In a comprehensive analysis of this research, Rosich (2007) concluded that while blatant and overt discrimination has diminished over the past few decades, the biases that remain have powerful consequences, even though they often are subtler and harder to tease out. Even slight acts of racial discrimination throughout the stages of processing in the criminal justice system can have a cumulative effect, resulting in significant differences in racial outcomes. For example, recent research suggests that, in general, African Americans have higher rates of being stopped, handcuffed, and searched by police. They're arrested and convicted at higher rates for offenses ranging from misdemeanors to murder. And they're sentenced to more time than whites, even when criminal history, education, age, and other factors are similar (U.S. Sentencing Commission, 2017; see, for example, Alexander, 2012; Hetey, Monin, Maitreyi, & Eberhardt, 2016; Stevenson & Mayson, 2018).

The War on Drugs policies of the 1980s (see below) led to a massive increase in the American prison population. Black men, especially those with less formal education, were primarily affected (Neal & Rick, 2014). Since 2009, the prison population has declined due to policy reversals and decreased crime. The incarceration rate for African American men dropped faster than it did for whites, helping to shrink that racial incarceration gap by about 17%. Women's racial incarceration gap declined more dramatically, in part because the incarceration rate for white women increased (The Sentencing Project, 2015, p. 2). Even with this progress, African Americans are five times more likely to be incarcerated than whites (Gramlich, 2018; Nellis, 2016). Since incarceration profoundly affects other life experiences, including family life, housing, employment, and the right to vote, it follows that black Americans would feel those effects more often (Alexander, 2012).

Education is a key factor affecting imprisonment. Pettit and Western (2004) studied men born between 1965 and 1969 and found that 20% of African Americans, compared with 3% of whites, were imprisoned by the time they were 30 years old. Nearly 60% of the African American men in this cohort who didn't complete high school went to prison. Similarly, a 2010 study found that nearly a third of black men, then aged 26–29, had dropped out of high school or been otherwise institutionalized as youth (Neal & Rick, 2014, p. 3). By late 2015, 9.1% of black men aged 20–34 were incarcerated compared to 1.6% of white men of the same age, a slight decrease from 1985 rates. Men with lower levels of education suffered disproportionate rates of incarceration, and the racial incarceration gap between blacks and whites was significantly bigger for those who didn't graduate high school (Pettit & Sykes, 2017, p. 25).

Youth incarceration rates reflect these general patterns: decreasing but with continuing racial disparities. In 2014, just over a million children were arrested; 34% were black—2.5 times the rate for whites (relative to population size). Additionally, black youth were more likely to go to prison rather than community-based residential programs and they received adult sentences nine times more frequently than whites (Children's Defense Fund, 2017, pp. 32–33). Once they left the juvenile system, about two thirds dropped out of school, which led to a greater chance of incarceration (Aizer & Doyle, 2015; Children's Defense Fund, 2017, p. 29).

The War on Drugs

Perhaps the most important reason for racial differences in adult incarceration rates is that, since the early 1980s, black men have been much more likely than white men to be penalized by America's "get tough" policy on drugs, especially crack cocaine. Crack is a cheap, smokable form of powdered cocaine used disproportionately by people of color from impoverished neighborhoods. As concern about a crack epidemic spread, police actively targeted inner-city areas using SWAT teams and "stop and frisk" methods that one federal judge recently called a "policy of indirect racial profiling" that violated constitutional rights (Goldstein, 2013). Street-level dealers (mostly young black men) felt the brunt of the anti-drug campaign, though it produced little decline in the number of people either dealing or using (Cooper, 2015).

Originally, people thought that crack was much more addictive than powdered cocaine and sentencing guidelines reflected this idea. For example, until 2010, federal law required a mandatory five-year prison term for possession of five grams of crack. A person would need to have one hundred times more powdered cocaine (500 grams) for a comparable sentence (Rosich, 2007). Thus, although it may have seemed race-neutral, the "war on drugs" produced significant racial disparities to such an extent that they constituted a form of institutional discrimination. The result was that many more poor minorities were (and still are) serving lengthy prison sentences compared to whites, who tend to use the powdered form of cocaine.

In 2010, the sentencing disparity was reduced by congressional action, and the mandatory five-year prison term for simple possession of crack cocaine was eliminated (Eckholm, 2010), yet Figure 5.1 illustrates the much higher drug arrest rate for blacks since the early 1980s. Notice that the arrest rate for African Americans spiked in the late 1980s, when the war on drugs began.

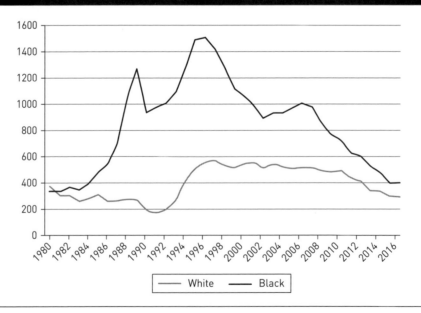

FIGURE 5.1 ■   Drug Abuse Arrests for Juveniles Age 10–17 by Race, 1980–2016

Source: National Center for Juvenile Justice (2018). "Juvenile Arrest Rates by Offense, Sex, and Race."

One national study, in 2010, focused on marijuana arrests and found huge racial disparities in every state except Hawaii. Overall, African Americans were roughly 3.7 times more likely to be arrested. Is this because black Americans use the drug more than white Americans? Decidedly not. It showed virtually no difference in drug use rates between racial/ethnic groups (American Civil Liberties Union, 2013, p. 9). In fact, a national survey conducted by the National Institutes of Health found that among youth, African Americans how lower usage rates of "nearly all drugs" compared with whites or Hispanics (Johnston, O'Malley, Bachman, & Schulenberg, 2012, p. 104).

So, what explains the huge racial disparity in arrests? African Americans are more likely to be policed, watched, stopped and frisked, and profiled than whites. Their greater vulnerability to arrest for marijuana, a relatively minor offense, is echoed in patterns throughout the criminal justice system. They go to prison on drug possession charges about five times more than whites; they're also exonerated from wrongful convictions 12 times as often (Gross, Possley, & Stephens, 2017).

In her important thought-provoking book, *The New Jim Crow: Mass Incarceration in the Age of Colorblindness*, Alexander (2012) argues that the massive racial disparities in the war on drugs amount to a new racial control system that's halted civil rights–era advances. Millions of black men convicted under the racially biased drug laws aren't only sent to prison; they also carry the stigma of a felony conviction their entire lives. Their prospects for legitimate employment are low, most lose the right to vote, and they're ineligible for many government programs, including college loans. Their families and communities are also affected. We'll talk about several of these issues later in the chapter.

Racial Profiling

Racial profiling happens when the police use a person's race to help decide if they're suspicious or dangerous (R. Kennedy, 2001, p. 3). This practice is significant because it lays the foundation for other racial inequalities in the criminal justice system, including incarceration. It's like the first domino that gets knocked over, causing the others to fall.

Earlier, we reported some findings from the 2017 DIA surveys that compared people's experiences across five racial/ethnic groups. Sixty percent (60%) of black participants reported that they or a family member had been "unfairly stopped" or "unfairly treated" by the police because of race; that's 10 times higher than whites (6%; NPR et al., 2018, p. 9). Almost two thirds of blacks (67%) living in the suburbs reported being "unfairly stopped" or "unfairly treated" by police compared with about half (49%) in urban areas (NPR et al., 2017a, p. 8), perhaps seeming "more suspicious" in the suburban context. Another national survey found that 17% of young black men felt "treated unfairly" by police within the previous 30 days (Newport, 2013). Some argue that humiliating encounters with police (e.g., being questioned for "driving while black") are so common, they're almost an unwelcome rite of passage for black men (Butler, 2018; Coates, 2015; R. Kennedy, 2001, p. 7).

Whether by policy or informal mechanisms, the tendency to focus on African Americans and to follow, stop, and question them disproportionately is a form of discrimination that generates resentment and increases the distrust and fear many African Americans feel toward their local police forces (Hall, Hall, & Perry, 2016). For example,

61% of black respondents in the DIA survey felt that local police were "more likely to use unnecessary force on a Black person than on a white person in the same situation." Because of concerns, 27% of African Americans limited their activities (e.g., driving) to avoid contact with police and 31% didn't call the police, even when needed; the rate for whites (2%) was 15 times lower (NPR et al., 2017a, p. 17)

Data support some of these concerns: Black boys and men (15–34 years old) are killed in officer-related shootings at significantly higher rates than others (9–16 times more, depending on the data used; Fryer, 2018; see also Arthur, Dolven, Hamilton, McCann, & Sherman, 2017; Kindy, Fisher, Tate, & Jenkins, 2015; Swain, Laughland, Lartey, & McCarthy, 2015). In a 2016 survey of more than 8,000 police officers in America, almost half (42%) said they "nearly always or often have serious concerns about their safety" and this may lead to hypervigilance, which may play a role in these shootings. However, black officers were about twice as likely as white officers (57% vs. 27%) to say that recent deaths of blacks during encounters with police are signs of broader problems, not isolated incidents (Morin, Parker, Stepler, & Mercer, 2017).

Increasing Class Inequality

As black Americans moved out of the rural South and as the repressive force of de jure segregation receded, social class inequality within the African American population increased. Since the 1960s, the black middle class has grown, but poverty continues to be a serious problem for African Americans.

The Black Middle Class

A small black middle class, based largely on occupations and businesses serving only the African American community, had existed since before the Civil War (Frazier, 1957). Has this more affluent segment benefited from increasing societal acceptance, civil rights legislation, and affirmative action programs? Has the black middle class continued to increase in size and affluence?

The answer appears to be no. Any progress made since the civil rights era seems to have been wiped out by the economic downturn that began in 2007.

The size and prosperity of the black middle class was always less than people assume. Between 1996 and 2002, the percentage of middle- and upper-class African Americans never exceeded 25% of the black population. For whites, it was 60%—more than twice the size of blacks (Kochhar, 2004). Oliver and Shapiro (2006) studied racial differences in wealth, which includes income and all other financial assets (e.g., home value, cars, savings, other property). Prior to the 2007 economic crisis, the African American middle class was smaller than the white middle class and much less affluent.

Figure 5.2 compares the wealth of African Americans and whites, using two different definitions of middle class and two different measures of wealth. Middle-class status is defined first in terms of level of education, with a college education indicating middle-class status, and second in terms of occupation, with a white-collar occupation indicating middle-class status.

Wealth is defined first by net worth which includes all assets (e.g., houses, cars) minus debt. The second measure, net financial assets, is the same as net worth but excludes the value of a person's home and cars. Net financial assets are a better gauge of the resources

FIGURE 5.2 ■ Wealth by Definition of the Middle Class by Race

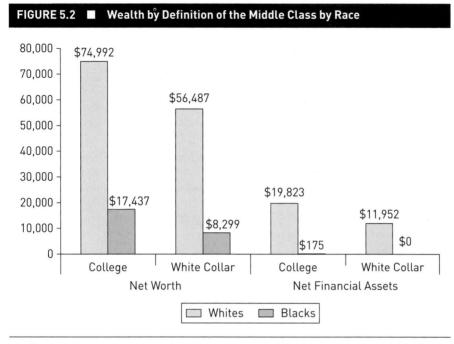

Source: Based on Oliver and Shapiro (2006, p. 96).

available to invest in children's education or financing a new business (Oliver & Shapiro, 2006, pp. 60–62).

By either definition, the black middle class was at a distinct disadvantage. You can see the huge differentials in net worth between African Americans and whites and even greater differences in net financial assets. Note that the figure for net financial assets of African Americans in white-collar occupations is exactly zero. Once their equity in houses and cars is subtracted, they have no wealth at all, a statistic that strongly underscores the greater precariousness of middle-class standing for African Americans.

The bad economic times that began in 2007 affected virtually all Americans, but they've been disproportionally hard on African Americans. In 2016, the median wealth of white households was $171,000, well below the levels for 2007 but 10 times greater than black households ($17,000) (Kochhar & Cilluffo, 2017. See also Kochhar, Fry, & Taylor, 2011; Pew Research Center, 2016, p. 25; Shapiro, Meschede, & Osoro, 2013, p. 2).

These economic differences are due partly to discrimination in the present and partly to the racial gaps in income, wealth, and economic opportunity inherited from past generations. Racial differences in homeownership are a key component of the racial wealth gap (Shapiro et al., 2013, p. 4). The greater economic marginality of the black middle class today is a form of past-in-present institutional discrimination. White parents (and grandparents) enjoyed much higher rates of homeownership, which allowed them to finance their children's college education and subsidize business ventures and other home mortgages (Oliver & Shapiro, 2006). Institutional discrimination such as redlining (see Chapter 4) meant that black parents (and grandparents) didn't have this same resource and advantage.

Not only is their economic position more marginal, but middle-class blacks commonly report that they're unable to escape the narrow straitjacket of race. No matter what their level of success, occupation, or professional accomplishments, many people still see race—blackness—as their primary defining characteristic (Benjamin, 2005; Cose, 1993; Hughes & Thomas, 1998). Without denying the advances of some, many analysts argue that the stigma of race still sharply limits African Americans' life chances. (We'll discuss this in upcoming sections.)

Some people express concern that greater class differentiation within the African American community may decrease its solidarity and cohesion. More income inequality among blacks exists than ever before; the urban poor are at one extreme and some of the wealthiest people in the world are at the other. If the black middle class increases, will class divisions grow as they have for whites? If so, will this further marginalize impoverished blacks, especially those in poor urban areas?

Urban Poverty

African Americans have become an urban minority group, and their fate is inextricably bound to that of America's cities (Figure 4.2). In other words, we can't successfully address black–white relations without dealing with urban issues, and vice versa.

As you saw in Chapter 4, automation and mechanization in the workplace eliminated many manual labor jobs that sustained city dwellers in earlier decades (Kasarda, 1989). The manufacturing (secondary) segment of the labor force has shrunk, and the service sector has continued to expand. The more-desirable jobs in the service sector have increasingly demanding educational prerequisites. The service sector jobs available to people with lower educational credentials pay low wages—often less than what's needed for essentials; they offer low security and few (if any) benefits or opportunities for advancement. This form of past-in-present institutional discrimination is a powerful disadvantage for colonized groups such as African Americans, who were excluded from educational opportunities for centuries.

Furthermore, many blue-collar jobs that escaped automation have migrated from cities. Industrialists have moved their businesses to areas where labor is cheaper, unions have less power, and taxes are lower. This movement to the suburbs and to the Sunbelt has been devastating for people living in city centers (Wilson, 1996). Historically, poor transportation systems, the absence of affordable housing (and housing discrimination and segregation, specifically) combined to keep poor blacks (and other people of color) confined to center-city neighborhoods, distant from opportunities for jobs and economic improvement (Feagin, 2001, pp. 159–160; Kasarda, 1989; Massey & Denton, 1993).

Sociologist Rogelio Saenz (2005) studied the 15 largest metropolitan areas in America and found that blacks were much more likely than whites to live in highly impoverished neighborhoods, cut off from the "economic opportunities, services, and institutions that families need to succeed" (para. 2). Their greater vulnerability and social and geographical isolation was pervasive. In addition to higher rates of poverty and unemployment, Saenz found substantial differences in their access to resources that most people of higher economic means take for granted (e.g., cars, phones). For example, blacks were three times less likely to have a car and thus had no independent means to get to jobs outside city centers and they were up to eight times less likely to have a telephone. By 2013, that latter reality had improved: 92% of African Americans owned cell phones and 56% had smartphones (Smith, 2014).

After some improvements in the late 20th century, the racial concentration of poverty increased. Since 2000, the percentage of African Americans living in "high poverty neighborhoods" (with more than 40% of the population living below the poverty level) increased from 19% to 25%. Comparatively, only about 8% of whites did (Jargowsky, 2015, p. 6).

Some of these industrial and economic forces affect all poor urbanites, not only minority groups or African Americans specifically. The dilemmas facing many African Americans isn't only due to racism or discrimination; the impersonal forces of evolving industrialization and social class structures matter as well. However, when immutable racial stigmas and centuries of prejudice (even disguised as modern racism) are added to these economic and urban developments, the forces limiting and constraining many African Americans become extremely formidable.

For more than 60 years, impoverished African Americans were increasingly concentrated in narrowly delimited urban areas ("the ghetto") where poverty was compounded and reinforced by other problems, including joblessness, high school dropout rates, crime, drug use, and teenage pregnancy, and inadequate support to move up the economic ladder. These increasingly isolated neighborhoods were fertile grounds for the development of oppositional cultures, which reject or invert the values of the larger society. The black urban counterculture may be most visible in music, fashion, and other forms of popular culture, but it's also manifested in a widespread lack of trust in the larger society, especially whites. An **urban underclass**, barred from the mainstream economy and the primary labor force and consisting largely of poor African Americans and other minority groups of color, has become a prominent and perhaps permanent feature of the American landscape (Kasarda, 1989; Massey & Denton, 1993; Wilson, 1987, 1996, 2009).

Consider this comparison between today's African American underclass and black southerners under de jure segregation:

- In both eras, a large segment of the African American population was cut off from opportunities for success and growth.

- In the earlier era, African Americans were isolated in rural areas; now, they're more likely to be in urban areas, especially city centers.

- Historically, escape from segregation was limited primarily by political and legal restrictions and blatant racial prejudice; escape from poverty in the present is limited by economic and educational deficits and a subtler and amorphous prejudice.

The result is the same: Many African Americans remain a colonized minority group— isolated, marginalized, and burdened with a legacy of powerlessness and poverty.

Modern Institutional Discrimination

The processes that maintain contemporary racial inequality are indirect and sometimes difficult to measure and document. They often flow from blatant racial discrimination of the past but aren't overtly racial today. They operate through a series of cumulative effects that tend to filter black Americans into less-desirable positions in education, housing, the criminal justice system, and the job market. To better understand this, we'll consider two areas in which racial class inequalities are perpetuated: employment networks that were closed in the past and remain shut today and the greater vulnerability of the black community to economic hardships in the larger society.

Closed Networks and Racial Exclusion

Royster (2003) dramatically illustrated the continuing importance of race as a primary factor in the perpetuation of class inequality through her extensive interviews with black and white graduates of a Baltimore trade school. Her respondents had all completed the same curricula and earned similar grades, so they were nearly identical in terms of work credentials. Yet, the black graduates were employed less often in the trades for which they had been educated, had lower wages and fewer promotions, and experienced longer periods of unemployment. Virtually every white graduate found secure and reasonably lucrative employment. The black graduates, in stark contrast, were usually unable to stay in the trades and became low-skilled, low-paid service sector workers instead.

The differences couldn't be explained by training or personality characteristics. What really mattered was not *what* you know but *who* you know. White graduates had access to networks of referrals and recruitment that linked them to the job market in ways that weren't available to black graduates. In job searches, whites were assisted more fully by their instructors and were able to use intraracial networks of family and friends, connections so powerful that they "assured even the worst [white] troublemaker a solid place in the blue-collar fold" (Royster, 2003, p. 78). Though not specifically about race, Rivera's (2015) analysis of elite students uncovered a similar process. Parents and students used their social networks to share important information about opportunities (e.g., internships) and to broaden connections, both of which provided an advantage to get into elite colleges or work in the most desirable jobs (p. 7).

Similarly, DiTomaso (2013) interviewed 246 working- and middle-class whites and found that more than two thirds (70%) of their jobs came from personal networks (e.g., friends, neighbors, family). Given that white social networks are overwhelmingly white, it stands to reason that blacks are excluded from these employment networks. Others got jobs as the result of favors. DiTomaso argues that such favors, within informal networks, have the same effect as overt discrimination.

Employment is particularly important for recent college graduates, not only for income but also because it provides crucial development opportunities for skills and professional networks (the latter can also help develop informal networks). Economists say professional networks affect earnings over one's lifetime (Ross, 2014). This is significant because even when black students graduate from college, their unemployment rates are higher than those of whites (Jones & Schmitt, 2014; Ross, 2014). Thus, their potential for future income is decreased more intensely.

These results run contrary to some deeply held American values, most notably the widespread, strong belief that success in life comes from individual effort and self-discipline. A recent survey documents the strength of this faith. Researchers asked a representative sample of adult Americans whether they thought people got ahead by hard work, luck, or a combination of the two. More than two thirds (69%), said "hard work," and another 20% chose "hard work and luck equally" (National Opinion Research Council, 1972–2016). This overwhelming belief in the importance of individual effort echoes human capital theory and other traditional sociological perspectives on assimilation discussed in Chapter 2.

Royster's (2003), DiTomaso's (2013), and Rivera's (2015) research demonstrates that the American faith in the power of hard work alone is simply wrong. To the contrary, access to jobs is influenced by networks of personal relationships that are decidedly not open to everyone. These subtle patterns of exclusion and closed intraracial networks are more difficult to document than the blatant discrimination that was at the core of Jim Crow segregation, but they can be just as devastating in their effects and just as powerful as mechanisms for perpetuating racial gaps in income and employment.

The Differential Impact of Hard Times

Because of their greater vulnerability, African Americans (and other racial minorities) are more likely to suffer from the widespread economic problems that affect society. They'll feel the impact earlier and more deeply, and they'll be the last to recover. As you've seen, the 2007 recession affected almost everyone in some way (e.g., job loss, loss of health care coverage, increasing poverty, home foreclosures). How did it affect African Americans?

Consider the unemployment rate, which generally runs twice as high for blacks as for whites. During the 2007 recession, unemployment increased for all groups. However, as Figure 5.3 shows, the unemployment rate for blacks rose at a steeper angle and went to a

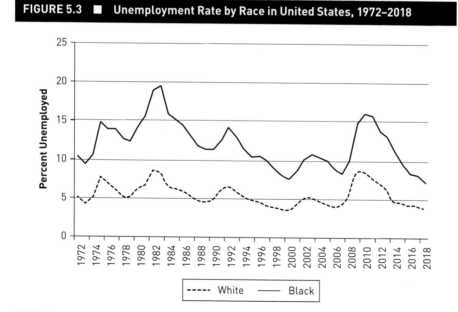

FIGURE 5.3 ■ Unemployment Rate by Race in United States, 1972–2018

Source: 1972–2013 (U. S. Bureau of Labor Statistics, 2013), 2014–2016 (U.S. Bureau of Labor Statistics, 2016), 2017–2018 (U.S. Bureau of Labor Statistics, 2018).

much higher peak. The highest rate for whites was 8.7%, about 55% of the peak rate of 15.8% for blacks. Also, the white unemployment rate leveled off and began decreasing somewhat earlier than the rate for African Americans.

Additionally, the recession disproportionately affected African American homeownership and unemployment rates. For most Americans, homeownership both reflects and provides a crucial source of wealth. For example, people can take out business and school loans using their houses as collateral. Therefore, homeownership can help families achieve upward social mobility (Oliver & Shapiro, 2008, p. A9).

In addition to the influence of redlining on residential segregation, Oliver and Shapiro (2008) found that black Americans and other minority groups of color were more than three times as likely as whites to be victimized by toxic subprime home loans and more than twice as likely to suffer foreclosure as a result. Subprime home loans were new financial instruments that enabled many previously ineligible people to qualify for home mortgages. Predatory lenders marketed the loans especially to more vulnerable populations, and the deals had hidden costs, higher interest rates, and other features that made keeping up with payments difficult. One result of the housing market's collapse was "the greatest loss of financial wealth" in the African American community (Coates, 2014; Oliver & Shapiro, 2008, p. A11). By 2017, only 43% of African Americans were home owners versus 72% of whites (U.S. Census Bureau, 2017a, p. 9).

Thus, a group that was already more vulnerable and economically marginalized suffered the greatest proportional loss—an economic collapse that will take years to recover from. Societal disasters such as the recent recession aren't shared equally by everyone; they're especially severe for the most vulnerable groups with the most tenuous connections to prosperity and affluence. Though it may not be obvious, this persistent racial inequality reflects decades of blatant, direct, state-supported segregation in America's past.

The Family Institution and the Culture of Poverty

African American family life has been a continuing source of public concern and controversy. Some analysts see African American families as structurally weak compared to white families. They assert that particular family forms are the cause of African Americans' problems, such as persistent poverty. The most famous study in this tradition was the 1965 Moynihan Report, which focused on African Americans' higher rates of divorce, separation, desertion, and children born to unmarried women (compared to whites). Moynihan asserted that these factors indicated a crumbling black family structure that would perpetuate a cycle of poverty for generations (p. iii). Of course, family structure is not monolithic, there is no "one" family for any race or ethnic group, though we see patterns ebb and flow over time and place. Today, for example, the aspects of family life that concerned Moynihan are even more pronounced in both black and white heterosexual couples. To illustrate, Figure 5.4 compares the percentage of households headed by women (black and white) with the percentage of heterosexual households headed by married couples. (Note that the trends seem to have stabilized since the mid-1990s.)

The Moynihan Report implicitly located the problems associated with urban poverty within the African American community, particularly African American families.

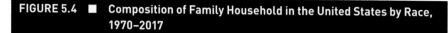

FIGURE 5.4 ■ Composition of Family Household in the United States by Race, 1970–2017

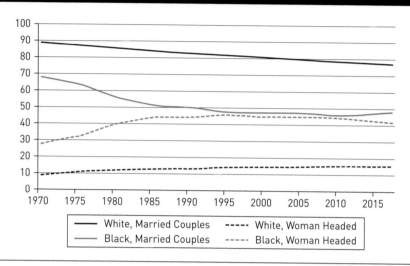

—— White, Married Couples	----- White, Woman Headed
—— Black, Married Couples	----- Black, Woman Headed

Source: U.S. Census Bureau (1978, p. 43), U.S. Census Bureau (2007, p. 56), U.S. Census Bureau (2017e).

He saw the black family as "broken" and in need of being fixed. Moynihan's argument is consistent with the idea of a **culture of poverty** or the belief that poor people have maladaptive beliefs, values, norms, and other qualities that make and keep them poor. We'll discuss this idea more in Chapter 7, but to summarize, poverty encourages **fatalism** or the sense that your destiny is beyond your control. As a result, you focus on the present, not the future. If you can't guarantee what happens in the future, why not enjoy life now? The supposed desire for instant gratification among the poor features prominently in this theory and is juxtaposed with the ability to defer gratification (thought to be essential for middle-class success). According to this theory, other problematic characteristics of the poor include tendencies toward violence, school failure, authoritarianism, alcoholism, and family desertion by men (Lewis, 1959, 1965, 1966; for a recent reprise of the debate over the culture of poverty concept, see Small, Harding, & Lamont, 2010; Steinberg, 2011).

Belief in a culture of poverty leads to the conclusion that if the poor could adopt "good" (i.e., white, middle-class) values and norms, they wouldn't suffer from the problems of urban poverty. Note that this approach is consistent with the traditional assimilationist perspective and human capital theory.

Another perspective, more consistent with the theories in this book, sees African American family structure as the *result* of urban poverty rather than a *cause* of it. For example, in impoverished neighborhoods, the number of men able to economically support their families has been reduced by high rates of unemployment, incarceration, and mortality (e.g., through violence). These conditions are, in turn, created by the concentration of urban poverty and the growth of the "underclass" (Massey & Denton, 1993; Wilson, 1996, 2009).

Even when men are available, they may not bring enough human or social capital to the table for marriage to "make sense." For example, both Boo (2001b) and Edin and Kefalas (2005) suggest that young, poor black (and Latina) girls and women want to marry, but many do a cost–benefit analysis before settling down. If a man was (or may be) unemployed or incarcerated, they may drain family resources rather than contribute to them. Similarly, Boo (2001a) shows how "welfare reform" disincentivized marriage (and even cohabitation) by cutting off forms of government aid once single women became partnered. Thus, with a smaller pool of eligible partners, impoverished women became heads of households, responsible for all aspects of family life.

Stack's (1974) ethnography of a poor, black, urban community challenged Moynihan's general assumptions. Because she became a participant in the community, she was able to view it in the long term and from an insider perspective. She argued that participants used adaptive strategies to cope with issues of poverty. Community members defined *family* broadly to include fictive kin (those you "adopt" as family), people moved around as necessity dictated, and members engaged in a lot of "swapping" as needed, sharing resources (food, money) and even long-term child care in creative, collaborative ways. From an outsider's perspective, such as Moynihan's, these families may have seemed disorganized and lacking in self-sufficiency. Stack shows they definitely didn't suffer from fatalism.

Census data shows the effect of intersecting gender, race, and marital statuses on family income. In 2016, 9.3% of men lived in poverty; the rate for women was 12.8%. That may not seem much, but women's rate is 38% higher than men's (a gender effect). About 1 in 10 (9.7%) of white women are poor. The rate is more than double for black women; more than 1 in 5 (21.4%) are poor (a race effect). More than a third (35.3%) of all single-women–headed households are poor—including 11% of them who work full-time (an effect of having only one income). Given the intersection of these three variables, it may not surprise you that families headed by single black mothers have higher rates of poverty (38.8%) compared to households headed by single white mothers (30.2%; National Women's Law Center, 2017, pp. 1–3).

Woman-headed families tend to be poor not because they're weak but because of the lower wages accorded to women generally and to African American women in particular (see Figure 5.5). Note that Figure 5.5 includes only full-time, year-round workers and that wages are in 2017 dollars (to control for the effects of inflation). Black woman workers have the lowest wages throughout this period. Also note that the gap between black women and white men has narrowed over the years. In 1955, black women earned about a third of what white men earned. In 2017, the gap stood at about 66% (after shrinking to just under 70% in 2005), largely because men's wages (for African Americans and whites) have been relatively flat since the 1970s, while women's wages (for whites and African Americans) have risen. This pattern reflects the impact of deindustrialization: the shift from manufacturing, which has eliminated many blue-collar jobs, and the rise of employment sectors in which women tend to be more concentrated.

The poverty associated with woman-headed households reflects the interactive effects of sexism and racism on black women, not some weakness in the black family. African American poverty results from the complex forces of past and present institutional discrimination, racism and prejudice, the precarious position of African American women in the labor force, and continuing urbanization and industrialization. The African American family doesn't need "fixing." The attitudes and values of the urban underclass

FIGURE 5.5 ■ Median Income for Full-Time, Year-Round Workers by Race and Gender, 1955–2017

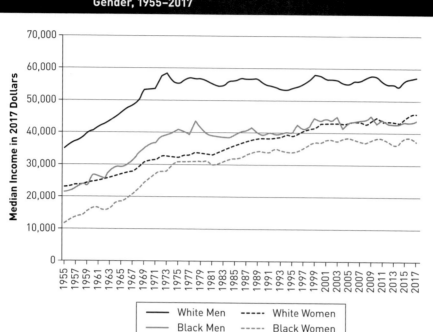

Source: U.S. Census Bureau (2017f).

are more the results of impoverishment than they are the causes. The solution to African American urban poverty lies in fundamental changes in the urban industrial economy and sweeping alterations in the distribution of resources and opportunities.

Mixed Race and New Racial Identities

As you've learned, Americans traditionally see race as a simple dichotomy: People are either black or white. Historically, the social convention of the "one-drop rule" meant that people of mixed racial descent were classified as black. To illustrate, consider the life of Gregory "Billy" Williams, a boy growing up in the segregated South in the late 1940s and early 1950s. When Billy was 10, his father revealed that he was "half-colored." Under the one-drop rule, that made Billy black. He at first refused to believe his father: "I'm not colored, I'm white! I look white! I've always been white! I go to the 'whites only' school, 'whites only' movie theaters, and 'whites only' swimming pool" (Williams, 1995, p. 34). Gradually, he came to realize that his life—not only his opportunities and his relations with others but his very identity—had been transformed by his father's revelation.

Historically, people like Williams had few choices: Others classified him as black, and the rigid social conventions of the day forced him to accept that identity, with all its implications. Today, five decades after the formal end of Jim Crow, Americans are confronting the limitations of this dichotomous racial convention. Multiracial people are increasing in number and some are the most well-known people in America, or even in the world. President Obama is one example; others include singers Alicia Keys and Mariah Carey, Yankees baseball star Derek Jeter, actor Halle Berry, and professional golfer Tiger Woods (who calls himself *Cablanasian*: Caucasian, black, Native American, and Asian).

How do people of multiracial descent define themselves today? How do others define them? Have the old understandings of race become irrelevant? Ideas are changing rapidly, especially among young people.

One important study illustrates some possible identities for mixed-race individuals. Rockquemore and Brunsma (2008) interviewed several hundred multiracial college students and narrowed their sample to people with one white and one black parent. Their sample isn't representative; their findings might not apply to all biracial Americans. Nevertheless, their study provides insights into the conceptually complex and highly variable nature of multiracial identity (p. 50).

1. The most common racial identity was the *border identity*. These respondents (58% of the sample) didn't consider themselves *black* or *white*. They saw themselves as members of a third, separate category linked to both groups. One respondent declared, "I'm not black, I'm biracial" (Rockquemore & Brunsma, 2008, p. 43). The authors make a further distinction:

    a. Some people's border identities are "validated" or accepted by others, such as family and friends and the community.

    b. Some border identities are "unvalidated" by others. These individuals see themselves as biracial but others classify them as black. For example, one respondent said, "I consider myself biracial but I experience the world as a black person" (p. 45). This disconnect may result from persistent traditional dichotomous ways of thinking about race, which makes it hard for some people to recognize or understand the category of *biracial*. People in this category are of special interest because of the tensions created by the conflict between their self-image and the way others define them.

2. The second most common identity was the *singular identity*. These individuals saw themselves as exclusively black (13%) or exclusively white (3%). Singular identity is most consistent with Americans' traditional constructions of race. The authors argue that the fact that this identity is *not* the most common illustrates the complexity of racial identity for biracial people.

3. A third identity was the *transcendent identity* (15%). These respondents rejected the whole notion of race, including traditional categories of *black* and *white*. They wanted people to see them as unique individuals and didn't want to be placed in a category, especially because of assumptions related to those categories (e.g., character, intelligence). These respondents constantly battled to avoid classification. One respondent's remarks are illustrative:

    > I'm just John, you know? . . . I'm a good guy, just like me for that. . . . When I came here (to college), it was like I was almost forced to look at other people as being white, black, Asian, or Hispanic. And so now, I'm still trying to go, "I'm just John," but uh, you gotta be something. (Rockquemore & Brunsma, 2008, p. 49)

4. The final racial identity is the least common (4%) but perhaps the most interesting: *protean*. These individuals' racial identity changes as they move between groups and across different social contexts. They slip effortlessly from one to the other and are accepted by both groups as members. It's common for people to adjust their *behavior* in different situations (e.g., a fraternity party vs. a family Thanksgiving dinner), but these individuals also change their *identity* and adjust who they are to different circumstances. Respondents with the protean identity felt empowered by their ability to fit in with diverse groups and felt they possessed a high degree of "cultural savvy" (p. 47) which, in an increasingly diverse, multicultural, and multiracial society, is a strength.

What can we conclude? Ideas about race as a dichotomy (e.g., the one-drop rule) live on but in weakened forms. Racial identity is evolving and becoming more complex. Similar to other aspects of self-identity, racial identity isn't permanent or fixed; it's contingent on social context. Biracial people have choices about identity and they're contingent on different factors (such as personal appearance) but they're always made in the context of a highly race-conscious society with long and strong traditions of racism and prejudice (Rockquemore & Brunsma, 2008).

QUESTIONS FOR REFLECTION

12. This section examined several issues and trends in contemporary black–white relations. In your opinion, which of these is most important? Why?

13. To what extent do black and white Americans live in different worlds? Is it fair to characterize contemporary black–white relations as "continuing separation"? Why or why not?

14. How has the social construction of race in America evolved since slavery? How is that related to wider social changes? How has that affected racial identity?

PREJUDICE AND MODERN RACISM

Some of the strongest evidence that traditional, overt antiblack prejudice is declining comes from public opinion research. Figure 5.6 uses survey data from representative samples of Americans to show the dramatic decline since the mid-20th century. In 1942, the vast majority—more than 70%—of white Americans thought that black and white children should attend different schools. Forty years later, in 1982, support for separate schools had dropped to less than 10%. Similarly, support for the right of white people to maintain separate neighborhoods declined from 65% in 1942 to 18% in the early 1990s.

The overall trend is unmistakable: There's been a dramatic decline in support for prejudiced statements since World War II. In the early 1940s, most white Americans supported prejudiced views. In recent years, only a small portion did.

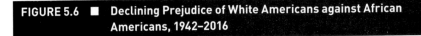

FIGURE 5.6 ■ Declining Prejudice of White Americans against African Americans, 1942–2016

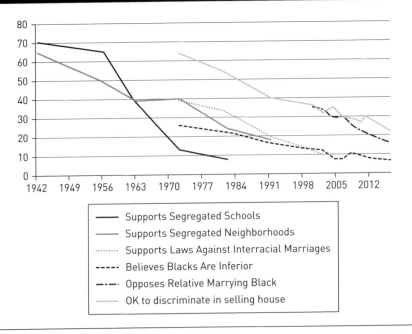

Source: Data for 1942, 1956, and 1963: Hyman and Sheatsley (1964). Data for 1972 to 2016: National Opinion Research Council (NORC) (1972–2016).

However, you shouldn't accept this information at face value. First, the survey items also show that prejudice has not vanished. A percentage of the white population continues to endorse highly prejudicial sentiments. Second, the polls show what people *say* they think, which can be different from what they *truly* believe. Figure 5.6 may document a decline in people's willingness to admit their prejudice as much as it does an actual change in attitudes.

Another possibility is that the figure is misleading—that prejudice remains substantial but takes new forms that we refer to as *symbolic, color-blind,* or *modern* racism (see Chapter 1). Rather than the overt hostilities of the past, modern racism is a more subtle, complex, and indirect way of thinking or expressing negative feelings about minority groups or about one's opposition to changes in dominant–minority relations (see Bobo, 1988, 2001; Bobo, Charles, Krysan, & Simmons, 2012; Bonilla-Silva, 2001, 2006; Kinder & Sears, 1981; Kluegel & Smith, 1982; McConahay, 1986; Sears, 1988; for a review, see Quillian, 2006).

Modern racists have negative feelings (the affective aspect of prejudice) toward minority groups; however, they reject the idea of biological inferiority and don't think in terms of traditional stereotypes. Instead, modern racists express their prejudice indirectly and subtly. The attitudes that define modern racism are generally consistent with some tenets of the traditional assimilation perspective, especially human capital theory and the Protestant ethic—the traditional American value system that stresses individual responsibility and the importance of hard work. Modern racists believe the following:

- They aren't prejudiced.

- Serious racial, ethnic, or religious discrimination in American society no longer exists.

- Because discrimination no longer exists, efforts to reduce inequality—such as affirmative action—are unjustified and unfair. Minority groups—especially African Americans—have already gotten more than they deserve (Sears & Henry, 2003).

- Any remaining racial or ethnic inequality is the fault of minority group members who suffer from largely self-imposed cultural disadvantages (for example, people who don't "make it" simply don't work hard enough).

The last tenet is particularly important: Traditional racists explained racial inequality as the result of "racial inferiority" or biological deficiencies. Modern racists explain it as the result of cultural deficiencies. For example, many people took President Obama's election in 2008 (and in 2012) as a sign that America is post-racial and that race no longer matters, despite "substantial evidence to the contrary" (Dawson & Bobo, 2009, p. 247). If America is post-racial, then racial inequality must be the result of minority groups' values and behaviors, not the powerful historical processes and policy choices of the dominant group. In other words, the problems of inequality lie with *them*—the people experiencing the inequality—not society (Bonilla-Silva, 2017; Dawson & Bobo, 2009; Schorr, 2008; see Chavez-Dueñas, Adames, & Organista, 2013).

To illustrate the difference between traditional prejudice and modern racism, consider the results of a recent survey administered to a representative sample of Americans (National Opinion Research Council, 1972–2016). Researchers asked people to choose up to four reasons why black people, on average, have "worse jobs, income, and housing than white people." Respondents could choose as many explanations as they wanted.

One explanation, consistent with traditional or overt antiblack prejudice, attributed racial inequality to the genetic or biological inferiority of African Americans ("The differences are mainly because blacks have less inborn ability to learn"). Less than 7% of the white respondents chose this explanation. A second explanation attributed continuing racial inequality to discrimination, and a third to the lack of opportunity for an education. Of white respondents, 38% chose the former and 50% chose the latter.

A fourth explanation, consistent with modern racism, attributes racial inequality to a lack of effort by African Americans ("The differences are because most blacks just don't have the motivation or willpower to pull themselves up out of poverty"). Of the white respondents, 42% chose this explanation, the second most popular of the four.

Thus, the survey found support for the idea that racial inequality resulted from discrimination and lack of educational opportunities, views that are consistent with the analysis in this book. It found relatively little support for traditional antiblack prejudice based on biological stereotypes.

However, the second most endorsed explanation was that continuing racial inequality lies within the African American community, not society. This suggests that African Americans could solve their own problems but aren't willing to do so.

Modern racism ignores centuries of historic oppression and continuing institutional discrimination. This thinking contributes to stereotypes about minority group members (e.g., "they're lazy"), which encourages the expression of negative attitudes and actions against them.

Modern racism is consistently correlated with opposition to policies and programs intended to reduce racial inequality (Bobo, 2001, p. 292; Quillian, 2006). In the 2016 survey summarized earlier, for example, respondents who blamed continuing racial inequality on the lack of motivation or willpower of blacks—the "modern racists"—were the least likely to support affirmative action programs and government help for blacks (see Figure 5.7). In fact, they're less supportive than traditional racists who chose the "inborn ability" explanation.

Many researchers argue that modern racism has taken the place of traditional, overt prejudice. If this is correct, then America's "report card" on declining racial hostility is mixed. We shouldn't understate the importance of the fading of overt prejudice. Yet, we can't ignore evidence that antiblack prejudice has changed forms rather than declined in degree. Subtle and diffuse prejudice may be preferable to the blunt and vicious kind, but it shouldn't be mistaken for the demise of prejudice.

How can we address the pervasive problems of racial inequality in the present atmosphere of modern racism? Many people advocate a "color-blind" approach: individuals, organizations, and institutions should ignore race and treat everyone the same. This approach seems sensible to many people because, at first glance, there aren't obvious limits on African Americans' life chances like there were under slavery or Jim Crow.

FIGURE 5.7 ■ White American's Level of Support for Government Intervention Based on Explanation of Racial Inequality, 2016

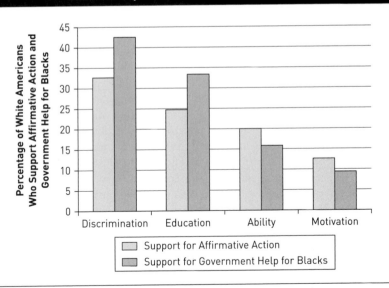

Source: NORC (1972–2016).

Others see a color-blind approach as doomed to fail. They argue that to end racial inequality and deal with the legacy of racism, society must use race-conscious programs that explicitly address the problems of race and racism. They assert that color-blind strategies amount to inaction, which will perpetuate (or widen) the present racial equality gap.

ASSIMILATION AND PLURALISM

In this section, we'll use the major concepts from Gordon's model of assimilation to assess the current status of African Americans. We can't address everything in this book, so consider these section overviews worthy of further exploration.

Acculturation

The Blauner hypothesis states that the culture of groups created by colonization will be attacked, denigrated, and, if possible, eliminated. Evidence seems to validate this assertion. As discussed in the Assimilation section of Chapter 3, slavery took African culture(s) from enslaved people and their descendants. As a relatively powerless, colonized minority group, slaves had few opportunities to preserve their heritage, though researchers have found traces of it in kinship systems, music, folklore, language, foodways, philosophies, and other dimensions of culture (see Levine, 1977; Stuckey, 1987).

Cultural domination continued under Jim Crow, albeit through a different structural arrangement. Under slavery, slaves and their owners worked near one another and interracial contact was common. Under de jure segregation, intergroup contact between blacks and whites diminished. After slavery ended, African Americans had more autonomy to create their own communities with distinct cultures. Since then, African Americans have continued to share and create a common culture with the dominant society while creating room to explore their unique cultural traditions.

The Black Power movement of the 1960s may have slowed (or even reversed) the acculturation process. Since then, African Americans have become increasingly interested in African culture and in celebrating the innumerable contributions of African Americans to America. For example, millions of people celebrate Kwanzaa, a holiday designed in the late 1960s to connect African Americans to African heritage. Likewise, after the 1976 mini-series, *Roots,* some couples incorporated "jumping the broom," into their weddings. This tradition recently reappeared on the popular television shows *Grey's Anatomy* and *This Is Us.*

The resurgence of Afrofuturism is another exciting expression of this trend. Think of Afrofuturism as a sci-fi approach to exploring alternate realities for black people (and others) around the world where past, present, and future blur and where white domination doesn't exist. The comic book/film, *Black Panther,* Kendrick Lamar's "All the Stars" video (featuring SZA), and the amazing story of Janelle Monáe's alter-ego, Cindi Mayweather (who lives 600 years in the future) are just some examples. Afrofuturism is about creation. Then again, similar traditions and contributions have existed all along, in different forms (e.g., Parliament/Funkadelic, Sun Ra); so, they may not be signs of stalled acculturation. Indeed, their recognition by the dominant culture may signal some degree of its willingness to move toward increased racial equality.

Secondary Structural Assimilation

Structural assimilation (*integration*) involves two phases. *Secondary* structural assimilation refers to integration in more public areas (e.g., the job market, schools, and political institutions). In the next sections, we'll assess structural assimilation by comparing different groups' residential patterns, income distributions, job profiles, political power, and education. Later, we'll discuss *primary* structural assimilation in intimate associations, such as friendship and intermarriage.

Residential Patterns

After a century of movement out of the rural South, African Americans today are highly urbanized and much more spread out across the nation. As you saw in Chapter 4 (see Figures 4.1 and 4.2), about 90% of African Americans are urban, and a slight majority of African Americans continue to live in the South. About 35% of African Americans now live in the Northeast and Midwest, overwhelmingly in urban areas. Figure 5.8 shows the concentration of African Americans in the states of the old Confederacy, the urbanized East Coast corridor from Washington, DC, to Boston, the industrial centers of the Midwest, and, to a lesser extent, California.

Residential segregation between African Americans and whites peaked toward the end of the Jim Crow era, in the 1960s and 1970s. In recent decades, it's decreased (Logan & Stults, 2011). Figure 5.9 uses census data from 1980–2010 to show residential segregation between white and black Americans. We also include residential segregation scores between white and Hispanic Americans and white and Asian Americans. We'll focus on black Americans here and discuss the other groups in Chapters 7 and 8, respectively.

Figure 5.9 uses a statistic called the **dissimilarity index**, which shows the degree to which groups are *not* evenly spread across neighborhoods or census tracts. Specifically, the index is the percentage of each group that would have to move to a different tract to achieve integration. A score above 60 indicates extreme segregation.

People seeking evidence of improved relations between blacks and whites ("the glass is half-full") should note the falling scores for racial residential segregation between 1980 and 2010 and, especially, that the dissimilarity index dipped to slightly below 60 in the most recent year. However, people with a "glass is half-empty" mind frame might notice that racial residential segregation continues and that African Americans are much more segregated from whites than the other two groups.

The Great Migration did little to end residential segregation, which tends to be highest in the older industrial cities of the Northeast and upper Midwest. In fact, the five most residentially segregated large metropolitan areas in 2010 weren't in southern or border states but were (in rank order) in Detroit, Milwaukee, New York, Newark, and Chicago (Logan & Stults, 2011, p. 6).

Military service didn't help much, either. Post-WWII, many white families took advantage of the G.I. Bill's extremely low interest rates, which made first-time home purchases possible for substantial numbers of Americans. Though not explicitly racist, this federal program was enacted on the local level, and most banks (or their individual representatives) would not do business with African Americans, essentially stripping them of this benefit (Coates, 2014). As America's first suburbs rose, black veterans and their families were shut out.

Legend:
50% to 86%
25% to 49.9%
10% to 24.9%
5% to 9.9%
Less than 5%
Percent of Total U.S. Population 13.6%

Source: Rastogi, Johnson, Hoeffel, and Drewery, 2011, p. 11.

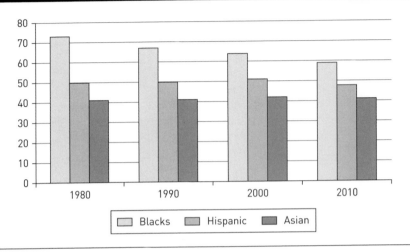

FIGURE 5.9 ■ Residential Segregation for Black Americans, Hispanic Americans, and Asian Americans, 1980–2010

Source: Logan and Stutts (2011, p. 5). "The Persistence of Segregation in the Metropolis: New Findings from the 2010 Census." Census Brief prepared for Project US2010. http://www.s4.brown.edu/us2010.

As you've learned, continuing patterns of residential segregation are reinforced by many practices, including racial steering by real estate agents (guiding clients to same-race housing areas) and barely disguised discrimination. Discriminatory banking practices continue as well. For example, in 2016, the Department of Justice and the Consumer Financial Protection Bureau charged a Mississippi-based bank with denying personal and business loans for African Americans twice as often as comparable whites. Additionally, the bank "structur[ed] its business to avoid and discourage consumers in minority neighborhoods from accessing mortgages" (Lane, 2016). There's no sign saying, "Keep out!" as in the past; however, the effects are similar.

Contrary to popular beliefs among whites, personal preference for living in same-race neighborhoods plays a small role in these patterns. Studies generally find that African Americans prefer to live in areas split 50/50 between African Americans and whites; however, whites much prefer neighborhoods with low percentages of African Americans or Latinos (e.g., see Havekes, Bader, & Krysan, 2016; Krysan & Farley, 2002, p. 949; Lewis, Emerson, & Klineberg, 2011). The social class and income differences between African Americans and whites are also relatively minor factors in perpetuating residential segregation, as the members of the black middle class are as likely to be segregated as the poor (Stoll, 2004, p. 26; see also Dwyer, 2010).

According to the National Fair Housing Alliance (2018), 50% of African Americans live in neighborhoods without white residents. The "average white person" lives in neighborhoods that are filled, overwhelmingly, with white residents (p. 6). As we've said previously, one's home is an indicator of economic health, but it also can create economic wealth. One's neighborhood affects quality of life in many ways through access (or lack thereof) to community resources such as parks, public transportation, grocery stores, job opportunities, medical facilities, and access to neighborhood networks. Combined, they have a profound impact on present-day quality of life. Additionally, as groundbreaking economic research is beginning to show, the "hyper-local setting" within a half-mile of a child's home exerts a powerful influence on future educational and economic success as an adult (Badger & Bui, 2018; Chetty, Friedman, Hendren, Jones, & Porter, 2018). If our neighborhoods remain segregated, what's the net effect for African Americans?

School Integration

In 1954, the year of the landmark *Brown* desegregation decision, the great majority of African Americans lived in states operating segregated school systems. Compared with white schools, Jim Crow schools were severely underfunded and had fewer qualified teachers, shorter school years, and inadequate physical facilities. School integration was one of the most important goals of the civil rights movement in the 1950s and 1960s and, aided by pressure from the courts and the federal government, considerable strides were made toward this goal for several decades.

In recent decades, however, pressure from the federal government has eased, and school integration is slowing and, in many areas, has even reversed. The high point in the desegregation of public schools was in 1988, three decades ago. In that year, less than 6% of public schools were "intensely segregated" with 90% to 100% nonwhite students. In the decades following, this percentage has tripled to over 18% (Ordfield, Ee, Frankenberg, & Siegel-Hawley, 2016, p. 3).

We haven't achieved the goal of school desegregation; indeed, black children (and those of other minority groups of color) are increasingly concentrated in schools segregated by social class and by race. Figure 5.10 shows that since the 2000–2001 school year, the percentage of black students that attended "high poverty" schools increased from 32% to 48%. Thus, poor African American students appear doubly isolated: by social class and by race. This increasing economic and racial separation is a deep betrayal of the philosophy and goals of the civil rights movement and of democracy generally.

What accounts for the failure to integrate public schools? One significant cause is the declining white population in general (see Figure 1.1) and in public schools in particular. In the 2013–2014 school year, whites were 50% of all students, down from almost 80% in the early 1970s (Orfield et al., 2016, p. 2).

Another cause is the widespread residential segregation mentioned previously. The challenges for school integration are especially evident in those metropolitan areas that consist of a largely black-populated inner city surrounded by largely white-populated rings of suburbs.

Without a renewed commitment to integration, American schools will continue to resegregate. This is a particularly ominous trend because it directly affects the quality of education. Years of research demonstrate that integrated schools—by social class and race—are related to better educational experiences, improved test scores, and other outcomes (e.g., see Orfield et al., 2016).

The black–white gap in educational attainment has generally decreased over the past several decades. Figure 5.11 displays the change from 1940 to 2017 in the percentage of the population older than 25 years with high school diplomas by race and gender; there is a dramatic decline in racial differences. Given the increasing demands for higher educational credentials in the job market, it's ironic that the nation has nearly achieved racial

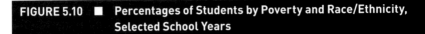

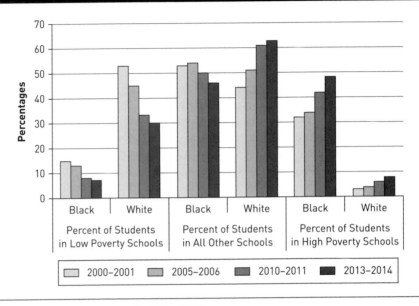

FIGURE 5.10 ■ **Percentages of Students by Poverty and Race/Ethnicity, Selected School Years**

Source: U.S. Government Accountability Office (2016).

equality in high school education at a time when this credential matters less. On the positive side, 61% of African Americans in one national survey reported being "encouraged to apply to college while growing up." Unfortunately, of those who "applied to or attended college," more than one third (36%) reported discrimination based on their race (NPR et al., 2017a, p. 6).

Similarly, Figure 5.12 shows a narrowing gap for college graduation rates. In 1940, white men held a distinct advantage over all other race/gender groups: They were about three times more likely than African American men and women to have a college degree. By 2017, the advantage of white men had shrunk, but they were still about 1.5 times more likely than black men and women to have a college degree. These racial differences grow larger with more advanced degrees, however, and these differences will be increasingly serious in an economy in which more desirable jobs more frequently require advanced education.

Political Power

Two trends have increased the political power of African Americans since World War II. One is the movement out of the rural South, a process that concentrated African Americans into areas in which it was easier to register and vote. As the black population outside the South grew, so did their national representation. The first African American representative to Congress (other than those elected during Reconstruction) was elected in 1928. Yet, by 1954, only three African Americans had been elected to serve in the House of Representatives (Franklin, 1967, p. 614).

FIGURE 5.11 ■ High School Graduation Rates for People 25 Years and Older in the United States, 1940–2017

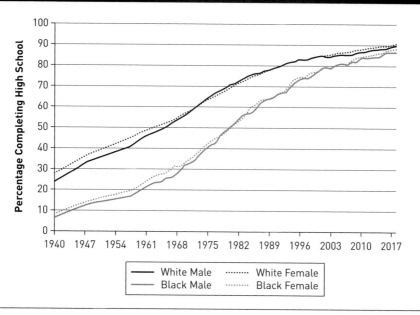

Source: U.S. Bureau of the Census (2018b).

FIGURE 5.12 ■ College Graduation Rates of People 25 Years and Older in the United States, 1940–2017

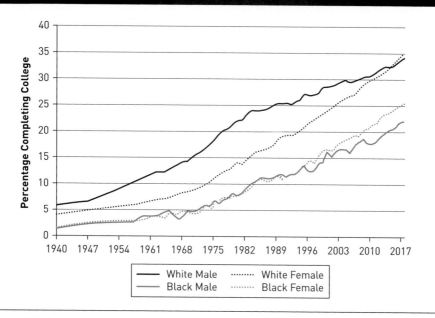

Source: U.S. Bureau of the Census (2018b).

In 1993, Carol Moseley Braun made history as she became the first black woman senator in America. When Barack Obama was elected to the Senate in 2004, he was only the fifth African American senator since Reconstruction to serve in that role. Since then, five more African Americans have been elected to the Senate: Roland Burris (Illinois, 2009), Tim Scott (South Carolina, 2013), Mo Cowan (Massachusetts, 2013), Corey Booker (New Jersey, 2013), and Kamala Harris (California, 2017). A record 51 African Americans are serving in the 115th Congress during the current session (2017–2019): three in the Senate and 48 in the House of Representatives (History, Art, & Archives, 2008), including seven new black House members.

The number of African American elected officials at all levels of government has increased over time. Both Colin Powell and Condoleezza Rice have served as Secretary of State, the highest governmental office ever held by an African American (along with Supreme Court Justice and excluding the presidency). Since Bill Clinton took office, African Americans have filled about 12% of appointed Cabinet positions.

At the state level are several new black Attorneys General, Lieutenant Governors, and county judges (Dovere, 2018). In 1989, Douglas Wilder (Virginia) became the first African American to be elected to a state governorship—only one of four ever elected in American history as of this writing (Brown & Atske, 2019). African American communities are virtually guaranteed some political representation because of their high degree of geographical concentration at the local level. Today, most large American cities, including Los Angeles, Chicago, Atlanta, New York, and Washington, DC, have elected African American mayors.

Another trend that has increased black political power is the dismantling of the institutions and practices of disenfranchisement that operated during Jim Crow segregation (Chapter 4). Since the 1960s, the number of African Americans in the nation's voting-age population has increased from slightly less than 10% to about 13%. But this increasing potential for political power has not always been fully mobilized in the past, and actual turnout has generally been lower for blacks than for whites. In the hotly contested presidential races between 2000–2016, however, many organizations (e.g., the NAACP) made a concerted and largely successful effort to increase turnout among African Americans. In the 2000–2008 elections, black turnout was comparable to whites, and in the 2012 presidential election, the black turnout (66.2%) was slightly larger than the white turnout (64.1%; File, 2013). However, after steadily increasing from 1996 through 2012, the African American turnout dropped sharply to 59.6% in the Trump–Clinton election of 2016, six percentage points below white voters (Krogstad & Lopez, 2017).

Overall, black American political power has increased over the past several decades at all levels. One potentially ominous threat to this trend is the growth of voting restrictions since the 2013 Supreme Court ruling on the VRA. Shortly after the decision, Texas announced that a voter identification law, previously blocked, would go into effect immediately (Liptak, 2013), and North Carolina passed one of the most restrictive laws since the Jim Crow era (Brennan Center for Justice, 2013). The courts declared the latter unconstitutional on the grounds that it "target[ed] African Americans with almost surgical precision" (Vicens, 2016; also see Liptak & Wines, 2017).

Well over half the states have considered or have passed various measures that could decrease the size of the electorate generally and disproportionately lower the impact of the African American vote. For example, many states may require voters to show a government-issued photo ID—such as a driver's license or passport—before allowing them to cast a ballot. For many reasons (e.g., their relative poverty) African Americans—and other minority groups of color—are less likely to possess official forms of identification. Other states have ended same-day voter registration and shortened early voting periods (Brennan Center for Justice, 2018). As a result, some people will face additional challenges getting to and from polling places and getting time off from work to vote.

Proponents of restrictive voting measures argue that they prevent voter fraud. As is typical of modern institutional discrimination, the new laws don't specifically mention minority groups. Fresh's (2018) analysis suggests that the Supreme Court's 2013 decision will decrease black voter registration the most while also decreasing white voter registration and general voter turnout. Groups with lower rates of voting (e.g., racial minorities, senior citizens, younger voters, lower-income people) will likely feel greater marginalization from the political system than others (e.g., white, affluent college graduates). This spate of new restrictive legislation affects them disproportionately, making them less likely to participate in the democratic process (Pew Research Center, 2014a; see Brennan Center for Justice, 2018).

Finally, we'd note that many formerly incarcerated people lose their right to vote. Thus, the high and disproportionate incarceration of black people not only affects their democratic rights but the group's overall political power.

Jobs and Income

African American integration in the job market and subsequent income follows the patterns that we've documented in other areas of social life: The situation has improved since Jim Crow, but it's stopped well short of equality. White men are much more likely to be employed in the highest-rated and most lucrative occupations, while African American men are overrepresented in the service sector and in unskilled labor (U.S. Census Bureau, 2015a). One comprehensive analysis of race/gender employment trends found that, after some gains following the landmark legislation of the mid-1960s, gains for black men and women (and white women) were slight, and whites, especially men, continue to disproportionally fill better jobs and earn higher wages (Stainback & Tomaskovic-Devey, 2012, pp. 155–177).

Although huge racial gaps continue, the current occupational distribution for African Americans has significantly improved. Some might say this progress has been rapid, given that as recently as the 1930s, most African American men worked as unskilled agricultural laborers (Steinberg, 1981, pp. 206–207). Likewise, African American women's employment has improved. In the 1930s, about 90% of employed African American women worked in agriculture or in domestic service (pp. 206–207). Those rates dropped dramatically. Today, most African American women are employed in the two highest occupational categories, although typically at the lower levels. For example, in the "managerial and professional" category, women are typically concentrated in lower-income occupations, such as nursing or teaching (see Figure 4.4), while men are more likely to be physicians and lawyers.

Figure 5.13 depicts the racial income gap in terms of the median—the average difference between "typical" white and black families. The racial income gap reflects racial differences in education, which influences occupational options and, therefore, wages. The graph presents two kinds of information. First, follow the solid lines from the left vertical axis toward the right, which shows changes in the median household incomes for the groups from 1967 to 2017. You'll notice that median household income for both groups generally moved together, trending upward until the turn of this century. Incomes flattened and then fell, reflecting hard economic times after 2000 and especially after the 2007 global economic crisis. Beginning around 2014, household incomes began to rise again, with white income rising more rapidly. Also note that black household income stayed well below white household income throughout this period. In the late 1960s, for example, black household income was about 58% of white household income.

The dotted line shows the percentage of black to white household income over time. (Note that incomes are presented in 2017 dollars, which adjusts for inflation.) The gap remained relatively steady through the 1980s but closed during the boom years of the 1990s. Since the turn of the century, it's widened again, especially in recent years. The gap was smallest in 2000 (68%) and, in the most recent year for which data was available (2017), it was 62%, reflecting the differential effects of the recession on minority groups of color, as we discussed previously.

Figure 5.14 supplements this information by comparing the distribution of income within each racial group for 2017. It also highlights the different percentages for each

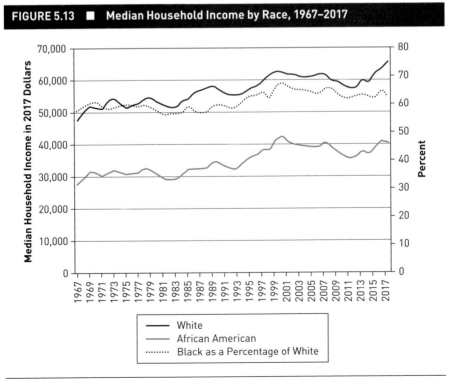

FIGURE 5.13   ■   Median Household Income by Race, 1967–2017

Legend:
——— White
——— African American
········ Black as a Percentage of White

Source: U.S. Bureau of the Census (2018c).

FIGURE 5.14 ■ Distribution of Household Incomes for White and Black Americans, 2017

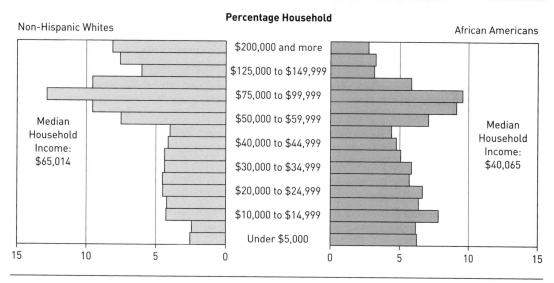

Percentage Household

Non-Hispanic Whites

African Americans

$200,000 and more
$125,000 to $149,999
$75,000 to $99,999
$50,000 to $59,999
$40,000 to $44,999
$30,000 to $34,999
$20,000 to $24,999
$10,000 to $14,999
Under $5,000

Median Household Income: $65,014

Median Household Income: $40,065

15   10   5   0   0   5   10   15

Source: U.S. Bureau of the Census (2018d).

group in low-, middle-, and upper-income categories. To read this graph, notice a few things: (1) income categories are arranged from the top (highest income category) to the bottom (lowest income category); (2) the horizontal axis (on the bottom) has a zero point in the middle of the graph; (3) the horizontal bars represent the percentage of households in each income category. Data for non-Hispanic whites are to the left of the zero point. Information for blacks is on the right of the zero point.

Starting at the bottom, notice that the bars representing black households (on the right side) are considerably wider than those for white households (on the left side). This reflects African Americans' greater concentration in lower-income brackets. For example, 12.4% of black households were in the lowest two income categories (less than $10,000), which is 2.5 times higher than the rate for white households (4.9%) in this income category.

As you read upward, notice the clustering of black and white households in the $50,000 to $124,000 category—income ranges associated with middle and upper-middle-class life-styles. White households are overrepresented in these income categories compared to blacks (39.4% and 31.7%, respectively). Racial differences are even more dramatic in the two highest income ranges: About 15.6% of white households had incomes greater than $150,000 versus only 6.1% of black households. In sum, while African Americans are at all income levels, this data convincingly refutes the notion, common among modern racists and others, that no important racial inequalities exist in America today.

Finally, poverty affects African Americans at much higher rates than it does white Americans. Figure 5.15 shows the percentage of white and black American families living below the federally established, "official" poverty level from 1967–2017. Historically, the poverty rate for African American families ran about two to three times higher than the

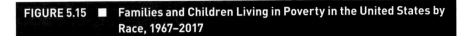

FIGURE 5.15 ■ Families and Children Living in Poverty in the United States by Race, 1967–2017

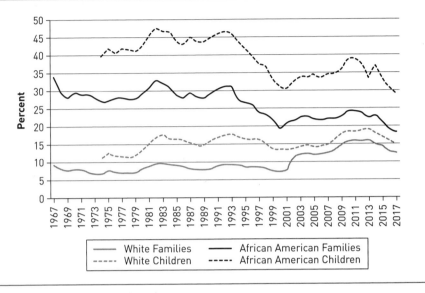

Source: U.S. Bureau of the Census (2018a).

Note: Family poverty rates and child poverty rates are computed using different units of analysis. Family rates represent the percentage of all families below the poverty line. The rates for children are the percentage of all people younger than 18 in poverty.

rate for whites. However, the gap has narrowed in the last several years. In 2017, the poverty rate for black families was 1.5 times higher than the rate for white families.

Note that a dramatic decrease in black poverty happened during the boom years of the 1990s, only to be followed by rising rates after 2000. The poverty rates for both groups trended upward between 2000 and 2012 before decreasing in recent years. Tragically, children's poverty rates—especially African American children—continue to be extremely high. Like Figures 5.13 and 5.14, this graph refutes the notion that serious racial inequality is a thing of the past.

Primary Structural Assimilation

Interracial contact in the more public areas of society (e.g., schools, workplaces), is more common today. As Gordon's model of assimilation predicts, this public contact has led to increases in more intimate contacts across racial lines. To illustrate, McPherson, Smith-Lovin, and Brashears (2006) looked at changing intimate relationships among Americans by asking a nationally representative sample about the people with whom they discuss important matters. Although the study didn't focus on black–white relations per se, the researchers found that between 1984 and 2004, the percentage of whites who included African Americans as intimate contacts increased from 9% to more than 15%. From one perspective, this increase is encouraging because it suggests progress toward a more integrated, racially unified society. Alternatively, the relatively low percentages may feel discouraging because they suggest that about 85% of white Americans maintain interpersonal networks of friends and acquaintances of the same race only.

In 2016, Cox, Navarro-Rivera, and Jones found similar patterns in people's social networks. They asked participants to name the people with whom they discussed important matters and then to identify each person by race. The vast majority of white respondents maintained racially homogenous networks: 91% of their close contacts were white. Black respondents reported less (but relatively high) racial exclusiveness: 83% of their close contacts were black. This difference in the racial composition of social networks results, partly, from population sizes: Because white Americans outnumber black Americans by far, they have more choices for friends and acquaintances and, as the dominant group, they can more easily maintain racial exclusiveness. (Note that one doesn't need to "intend" to have race-exclusive networks. Partly they result from segregation in neighborhoods, schools, etc.)

Fisher (2008) studied interracial friendships on 27 college campuses across the nation and found similar patterns. First-year students were interviewed at the end of their second semester and asked about the group membership of their 10 closest friends on campus. Cross-group friendships were common, but white students had the least diverse circles of friends. For whites, 76% of their friends were also white, a much higher percentage of in-group exclusiveness than Asian students (51%), Hispanic students (56%), and black students (27%).

Obviously, these percentages reflect the racial composition of the campuses (all were majority white). But it's significant that the study found that cross-group choices were positively related to more tolerant attitudes and a history of having a friend from another group in high school. Most interesting, perhaps, was that cross-group choices were positively related to greater campus diversity. This finding supports the contact hypothesis and Gordon's assertion that integration at the secondary level leads to integration at the primary level.

Consistent with the decline in traditional, overt prejudice, Americans are much less opposed to interracial dating and marriage today. As noted in Chapter 1, a recent national poll (Livingston & Brown, 2017) found that 9% of Americans felt that interracial marriage is "a bad thing" for society. Almost 40% felt interracial marriages were "a good thing" (up from 24% in 2010) and the majority (52%) felt that it didn't "make much difference" (p. 24). Support for interracial marriage was especially high among young people (54% of 18- to 29-year-olds said it was "a good thing" vs. only 26% of respondents over 65), the college educated (54% of the college educated said it was "a good thing" vs. only 26% of respondents with a high school degree), and urbanites (45% of city dwellers said it was "a good thing" vs. only 24% of rural respondents; p. 25).

Behavior follows attitudes, so you're probably not surprised that rates of interracial dating and marriage are increasing. Several studies find that interracial dating is increasingly common (see Keels & Harris, 2014; Wellner, 2007), and the number of marriages between African Americans and whites is increasing, although still a tiny percentage of all marriages. In 1970, the U.S. census recorded 65,000 black–white married couples (including persons of Hispanic origin). That's about 0.10% of all married couples. By 2010, that increased 8.5 times (to 558,000), which is still less than 1% (0.9%) of all married couples (U.S. Census Bureau, 2012a, p. 54; see also Livingston & Brown, 2017).

Finally, a study comparing intermarriage based on the 1980 and 2008 censuses found a trend toward decreasing in-marriage, particularly for black men, as shown in Table 5.1. Also, most black men in interracial marriages married white people (14.4%) and Hispanics (4.8%). Black women in interracial marriages showed a similar pattern: 6.5% were married to whites and 2.3% to Hispanics.

TABLE 5.1 ■ Percentage Married to a Person of the Same Race, 1980 and 2008				
	Whites		African Americans	
Year	Men	Women	Men	Women
1980	96%	95%	93%	97%
2008	93%	92%	77%	88%

Source: Qian and Lichter (2011, p. 1072).

QUESTIONS FOR REFLECTION

15. Which dimensions of acculturation and integration for African Americans are most important? Why?

16. What evidence can you cite for the claim that "black–white relations are the best they've ever been"? What evidence can you cite against this claim?

FOCUS ON CONTEMPORARY ISSUES
DOES THE ELECTION OF PRESIDENT OBAMA MEAN THAT AMERICA IS POST-RACIAL?

The election of President Barack in 2008 led many people to conclude that America had rejected racism and finally become a "post-racial" society in which race was irrelevant. Others warned that reports about the death of racism were vastly exaggerated and that the triumph of one person—even one as significant as the president—doesn't represent the situation of black Americans generally or that of other minority groups.

Which view seems more accurate? We can't fully address this topic in merely a few paragraphs, but we can offer some important points that suggest that America is far from being post-racial.

First, race figured prominently in the presidential campaign, although its effects tended to be below the surface. The Obama campaign knew that they had to avoid the controversial topic of American racism if their candidate was to be successful. They de-emphasized his racial identity, presenting him as a candidate who happened to be black, not "the black candidate." Additionally, Obama avoided discussion on racially charged issues (e.g., civil rights, affirmative action, the war on drugs) and focused on issues of broad concern instead (e.g., the economy, wars in Iraq and Afghanistan, health care). His strategy was to discuss race "only in the context of other issues" (Ifill, 2009, p. 53).

This strategy couldn't defuse all of people's concerns, fears, and anxieties triggered by Obama's race. Given traditional stereotypes about whites and blacks, the campaign wanted people to see Obama as a multiracial person and as "more white," which has positive associations. They wanted to contain negative associations related to his blackness.

The most potentially disastrous racial episode during the campaign linked Obama with Pastor Jeremiah Wright, a flamboyant minister of a Chicago church that Obama had attended. A YouTube video in which Wright strongly condemned America for its treatment of blacks and other people of color surfaced and threatened to sink Obama's candidacy by associating him with what most whites would see as angry, militant racialized rhetoric.

Forced to confront American racism openly, Obama crafted a speech acknowledging racism past and present, but he rejected Reverend Wright's views as distorted, saying that Wright elevated "what is wrong with America above all that we know is right with America" (Obama, 2008). The speech successfully defused the immediate issue, but issues of race continued to lurk in the background of the campaign. There was a persistent tendency to label Obama as something other than a "true American"—as a Muslim, a Kenyan, an outsider, a terrorist, a revolutionary, or an angry black man. His campaign provided evidence to refute those claims. The campaign was, in part, successful because it was able to portray him as "white-assimilated, acceptable, multiracial, and thus less black (or not really black)" (Wingfield & Feagin, 2010, p. 219). Thus, the first black president in American history owed his success to many people's perception of him as not "really" black.

Second, support for Obama on Election Day was highly racialized. The candidate built a broad coalition of supporters, including the young, first-time voters, low-income voters, liberals, Democrats, and women. However, his staunchest support came from the black community. Obama actually lost among white voters by a considerable margin (55% voted for McCain, the Republican candidate) but he attracted 95% of black voters.

Furthermore, perceptions of Obama's effectiveness remained highly racialized. Weekly surveys showed that the percentage of whites who approved of the job he was doing varied between 30% and 40%, while approval ratings among blacks typically ran between 80% and 90 (Gallup, 2012). In January 2017, as he was preparing to leave office, those numbers had increased: 49% of whites and 91% of blacks approved of the job he did (Gallup, 2017b). Thus, his support in the black community was roughly two to three times his support in the white community.

Finally, and most detrimental to the argument that America is post-racial, the racial gaps that existed when Obama took office have persisted, as figures in this chapter show. Racial issues regularly animate public discourse, and prejudice, racism, and discrimination have increased and become more overt since the election of Donald Trump.

IS THE GLASS HALF-EMPTY OR HALF-FULL?

The contemporary situation of African Americans is what we might expect for a group so recently released from exclusion and subordination. Figure 5.16 shows the length of the periods of subjugation and the brevity of time since the fall of Jim Crow—information that's easy to forget. Overall, life for African Americans improved vastly during the last half of the 20th century in virtually every area. Yet, as the data in this chapter show, racial progress has stopped well short of equality, sometimes even reversing course.

In assessing the present situation, one might stress the improved situation of the group (the glass is half-full) or the challenges that remain before full racial equality and justice are achieved (the glass is half-empty). While African Americans have occupied the highest levels of American society (e.g., Oval Office, Supreme Court), a large percentage have merely shifted from rural peasantry to urban poverty, still facing many formidable and deep-rooted problems.

The situation of African Americans is intimately connected to the changing economy and the plight of city centers. It is the consequence of approximately 400 years of prejudice, racism, and discrimination and it also reflects broader social forces, such as urbanization and industrialization.

Consistent with their origin as a colonized minority group, African Americans' relative poverty and powerlessness has persisted long after some minority groups have achieved equality and acceptance (e.g., the descendants of the white European immigrants who arrived from the 1820s through 1920s).

Whites enslaved African Americans to meet the labor demands of an agrarian economy. Blacks became rural peasants under Jim Crow segregation, were excluded from the opportunities created by early industrialization, and remain largely excluded from the better jobs in the emerging post-industrial economy.

Progress toward racial equality has slowed since the heady days of the 1960s, and in many areas, earlier advances seem hopelessly stagnated. Public opinion polls indicate

FIGURE 5.16   ■   Time Line of American Slavery and Segregation

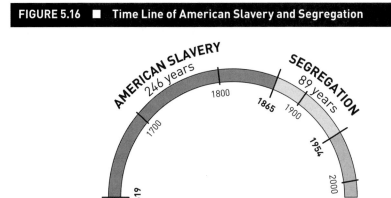

Source: Illustration by Benjamin Jancewicz, Zerflin, 2015.

little support or sympathy for African Americans and the issues they face. Traditional prejudice has declined, only to be replaced by modern racism. Biological racism has been replaced with indifference to racial issues or with victim blaming. And the court of public opinion often holds African Americans responsible for what centuries of structural oppression has wrought.

Nevertheless, contemporary African Americans, as a group, have experienced real improvements in their lives. Compared with their counterparts during Jim Crow, they are, on average, more prosperous and more politically powerful. They have increased opportunities to develop their interests and skills through formal education. They can work in diverse professions and be recognized for their contributions. Media portrayals of African Americans are increasingly diverse, realistic, and complex, not merely stereotypical. Indeed, it's worth noting that *Get Out* (2017) and *Black Panther* (2018) earned critical acclaim and broke box office records and were created by people of color, featuring people of color, telling stories that offered powerful critiques of white supremacy and colonialism. Related to this, beauty ideals have expanded to include diverse skin tones, body shapes, hair textures, and facial features. (That's if you see the glass as half-full.)

However, the increases in average income and education and the glittering success of the few obscure the complex, interrelated problems experienced by many—unemployment, a failing educational system, residential segregation, poverty, racism, and continuing discrimination persist as seemingly inescapable realities for millions of African Americans. Crime, drugs, violence, poor health care, malnutrition, incarceration, and other factors compound these problems, which may grow worse without the commitment of will and the resources to solve them. (That's if you see the glass as half-empty.)

Given what can feel like a depressing situation, it's not surprising that African Americans (and their allies) feel anger and resentment and are embracing pluralistic, nationalistic thinking as a result. Black nationalism and Black Power offer powerful ideas and hope for the widespread development and autonomy of African Americans as a community. Yet, without the support to bring them to fruition, these ideas remain largely symbolic.

We could characterize the situation of the African American community in the early 21st century as a combination of partial assimilation, structural pluralism, and inequality that reflects the continuing effects of being a colonized group. Contemporary problems are less visible than in earlier eras (or perhaps they're better hidden from the average white middle-class American). Responsibility is more diffused, and the moral certainties in opposition to slavery or to Jim Crow laws are long gone. Modern racism and institutional discrimination are less dramatic and more difficult to measure than an overseer's whip, a lynch mob, or a sign that reads "Whites Only." However, as you've learned, they're as real and as deadly in their consequences.

As we end this chapter, we want to encourage you to see the glass as half-full and to feel hopeful about the present and the future. College students and other young people were at the heart of the civil rights movement (and other justice movements, too). They dismantled Jim Crow in creative, powerful, nonviolent ways, and they did it with courage and dignity. Let them inspire you to forge ahead in community with one another, doing the work that needs to be done to bring America closer, each day, to equality and justice for all.

Main Points

- At the beginning of the 20th century, the racial oppression of African Americans took the form of a rigid competitive system of group relations and de jure segregation. This system ended because of changing economic and political conditions, changing legal precedents, and a mass protest movement started by African Americans.

- The Supreme Court decision in *Brown v. Board of Education of Topeka* (1954) was the single most powerful decision against legalized segregation. The civil rights movement pursued a nonviolent direct action campaign in the South that challenged and defeated Jim Crow. Congress delivered the final blows to de jure segregation in the 1964 Civil Rights Act and the 1965 Voting Rights Act.

- Outside the South, African American concerns centered on access to education, jobs, housing, health care, and other opportunities. African Americans expressed their frustration in the urban riots of the 1960s. The Black Power movement addressed the massive problems of racial inequality that remained after the civil rights movement defeated Jim Crow.

- Black–white relations since the 1960s have been characterized by continuing inequality, separation, and hostility, along with substantial improvements in status for some African Americans. Class differentiation within the African American community is greater than ever before.

- Many people perceive some African American family forms as weak, unstable, and a cause of continuing poverty. Some claim that African Americans (and others) possess a culture of poverty that discourages upward mobility. Structural (and other) theories see African American family forms (e.g., women-headed households) as *resulting* from poverty, not *causing* it.

- Subtler forms of antiblack prejudice and discrimination (modern racism and institutional discrimination) have replaced traditional forms of overt antiblack prejudice and discrimination.

- African Americans are largely acculturated, but centuries of separate development have created a unique black experience in American society.

- Though many African Americans have experienced real improvements in life, secondary structural assimilation, overall, remains low. Evidence of racial inequalities in residence, schooling, politics, jobs, income, unemployment, and poverty is massive and underlines the realities of the urban underclass.

- In the area of primary structural assimilation, interracial interaction and friendships are rising. Interracial marriages are increasing, although they remain a tiny percentage of all marriages.

- Compared with the start of the 20th century, African Americans have experienced improved quality of life, overall, but the distance to true racial equality remains significant.

Applying Concepts

The table below lists 10 metropolitan areas from across the nation in alphabetical order. Which ones do you think have the most racial residential segregation? Cities in the South? Cities in the Northeast or the West? Cities with a higher or lower black population? What's your best guess and why? Rank order them, accordingly, from 1 (most segregated) to 10 (least segregated).

	City	Region	Percentage Black, 2010*	Rank
1	Atlanta, Georgia	South	32%	
2	Baltimore, Maryland	Border	29%	
3	Boston, Massachusetts	Northeast	7%	
4	Dallas–Fort Worth, Texas	Southwest	15%	
5	Kansas City, Kansas	Midwest	13%	
6	Pittsburgh, Pennsylvania	Northeast	8%	
7	Richmond, Virginia	South	38%	
8	San Diego, California	West	5%	
9	San Francisco, California	West	8%	
10	Washington, DC	South/Border	26%	

*Percentage in entire metropolitan area, including suburbs.

Source: Data from U.S. Census Bureau (2012c, p. 31).

Turn the page to see the actual ranks and scores.

Review Questions

1. What led to the end of de jure segregation? When answering, address broad social changes (e.g., industrialization) as well as changes created by collective action.

2. Compare the civil rights movement to the Black Power movement. How were they similar? How were they different? How does Black Lives Matter compare to the earlier movements? When answering, consider philosophies, tactics, leaders, and the greater social context.

3. Explain the most critical issues related to black–white relations since the 1960s, including (a) the relationship between the criminal justice system and the black community, (b) class and gender inequality

within the black community, (c) family forms, (d) new racial identities, (e) prejudice, and (f) individual and institutional forms of discrimination.

4. Analyze the contemporary situation of African Americans using the concepts of *assimilation* and *pluralism*, especially in terms of acculturation, secondary structural assimilation, and primary structural assimilation.

5. Are African American women a minority group within a minority group? Explain.

6. An old saying is, "When America catches a cold, African Americans get pneumonia." Based on this chapter, would you say that's mostly true or untrue? Why? Use evidence from this chapter (and others) in your answer.

7. What are the implications of increasing class differences among African Americans?

8. Regarding contemporary black–white relations, is the glass half-empty or half-full? Discuss at least three areas of social life (e.g., education) when answering.

Answers to Applying Concepts

Here are the 10 metro areas listed from most to least segregated. Many American cities are more segregated than Pittsburgh; some are less segregated than San Diego. These 10 cities were selected to represent many regions and race relations histories and can't, of course, represent America as a whole.

	City	Score (Dissimilarity Index)
1	Pittsburgh, Pennsylvania	64.9
2	Baltimore, Maryland	62.2
3	Kansas City, Kansas	57.7
4	Boston, Massachusetts	57.6
5	Washington, DC	56.1
6	Atlanta, Georgia	54.1
7	San Francisco, California	50.5
8	Richmond, Virginia	49.6
9	Dallas–Fort Worth, Texas	47.5
10	San Diego, California	38.6

Source: Data from Glaeser and Vigdor (2012).

Internet Learning Resources

SAGE edge™ offers teachers and students easy-to-use resources for review, study, and further exploration. See **http://edge.sagepub.com/diversity6e**

Note

1. This incident is the basis for the 2013 feature-length film *Fruitvale Station*.

6

NATIVE AMERICANS

From Conquest to Tribal Survival in a Postindustrial Society

Lorinda announced that the [Blessing Way ceremony for Lynette's unborn child] was about to start . . . [so we] walked into the hoghan. A single light bulb lit the room dimly. Couches, futon mattresses, and large pillows were set against the walls for the night's sing. A coffee-maker, microwave, and crock-pot sat on a folding table against the northern wall for the midnight eating. This was the same Navajo adaptation I'd grown up seeing, the age-old ritual with modern technology.

The hataałii [shaman or healer] sat against the western wall. . . . He wore thick silver bracelets and a silk bandana across his brow, the knot tied off at his right temple in traditional style. A basket of tádídíín [corn pollen] sat at his left.

[There were] gifts: . . . a stethoscope, that the baby would have good health and might be a healer; . . . a pair of running shoes, that the child would be a strong runner; dollar bills . . . to wish the child a wealthy life; cowboy boots and work gloves so that the child would be a hard worker. . . .

The hataałii spoke in quiet Navajo as he passed the basket of tádídíín to Dennis, who sprinkled the yellow pollen at each corner of the hoghan, first East, South, West, then North. Then he passed the basket around the room in a clockwise order; when it came to me, I did what the others had done: I placed a pinch inside my lower lip, pressed a second pinch to my forehead, then spread the pollen in the air in a small arch to resemble the rainbow that promises life and beauty.

The hataałii began the sing. Brandon and the two burly men entered the chant with accenting rhythms as articulate as wind chimes, but with the resonance of distant thunder. . . .

Lorinda leaned forward and rocked slowly, speaking her own prayer: I heard the word hózhó sung many times. There is no English equivalent, but mostly it means "beautiful harmony." Christians might call it grace.

—Jim Kristofic (2011, pp. 183–184)

At the end of first grade, Jim Kristofic found himself moving from western Pennsylvania to the Navajo reservation in Arizona, where his mother had taken a job as a nurse. Like many Americans, he had little information about Indigenous people before getting to know them. As the new boy in school, he was initially rejected and bullied by the Navajo kids. Eventually, he developed a deep respect for and understanding of the "Rez," the people, and the Navajo way of life. In the previous passage, he gives us a glimpse into a sacred Navajo ceremony called the *Blessing Way* that has been practiced for centuries. Can ancient traditions such as this—and the Indigenous people that practice them—survive in the modern world?

I n Chapter 3, we discussed the contact period for Native Americans, which began in the earliest colonial days and lasted nearly 300 years. It ended with the final battles of the Indian Wars in the late 1800s. During that time, the many diverse Indian[1] nations fought to preserve their cultures and to keep their land. The tribes had enough power to win many battles, but they eventually lost all of the wars. Nichols (1986, p. 128) suggests that the diversity of Native communities (including 250 different languages) contributed to the challenges of fighting whites (Reagan, 2018, p. 239). The superior resources of the burgeoning white society made the eventual defeat of Native Americans almost inescapable (Diamond, 1998).

By 1890, the last of the tribes had been conquered, their leaders had been killed or were in custody, and their people were living on U.S. government–controlled reservations. By the start of the 20th century, Native Americans were, in Blauner's (1972) terms, a conquered and colonized minority group. Like African Americans on slave plantations,

Native people living on reservations lived, by law, under a paternalistic system controlled by federally mandated regulations. Because the reservation system greatly weakened tribal governments, most lived under the supervision of U.S.–appointed Indian agents who temporarily lived on the reservations and who supervised their acculturation into U.S. society in detail, for example, by governing everything—including hair length, clothing, and language (Nichols, 1986, p. 135). Between 1890 and the present, as Jim Crow segregation, Supreme Court decisions, industrialization, and urbanization shaped the status of other minority groups, Native Americans lived on the fringes of development and change and had weaker links to the larger society than other groups. Thus, they were marginalized, relatively powerless, and isolated geographically and culturally. While other minority groups have maintained a regular presence in the national headlines, Native Americans have been generally ignored and unnoticed, except perhaps as mascots for sports teams (e.g., Washington Redskins, Atlanta Braves) or because of recent protests at the Standing Rock Reservation about the Dakota Access Pipeline (DAPL).

The last decades of the 20th century witnessed some improvement in the status of Native Americans in general, and some tribes, especially those with casinos and other gaming establishments, made notable progress toward parity with national standards (Spilde & Taylor, 2013; Taylor & Kalt, 2005). Also, the tribes now have more control over their own affairs, and many have effectively used their increased autonomy and independence to address problems in education, health, joblessness, and other matters. Despite the progress, large gaps remain between Native Americans and other groups, especially whites, in virtually every area of social and economic life. For example, some Native Americans living on reservations are among the poorest groups in the United States.

In this chapter, we'll discuss the history of Native Americans up to the present and explore recent progress and persistent problems. Some of the questions we'll discuss include the following: How does the situation of Native Americans compare with that of other colonized and conquered minority groups? What accounts for the inequalities this group has faced for much of the past century? How can we explain improvements, especially since the 1990s? What key problems remain? What strategies could close the remaining gaps between Native Americans and the larger society?

SIZE OF THE GROUP

How many Native Americans live in the United States? This question has several answers, partly because of the social and subjective nature of race and group membership. Historically and today, the U.S. government and individual tribes have defined the status of "Indian" in different ways. Sometimes those definitions have been based on specific percentages of "Indian blood" (Cohen, 1945, p. 5). At other times, the government and the tribes have defined Indian status broadly, even including individuals who joined tribal communities through marriage (Nichols, 1986, p. 128).

The answer also varies because of the way the Census Bureau collects information. As with other racial and ethnic groups, the Census Bureau's categories for Native Americans have changed over time. As you recall from Chapter 1, the 2000 census was the first time people could claim membership in more than one racial or ethnic category.

If we define Native Americans as consisting of people who identify themselves as *only* Native American, we'll get one estimate. If we include people who claim mixed racial ancestry, then our estimate of group size will be much larger. Table 6.1 shows this difference in size.

If you look at the top row of Table 6.1, you'll see that about 5.6 million people claimed at least *some* Native American or Alaska Native ancestry; if we define the group

TABLE 6.1 ■ Native Americans and Alaska Natives, 2016		
	Alone	Alone or in Combination (Two or More Groups)
All Native Americans and Alaska Natives	2,597,817	5,609,575
Native Americans	2,071,267	4,904,556
Alaska Natives	120,829	185,157
Ten Largest Tribal Groupings for Native Americans		
	One Tribe Reported	Two or More Tribes
Cherokee	282,096	1,112,052
Navajo	314,169	374,476
Choctaw	94,961	244,515
Sioux	124,980	208,592
Chippewa	115,320	200,785
Blackfeet	28,688	167,695
Apache	70,314	144,395
Iroquois	44,025	109,412
Creek	42,469	101,580
Lumbee	69,805	87,561
Largest Tribal Groupings for Alaska Natives		
Yup'ik	36,137	43,747
Inupiat	29,227	41,659
Tlingit-Haida	15,608	28,681
Alaskan Athabascan	15,092	25,849

Note: People with unspecified tribal groupings are omitted in lists of largest groupings.

Source: U.S. Census Bureau (2016b).

FIGURE 6.1 ■ Native American and Alaska Native Population, 1900–2016

Sources: For data for 1900 to 1990 (Thornton, 2001, p. 142), for 2000 and 2010 (Norris, Vines, & Hoeffel, 2012; U.S. Census Bureau, 2007, p. 14; U.S. Census Bureau, 2010), for 2016 (U.S. Census Bureau, 2016b).

as people who select *only* Native American, the group is less than half that size. By either count, Native Americans are a small minority of the U.S. population—1.7% at most. Table 6.1 presents information for the 10 largest tribal groupings of Native Americans and for the four largest tribal groupings of Alaska Natives, but these categories only hint at the diversity of the group. We present them as separate groups because their vastly different geographical locations shaped the contact situation and, therefore, their group histories and also because tribal affiliation continues to matter to many members of this group (National Congress of American Indians, n.d.).

As you'll see in Figure 6.1, the Native American population has grown rapidly over the past several decades, but this fact needs to be seen in the full context of history. As you learned in Chapter 3, in 1492, there were anywhere from several million to 10 million or more Native Americans living in what is now the continental ("Lower 48") United States (Mann, 2011). By 1900, fewer than 250,000 Native Americans remained due to deaths during the contact period from disease, battles, and starvation due to loss of land (and, therefore, the ability to hunt animals and gather plants, and nuts, and other resources).

Recent population growth is largely the result of changing definitions of race in the larger society and people's greater willingness to claim Indian ancestry (Wilson, 2000). This pattern also underscores the social character of race.

NATIVE AMERICAN CULTURES

The relationships between Native Americans and Anglo Americans have been shaped by vast differences in culture between the two groups (e.g., beliefs, values, norms, language).

These differences have hampered communication in the past and continue to do so in the present. Although we're discussing Native Americans as a group, as we noted in Chapter 3, there were (and are) almost 600 different tribes, each with its own heritage, social structure, and geography (National Congress of American Indians, n.d.; Regan, 2018). A comprehensive analysis of Native American cultures that takes such diversity into account is beyond the scope of this text. However, as Regan (2018) notes, we can identify some common cultural characteristics.

Agriculture, Views on Nature, and Land Ownership

Before exploring the content of Native American culture, recall Lenski's arguments about how subsistence technology profoundly shapes societies. Many Native American tribes that existed in what is now the U. S. relied on hunting, fishing, and gathering to satisfy their basic needs while others cultivated gardens rich with squash, corn, beans, oil-rich seeds, and other plants (George-Kanentiio, 2000; Nabhan, 2002; Nash & Strobel, 2006; Nelson, 2008; Park, Hongub, & Daily, 2016; Wessell, 1986).

In 1607, when the colonists arrived in Virginia, their survival was due, in part, to Native Americans' crops and seeds as well as their willingness to share their knowledge about how to cultivate crops in the new world (Smith, 2013, p. xv). Nevertheless, the food supply was unreliable and Native Americans and colonists often lived on the edge of hunger and want.

As is typical at the hunting-and-gathering level of development, Native American societies tended to be more oriented toward groups (e.g., the extended family, clan, or tribe) than toward individuals. Such communities stressed the values of sharing and cooperation, which enabled them to maintain strong bonds of cohesion and solidarity. In such communities, people subordinated self-interests to those of the group (Regan, 2018).

In traditional Native American cultures, the universe is a unity and humans are part of a larger reality, no different from or more important than other animals, plants, trees, and the earth itself. Because the natural world is connected to the spiritual world, many Native American tribes sought to live in harmony with nature (Regan, 2018, p. 240).

This framework influenced Native American beliefs about property, which differed from European thinking. Contrary to some stereotypes, Native Americans owned personal possessions. For example, Lakota men owned their horses, clothing, weapons, and spiritual objects. Many Indigenous Alaskan women marked stored fish to indicate ownership. The Great Law of the Iroquois says, "women shall be considered the Progenitors of the Nation. They shall own the land and soil" (cited from K. Anderson, 2016, p. 37). This phrasing shows the importance of communal ownership. Thus, when Tecumseh (a Shawnee chief) was angry when he discovered that several tribal members had sold land to settlers. He explained why this was problematic to Governor William Henry, saying

[the] Great Spirit . . . made them, to keep it, to traverse it, to enjoy its productions. . . . It never was divided, but belongs to all for the use of each. For no part has a right to sell, even to each other, much less to strangers—those who want all, and will not do with less. (Tecumseh, 1810, as cited in Drake, 1845, p. 121)

Native Americans had a system of land tenure, similar to the English common gardens with which colonists may have been familiar (Banner, 2005; Craven, 1970, p. 107). Land was often given to people who had land use rights, but anyone could hunt or gather on unallocated land (Banner, 2005, p. 37). According to one Creek chief, "We have no suits about land titles because the title is not disputable" (p. 266).

Gender and Social Structure

Egalitarianism, respect, and the worth of every person were other important values that organized many traditional Native American communities. Most tribes had a gendered division of labor that reflected these values. For example, Choctaw men and women did food-related work: Men hunted for food and women produced and distributed it (K. Anderson, 2016). This division of labor was often flexible, allowing people to choose work based on their gender identity and skills. For example, among the Yuma (or Quechan), a woman who had a dream about fighting could fight alongside the men (Allen, 1992; K. Anderson, 2016, p. 35).

Women in many Indigenous communities occupied important economic, political, and religious positions and had much greater freedom than colonial women (who the law defined as men's dependents; K. Anderson, 2016; George-Kanentiio, 2006; Hartman, n.d.). Among the Iroquois, a council of older women appointed tribal chiefs and had veto power over their decisions. Women could also impeach chiefs that didn't make decisions in the interests of the group or live up to their standards and women made decisions about going to war (Allen, 1992; Amott & Matthaei, 1991; George-Kanentiio, 2006; Mann, 2008).

The colonists and Native Americans thought differently about gender in other ways, too. The colonists believed that one's gender came from God and that gender relations on earth should model the biblical account of Adam and Eve. Colonists saw gender as binary: girl/woman or boy/man. They linked gender to biological sex (e.g., anatomy) and saw women and men as having essential differences. In their interpretation of Genesis, God made woman from man. Thus, in colonial families, men were expected to be patriarchs ("fathers") who would rule families like God—with ultimate power and authority. Women and children were to be subservient.

However, many Native Americans' creation accounts were woman-centered and emphasized women's ability to give birth. For example, the Iroquois tell of Sky People who lived happily and for whom death did not exist. When a pregnant Sky Woman fell toward earth, the birds caught her. She, together with other animals, created the world. Because women are central to creation, Native Americans considered them central to everything (Allen, 1992; K. Anderson, 2016; Nash & Strobel, 2006, p. 40).

Native Americans saw gender, sex, and sexual orientation as distinct, which allowed for gender expression beyond the girl/woman and boy/man dichotomy. Researchers have documented as many as 130 tribal communities that welcomed **two-spirit** people who identify as both genders simultaneously or who identify outside of the Western gender binary. Some people also use *two-spirit* to include nonheterosexual orientations (e.g., lesbian/gay, queer; Lang, 2010; Roscoe, 1991, p. 5; Thomas, 1997).

Gender varied by tribal community. The *nádleehí* (Navajo), for example, had four genders. Two were *cisgender*, meaning their biological sex is congruent with their gender (for example, a female who identifies and lives as a girl/woman). However, a person's sex didn't have to "match" in that way. For example, a person could be accepted as a woman though biologically male (Estrada, 2011; Lang, 2010; Mirandé, 2017; Thomas, 1997).

Westerners didn't approve of these gender ideologies or practices. Leaders of the dominant group usually ignored women tribal leaders and imposed Western notions of patriarchy onto the tribes (Amott & Matthaei, 1991, p. 39). According to Kim Anderson (2016), George Washington planned "to turn Native men into industrious, republican farmers and women into chaste, orderly housewives" (p. 38).

In summary, Native Americans' views about gender, sexuality, and family led to many misunderstandings and conflicts with the dominant group. More importantly, their views about land ownership and nature, combined with a lack of power and inexperience with deeds, titles, contracts, and other Western legal concepts, made it difficult for them to defend their resources from Anglo Americans.

QUESTIONS FOR REFLECTION

1. Why are there different size estimates for the Native American and Alaska Native populations? How do these differences support the idea that ethnicity, like race and gender, are social constructions?

2. Describe the colonists' and Native Americans' beliefs about gender and nature (e.g., land, animals). How did each group's ideas shape social life? How did their differing worldviews and practices contribute to tensions between the groups?

3. Consider what you've learned so far about Native Americans. What surprised you the most? What was most important to understand? Why?

RELATIONS WITH THE FEDERAL GOVERNMENT AFTER THE 1890s

By the end of the Indian Wars in 1890, Native Americans had few resources with which to defend their self-interests. In addition to being confined to the reservations, most Native American groups were scattered throughout the western two thirds of the United States and split by cultural and linguistic differences. Politically, the power of the group was further limited by the fact that most Native Americans were not U.S. citizens and most tribes lacked a cultural basis for understanding democracy as it was practiced in the larger society.

Economically, Native Americans were among the most impoverished groups in society. Reservation lands were generally poor quality, traditional food sources such as buffalo and other game had been destroyed, and traditional hunting grounds and gardening plots had been lost to white farmers and ranchers. The tribes had few means of satisfying even their most basic needs. Many became totally dependent on the federal government for food, shelter, clothing, and other necessities.

Prospects for improvement seemed slim. Most reservations were in remote areas, far from sites of industrialization and modernization (see Figure 6.2), and Native Americans had few of the skills (knowledge of English, familiarity with Western work habits and routines) that would have enabled them to compete for a place in the increasingly urban and industrial American society of the early 20th century. Off the reservations, racial prejudice and strong intolerance limited them. On the reservations, they were subjected to policies designed either to maintain their powerlessness and poverty or to force them to Americanize. Either way, the future of Native Americans was in serious jeopardy, and their destructive relations with white society continued in peace as they had in war.

Reservation Life

As would be expected for a conquered and still hostile group, the reservations were intended to closely supervise Native Americans and maintain their powerlessness. The federal government developed many paternalistic policies designed to coercively acculturate the tribes.

FIGURE 6.2 ■ Native American Reservations in the United States

Source: U.S. Parks Service (n.d.).

Paternalism and the Bureau of Indian Affairs

The reservations were run not by the tribes, but by an agency of the federal government: the **Bureau of Indian Affairs (BIA)** of the U.S. Department of the Interior. The BIA and its local superintendent controlled virtually all aspects of everyday life, including the reservation budget, the criminal justice system, and the schools. The BIA (again, not the tribes) even determined tribal membership.

The traditional leadership structures and political institutions of the tribes were ignored as the BIA executed its duties with little regard for, and virtually no input from, the people it supervised. The BIA superintendent of the reservations "ordinarily became the most powerful influence on local Indian affairs, even though he was a government employee, not responsible to the Indians but to his superiors in Washington" (Spicer, 1980, p. 117). The superintendent controlled the food supply and communications with the world outside the reservation and used it to reward cooperative tribal members and punish those who were not.

Coercive Acculturation: The Dawes Act and Boarding Schools

Consistent with Blauner's hypothesis, Native Americans on the reservations were subjected to coercive acculturation or forced Americanization. Their culture was attacked, their languages and religions forbidden, and their institutions circumvented and undermined. The centerpiece of U.S. Indian policy was the **Dawes Allotment Act of 1887**, a deeply flawed attempt to impose white definitions of land ownership by dividing Native American land into smaller units that the government gave to individuals, thus weakening and circumventing the tribe.

The intention was to give each Indian family the means to survive as their white neighbors did and to encourage Native people to assimilate into the larger white society. Once the U.S. government allotted the land, it sold the rest to non-Native settlers. By allotting land to families and individuals, the legislation destroyed the broader kinship, clan, and tribal social structures and replaced them with Western systems that emphasized individualism and profit (Cornell, 1988, p. 80). In many ways, this policy attacked Native American cultures by reorganizing tribal communities.

The U.S. government allotted about 140 million acres to Native Americans in 1887. By the 1930s, nearly 90 million of those acres—almost 65%—had been lost. Most of the remaining land was desert or otherwise nonproductive and would not be able to support their communities. From the standpoint of the Indian nations, the Dawes Allotment Act was a disaster and a further erosion of their limited resources (for more details, see Josephy, 1968; Lurie, 1982; McNickle, 1973; Treuer, 2019; Wax, 1971).

Additionally, coercive acculturation operated through a variety of other avenues. Whenever possible, the BIA sent Native American children to boarding schools, sometimes hundreds of miles away from parents and other kin, where they were required to speak English, convert to Christianity, and become educated in the ways of Western civilization, such as dressing in Western-style clothing (Jacobs, 2009). Consistent with the Blauner (1972) hypothesis, tribal languages, dress, and religion were forbidden, and to the extent that native cultures were mentioned at all, they were attacked and ridiculed. Children of different tribes were mixed together as roommates to speed the acquisition of English. When school wasn't in session, children were often boarded with local white families, usually as unpaid domestic helpers or farmhands, and prevented from visiting their families and revitalizing their tribal ties (Hoxie, 1984; Spicer, 1980; Wax, 1971).

The Indian Reorganization Act (IRA)

By the 1930s, the failure of the reservation system and the policy of forced assimilation had become obvious to all who cared to observe. The quality of life for Native Americans had not improved, and there was little economic development, as well as fewer job opportunities, on the reservations. Health care was woefully inadequate, and education levels lagged far behind national standards.

The plight of Native Americans eventually found a sympathetic ear in the administration of Franklin D. Roosevelt, who was elected president in 1932, and John Collier, the man he appointed to run the BIA. Collier was knowledgeable about Native American issues and concerns and was instrumental in securing the passage of the **Indian Reorganization Act (IRA)** in 1934.

This landmark legislation contained a number of significant provisions for Native Americans and broke sharply with the federal policies of the past. In particular, the IRA rescinded the Dawes Act of 1887 and the policy of individualizing tribal lands. It also provided means by which the tribes could expand their landholdings. Many of the mechanisms of coercive Americanization in the school system and elsewhere were dismantled. Financial aid in various forms and expertise were made available for the economic development of the reservations. In perhaps the most significant departure from earlier policy, the IRA proposed an increase in Native American self-governance and a reduction of the paternalistic role of the BIA and other federal agencies.

Although sympathetic to Native Americans, the IRA had its limits and shortcomings. Many of its intentions were never realized, and the empowerment of the tribes wasn't unqualified. The move to self-governance generally took place on the dominant group's terms and in conformity with the values and practices of white society. For example, the proposed increase in the decision-making power of the tribes was contingent on their adoption of Anglo American political forms, including secret ballots, majority rule, and written constitutions. These were alien concepts to those tribes that selected leaders by procedures other than popular election (e.g., leaders might be chosen by councils of elders) or that made decisions by open discussion and consensus building (i.e., decisions required the agreement of everyone with a voice in the process, not a simple majority). The incorporation of these Western forms illustrates the basically assimilationist intent of the IRA.

The IRA had variable effects on Native American women. In tribes dominated by men, the IRA gave women new rights to participate in elections, run for office, and hold leadership roles. In other cases, new political structures replaced traditional ones, some of which, as in the Iroquois culture, had given women considerable power. Although the political effects were variable, the programs funded by the IRA provided opportunities for women on many reservations to receive education and training for the first time. Many of these opportunities were oriented toward domestic tasks and other roles traditionally done by Western women, but some prepared Native American women for jobs outside the family and off the reservation, such as clerical work and nursing (Evans, 1989, pp. 208–209).

In summary, the IRA of 1934 was a significant improvement over prior federal policies but was bolder and more sympathetic to Native Americans in intent than in implementation. On the one hand, not all tribes could take advantage of the opportunities provided by the legislation, and some ended up being further victimized. For example, in the Hopi tribe, located in the Southwest, the Act allowed a Westernized group of Native Americans to be elected to leadership roles, with the result that dominant group firms were allowed to have access to the mineral resources, farmland, and water rights controlled by the tribe. The resultant development generated wealth for the white firms and their Hopi allies, but most of the tribe continued to languish in poverty (Churchill, 1985, pp. 112–113). On the other hand, some tribes prospered (at least comparatively speaking) under the IRA. One impoverished, landless group of Cherokee in Oklahoma acquired land, equipment, and expert advice through the IRA, and between 1937 and 1949, they developed a prosperous, largely debt-free farming community (Debo, 1970, pp. 294–300). Many tribes remained suspicious of the IRA, and by 1948, fewer than 100 tribes had voted to accept its provisions.

The Termination Policy

The IRA's stress on the legitimacy of tribal identity seemed un-American to many Anglos. The federal government faced constant pressure to return to an individualistic policy that encouraged (or required) Americanization. Some viewed the tribal structures and communal property-holding patterns as relics of an earlier era and as impediments to modernization and development. Not incidentally, some whites still coveted the remaining Indian lands and resources, which could be more easily exploited if property ownership were individualized.

In 1953, the assimilationist forces won a victory when Congress passed a resolution calling for an end to the reservation system and to the special relationships between the tribes and the federal government. The proposed policy, called **termination**, was intended to get the federal government "out of the Indian business." It rejected the IRA and proposed a return to the system of private land ownership imposed on the tribes by the Dawes Act. Horrified at the notion of termination, the tribes opposed the policy strongly and vociferously. Under this policy, all special relationships—including treaty obligations—between the federal government and the tribes would end. Tribes would no longer exist as legally recognized entities, and tribal lands and other resources would be placed in private hands (Josephy, 1968, pp. 353–355).

The government terminated about 100 tribes, most of them small. In virtually all cases, the termination process was administered hastily, and fraud, misuse of funds, and other injustices were common. The Menominee of Wisconsin and the Klamath on the West Coast were the two largest tribes that were terminated. Both suffered devastating economic losses and precipitous declines in quality of life. Neither tribe had the business or tax base needed to finance the services (e.g., health care and schooling) formerly provided by the federal government, and both were forced to sell land, timber, and other scarce resources to maintain minimal standards of living. Many poor Native American families were forced to turn to local and state agencies, which placed severe strain on welfare budgets. The experience of the Menominee was so disastrous that, at the concerted request of the tribe, reservation status was restored in 1973; for the Klamath, it was restored in 1986 (Raymer, 1974; Snipp, 1996, p. 394; Treuer, 2019, pp. 263–267).

Relocation and Urbanization

At about the same time the termination policy came into being, the government established various programs to encourage Native Americans to move to urban areas. The movement to cities had already begun in the 1940s, spurred by the availability of factory jobs during World War II. In the 1950s, the movement was further encouraged with programs of assistance and by the declining government support for economic development on the reservation, the most dramatic example of which was the policy of termination (Green, 1999, p. 265). Centers for Native Americans were established in many cities, and various services (e.g., job training, housing assistance, English instruction) were offered to assist in the adjustment to urban life.

Figure 6.3 shows the urbanization of the Native American population. Note the rapid increase in the movement to cities beginning in the 1950s. More than 70% of all Native Americans are now urbanized, and since 1950, Indians have urbanized faster than the general population. Nevertheless, Native Americans are still the least urbanized minority group. The population as a whole is about 80% urbanized; in contrast, African Americans are about 90% urbanized (see Figure 5.8).

Like African Americans, Native Americans arrived in the cities after the mainstream economy began to de-emphasize blue-collar or manufacturing jobs. Because of their relatively low average levels of educational attainment and their racial and cultural differences, Native Americans in cities tended to encounter the same problems African

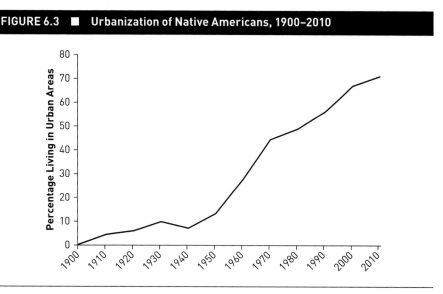

FIGURE 6.3 ■ Urbanization of Native Americans, 1900–2010

Source: For 1900–1990 (Thornton, 2001, p. 1420), for 2000 and 2010 (U.S. Bureau of the Census, 2013f).

Americans and other minority groups of color experienced: high rates of unemployment, inadequate housing, and all the other travails of the urban underclass.

Native American women also migrated to cities in considerable numbers. The discrimination, unemployment rates, and poverty of the urban environment often made it difficult for Native American men to be the "breadwinner" of their families. Therefore, women sought employment to financially support their families. The difficulties inherent in combining child rearing and a job outside the home were compounded by isolation from the support networks provided by extended family and clans back on the reservations. Nevertheless, one study found that Native American women in cities continued to practice their traditional cultures and maintain the tribal identity of their children (Joe & Miller, 1994, p. 186).

Native Americans living in cities are, on average, better off than those living on reservations, where unemployment can reach 80% or even 90%. The improvement is relative, however. Although many individual Native Americans prosper in the urban environment, income figures for urban Native Americans are comparable to those of African Americans and well below those of whites. Native American unemployment rates run much higher than the national average. For example, in the first half of 2010, unemployment for all Native Americans was about 15%, comparable to the rate for African Americans (see Figure 5.3) and 67% higher than that of whites (Austin, 2010). Thus, moving to cities often meant trading rural poverty for the urban variety, with little net improvement in life chances.

Native Americans will probably remain more rural than other minority groups for years to come. Despite the poverty and lack of opportunities for schooling and jobs, the reservation offers some advantages in services and lifestyle. On the reservation, people may have opportunities for political participation and leadership roles that aren't available in cities where Native Americans are a tiny minority. Reservations also offer kinfolk, friends, religious services, and tribal celebrations (Snipp, 1989, p. 84). Lower levels of education, work experience, and financial resources combine with the prejudice, discrimination, and racism of the larger society to lower the chances of success in cities and will probably sustain a continuing return to the reservations.

Although the economic benefits of urbanization have been slim for the group as a whole, other advantages have accrued from life in cities. It was much easier to establish networks of friendship and affiliation across tribal lines in the cities, and urban Indians have been one of the sources of strength and personnel for a movement of protest that began early in the 20th century. Virtually all the organizational vehicles of Native American protest have had urban roots.

Self-Determination

The termination policy aroused so much opposition from Native Americans and was such an obvious disaster that the pressure to push tribes to termination faded in the late 1950s, although the act itself wasn't repealed until 1975. Since the 1960s, federal Indian policy has generally returned to the tradition set by the IRA. Termination and forced assimilation continue to be officially rejected, and within limits, the tribes have been granted more freedom to find their own way of relating to the larger society at their own pace.

Several federal programs and laws have benefited the tribes during the past few decades, including the antipoverty and "Great Society" campaigns launched in the 1960s. In 1970, President Richard Nixon affirmed the government's commitment to fulfilling treaty obligations and the right of the tribes to self-governance. The Indian Self-Determination and Education Assistance Act was passed in 1975. This legislation increased aid to reservation schools and Native American students and increased tribal control over the administration of the reservations, from police forces to schools to road maintenance.

The Self-Determination Act primarily benefited the larger tribes and those that had well-established administrative and governing structures. Smaller and less-organized tribes have continued to rely heavily on the federal government (Snipp, 1996, p. 394). Nonetheless, in many cases, this new phase of federal policy has allowed Native American tribes to plot their own courses free of paternalistic regulation and, just as important, it gave them the tools and resources to address their problems and improve their situations. Decision making was returned to local authorities, who were "held more accountable to local needs, conditions, and cultures than outsiders" (Taylor & Kalt, 2005, p. xi).

In the view of many, self-determination is a key reason for the recent improvements in the status of Native Americans. We'll look at some of these developments after examining the Native American protest movement.

PROTEST AND RESISTANCE

Early Efforts

As BIA-administered reservations and coercive Americanization came to dominate tribal life in the early 20th century, new forms of Indian activism appeared. The modern protest movement was tiny at first and, with few exceptions, achieved a measure of success only in recent decades. In fact, the Native American protest movement in the past wasn't so much unsuccessful as simply ignored. The movement has focused on several complementary goals: protecting Native American resources and treaty rights, striking a balance between assimilation and pluralism, and finding a relationship with the dominant group that would permit a broader array of life chances without sacrificing tribal identity and heritage.

Formally organized Native American protest organizations have existed since the 1910s, but the modern phase of the protest movement began during World War II. Many Native Americans served in the military or moved to cities to take jobs in aid of the war effort and were thereby exposed to the world beyond the reservation. Also, political activism on reservations, which had been stimulated by the IRA, continued through the war years, as the recognition of problems common across tribal lines grew.

These trends helped stimulate the founding of the National Congress of American Indians (NCAI) in 1944. This organization was pan-tribal (i.e., included members from many different tribes); 50 different tribes and reservations attended its first convention (Cornell, 1988, p. 119). The leadership consisted largely of Native Americans educated and experienced in the white world. However, the NCAI's program stressed the importance of preserving traditional tribal institutions and cultural practices as well as protecting Indian welfare. An early victory for the NCAI and its allies came in 1946, when the federal government created an Indian Claims Commission. This body was authorized to hear claims brought by the tribes with regard to treaty violations. The commission has since settled hundreds of claims, resulting in awards of millions of dollars to the tribes (Weeks, 1988, pp. 261–262).

In the 1950s and 1960s, the protest movement was further stimulated by the threat of termination and by the increasing number of Native Americans living in the cities who developed friendships across tribal lines. Awareness of common problems, rising levels of education, and the examples set by the successful protests of other minority groups also increased readiness for collective action.

Red Power

By the 1960s and 1970s, Native American protest groups were finding ways to express their grievances and problems to the nation. The Red Power movement, similar to the Black Power movement (see Chapter 5), encompassed a coalition of groups, many considerably more assertive than the NCAI, and a varied collection of ideas, most of which stressed self-determination and pride in race and cultural heritage. Red Power protests included a "fish-in" in Washington in 1965, an episode that also illustrates the nature of Native American demands. The state of Washington had tried to limit the fishing rights of several different tribes because the supply of fish was diminishing and needed to be protected. The tribes depended on fishing for subsistence and survival, and they argued that their right to fish had been guaranteed by treaties signed in the 1850s and it was the pollution and commercial fishing of the dominant society that had depleted the supply of fish. They organized a "fish-in" in violation of the state's policy and were met by a contingent of police officers and other law officials. Violent confrontations and mass arrests ensued. Three years later, after a lengthy and expensive court battle, the tribes were vindicated, and the U.S. Supreme Court confirmed their treaty rights to fish the rivers of Washington (Nabakov, 1999, pp. 362–363).

Another widely publicized episode took place in 1969, when Native Americans from various tribes occupied Alcatraz Island in San Francisco Bay, then the site of a closed federal prison. The protesters acted based on an old law granting Native Americans the right to reclaim abandoned federal land. The occupation of Alcatraz was organized in part by the American Indian Movement (AIM), founded in 1968. More militant and radical than the previously established protest groups, AIM uncompromising and courageously confronted the BIA, the police, and other forces they saw as repressive. With the backing of AIM and other groups, the activists occupied Alcatraz for nearly four years and generated significant publicity for the Red Power movement and the difficulties facing Native Americans.

In 1972, AIM helped organize a march on Washington, DC, called the Trail of Broken Treaties. Marchers came from many tribes and represented both urban and reservation Indians. The intent of the marchers was to dramatize the problems of the tribes. The leaders offered a 20-point position paper that demanded the abolition of the BIA, the return of illegally taken land, and increased self-governance for the tribes, among other things. When they reached Washington, some of the marchers forcibly occupied the BIA offices. Property was damaged (by which side is disputed), and records and papers were destroyed. The marchers eventually surrendered, and none of their demands were met.

The following year, AIM occupied the village of Wounded Knee in South Dakota to protest the violation of treaty rights. Wounded Knee was the site of the last armed confrontation between Native Americans and whites in 1890 and was selected by AIM for its deep symbolic significance. The occupation lasted more than two months and involved several armed confrontations with federal authorities. Again, the protest ended without the federal government meeting any of the demands made by the Native American leadership (Olson & Wilson, 1984, pp. 172–175).

FOCUS ON CONTEMPORARY ISSUES
WERE NATIVE AMERICANS THE VICTIMS OF GENOCIDE?

By 1900, Native Americans had lost at least 75% of their population base and numbered fewer than 250,000 people. There's no question that Native Americans suffered untold horrors during the contact period, but does it constitute genocide? Was there a deliberate attempt to destroy Native Americans and their culture(s)? Or was the population loss simply a tragic, unavoidable result of a clash of civilizations?

According to a resolution adopted by the United Nations in 1948, *genocide* consists of acts "committed with the intent to destroy, in whole or in part, a national, ethnic, racial, or religious group" (United Nations, 1948). In addition to killing, it includes other actions such as serious bodily or mental harm or the creation of conditions designed to destroy the group.

The concepts you've learned so far apply to the discussion of genocide, since genocide involves a dominant–minority group situation in which the dominant group views the minority group with contempt, racism, or extreme prejudice. Power, a key component in the Noel hypothesis, is an essential element in genocide. To pursue the mass extermination of the minority group, the dominant group must have power.

Before addressing Native Americans, let's briefly consider some well-known historical examples of genocide to provide some comparison and context. Unfortunately, there are many instances from which to draw.

As you learned in Chapter 2, the best-known genocide was the effort of German Nazis to exterminate Jews, Slavs, Gypsies, and other "inferior" groups before and during World War II. They systematically killed millions of people, including 6 million Jews. This massive, highly bureaucratized, and rationally organized genocide was motivated and "justified" by deep racism and anti-Semitism. Nazi ideology demonized Jews and characterized them as a separate, lesser, contemptible race that had to be destroyed for the good of all "proper" Germans and for the health of the Third Reich.

A more recent genocide occurred in the early 1990s in the tiny African nation of Rwanda. The two main ethnic groups, Hutus and Tutsis, had a long history of mutual enmity that had been exacerbated by their German and Belgian colonial rulers' policy of "divide and conquer." The colonizers gave the Hutus a privileged status, and their greater power continued after Rwanda

(Continued)

(Continued)

became independent in 1962. The sporadic clashes between the tribal groups blossomed into full-blown genocide in 1994, prompted by a Tutsi-led rebellion and the death of the Hutu president of Rwanda in a plane crash that people thought resulted from Tutsi sabotage.

The slaughter that ensued resulted in the deaths of approximately 800,000 Tutsis (perhaps many more), including pregnant women, children, and the elderly. Much of the killing was done by "regular people" such as neighbors and acquaintances with bare hands or machetes. Hutu-controlled radio encouraged the killing by characterizing the Tutsi as "cockroaches" and worse (see Gourevitch, 1999). This language expresses the dominant group's prejudice and contempt for the minority group. Further, it erases the humanity of the victimized group, maximizing their "otherness," which facilitates their murder.

How does the history of Native Americans compare? As noted previously, genocide must include an intention to exterminate the group, as opposed to, for example, killing enemy combatants in battle. The Nazis openly expressed the desire for the "final solution," the extermination of the Jewish people. Hutus that led the Rwandan genocide meant to annihilate the Tutsi. What was the intent of whites regarding Indigenous people?

Some whites clearly wanted to eliminate Native Americans. For example, in 1864, troops under the command of Colonel John Chivington attacked a Cheyenne village near Sand Creek, Colorado. They killed several hundred Indians, most of them women, children, and old men. The incident is sometimes called the Massacre at Sand Creek, but what makes it a candidate for genocide is Chivington's motivation. He said: "My intention is to kill all Indians I come across," including babies and infants, because 'nits make lice' (Churchill, 1997).

However, some whites expressed sympathy for the plight of Native Americans and outrage over incidents such as Sand Creek (Lewy, 2004). Some researchers have noted that, in the 19th century, such sentiments were strongest in places furthest from battle. Nevertheless, there's no reason to suspect its sincerity. (That said, as in the case of the Dawes Act or other policies, sympathy without understanding of Native American culture was often harmful.) So, while it is abundantly clear that some—perhaps most—whites wanted to exterminate all Native Americans, that sentiment wasn't unanimous.

Additionally, we must consider the reasons for Native American population loss. Diseases brought by European colonists caused much of the population decline. While there were some instances of "biological warfare," such as deliberately infecting Indians with smallpox, for the most part, diseases simply took their toll unguided by intention or deliberate plan (Lewy, 2004).

Some people argue that the intent to exterminate was implicit in the coercive, one-sided assimilation that was the centerpiece of policies such as the Dawes Act and institutions such as Indian boarding schools. If these policies had succeeded, they would have completely destroyed the Native American way of life, even if some descendants of the tribes survived. We could view deliberate attempts to destroy the food base (e.g., by slaughtering buffalo herds on the Great Plains) and to move Indian tribes from their homelands as attempts to create living conditions so impoverished and horrific that they would result in a massive loss of life. The intention to exterminate does not have to be overtly stated to be effective or to have that result.

It's important to use the term *genocide* judiciously, lest we dilute its significance through overuse. However, it's also important to be clear about what happened to Native Americans and not minimize their experiences of tremendous suffering and loss. Did Europeans carry out a genocide against Indigenous people? Scholars, activists, and others have made that case for classifying it as genocide (see, for example, Churchill, 1997; Stannard, 1992). Others argue that the case for genocide is weakened by the fact that most of the population loss was caused by the impersonal spread of disease, not by intentional physical assault or other forms of violence (Lewy, 2004).

Did Native Americans, as a group, nearly disappear? Yes. Was there intent to exterminate this group? Yes—at least among many dominant group members. Did the U.S. government create conditions for the conquered tribes that were so desperate that they resulted—directly or indirectly—in widespread loss of life? Yes, in many instances and for many years. The story of Native Americans doesn't feature state-sponsored slaughter like the Nazi Holocaust or the bloody person-to-person violence of the Rwandan genocide. Perhaps Native Americans did not experience genocide by the literal letter of the law. The results, however, are the same.

In 2016, Native Americans carried out their biggest protest of the last 40 years in opposition to the DAPL, a 1,172-mile oil pipeline running through North Dakota and parts of Illinois (Dakota Access, LLC, n.d.; Healy, 2016a; McCown, 2018). The first proposed route threatened populous (mostly white) residential areas and city water systems, leading the U.S. Corps of Engineers to recommend an alternate route approximately one-half mile north of the Standing Rock Sioux Reservation on land taken from them in 1958 (McKibben, 2016; Meyer, 2017a).

DAPL was fast-tracked and received exemptions from the National Environmental Policy Act and the Clean Water Act. The company behind DAPL, Energy Transfer Partners (ETP), said it would create thousands of jobs and be safer than other pipelines (McKibben, 2016; Meyer, 2017a; Mufson, 2016). The Standing Rock Sioux (SRS) expressed concerns about the potential impact of an oil spill. Several federal agencies were apprehensive, too; for example, the Department of the Interior said the pipeline's location was a "serious concern" (Sammon, 2016).

The Great Sioux Nation tribes, including the Sioux, Lakota, Oglala, and others, argued that the pipeline threatened 380 archeological and sacred sites, including burial grounds, along its route (Matas, 2016). Therefore, it threatened Native American culture(s) (McKibben, 2016). Thousands of Native Americans from more than 100 tribes, and other Indigenous people from around the world, began living at three protest camps in North Dakota (McKibben, 2016; Sammon, 2016). Nonindigenous people gave them support, including 2,100 U.S. military veterans offering to act as human shields in the wake of the U.S. government's militarized police force (Healy, 2016b; Veterans for Standing Rock, n.d.). Thousands more protested around the world and donated money to help with legal fees and supplies (e.g., blankets, generators, eye protection against tear gas). More than a million people signed petitions asking the U.S. government to end the project and banks to stop funding it (Amazon Watch, 2017). Tensions between protestors and law enforcement often ran high, with police turning to pepper spray, dogs, tear gas, and water cannons to quell protests. Hundreds of people were arrested and injured (Healy, 2016a) and the governor of North Dakota called in the National Guard (Sammon, 2016).

The DAPL conflict illustrates familiar concerns about land treaties, Native American sacred sites, and cultural preservation. Calling themselves *water protectors*, the tribes repeatedly sued the federal government, ETP, and its subsidiaries to prevent the pipeline's construction. They argued that the land is theirs—and sacred—noting that the U.S. Government had broken the 1851 and 1868 Laramie Treaties that gave them the land west of the Missouri River (McKibben, 2016).

In September 2016, a court order temporarily halted construction; however, a federal judge rejected the SRS's petition to end construction. In response, the U.S. Department of the Interior, the Department of Justice, and the Department of the Army asked ETP to voluntarily halt construction until it could confirm if DAPL would break National Environmental Policy Act rules. The SRS made other efforts to halt construction, each rejected by the courts. ETP ignored these requests (Sammon, 2016). In June 2017, a judge ruled that the federal investigation of "the impacts of an oil spill on fishing rights, hunting rights, or environmental justice" was "particularly deficient" and ordered a new study (Meyer, 2017a). Protests and legal efforts to stop construction continued, but the pipeline was built; it now carries about 500,000 barrels of crude oil per day (Dakota Access, LLC, n.d.; Hand, 2017; Healy, 2016a; Hult, 2017; McCown, 2018; Sawyer, 2017).

PROTEST AND PRESERVATION OF NATIVE AMERICAN CULTURES

Ironically, the struggle for Red Power encouraged assimilation as well as pluralism. The movement linked members of different tribes and encouraged them to find common ground, often in the form of a collective Native American culture. Inevitably, the protests were conducted in English, and the grievances were expressed in ways that were understandable to white society, thus increasing the pressure to acculturate even while arguing for the survival of the tribes. Furthermore, successful protest required that Native Americans be fluent in English, trained in the law and other professions, skilled in dealing with bureaucracies, and knowledgeable about the formulation and execution of public policy. Native Americans who became proficient in these areas thereby took on the characteristics of their adversaries (Hraba, 1994, p. 235).

As the pan-tribal protest movement forged ties between members of diverse tribes, the successes of the movement along with changing federal policy and public opinion encouraged a rebirth of commitment to tribalism and "Indianness." Native Americans were simultaneously stimulated to assimilate (by stressing their common characteristics and creating organizational forms that united the tribes) and to retain a pluralistic relationship with the larger society (by working for self-determination and enhanced tribal power and authority). Thus, part of the significance of the Red Power movement was that it encouraged pan-tribal unity and tribal diversity (Olson & Wilson, 1984, p. 206). Today, Native Americans continue to seek ways of existing in the larger society that merges assimilation with pluralism.

Table 6.2 summarizes this discussion of federal policy and Indian protest. The left column shows the four major policy phases since the end of overt hostilities in 1890.

TABLE 6.2 ■ Federal Indian Policy and Indian Response				
Period	**Economic Impact**	**Political Impact**	**Tribal Response**	**Government Approach**
Reservation late 1800s–1930s	Land loss (Dawes Act) and welfare dependency	Government control of reservation and coerced acculturation	Some resistance; growth of religious movements	Individualistic; creation of self-sufficient farmers
Reorganization (IRA) 1930s and 1940s	Stabilized land base and supported some development of reservation	Established federally sponsored tribal governments	Increased political participation in many tribes; some pan-tribal activity	Incorporated tribes as groups; creation of self-sufficient "Americanized" communities
Termination and Relocation late 1940s–early 1960s	Withdrawal of government support for reservations; promotion of urbanization	New assault on tribes; new forms of coercive acculturation	Increased pan-tribalism; widespread and intense opposition to termination	Individualistic; dissolved tribal ties and promoted incorporation into the modern, urban labor market
Self-Determination 1960s to present	Developed reservation economies; increased integration of Indian labor force	Support for tribal governments	Greatly increased political activity	Incorporated tribes as self-sufficient communities with access to federal programs of support and welfare

Source: Based on Cornell, Kalt, Krepps, and Taylor (1998, p. 5).

The next two columns show the thrust of the government's economic and political policies, followed by a brief characterization of tribal response. The last column shows the changing bases for federal policy, sometimes aimed at weakening tribal structures and individualizing Native Americans, and sometimes (including most recently) aimed at working with and preserving tribal structures.

QUESTIONS FOR REFLECTION

4. What are the major phases in Indigenous–white relations since the 1890s? What laws and federal policies shaped these changes? How did Indigenous Americans respond?

5. Compare the Red Power movement with the Black Power movement. How were the similarities and differences shaped by the groups' situations?

CONTEMPORARY NATIVE AMERICAN–WHITE RELATIONS

Conflicts between Native Americans and the larger society are far from over. Although the days of deadly battle are (with rare exceptions) long gone, the remaining issues are serious, difficult to resolve, and, in their own way, still matters of life and death. Native Americans face enormous challenges in their struggle to improve their status, but—largely because of their greater freedom from stifling federal control since the 1970s—they also have some resources, some opportunities, and leadership that is talented and resourceful (Bordewich, 1996, p. 11).

Natural Resources

Ironically, land allotted to Native American tribes in the 19th century sometimes turned out to be rich in resources that became valuable in the 20th century. These resources include oil, natural gas, coal, and uranium—basic sources of energy in the larger society. In addition (and despite the devastation wreaked by the Dawes Act of 1887), some tribes hold titles to water rights, fishing rights, woodlands that could sustain a timber industry, and wilderness areas that could be developed for camping, hunting, and other forms of recreation. These resources are likely to become more valuable as the earth's natural resources and undeveloped areas are further depleted in the future.

The challenge Native Americans face is to retain control of these resources and to develop them for their own benefit. Threats to the remaining tribal lands and assets are common. Mining and energy companies continue to cast envious eyes on Native American land, and other tribal assets are coveted by real estate developers, fishers (recreational as well as commercial), backpackers and campers, and cities facing water shortages (Harjo, 1996).

Some tribes have succeeded in developing their resources for their own benefit, in part because of their increased autonomy and independence since the passage of the 1975 Indian Self-Determination Act. For example, the White Mountain Apaches of Arizona own a variety of enterprises, including a major ski resort and a casino (Cornell & Kalt, 1998, pp. 3–4). On many other reservations, however, even richer stores of resources lie dormant, awaiting the right combination of tribal leadership, expertise, and development capital.

On a broader level, tribes are banding together to share expertise and negotiate more effectively with the larger society. For example, 25 tribes founded the Council of Energy Resource Tribes in 1975 to coordinate and control the development of the mineral resources on reservation lands. Since its founding, the council has successfully negotiated a number of agreements with dominant group firms, increasing the flow of income to the tribes and raising their quality of life (Cornell, 1988; Snipp, 1989). The council now encompasses more than 50 tribes and several Canadian First Nations (Council of Energy Resource Tribes, n.d.).

Attracting Industry to the Reservation

Many efforts to develop the reservations have focused on creating jobs by attracting industry through such incentives as low taxes, low rents, and a low-wage pool of labor—not unlike the package of benefits offered to employers by less-industrialized nations in Asia, South America, and Africa. With some notable exceptions, these efforts have not been particularly successful (for a review, see Cornell, 2006; Vinje, 1996). Reservations are often so geographically isolated that transportation costs become prohibitive. The jobs that have materialized are typically low wage and have few benefits; often, non-Indians fill the more lucrative managerial positions. Thus, the opportunities for building economic power or improving the standard of living from these jobs are sharply limited. These new jobs may transform "the welfare poor into the working poor" (Snipp, 1996, p. 398), but their potential for raising economic vitality is low.

To illustrate the problems of developing reservations by attracting industry, consider the Navajo, the second-largest Native American tribe. The Navajo reservation spreads across Arizona, New Mexico, and Utah and encompasses about 20 million acres, an area a little smaller than either Indiana or Maine (see Figure 6.2). The reservation seems huge on a map, but much of the land is desert not suitable for farming or other uses. As they have for the past several centuries, the Navajo today rely heavily on the cultivation of corn and sheepherding for sustenance.

Most wage-earning jobs on the reservation are with the agencies of the federal government (e.g., the BIA) or with the tribal government. Tourism is a large industry, but the jobs are typically low wage and seasonal. There are reserves of coal, uranium, and oil on the reservation, but these resources have not generated many jobs. In some cases, the Navajo have resisted the damage to the environment that would be caused by mines and oil wells because of their traditional values and respect for the land. When exploitation of these resources has been allowed, the companies involved often use highly automated technologies that generate few jobs (Oswalt & Neely, 1996, pp. 317–351).

COMPARATIVE FOCUS
AUSTRALIAN ABORIGINES AND NATIVE AMERICANS

Each colonization situation has a unique history, but similar dynamics are at work. To illustrate, we'll compare the effect of European colonization on Australian Aborigines to the effect on Indigenous peoples of North America.

Australia came under European domination in the late 1700s, nearly two centuries after colonization of what would become the United States. Despite the time difference, the contact situations have commonalities: (1) Great Britain was the colonial power, (2) first contact occurred in the preindustrial era, and (3) indigenous groups were spread thinly across vast geographical areas and they lacked resources and technological development compared to the British (Diamond, 1998).

Aboriginal peoples lived in Australia 50,000 to 65,000 years before the British arrived. They were nomadic hunter–gatherers who lived in groups of 30 to 50 people connected by marriage or kinship and organized into 500 to 600 nations. Aborigines shared a common culture, including a belief system called *the dreaming* that explained the world and offered a moral

(Continued)

(Continued)

framework (Australian Government, 2015; Bodley, 2013, p. 41; Pettit, 2015).

Although early relations between the English and the Aborigines were hospitable, competition for land and other resources soon led to conflict (Pettit, 2015; Reynolds, 2006). The British equated *blackness* with inferiority (Smithers, 2008) and saw the Aborigines as savages. They disliked much about them; for example, Aborigines' use of spears to hunt, bodily adornment, nomadic ways, and their lack of desire for material wealth (Buchanan, 2005; Grey, 1841).

The contact situation became violent and included massacres, rape, and the forcible removal of indigenous people from their land. The Aborigines fought back but lacked British firepower. Disease, violence, loss of land, and malnutrition killed 90% to 95% of the Aboriginal population. Many people consider it genocide (Clements, 2014; Reynolds, 2006, p. 127).

The British pushed the remaining Aborigines into missions, reserves, and stations. Church-established missions attempted to "civilize" Aborigines. The government created unmanaged reserves where Aborigines could live as they had prior to colonization. Eventually, the government provided blankets and basic food—less out of concern for Aborigines' well-being than to keep Aborigines from killing settlers' cattle in "white areas". Government-supervised stations provided housing and basic job training (e.g., as servants; Choo, 2016; Commonwealth of Australia, 1997). However, station conditions were "appalling" and Aborigines suffered from malnutrition and poor health (Berndt & Berndt, 1987, p. xi; Peterson, 2005).

Between 1905 and 1969, the government took approximately 100,000[2] "half-caste" children from their families by "persuasion and threats" (Commonwealth of Australia, 1997, p. 34). Today, they are called the *Stolen Generation*. The stated goals of child removal laws were to protect "neglected" children, teach them "European values and work habits," and make them employable (p. 2).

The government focused on half-caste children that it believed it could absorb into the white population. It hoped that over time, "full-blooded natives" would be "eliminated." To ensure they "never saw their parents or families again," they changed children's names and took them far from home (Commonwealth of Australia, 1997, p. 24). Their lives were strictly controlled—for example, their hair was cut and their possessions taken. They worked during the day or went to school. At sundown, they were "locked up in dormitories" to discourage running away (p. 116). Breaking even minor rules resulted in the "strap" or being "put into jail" (e.g., solitary confinement; p. 71).

At the start of the 20th century, the Aboriginal (and Torres Strait Islander Australian) population was less than 100,000. In 2014, it was 686,800—about 3% of Australia's population. Numbers have increased, partly because of higher birth rates but also because changing attitudes make it easier for people to claim their Aboriginal heritage. Sixty-two percent of Aboriginal people identified with "a clan, tribal, or language group." Just over 1 in 3 (35%) live in cities while about 1 in 5 (21%) live in remote areas (Australian Bureau of Statistics, 2016).

Compared with the general population, Aborigines have less access to health care and higher rates of alcoholism, malnutrition, unemployment, and suicide. Their life expectancy is 12 years lower and 65% of the Aboriginal population reported long-term health problems. Only 26% had completed 12th grade (up from 20% in 2008) and 18% lived in overcrowded housing. More than one third (39%) reported experiencing discrimination (Australian Bureau of Statistics, 2016).

The issues facing the Australian Aborigines include the preservation of their culture and identity, self-determination and autonomy, the return of stolen lands, and an end to discrimination. Their history and their present situation support the Blauner and Noel hypotheses.

QUESTIONS FOR REFLECTION

6. Compare the contact situations of Native Americans and Australian Aborigines. In what ways were they colonized minorities?

7. Compare the contemporary situations of Native Americans and Australian Aborigines. Why do these differences exist?

8. What similarities and differences exist between the experiences of African Americans and Australian Aborigines? Between Australian Aborigines and racial minorities in Brazil? (See the Chapter 5 Comparative Focus.)

Figures 6.4 and 6.5 contrast Navajo income, poverty, and education with those of the general U.S. population. The poverty rate for the Navajo is almost three times greater than the national norm, and they are below national standards in terms of education, especially in terms of college education. Also, the median household income for the Navajo is only about 67% of household income for all Americans, and their per capita income is only 52% of the national norm.

FIGURE 6.4 ■ Poverty Rates and Educational Attainment for the Total Population, American Indians and Alaska Natives (AIAN), Navajo, and Choctaw, 2016

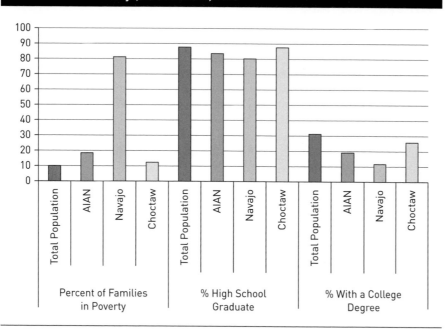

Source: U.S. Census Bureau (2017a).

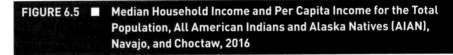

FIGURE 6.5   ■   Median Household Income and Per Capita Income for the Total Population, All American Indians and Alaska Natives (AIAN), Navajo, and Choctaw, 2016

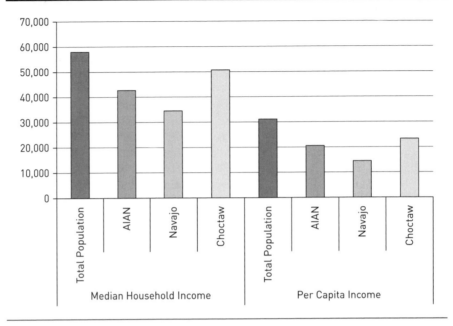

Source: U.S. Census Bureau (2017a).

However, some tribes have managed to achieve relative prosperity by bringing jobs to their people. The Choctaw Nation of Mississippi, for example, is one of the 10 largest employers in the state. Tribal leaders have been able to attract companies such as McDonald's and Ford Motor Company by promising (and delivering) high-quality labor for relatively low wages. The tribe runs many business enterprises, including two casinos. Incomes have risen; unemployment is relatively low; the tribe has built schools, hospitals, and a television station; and it administers numerous other services for its members (Mississippi Band of Choctaw Indians, 2017).

The poverty rate for the Choctaw is about one third that of the Navajo (although still higher than the national norm), and their educational level approaches the national standard for high school education and is much closer to the national standard for college education than are those of the Navajo or Native Americans generally. Median household income for the Choctaw is almost 90% of the national norm and more than $16,000 greater than the median income for the Navajo.

The Choctaw are not the most affluent tribe, and the Navajo are far from being the most destitute. They illustrate the mixture of partial successes and failures that typify efforts to bring prosperity to the reservations; together, these two cases suggest that attracting industry and jobs to the reservations is a possible—but difficult and uncertain—strategy for economic development.

It is worth repeating that self-determination—the ability of tribes to control development on the reservation—seems to be one of the important keys to success. Tribes such as the Choctaw have, in a sense, developed ethnic enclaves (see Chapter 2) in which they can capitalize on local networks of interpersonal relationships. As with other groups that have followed this strategy, success in the enclave depends on solidarity and group cohesion, not Americanization and integration (see Cornell, 2006).

Broken Treaties

For many tribes, the treaties signed with the federal government in the 19th century offer another potential resource. These treaties were often violated by white settlers, the military, state and local governments, the BIA, and other elements and agencies of the dominant group, and many tribes are pursuing this trail of broken treaties and seeking compensation for the wrongs of the past. For example, in 1972, the Passamaquoddy and Penobscot tribes filed a lawsuit demanding the return of 12.5 million acres of land—an area more than half the size of Maine—and $25 billion in damages. The tribes argued that this land had been illegally taken from them more than 150 years earlier. After eight years of litigation, the tribes settled for a $25 million trust fund and 300,000 acres of land. Although far less than their original demand, the award gave the tribes control over resources that could be used for economic development, job creation, upgrading educational programs, and developing other programs that would enhance human and financial capital (Worsnop, 1992, p. 391).

Virtually every tribe has similar grievances and, if pursued successfully, the long-dead treaty relationship between the Indian nations and the government could be a significant fount of economic and political resources. Of course, lawsuits require considerable (and expensive) legal expertise and years of effort before they bear fruit. Because there are no guarantees of success, this avenue has some sharp limitations and risks.

Gaming and Other Development Possibilities

Another resource for Native Americans is the gambling industry, the development of which was made possible by federal legislation passed in 1988. There are currently almost 500 tribally owned gaming establishments (National Indian Gaming Commission, 2018a), and the industry has grown many times over, from almost $5 billion in revenue in 1995 to over $32 billion in 2017 (National Indian Gaming Commission, 2018b). Figure 6.6 charts the growth in revenue from gaming on Native American reservations from 1995 to 2017.

Most operations are relatively small in scale. The 21 largest Indian casinos—about 5% of all Indian casinos—generate almost 40% of the total income from gaming, and the 74 smallest operations—about 17% of all Indian casinos—account for less than 1% of the income (National Indian Gaming Commission, 2011).

The single most profitable Indian gambling operation is the Foxwoods Casino in Connecticut, operated by the Pequot tribe. The casino is one of the largest in the world and generates more revenue than the casinos of Atlantic City. The tribe uses casino profits to benefit tribal members in many ways, including repurchasing tribal lands and providing housing assistance, medical benefits, educational scholarships, and

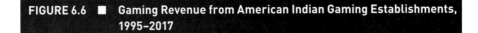

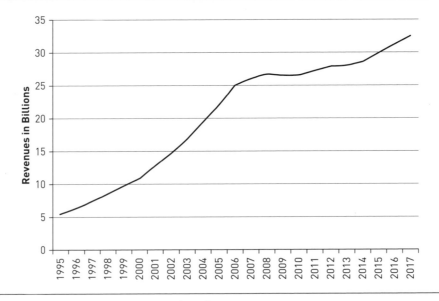

FIGURE 6.6 ■ Gaming Revenue from American Indian Gaming Establishments, 1995–2017

Source: National Indian Gaming Commission (2018b).

public services such as a tribal police force. Other tribes use gambling profits to buy restaurants and marinas and to finance the development of outlet malls, manufacturing plants, and other businesses (Bordewich, 1996; Spilde, 2001).

The power of gaming to benefit the tribes is suggested by the information displayed in Table 6.3, which shows that on a number of indicators, both gaming and nongaming reservations enjoyed significant improvements in their quality of life in the last decade of the 20th century, but the gaming reservations improved more rapidly. For example, all

TABLE 6.3 ■ Various Indicators of Improvement on Gaming vs. Nongaming Reservations, 1990–2000

Indicator	Nongaming	Gaming	United States
Per capita income	+21%	+36%	+11%
Family poverty	−7%	−12%	−1%
Unemployment	−2%	−5%	−1%
High school graduates	−1%	+2%	−1%
College graduates	+2%	+3%	+4%

Source: Adapted from Taylor and Kalt (2005, p. xi). Copyright 2011 The Harvard Project on American Indian Economic Development and Harvard University. All Rights Reserved.

reservations increased their per capita income faster than the nation as a whole (+11%), but gaming reservations improved faster (+36%) than nongaming reservations (+21%). (For a more pessimistic view of the benefits of gaming, see Guedel, 2014.)

Various tribes have sought other ways to capitalize on their freedom from state regulation and taxes. Some have established small but profitable businesses selling cigarettes tax free. Also, because they are not subject to state and federal environmental regulations, some reservations are exploring the possibility of housing nuclear waste and other refuse of industrialization—a somewhat ironic and not altogether attractive use of the remaining Indian lands.

Clearly, the combination of increased autonomy, treaty rights, natural resources, and gambling means that Native Americans today have an opportunity to dramatically raise their standards of living and creatively take control of their own destinies. Some tribes have enjoyed enormous benefits, but for others, these assets remain merely a potential waiting to be actualized. Without denying the success stories or the improvements in recent years, the lives of many Native Americans continue to be limited by poverty and powerlessness, prejudice, and discrimination. We document these patterns in the next section.

Prejudice and Discrimination

Anti-Indian prejudice has been a part of American society since first contact. Historically, intense negative feelings (e.g., hatred, contempt) have been widespread, particularly during the heat of war. As you might expect, stereotypes of Native Americans have been common, too. During periods of conflict, one stereotype that seems particularly strong equates Native Americans with bloodthirsty, ferocious, cruel savages who are capable of all types of atrocities. A stereotype that juxtaposes that of the savage is "the noble Red Man" who lives in complete harmony with nature and who symbolizes goodwill and pristine simplicity (Bordewich, 1996, p. 34). Although the first stereotype tended to fade away as hostilities drew to a close, the latter image retains a good deal of strength in modern, popular culture's depictions of Native Americans and among environmentalist and new age spiritual organizations.

Many studies document the continued stereotyping of Native Americans in film, television, textbooks, cartoons, YouTube videos, and other places (for example, as "bucks" and "squaws," complete with headdresses, bows, tepees, war chants, and other symbols perceived as "Indian"; e.g., see Aleiss, 2005; Bird, 1999; Meek, 2006; Rouse & Hanson, 1991). These ideas become reproduced in other contexts such as Halloween or college parties, sporting events, or Thanksgiving reenactments. Most importantly these oversimplified, inaccurate portrayals obliterate the diversity of Native American culture and, as with any stereotype, can harm real people and prevent intergroup understanding.

The persistence of stereotypes and the extent to which they have become enmeshed in modern culture is illustrated by continuing controversies surrounding the names of athletic teams (e.g., the Washington Redskins, the Cleveland Indians, and the Atlanta Braves) and the use of Native American mascots, tomahawk "chops," and other practices offensive to many Native Americans. Protests have been held at athletic events to increase awareness of these derogatory depictions. These stereotypes have given rise to awareness campaigns such as "Not a Mascot" (#NotaMascot) and "Culture Not a Costume." Unfortunately, as was the case so often in the past, these protests have been attacked, ridiculed, or simply ignored. (To learn more, see this book's companion website, http://edge.sagepub.com/diversity6e)

Native Americans are often referred to in the past tense, as if they don't exist. Many history books begin the study of American history in Europe or with the "discovery" of America, omitting the millennia of civilization prior to the arrival of European explorers and colonizers. Contemporary portrayals of Native Americans, such as in the movie *Dances with Wolves* (Costner, 1990), are more sympathetic but still treat the tribes as part of a bucolic past forever lost, not as people with real problems in the present.

Relatively few studies of anti-Indian prejudice exist within the social science literature. Therefore, it is difficult to fully understand the changes that may have occurred over the past several decades. We don't know whether there has been a shift to more symbolic or modern forms of anti-Indian racism (as there has been for antiblack prejudice) or whether the stereotypes of Native Americans have declined in strength or changed in content.

One of the few records of national anti-Indian prejudice over time is that of social distance scale results (see Table 1.2). When the scales were first administered in 1926, Native Americans were ranked in the middle third of all groups (18th out of 28), near the same level as Southern and Eastern Europeans and slightly above Mexicans, another colonized group. The ranking of Native Americans remained stable until 1977, when there was a noticeable rise in their position relative to other groups. In the most recent polls, the rankings of Native Americans have remained stable, near the same level as Jews and Poles but below African Americans. These shifts may reflect a decline in levels of prejudice, a change from more overt forms to more subtle modern racism, or both. Remember, however, that the samples for the social distance research were college students, for the most part, and the results don't necessarily reflect trends in the general population (see also Hanson & Rouse, 1987; Smith & Dempsey, 1983).

Additionally, research is unclear about the severity or extent of discrimination against Native Americans. Certainly, the group's lower average levels of education limit their opportunities for upward mobility, choice of occupations, and range of income. This is a form of institutional discrimination in the sense that the opportunities to develop human capital are much less available to Native Americans than to much of the rest of the population.

In terms of individual discrimination or more overt forms of exclusion, there is simply too little evidence to sustain clear conclusions (Snipp, 1992, p. 363). The situation of Native American women is under-researched, but Snipp reports that, similar to their counterparts in other minority groups and the dominant group, they "are systematically paid less than their male counterparts in similar circumstances" (p. 363).

The very limited evidence available from social distance scales suggests that overt anti-Indian prejudice has declined, perhaps in parallel with antiblack prejudice. A great deal of stereotyping remains, however; and demeaning, condescending, or negative portrayals of Native Americans are common throughout the dominant culture. Institutional discrimination is a major barrier for Native Americans, who have not had access to opportunities for education and employment.

QUESTIONS FOR REFLECTION

9. Consider the issues of contemporary Native American–white relations addressed in this section. Which of these seems most important and why?

10. What is the single most important force shaping the situation of Native Americans over the past century? Why?

11. Compare antiblack prejudice with anti-Indian prejudice. How and why are the two forms of prejudice different? How has that prejudice influenced unique forms of discrimination? What similarities are useful to discuss?

12. Was the colonization of America a Native American genocide? Explain.

ASSIMILATION AND PLURALISM

In this section, we continue to assess the situation of Native Americans today using the same conceptual framework used in Chapter 6. Once again, please regard this material as an overview and as starting points for further research.

Compared with other groups, information about Native Americans is scant. Nonetheless, a relatively clear picture emerges. The portrait stresses a mixed picture: improvements for some, combined with continued colonization, marginalization, and impoverishment for others. Similar to African Americans, Native Americans can be found at every status and income level in the United States, but Indians living on reservations continue to be one of the most impoverished, marginalized groups in society. Native Americans as a group face ongoing discrimination and exclusion and continue the search for a meaningful course between assimilation and pluralism.

Acculturation

Despite more than a century of coercive Americanization, many tribes have been able to preserve at least a portion of their traditional cultures. For example, many tribal languages continue to be spoken on a daily basis. About 20% of American Indians and Alaska Natives (AIAN) speak a language other than English at home, about the same percentage as the total population. Figure 6.7 suggests the extent of language preservation. For many tribes, less than 10% of their members speak the tribal language at home. Some tribes, however, continue to speak their native language, including about 25% of Apache and half of Navajo.

While some Native American languages have survived, it seems that even the most widely spoken of these languages is endangered. One study (Krauss, 1996) estimates that only about 11% of the surviving 200 spoken languages are being taught by parents to their children in the traditional way and that most languages are spoken on a daily basis only by the older generation. Few, if any, people are left who speak only a tribal language. Treuer (A. Treuer, 2012, p. 80) reports that only 20 tribal languages in the U. S. and

Canada are spoken by children in significant numbers. If these patterns persist, Native Americans' languages will disappear as the generations change. A number of tribes have instituted programs to try to renew and preserve their language, along with other elements of their culture, but the success of these efforts is uncertain (Schmid, 2001, p. 25; see also D. Treuer, 2012, pp. 300–305).

Traditional culture is retained in other forms besides language. Religions and value systems, political and economic structures, and recreational patterns have all survived the military conquest and the depredations of reservation life, but each pattern has been altered by contact with the dominant group. Cornell (1987), for example, argues that the strong orientation to the group rather than the individual is being significantly affected by the "American dream" of personal material success.

The tendency to filter the impact of the larger society through continuing vital Native American culture is also illustrated by the Native American Church, an important Native American religion with more than 100 congregations across the nation.

This religion combines elements from both cultures, and church services freely mix Christian imagery and the Bible with attempts to seek personal visions by using peyote, a hallucinogenic drug. The latter practice is consistent with the spiritual and religious traditions of many tribes but clashes sharply with the laws and norms of the larger society. The difference in traditions has generated many skirmishes with the courts, and as recently as 2004, the right of the Native American Church to use peyote was upheld by the Supreme Court of Utah ("Utah Supreme Court Rules," 2004).

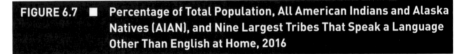

FIGURE 6.7 ■ Percentage of Total Population, All American Indians and Alaska Natives (AIAN), and Nine Largest Tribes That Speak a Language Other Than English at Home, 2016

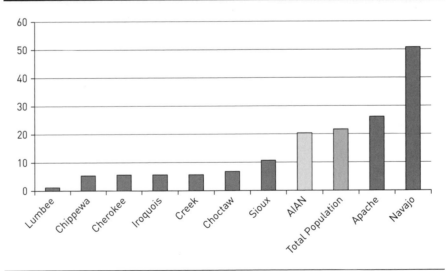

Note: Data for Blackfeet not available.

Source: U.S. Census Bureau (2017a).

Native Americans have been more successful than African Americans in preserving their traditional cultures, a pattern that is partly explained by the differences in the relationship between each minority group and the dominant group. African Americans were exploited for labor, whereas the competition with Native Americans involved land. African cultures could not easily survive because the social structures that transmitted the cultures and gave them meaning were largely destroyed by slavery and sacrificed to the exigencies of the plantation economy.

In contrast, Native Americans confronted the dominant group as tribal units, intact and whole. The tribes maintained integrity throughout the wars and throughout the reservation period. Tribal culture was attacked and denigrated during the reservation era, but the basic social unit that sustained the culture survived, albeit in altered form. The fact that Native Americans were placed on separate reservations, isolated from one another and the "contaminating" effects of everyday contact with the larger society, also supported the preservation of traditional languages and culture (Cornell, 1990).

The vitality of Indian cultures may have increased in the current atmosphere of greater tolerance and support for pluralism in the larger society, combined with increased autonomy and lower government regulation on the reservations. However, a number of social forces are working against pluralism and the continuing survival of tribal cultures. Pan-tribalism may threaten the integrity of individual tribal cultures as it represents Native American grievances and concerns to the larger society. Opportunities for jobs, education, and higher incomes draw Native Americans to more-industrialized urban areas and will continue to do so as long as the reservations are underdeveloped. Many aspects of the tribal cultures can be fully expressed and practiced only with other tribal members on the reservations. Thus, many Native Americans must make a choice between "Indian-ness" on the reservation and "success" in cities. The younger, more educated Native Americans will be most likely to confront this choice, and the future vitality of traditional Native American cultures and languages will hinge on which option they choose.

Secondary Structural Assimilation

This section assesses the degree of integration of Native Americans into the various institutions of public life, following the general outlines of the parallel section in Chapter 5.

Residential Patterns

Since the Indian Removal Act of 1830 (see Chapter 3), Native Americans have been concentrated in the western two thirds of the nation, as illustrated in Figure 6.8, although some pockets of population still can be found in the East. The states with the largest concentrations of Native Americans—California, Oklahoma, and Arizona—together include about 30% of all Native Americans. As Figure 6.8 illustrates, most U.S. counties have few Native American residents. The population is concentrated in eastern Oklahoma, the upper Midwest, and the Southwest (Norris et al., 2012, p. 8).

Because Native Americans are such a small, rural group, it is difficult to assess the overall level of residential segregation. An earlier study using 2000 census data found that they were less segregated than African Americans and that the levels of residential segregation had declined since 1980 (Iceland, Weinberg, & Steinmetz, 2002, p. 23). More detailed data from the 2000 census for the 10 metropolitan areas with the highest

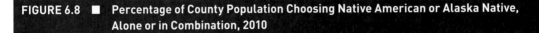

FIGURE 6.8 ■ Percentage of County Population Choosing Native American or Alaska Native, Alone or in Combination, 2010

Source: Norris, Vines, and Hoeffel (2012). Data from: U.S. Census Bureau, 2010 Census Redistricting Data (Public Law 94–171) Summary File, Table P1.

number of Native American residents show that residential segregation was "extremely high" (dissimilarity index at or above 60) in four of the cities (New York City, Phoenix, Albuquerque, and Chicago) but lower than the levels of black–white segregation. Also, a couple of the cities (Oklahoma City and Tulsa) had low scores, or a dissimilarity index at or below 30 (Social Science Data Analysis Network, n.d.).

What can we conclude? It seems that residential segregation for Native Americans is lower than it is for African Americans. However, it is difficult to declare firm conclusions because of the small size of the group and the fact that 30% of Native Americans live on rural reservations, where the levels of isolation and racial segregation are quite high.

School Integration and Educational Attainment

As a result of the combined efforts of missionaries and federal agencies, Native Americans have had a long but not necessarily productive acquaintance with Western education. Until the past few decades, schools for Native Americans were primarily focused on Americanizing children, not so much on educating them.

For many tribes, the percentage of high school graduates has increased in the recent past, but Native Americans' graduation rates are still somewhat below national rates and the rates of non-Hispanic whites, as shown in Figure 6.9. The differences in schooling are especially important because the lower levels of educational attainment limit mobility and job opportunities in the postindustrial job market.

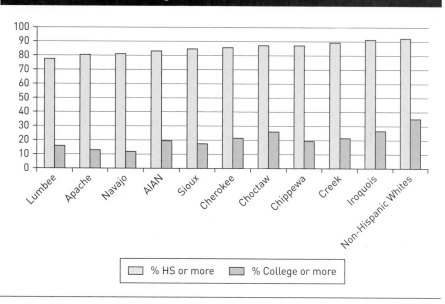

FIGURE 6.9 ■ Educational Attainment for Non-Hispanic Whites, All AIAN, and the Nine Largest Tribes, 2016

Source: U.S. Census Bureau (2018).

Note: Data for Blackfeet not available.

One positive development for the education of Native Americans is the rapid increase in tribally controlled colleges. There are now 37 tribal colleges: All offer two-year degrees, six offer four-year degrees, and two offer master's degrees. These institutions are located on or near reservations; some have been constructed with funds generated in the gaming industry. They are designed to be more sensitive to the educational and cultural needs of the group, and tribal college graduates who transfer to four-year colleges are more likely to graduate than are other Native American students (Pego, 1998; see also His Horse Is Thunder, Anderson, & Miller, 2013).

An earlier study found that Native American schoolchildren were less segregated than African American schoolchildren in the 2005–2006 school year but that the levels of racial isolation might be increasing (Fry, 2007). Again, it is difficult to assess trends because of the small size of the group and their concentration in rural areas.

Political Power

The ability of Native Americans to exert power as a voting bloc or otherwise directly affect the political structure is limited by group size; they are a tiny percentage of the electorate. Furthermore, their political power is limited by their lower-than-average levels of education, language differences, lack of economic resources, and fractional differences within and between tribes and reservations. The number of Native Americans holding elected office is minuscule, far less than 1% (Pollard & O'Hare, 1999). In 1992, however, Ben Nighthorse Campbell of Colorado, a member of the Northern Cheyenne tribe, was elected to the U.S. Senate and served until 2005.

Jobs and Income

Some of the most severe challenges facing Native Americans relate to work and income. The problems are especially evident on the reservations, where jobs have traditionally been scarce and affluence rare. As mentioned previously, the overall unemployment rate for Native Americans is about double the rate for whites. For Indians living on or near reservations, however, the rate is much higher, sometimes rising to 70% or 80% on the smaller, more-isolated reservations (U.S. Census Bureau, 2010).

Nationally, Native Americans are underrepresented in the higher-status, more lucrative professions and overrepresented in unskilled labor and service jobs (U.S. Census Bureau, 2010). Similar to African Americans, Native Americans who hold white-collar jobs are more likely than whites to work in lower-income occupations, such as typist or retail salesperson (Ogunwole, 2006, p. 10).

Figure 6.10 shows the median household income in 2016 for non-Hispanic whites, all AIAN, and the 10 largest tribes. The median household income for AIAN is about 67% of that of non-Hispanic whites. There is a good deal of variability among the tribes, but again, none approach the incomes of non-Hispanic whites.

These income statistics reflect lower levels of education as well as the interlocking forces of past discrimination and lack of development on many reservations. The rural isolation of much of the population and their distance from the more urbanized centers of economic growth limit possibilities for improvement and raise the likelihood that many reservations will remain the rural counterparts to urban underclass ghettos.

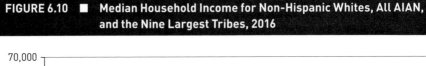

FIGURE 6.10 ■ Median Household Income for Non-Hispanic Whites, All AIAN, and the Nine Largest Tribes, 2016

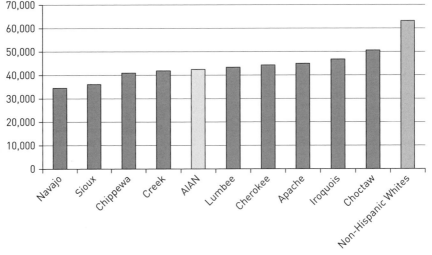

Source: U.S. Census Bureau (2018).

Note: Date for Blackfeet not available.

FIGURE 6.11 ■ Distribution of Household Income for Non-Hispanic Whites and American Indians and Alaska Natives (AIAN), 2016

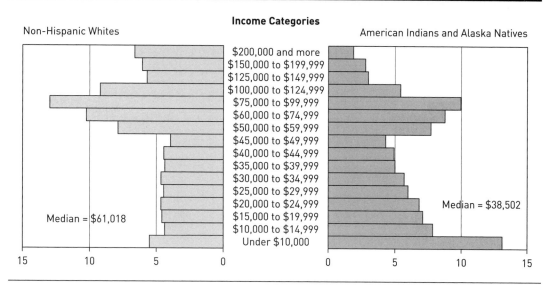

Source: U.S. Census Bureau (2018).

Figure 6.11 supplements the information in Figure 6.10 by displaying the distribution of income for all AIAN compared with non-Hispanic whites. This type of graph was introduced in Chapter 6 (which covered African Americans) and its format is similar to the format of Figure 5.14. In both graphs, the pattern of income inequality is immediately obvious. Starting at the bottom, you'll see that Native Americans and Alaska Natives are overrepresented in the lowest-income groups, as were African Americans. For example, over 13% of AIAN have incomes less than $10,000—this is more than double the percentage for whites (5.5%) in this range.

Moving up the figure through the lower- and middle-income brackets, you can see that AIAN households continue to be overrepresented. There is a notable clustering of both groups in the $50,000 to $100,000 categories, but it's whites who are overrepresented at these higher-income levels. The income differences are especially obvious at the top of the figure. For example, almost 13% of non-Hispanic white households are in the two highest income categories, compared with only 4.6% of AIAN households. Figure 6.11 also shows the median household incomes for the two groups: The figure for non-Hispanic whites is more than $22,000 higher than that of AIAN.

Finally, Figure 6.12 shows the poverty levels for non-Hispanic whites, all AIAN, and the nine largest tribes. The poverty rate for all AIAN families is about triple the rate for non-Hispanic whites, and five of these tribes have an even higher percentage of families living in poverty. The poverty rates for children show a similar pattern, with very high rates for the Lumbee, Navajo, and Sioux. As a whole, this information on income and poverty shows that despite the progress Native Americans have made over the past several decades, a sizable socioeconomic gap persists.

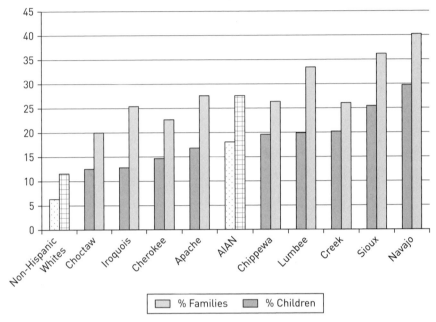

FIGURE 6.12 ■ Family and Children Poverty Rates for Non-Hispanic Whites, All AIAN, and Nine Largest Tribes, 2016

Note: Family and child poverty rates are computed using different units of analysis. Family rates represent the percentage of all families in the group that are below the poverty line while the rates for children are the percentage of all people younger than 18 in the group who live in poverty.

Source: U.S. Census Bureau (2018).

Note: Data for Blackfeet not available.

Primary Structural Assimilation

Rates of out-marriage for Native Americans are quite high compared with other groups, as displayed in Table 6.4. While the overwhelming majority of whites were married to other whites in both years, a little more than 40% of Native Americans had marriage partners within the group. This pattern is partly the result of the small size of the group. As less than 1% of the total population, Native Americans are numerically unlikely to find dating and marriage partners within their own group, especially in those regions of the country and urban areas where the group is small in size. For example, an earlier study found that in New England, which has the lowest relative percentage of Native Americans of any region, more than 90% of Indian marriages were to partners outside the group. But even in the mountain states, which have a greater number of Native Americans who are also highly concentrated on reservations, only about 40% of Indian marriages involved partners outside the group (Snipp, 1989, pp. 156–159). Also, the social and legal barriers to Native American–white intermarriages have been comparatively weak (Qian & Lichter, 2011).

TABLE 6.4 ■ Percentage Married to a Person of the Same Race, 1980 and 2008				
	Whites		**Native Americans**	
Year	**Men**	**Women**	**Men**	**Women**
1980	96%	95%	41%	43%
2008	93%	92%	43%	42%

Source: Adapted from Qian and Lichter (2011). Copyright © 2011 National Council on Family Relations. Reprinted with permission.

QUESTIONS FOR REFLECTION

14. This section examined a variety of dimensions of acculturation and integration for Native Americans. Which seems most important? Why?

15. In which of these areas has there been the most progress over the past 50 years? Explain.

COMPARING MINORITY GROUPS

Comparing the experiences of Native Americans with those of other groups will further our understanding of the complexities of dominant–minority relationships and permit us to test the explanatory power of the concepts and theories that are central to this text. No two minority groups have had the same experiences, and our concepts and theories should help us understand their differences and similarities. We'll make it a point to compare groups in each of the chapters in this part of the text. We begin by comparing Native Americans with African Americans.

First, note the differences in the stereotypes attached to the two groups during the early years of European colonization. While Indians were seen as cruel savages, African Americans under slavery were seen as lazy, irresponsible, and in constant need of supervision. The two stereotypes are consistent with the outcomes of the contact period. The supposed irresponsibility of blacks under slavery helped justify their subordinate, highly controlled status, and the alleged savagery of Native Americans helped justify their near-extermination by white society.

Second, both African Americans and Native Americans were colonized minority groups, but their contact situations were governed by very different dynamics (competition for labor vs. land) and a very different dominant-group agenda (the capture and control of a large, powerless workforce vs. the elimination of a military threat). These differing contact situations shaped subsequent relationships with the dominant group and the place of the groups in the larger society.

For example, consider the situations of the two groups a century ago. At that time, the most visible enemy for African Americans was de jure segregation, the elaborate system of repression in the South that controlled them politically, economically, and socially (see Chapters 4 and 5). In particular, the southern system of agriculture needed the black population—but only as a powerless, cheap workforce. The goals of African Americans centered on assimilation, equality, and dismantling this oppressive system.

Native Americans, in contrast, were not viewed as a source of labor and, after their military defeat, were far too few in number and too dispersed geographically to constitute a political threat. Thus, there was little need to control them in the same way African Americans were controlled. The primary enemies of the tribes were the reservation system, various agencies of the federal government (especially the BIA), rural isolation, and the continuing attacks on their traditional cultures and lifestyles, which are typical for a colonized minority group. Native Americans had a different set of problems, different resources at their disposal, and different goals in mind. They always have been more oriented toward a pluralistic relationship with the larger society and preserving what they could of their autonomy, their institutions, and their heritage. African Americans spent much of the 20th century struggling for inclusion and equality; Native Americans were fighting to maintain or recover their traditional cultures and social structures. This difference in goals reflects the different histories of the two groups and the different circumstances surrounding their colonization.

PROGRESS AND CHALLENGES

What does the future hold for Native Americans? Their situation has certainly changed over the past 100 years, but is it *better* or merely *different* (as is the case for large numbers of African Americans)? As the group grows in size and improves its status, the answer may be a little of both. To reach some conclusions about this question, we'll review several aspects of the situation currently facing Native Americans as a group. Additionally, we'll assess the usefulness of our theoretical models and concepts for understanding them.

Since the 1960s, the decline of intolerance in society, the growth of pride in ancestry in many groups (e.g., Black Power), and the shift in federal government policy to encourage self-determination have all helped spark a reaffirmation of commitment to tribal cultures and traditions. Similar to the Black Power movement, the Red Power movement asserted a distinct and positive Indian identity, a claim for the validity of Native American cultures within the broad framework of the larger society. During the same period, the favorable settlements of treaty claims, the growth in job opportunities, and the growth of the gambling industry have enhanced the flow of resources and benefits to some reservations. In popular culture, Native Americans have enjoyed a strong upsurge of popularity and sympathetic depictions. This enhanced popularity accounts for much of the growth in population size as people of mixed ancestry resurrect and reconstruct their Indian ancestors and their own ethnic identities.

Linear or simplistic views of assimilation don't fit the current situation or the past experiences of Native Americans very well. Some Native Americans are intermarrying with whites and integrating into the larger society; others strive to retain a tribal culture in the midst of an urbanized, industrialized society; still others labor to use the profits from gaming and other enterprises for the benefit of the tribe. Members of the group can be found at every degree of acculturation and integration, and the group seems to be moving toward assimilation in some ways and away from it in others.

From the standpoint of the Noel and Blauner hypotheses, Native Americans have struggled with conquest and colonization, experiences made more difficult by the loss of so much of their land and other resources and by the concerted, unrelenting attacks on their culture and language. The legacy of conquest and colonization was poor health and housing, an inadequate and misdirected education system, and slow (or nonexistent) economic development. For most of the 20th century, Native Americans were left to survive as best they could on the margins of the larger society, too powerless to establish meaningful pluralism and too colonized to pursue equality.

Today, one key to further progress for some members of this group is economic development on reservation lands and the further strengthening of the tribes as functioning social units. Some tribes do have assets—natural resources, treaty rights, and the gambling industry—that could fuel development. However, they often don't have the expertise or the capital to finance the exploitation of these resources. They must rely, in whole or in part, on non-Indian expertise and white-owned companies and businesses. Thus, non-Indians, rather than the tribes, may be the primary beneficiaries of some forms of development (this would, of course, be quite consistent with American history). For those reservations for which gambling isn't an option and for those without natural resources, investments in human capital (primarily education) may offer the most compelling direction for future development.

Urban Indians face the same patterns of discrimination and racism that confront other minority groups of color. Members of the group with lower levels of education and job skills face the prospect of becoming part of a permanent urban underclass. More educated and more skilled Native Americans share with African Americans the prospect of a middle-class lifestyle that is more partial and tenuous than that of comparable segments of the dominant group.

The situation of Native Americans today is vastly superior to the status of the group a century ago, and this chapter has documented the notable improvements that have occurred since 1990. Given the depressed and desperate conditions of the reservations in the early 20th century, however, it would not take much to show an improvement. Native Americans are growing rapidly in numbers and are increasingly diversified by residence, education, and degree of assimilation. Some tribes have made dramatic progress over the past several decades, but enormous problems remain both on and off the reservations. The challenge for the future, as it was in the past, is to find a course between pluralism and assimilation, between pan-tribalism and traditional lifestyles, which will balance the issues of quality of life against the importance of retaining an Indian identity.

Main Points

- Native American and Anglo American cultures are vastly different. These differences have hampered communication and understanding between the groups, usually in ways that harmed Native American communities.

- In the early 20th century, the BIA enforced a paternalistic reservation system that resulted in widespread poverty and powerlessness, rural isolation, and marginalization among Native American communities. Key legislation such as the IRA (1934) and termination and relocation policies further harmed tribal communities. Native Americans continued to lose land and other resources.

- Native Americans have organized protest movements since the early 20th century, including the Red Power movement. Native American protests achieved some successes. They were partly assimilationist, even though they pursued some pluralistic goals and greater autonomy for the tribes.

- Beginning in the 1970s, federal policies allowed for increased self-determination for tribal communities.

- As a group, Native Americans and Alaska Natives have experienced some improvements in quality of life, especially since the 1970s, but progress has been uneven and enormous challenges remain.

- Some tribes have valuable natural resources, including oil, coal, clean water, and timber, which they sometimes use to improve their situation.

- Some tribes use legal means to regain resources and opportunities taken from them by the government through broken treaties.

- Some tribes (e.g., the Choctaw Nation of Mississippi) have attracted industry, but many reservations are too remote and inaccessible to be viable sites for development and good jobs. The gaming industry has benefited some tribes and has the potential to benefit others.

- Prejudice and discrimination still limit the opportunities for Native Americans and Alaska Natives. Anti-Indian prejudice has shifted to subtler, modern forms.

- Institutional discrimination and access to education and employment remain major problems confronting Native Americans.

- Native Americans began to urbanize rapidly in the 1950s but remain less urbanized than the U.S. population. They are the least urbanized American minority group.

- Native Americans have retained more of their culture than African Americans. Tribal languages are still spoken on some reservations. However, the forces of pan-tribalism and the attractions of education and jobs in the larger society work against traditional cultures.

- Native Americans' origin as a colonized minority group, their history of competition with the dominant group, and their recent history on the reservations shape their current situation.

- Despite recent improvements, the overall secondary structural assimilation of Native Americans remains low. Inequalities persist in schooling, jobs, income, unemployment, and poverty levels.

- In terms of primary structural assimilation, intermarriages are high, largely because of their small group size relative to other groups.

- Indigenous people experience problems similar to those faced by other colonized minority groups as they try to raise their quality of life while continuing their commitment to tribal communities and Indian identity.

Applying Concepts

In this chapter, we've shown some of the diversity within the Native American population. To test your general knowledge about Native Americans as a group, here is a true/false quiz. You'll be able to answer some questions from the chapter information, but others ask you to consider ideas that you might have heard about Native Americans from popular culture or friends. How well do you think most Americans would do on this quiz? Why?

1. Native Americans have their college expenses paid for by their tribes or by the federal government.

2. Pocahontas was an Indian princess.

3. Native Americans scalped their slain enemies.

4. The term *powwow* is a derogatory, stereotypical term that shouldn't be used by non-Native people.

5. Native Americans practiced slavery and Native Americans were enslaved much like African Americans.

6. Native Americans use peyote in religious ceremonies.

7. Native Americans are getting rich from casinos.

8. Anyone with an Indian ancestor is automatically a member of that tribe.

9. Native Americans were always considered U.S. citizens.

10. Indian tribes are sovereign nations.

Review Questions

1. What were the most important cultural differences between Native American tribes and the dominant society? How did these affect relations between the two groups?

2. Compare and contrast the effects of paternalism and coercive acculturation on Native Americans after the end of the contact period with the effects on African Americans under slavery. What similarities and differences existed in the two situations? Which system was more oppressive and controlling? How did these different situations shape the futures of the groups?

3. How did federal Indian policy change over the course of the 20th century? What effects did these changes have on the tribes? Which were more beneficial? Why? What was the role of the Indian protest movement in shaping these policies?

4. What options do Native Americans have for improving their position in the larger society and for developing their reservations? Which strategies seem to have the most promise? Which seem less effective? Why?

5. Compare and contrast the contact situations of Native Americans, African Americans, and Australian Aborigines. What are the most crucial differences in their situations? What implications did these differences have for the development of each group's situation after the initial contact?

6. Characterize the present situation of Native Americans in terms of acculturation and integration. How do they compare with African Americans? What factors in the experiences of the two groups might help explain contemporary differences?

7. What gender differences can you identify in the experiences of Native Americans? How do these compare with the gender differences in the experiences of African Americans?

8. Given the information in this chapter, speculate about the future of Native Americans. Are Native American cultures and languages likely to survive? What are Native Americans' prospects for achieving equality?

9. Given their small size and marginal status, recognition of their situations and problems continues to be a central struggle for Native Americans. What are some ways the group can build a more realistic, informed, and empathetic relationship with the larger society, the federal government, and other authorities? Are there lessons in the experiences of other groups or in the various protest strategies followed in the Red Power movement?

Answers to Applying Concepts[3]

1. False. Some tribes offer scholarships to members, and the number of tribal colleges has increased. Approximately 19% of Native Americans have a college degree.

2. False. Pocahontas was the daughter of Powhatan, the paramount chief of a large confederation of tribes in the Tidewater, Virginia area. She was held in high regard, but she wasn't a *princess* (which is a British royal title).

3. True. Archaeological evidence dating to pre-Columbian times suggests that some groups practiced scalping; however, the type and prevalence varied. Europeans transformed this indigenous practice into a kind of bounty hunting by encouraging native people to scalp Indians who were hostile to European interests (see Axtell & Sturtevant, 1980).

4. True. Powwows are festivals that celebrate and preserve Native American culture and traditions, including sacred ones. Thus, using the phrase "have a powwow" to indicate a chat, meeting, or negotiation would be factually incorrect and some people would see that phrase as inappropriate or insensitive.

5. True. Before colonization, some tribes enslaved Native Americans as war captives to provide labor (including reproductive labor). However, they often became integrated into tribes (e.g., through marriage). Rushforth notes that "indigenous slavery moved captives 'up and in' toward full, if forced, assimilation" (2012, p. 66). For the Comanche, enslavement practices were strategic—to gain numbers. However, they "never drew a hard line between masters and slaves, and they possessed neither the necessary means to enforce unconditional submission nor a racist ideology to mentally suppress the slave population" (Hämäläinen, 2008, p. 251).

   Native enslavement practices changed as the British and Spanish systems of slavery developed. Eventually, it became more lucrative for Native Americans to sell, rather than enslave, other Native Americans. However, widespread enslavement of Native Americans in the U.S. colonies was problematic. Many Native Americans died due to a lack of immunity to European diseases, reducing the potential labor pool. Additionally, Native Americans could escape more easily than African slaves because they possessed knowledge of the area and could often get help from other Indigenous people (Lowcountry Digital History Initiative at the College of Charleston, n.d.). Because of this flight risk, slave traders often took Native Americans to Brazil to be sold. As the U.S. system of slavery developed, some tribes, especially those in the Southeast, began to enslave Africans (Snyder, 2010) while others offered sanctuary to runaway African slaves. For example, researchers estimate that thousands of "Maroons" lived with Native Americans in the Great Dismal Swamp (Sayers, Burke, & Henry, 2007). In short, Native Americans enslaved other Native Americans and, at times, Africans. However, it was quite different from the chattel-oriented slave system developed in the U. S. (also see Madley, 2016; Reséndez, 2016; Treuer, 2012).

6. True. For example, the Native American Church uses peyote as part of its rituals.

7. False. While some tribes earn a lot of money from casinos, many don't. See the relevant sections of this chapter.

8. False. Tribes have specific rules about membership eligibility; an Indian ancestor is no guarantee of acceptance.

9. False. The Fourteenth Amendment did not apply to all Native Americans. The Indian Citizenship Act of 1924 granted citizenship; however, it didn't guarantee all rights to Native people. For example, some states refused to give Native Americans the right to vote.

10. False. However, a variety of laws provide tribes with considerable autonomy to govern their own tribal communities.

Internet Learning Resources

SAGE edge™ offers teachers and students easy-to-use resources for review, study, and further exploration. See **http://edge.sagepub.com/diversity6e**

Notes

1. Columbus used the term *Indian* because he thought he had landed in India. We use *Native American*—rather than *American Indian*—to emphasize that such people are indigenous to the area that became the United States, including Alaska. Similarly, people debate the language of *tribes*, *nations*, or *communities*. Different indigenous people prefer different terms. As with other racial and ethnic groups, these labels highlight their socially constructed nature.

2. The Australian government's report notes that it's hard to estimate a number because many institutions didn't keep records or didn't record children's family history information as Aboriginal. It "conclude[d] with confidence that between one in three and one in ten Indigenous children were forcibly removed from their families and communities in the period from approximately 1910 until 1970 . . . and not one Indigenous family has escaped the effects of forcible removal" (Commonwealth of Australia, 1997, p. 3).

3. Answers vary by tribal community and geographic region.

HISPANIC AMERICANS

Colonization, Immigration, and Ethnic Enclaves

Graham Avenue in [Brooklyn] was the broadest street I'd ever seen. . . . Most of these stores were . . . run by Jewish people [and] there were special restaurants called delis where Jewish people ate. . . . We didn't go into the delis because, Mami said, they didn't like Puerto Ricans in there. Instead, she took me to eat pizza.

"It's Italian," she said.

"Do Italians like Puerto Ricans?" I asked as I bit into hot cheese and tomato sauce that burned the tip of my tongue.

"They're more like us than Jewish people are," she said, which wasn't an answer.

In Puerto Rico, the only foreigners I'd been aware of were Americanos. In two days in Brooklyn, I had already encountered Jewish people, and now Italians. There was another group of people Mami had pointed out to me: Morenos [African Americans]. But they weren't foreigners, because they were American. They were black, but they didn't look like Puerto Rican negros. They dressed like Americanos but walked with a jaunty hop that made them look as if they were dancing down the street, only their hips were not as loose as Puerto Rican men's were. According to

Mami, they too lived in their own neighborhoods, frequented their own restaurants, and didn't like Puerto Ricans.

"How come?" I wondered, since in Puerto Rico, all of the people I'd ever met were either black or had a black relative somewhere in their family. I would have thought morenos would like us, since so many of us looked like them.

"They think we're taking their jobs."

"Are we?"

"There's enough work in the United States for everybody," Mami said.

—Esmeralda Santiago (1993)

Esmeralda Santiago moved from Puerto Rico to Brooklyn the summer before eighth grade. New York City, and the variety of different groups she encountered there, felt so different from Puerto Rico. Puerto Ricans have been U.S. citizens since 1917 but often live in a different cultural world. Like many Puerto Ricans who move to the mainland, Esmeralda had to adjust to all sorts of things, including ideas about race. At times, it felt overwhelming.

Just as Esmeralda was changed by her experience with the culture on the mainland, fast-growing and diverse Hispanic American groups are changing the United States. It makes many people wonder what America will look like in a few decades.

Hispanic Americans are 18% of the U.S. population, making them the nation's largest minority group. Not all Hispanic American groups are newcomers; some lived in North America long before European colonists founded Jamestown. Historically, they've been concentrated in the West and the South (particularly in California, Texas, and Florida), reflecting the Mexican and Spanish histories of those areas. Like the larger society, these groups are always changing. They share a language and some cultural traits, but they're diverse and distinct from one another. Generally, as we'll discuss, Hispanic Americans don't think of themselves as one group. The 2014 National Survey of Latinos showed that only 25% considered themselves *Hispanic* or *Latino* (Parker, Horowitz, Morin, & Lopez, 2015). An earlier study found that 51% identified themselves by their country of origin (e.g., *Cuban American*). Nearly one fourth (21%) saw themselves simply as *American*. Identity varied based on the respondent's primary language, generation, and education. First-generation Latinos prefer to identify with their countries of origin while *American* is most popular with the third and higher generations, a pattern that suggests acculturation (Taylor, Lopez, Martinez, & Velasco, 2012, p. 9–13).

In recent decades, the Hispanic American population has grown rapidly and expanded into every region of the country (Ennis, Rios-Vargas, & Albert, 2011, p. 6; Gutiérrez, n.d.). As they join more communities, they're remaking America—just as African Americans, white ethnic groups, Native Americans, and Asian Americans have (and still are). Some Americans are excited about these changes. For the first time in many places, people are getting the opportunity to meet Hispanics from other countries (and Puerto Rico) and learn about diverse cultures. They're hearing Spanish in their communities and enjoying new foods like pozole, sofrito, Ropa Vieja, and tostones in their grocery stores and restaurants. However, some people worry that Latinos will change America too much and in negative ways (e.g., job competition). These fears are, in part, what's caused an increase in prejudice and discrimination toward Latinos over the last several years.

In this chapter, we'll explore the development of Hispanic American groups over the past century or so, examine their relationship to the larger society, and assess their current status. We focus on the largest groups: Mexican Americans, Puerto Ricans, and Cuban Americans. (We'll cover smaller Hispanic groups such as Dominicans and Colombians in Chapter 9.)

Table 7.1 shows the 10 largest Latino groups in 2017. The largest group, Mexican Americans, comprises over 11% of the U.S. population (and almost two thirds of all Hispanic Americans). Figure 7.1 displays the relative size of the 10 largest Latino groups.

| FIGURE 7.1 ■ Relative Size of Hispanic American Groups by Country or Territory of Origin, 2017 |

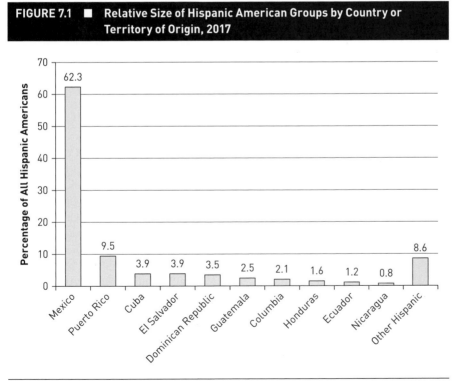

Source: U.S. Bureau of the Census (2018a).

Note: *Other Hispanics* include Costa Ricans, Venezuelans, Argentinians, Bolivians, and many others.

FIGURE 7.2 ■ **Percentage Foreign Born for Total Population, All Hispanic Americans, and the 10 Largest Groups, 2017**

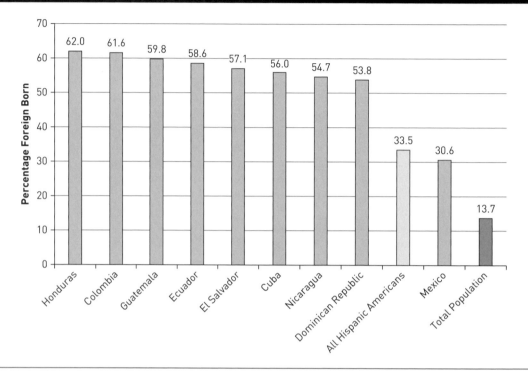

Source: U.S. Bureau of the Census (2018a).

Latino groups are growing, partly because of their relatively high birth rates (which is related to religious beliefs about contraception and abortion), but mainly because of immigration (Cohn, 2010). As Table 7.1 shows, between 1990 and 2017, the Mexican American population increased by 2.7 times. The Latino population grew 2.6 times—double the growth rate for the U.S. population (1.3 times). Today, 18.1% of Americans are of Hispanic descent. Researchers expect that level to increase to approximately 29% by 2060 (see Figure 1.1). One result of immigration is that most (53.8% and higher) of the smaller Hispanic American groups (e.g., Honduran, Colombian) are foreign-born or first-generation Americans (see Figure 7.2).

It is appropriate to discuss Hispanic Americans at this point because they include colonized and immigrant groups. Based on Blauner's typology, we'd expect the more colonized Hispanic groups to share commonalities with other colonized groups (i.e., African Americans, Native Americans). Likewise, we'd expect Hispanic groups whose experiences lie closer to the "immigrant" end of the continuum to follow different pathways of adaptation compared with colonized groups. We'll test these ideas by reviewing the groups' histories and by analyzing their current patterns of acculturation and integration.

Country of Origin	1990	2000	2017	Growth (Number of Times Larger, 1990–2017)	Percentage of Total Population, 2017
TABLE 7.1 ■ Size and Growth of All Hispanic Americans and the 10 Largest Groups by Origin, 1990–2017					
Total Hispanic American	22,355,990	35,305,818	58,846,134	2.6	18.1%
Mexico	13,496,000	20,640,711	36,668,018	2.7	11.3%
Puerto Rico*	2,728,000	3,406,178	5,588,664	2.0	1.7%
Cuba	1,044,000	1,241,685	2,315,863	2.2	<.1%
El Salvador	565,081	655,165	2,310,784	4.1	<.1%
Dominican Republic	520,521	764,945	2,081,419	4.0	<.1%
Guatemala	268,779	372,487	1,456,965	5.4	<.1%
Colombia	378,726	470,684	1,222,960	3.2	<.1%
Honduras	131,066	217,569	945,916	7.2	<.1%
Ecuador	191,198	260,559	735,185	3.8	<.1%
Nicaragua	202,658	177,684	444,585	2.2	<.1%
Percentage of U.S. Population	9.0%	12.5%	18.1 %		
Total U.S. Population	248,710,000	281,421,906	325,719,178	1.3	

Sources: For 1990 (U.S. Census Bureau, 1990), for 2000 (Ennis et al., 2011, p. 3), for 2016 (U.S. Census Bureau, 2017a).

*Living on mainland only

Before moving on, it's important to address some additional issues:

- Hispanic Americans are partly an ethnic minority group (identified by cultural characteristics such as language) and partly a racial minority group (loosely identified by physical appearance). Everyone's physical characteristics reflect one's genetic makeup. For example, the original inhabitants of Puerto Rico (the Taíno people) descend from two groups: the Arawak and the Kalinago (formerly called the *Caribe*). Spanish colonizers brought enslaved Africans to the island. They also brought diseases which, together with violence and loss of land, decimated the indigenous population (Taíno Museum, 2017). Today, genomic testing shows Puerto Ricans with European (54%), African (29%), and Indigenous (17%) ancestries, which reflects the "considerable intermarriage between groups" (National Geographic Society, 2017). In contrast, Mexican Americans primarily have Native American (67%) and European (17%) ancestries, among others.

- Latinos—even those who are completely acculturated—may experience discrimination based on people's perceptions of their race and culture. This suggests that some people don't see Latinos as part of American society.

- As we discussed in Chapter 6, group names are important because they reflect power dynamics (e.g., *Native Americans, Indigenous Americans,* and *American Indians*). Similar debates exist about the terms *Hispanic* and *Latino.* Colonizing nations created both labels. *Hispanic* emphasizes Spanish (European) heritage but doesn't acknowledge the cultural roots of Latin American groups in African and Native American civilizations. *Latino* is short for *Latino Americano* and stresses the geographic origins of Latin American groups, thereby excluding people of Spanish (European) origin. Neither Latino nor Hispanic applies well to other groups (e.g., many Brazilians are of Portuguese descent). These labels highlight the social construction of race and ethnicity. Because no term encompasses everyone, we use them interchangeably.

If 2 or more groups come together in a situation characterized by ethnocentrism, competition, and diff in power, then some form of racial or ethnic stratification will result

MEXICAN AMERICANS

In Chapter 3, we applied the Noel and Blauner hypotheses to Mexican Americans. Europeans colonized Mexicans in the 19th century to use as cheap labor in the Southwest. In the competition for control of land and labor, Mexicans—and by extension, Mexican Americans—became a minority group. The contact situation left them with few resources.

By the dawn of the 20th century, the situation of Mexican Americans resembled that of Native Americans. Both groups were small (about 0.5% of the U.S. population; Cortes, 1980, p. 702). Both differed from the dominant group in culture and language, and both were impoverished, relatively powerless, and isolated in rural areas distant from the centers of industrialization and modernization.

In other ways, Mexican Americans resembled African Americans in the South: Both groups supplied much of the labor for the agricultural economy and were limited to low-paying occupations and subordinate social status. Anglo Americans colonized all three groups and, at least in the early decades of the 20th century, these groups lacked the resources to end their exploitation and protect their cultural heritages from continual attack by the dominant society (Mirandé, 1985, p. 32). One important difference was that, because of the proximity of Mexico and the ease of travel across the border, it was much easier for Mexican Americans to maintain a distinct cultural heritage.

Cultural Patterns

Besides language, Mexican American and Anglo American cultures differ in several ways. Whereas Anglo American society is largely Protestant (47%), the majority (61%)

of Mexican Americans are Catholic—down from 71% in 2010 (Pew Research Center, 2015). Almost a quarter (23%) are unaffiliated with a specific faith (López, 2015d).

Another area of difference relates to what some researchers call the "culture of poverty" (see Chapter 5). This idea emerged from anthropological research, primarily by Oscar Lewis, within different Hispanic communities in Cuba, Puerto Rico, Mexico, and New York (see Lewis, 1959, 1965, 1966). Lewis claimed that a specific culture existed among the poor that made it hard for them or their children to escape poverty. Lewis said the culture of poverty influenced people's families and mindsets. However, Lewis put this into context saying that "the culture of poverty is both an adaptation and a reaction of the poor classes to their marginal position in a class-stratified, highly individualistic, capitalistic society" (1965, p. xliv). Many people overlook this connection to the broader economic system and interpret his research to be about the culture of specific groups, including Mexican Americans.

In fact, contemporary research shows little difference between the values of Mexican Americans and other Americans of similar social class, educational background, length of residence in the U. S., urban versus rural residence, and other factors (e.g., see Buriel, 1993; Moore & Pinderhughes, 1993; Pew Hispanic Center, 2005, p. 20; Valentine & Mosley, 2000). For example, Taylor et al. (2012, pp. 18–19) found that 75% of Latinos agreed that most people can "get ahead with hard work"—perhaps the central value in the American creed—compared with only 58% of the non-Hispanic population.

Another cultural difference involves **machismo**, a value system that stresses men's dominance, honor, virility, and violence. Stereotypical views of machismo emphasize its negative aspects and often fail to recognize positive ones, such as being a good provider and father (Arciniega, Anderson, Tovar-Blank, & Tracey, 2008; Falicov, 2010) Yet, similar attitudes exist in many cultures, including Anglo American cultures (Moore & Pachon, 1985).

Some cultural differences (e.g., language) have inhibited communication with the dominant group and have served as the basis for excluding Mexican Americans from the larger society. However, the differences have also provided a basis for group solidarity that has sustained identity-based activism among Mexican Americans. As you'll see in the next section, part of the divide between groups has to do with feelings about immigration.

Immigration

Although Mexican Americans originated as a colonized minority group, immigration has shaped their situation since the early 1900s (and especially since the 1960s). Figure 7.3 shows the numbers of legal Mexican immigrants to the United States. Conditions in Mexico explain the fluctuations in immigration rates: the varying demand for labor in the low-paying, unskilled sector of the U.S. economy; broad changes in North America and the world; and changing federal immigration policy. As you will see, competition, one of the key variables in Noel's hypothesis, has shaped the relationships between Mexican immigrants and the larger American society.

Push and Pull

European immigration was propelled by industrialization, urbanization, and rapid population growth (see Chapter 2). Similar social forces, both domestic and global, encouraged Mexican immigration.

FIGURE 7.3 ■ Legal Immigration from Mexico, 1905–2017

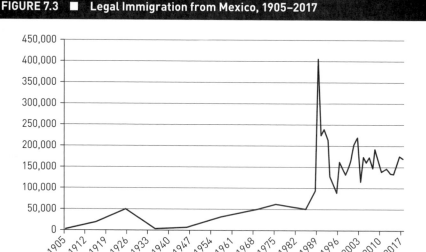

Source: U.S. Department of Homeland Security (2018a, 2018b).

Notes:

1. The high number of immigrants in the late 1980s and early 1990s was the result of people already in the U.S. legalizing their status under the provisions of the Immigration Reform and Control Act (IRCA).
2. Values are averages per year during each decade until 1989.

At the heart of the immigration lies a simple fact: The almost 2,000-mile-long border between Mexico and the U. S. is the longest continuous point of contact between a less-industrialized nation and a more-industrialized nation in the world. For more than a century, the United States has developed faster than Mexico, moving from an industrial to a postindustrial society and sustaining a substantially higher standard of living. The continuing wage gap between the two nations has made even unskilled work in the North attractive to millions of Mexicans (and Central and South Americans). Many Mexicans need work, and jobs in the U. S. pay more—often much more—than the wages south of the border. To lend some numerical perspective to the size of the immigration, over 36 million people of Mexican descent live in America. Although many have had family in what is now the United States for centuries, about 33% are first generation (see Table 7.1 and Figure 7.2).

Conditions in Mexico, Fluctuating Demand for Labor, and Federal Immigration Policy

For more than a century, Mexico has served as a reserve pool of cheap labor for American businesses, agricultural interests, and other groups. The volume of immigration primarily reflects changing economic conditions in America. Just as air flows from high to low pressure, people move from areas of lower opportunities to those with higher economic opportunities. The flow isn't continuous: Immigration increases when times in the U. S. are good and decreases when they're bad. Federal policies and actions reinforce the pattern. Table 7.2 presents a summary of the most important events in the complex

TABLE 7.2 ■ Significant Dates in Mexican Immigration

Dates	Event	Result	Effect on Immigration from Mexico
1910	Mexican Revolution	Political turmoil and unrest in Mexico	Increased
Early 20th century	Mexican industrialization	Many groups (especially rural peasants) displaced	Increased
1920s	Passage of National Origins Act of 1924	Decreased immigration from Europe	Increased
1930s	Great Depression	Decreased demand for labor and increased competition for jobs leads to repatriation campaign	Decreased, many return to Mexico
1940s	World War II	Increased demand for labor leads to Bracero Guest Worker Program	Increased
1950s	Concern over undocumented immigrants	Operation Wetback	Decreased, many return to Mexico
1965	Repeal of National Origins Act	New immigration policy gives high priority to close family of citizens	Increased
1986	IRCA	Undocumented immigrants given opportunity to legalize status	Many undocumented immigrants gain legal status
1994	NAFTA	Many groups in Mexico (especially rural peasants) displaced	Increased
2007	Recession in the U. S.	Widespread unemployment in the U. S., job supply shrinks	Decreased
2010–2015	U.S. economy begins a gradual recovery	Job supply in U. S. expands	Increased

history of Mexican immigration to the United States along with some comments about their effects.

Prior to the early 1900s, the volume of immigration was generally low and largely unregulated. In 1904, President Teddy Roosevelt created the U.S. Immigration Service (Johnson, 2014) but people continued to cross the border—in both directions—as the need arose, informally and without restriction. The volume of immigration and concern over controlling the border increased with the increase of political and economic turmoil in Mexico in the early 20th century, but still remained a comparative trickle.

Immigration increased in the 1920s when federal legislation curtailed the flow of cheap labor from Europe. In 1924, the government established the U.S. Border Patrol to prevent illegal immigration; at that time, it focused on Canada, fearing that illegal liquor was being smuggled in during prohibition (Johnson, 2014). When the Great Depression brought hard times in the 1930s, many Mexicans voluntarily returned home.

As competition for jobs increased, efforts began to expel Mexicans by force, as the Noel hypothesis would predict.

The federal government instituted a **repatriation** campaign aimed specifically at deporting undocumented Mexican immigrants. These efforts also intimidated many legal immigrants and U.S.–born Mexican Americans into moving to Mexico. As a result, the Mexican American population of the U. S. declined by about 40% (Cortes, 1980, p. 711).

Soon after the Depression ended, America mobilized for World War II. With so many American men abroad, employers needed workers. Thus, in 1942, the government created the Bracero Program to permit contract laborers, usually employed in low-skill jobs (e.g., agriculture), to work in the U. S. for a limited time. When their contracts expired, the workers were required to return to Mexico (Budech, 2014).

The Bracero Program continued for several decades after the war and was a crucial source of labor for the growing American economy. In 1960 alone, **braceros** supplied 26% of the nation's seasonal farm labor (Cortes, 1980, p. 703). The program generated millions of dollars of profit for growers and other employers because they were paying braceros much less than they would have paid American workers (Amott & Matthaei, 1991, pp. 79–80).

While the Bracero Program allowed Mexican immigration, other programs and agencies worked to deport undocumented immigrants, large numbers of whom entered America with the braceros. These efforts reached a peak in the early 1950s with **Operation Wetback**, a federal program that led to the deportations of almost four million Mexicans (Grebler, Moore, & Guzman, 1970, p. 521). During Operation Wetback, raids on Mexican American homes and businesses were common, and authorities often ignored their civil and legal rights. In an untold number of cases, U.S. citizens of Mexican descent were deported along with undocumented immigrants. These violations of civil and legal rights have been a continuing grievance of Mexican Americans (and other Latinos; Mirandé, 1985, pp. 70–90).

The overtly racist national immigration policy incorporated in the 1924 National Origins Act (see Chapter 2) was replaced in 1965 by a new policy that gave a high priority to immigrants who were close kin to U.S. citizens. The immediate family (parents, spouses, and children) of U.S. citizens could enter without numerical restriction. Some numerical restrictions were placed on the number of immigrants from each sending country but about 80% of these restricted visas were reserved for other close relatives of citizens. The remaining 20% of the visas went to people who had skills needed in the labor force (Bouvier & Gardner, 1986, pp. 13–15, 41; Rumbaut, 1991, p. 215). Immigrants have always tended to move along chains of kinship and other social relationships, and the 1965 policy reinforced that pattern. As immigrants became citizens, they sent for family, and the rate of immigration began to increase (see Figure 7.3).

Most of the Mexican immigrants, legal and undocumented, who have arrived since 1965 continue the pattern of seeking work in the low-wage, unskilled sectors of the labor market, especially in the fields and cities of the Southwest. For many, work is seasonal or temporary, and it follows agricultural patterns, with migrants moving to the South in the fall and North in the spring. When the work ends, they often return to Mexico, commuting across the border as they've done for decades in a pattern of circular migration (Passel & Cohn, 2017).

In 1986, Congress attempted to deal with undocumented immigrants, most of whom were thought to be Mexican, by passing the Immigration Reform and Control Act (IRCA). This legislation allowed undocumented immigrants who had been in the country continuously since 1982 to legalize their status. According to the U.S. Immigration and Naturalization Service (1993), about 3 million people—75% of them Mexican—did so. However, the program didn't decrease undocumented immigration (p. 17). In 1988, when the amnesty period ended, almost 3 million undocumented immigrants were living in the United States. By 2015, 11 million undocumented immigrants were in the U. S., down from a high of 12 million in 2007 (Passel & Cohn, 2017).

Recent Immigration from Mexico

Mexican immigration to the U. S. continues to reflect the differing level of development and standard of living between the two societies. Mexico is still a more agricultural nation and has a lower standard of living, as measured by average wages, housing quality, health care, and many other criteria. To illustrate, the gross national income per capita for Mexico in 2016 was $16,383—much higher than in 2002 but nowhere near the comparable figure for the United States at $56,180. About half of the Mexican population (53.2%) lives in poverty (World Bank, 2013). Almost half (48%) of Mexican immigrants come to enjoy a better life in America (Gonzalez-Barrera, 2015). Opportunities for work in Mexico are scarce; 60% of Mexicans express dissatisfaction with the state of their economy (Pew Research Center, 2014a), and many Mexicans are drawn to the U. S. in the hopes of finding employment or better wages. The average length of schooling in Mexico is about 8.6 years; thus, Mexican immigrants have much lower levels of job skills than U.S. citizens and compete for work in the lower levels of the U.S. job structure (United Nations Development Programme Human Development Reports, 2016). Furthermore, 79% cite crime and illegal drugs (72%) as significant problems in their homeland (Pew Research Center, 2015). Since 2006, 80,000 people have been killed in Mexico due to organized crime–related incidents (CNN Library, 2017).

The globalization of the Mexican economy reinforces people's drive to immigrate. Historically, the Mexican government insulated its economy from foreign competition through tariffs and barriers. Over the past several decades, Mexico, like many less-industrialized nations, has abandoned these protections. The result has been a flood of foreign agricultural products (especially cheap corn), manufactured goods, and capital, which (while helpful to parts of the economy) has disrupted social life and forced many Mexicans, especially the poor and rural dwellers, out of their traditional way of life (see Johnson, 2011).

The 1994 North American Free Trade Agreement (NAFTA) brought some of the most significant changes to Mexican society. As discussed in Chapter 1, NAFTA united Mexico, Canada, and the U. S. into a single trading zone. U.S. and Canadian companies began moving their manufacturing operations to Mexico, attracted by lower wages, less-stringent environmental regulations, and weak labor unions. They built factories, called *maquiladoras,* along the border and brought many jobs. However, between 2 million and 2.5 million Mexican jobs were actually lost, offsetting any gains. Families—especially rural ones—were driven out of the agricultural economy because they couldn't compete with agribusinesses (Faux, 2004; Johnson, 2011). Mexican wages declined and costs rose, increasing the already large number of Mexicans living in poverty. Many men from rural communities left to find work in the United States, leaving nearly empty villages or ones populated only by women and children (Johnson, 2011).

Thus, globalization (and NAFTA in particular) reinforced the long-term relationship between the two nations. Mexico, similar to other nations of the less-industrialized South, continues to produce a supply of unskilled, less-educated workers, while the U. S., similar to other nations of the more-industrialized North, desires cheap labor. Compared with what is available at home, the wages in America are quite attractive, even when the jobs are at the margins of the mainstream economy or in the underground economy (e.g., day laborers paid off the books, illegal sweatshops, and sex work) and even when the journey requires Mexican immigrants to break American laws, pay large sums of money to "coyotes" to guide them across the border, and live in fear of immigration authorities.

The movement of Mexicans that began in the 1960s and accelerated in the 1990s was the largest immigration from a single nation to America in history (Passel, Cohn, & Gonzalez-Barrera, 2012, p. 6). Some 12 million people, about 51% unauthorized, crossed the border during this period.

More recently, the historic trend has reversed. Between fiscal years 2000–2017, almost 13 million people were apprehended at the southern border. Between 2000–2007, an average of 1,057,711 people entered illegally per year. Between 2011–2017, it dropped to 374,620 people per year, on average (United States Border Patrol, n.d.). Multiple factors affected this decline, including enhanced border enforcement, increasing dangers of crossing illegally, and Mexico's declining birthrate (Passel, Cohn, & Gonzalez-Barrera, 2013, p. 6). However, the most significant factor was the 2008 collapse of the housing market and the resulting economic recession (Gonzalez-Barrera, 2015). Between 2008–2009, apprehensions decreased by 164,140 over the prior year. Since 2018, U.S. immigration policy has tightened, and NAFTA was reconfigured into the United States–Mexico–Canada Agreement (USMCA). Tensions between the governments of Mexico and America have intensified, and prejudice and discrimination toward Hispanics has increased. These factors, for now, suggest that immigration will not increase.

The Continuing Debate over Immigration Policy

Immigration has become a hotly debated issue in the United States. How many immigrants should we admit? From which nations? With what skills? Should the relatives of U.S. citizens continue to receive priority? If so, which ones? What about people fleeing war or violence? And what should we do about unauthorized immigrants? Though they apply to other immigrant groups, when Americans discuss these questions, they're mainly thinking about immigration along our southern border.

In addition to Mexican immigration, the U.S. southern border is, increasingly, crossed by Guatemalans, Hondurans, and Salvadorans. In 2017, the Border Patrol apprehended 175,978 of them. They're fleeing war, organized crime and gangs, domestic violence, human trafficking, and starvation (Bolter, 2017; Meyer & Isacson, n.d.; United States Border Patrol, 2017, p. 1). Their plight became well known in 2018, when several large groups of them, primarily Hondurans, began the journey of more than 2,000 miles north in caravans. These large groups, typically more than 1,000 people, have been organized by nonprofit groups. They travel together to avoid murder, kidnapping, rape, and robbery along the route (Kinosian & Holpuch, 2018). In response, the federal government sent thousands of troops to reinforce and patrol the border.

One concern that most people can agree on is the number of unaccompanied children trying to cross. In 2014, Border Patrol apprehended 68,541 of them. By 2016, that number had decreased to 59,692 (Johnson, 2016; see Figure 7.4). Those numbers have declined because the U. S. pushed Mexico to crack down on non-Mexican Latinos crossing into Mexico (Meyer & Isacson, n.d.). Nevertheless, the number of children migrating alone is staggering and suggests their desperation.

In 2018, people raised similar concerns about the government separating migrant children from their parents and putting more than 2,000 of them in detention centers while waiting to be placed in foster care (Dickerson, 2017b; Nixon, 2018). Concerns about children's safety intensified after 1,500 of them got "lost" in the system (Jordan, 2018; Nixon, 2018).

The federal government has attempted to reduce the flow of immigrants by increasing the Border Patrol's budget, which, in 2014, increased to $3.5 billion (Johnson, 2014). That money will be used to extend, maintain, and patrol the southern border wall in particular (see Table 7.3). As federal policies tighten, expenses will increase. The proposed Department of Homeland Security budget for 2019 is 22% higher than 2017, including $14.2 billion for customs and border protection and $8.3 billion for Immigration and Customs Enforcement (ICE).

FIGURE 7.4 ■ Border Patrol Apprehensions of Unaccompanied Minors

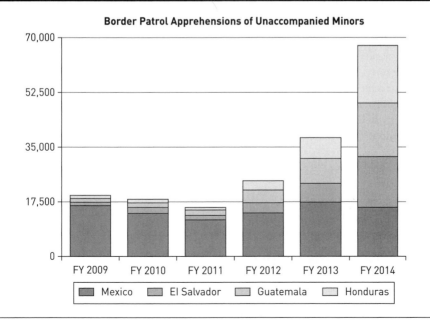

Source: Meyer and Isacson (n.d.). "Border Security, Migration, and Humanitarian Concerns in South Texas." https://www.wola.org/files/1502_stx/index.html. Data from U.S. Customs and Border Protection.

excessive budget in 14 years

Immigration expansion

TABLE 7.3 ■ Growth in Border Patrol Resources, Fiscal Years 2000–2014		
	2000	**2014**
Border Patrol agents dedicated to the southwest border	8,619	18,127
Fence (miles)	77	700
"Strategically placed" all-weather roads (miles)	17	145.7
Underground sensors	"few"	11,863
Aircraft	56	107
Aerial surveillance vehicles (unstaffed)	0	8
Boats	2	84
Mobile video surveillance systems	"little if any"	178
Remote video surveillance systems	140	273
Night vision goggles	n/a	9,255
Thermal imaging capabilities	little or none	Over 600

Source: Johnson (2014).

Communities across the nation wonder about how to respond to immigration issues. Some citizens support measures to close the borders through bigger, thicker walls; surveillance; and even the use of deadly force. Others ponder ways to allow newcomers into the U. S. without negatively affecting schools, employment, medical facilities, or housing markets. Some raise fiscal and humanitarian concerns (Washington Office on Latin America, 2017), noting, for example, the estimated 7,216 migrants who died trying to cross the border between 1998 and 2017 (U.S. Border Patrol, 2017)—estimates that are probably low because finding bodies is difficult (International Organization for Migration, 2014) and because federal statistics often don't include bodies recovered by local officials (O'Dell, González, & Castellano, 2018).

Although many issues still divide the nation, most Americans support immigration. In 2017, 71% of people consistently said that immigration is a "good thing" and only 23% said it's a "bad thing" (see Figure 7.5). Similarly, over the past decade, public opinion polls show that about 40% to 50% of Americans want to decrease immigration. However, an almost equal percentage (30%–40%) favor keeping present levels. A 2016 Gallup Poll yielded comparable results: 38% of Americans wanted to decrease immigration and 38% wanted to keep the current level. Interestingly, 21% wanted to *increase* immigration (Morales, 2010; Newport, 2016).

Should undocumented immigrants be deported immediately, or should some provision be made for them to legalize their status, as was done in the IRCA of 1986? If the latter, should the opportunity to attain legal status be extended to all or only to immigrants who meet certain criteria (e.g., those with steady jobs and clean criminal records)? Many feel that amnesty is unjust because immigrants who entered illegally have broken

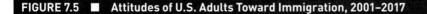

FIGURE 7.5 ■ Attitudes of U.S. Adults Toward Immigration, 2001–2017

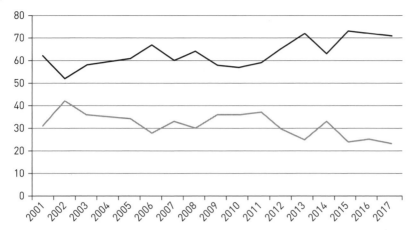

ACTUAL QUESTION: On the whole, do you think immigration is a good thing or a bad thing for this country today?

——— Immigration is a good thing for the United States

·········· Immigration is a bad thing for the United States

Source: Newport (2016). "In US, Support for Decreasing Immigration Holds Steady," Gallup Polls, http://www.gallup.com/poll/194819/support-decreasing-immigration-holds-steady.aspx.

the law and should be punished. Others point to the economic contributions of these immigrants and the damage to the economy that would result from mass expulsions. Still others worry about the negative impact undocumented immigrants may have on the job prospects for the less-skilled members of the larger population, including the urban underclass that is disproportionately populated by minority group members. (We address some of these issues later in this chapter and in Chapters 8 and 9.)

Immigration, Colonization, and Intergroup Competition

We conclude this discussion by focusing on three points about Mexican immigration to the United States. First, powerful political and economic interests in the U. S. stimulate and sustain migration from Mexico. Systems of recruitment and networks of communication and transportation have been established to provide a predictable labor source that benefits U.S. employers. The movement of people back and forth across the border was established long before current efforts to regulate it. Depending on U.S. policy, this immigration is sometimes legal and encouraged and sometimes illegal and discouraged. Nevertheless, it has flowed for decades in response to opportunities for work in the North (Gonzalez-Barrera & Lopez, 2013; Portes, 1990, pp. 160–163).

Second, Mexican immigrants enter a social system where the group's colonized status has been established. The paternalistic traditions and racist systems of the 19th century shaped the positions available to Mexican immigrants in the 20th century. Despite the streams of new arrivals, Mexican Americans are largely treated as a colonized group and

Due to political and economic competition, Mexican-Americans are exploited and discriminated against

the history of the group in the 20th and 21st centuries closely parallels those of African Americans and American Indians. Thus, we might think of Mexican Americans as a colonized minority group with a large number of immigrants or as an immigrant group that incorporates a strong tradition of colonization.

Third, this brief review of the twisting history of U.S. policy on Mexican immigration should remind us that prejudice, racism, and discrimination increases as competition and the sense of threat between groups increases. The qualities that make Mexican labor attractive to employers have caused bitter resentment among segments of the Anglo population that feel that their jobs and financial security are threatened. Often caught in the middle, Mexican immigrants and Mexican Americans haven't had the resources to avoid exploitation by employers or rejection and discrimination by others. We can understand the changing efforts to regulate immigration in terms of competition, power differentials, and prejudice.

QUESTIONS FOR REFLECTION

1. How do Mexican American and Anglo cultures vary? How have these differences shaped relations between the groups?

2. Why has the volume of immigration from Mexico to the U. S. fluctuated over time?

Developments in the United States

As the flow of immigration from Mexico fluctuated with the need for labor, Mexican Americans struggled to improve their status. In the early decades of the 20th century, similar to other colonized minority groups, they faced a system of repression and control that gave them few rights and little political power.

Continuing Colonization and Gender Patterns

Early in the 20th century, Mexican Americans were largely limited to less desirable, low-wage jobs. Split labor markets, in which employers paid Mexican Americans less than Anglos for the same jobs, were common. Additionally, the workforce was split further by gender, with Mexican American women filling the worst and lowest-wage jobs (Takaki, 1993, pp. 318–319).

Men's jobs often took them away from their families to work in the mines and fields. In 1930, 45% of all Mexican American men worked in agriculture and 28% in unskilled nonagricultural jobs (Cortes, 1980, p. 708). Economic necessity often forced women to enter the job market. Employers typically paid them less than Mexican American men or Anglo women. In addition to job responsibilities, Mexican American women had to maintain their households and raise their children, often facing these tasks without partners (Baca Zinn & Eitzen, 1990, p. 84).

Immigrant women have increasingly worked outside the home, but historically, their employment was limited to agriculture, domestic service, and the garment industry (Amott & Matthaei, 1991; Cortes, 1980). In 1930, Hispanic women were concentrated in farm work (21%), unskilled manufacturing jobs (25%), and domestic and other service work (37%; Amott & Matthaei, 1991, pp. 76–77).

By 2015, 12 million immigrant women held jobs in the U.S., making them 7% of the labor force. Just over half (50.8%) came from Latin America, and of those, 2.8 million (23.8%) came from Mexico ("The Impact on Immigrant Women," 2017; see Figure 7.6). Nearly a third (32.5%) of immigrant women are employed in "pink-collar" personal service jobs such as housekeepers, health aides, cashiers, and building cleaners. These jobs have low pay, offer few benefits, and have little autonomy and room for advancement (Stallard, Ehrenreich, & Sklar, 1983, p. 19). In 2015, 20.4% of immigrant women workers earned poverty-level wages of $11,770 per year. Another fifth (21%) earned more than $11,770 but less than $20,000. Most of these women (62%) were Latin American, primarily from Mexico ("The Impact on Immigrant Women," 2017).

As the United States industrialized and urbanized during the century, employment patterns became more diversified. Mexican Americans found work in manufacturing, construction, transportation, and other sectors of the economy. Some Mexican Americans, especially those of the third generation or later, moved into middle- and upper-level occupations, and some moved out of the Southwest. Today, Mexican Americans are at all levels of affluence and poverty; however, they're disproportionately concentrated in lower-level occupations and face higher levels of poverty (especially more recent immigrants). For example, in 2017, Mexican Americans were twice as likely to work in agriculture and construction (17.6%) as non-Hispanic whites (8.4%) and only half as

FIGURE 7.6 ■ Foreign-Born Women Workers by Country of Origin, 2015

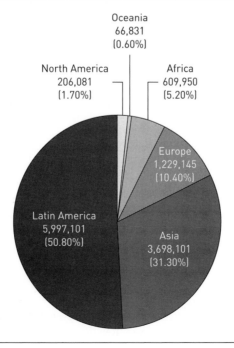

Oceania
66,831
(0.60%)

North America
206,081
(1.70%)

Africa
609,950
(5.20%)

Europe
1,229,145
(10.40%)

Latin America
5,997,101
(50.80%)

Asia
3,698,101
(31.30%)

Source: Adapted from American Immigration Council.

likely to be in management positions (19.4% vs. 42.8%). Mexican American households' median income was $16,257 less than non-Hispanic whites ($49,439 vs. $65,696) and Mexican American families were almost three times more likely to be in poverty (17.8% vs. 6.2%; U.S. Bureau of the Census, 2018a).

Similar to African Americans in the segregated South, laws and customs concerning Mexican Americans excluded them from the institutions of the larger society for much of the 20th century. There were separate (and unequal) school systems for Mexican American children, and in many communities, Mexican Americans were disenfranchised and accorded few legal or civil rights. There were "whites only" primary elections modeled after the Jim Crow system, and residential segregation was widespread. The police and the court system generally supported or ignored the rampant discrimination against the Mexican American community, and discrimination in the criminal justice system and civil rights violations have been continual grievances of Mexican Americans throughout the century.

Protest and Resistance

Like all minority groups, Mexican Americans have attempted to improve their collective position whenever possible. Their activism stretches back to the original contact period in the 19th century (Cortes, 1980). Similar to African Americans, Mexican Americans' early protest organizations were integrationist and reflected the assimilationist values of the larger society. For example, one of the earlier and more significant groups was the League of United Latin American Citizens (LULAC), founded in 1929. LULAC promoted Americanization and greater educational opportunities for Mexican Americans. It worked to expand civil and political rights for Mexican Americans and fought against racial discrimination in various ways (Moore, 1970); for example, by fighting for employment rights, including the right to join unions that had previously barred Mexican Americans and other immigrants (Grebler et al., 1970). Since the early 19th century, LULAC has organized unions, particularly in agriculture and mining, and when excluded by Anglo labor unions, it often formed its own. Additionally, members of LULAC have held important leadership roles in the labor movement.

The number and variety of groups working for Mexican American equality increased as the 20th century progressed. During World War II, Mexican Americans served in the U.S. armed forces in Europe. After the war ended, they returned to the U. S.; they were frustrated that the country they fought for didn't treat them equally under the law. As with other minority groups, this experience of broader rights and greater respect in Europe increased their impatience with the constraints they experienced in the United States. Inspired to make changes, they founded new Mexican American organizations, including the Community Service Organization and the American GI Forum. Compared with older organizations like LULAC, the new groups were less concerned with assimilation. They hoped to increase Mexican American political power and address numerous community problems (Grebler et al., 1970, pp. 543–545).

El Movimento and Chicanismo

The 1960s were a time of intense activism for many minority groups, including Mexican Americans. They created a civil rights movement—*El Movimento*—around the same time as the Black Power and Red Power movements. It was guided by an ideology called ***Chicanismo,*** somewhat similar to Black Power (see Chapter 5). Activists saw the inequalities that separated Mexican Americans from the larger society as resulting from deep-rooted, continuing racism and cumulative effects of decades of exclusion and institutional discrimination. They believed the solution to these problems lay in group empowerment, increased militancy, and group pride—not in assimilation to a culture that had supported their exploitation (Acuña, 1988; Grebler et al., 1970; Moore, 1970).

They rejected negative stereotypes of Mexican Americans and proclaimed a powerful and positive group image tied to their Mesoamerican heritage. Many Mexicans began to describe themselves as **Chicano/Chicana,** which, prior to the Chicano movement, was a derogatory term. Other minority groups underwent similar name changes. These changes weren't superficial—they showed fundamental shifts in group goals and a desired relationship with the larger society. The new names came from the minority groups, not from the dominant group, and they expressed the pluralistic themes of group pride, self-determination, militancy, and increased resistance to exploitation and discrimination.

Organizations and Leaders of the Chicano Movement

The Chicano movement saw the rise of many new groups and leaders: Reies López Tijerina, who formed the *Alianza Federal de Mercedes* (Federal Alliance of Land Grants) in 1963, was one of the most important. This group sought to rectify the unjust, illegal seizure of land from Mexicans during the 19th century. The Alianza occupied federal lands to bring attention to their cause. Because of his activities, Tijerina spent several years in jail. In the 1970s, the movement eventually lost its strength and faded from view.

Another prominent Chicano leader was Rodolfo Gonzalez, who founded the Crusade for Justice in 1965. This organization focused on violations of civil and legal rights, including discrimination by the criminal justice system. At a 1969 symposium on Chicano liberation, Gonzalez expressed some of the nationalistic themes of Chicanismo and the importance of creating a power base within the group (as opposed to assimilating or integrating):

> Where [whites] have incorporated themselves to keep us from moving into their neighborhoods, we can also incorporate ourselves to keep them from controlling our neighborhoods. We . . . have to understand economic revolution. . . . We have to understand that liberation comes from self-determination, and . . . start to use the tools of nationalism to win over our barrio brothers. . . . We have to understand that we can take over the institutions within our community. We have to create the community of the Mexicano here in order to have any type of power. (Moquin & Van Doren, 1971, pp. 381–382)

José Angel Gutiérrez, organizer of the party *La Raza Unida* (The People United), was another important leader. This organization worked to register and educate voters and create a political alternative to the Democrats and Republicans. Its most notable success was in Crystal City, Texas, where, in 1973, its entire slate of candidates was elected to office (Acuña, 1988).

The best-known Chicano leader of the 1960s and 1970s is César Chávez, who founded the National Farm Workers Association (NFWA). Recognizing connections between workers, the NFWA joined the Filipino workers' union and became the United Farm Workers (UFW) the first union to successfully represent migrant workers (Rojas, 2011). Chávez was as much a labor leader as a leader of the Mexican American community, and the UFW sought to protect and advance the rights of African American, Asian American, and Anglo American workers. Migrant farm workers had few economic or political resources, and the migratory basis of their work isolated them in rural areas and made them difficult to contact. In the 1960s (and still today), many were undocumented immigrants who spoke little or no English and returned to the cities or to their countries of origin at the end of the season. As a group, farm workers were nearly invisible in the social landscape of the U. S. in the 1960s. Thus, organizing this group was a demanding task. Chávez's success is one of the more remarkable studies in social movement organization.

Similar to Dr. Martin Luther King Jr., Chávez studied the nonviolent protest tactics and philosophy of Gandhi. In 1965, Chávez applied Gandhi's (and King's) tactics to organize a grape-pickers' strike and a national consumer boycott of grapes that lasted for five years and ended when the growers recognized the UFW as the legitimate representative of farm workers. This major victory for the UFW led to significant improvements for workers.

Gender and the Chicano Protest Movement

Similar to African American women involved in the civil rights movement, Chicana women encountered sexism within the Chicano movement. Activist Sylvia Gonzales described their dilemmas:

> Along with her male counterparts, she attended meetings, organized boycotts, did everything asked of her. . . . But, if she [tried to assume leadership roles] she was met with the same questioning of her femininity which the culture dictates when a woman is not self-sacrificing and seeks to fulfill her own needs. . . . The Chicano movement seemed to demand self-actualization for only the male members of the group. (cited in Amott & Matthaei, 1991, p. 83)

Despite having to fight to participate, Chicanas were key to the movement's success. Dolores Huerta and Jessie Lopez De La Cruz were central figures. With Chávez, Huerta built the NFWA and she organized the grape-pickers strike. Her intellect and fortitude made her a strong negotiator with farm owners and politicians, and she was able to build coalitions between workers and community members. Popularly, she's also known for the phrase, "Sí, se puede" (loosely meaning "yes, we can"), later adopted by Obama's presidential campaign. Lopez De La Cruz is best known for helping ban the mandated use of *el cortito*, a short-handled hoe requiring workers to stoop and twist all day, leading to long-term pain and disability. It was particularly hard on children's bodies (Beagle, 2016; Davis, 2008).

Chicanas in El Movimento possessed an intersectional view on civil rights. They made significant contributions to the movement and fought against "the triple burden of racial, gender, and economic discrimination" (Beagle, 2016, p. 118) by organizing poor communities and working for welfare reform. Without women such as Huerta, Lopez De La Cruz, Maria Luisa Rangel, Juanita Valdez, Herminia Rodriguez and many others, the group would not have flourished and made as significant an impact.

Mexican Americans and Other Minority Groups

Similar to the Black Power and Red Power movements, Chicanismo faded from public view in the 1970s and 1980s. The movement could claim some successes, but a key victory was in raising awareness in the larger society about Mexican Americans' problems and grievances. Today, many Chicanos continue to face poverty, powerlessness, and exploitation. The less-educated, urbanized group members share the prospect of becoming a part of a permanent urban underclass.

As with African Americans, internal and external forces have largely excluded Chicanos from major social institutions, which has limited their ability to pursue their self-interests. Continuing immigration from Mexico has increased the group's size, but many immigrants lack resources that can be translated immediately into economic or political power.

Unlike European immigrants who settled in the urban centers of the industrializing East Coast, Mexican Americans tended to live in rural areas, distant from opportunities for education and skill development that could lead to upward mobility. They were (and are) a vitally important source of labor in agriculture and other segments of the economy. Many people see their primary value as economic. That is, because of their powerlessness and lack of resources, they'll work long hours for low wages, which creates greater profit for employers. As Chicanos moved to the cities, they've tended to remain a colonized, exploited labor force concentrated at the lower end of the stratification system. That is, the challenges created by past discrimination are reinforced by present-day discrimination, allowing the cycles of poverty and relative powerlessness to continue.

Nevertheless, the constant movement of people back and forth across the border kept Mexican culture and the Spanish language alive. Unlike African Americans under slavery, Chicanos weren't cut off from their homeland, which made it easier for Mexican American culture to survive. Clearly, the traditional model of assimilation—which was based largely on the experiences of European immigrant groups—doesn't effectively explain Mexican Americans' experiences. They've had less social mobility than European immigrant groups but have maintained their traditional culture more completely. Similar to African Americans, Mexican Americans are split along social class lines. Although many Mexican Americans (particularly of the third generation and later) have acculturated and integrated, a large part of the group still fills the same economic role as their ancestors: as an unskilled labor force for the development of the Southwest, augmented with new immigrants at the convenience of U.S. employers. For the less educated and for recent immigrants, cultural and racial differences can increase their social visibility, mark them for exploitation, and rationalize their continuing exclusion from the larger society.

QUESTIONS FOR REFLECTION

3. Are Mexican Americans a colonized or immigrant minority group? Both? Neither? Why?

4. Compare Chicanismo with Black and Red Power. How and why did these protest movements differ? Describe the key ideas, leaders, and organizations of Mexican American protest.

PUERTO RICANS

Puerto Rico ("Rich Port") became a U.S. territory in 1898 after Spain's defeat in the Spanish–American War. While rich in natural resources, the island was small, relatively impoverished, and powerless compared with the United States. In 1900, the Foraker Act made Puerto Rico the first unincorporated territory of the U. S. and instituted a civil government (Santiago, 2001). It also replaced people's Spanish citizenship with a Puerto Rican one and sought to make English the official language (Foraker Act, 1900; Leonard & Lugo-Lugo, 2015). In 1914, the Puerto Rican House of Delegates unanimously voted for independence from the United States, but Congress rejected this idea (Gonzalez, 2011). A year later, Puerto Rico's governor asked Congress to give the island greater autonomy. Instead, Congress responded with the Jones-Shafroth Act, which designated island-born residents as U.S. citizens and created a bill of rights and a three-branch government that many Puerto Ricans didn't want (Leonard & Lugo-Lugo, 2015).

This complex, often-contested relationship has continued. Puerto Ricans aren't "foreigners"; however, the U.S. government hasn't given them the rights of *full* American citizenship (Santiago, 2001). Puerto Ricans still debate their status as a U.S. territory. Many want statehood while others want independence (Robles, 2017). When evaluating the situation of contemporary Puerto Ricans, remember that the first contact between Puerto Ricans and the United States occurred in an atmosphere of war and conquest. Further, by the time Puerto Ricans migrated to the mainland in large numbers, their relationship to U.S. society was largely that of a colonized minority group, and they've generally retained that status on the mainland.

Migration (Push and Pull) and Employment

At the time of contact, Puerto Rico's population was primarily rural and supported itself with subsistence farming and by exporting coffee and sugar. As the 20th century progressed, U.S. firms invested in the island's economy, especially the sugarcane industry. These agricultural endeavors increasingly took much of the land, forcing people to move to the cities as opportunities for economic survival in rural areas declined (Portes, 1990, p. 163).

Movement to the mainland increased slowly until the 1940s. In 1900, about 2,000 Puerto Ricans lived on the American mainland. By World War II, that number had increased to 70,000. During the 1940s, the number of Puerto Ricans on the mainland increased more than fourfold to 300,000, and during the 1950s, it nearly tripled to 887,000 (U.S. Commission on Civil Rights, 1976, p. 19).

This sudden population growth resulted from a combination of circumstances. First, because Puerto Ricans are U.S. citizens, international boundaries or immigration restrictions didn't impede their movements. Second, unemployment was a major problem on the island. The sugarcane industry continued to displace the rural population, urban unemployment was high, and the population continued to grow. By the 1940s, a considerable number of Puerto Ricans were available to work off the island and, similar to Chicanos, could serve as a cheap labor supply for U.S. employers.

Third, Puerto Ricans were pulled to the mainland by the same labor shortages that attracted Mexican immigrants during and after World War II. Whereas the latter responded to job opportunities in the West and the Southwest, Puerto Ricans moved to the Northeast. The job profiles of these two groups were similar: Both were concentrated in the low-wage, unskilled sector of the job market. However, the Puerto Rican migration began decades after the Mexican migration, at a time when the U. S. was much more industrialized and urbanized. Therefore, Puerto Ricans were more concentrated in urban labor markets than Mexican immigrants (Portes, 1990, p. 164).

In the late 1940s, affordable air travel between San Juan and New York City facilitated movement between the island and the mainland. New York had been the major center of settlement for Puerto Ricans on the mainland even before annexation. Puerto Ricans established a small community in the city and, similar to many other immigrant groups, created organizations and networks to help newcomers with housing, jobs, and other transition issues. Although they eventually dispersed to other regions and cities, Puerto Ricans on the mainland remain centered in New York City; 53% resided in the Northeast, with 23% in New York alone (Brown & Patten, 2013, p. 2).

Economics and jobs were at the heart of the Puerto Rican migration to the mainland that followed the cycle of boom and bust, just as they were for Mexican immigrants. The 1950s, the peak decade for Puerto Rican migration, was a period of rapid U.S. economic growth. Migration was encouraged, and job recruiters traveled to the island to attract workers. By the 1960s, however, the supply of jobs in Puerto Rico expanded appreciably, reducing the average number of migrants from the peak of 41,000 per year in the 1950s to about 20,000 per year. In the 1970s, the U.S. economy faltered, unemployment grew, and the flow of Puerto Rican migration reversed itself, with the number of returnees exceeding the number of migrants in various years (U.S. Commission on Civil Rights, 1976, p. 25). However, movement to the mainland has continued, and in 2017, about 5.5 million Puerto Ricans (about 60% of all Puerto Ricans), were living on the mainland. In 2016, 3.2 million lived in Puerto Rico (see Table 7.1; Krogstad, Starr, & Sandstrom, 2017).

A major factor affecting recent migration was a devastating Category 5 hurricane that hit Puerto Rico in 2017. It ravaged the natural environment and much of the island's infrastructure, including buildings, roads, water systems, and the electrical grid. The storm closed schools, medical facilities, and businesses, and it destroyed vast amounts of agriculture—all of which radically affected life in Puerto Rico. By most counts, the federal response was inadequate. For months, many Puerto Ricans lacked essential items such as safe drinking water, shelter, medical supplies, power, and cell phone service (Holmes, 2017).

In estimating the death toll, Puerto Rican and federal officials focused on immediate deaths such as drowning, claiming about 64 people died from the storm. However, researchers, such as those from the Washington University Milken Institute School of Public Health (2018), took a different approach. They collected statistics and interviewed funeral directors, medical staff, and others to calculate and compared death rates pre- and post-hurricane. They also counted indirect deaths (for example, if someone died because their ventilator didn't work because they had no electricity). Their report put the death toll at 2,975 people (Fink, 2018).

Reconstruction has been slow, and mental health professionals suggest that most Puerto Ricans suffer some degree of post-traumatic stress disorder. Research suggests that more than 130,000 people have left the island. This mass migration will surely change the island and the American mainland in ways that we don't yet understand (Alvarez, 2017; Dickerson, 2017a; Holmes, 2017; Meyer, 2017b).

Transitions

Although Puerto Ricans aren't immigrants, the move to the mainland involves a change in culture, including language (Fitzpatrick, 1980). Despite more than a century of political affiliation, Puerto Rican and Anglo cultures differ along many dimensions. Puerto Ricans are overwhelmingly Catholic, but their religious practices and rituals on the mainland are quite different from those on the island. Mainland Catholic parishes often reflect the traditions and practices of other cultures and groups. On the island, "Religious observance reflects the spontaneous and expressive practices of the Spanish and the Italian and not the restrained and well-organized worship of the Irish and Germans" (p. 865). Also, a shortage of Puerto Rican priests and Spanish-speaking clergy exists on the mainland. Although the overwhelming majority of Latinos are Catholic, only about 6% of Catholic priests are Latinos (Olivo & Eldeib, 2013). Thus, members of the group often feel estranged from and poorly served by the Church (Fitzpatrick, 1987).

Like most Caribbean people, Puerto Ricans construct race as a continuum of possibilities and combinations, not as a simple dichotomy between white and black. Compared with the U.S. mainland, slavery in Puerto Rico was less monolithic and total, and the island had no periods of systematic, race-based segregation like the Jim Crow system. Additionally, Puerto Rico has a long history of racial intermarriage. Thus, although racial prejudice exists in Puerto Rico, it never has been as categorical as on the mainland (Grant-Thomas & Ofield, 2008, p. 167; Hollinger, 2003).

In Brazil (see Chapter 5), social class can affect perceptions of skin color. Puerto Ricans also possess a more nuanced view of race. For example, people might call an upper-class woman *blanquita* (Grant-Thomas & Ofield, 2008). Roughly translated as "little white woman," this term simultaneously constructs race, class, and gender. Other labels construct ethnicity in relation to geographic location. For example, *Nuyoricans* (Puerto Rican New Yorkers) are different from *Boricuas* (Puerto Ricans from the island, not the mainland).

Coming from this perspective, some Puerto Ricans find the Anglo American way of thinking about race to be disconcerting. For example, a study of Puerto Rican college students in New York City found dramatic differences between people's personal racial identification and their perceptions of how Anglos labeled them. When asked for their racial identification, most students classified themselves as *tan*; one third said *white* and only 7% said *black*. When asked how they thought Anglos classified them, nobody said *tan*. Fifty-eight percent said *white* and 41% said *black* (Rodriguez, 1989, pp. 60–61; see also Rodriguez & Cordero-Guzman, 1992; Vargas-Ramos, 2005).

Another study documented dramatic differences in the terms Puerto Rican women use to express racial identity based on their location. Women on the island identified themselves primarily by skin color: black, white, or *trigueña* ("wheat-colored"). Mainland women identified themselves in nonracial terms, such as *Hispanic, Latina, Hispanic American*, or *American*. Researchers argue that these latter terms serve to deflect the stigma associated with black racial status on the mainland (Landale & Oropesa, 2002). As with other social constructs, racial labels are contextual. For example, Goudreau (2000) notes that a woman might be called "*trigueña, negra, india, de color o blanquita* (copper color, black, Indian, colored, or white) by different people in different moments" (p. 45, c.f. Grant-Thomas & Orfield, 2008, p. 167).

In the U. S., where race is less fluid, Puerto Ricans may feel that they have no clear place or may favor one aspect of their racial or ethnic identity over others (Quiros, 2009). Schachter's (2016) research suggests that whites viewed nonwhite people as dissimilar— symbolically not fully American. A recent example of this happened when U.S.–born Sonia Sotomayor was named to the U.S. Supreme Court. Some questioned whether her "immigrant background" would interfere with her ability to uphold the Constitution (Greenberg, 2015). The negative racial perceptions and stereotypes of the dominant culture threaten Puerto Ricans to the extent that they can be victimized by the same types of discrimination and disadvantages that affect African Americans, Native Americans, and other minority groups. Institutionalized racial barriers can be extremely formidable; they may combine with cultural and linguistic differences to sharply limit opportunities and mobility for Puerto Ricans.

Puerto Ricans and Other Minority Groups

Puerto Ricans arrived in Northeast cities long after the great wave of European immigrants and several decades after African Americans began migrating from the South. They've often competed with other minority groups for housing, jobs, and other resources. In some neighborhoods and occupational areas, a pattern of ethnic succession can be seen in which Puerto Ricans have replaced other groups that have moved out (and sometimes up).

Because of their more recent arrival, Puerto Ricans on the mainland didn't experience the more repressive paternalistic or rigid competitive systems of race relations such as slavery or Jim Crow. However, the subordinate status of the group is manifested in their occupational, residential, and educational profiles and by the institutionalized barriers to upward mobility that they face.

Similar to Mexican Americans, Puerto Ricans on the mainland combine elements of immigrant and colonized minority experiences. The movement to the mainland is voluntary in some ways, but in others, it's strongly motivated by the transformations in the island economy that resulted from modernization and U.S. domination. Like Chicanos, Puerto Ricans tend to enter the labor force at the bottom of the occupational structure and face similar problems of inequality and marginalization.

Like other urban minority groups of color, Puerto Ricans find their fate to be dependent on the future of the American city, particularly concerning problems of employment, poverty, failing educational systems, and crime. Without improvement in those areas, a segment of the group is at risk of becoming part of the permanent urban underclass.

Since 2005, a historic number of people (almost half a million) have left Puerto Rico for the mainland because of economic recession (Krogstad et al., 2017). Given the island's current infrastructure and financial problems, we expect more islanders to migrate to the mainland. That said, Puerto Rican culture is strong and it's continually reinvigorated by the considerable movement back and forth between the island and the mainland.

QUESTIONS FOR REFLECTION

5. Would you say that Puerto Ricans are more an immigrant or colonized minority group? Why?

6. What are some of the key differences between Puerto Rican and Anglo cultures? How have these differences shaped relations between the groups?

CUBAN AMERICANS

The contact period for Cuban Americans, as for Puerto Ricans, dates to the Spanish–American War of 1898. Although Cuba was a Spanish colony, the U. S. had been involved in Cuban politics and economics for decades prior to the war. The U. S. invaded Cuba in 1898 and maintained a military force there until 1902, when Cuba became an independent nation. (U.S. troops occupied the island twice more: from 1906–1909 and 1917–1922.) Today, the U. S. still operates a military base at Guantanamo.

The development of a Cuban American minority group in the U. S. bears little resemblance to the experience of Mexican Americans or Puerto Ricans. Until the 1950s, few Cubans immigrated to America, even during times of labor shortages, and Cuban Americans were a very small group, numbering no more than 50,000 (Perez, 1980, p. 256).

Immigration (Push and Pull)

The conditions for a mass immigration emerged in the 1950s, when a revolution brought Fidel Castro to power in Cuba. Castro's government was decidedly anti-American and began to restructure Cuban society along socialist lines. The middle and upper classes, who had become Americanized in their attitudes and lifestyles, could no longer do business as usual and quickly began to lose political and economic power. Thus, the first Cuban immigrants to the U. S. were elites. Most were affluent, powerful, and white; their resources made it possible for them to leave (Pedraza, 1998; Portes, 1990).

America was a logical destination. Cuba is only 90 miles from southern Florida, and many Cubans had had prior social, cultural, and business ties pulling them toward the United States. Some exiles saw Florida as an ideal spot from which to launch a counterrevolution. Most importantly, the American government saw them as refugees fleeing Communist tyranny (the immigration occurred at the height of the Cold War) and, thus, welcomed them warmly.

More than 215,000 Cubans arrived during this first wave of immigration, which ended in 1962 after an escalation of hostile relations, including the failed Bay of Pigs invasion, resulted in the cutoff of direct contact between Cuba and the United States. Nevertheless, many of these migrants hoped to return to Cuba (Pedraza, 1998).

The second wave of immigrants came after the Cuban government seized 55,000 small businesses (Pedraza, 1998). After contact between the U. S. and Cuba resumed in 1965, U.S.–sponsored "Freedom Flights" brought 300,000 more Cubans to America. When the flights ended in 1973, immigration slowed to a trickle (Rusin, Zong, & Batalova, 2015).

In 1980, Castro permitted another period of immigration, during which about 124,000 Cubans crossed to Florida using boats of every shape, size, and degree of seaworthiness. Sometimes people call them *marielitos*, after the port of Mariel from which many departed. Most Americans called them "Cuban boat people." Most of these immigrants were young, working class, single, black men. Castro called them "scum" ("Flight from Cuba," 1994; Pedraza, 1998). Many were convicted criminals. However, this wave also included political prisoners and people who had been imprisoned for being gay or for having mental illnesses. The *marielitos* generated a great deal of controversy in the U. S. and their reception was decidedly less favorable than it was for the prior waves. Even some in the established Cuban American community distanced itself from the *marielitos*, who were born after the revolution and with whom they lacked kinship or friendship ties (Portes & Shafer, 2006, pp. 16–17).

In 1992, in hopes of pushing Cubans to overthrow Castro, the U.S. government escalated its embargo. Cubans, who already found it difficult to obtain necessities, became desperate and tried to flee. An initial government crackdown led to mass rioting. Eventually, Castro temporarily lifted the travel ban and more than 32,000 Cubans left on anything that would float, including homemade rafts and old tires. Boats were often overcrowded and didn't have water or life jackets. At least 16,000 people died making the perilous journey (Ackerman, n.d.; Pedraza, 1998; Taylor, 2014).

When Raul Castro became Cuba's leader in 2006, a new relationship between the U. S. and Cuba began. In 2014, the U.S. government began allowing small numbers of U.S. citizens to travel to Cuba and, in 2015, took Cuba off its terrorism list, where it had been since 1982. Embassies opened in both nations. However, since 2016, U.S. relations with Cuba have been under scrutiny and trade and travel restrictions have tightened. How things unfold in the future will affect Cubans' lives for better or worse, which may encourage them to stay in Cuba or pull them to the United States (Corral, Negrete, Nesmith, & Anaagasti, 2016; Kahn, 2017; *Los Angeles Times* Editorial Board, 2015; Sopel, 2015).

Regional Concentrations

The overwhelming majority of Cuban immigrants settled in southern Florida, especially in Miami and the surrounding Dade County. Today, Cuban Americans remain one of the most spatially concentrated minority groups in the U. S., with 68% of all

Cuban Americans residing in Florida (López, 2015b). This dense concentration has led to many disputes between the Hispanic, Anglo, and African American communities in the area. Issues have centered on language, jobs, and discrimination by the police and other governmental agencies. The conflicts often have been intense and, on more than one occasion, have erupted into violence and civil disorder.

Socioeconomic Characteristics

Because early immigrants included large numbers of professionals, landowners, and businesspeople, Cubans are unusually affluent and well-educated compared with other Latin American immigrants. Today, Cuban Americans rank higher than other Latino groups on many dimensions, which is reflective of the educational and economic resources they brought with them and the favorable reception they enjoyed in America (Portes, 1990).

These assets gave Cubans an advantage over Chicanos and Puerto Ricans, but the differences between the three Latino groups run deeper and are more complex than a simple accounting of initial resources would suggest. Cubans adapted to U.S. society in a way that is fundamentally different from the experiences of the other two Latino groups.

The Ethnic Enclave

Most of the minority groups we've discussed to this point have been concentrated in the unskilled, low-wage segments of the economy in which jobs are insecure and have few, if any, opportunities for upward mobility. Many Cuban Americans bypassed this sector of the economy and much of the discrimination and limitations associated with it. Like several other groups, such as Jewish Americans, Cuban Americans are an *enclave* minority, a social, economic, and cultural sub-society. Located in a specific geographical area or neighborhood inhabited solely or largely by members of the group, the enclave encompasses sufficient economic enterprises and social institutions to permit the group to function as a self-contained entity, largely independent of the surrounding community (see Chapter 2).

The first-wave Cubans brought with them considerable human capital and business expertise. Although much of their energy was focused on ousting Castro and returning to Cuba, they generated enough economic activity to sustain restaurants, shops, and other small businesses that catered to the exile community.

As the years passed and the hope of a return to Cuba dimmed, the enclave economy grew. Between 1967 and 1976, the number of Cuban-owned firms in Dade County increased ninefold from 919 to about 8,000. Six years later, it was 12,000. Most of these enterprises were small, but some factories employed hundreds of workers (Portes & Rumbaut, 1996, pp. 20–21). By 2001, more than 125,000 Cuban-owned firms existed in the U. S., and the rate of Cuban-owned firms per 100,000 people was four times greater than the rate for Mexican Americans and 14 times greater than the rate for African Americans (Portes & Shafer, 2006, p. 14).

Cuban-owned firms have become integrated within local economies and increasingly competitive with other firms involved in construction, manufacturing, finance, insurance, real estate, and an array of other activities in the larger society. The growth of economic enterprises has been paralleled by a growth in the number of other types of groups and organizations and in the number and quality of services available (e.g., schools, law firms, medical care). The enclave has become a largely autonomous community capable of providing for its members from cradle to grave (Logan, Alba, & McNulty, 1994; Peterson, 1995; Portes & Bach, 1985, p. 59).

That the group controls the enclave economy is crucial; this differentiates the ethnic enclave from "the ghetto" or other impoverished and segregated neighborhoods. In ghettos, members of other groups typically control the local economy; the profits, rents, and other resources flow out of the neighborhood. In the enclave, profits are reinvested into the neighborhood. By staying within the enclave, group members can avoid the discrimination and limitations experienced within the larger society and can apply their skills, education, and talents in an atmosphere free from language barriers and prejudice. Those who might wish to venture into business for themselves can use the networks of cooperation and mutual aid for advice, credit, and other forms of help. Thus, the ethnic enclave provides a platform from which Cuban Americans can pursue economic success independent of their degree of acculturation or English language ability.

The effectiveness of the ethnic enclave as a pathway for adaptation is illustrated by a study of Cuban and Mexican immigrants who entered the United States in 1973. At the time of entry, the groups were comparable in levels of skills, education, and English language ability. Researchers interviewed group members on several different occasions, and although they remained comparable on many variables, dramatic differences between the groups existed that reflected their different positions in the labor market. Most of the Mexican immigrants were employed in the low-wage job sector. Less than 20% were self-employed or employed by someone of Mexican descent. Conversely, 57% of the Cuban immigrants were self-employed or employed by other Cubans in the enclave economy. Among the subjects in the study, self-employed Cubans reported the highest monthly incomes ($1,495), and Cubans otherwise employed in the enclave earned the second-highest monthly incomes ($1,111). Mexican immigrants employed in small, non-enclave firms earned the lowest monthly incomes ($880); many worked as unskilled laborers in seasonal, temporary, or otherwise insecure jobs (Portes, 1990, p. 173; see also Portes & Bach, 1985).

A more recent study confirms the advantages that accrue from forming an enclave. Using 2000 census data, Portes and Shafer (2006) compared the incomes of several groups in the Miami–Fort Lauderdale metropolitan area, including the original Cuban immigrants (who founded the enclave), their children (the second generation), Cuban immigrants who arrived after 1980 (the *marielitos* and others), and several other groups. Figure 7.7 shows some of the results of the study for men.

The far-left bar in Figure 7.7 shows that the founders and primary beneficiaries of the Cuban enclave are the self-employed, pre-1980 Cuban immigrants. Their income is higher than for all other Cuban groups included in the graph and only slightly less than for non-Hispanic whites (not shown). The sons of the founding generation (U.S.–born Cuban Americans) also enjoy a substantial benefit, both directly (through working in the enclave firms started by their fathers) and indirectly (by translating the resources of their families into human capital, including education, for themselves). The incomes of post-1980 Cuban immigrants are the lowest on the graph and comparable to incomes for non-Hispanic blacks (not shown).

FIGURE 7.7 ■ Family Incomes for Self-Employed and Wage/Salaried Men Workers from Three Cuban American Groups, 2000

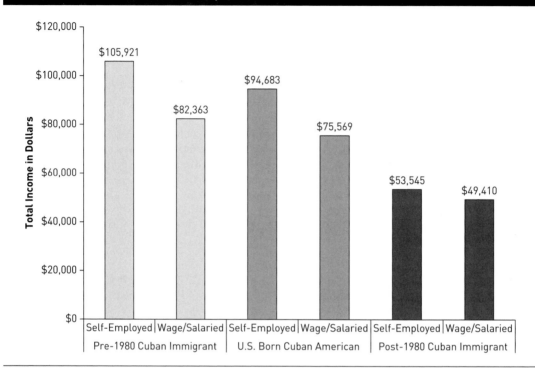

Source: Portes and Shafer (2006, p. 42). "Revisiting the Enclave Hypothesis: Miami Twenty-Five Years Later." The Center for Migration and Development, Princeton University, p. 42.

The ability of most Hispanic (and other) immigrants to rise in the class system and compete for place and position is constrained by discrimination and their lack of economic and political power. Cuban immigrants in the enclave don't need to expose themselves to American prejudices or to rely on its job market. They constructed networks of mutual aid, which helped them find opportunities more consistent with their ambitions and qualifications.

The link between the enclave and economic equality (an aspect of secondary structural integration) challenges the predictions of some traditional assimilation theories and the understandings of many Americans. Some leaders of other groups have long recognized this pattern. For example, you learned about similar themes of self-help, self-determination, nationalism, and separation within the Black Power, Red Power, and Chicanismo movements.

However, ethnic enclaves aren't a panacea for all immigrant or minority groups. They develop only under certain limited conditions—namely, when business and financial expertise and reliable sources of capital are combined with a disciplined labor force willing to work for low wages in exchange for on-the-job training, future assistance and loans, or other delayed benefits. Enclave enterprises usually start on a small scale and cater only to other group members. Thus, the early economic returns are small, and prosperity follows only after years of hard work, if at all. Most importantly, the eventual success and expansion beyond the boundaries of the enclave depends on the persistence of strong ties of loyalty, kinship, and solidarity. The pressure to assimilate might easily weaken these networks and the strength of group cohesion (Portes & Manning, 1986).

Cuban Americans and Other Minority Groups

The adaptation of Cuban Americans contrasts sharply with the experiences of colonized minority groups and with the traditional view of how immigrants are "supposed" to acculturate and integrate. Cuban Americans are neither the first nor the only group to develop an ethnic enclave, and their success has generated prejudice and resentment from the dominant group and from other minority groups. Puerto Ricans and Chicanos have been stereotyped as lazy, unmotivated, criminals, clowns, or "Latin lovers" (Mastro, Behm-Morawitz, & Ortiz, 2007). Yet, people stereotype higher-status Cuban Americans as too successful, too clannish, and too ambitious. The former stereotype commonly emerges to rationalize exploitative relationships; the latter expresses disparagement and a sense of group rejection in the struggle to acquire resources. Nonetheless, Cuban stereotypes are an exaggeration and a misperception that obscures the fact that poverty and unemployment are major problems for many members of this group, especially for the post-1980 immigrants.

QUESTIONS FOR REFLECTION

7. Would you say that Cuban Americans are more an immigrant or colonized minority group? Why?

8. Are Cuban Americans an enclave minority? What are the most important advantages enjoyed by enclave minority groups? Are there any disadvantages?

PREJUDICE AND DISCRIMINATION

The American tradition of prejudice against Latinos was born in the 19th-century conflicts that created minority group status for Mexican Americans. The themes of the original anti-Mexican stereotypes and attitudes were consistent with the type of contact situation: As Mexicans were conquered and subordinated, they were characterized as inferior, lazy, irresponsible, low in intelligence, and dangerously criminal (McWilliams, 1961). Prejudice and racism, supplemented with the echoes of the racist ideas and beliefs brought to the Southwest by many Anglos, helped justify and rationalize the colonized, exploited status of the Chicanos.

These prejudices were incorporated into the dominant culture and transferred to Puerto Ricans when they arrived on the mainland. However, this stereotype doesn't fit the situation of Cuban Americans very well. Instead, their affluence has been exaggerated and perceived as undeserved or achieved by unfair or un-American means, a characterization similar to the stereotype of Jews but just as prejudiced as perceptions of Hispanic inferiority.

Some evidence suggests that the level of prejudice against Latinos has been affected by the decline of explicit American racism. For example, social distance scales show a decrease in the scores for Mexicans, although their relative ranking remains fairly stable. (See Chapters 1 and 5.)

However, anti-Latino prejudice and racism tend to increase during times of high immigration. Considerable (though largely anecdotal evidence) suggests that the surge of immigration that began in the 1990s sparked high levels of anti-Latino prejudice in areas along the U.S.–Mexican border. Extreme racist rhetoric was common, and the media prominently featured hate group activities. Many people see extensions of these views in Arizona's recent policies, including a state-mandated ban on ethnic studies programs in public schools and its widely debated State Bill 1070 that, in part, allowed police to check anyone for proof of citizenship. In 2012, the Supreme Court upheld this part of the bill but struck down three other provisions, and in 2014, a federal judge rejected those other provisions. At any rate, the level of immigrant bashing and anti-Latino sentiment along the border and in other parts of the United States demonstrates that American prejudice, although sometimes disguised as a subtle modern racism, is alive and well.

Although immigration rates from Mexico and Latin America tended to decrease in recent years, prejudicial sentiments were a prominent feature of President Trump's presidential campaign and the early days of his administration. As you've learned, prejudice isn't always a direct response to threat and group competition but can be motivated by cultural and personality factors (see Chapter 1). Anti-Hispanic and anti-immigration sentiments were frequently expressed during Mr. Trump's presidential campaign. In fact, his campaign began with a speech associating undocumented Mexican immigrants with drug dealers and rapists, and one of the most prominent features of his campaign rhetoric was a promise to build a wall along the U.S.–Mexican border.

Furthermore, one of Trump's first acts as president was to initiate a ban on immigrants from seven predominantly Muslim nations (Singhvi & Parlapiano, 2017). This ban was overturned in the courts, but in June 2018, the Supreme Court ruled that a revised policy was constitutional (Liptak & Shear, 2018).

In Chapter 4, we mentioned that audit studies have documented the persistence of discrimination against African Americans in the housing and job markets; many of the same studies also demonstrate anti-Hispanic biases (see Quillian, 2006, for a review). Discrimination of all kinds, institutional and individual, against Latino groups has been common. However, it hasn't been as rigid or as total as the systems that controlled African American labor under slavery and segregation. However, discrimination against Latinos persists across the United States. Because of their longer tenure in the U. S. and their original status as a rural labor force, Mexican Americans probably have been more victimized by the institutionalized forms of discrimination than have other Latino groups.

ASSIMILATION AND PLURALISM

As with previous chapters, we'll use the central concepts of this book to review the status of Latinos in the United States. Where relevant, we'll compare the major Latino groups and the minority groups discussed in previous chapters.

Acculturation

Latinos are highly variable in their extent of acculturation but are often seen as slow to change, learn English, and adopt Anglo customs. However, research shows that Hispanics follow many of the same patterns of assimilation as the European groups that arrived between the 1820s and 1920s (Chapter 2). For example, language acculturation for Hispanic groups, as for immigrants from Europe in the past, increases over the generations (see Figure 7.8). Furthermore, one recent study showed that English proficiency is greater among the native-born, the more educated, and those who have lived in the U. S. longer—trends that are quite consistent with the traditional model of assimilation. The researchers also found that the majority of Hispanics speak English only (25%) or are bilingual (36%) and the percentage who mainly speak English increases with the generations: 42% of second-generation Hispanics speak mainly English, as do 76% of the third generations or later (Krogstad & Gonzalez-Barrera, 2015; see also, Espinosa & Massey, 1997; Goldstein & Suro, 2000; Valentine & Mosley, 2000).

Similarly, an earlier study found that Anglo and Latino values become virtually identical as length of residence increases, generations pass, and English language ability increases. For example, the values of predominantly Spanish speakers (who were mostly foreign-born or first generation) are distinctly different from those of non-Latinos, especially on a survey item that measures support for the statement, "Children should live with their parents until they are married." Virtually all the predominantly Spanish speakers supported the statement, but English-speaking Latinos showed the more

FIGURE 7.8 ■ Primary Language by Generation for Hispanic Americans, 2012

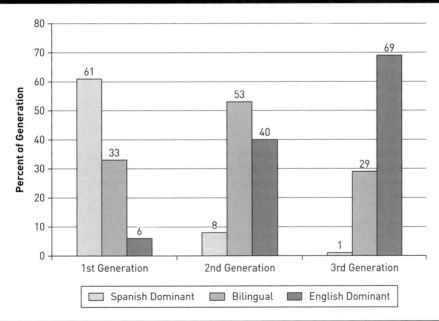

Source: Taylor, Lopez, Martinez, and Velasco (2012). "When Labels Don't Fit: Hispanics and their Views of Identity" http://www.pewhispanic.org/2012/04/04/when-labels-dont-fit-hispanics-and-their-views-of-identity/

individualistic values of Anglos. A similar acculturation to American values occurred for the other three items that researchers studied (Pew Hispanic Center, 2004).

A more recent study (Pew Research Center, 2014b) found similar acculturation trends on the "hot-button" issues of same-sex marriage and abortion (see Table 7.4). The attitudes of Hispanic Americans born in the U. S. are far more similar to the general public than are those of foreign-born Hispanic Americans.

Even while acculturation continues, however, immigration revitalizes Hispanic culture and the Spanish language. Assimilation is a slow process that can require decades or generations to complete. In contrast, immigration can be fast, often accomplished in less than a day. Thus, even as Hispanic Americans acculturate and integrate, Hispanic culture and language are sustained and strengthened. What people perceive as slow acculturation for these groups is mostly the result of fast and continuous immigration.

Furthermore, colonized minority groups such as Chicanos and Puerto Ricans weren't encouraged to assimilate in the past. Valued primarily for the cheap labor they supplied, they were seen as inferior, undesirable, and unfit for integration. For much of the 20th century, Latinos were excluded from the institutions and experiences (e.g., school) that could have led to greater equality and higher rates of acculturation. Prejudice, racism, and discrimination combined to keep most Latino groups away from the centers of modernization and change and away from opportunities to improve their situation.

Finally, for Cubans, Dominicans, Salvadorans, and other groups, cultural differences reflect that they're largely recent immigrants. Their first generations are alive and well. As is typical for immigrant groups, they keep their language and traditions alive.

Secondary Structural Assimilation

In this section, we review the situation of Latinos in the public areas and institutions of American society. We follow the same format as the previous two chapters, beginning with where people live.

Residence

Figure 7.9 shows the geographic concentrations of Latinos in 2010. The legacies of the varied patterns of entry and settlement for the largest groups are evident. The higher

TABLE 7.4 ■ Opinions on Same-Sex Marriage and Abortion			
	Percentage in Favor		
Item	**General Public**	**U.S.–Born Hispanics**	**Foreign-Born Hispanics**
"Gays and lesbians should be allowed to legally marry."	50%	58%	39%
"Abortion should be legal in all or most cases."	54%	49%	33%

Source: Pew Research Center (2014b).

50% to 95.7%
25% to 49.9%
15% to 24.9%
5% to 14.9%
Less than 5%

*Percent of Total U.S.
Population 16.3%*

Source: Ennis, Rios-Vargas, & Albert (2011, p. 10); U.S. Census Bureau (2011b).

concentrations in the Southwest reflect the presence of Mexican Americans, those in Florida are the result of the Cuban immigration, and those in the Northeast display the settlement patterns of Puerto Ricans.

Figure 7.10 highlights the areas of the nation where the Latino population is growing fastest. A quick glance at the map reveals that many of the high-growth areas are distant from the traditional points of entry for these groups. In particular, the Latino population is growing rapidly in parts of New England, the South, the upper Midwest, the Northwest, and even Alaska. This population movement is a response to (among many other forces) the availability of jobs in factories, mills, chicken-processing plants and slaughterhouses, farms, construction, and other low-skilled areas of the economy.

Within each of these regions, Latino groups are highly urbanized (see Figure 7.11). Except for Mexican Americans, more than 90% of each of the 10 largest Hispanic American groups live in urban areas, and this percentage approaches 100% for some groups. Mexican Americans are more rural than the other groups, but the percentage of the group living in rural areas is tiny today, in sharp contrast to their historical role as an agrarian workforce.

In Figure 5.9, you saw the extent of residential segregation for Hispanic Americans based on a dissimilarity index. Residential segregation is much lower for Hispanics than for African Americans: None of the scores for Hispanics approach the "extreme" segregation denoted by a dissimilarity index of 60 or more.

Contrary to the decreasing levels of black–white segregation, Hispanic–white residential segregation has held steady, with minor increases or decreases. Among other

FIGURE 7.10 ■ Rate of Growth of Latino Population by County, 2007–2014

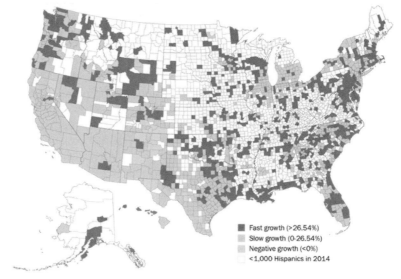

Fast growth (>26.54%)
Slow growth (0-26.54%)
Negative growth (<0%)
<1,000 Hispanics in 2014

Source: Stepler and Lopez (2016).

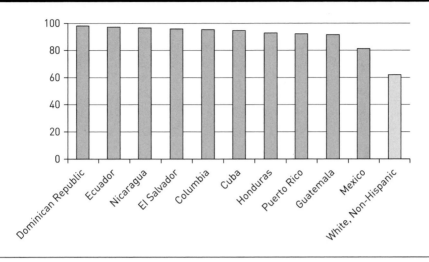

FIGURE 7.11 ■ **Percentage Living in Urban Areas for Non-Hispanic Whites and the 10 Largest Hispanic Groups, 2000**

Source: U.S. Census Bureau (2000b).

Note: An *urban area* is defined as an area with a minimal population density of 1,000 persons per square mile and a maximum population of 50,000.

factors, this reflects high rates of immigration and chain patterns of settlement, which concentrate newcomers in ethnic neighborhoods. That is, levels of residential segregation for Hispanics remain relatively steady because weakening barriers to integration in the larger society are counteracted by the continuing arrival of newcomers, who tend to settle in predominantly Hispanic neighborhoods.

Education

Figure 7.12 uses data from the U. S. General Accountability Office to display the extent of school segregation for Hispanic Americans across four different school years in three types of schools: *low poverty, high poverty,* and *all other schools.* If you look at each of the far right bars that represents the 2013–2014 school year, you'll see that Hispanics are increasingly likely to attend high-poverty schools. By 2013–2014, almost half (48%) of Hispanic students were in high-poverty schools, up from 35% in 2000–2001. In contrast, only 8% of white students were in high-poverty schools, up from 3% in 2000–2001. The data show that school segregation, by ethnicity and class, is increasing over time. Also note that these patterns are virtually identical to those for African Americans (see Figure 5.10)

As we explained in Chapter 5, the increasing concentrations of students by social class and race or ethnicity reflect persistent residential segregation by race, which, as you know, is closely linked with social class. These trends also reflect the decreasing percentage of whites in the population and the increasing percentage of Hispanics.

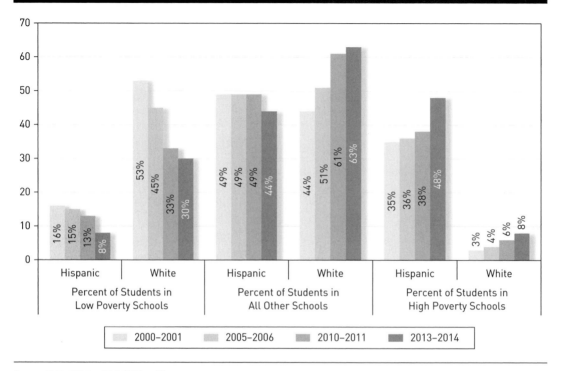

FIGURE 7.12 ■ Percentages of Students by Poverty and Race/Ethnicity, Selected School Years

Source: United States GAO, 2016. p. 59.

COMPARATIVE FOCUS
IMMIGRATION AROUND THE WORLD VERSUS THE UNITED STATES

Immigration in the world is at record levels. In 2017, 258 million people lived outside their birth countries. That's a 49% increase since 2000 (United Nations, 2017, p. 1). In 2017, about 60% of the world's migrants lived in Asia (79.6 million) or Europe (77.9 million) compared with 50 million in America (p. 5). Germany and the Russian Federation each had about 12 million migrants. The United Kingdom had almost 9 million people (p. 6).

The immigrant stream also included refugees and asylum seekers spurred by civil war, famine, genocide, political unrest, and other forms of violence, such as human trafficking. In 2017, 25.9 million migrants were refugees fleeing war, famine, and persecution—the highest number since World War II (United Nations, 2017 p. 8). In 2017, Turkey hosted the most refugees of any country in the world—3.1 million (p. 7), up from 1.6 million in 2014. The 2017 United Nations International Migration Report (p. 6) said that the next top hosting countries were "Jordan (2.9 million), the State of Palestine (2.2 million), Lebanon (1.6), Pakistan (1.4 million), Germany (1.3 million), and Uganda (1.2 million)." In 2017, the U. S. took in 53,716 refugees (López, Bialik, & Radford, 2018), down from 84,995 in 2016 (López & Bialik, 2017).

The advanced industrial nations of the world were prime destinations for immigrants. The immigrant stream to Europe included people from all walks of life. The most prominent immigration flows included movement from Turkey to Germany, from Africa to Spain and Italy, and from many former British colonies (e.g., Jamaica, India, Nigeria) to the United Kingdom. This immigration was primarily an economic phenomenon motivated by the search for jobs and survival, though they may have had to live at the margins of society to do so. Most Western European nations have very low birth rates, and researchers expect population declines in some countries (e.g., Germany and Italy) in coming decades which will create labor shortages and attract immigrants to Western Europe for decades to come (Population Reference Bureau, 2014, p. 11).

In terms of numbers, the volume of immigration to Europe is smaller than the flow to America, but its proportional impact is comparable. About 13.5% of the American population is foreign-born. That's three times more than in the 1970s, when immigrants were 4.7% of the population. However, it's not the high we had in 1890, when 14.8% of the American population was foreign-born (López et al., 2018). Many European nations (including Belgium, Germany, and Sweden) have similar profiles (Dumont & LeMaitre, 2011).

Germany has one of the largest immigrant communities of any European nation. In the 1960s, it began allowing large numbers of immigrants to enter as temporary guest workers to help staff its expanding economy. Germany saw no need to encourage acculturation and integration because they expected people to return to their homeland when they were no longer needed. However, many settled permanently, and many of their millions of descendants today speak only German and have no knowledge of or experience with their "homeland." Although acculturated, they aren't fully integrated. In fact, the government denied them citizenship until recently.

In recent years, immigration has generated major debates about how to handle newcomers and manage a pluralistic society, including national language policy, the limits of religious freedom, and criteria for citizenship. Citizens in the European Union have expressed discontent about immigrants, including refugees, through protests and policies (Connor & Krogstad, 2016). Greeks, Swedes, and Italians express the highest dissatisfaction, reflecting the large proportions of refugees in their countries. They're concerned that immigrants will take jobs and other social services such as education. Additionally, they fear the possibility of increased crime and terrorism (the latter concern is linked with negative attitudes about Muslims) (Poushter, 2016). These realities have resulted in increased nationalism, perhaps best exemplified by Britain's decision to exit ("Brexit") the European Union (Stokes, 2016).

Increasingly, many nations wrestle with the essential meaning of national identity and issues of inclusion and diversity: What should it mean to be German, French, British, Dutch, or American? How much diversity can be accepted before national cohesion is threatened? What is the best balance between assimilation and pluralism?

QUESTIONS FOR REFLECTION

9. What is the most important idea you learned in this section? What surprised you most? What are you now curious to know, based on what you read?

10. What similarities and differences do you see between immigration to American and Europe?

(Continued)

(Continued)

11. Is the U. S. more or less successful in its approach to immigration than European nations? Why?

12. Consider issues facing immigrants generally and refugees in particular. If you were in charge of immigration policy, what would you want it to look like and why? (We realize the reality and the vision may be two different things. For now, focus on the ideas.) How might your views compare with a refugee who was fleeing war or an immigrant leaving their country because they couldn't find work? What do your answers say about your social location?

Levels of education for Hispanic Americans have risen in recent years but are far below national standards (see Figure 7.13). Hispanic Americans in general and all subgroups, except Colombian Americans, fall well below non-Hispanic whites for high school education. Note that 64% of Mexican Americans and a little more than half of Honduran, Salvadoran, and Guatemalan Americans have completed high school. At the college level, Colombian and Cuban Americans approximate national norms, but the other groups and Hispanic Americans as a whole are far below non-Hispanic whites.

The lower levels of education for Mexican Americans and Puerto Ricans are the cumulative results of decades of systematic discrimination and exclusion. These levels have been further reduced by the high percentage of recent immigrants from Mexico, the Dominican Republic, El Salvador, and other nations that have modest educational backgrounds.

FIGURE 7.13 ■ Education Attainment for All Hispanic Americans, Non-Hispanic Whites, and the 10 Largest Hispanic American Groups, 2017

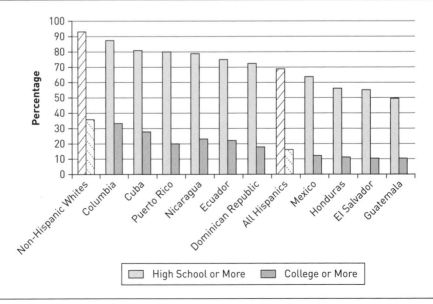

Source: U.S. Census Bureau (2018a).

Given the role that educational credentials have come to play in the job market, these figures are consistent with the idea that assimilation may be segmented for some Hispanic groups (see Chapters 2 and 9), who may contribute in large numbers, along with African Americans and Native Americans, to the growth of an urban underclass.

Political Power

The political resources available to Latinos have increased over the years, but the group is still proportionally underrepresented. Nationally, Hispanic Americans rose from about 6% of those eligible to vote in 1996 to almost 12% in 2016 (Krogstad, 2017). However, this increase in potential political power was limited by low rates of registration and low voter turnout: Less than half (48%) of Hispanic Americans eligible to vote cast a ballot in the 2016 presidential election (U.S. Bureau of the Census, 2017g). The impact of the Latino vote on national politics will increase as the group grows, but participation is likely to remain lower than that of other groups for some time because of the large percentage of noncitizens and recent, non-English-speaking immigrants in the group.

At the national level, 45 Hispanic Americans serve in the U.S. Congress; this is more than double the number in 1990 and about 8% of the total membership. There are 40 Hispanic members of the House of Representatives (29 of them are Democrats; 10 are women) and 5 senators (3 of them are Republicans; one is a woman; Manning, 2017). On the local and state levels, the number of public officials identified as Hispanic increased by more than 65% between 1985 and 2008 (from 3,147 to 5,240; U.S. Census Bureau, 2011, p. 259).

Although Latinos are still underrepresented, these figures suggest that they'll become increasingly important in American political life as their numbers increase and their rates of naturalization rise. Even with a relatively small turnout, Hispanic voters were an important part of the coalition that elected President Barack Obama in 2008 and 2012. Not surprisingly, Hispanic voters voted overwhelmingly for Hillary Clinton (the Democratic candidate) in 2016; only 28% voted for Trump (Krogstad & Lopez, 2016). However, it seems probable that the competition between the Republican and Democratic parties for this growing segment of the electorate will continue.

Jobs and Income

The economic situation of Latinos is quite mixed. Many Latinos, especially those whose families have been in the U. S. for several generations, are doing "just fine. They've, in ever increasing numbers, accessed opportunities in education and employment and have carved out a niche of American prosperity for themselves and their children" (Camarillo & Bonilla, 2001, pp. 130–131). For others, however, the picture isn't as promising. They face the possibility of becoming members of an impoverished, powerless, and economically marginalized urban underclass, similar to African Americans and other minority groups of color.

Occupationally, Latinos who are recent immigrants with modest levels of education and job skills are concentrated in the less desirable, lower-paid, unskilled service segments of the job market. Those with higher levels of human capital and education compare more favorably with the dominant group.

Unemployment, low income, and poverty continue to be issues for all Hispanic groups. Figure 7.14 compares median household incomes for non-Hispanic whites and all Hispanic Americans across a 46-year period. The size of the income gap fluctuates but generally remains in the 70% range. In the most recent years, however, it has risen slightly to 74%.

As a group, Latinos historically have been intermediate between African Americans and whites in the stratification system; this is reflected by the fact that the Hispanic–white income gap is smaller than the black–white income gap, which was 62% in 2017 (see Figure 5.14). This smaller gap also reflects the more favorable economic circumstances of Hispanics (especially those more "racially" similar to the dominant group) who have been in the U. S. for generations and are thoroughly integrated into the mainstream economy.

Figure 7.15 shows that there is a good deal of income variability from group to group but that Hispanic Americans in general and all subgroups have, on average, dramatically lower median household incomes than non-Hispanic whites, especially the groups with large numbers of recent immigrants who bring low levels of human capital.

Figure 7.16 supplements the information on median income by displaying the overall distribution of income for Hispanic Americans and non-Hispanic whites for 2016. Although Latinos are represented at all income levels, the figure shows a greater concentration (wider bars) of Hispanics in the lower-income categories and a lower

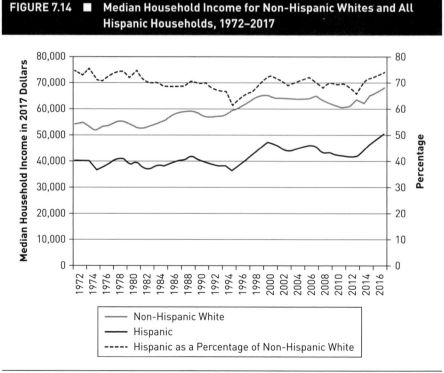

FIGURE 7.14 ■ **Median Household Income for Non-Hispanic Whites and All Hispanic Households, 1972–2017**

Legend:
——— Non-Hispanic White
——— Hispanic
----- Hispanic as a Percentage of Non-Hispanic White

Source: U.S. Census Bureau (2018a).

FIGURE 7.15 ■ Median Household Income for All Hispanic Americans, Non-Hispanic Whites, and the 10 Largest Hispanic American Groups, 2017

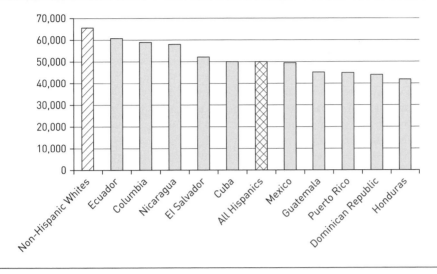

Source: U.S. Census Bureau (2018a). American Community Survey, 2017. One Year Estimates.

FIGURE 7.16 ■ Distribution of Household Income for Non-Hispanic Whites and Hispanic Americans, 2016

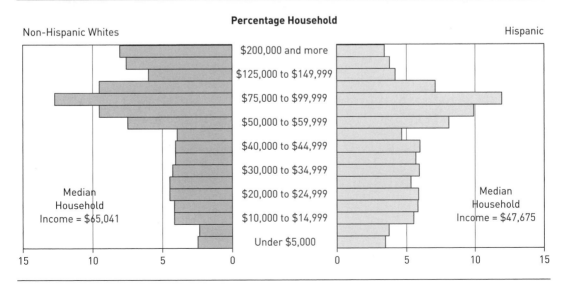

Source: U.S. Census Bureau (2018a).

concentration (narrower bars) in the income groups at the top of the figure. There is a noticeable concentration of both groups in the $50,000 to $125,000 categories, and the percentage of both groups in this income range is comparable (39% to 37%). In the three highest income categories, however, the percentage of whites is double that of Hispanic Americans (22% to 11%).

Figure 7.17 finishes the socioeconomic profile for Latinos. It shows varying levels of poverty, a pattern that is consistent with prior information on income and education. The poverty rate for all Hispanic families is almost three times the rate for non-Hispanic white families but lower than that of African Americans (see Figure 5.15). However, considerable diversity exists across the groups. The poverty rates for Colombians, Ecuadorans, Nicaraguans, and Cubans are closest to that of non-Hispanic whites; Hondurans and Guatemalans are the most impoverished. For all groups, children have higher poverty rates than families.

These socioeconomic profiles reflect the economic diversity of Latinos. Some are "doing just fine," but many are concentrated in the low-wage sector of the economy. As a group, Cuban Americans rank higher than Mexican Americans and Puerto Ricans—the two other largest groups—on virtually all measures of wealth and prosperity. As we saw previously, this relative prosperity is even more pronounced for the earlier immigrants from Cuba and their children.

FIGURE 7.17 ■ Poverty Rates for All Hispanic Americans, Non-Hispanic Whites, and the 10 Largest Hispanic Groups, 2017

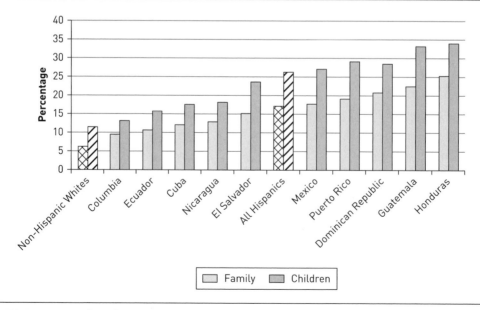

Source: U.S. Census Bureau (2018a). American Community Survey, 2017. One Year Estimates.

Note: Researchers use different units of analysis to calculate family and child poverty rates. Family rates represent the percentage of families below the poverty line. Child poverty rates represent the percentage of people under 18 who live in poverty.

The income gap and the level of economic distress would be higher if we focused on recent immigrants, especially undocumented immigrants, who are concentrated in the informal economy. Such workers are paid less than minimum wage and off the books by their employers. As discussed previously, recent immigrants typically live as frugally as possible to maximize the money they can send home by living 5 or even 10 people to a room, for example. Because they tend to live off the radar, they're less likely to be included in the data-gathering efforts that supply the information for the figures in this chapter. If they were included, the average wages for virtually all Latino groups would decrease and, thus, the rates of poverty would increase.

Gender and Inequality

As you've seen, the labor market is differentiated by race and ethnicity. It's also segmented by gender. Hispanic women—like minority group women in general—are among the lowest paid, least-protected, and, therefore, most-exploitable segments of the American labor force. The impact of poverty is especially severe for Latino women because they often find themselves taking sole responsibility of caring for their children. In 2016, about 20% of all Hispanic American households were headed by women versus about 13% in the total population. This percentage ranged from a low of 16% for Cuban Americans to a high of about 31% for Dominicans (U.S. Census Bureau, 2016a). This pattern results from many factors, including Latino men's status in the labor force. The jobs available to Latino men often don't pay enough to support a family because many jobs are seasonal, temporary, low wage, or otherwise insecure.

Women-headed Latino families face a triple economic burden: They only have one wage earner whose potential income is often limited by discrimination against women *and* Latinos. These multiple disadvantages result in an especially high rate of poverty. Whereas 21% of non-Hispanic white, woman-headed households fall below the poverty line, it's almost 36% for Hispanic households headed by women (U.S. Census Bureau, 2016a).

Summary

The socioeconomic situation of Latinos is complex, diversified, and segmented. Many Latinos have successfully entered the mainstream economy, but others face poverty and exclusion. Highly concentrated in deteriorated urban areas, some people in these groups, like other minority groups of color, face the possibility of permanent poverty and economic marginality.

Primary Structural Assimilation

Overall, the extent of intimate contact between Hispanic Americans and the dominant group probably has been higher than for either African Americans or American Indians (e.g., see Quillian & Campbell, 2003; Rosenfield, 2002). This pattern may reflect the fact that Latinos are partly ethnic minority groups and partly racial minority groups. Some studies report that contact is greater for the more affluent social classes, in the cities, and for the younger generations (who may be more Americanized; Fitzpatrick, 1976; Grebler et al., 1970, p. 397; Rodriguez, 1989, pp. 70–72). Yet, the extent of contact probably has been decreased by the rapid increase in immigration and the tendency of the first generation to socialize more with co-ethnics.

Rates of intermarriage are higher for Latinos than for African Americans, but both are low. Black and white interracial couples make up less than 1% of all marriages, and the comparable figure for Latinos is 4% of all marriages (U.S. Census Bureau, 2012c, p. 54).

Table 7.5 shows that rates of in-marriage for Hispanics are lower than those for whites. This is partly a function of simple arithmetic: The larger group (white Americans) is more likely to find partners within the group. However, note that the rate of Latino in-marriage is also lower than that of blacks (see Table 5.1), a group of about the same size. This pattern may reflect the tenacity of racial (vs. ethnic) barriers to integration in this institutional area.

Also note that nativity affects rates of in-marriage for Latinos. In both years, the foreign-born were more likely to marry within the group than were the U.S.–born. This pattern, like so many others, reflects the high rates of immigration and the tendency of recent immigrants to socialize within the ethnic subcommunity. For both years, Hispanics who married outside their group were most likely to marry whites.

Finally, a 2017 study found that, for recently married couples, Hispanics were more likely to cross group boundaries (27%) than blacks (16%). However, the percentage of Hispanic newlyweds marrying across group lines was virtually the same as in 1980 (26%) while the percentage for black newlyweds had increased dramatically from 5% to 18%. While these patterns and percentages varied by level of education, age, and urban versus rural residence, the overall trend is toward more diversity and, thus, an increasing percentage of "mixed-race" individuals (Livingston & Brown, 2017).

QUESTIONS FOR REFLECTION

13. This section examined several dimensions of acculturation and integration for Hispanic Americans. Which is most important? Why?

14. Which Hispanic groups have been more successful in U.S. society and why? Do you agree with the definitions of *success* used in this section? What other definitions might be useful, and how might these change your ideas about which group is most successful?

TABLE 7.5 ■ Percentage of Whites and Latinos Married to a Person of the Same Group, 1980 and 2008

| | Whites | | Latinos | | | |
| | | | Men | | Women | |
Year	Men	Women	Foreign-Born	U.S.–Born	Foreign-Born	U.S.–Born
1980	96%	95%	80%	67%	84%	70%
2008	93%	92%	83%	58%	83%	59%

Source: Qian and Lichter (2011, p. 1072).

ASSIMILATION AND HISPANIC AMERICANS

As test cases for what we've called the *traditional* view of American assimilation, Latinos fare poorly. Almost two centuries after the original contact period, Mexican Americans tend to be concentrated in the low-wage sector of the labor market, a source of cheap labor for the dominant group's economy. Puerto Ricans, who are more recent arrivals, occupy a similar profile and position.

The fundamental reality faced by both groups, in their histories and in their present situations, is their colonized status in American society. While many Mexican Americans and Puerto Ricans have risen in the social class and occupational structure of the larger society, others share many problems with urban minority groups of color.

Traditional views of the nature of assimilation likewise fail to describe the experiences of Cuban Americans. They're more prosperous, on average, than either Mexican Americans or Puerto Ricans, but they became successful by remaining separate and developing an ethnic enclave in southern Florida.

There is no single Hispanic American experience or pattern of adjustment to the larger society. We've focused mainly on three of the many Hispanic groups in the U. S., and the diversity of their experiences suggests the variety and complexity of what it means to be a minority group in the United States. Additionally, their experiences illustrate some of the fundamental forces that shape minority group experiences: the split labor market and the American appetite for cheap labor, the impact of industrialization, the dangers of a permanent urban underclass, the relationships between competition and levels of prejudice and rejection, and the persistence of race as a primary dividing line between people and groups.

FOCUS ON CONTEMPORARY ISSUES
HISPANIC AMERICANS AND THE EVOLUTION
OF THE AMERICAN RACIAL ORDER

The U. S. has, virtually since its birth, been organized into two communities: black and white, separate and unequal (Hacker, 1992). The perception that *only* two races exist reinforces this structural relationship. What will happen as groups that are neither black nor white— Latinos, Asian Americans, and others—continue to grow in numbers and significance?

One possibility, called the *whitening* thesis, hypothesizes that Latinos (and Asian Americans) eventually will be accepted as white, while African Americans remain relegated to the perpetual black (Vasquez, 2014). An opposing position, called the *browning* thesis, predicts that all "peoples of color" will band together and threaten white dominance in society. Below, we

(Continued)

(Continued)

consider both views as well as a third possible future for U.S. race relations.

Whitening

In this model, Latinos and Asian Americans will become part of the white American racial group while African Americans will remain disproportionately unequal, powerless, and marginalized. The racial identities of Latinos and Asians will become "thinner," declining in salience as they increasingly access the privileges of whiteness, much like the Irish and Italians before them. As they assimilate, their "white" racial identity will gain prominence and their sense of ethnicity will become largely symbolic.

This prediction is consistent with Gordon's assimilation model and the notion that immigrants move through a series of stages and become more incorporated into the dominant society in a relatively linear fashion. Once a group has completed acculturation, integration, and intermarriage, they'll begin to racially identify with the dominant group.

Yancey (2003) tested the whitening thesis on a nationally representative data set, and his analysis places Latinos and Asian Americans in the middle stages of assimilation because their residential patterns, marital patterns, and several key political beliefs align more closely with white Americans than with black Americans. If Gordon's model holds true, these groups will come to identify as white over the next several generations.

Another research project (Murguia & Foreman, 2003) focused on Mexican Americans and found that they tend to prefer spouses, neighbors, coworkers, and friends who are either Puerto Rican or white, not black. The researchers also found that Mexican Americans tend to endorse modern racism (the belief that racism isn't much of a barrier to success and that people of color are largely responsible for their own hardships; see

Chapter 3). This consistency with the dominant ideology also positions Mexican Americans on the path to whiteness.

Finally, an important part of the whitening process requires distancing oneself from the perpetually stigmatized black group. To the extent that a whitening process occurs for Latino and Asian Americans, these groups will tend to use both traditional and modern anti-black racism to emphasize their differences and align themselves more with the attitudinal and cultural perspectives of the dominant group. We discussed this type of dynamic in our coverage of the racial identity of Puerto Ricans who came to the mainland.

Browning

The browning thesis argues that whites will gradually lose their dominant status as Latino and Asian American groups increase in size. The balance of power will tip toward nonwhite groups, who will use their greater numbers to challenge whites for better positions in society.

Some theorists see the loss of white dominance negatively—as a threat to Anglo American culture. For example, political scientist Samuel Huntington (2004) ascribes to this version of the browning thesis (see the Current Debates for this chapter at http://edge.sagepub.com/diversity6e). Some proponents of this perspective argue that Latinos are unassimilable due to their alleged unwillingness to learn English and absorb other aspects of U.S. culture, a view based largely on nativism, ethnocentrism, and prejudice and refuted by much of the evidence in this chapter (e.g., see Figure 7.8). Nevertheless, this version of the browning thesis has gained momentum in popular culture and on some talk radio and cable TV shows. This idea also manifests itself in the political arena in debates over immigration policy and in the movement to make English America's official language (see Chapter 2).

Some sociologists offer a different version of the browning thesis. For example, Feagin and O'Brien (2004) put a positive spin on the declining white numerical majority. They believe that as nonwhite groups grow in size, whites will be forced to share power in a more democratic, egalitarian, and inclusive fashion. This shift will be more likely if minority groups forge alliances with one another, as suggested by studies of generational differences in immigrants' racial attitudes. Specifically, this research suggests that native-born or second-generation Latinos and Asian Americans express more solidarity with African Americans than foreign-born and recently arrived members of their group (Murguia & Foreman, 2003). In contrast to the whitening thesis, this view of the browning thesis expects Latinos and Asian Americans to embrace a more color-conscious worldview and find ways to leverage their growing numbers in alliance with African Americans to improve their status.

This version of the browning thesis also adopts a more global perspective. It recognizes that the world is occupied by many more people of color than by whites of European descent and that the growing numbers of nonwhites in the U. S. can be an important resource in the global marketplace. For example, people around the world commonly speak several languages. Because most Americans are monolingual, they're disadvantaged in a global marketplace. The U. S. might improve its position if it encourages the fluent bilingualism of its Latino, Asian American, and other citizens, rather than insisting on English only.

Something Else?

Another group of scholars challenges the browning and the whitening theses and foresees a three-way racial dynamic. These scholars focus on the tremendous diversity within the Latin and Asian American communities in the U. S. in terms of relative wealth, skin color and other "racial" characteristics, religion, and national origins. This diversity leads them to conclude that only some Latino and Asian Americans will "whiten."

For example, Bonilla-Silva (2003) envisions a future racial trichotomy: whites, honorary whites, and the collective black. In this schema, well-off and light-skinned Latinos and Asians wouldn't become white but would occupy an intermediary status as "honorary whites." This status would afford them much of the privilege and esteem not widely accorded to people of color, but it would still be a conditional status, which potentially could be revoked in times of economic crisis or at any other time when those in power found it necessary. Bonilla-Silva predicts that groups such as Chinese Americans and lighter-skinned Latinos would fit into the honorary white category, while darker-skinned Latinos and Asians would fit into the collective black category, along with, of course, African Americans.

Murguia and Foreman's (2003) study of Mexican Americans illustrates this process. They point out that skin color and educational levels make a difference in whether Latinos ally with African Americans. Mexican Americans with darker skin and higher educational levels and those born in the U. S. are less likely to hold the antiblack stereotypes of the larger culture and are more likely to recognize the racism in their own lives. Such attitudes and awareness may form the basis of future alliances between some Latinos, Asian Americans, and African Americans.

How will the Racial Order Evolve?

Will America become "browner" or "whiter"? In the face of high levels of immigration and the growing importance of groups in the "racial middle"—those that are neither black nor white—it seems certain that the traditional, dichotomous black–white racial order cannot persist. What will replace it? Whichever thesis proves correct, it seems certain that new understandings of race and new relationships among racial groups will emerge in the coming decades.

Main Points

- Latinos are a diverse and growing part of American. society and include distinct groups; the three largest are Mexican Americans, Puerto Ricans, and Cuban Americans. These groups generally don't think of themselves as a single entity.

- Latinos have some characteristics of colonized groups and some of immigrant groups. Similarly, these groups are racial minorities in some ways and ethnic minorities in others.

- Since the beginning of the 20th century, Mexico has provided a reserve labor force that helped develop the U.S. economy. Immigrants from Mexico entered a social system in which the colonized status of the group was already established. Mexican Americans have been a colonized minority group, despite the large numbers of immigrants in the group, and have been systematically excluded from opportunities for upward mobility by institutional discrimination and segregation.

- A Mexican American protest movement has been continuously seeking to improve the status of the group. In the 1960s, a more intense and militant movement emerged, guided by the ideology of Chicanismo. Puerto Ricans started moving to the mainland in large numbers only in the 1940s and 1950s. The group is concentrated in the urban Northeast, in the low-wage sector of the job market.

- Cubans began immigrating after Castro's revolution in the late 1950s. They settled primarily in southern Florida, where they created an ethnic enclave.

- Anti-Hispanic prejudice and discrimination seem to have declined, mirroring the general decline in explicit, overt racism in American society. Recent high levels of immigration seem to have increased anti-Hispanic prejudice and discrimination, however, especially in the borderlands and other areas with large numbers of immigrants.

- Levels of acculturation are highly variable from group to group and generation to generation. Acculturation increases with length of residence, but the vitality of Latino cultures has been sustained by recent immigration.

- Secondary structural assimilation varies from group to group. Poverty, unemployment, lower levels of educational attainment, and other forms of inequality continue to be major problems for Hispanic groups, even the relatively successful Cuban Americans.

- Primary structural assimilation with the dominant group is greater for Hispanic Americans than for African Americans.

Applying Concepts

As a child, Jane Hill used "mock Spanish" phrases such as "no problemo" and "buenos nachos." *Mock Spanish* is different from *Spanglish*, which blends English and Spanish into a new language and is used by bilingual speakers in the Southwest borderlands, sometimes as a kind of light-hearted banter. For example, in Spanglish "el menu de lonche" blends *el menu* (Spanish) with the phonetic *lonche* (Gonzalez, 2001). Mock Spanish also differs from *code switching*, which is when bilingual speakers alternate between two languages during a conversation (Leslie, 2016; Montes-Alcalá, 2000, p. 218; Price, 2010).

Now a linguistic anthropologist, Hill (1995) and others argue that mock Spanish, a seemingly innocent butchering of Spanish, is actually a subtle form of racism that relies on and reinforces negative stereotypes of Hispanics for its humor (Zentella, 2003, p. 52). For example, "Es no my yob" builds on the stereotype of Latinos as lazy. Likewise, "bad hombres" depends on the speaker and the listener knowing (and, perhaps believing) the stereotype of Latino men as violent, criminal, or deviant.

Hill (1995) and Zentella (2003) argue that mock Spanish reveals a linguistic double standard: English speakers who misuse Spanish generally do so without consequence. However, Anglo Americans often disparage Spanish speakers for using English incorrectly. Indeed, English-only legislation suggests that speaking Spanish is problematic.

Does mock Spanish reduce Spanish-speaking people to caricatures? Does it parallel the use of Indian mascots (see Chapter 6)? Explain. Next, look at the examples of mock Spanish below. Do they rely on and perpetuate stereotypes? Or are they "just fun"? Where do you think these phrases are taken from?*

1. "My ears are too beeg for my head. My head ees too beeg for my body."

2. "I'll splain." "Ok splain."

3. "Nurse Espinosa and her nursitas want more dinero."

4. "I need a lift in your el trucko to the next towno."

5. "Correctomundo."

6. "First-o, take a finger to the cream. . . . The goal is to achieve 'El Messy Look.'"

Have you heard examples of mock Spanish spoken or seen it in greeting cards, magazines, newspapers, blogs, television, or movies (for example, "cinco de drinko" instead of Cinco de Mayo)? Can you identify the sources and the speakers?

*Some of these examples come from Teaching Linguistic Anthropology at (teach.linguistican thropology.org/tag/mock-Spanish).

Turn the page to find the answers.

Review Questions

1. You learned that Hispanic Americans "combine elements of the polar extremes [immigrant and colonized] of Blauner's typology of minority groups" and that they're "partly an ethnic minority group and partly a racial minority group." Explain these statements in terms of the rest of the material presented in the chapter.

2. What important cultural differences between Mexican Americans and the dominant society shaped the relationships between the two groups?

3. How does the history of Mexican immigration demonstrate the usefulness of Noel's concepts of differentials in power and competition?

4. Compare and contrast the protest movements of Mexican Americans, American Indians, and African Americans. What similarities and differences existed in Chicanismo, Red Power, and Black Power? How do the differences reflect the unique experiences of each group?

5. In what ways are the experiences of Puerto Ricans and Cuban Americans unique compared with those of other minority groups? How do these experiences reflect other changes, such as differences in contact situation?

6. The Cuban American enclave has resulted in diverse benefits for the group. Why don't other minority groups follow this strategy?

7. Describe the situation of the major Hispanic American groups in terms of acculturation and integration. Which groups are closest to equality? What factors or experiences might account for the differences between groups? In what ways might the statement "Hispanic Americans are remaining pluralistic even while they assimilate" be true?

Answers to Applying Concepts

1. This comes from the children's book, *Skippyjon Jones* (2003).

2. These lines come from the 1950s sitcom, *I Love Lucy*. Variations of this saying have been used in TV shows, movies, and other situations. For example, U.S. Senator Tom Coburn said, "You've got some 'splainin to do" to Justice Sonia Sotomayor during her U.S. Supreme Court confirmation hearing.

3. This example comes from the sitcom, *Scrubs*, when the nurses ask for a raise. Dr. Kelso, the hospital administrator, uses mock Spanish to make the nurses (nurse Espinosa, in particular) feel inferior. The hospital lawyer hears it and thinks, "Dr. Kelso and his racism."

4. Brad Pitt's character says this in the movie, *The Mexican*.

5. Samuel L. Jackson's character, Jules Winnfield, says this in the movie, *Pulp Fiction*.

6. This line comes from an Axe body spray commercial.

Internet Learning Resources

SAGE edge™ offers teachers and students easy-to-use resources for review, study, and further exploration. See **http://edge.sagepub.com/diversity6e**

8

ASIAN AMERICANS

Model Minorities?

I had flown from San Francisco . . . and was riding a taxi to my hotel to attend a conference on multiculturalism. My driver and I chatted about the weather and the tourists. . . . The rearview mirror reflected a white man in his forties. "How long have you been in this country?" he asked. "All my life," I replied, wincing. "I was born in the United States." With a strong Southern drawl, he remarked: "I was wondering because your English is excellent!" . . . I explained: "My grandfather came here from Japan in the 1880s. My family has been here for over a hundred years." He glanced at me in the mirror. Somehow, I did not look "American" to him; my eyes and complexion looked foreign.

—Ronald Takaki (1993, p. 2), professor of
Asian American studies

At the time of this brief conversation, Professor Takaki was a distinguished professor at a prestigious West Coast university and an internationally renowned expert in his area. It's possible that his family had been in the U. S. longer than the taxi driver's family. So why did the driver assume Takaki wasn't "from here"? And why was he surprised at Takaki's "excellent" English? The taxi driver probably meant no harm, but he's clearly making assumptions based on Takaki's appearance. He's not alone. As you'll learn, those few seconds of conversation reflect widely held beliefs that Asians aren't really "from here" [the United States] and aren't fully American. In other words, they're perceived as "outsiders."

Professor Takaki's interaction with the driver is one instance of the "othering," exclusion, or stigmatization that Asian Americans, like other peoples of color, experience. The perception that Asians are outsiders has also led to significant discrimination, such as the 19th-century anti-Chinese campaign in California and the 1922 Supreme Court decision (*Takao Ozawa v. U.S.*) that declared Asians ineligible for U.S. citizenship. Stereotypes about Asian Americans can be positive, such as the view that they're "model minorities," but othering is real, painful, and consequential (Wu, 2015).

We begin this chapter with an overview of Asian American groups and then briefly examine the traditions and customs they brought with them to America. We'll primarily focus on the two oldest groups, Chinese Americans and Japanese Americans. (We'll address smaller groups in Chapter 9.) Additionally, we'll examine whether people's perception that Asian Americans in general and Chinese and Japanese Americans in particular are "model minorities": successful, affluent, highly educated people who don't suffer from the problems usually associated with minority group status. How accurate is this view?

Do the concepts and theories that have guided our discussion so far, particularly Blauner's and Noel's hypotheses, apply to Asian Americans? Have Asian Americans forged a pathway to upward mobility that other groups could follow? Does the relative success of Asian Americans mean that the United States is an open, fair, and just society and that the challenges facing other minority groups come solely from individual choices or abilities?

America is home to at least 30 different Asian American ethnic groups (U.S. Census Bureau, 2010). They vary culturally and physically and in their experiences in the United States. Some groups are relative newcomers, while others have roots in this country stretching back more than 200 years. As with Native Americans and Hispanic Americans, *Asian American* is a convenient label created by the larger society (and by government agencies such as the U.S. Census Bureau) that, unfortunately, de-emphasizes distinctions between the groups. Table 8.1 displays information about the size and growth rates of the 10 largest Asian American groups between 1990 and 2017. Figure 8.1 provides a visual snapshot of each group's size.

Several features of Table 8.1 are worth noting. First, even when combined, Asian Americans are only 6.7% of the total U.S. population. In contrast, African Americans and Hispanic Americans constitute 13% and 16% of the population, respectively (Brown, 2014).

Second, most Asian American groups have grown dramatically since 1965 because of high rates of immigration stemming from changes in immigration policies. Additionally, these groups grew faster than the total population between 1990 and 2017. Japanese Americans had the slowest growth rate (1.7 times), largely because Japanese immigration has been low in recent decades. However, the number of Asian Indians more than quintupled, and the other groups doubled or tripled their populations.

TABLE 8.1 ■ Size and Growth of Asian Americans* and the 10 Largest Asian American Groups by Nation of Origin, 1990–2017					
Group	1990	2000	2017	Growth (Number of Times Larger), 1990–2017	Percent of Total Population, 2017
Total Asian American	6,908,638	11,070,913	21,646,070	3.1	6.7%
China	1,645,472	2,879,636	5,219,184	3.2	1.6%
India	815,447	1,899,599	4,402,362	5.4	1.4%
Philippines	1,406,770	2,364,815	4,037,564	2.9	1.2%
Vietnam	614,547	1,223,736	2,104,217	3.4	<1%
Korea	798,849	1,228,427	1,887,914	2.4	<1%
Japan	847,562	1,148,932	1,466,514	1.7	<1%
Pakistan	N/A	204,309	500,433	--	<1%
Cambodia	147,411	206,052	331,733	2.3	<1%
Hmong**	90,082	186,310	309,564	3.4	<1%
Laos	149,014	198,203	265,138	1.8	<1%
Percent of U.S. Population	2.8%	3.9%	6.7%		
Total U.S. Population	248,710,000	281,422,000	323,127,515	1.3	

*Asian Americans, alone and in combination with other groups.
**The Hmong come from various Southeast Asian nations, including Laos and Vietnam.

Sources: For 1990: U.S. Bureau of the Census, 1990); for 2000: U.S. Bureau of the Census, 2000b); for 2017: U.S. Bureau of the Census, 2018a).

Researchers expect this rapid growth to continue for decades, and the impact of the Asian American population on everyday life and American culture will increase accordingly. As you saw in Figure 1.1, by 2060, 1 out of every 10 Americans will likely be of Asian descent. If projections hold, by 2065, no group will be a majority of the population: Non-Hispanic whites will be 45% of the population, Hispanics will be 28%, and African Americans will be 15% (U.S. Census Bureau, 2017a).

Today, more than half (58.1%) of the U.S. Asian population is foreign-born (López, Ruiz, & Patten, 2017) and, like Hispanic American groups, most Asian American groups have a high percentage of foreign-born members (see Figure 8.2). Even the group with the smallest percentage of foreign-born members, Japanese Americans, has almost double the national norm for foreign-born members (24.2% compared with 13.2%, respectively).

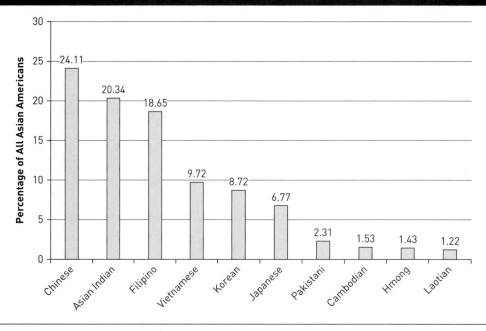

FIGURE 8.1 ■ Relative Sizes of Asian American Groups, 2017

Source: U.S. Census Bureau (2018a). American Community Survey, 2017.

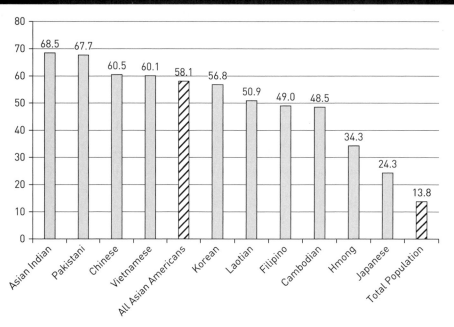

FIGURE 8.2 ■ Percentage Foreign-Born for All Asian Americans, Total Population, and the 10 Largest Asian American Groups, 2017

Source: U.S. Census Bureau (2018a). American Community Survey, 2017.

In Chapter 7, you learned that most Hispanic Americans identify themselves in terms of their family's country of origin. The same is true of Asian Americans. According to a recent survey, about 62% describe themselves in terms of their country of origin (e.g., *Chinese American*), about 20% describe themselves as *Asian American*, and 14% describe themselves as *American*. There are large differences in self-description across groups. On average, almost 70% of the foreign-born population (vs. 43% of the native-born population) describe themselves in terms of their country of origin (Pew Research Center, 2013, pp. 88–89).

ORIGINS AND CULTURES

Asian cultures predate the founding of America by thousands of years and each culture has its own history. Asians vary politically, economically, and culturally. They speak many different languages and practice diverse religions, including Buddhism, Islam, Hinduism, Confucianism, and Christianity. Asian American immigrants bring this diversity to the United States. Although no two Asian cultures are the same, they share some similarities. These cultural traits have shaped Asian Americans beliefs and actions as well as the perceptions of dominant group members. Thus, they're foundational to Asian American experiences in this country.

Asian cultures tend to stress group membership over individual self-interest. For example, Confucianism, the dominant ethical and moral system in traditional China (around the 10th or 11th century), encouraged people to see themselves as part of larger social systems (including status hierarchies). Kinship relations with family members organized daily life (Lyman, 1974). The family or clan often owned the land on which they depended for survival, and kinship ties determined inheritance patterns. The clan also performed other crucial social functions, including arranging marriages, settling disputes, and organizing festivals and holidays.

The Chinese and Japanese both value group loyalty, conformity, respect for others (especially "superiors"), sensitivity to others' opinions and judgments, avoidance of public embarrassment ("saving face"), and not offending others. This Japanese proverb reflects these ideas: "The nail that sticks up must be hammered down" (Whiting, 1990, p. 70). These cultural tendencies contrast sharply with Western values and norms. For example, Western cultures encourage individuals to develop and follow their conscience. That is, one's personal morality, such as ideas of guilt versus shame, should guide personal behavior (Benedict, 1946).

A possible manifestation of this tendency to seek harmony and avoid confrontation was documented by Chou and Feagin (2008) in interviews with Asian Americans from a variety of groups. Participants commonly used "compliant conformity" to cope with white racism, discrimination, and rejection (p. 222). They expressed the belief that their conformity and hard work would bring recognition and acceptance from the larger society. Respondents' parents, even those who had personally experienced substantial discrimination, commonly pressured their children to conform to Anglo values and norms in the hope that their children's success (e.g., in school) would protect them from negative treatment and stereotyping. However, complying with racism rather than challenging it ultimately sustains white prejudicial values and the American racial hierarchy. Thus, this strategy has had limited success (at best).

Men dominated traditional Asian cultures. For example, in traditional China, a woman was expected to serve her father first, then her husband, and, if widowed, her eldest son. Confucianism decreed that women should practice the Four Virtues: chastity and obedience, shyness, a pleasing demeanor, and domestic skill (Amott & Matthaei, 1991, p. 200). High-status women symbolized their subordination and their social class through foot binding. The ideal foot, just 3–4 inches long, was considered beautiful and erotic. To achieve this look, young girls, usually between 4 and 10 years old, underwent a painful practice that involved breaking the arch bones so that the toes could be bent under the foot. The full process usually took about two years to complete. During that time, girls would wrap and unwrap their feet every few weeks to modify their shape and size and keep them artificially small. As with many beauty practices, the goal was (at least in part) to attract the best mate possible. In this case, people believed that the smaller the foot, the better the husband (more economically well-off) that a girl or woman could attract (Foreman, 2015). Because it was somewhat immobilizing, foot binding made women more dependent on their husbands. Bound feet symbolically suggested that they didn't need to do poor women's work. Indeed, it tethered many women to home and family (Jackson, 2000; Takaki, 1993).

Until recently, it was widely believed that only elite girls and women practiced foot binding. However, recent research shows that some poor girls also bound their feet. Bossen and Gates (2017) interviewed 1,800 elderly women across China and learned that foot binding not only helped these girls achieve a beauty ideal (and, hopefully, a good husband), it also facilitated their economic contributions to their families. The women reported that during this time, their mothers would have them sit and weave, sew, or make products that could be sold.

Asian Americans in the U. S. modified these patriarchal values and traditional traits. For groups with longer histories in America, such as Chinese Americans and Japanese Americans, their effects may be slight. However, for more recently arrived groups, the effects of these cultural traditions are typically more powerful.

The cultural and religious differences among Asian American groups also reflect the recent histories of each sending nation. For example, Vietnam was a Chinese colony for 1,000 years, and between 1887 and 1945, it was a French colony. Although China has heavily influenced Vietnamese culture, many Vietnamese are Catholic because of the French efforts to convert them. Western nations also colonized the Philippines and India—the former by Spain and then the United States, and the latter by Great Britain. Thus, many Filipinos are Catholic, and many Asian Indian immigrants speak English and are familiar with Anglo culture.

These examples are the merest suggestion of the diversity between Asian American groups. Additionally, we see tremendous diversity *within* each group when we take other social statuses into account (e.g., gender, class, sexual orientation, age). In fact, Asian Americans, who share little more than a slight physical resemblance and some broad cultural similarities, are much more diverse than Hispanic Americans, who are overwhelmingly Catholic and share a common language and a historical connection with Spain (Min, 1995).

QUESTIONS FOR REFLECTION

1. What are some key differences between Asian and Anglo cultures? How have these differences shaped relations between the groups?

2. Which group do you think is the most diverse and why: African Americans, Native Americans, Hispanic Americans, or Asian Americans? Given their levels of diversity and similarity, what are the pros and cons of discussing each of these groups as individual entities?

CONTACT SITUATIONS AND THE DEVELOPMENT OF THE CHINESE AMERICAN AND JAPANESE AMERICAN COMMUNITIES

China and Japan were the earliest Asian groups to arrive in America in substantial numbers. Their contact situations shaped their histories and affected the present situation of all Asian Americans in many ways. As you'll see, the contact situations for Chinese Americans and Japanese Americans featured massive hostility and discrimination. Both groups coped with racism from the larger society by forming enclaves, a strategy that, similar to Cuban Americans, produced some major benefits for their descendants.

Chinese Americans

Early Immigration and the Anti-Chinese Campaign

Immigrants from China began arriving in the early 1800s. Generally, they were motivated by the same kinds of social and economic forces that have inspired immigration everywhere. Rapid population growth and European colonization disrupted traditional social relations and pushed Chinese immigrants to leave their homeland (Chan, 1990; Lyman, 1974; Tsai, 1986). Simultaneously, they were pulled to America's West Coast by the 1849 gold rush and by other opportunities that arose as the West developed. By 1852, more than 20,000 Chinese immigrants lived in California in relative harmony with whites, though that changed as economic conditions deteriorated.

The Noel hypothesis (Chapter 3) offers a useful way to analyze the contact situation between Chinese and Anglo Americans in the mid-19th century. Remember that Noel argues that racial or ethnic stratification occurs when a contact situation has three conditions: ethnocentrism, competition, and a differential in power. Once all three conditions were met on the West Coast, whites started a vigorous campaign against the Chinese and pushed them into a subordinate, disadvantaged position. For example, in 1862, Congress passed what became known as the Anti-Coolie Act (or the Chinese Police Act). The law required Chinese immigrants to pay a hefty monthly tax to work in California. By some estimates, the tax was between 60% to 80% of their wages. Police impounded and auctioned the belongings of those who couldn't pay and held employers liable after that (Odo, 2002; Soennichsen, 2011, p. 121).

Ethnocentrism based on racial and cultural differences existed at first contact. However, competition for jobs between Chinese immigrants and native-born workers was muted by a robust, rapidly growing economy. At first, politicians, newspaper editorial writers, and business leaders praised the Chinese for their industriousness and tirelessness (Tsai, 1986). Before long, however, the economic boom slowed, and the supply of jobs dwindled. The gold rush petered out, and the transcontinental railroad, which thousands of Chinese workers helped build, was completed in 1869. Anglo Americans continued migrating from the East, and competition for jobs and other resources increased. As the West Coast economy changed, whites began to see the Chinese as a threat.

In 1870, the Chinese were a small group of only about 100,000. The law didn't allow them to become citizens. Hence, they controlled few power resources with which to withstand these attacks. During the 1870s, whites limited their competition by forcing Chinese workers out of most sectors of the mainstream economy. Yet, hostilities lingered and an anti-Chinese campaign of harassment, discrimination, and violent attacks began. In Los Angeles, for example, a mob of "several hundred whites shot, hanged, and stabbed 19 Chinese to death" in what is now called the 1871 Chinese Massacre (Tsai, 1986, p. 67). Other attacks against the Chinese occurred in Denver, Seattle, Tacoma, and Rock Springs, Wyoming (Lyman, 1974). Denis Kearney, head of the Workingman's Party (WP) labor organization, fanned resentments by speaking of Chinese men as "cheap working slave[s]" who created unfair competition for jobs. The WP adopted the motto, "The Chinese must go!" which Kearney would say at the end of every speech. He encouraged white workers to take matters into their own hands because the government was run by "money men" who didn't care about the "poor [white, man] Laborer" (Kearney & Knight, 1978).

In 1882, the anti-Chinese campaign experienced its ultimate triumph when the U.S. Congress passed the **Chinese Exclusion Act**, banning virtually all Chinese immigration. The act was one of the first restrictive immigration laws aimed solely at the Chinese. It established a rigid competitive relationship between the groups and, by excluding the Chinese from American society, it eliminated the perceived threat of Chinese labor. The primary antagonists of Chinese immigrants were native-born workers and organized labor. White owners of small businesses, feeling threatened by Chinese-owned businesses, also supported passage of the Chinese Exclusion Act (Boswell, 1986). Other social classes, such as the capitalists who owned larger factories, benefited from the continued supply of cheaper labor created by Chinese immigration. Conflicts such as the anti-Chinese campaign could be especially intense because they confounded racial and ethnic antagonisms with disputes between different social classes.

The ban on Chinese immigration remained in effect until World War II, when China was awarded a yearly quota of 105 immigrants in recognition of its wartime alliance with the United States. Large-scale immigration from China didn't resume until federal policy revision in the 1960s.

Population Trends and the "Delayed" Second Generation

Following the Chinese Exclusion Act, the number of Chinese people in the U. S. declined (see Figure 8.3) as some immigrants passed away or returned to China and weren't replaced by newcomers. The vast majority of Chinese immigrants in the 19th century had been young adult men, sojourners who intended to work hard, save money, and return home (Chan, 1990). After 1882, it was difficult for anyone from China—men or women—to enter the United States; therefore, the Chinese community in the U. S. remained dominated by men for many decades. At the end of the 19th century, for example, men outnumbered women by more than 25 to 1, and the gender ratio didn't approach parity for decades (Wong, 1995, p. 64; see also Ling, 2000). The scarcity of Chinese women in the U. S. delayed the second generation (the first generation born in the U. S.). It wasn't until the 1920s, 80 years after immigration began, that one third of all Chinese in America were native-born (Wong, 1995, p. 64).

The delayed second generation (immigrants' children) may have reinforced the exclusion of the Chinese American community, which began as a reaction to the overt discrimination by the dominant group (Chan, 1990). Children of immigrants are usually much more acculturated, and their language skills and greater familiarity with the larger society allowed them to speak for the group more effectively.

Second-generation Chinese Americans (and other Asian groups) were born U.S. citizens with legal and political rights not available to their parents, who were forbidden to become citizens. Thus, the decades-long absence of a more Americanized, English-speaking generation increased Chinese Americans' isolation.

The Ethnic Enclave

The Chinese became increasingly urbanized as the anti-Chinese campaign and rising racism took their toll. Forced out of towns and smaller cities, they settled in larger urban areas, especially San Francisco (which offered the safety of urban anonymity), and ethnic

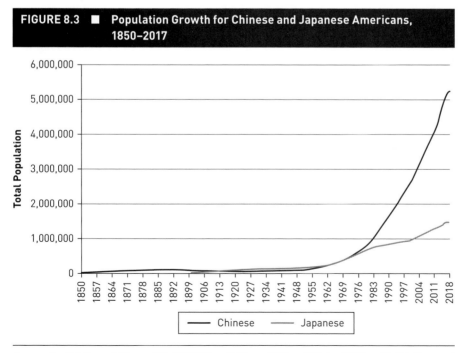

FIGURE 8.3 ■ Population Growth for Chinese and Japanese Americans, 1850–2017

Sources: Hoeffel, Rastogi, Kim, and Shahid (2012, p. 4); Kitano (1980, p. 562); Lee (1998, p. 15), U.S. Bureau of the Census (2018a). American Community Survey, 2017.

neighborhoods where they could practice "old ways" and minimize contact with Anglo society. Chinatowns had existed since the start of immigration, but they now took on added significance as safe havens from the storm of anti-Chinese venom. By withdrawing to these neighborhoods, the Chinese became an "invisible minority" (Tsai, 1986, p. 67).

These early Chinatowns were ethnic enclaves similar to those founded by Jews on the East Coast and Miami's Cuban community, and a similar process formed them. The earliest urban Chinese included merchants and skilled artisans who, similar to the early wave of Cuban immigrants, were experienced in commerce (Chan, 1990). They established businesses and retail stores, typically small in scope and modest in profits. As their population increased, the market for these enterprises became larger and more spatially concentrated. As people needed new services, the size of the cheap labor pool available to Chinese merchants and entrepreneurs increased, and Chinatowns became the economic, cultural, and social centers of the community.

Within the Chinatowns, elaborate social structures developed that mirrored traditional China in many ways. Residential segregation by whites helped preserve much of the traditional Chinese food, dress, language, values, norms, and religions of their homeland. The social structure was based on many types of organizations, including family and clan groups and *huiguan*, or associations based on the region or district in China from which the immigrants had come. These organizations performed various—often overlapping—social and welfare services, including settling disputes, aiding new arrivals from their regions, and facilitating the development of mutual aid networks (Lai, 1980; Lyman, 1974).

Life wasn't always peaceful in Chinatown; there were numerous disputes over control of resources and the organizational infrastructure. In particular, secret societies called *tongs* contested the control and leadership of the merchant-led *huiguan* and the clan associations. The American press sensationalized these sometimes-bloody conflicts as "Tong Wars," which contributed to the stereotypes of Asians as dangerous, exotic, and mysterious (Lai, 1980; Lyman, 1974).

Despite internal conflicts, American Chinatowns evolved into highly organized, largely self-contained communities, complete with their own leadership and decision-making structures. The Chinese Consolidated Benevolent Association (CCBA) functioned as the internal city government of Chinatown. Dominated by the larger *huiguan* and clans, the CCBA coordinated and supplemented the activities of the various organizations and represented community interests outside the enclave.

The local CCBAs, along with other organizations, fought the anti-Chinese campaign, speaking out against racial discrimination and filing numerous lawsuits to contest racist legislation (Lai, 1980). The lack of resources in the Chinese community and the fact that Chinese immigrants couldn't become citizens limited the effectiveness of protest efforts. China tried to mobilize international pressure against the treatment of the Chinese in America. However, China was colonized and dominated by other nations (including the United States). Additionally, internal turmoil further weakened China; therefore, it couldn't effectively help its citizens in the United States (Chan, 1990).

Survival and Development

The Chinese American community survived despite widespread poverty, discrimination, and the lack of women. Group members sought opportunities in other regions, resulting in Chinatowns developing in New York, Boston, Chicago, Philadelphia, and many other cities.

The patterns of exclusion and discrimination that began during the 19th-century anti-Chinese campaign were common throughout the nation and continued well into the 20th century. Chinese Americans responded by finding economic opportunity in areas where dominant group competition for jobs was weak, allowing them to remain an "invisible" minority. Very often, they started small businesses that either served other members of their own group (e.g., restaurants) or relied on the patronage of the public (e.g., laundries). The jobs these small businesses provided were the economic lifeblood of the community but were limited in the amount of income and wealth they could generate. Until recent decades, for example, most restaurants served primarily other Chinese, especially single men. Because their primary clientele was poor, the profit potential of these businesses was sharply limited. Laundries served the more affluent dominant group, but the returns from this enterprise declined as washers and dryers became increasingly common in homes throughout the nation. The population of Chinatown was generally too small to sustain more than these two primary commercial enterprises (Zhou, 1992).

As the decades passed, the enclave economy and the complex sub-society of Chinatown evolved. However, discrimination, combined with defensive self-segregation, ensured the continuation of poverty, limited job opportunities, and substandard housing. Relatively hidden from general view, Chinatown became the world where the second generation grew into adulthood.

The Second Generation

The immigrant generation generally retained its native language and customs. However, the second generation was much more influenced by the larger culture. The institutional and organizational structures of Chinatown were created to serve the older (mostly men) immigrant generation. But younger Chinese Americans looked beyond the enclave to fill their needs. They came in contact with the larger society through schools, churches, and voluntary organizations such as the YMCA.

This second generation of Chinese Americans abandoned many traditional customs and were less interested in the clan and regional associations that the immigrant generation had constructed. They founded organizations more compatible with their Americanized lifestyles (Lai, 1980).

Like other minority groups, World War II was an important watershed for Chinese Americans. During the war, opportunities outside the enclave increased; after the war, many of the 8,000 Chinese Americans who had served in the armed forces took advantage of the GI Bill to further their education (Lai, 1980). Thus, in the 1940s and 1950s, many moved out of the enclave to pursue opportunities. This group was mobile and Americanized, and with educational credentials comparable to the general population, they were prepared to seek success outside Chinatown.

In another departure from tradition, second-generation Chinese women pursued education. As early as 1960, the median years of schooling for Chinese American women was slightly higher than for Chinese American men (Kitano & Daniels, 1995) and as the century progressed, Chinese American women became more occupationally diverse. In 1900, three fourths of all employed Chinese American women were doing domestic work or working in manufacturing (usually in the garment industry or in canning factories). By 1960, less than 2% did domestic work, 32% were in clerical occupations, and 18% held professional jobs, often as teachers (Amott & Matthaei, 1991, pp. 209–211).

Men and women of the second generation achieved considerable educational and occupational success and helped establish the idea that Chinese Americans were a "model minority." A closer examination reveals, however, that anti-Chinese prejudice and discrimination continued to limit their life chances. Second-generation Chinese Americans earned less, on average, and had less-favorable occupational profiles than comparably educated white Americans, a gap between qualifications and rewards that reflects persistent discrimination. Kitano and Daniels (1995) conclude that although well-educated Chinese Americans could find good jobs in the mainstream economy, the highest, most lucrative positions—and those that required direct supervision of whites—were still unattainable (see Hirschman & Wong, 1984).

Furthermore, many Chinese Americans, including many who stayed in the Chinatowns to run the enclave economy as well as the immigrants who began arriving after 1965, didn't fit the image of success at all. A large percentage of them faced many of the same problems as members of colonized, excluded, exploited minority groups of color. For survival, they relied on low-wage jobs in the garment industry, the service sector, and the small businesses of the enclave economy, and they were beset by poverty and powerlessness, much like the urban underclass segments of other groups.

Thus, Chinese Americans were represented at both ends of the occupational structure spectrum (see Barringer, Takeuchi, & Levin, 1995; Min, 2006; Takaki, 1993; Wong, 1995; Zhou & Logan, 1989). A large percentage work in more desirable occupations, which offered some level of affluence, and this sustained the popular idea of Asian success. Others, less visible, were concentrated at the lowest levels. Because they were present at both poles or ends of the spectrum, researchers often describe Chinese Americans (as a group) as "bipolar."

Japanese Americans

Immigration from Japan increased shortly after the Chinese Exclusion Act of 1882 took effect, in part to fill the gap in the labor supply created by the restrictive legislation (Kitano, 1980). The 1880 census counted only a few hundred Japanese in the U. S., but the group increased rapidly. By 1910, the Japanese in America outnumbered the Chinese, and they remained the larger of the two groups until large-scale immigration resumed in the 1960s (see Figure 8.3).

The Anti-Japanese Campaign

The contact situation for Japanese immigrants resembled that of the Chinese. They immigrated to the same West Coast regions as the Chinese, entered the labor force in a similar position, and were also a small group with few power resources. Predictably, the feelings and emotions generated by the anti-Chinese campaign transferred to them. By the early 1900s, an anti-Japanese campaign to limit competition was in full swing. Efforts were being made to establish a rigid competitive system of group relations and to exclude Japanese immigrants in the same way the Chinese were barred (Kitano, 1980; Kitano & Daniels, 1995; Petersen, 1971).

Japanese immigration was partly curtailed in 1907 when a "gentlemen's agreement" was signed between Japan and the U. S. limiting the number of laborers Japan would allow to emigrate (Kitano & Daniels, 1995, p. 59). This policy remained in effect until the United States changed its immigration policy in the 1920s and barred Japanese immigration completely. The end of Japanese immigration is largely responsible for the slow growth of the Japanese American population throughout most of the 20th century (see Figure 8.3).

Most Japanese immigrants, similar to the Chinese, were young men laborers who planned to return to their homeland or, if married, to bring their wives to America once they were established (Duleep, 1988). The agreement of 1907 curtailed men's immigration, but because of a loophole, women could continue immigrating until the 1920s. Thus, the group of Japanese Americans had relatively equal numbers of women and men who would marry and begin families, and a second generation of Japanese Americans began appearing without much delay. By 1930, about half of all Japanese Americans were native-born; by the eve of World War II, a majority (63%) were U.S.–born (Kitano & Daniels, 1995, p. 59).

The anti-Japanese movement also attempted to dislodge the Japanese from agriculture. Many Japanese immigrants were skilled agriculturists, and farming was their most promising avenue for advancement (Kitano, 1980). In 1910, between 30% and 40% of all Japanese in California were engaged in agriculture; from 1900 to 1909, the number of independent Japanese farmers increased from fewer than 50 to about 6,000 (Jibou, 1988, p. 358).

Most of these immigrant farmers owned small plots of land, and they made up only a minuscule percentage of West Coast farmers. Nonetheless, their presence and relative success didn't go unnoticed and eventually stimulated discriminatory legislation, most notably the **Alien Land Act**, passed by the California legislature in 1913. This bill made foreign-born people ineligible for citizenship and, therefore, ineligible to own land. Given the West Coast population at the time, this law essentially applied to Asian immigrants. Somewhat surprisingly, the legislation didn't achieve its goal of dislodging the Japanese from the rural economy, who dodged the discriminatory legislation through various methods, mostly by putting land titles in the names of their American-born children, who were citizens by law (Jibou, 1988; Kitano, 1980).

The Alien Land Act was one part of a sustained campaign against the Japanese in the United States. In the early decades of this century, the Japanese were politically disenfranchised and segregated from dominant group institutions, such as schools and residential areas. They were discriminated against in movie theaters, swimming pools, and other public facilities. The Japanese were excluded from the mainstream economy and confined to a limited range of poorly paid occupations (Kitano & Daniels, 1988; see Yamato, 1994). In short, they experienced strong elements of systematic discrimination, exclusion, and colonization in their overall relationship with the dominant white society.

The Ethnic Enclave

Spurned and disparaged by the larger society, the Japanese, similar to the Chinese, constructed a separate sub-society. The immigrant generation, called **Issei** (from the Japanese word *ichi,* meaning "one"), established an enclave in agriculture and related enterprises, a rural counterpart of the urban enclaves constructed by other groups we've examined.

By World War II, the Issei had come to dominate a narrow but important segment of agriculture on the West Coast, especially in California. Although the Issei were never more than 2% of the total population of California, Japanese American–owned farms produced as much as 30% to 40% of various fruits and vegetables grown in that state. As late as 1940, more than 40% of the Japanese American population was involved directly in farming, and many more were dependent on the economic activity stimulated by agriculture, including the marketing of their produce. Other Issei lived in urban areas, where they were concentrated in a narrow range of businesses and services, such as domestic work and gardening, some of which catered to other Issei and some of which served the dominant group (Jibou, 1988, p. 362).

Japanese Americans in the rural and urban sectors maximized their economic clout by doing business with other Japanese-owned firms as often as possible. Gardeners and farmers purchased supplies at Japanese-owned firms, farmers used other group members to haul their produce to market, and businesspeople relied on one another and mutual credit associations (rather than dominant-group banks) for financial services. These networks helped the enclave economy to grow and also permitted the Japanese to avoid the hostility and racism of the larger society. However, these very same patterns helped sustain the stereotypes that depicted the Japanese as clannish and unassimilable. In the years before World War II, the Japanese American community was largely dependent for survival on networks of cooperation and mutual assistance, not on Americanization and integration.

The Second Generation (*Nisei*)

In the 1920s and 1930s, anti-Asian feelings continued to run high, and Japanese Americans continued to be excluded and discriminated against despite (or perhaps because of) their relative success. Unable to find acceptance in Anglo society, the second generation, called *Nisei*, established clubs, athletic leagues, churches, and a multitude of other social and recreational organizations within their own communities (Kitano & Daniels, 1995). These organizations reflected the high levels of Americanization of the Nisei and expressed values and interests quite compatible with those of the dominant culture. For example, the most influential Nisei organization was the Japanese American Citizens League, whose creed expressed an ardent patriotism that was to be sorely tested: "I am proud that I am an American citizen. . . . I believe in [American] institutions, ideas, and traditions; I glory in her heritage; I boast of her history, I trust in her future" (Kitano & Daniels, 1995, p. 64).

Although the Nisei enjoyed high levels of success in school, the intense discrimination and racism of the 1930s prevented most of them from translating their educational achievements into better jobs and higher salaries. Many occupations in the mainstream economy were closed to even the best-educated Japanese Americans, and anti-Asian prejudice and discrimination didn't diminish during the hard times and high unemployment of the Great Depression in the 1930s. Many Nisei were forced to remain within the enclave, and in many cases, jobs in the produce stands and retail shops of their parents were all they could find. Their demoralization and anger over their exclusion were eventually swamped by the larger events of World War II.

The Detention Centers

On December 7, 1941, Japan attacked Pearl Harbor, killing almost 2,500 Americans. The next day, President Franklin D. Roosevelt asked Congress for a declaration of war. The preparations for war stirred up a wide range of fears and anxieties among the

American public, including concerns about the loyalty of Japanese Americans. Decades of exclusion and anti-Japanese prejudice conditioned members of the dominant society to see Japanese Americans as sinister, clannish, cruel, unalterably foreign, and racially inferior. Fueled by the ferocity of the war itself and fears about a Japanese invasion of the mainland, the tradition of anti-Japanese racism laid the groundwork for a massive violation of civil rights.

Two months after the attack on Pearl Harbor, President Roosevelt signed Executive Order 9066, which led to the forced detention of Japanese Americans living on the West Coast. By the late summer of 1942, about 115,000 Japanese Americans, young and old, men and women—virtually the entire Japanese population from the West Coast— were forcibly transported to **detention centers,** where the government imprisoned them behind barbed-wire fences patrolled by armed guards. Most of these people were American citizens, yet the U.S. government made no attempt to distinguish between citizens and non-citizens. No trials were held, and no one was given the opportunity to refute the implicit charge of disloyalty. (The government forcibly detained approximately 11,500 German Americans and 3,000 Italian Americans, and others, including those abroad, but it wasn't a wide-sweeping roundup [Mak, 2017].)

The U.S. government gave families little time to prepare for removal and secure their homes, businesses, and belongings. Because the government only allowed them to bring what they could carry, most Japanese Americans had to abandon the majority of their possessions. Businesspeople sold their establishments (and everything in them) and farmers sold their land at panic-sale prices. Others locked up their stores and houses and walked away, hoping that the removal would be short-lived and their possessions undisturbed.

Their detention lasted for most of the war. At first, the government didn't permit Japanese Americans to serve in the armed forces, but eventually, more than 25,000 escaped the detention centers by volunteering for military service. Nearly all of them served in segregated units or in intelligence work with combat units in the Pacific Ocean. Two all-Japanese combat units served in Europe and became the most decorated units for their size in American military history (Asahina, 2007). Other Japanese Americans were able to get out of the detention centers by different means. Some, for example, agreed to move to militarily nonsensitive areas far away from the West Coast (and their former homes). Still, about half of the original internees remained when the detention centers closed at the end of the war (Kitano & Daniels, 1988).

The strain of living in the detention centers affected Japanese Americans in a variety of ways. Overcrowding, lack of privacy, and boredom were common complaints. For example, Manzanar, one of the biggest facilities, housed more than 11,000 people. Eight people lived in a 20-by-25-foot room with few furnishings, usually cots or blankets with straw. On each of its 36 blocks, "200 to 400 people . . . shared men's and women's toilets and showers [with no partitions and showers with no stalls]" (National Park Service, 2015a). Detention disrupted the traditional forms of family life, as people adapted to living in crowded barracks and dining in mess halls. Conflicts flared between people who counseled caution and temperate reactions to the incarceration and those who wanted to protest in more vigorous ways. Many of those who advised moderation were Nisei, intent on proving their loyalty by cooperating with the administration.

Despite the injustice and dislocations of the incarceration, the detention centers reduced the extent to which women were relegated to subordinate roles. Similar to Chinese women, Japanese women were expected to devote themselves to family care. In Japan, for example, the goal of women's education was to make them better wives and mothers, not expand their minds or skills. Living in small quarters and eating in mess halls freed women from some housework. Many took classes to learn more English and other skills. Additionally, almost all adults worked full-time running the detention centers, and U.S. citizens were eligible for a few paying jobs. The pay was low but about equal for men and women. (Japanese Americans and whites had unequal pay. For example, Japanese American teachers at Heart Mountain Relocation Center were paid about nine times less than white counterparts [Digital Public Library of America, n.d.].) Employment gave women a sense of self independent from their family. The younger women were able to meet young men on their own, weakening the tradition of family-controlled, arranged marriages (Amott & Matthaei, 1991).

Some Japanese Americans protested the incarceration from the start and brought lawsuits to end their forced relocation. Finally, in 1944, the Supreme Court ruled that detention was unconstitutional. As the detention centers closed, some Japanese American individuals and organizations sought compensation and redress for the economic losses the group had suffered. In 1948, Congress passed legislation to compensate Japanese Americans for lost wages and lost property. About 26,500 people filed claims and eventually settled for a total of about $38 million or about $1,434 per person (or about $15,041 in 2019 dollars)—much less than the actual economic losses for lost wages and property (Pippert, 1983).

Demand for meaningful redress and compensation continued. In 1980, Congress began studying the impact of the detention centers, and a 1982 report estimated total economic losses between $2.5 billion to $6.2 billion after adjusting for inflation. Further, it acknowledged that "the magnitude of the losses and injuries that come under the heading of 'pain and suffering' cannot be estimated objectively in an economic sense and we made no attempt to study them" (Pippert, 1983). In 1988, Congress passed a bill granting reparations of about $20,000 to each of the 60,000 survivors and acknowledged that the detention had resulted from "racial prejudice, war hysteria and the failure of political leadership." The law also acknowledged that the relocation program had been a grave injustice to Japanese Americans (Biskupic, 1989, p. 2879; Qureshi, 2013).

In 2004, the House of Representatives approved a National Day of Remembrance on February 19, the date Executive Order 9066 was signed. The Congressional record notes that though national security should be the highest priority,

> [we must] not again have a failure among our political leadership. We must not give in to war hysteria. We must not fall back to racial prejudice, discrimination and unlawful profiling. It is critical and important, more than ever, to speak up against possible unjust policies that may come before this body. (Congressional Record, 2007)

The detention devastated the Japanese American community and left it with few material resources. The emotional and psychological damage inflicted by this experience is incalculable. The fact that today, only seven decades later, the performance of Japanese Americans is equal or superior to national averages on measures of educational achievement, occupational prestige, and income is one of the more dramatic transformations in minority group history.

QUESTIONS FOR REFLECTION

3. What practical, emotional, and other consequences would living in detention centers have on you, your family, and the community?

4. Some people have called for detention centers for American Muslims as a preventative measure. Is this a reasonable, effective solution that could increase national security? If so, should we detain members of other groups that also have the potential to become radicalized or to harm the nation (e.g., white nationalists)? Explain. If you think this is a problematic plan, explain why.

5. Compare the forcible removal of Japanese Americans with that of Native Americans, with the legal segregation of black Africans under apartheid and African Americans under Jim Crow, and with the persecution of Jews, the Roma, and gays under the Third Reich in Germany.

Japanese Americans after World War II

In 1945, after their detention, Japanese Americans faced a very different world. About half the original internees remained when the detention centers closed. They stayed to avoid anti-Japanese prejudice that they feared on returning home. (After all, those feelings didn't end when the war did. See Table 1.2.) Many also stayed because they'd lost their businesses and property, which put them at risk for poverty (Robinson, 2012). The rest of the group scattered throughout the country and lived everywhere but the West Coast. The Japanese Americans who moved back to their former homes found their fields untended, their stores vandalized, their possessions lost or stolen. In some cases, there was no Japanese neighborhood to return to; for example, the Little Tokyo area of San Francisco had become inhabited by African Americans who had moved to the West Coast to take jobs in the defense industry (Amott & Matthaei, 1991).

Japanese Americans had changed, also. In the detention centers, the Issei had lost power to the Nisei. The English-speaking second generation had dealt with the camp administrators and held the leadership positions. Many Nisei had left the detention centers to serve in the armed forces or to find work in other areas of the country. For virtually every American minority group, the war brought new experiences and a broader sense of themselves, the nation, and the world. A similar transformation occurred for the Nisei. When the war ended, they were unwilling to rebuild the Japanese community as it was before.

Similar to second-generation Chinese Americans, the Nisei had a strong record of success in school, and they also took advantage of the GI Bill to further their education. When anti-Asian prejudice began to decline in the 1950s and the job market began opening, the Nisei were educationally prepared to take advantage of the resultant opportunities (Kitano, 1980).

The Issei-dominated enclave economy didn't reappear after the war. One indicator of the shift from an enclave economy was that the percentage of Japanese American women in California who worked as unpaid family laborers (i.e., worked in family-run businesses for no salary) declined from 21% in 1940 to 7% in 1950 (Amott & Matthaei, 1991, p. 231). Also, between 1940 and 1990, the percentage of Japanese Americans employed in agriculture declined from about 50% to 3%, and the percentage employed in personal services fell from 25% to 5% (Nishi, 1995, p. 116).

By 1960, Japanese Americans had an occupational profile very similar to whites except that they were actually overrepresented among professionals. Many were employed in the primary economy, not in the ethnic enclave. Many chose to work in stable careers (e.g., engineering, optometry, pharmacy, accounting) that didn't require extensive public contact or supervision by whites (Kitano & Daniels, 1988).

Within these limitations, the Nisei, their children (**Sansei**), and their grandchildren (**Yonsei**) enjoyed relatively high status, and their upward mobility and prosperity have contributed to the perception that Asian Americans are a model minority. An additional factor contributing to Japanese Americans' high status (and to the disappearance of Little Tokyos) is that, unlike the Chinese American community, the Japanese American community received few new immigrants. Therefore, the community hasn't needed to devote many resources to newcomers. Furthermore, recent Japanese immigrants tend to be highly educated professionals whose socioeconomic characteristics add to the perception of the group's success and affluence.

COMPARATIVE FOCUS
JAPAN'S "INVISIBLE" MINORITY

In Chapter 1, you learned two of the most important characteristics of minority groups. They are (1) objects of a pattern of disadvantage and (2) easily identifiable, either culturally or physically. These traits work in tandem: Members of the dominant group must be able to determine a person's group membership quickly and easily so the discrimination that is the hallmark of minority group status can be practiced.

Visibility is such an obvious precondition for discrimination that it almost seems unnecessary to state it. However, every generalization has an exception, and the members of at least one minority group, the Japanese *Barakumin*, have been victimized by discrimination and prejudice for hundreds of years but are virtually indistinguishable from the general population. How could this "invisible" minority come into being? How could the disadvantaged status be maintained through time?

The Barakumin were created centuries ago, when Japan was organized into a caste system based on occupation. The ancestors of today's Barakumin did work that brought them into contact with death (e.g., gravediggers) or required them to handle meat products (e.g., butchers). People regarded these occupations as very low in status, unclean, or polluted.

The dominant group forced the Barakumin to live in separate villages and to wear leather patches that raised their visibility. They were forbidden to marry outside their caste, and any member of the general population who touched a Barakumin person had to be ritually purified (Lamont-Brown, 1993).

The caste system was officially abolished in the 19th century, around the time Japan began to industrialize. Today, most observers agree that the Barakumin's situation has improved. However, the Barakumin maintain their minority status, and prejudice and discrimination against them continues, for example, in housing, employment, and education (Ball, 2009; Hanskins, 2014; Neary, 2003).

The Barakumin are a small group of about 1.2 million people, about 2% or 3% of Japan's population. The dominant group continues to see them as "filthy," "not very bright," and "untrustworthy"—stereotypical traits associated with other minority groups (Hanskins, 2014; Main, 2012).

The Barakumin situation might seem puzzling. If the group isn't distinguishable from the general population, why don't the Barakumin blend in? What keeps them attached to their group?

Some Barakumin are proud of their heritage and refuse to surrender to the dominant culture. They have no intention of trading their ethnic identity for acceptance or opportunity. For others, the ancient system of residential segregation makes it difficult to pass as anything other than Barakumin. Specifically, the Japanese have recorded family histories (including addresses) for centuries. Traditional Barakumin areas of residence are well known, and this information—not race or culture—creates group boundaries and forms the ultimate barrier to assimilation. Historically, anyone could review that information. Employers used it to screen out potential employees. Additionally, that telltale information would emerge when they apply to rent apartments or get home loans. Like other minority groups, some landlords refuse to rent to them, and banks have been reluctant to provide loans to them. Similarly, Japanese parents typically research information about

their child's fiancé to know who is joining the family. Thus, if any Barakumin attempted to marry outside their group, they would be discovered. In each of these cases, the Barakumin who could pass and blend in would be outed (see Main, 2012; Reber, 1998).

Historically, standard practice was to investigate someone going back five generations. Legislation in 1968 made it illegal for the public to access these records. Thus, in 1975, when an anonymous source revealed that more than 200 businesses had purchased lists of Barakumin information (e.g., family names, addresses, community names) for 5,300 Buraku districts, it became known as the "Buraku Lists Scandal." Nevertheless, such practices continue in new forms, such as hiring private detectives or using Google Earth records. As recently as 2014, more than one fourth (27%) of people surveyed said they wouldn't support their children marrying a Barakumin member (Buraku Liberation and Human Rights Research Institute, 2005; Hanskins, 2014; Okaki, 2016; Sunda, 2015).

Awareness of traditional Barakumin residential areas means that this group isn't really invisible: There's a way to determine group membership, a mark of who belongs and who doesn't. Consistent with our definition, this "birthmark" is the basis for a socially constructed boundary that differentiates *us* from *them* and for the discrimination and prejudice associated with minority group status.

Legislation in 2015 officially recognized discrimination against the Barakumin and mandated the government to help improve the group's situation; for example, by investigating discrimination complaints. However, the law leaves plenty of room for local communities to avoid implementing it. Similar to American minority groups, the Barakumin have created protest organizations dedicated to improving their lives. They've faced significant resistance but made some progress and will continue to fight for equality (Hanskins, 2014; Osaki, 2016; Sunda, 2015).

QUESTIONS FOR REFLECTION

6. In what ways are the Barakumin unique? What other minority groups are similarly invisible?

7. How does the experience of the Barakumin parallel that of visible minority groups in the U. S., such as African Americans and Asian Americans?

The Sansei and Yonsei are highly integrated into the occupational structure of the larger society. Compared with their parents, their connections with their ethnic past are more tenuous, and in their values, beliefs, and personal goals, they resemble dominant group members of similar age and social class (Kitano & Daniels, 1995; see also Spickard, 1996).

COMPARING MINORITY GROUPS

What factors account for the differences in the development of Chinese Americans and Japanese Americans and other racial minority groups? First, the dominant group didn't need to control Asian American labor as it did with African Americans in the 1600s and Mexican Americans in the 1800s. The Asian American contact situation featured economic competition (e.g., for jobs) during an era of rigid competition between groups (see Table 4.2). Whites saw Chinese Americans and Japanese Americans as a threat to security that they needed to eliminate, not as a labor pool they needed to control.

Second, unlike Native Americans, Chinese and Japanese Americans in the early 20th century presented no military danger to America; once the economic threat ended, people had little concern with their activities. Third, Chinese and Japanese Americans had the ingredients and experiences necessary to form enclaves. The groups were allowed to "disappear," but unlike other racial minority groups, the urban location of their enclaves left them with opportunities for starting small businesses and providing an education for the second and later generations. As many scholars argue, the mode of incorporation developed by Chinese Americans and Japanese Americans is the key to understanding the present status of these groups.

QUESTIONS FOR REFLECTION

8. What forces shaped Chinese and Japanese immigration? Compare these patterns with those of Hispanic immigration and European immigration between 1820 and 1920. What are the key differences and similarities?

9. Compare the development of the Chinese American community with the development of the Japanese American community. What are the most significant differences and similarities? What accounts for these patterns?

10. Are Japanese and Chinese Americans colonized or immigrant groups? Explain.

CONTEMPORARY IMMIGRATION FROM ASIA

Figure 8.4 displays the volume of immigration from Asia since 1900. Follow the black line from the left vertical axis; it represents the average number of immigrants per year for each period. Notice the decline—almost to zero—after the restrictive legislation of the 1920s. Also note the steep increases in the mid-1960s after changes in immigration policy. Since then, Asian immigration has steadily increased, making Asia the largest supplier of immigrants to America since 2009.

The gray line shows the percentage of all immigrants that were from Asia in each period. Notice that Asian immigration was rare—less than 5% of all immigrants—until the mid-1960s. The percentage increased until the 1980s; then it declined in the 1990s as the volume of immigration from Mexico and Central and South America skyrocketed.

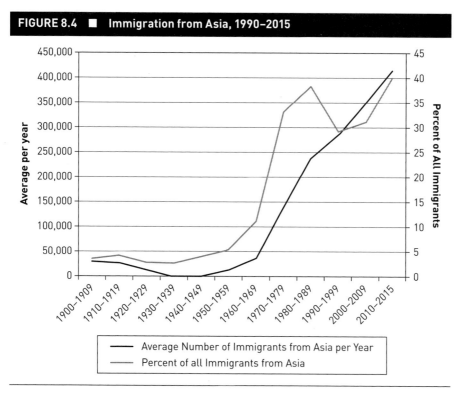

FIGURE 8.4 ■ Immigration from Asia, 1990–2015

— Average Number of Immigrants from Asia per Year
— Percent of all Immigrants from Asia

Source: U.S. Department of Homeland Security (2016).

The percentage has risen to about 40% in more recent years, reflecting the continued flow from Asia and the declining flow of Hispanics.

Figure 8.5 shows that Asian immigration since the 1950s has been heaviest from China, India, and the Philippines, though Korea and Vietnam have made sizable contributions. As noted previously, Japanese immigration has been relatively low since the initial influx more than a century ago (see Figure 8.3).

Similar to Hispanic immigrants, the sending nations (other than Japan) are less economically developed than the United States. Thus, the primary motivation for most of these immigrants is economic. However, unlike Hispanic immigration, the Asian immigrant stream includes a large contingent of highly educated professionals seeking opportunities to practice their careers and expand their skills.

These more-elite immigrants contribute to the image of "Asian success," but many Asian immigrants are less skilled and educated and are often undocumented. Thus, the stream of Asian immigrants includes people from the top and bottom of the educational and occupational hierarchies.

Of course, other factors besides economics attract Asian immigrants. For example, since the end of World War II, the U. S. has maintained military bases throughout the region (e.g., South Korea, Japan, the Philippines). Many Asian immigrants to the United States are married to American military personnel who were stationed in those parts of the world.

Additionally, American involvement in the war in Southeast Asia in the 1960s and 1970s created interpersonal ties and governmental programs that drew refugees from

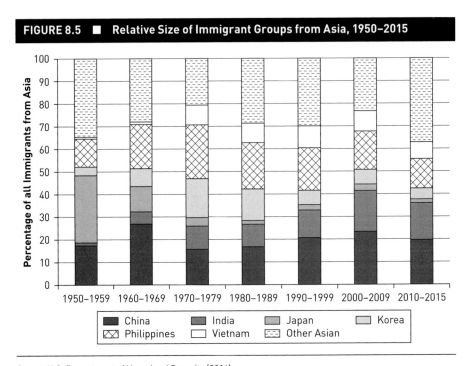

FIGURE 8.5 ■ Relative Size of Immigrant Groups from Asia, 1950–2015

Source: U.S. Department of Homeland Security (2016).

Vietnam, Cambodia, and Laos, many of whom were escaping war and living in refugee camps for years before immigrating to the U. S. Because of the conditions of their escape, few brought substantial human or material capital.

Among the refugee groups are the *Hmong*, people from Laos and other Southeast Asian nations who fought for the U. S. in the Vietnam War. They're a relatively small group of immigrants (see Table 8.1) and face some unique challenges in adjustment to American society. Their culture is very traditional and, in many ways, far removed from the contemporary United States.

Anthropologist Anne Fadiman illustrates the complex challenges the Hmong face in acculturating in her 1998 book about an epileptic Hmong girl, Lia Lee. Prior to the Vietnam War, the Hmong were at the hunter–gatherer level of subsistence technology. Therefore, Hmong immigrants brought little of what most Americans would call social or cultural capital with them. This was the case for Lia's family. Lia's parents loved her deeply and wanted to help her. According to traditional Hmong beliefs, spirits cause illness; illness should be treated by shamans (traditional healers) in the time-honored way. But the Lees lived in California, and the law mandated modern medicine so the Lees consulted with local doctors, who attempted to treat Lia with medicine. However, linguistic barriers and the Hmong religious and cultural beliefs made it difficult for the Lees to understand and follow medical instructions. Lia died at the age of 30 after being in a vegetative state for 26 years (Fox, 2012). This tragedy underscores the distance between the Hmong and the Western world and illustrates the challenges of acculturation for the Hmong (Fadiman, 1998). Contrary to the stereotypical image of Asian American success, the Hmong's socioeconomic profile is more consistent with America's colonized minority groups.

Another striking contrast occurs between the socioeconomic profiles of Indian Americans and Vietnamese Americans. This difference relates to their contact situations. Indian immigrants are at the "immigrant" end of Blauner's continuum. They tend to be highly educated and skilled and, therefore, able to compete for favorable positions in the occupational hierarchy. The Vietnamese, however, began their American experience as refugees fleeing war. Although they don't fit Blauner's "conquered or colonized" category, most Vietnamese Americans had to adapt to American society with few resources and few contacts with an established immigrant community. Today, their socioeconomic profile typically resembles that of non-Asian racial minorities. The figures at the end of this chapter illustrate the consequences of these vastly different contact situations.

QUESTIONS FOR REFLECTION

11. How did the motivation for immigration vary for the different Asian groups? How have these differences affected their relationship with American society and their experiences as immigrants?

12. How does each group's contact situation affect their acculturation?

PREJUDICE AND DISCRIMINATION

American prejudice against Asians first became prominent during the anti-Chinese movement of the 19th century. Whites saw the Chinese as a threat to American democracy and institutions and, especially, to its working class. They viewed the Chinese as racially inferior and subservient but also cruel, crafty, and threatening (Lai, 1980; Lyman, 1974). Their belief that the Chinese could never fully assimilate helped them justify the Chinese Exclusion Act (1882). Later in the 19th century, whites transferred many of these stereotypes and fears onto the Japanese and, in turn, to other groups as they arrived in America.

The social distance scores in Table 1.2 provide the only long-term record of anti-Asian prejudice in America. In 1926, the five Asian groups ranked in the bottom third, along with other racial and colonized minority groups. Twenty years later, in 1946, the Japanese fell to the bottom of the rankings, and the Chinese rose seven positions, changes that reflect America's World War II conflict with Japan and its alliance with China. This improvement for China suggests that anti-Chinese prejudice may have softened during the war as people made distinctions between "good" Asians (the Chinese) and "bad" Asians (the Japanese). Government propaganda and media helped to reinforce this distinction. For example, a 1941 *Time* magazine article offered tips: "The Chinese expression is likely to be more placid, kindly, open; the Japanese more positive, dogmatic, arrogant. . . . Japanese are nervous in conversation, [and] laugh loudly at the wrong time" ("How to Tell Your Friends," p. 33).

In recent decades, social distance scores for Asian groups have fallen, even though the group rankings have remained relatively stable. The falling scores probably reflect general increases in tolerance and the shift from blatant prejudice to modern racism. However, the relative position of Asians in the American hierarchy of group preferences has remained remarkably consistent since the 1920s. This stability may reflect the cultural nature of anti-Asian prejudice.

In Chapter 5, we told you about a survey that asked 3,453 Americans across demographic groups about their experiences of prejudice and discrimination "because of their race or ethnicity" (NPR, Robert Wood Johnson Foundation, & Harvard T. H. Chan School of Public Health, 2017b, p. 3). In 2012, Pew Research Center (2013), conducted two similar surveys among Asian Americans. The first asked a nationally representative sample of 3,511 Asian Americans from the six biggest ethnic groups (e.g., Chinese, Japanese, Indian, Korean) about their experiences. The second sought answers from Asian Americans of 14 smaller groups (e.g., Bhutanese, Cambodian). In the next few paragraphs, we'll compare the results between 2012 and 2017, some of which show significant and negative change.

In 2012, Asian Americans, overall, didn't see prejudice and discrimination as a major concern (Pew Research Center, 2013, p. 114). However, by 2017, awareness and concern seem heightened and, significantly, suggest a widespread pattern. In explaining these patterns, about two thirds (68%) of respondents saw people rather than policies and laws (14%) as the cause behind prejudice and discrimination (NPR et al., 2017b).

Competition for resources is a key component of prejudice and discrimination. The findings suggest a sense of increased competition over time. In 2012, only 12%

of respondents said that being Asian American "hurt" people's chances when "applying for jobs" (Pew Research Center, 2013, p. 111). By 2017, 45% of participants reported that Asian Americans "often" (4%) or "sometimes" (41%) faced discrimination when applying for jobs (NPR et al., 2017b). More than 1 in 4 (27%) reported "personally experiencing" discrimination when applying for jobs (p. 6).

Rates were similar when asked about promotions at work. In 2012, 15% of respondents said that being Asian American hurt people's chance for promotion (Pew Research Center, 2013, p. 111). In 2017, 49% of participants said that Asian Americans "often" (12%) or "sometimes" (37%) faced discrimination in promotion (p. 5). One fourth (25%) reported personally experiencing such discrimination (NPR et al., 2017b, p. 1).

In 2017, about one third (35%) of the respondents said they'd experienced "insensitive or offensive comments or negative assumptions" because of their race or ethnic group (NPR et al., 2017b, p. 9). Even more troubling are their experiences with overt hostility in the form of race- or ethnic-related slurs, which are more extreme than "insensitive comments." Between 2012 and 2017, the rate tripled from 10% in 2012 (p. 114) to 32% in 2017 (Pew Research Center, 2013, p. 1). To better understand these experiences, the nonprofit organization Asian Americans Advancing Justice (AAAJ) has been encouraging Asian Americans to report these experiences. One person described a man making machine gun sounds while screaming "YELLOW [n-word]" and threatening to "ship [their] remains back to where [they] come from." Others reported being told "go back where [you] came from" and "I hate your f****** race. We're in charge of this country now." These latter statements are particularly telling because they highlight the aggressor's negative feelings, their sense of power, and the assumption that the Asian American person wasn't "from here."

As you might expect, answers varied based on respondents' other social statuses. For example, in 2012, 19% of Asian Americans reported personally experiencing discrimination, regardless of whether they were U.S.–born or immigrants (Pew Research Center, 2013, p. 114). In 2017 (NPR et al., 2017b), U.S.–born Asian Americans reported higher levels of discrimination, both in general and personally, than immigrants. For example, 21% of Asian Americans reported experiencing threats or nonsexual harassment because of their race or ethnicity. However, the rate for U.S.–born Asian Americans was more than double the rate (36%) of immigrant Asian Americans (15%). U.S.–born Asian Americans reported sexual harassment at four times the rate of foreign-born Asian Americans, at 16% and 4%, respectively. Similarly, more than three times as many U.S.–born Asian Americans (20%) have experienced race-related violence, compared with 6% of foreign-born Asian Americans (p. 10). This pattern doesn't always occur. For example, foreign-born Asian Americans reported 17 times the rate of discrimination when seeking health care compared to U.S.–born Asian Americans (p. 7).

Variation also occurred by age. In 2012, 13% of Asian Americans over 55 years old reported personal experiences of discrimination based on their race or ethnicity. The rate was somewhat higher for younger age groups (23% for respondents ages 18 to 34; Pew Research Center, 2013, p. 114). Though the age categories in the 2017 survey aren't identical, we see a similar pattern by approximate age group and an increased rate across time. In 2017, more than one third (40%) of respondents 65 and over believed that Asian Americans experienced prejudice and discrimination due to their race, while about two thirds (68%) of 18- to 29-year-olds did (NPR et al., 2017b, p. 21). Overall, 61% of Asian

Americans said discrimination against their group happened in America. Rates were much higher for African Americans (92%), Latinos (78%), and Native Americans (75%; NPR et al., 2018, p. 4).

What might account for these differences across minority groups? One possibility is that Asian Americans downplay the extent of their negative experiences, following cultural norms to avoid confrontation and stress harmony.

Another possibility is that Asian Americans truly experience less discrimination than other racial minorities. Some researchers argue that Asian Americans (along with lighter-skinned, more-affluent Latinos) become "honorary whites," positioned between whites and blacks (and darker-skinned, less-affluent Latinos) in the American racial hierarchy. (See Chapter 7.) If so, we'd expect Asian Americans to be somewhat less victimized than blacks and some Hispanic Americans.

A final possibility, closely related to the second, is that Asian Americans benefit from positive stereotypes and are seen in a more favorable light than other racial minorities. The perception of Asian Americans as a model minority—polite, hardworking, smart, successful, and deferential—could explain lower levels of discrimination.

However, the model minority image is a stereotype, exaggerated and overstated. For some Asian American groups, the image is simply false. The media, politicians, and others have constructed and applied this label. It's not an identity Asian American groups themselves have developed or advocated—many strongly oppose it because it homogenizes Asian Americans as "all the same" and obscures problems that exist in Asian American communities.

Though positive, this stereotype can be problematic. For example, Zhang (2010) found that people's beliefs about Asian Americans as the model minority were in line with media portrayals. Respondents saw Asians as "nerds" and expected them to be more successful than other groups.

These ideas shape peer interactions. For example, being stereotyped as "high-achieving students who rarely fight back," makes Asian American students more likely to be bullied or teased at school compared with other students (Associated Press, 2005; Qin, Way, & Rana, 2008). Sue and colleagues (2007) found they also experienced high levels of microaggressions, the "brief and commonplace daily verbal, behavioral and environmental indignities, whether intentional or unintentional, that communicate hostile, derogatory or negative racial slights and insults" (p. 72). These incidents can be so subtle and common that some might barely notice them, yet they "potentially have harmful or unpleasant psychological impact on the target person or group" (p. 72).

The model minority myth can negatively affect college students, too. In the Chapter 1 Internet Activity, you learned about implicit bias—the idea that people have unconscious attitudes about groups of people (e.g., overweight people, feminists, old people), which influences how they behave toward those group members. For example, Harvard University has recently been involved in a lawsuit about discrimination against Asian American applicants. Implicit bias may have affected the admissions process in two ways. First, applicants' recommendations letters may emphasize stereotypical qualities (e.g., "hardworking," "serious about their studies"). These positive statements, without broader description, lack the "complexity of the description" that Harvard wants (Hartocollis, 2018b). Second, Harvard conducts face-to-face interviews with top applicants that show "patterns of stereotypical descriptions." Compared to whites, interviewers gave

Asian Americans 25% more "standard strong," ratings; although they typically had better academic scores than whites, they didn't have "special qualities that would warrant admission" (Hartocollis, 2018a).

Cumulatively, these experiences can psychologically harm individuals and groups (Sue et al., 2007, p. 72). If they believe the myth, students with poor academic performance could be harmed most often by thinking they're personally deficient (Masuda et al., 2009). Since Asian Americans have negative views toward seeking help, these effects can be magnified. Asian American students, especially those who accept the model minority myth, are also less likely to seek support such as therapy. Finally, it's worth mentioning that as Lee, Park, and Wong (2017) note, the model minority myth, when used to explain why other minority groups are less successful academically, harms other individuals and groups, too.

ASSIMILATION AND PLURALISM

In this section, we continue to assess the situation of Asian Americans today using the same conceptual framework as in the last three chapters.

Acculturation

The extent of acculturation of Asian Americans is highly variable across groups. Japanese Americans represent one extreme. They've been a part of American society for more than a century, and the current generations are highly acculturated. Immigration from Japan has been low and hasn't revitalized the traditional culture or language. Therefore, Japanese Americans are the most acculturated of the Asian American groups and have the lowest percentage of members who speak English "less than very well," as illustrated in Figure 8.6.

Filipino and Indian Americans also have low percentages of members who aren't competent English speakers, but for different reasons. The Philippines has had a strong American presence since the Spanish–American War of 1898, while India is a former British colony in which English remains an important language for higher education and of the educated elite.

Chinese Americans, in contrast, are highly variable in the extent of their acculturation. Many are members of families that have been American for generations and are highly acculturated. Others, including many recent undocumented immigrants, are newcomers with little knowledge of English or Anglo culture. This great variability within the group makes it difficult to characterize their overall degree of acculturation.

Also, note that the groups who are refugees from the 1960s and 1970s wars in Southeast Asia (Vietnamese, Cambodians, Hmong, and Laotians) are less acculturated. They, along with the Chinese and Koreans, have many foreign-born members (see Figure 8.2) and are still largely in their first generation.

Gender and Physical Acculturation: The Anglo Ideal

Anglo conformity can happen on levels, too. Many studies document the feelings of inadequacy and negative self-images that often result when minority group

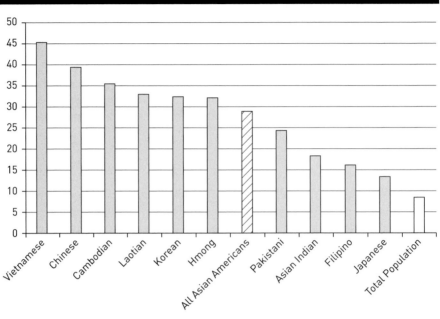

FIGURE 8.6 ■ Percentage of Asian American Groups That Speak English "Less Than Very Well," 2017

Source: U.S. Census Bureau (2018a). American Community Survey, 2017.

members—especially women—compare themselves with the Anglo standards of attractiveness and beauty that dominate U.S. culture.

Some research in this tradition are classics of the social science literature, including the "doll studies" of the 1930s and 1940s (Clark & Clark, 1940, 1950). The Clarks showed pairs of dolls to a sample of young African American children. The dolls were identical except that one was white and the other black. The Clarks asked the children several questions, including "Which doll is pretty?" "Which doll is nice?" "Which doll would you like to play with?" and "Which doll is ugly?" The children consistently showed a strong preference for the white doll, which suggested that they had internalized ideas about race, including white beauty standards. As a result, the Clarks expected them to develop negative self-perceptions. Contemporary projects inspired by the Clark doll study include a video, "A Girl Like Me" (2005), by then–17-year-old Kiri Davis[1], and a documentary by Chris Rock titled *Good Hair* (2009).

Asian American women, like most women in modern American society, are pressured by the cultural message that physical beauty should be among their most important concerns. As minorities, they're also subjected to the additional message that they're inadequate by Anglo standards and that some physical traits are unattractive and need to be fixed (Kaw, 1993). For example, many African American women spend millions of dollars on hair straightening and skin bleaching. Asian American women's attempts to meet Anglo beauty standards include cosmetic surgery to sculpt their noses, "open" their eyes, and make their legs longer.

Kaw (1993) conducted in-depth interviews with medical practitioners and with a small sample of Asian American women, most of whom had had surgery on their eyelids or noses. The women tended to see their surgeries as personal choices, not unlike putting on makeup. However, they consistently described their pre-surgical features negatively. They uniformly said "that 'small, slanty' eyes and a 'flat' nose" (p. 75) suggest a person who is dull and passive. One participant wanted to "avoid the stereotype of the Oriental bookworm" (p. 79). Similar to Chinese girls with bound feet, mothers encouraged surgeries, believing it would make their daughters more attractive to potential husbands and employers. Kaw concludes that racist stereotypes and patriarchal norms greatly influence Asian American women's decisions to undergo surgery: an attempt—common among all racial minority groups—to acculturate physically as well as culturally.

Secondary Structural Assimilation

We cover this topic in the order followed in previous chapters.

Residence

Figure 8.7 shows the regional concentrations of all Asian Americans in 2010. The tendency to reside on either coast and around Los Angeles, San Francisco, and New York City stands out clearly. Note the sizable concentrations in many metropolitan areas, including Chicago, Atlanta, Miami, Denver, and Houston.

The various Asian American groups are concentrated in different regions, with the vast majority of Filipino and Japanese Americans in the West, along with about half of Chinese and Vietnamese Americans. Asian Indians have the highest percentage living in the Northeast (30%), and Vietnamese Americans have the highest percentage in the South (32%), mostly concentrated on the Texas and Louisiana coasts to work in the fishing industry. The Hmong, alone among Asian American groups, are concentrated in the upper Midwest, especially in Wisconsin and Minnesota (Hoeffel et al., 2012, pp. 18–20).

Figure 8.8 shows that Asian Americans, similar to Hispanic Americans, are moving away from their traditional places of residence into new regions. Between 2000 and 2010, the Asian American population increased especially rapidly along the East and West Coast, in Arizona, and in some areas of the upper Midwest.

Between 2000 and 2010, the Asian population increased more than 50% in 30 of the 50 states, with eight more closely approaching the 50% mark. In seven states (including Arizona, Nevada, Delaware, and North Carolina) the Asian population increased by more than 75% (Hoeffel et al., 2012, p. 7).

Asian Americans, in general, are highly urbanized, reflecting the social conditions for recent immigrants and the appeal of ethnic neighborhoods, such as Chinatowns, with long histories and continuing vitality. As Figure 8.9 shows, all but two of the 10 largest Asian American groups were more than 90% urbanized in 2000, and several approach the 100% mark.

Asian Americans are also moving into the suburbs of metropolitan areas, most notably around Los Angeles, San Francisco, New York, and other cities with large concentrations of Asian Americans. For example, Asian Americans have been moving in large numbers to the San Gabriel Valley, just east of downtown Los Angeles. Once a bastion of white, middle-class suburbanites, these areas have taken on a distinctly Asian flavor. Monterey

FIGURE 8.7 ■ Distribution of Asian Americans, 2010 (Percentage of County Population)

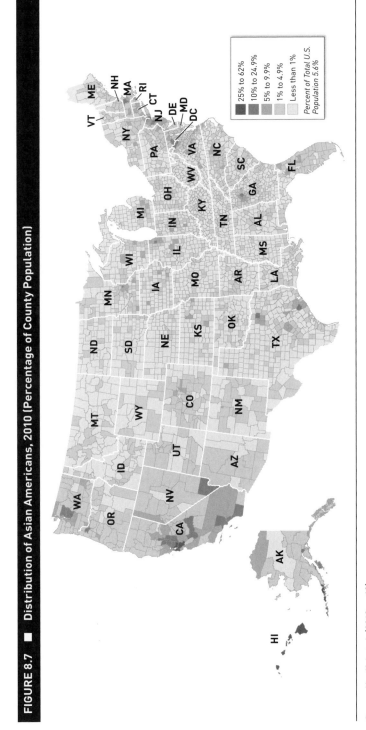

25% to 62%

10% to 24.9%

5% to 9.9%

1% to 4.9%

Less than 1%

Percent of Total U.S. Population 5.6%

Source: Hoeffel et al. (2012, p. 10).

FIGURE 8.8 ■ Percentage Change in Asian American Population, 2000–2010

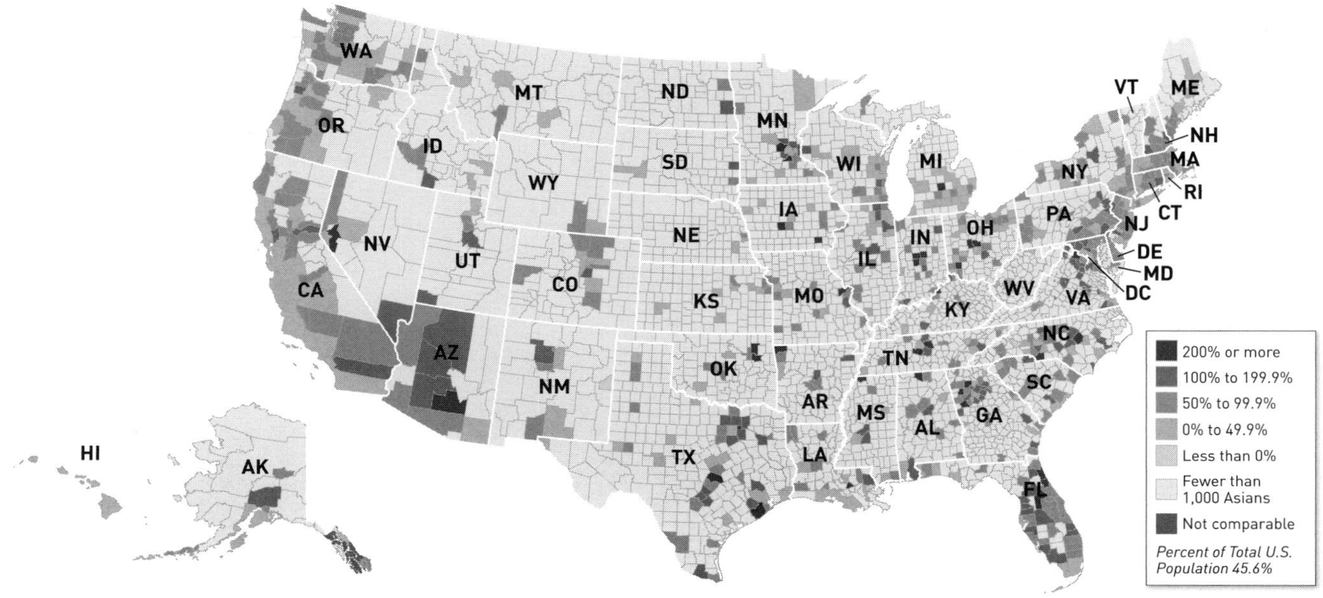

Legend:
- 200% or more
- 100% to 199.9%
- 50% to 99.9%
- 0% to 49.9%
- Less than 0%
- Fewer than 1,000 Asians
- Not comparable

Percent of Total U.S. Population 45.6%

Source: Hoeffel et al. (2012, p. 11).

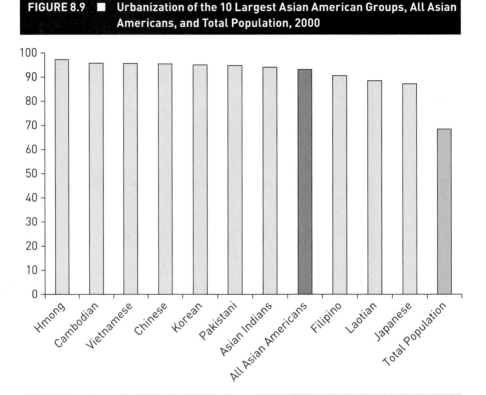

FIGURE 8.9 ■ Urbanization of the 10 Largest Asian American Groups, All Asian Americans, and Total Population, 2000

Source: U.S. Census Bureau (2000a).

Park, once virtually all white, is now majority Chinese American and people often refer to it as "America's first suburban Chinatown" or the "Chinese Beverly Hills" (Fong, 2002, p. 49; see also Chowkwanyun & Segall, 2012).

Historically, these areas have been off-limits to Asian Americans (and other minority groups). Explicitly racist policies, such as restrictive real estate covenants created and enforced by the dominant group, maintained the residential segregation by banning certain types of people from renting, leasing, buying, or residing in particular areas. Here's one example from Seattle's SeaTac neighborhood, enforced from 1937–1956:

> Nor shall the said property, or any part thereof, be used or occupied by any person of the Malay [Filipino] or any Asiatic race or descent, or any person of the races commonly known as the Negro race, or of their descent, and the grantee, his heirs, personal representatives or assigns shall not, at any time throughout said period, place any such person in the possession or occupancy of said property, excepting only employees in the domestic service. (Seattle Civil Rights and Labor History Project, n.d.)

Nevertheless, as shown in Figure 5.9, residential segregation for Asian Americans has been well below "high" (dissimilarity scores greater than 60) but tends to be slightly higher in cities with more concentrated Asian populations. The level of residential segregation is holding steady, reflecting high rates of immigration and the tendency of newcomers to settle close to other members of their group. These lower scores may reflect the more favored position for Asian Americans compared to blacks and darker-skinned Hispanic Americans.

Education

Asian American children experience less school segregation than Hispanic and black American children (Fry, 2007), although the extent of segregation for this population may have increased in recent years because of high rates of immigration and residential concentration, particularly in larger cities.

The extent of schooling for Asian Americans is very different from other U.S. racial minority groups, at least at first glance. Asian Americans, as a whole, compare favorably with society-wide standards for educational achievement, and they generally perform above those standards on many measures. Figure 8.10 shows that three of the 10 Asian American groups rank higher than non-Hispanic whites in high school completion, and six of 10 rank higher in college completion, a pattern reinforced by the high levels of education of many recent Asian immigrants.

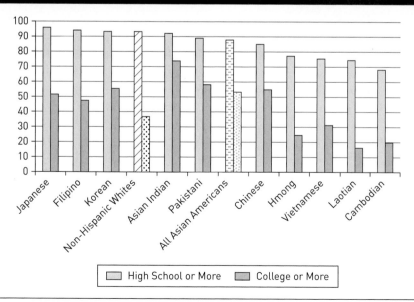

FIGURE 8.10 ■ Education Attainment for All Asian Americans, Non-Hispanic Whites, and the 10 Largest Groups of Asian Americans, 2017

Source: U.S. Census Bureau (2018a). American Community Survey, 2017.

At first glance, Figure 8.10 might suggest Asian American success, but note that several groups have relatively low educational attainment. While some groups (or at least some elements of some groups) are quite successful, others have profiles closer to those of colonized racial minority groups.

Figures 8.11 and 8.12 offer a more balanced view of Asian Americans' educational achievement. The former shows the percentage of each group with *less* than a high school education and includes Hispanic Americans, African Americans, Native Americans, and non-Hispanic whites for comparison. As you learned in Chapter 7, recent Hispanic immigrants tend to bring modest educational credentials—a point that can be made about several Asian American groups, all of which have a high percentage of foreign-born members and include many refugees from the wars in Southeast Asia. On this measure, the Southeast Asian groups actually fare worse than African Americans and Native Americans, both colonized racial minorities. This data presents a serious challenge to glib characterizations of Asian Americans as the always-successful model minorities.

Figure 8.12 further challenges the model minority image by comparing the educational attainment of Chinese Americans and non-Hispanic whites. Almost 55% of Chinese Americans hold college and graduate degrees, far outnumbering whites (35.8%). Note, however, that Chinese Americans are *also* disproportionately concentrated at the lowest level of educational achievement. About 15% of the group has less than a high school diploma, compared to about 7% of non-Hispanic whites. Many of these less-educated Chinese Americans are recent immigrants (many undocumented) who supply the unskilled labor force—in retail shops, restaurants, and garment industry sweatshops—at the lowest levels of the economy.

FIGURE 8.11 ■ Percentage of Hispanic Americans, Native Americans, African Americans, Non-Hispanic Whites, All Asian Americans, and the 10 Largest Asian Americans Groups with Less Than a High School Education, 2017

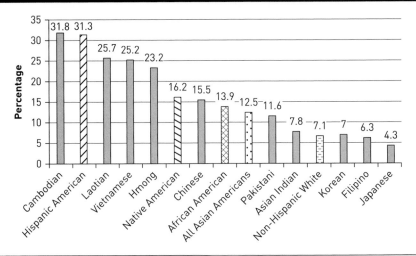

Source: U.S. Census Bureau (2018a). American Community Survey, 2017.

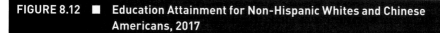

FIGURE 8.12 ■ Education Attainment for Non-Hispanic Whites and Chinese Americans, 2017

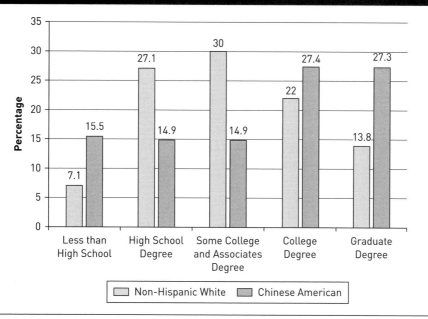

Source: U.S. Census Bureau (2018a). American Community Survey, 2017.

Assessments of Asian American success must also differentiate between the native-born and the foreign-born group members. The native-born are generally better educated. The foreign-born are split between highly educated professionals and those who bring low levels of human capital. For example, a recent survey showed that almost all (98%) U.S.–born Chinese Americans were high school graduates and 73% had college degrees. In contrast, only 77% of foreign-born Chinese Americans had finished high school and only 41% had earned a college degree (computed from Pew Research Center, 2013).

These examples illustrate that the image of Asian Americans' success should be balanced with the recognition that a full range of achievement exists within the group and that average levels of educational attainment for some groups are inflated by recent immigrants who are highly educated, skilled professionals.

Political Power

The ability of Asian Americans to pursue their group interests has been sharply limited by several factors, including the relatively small size of the population, institutionalized discrimination, and the same racist practices that limited the power resources of other minority groups of color. However, and contrary to the perception that Asian Americans are a "quiet" minority, the group has a long history of political action, including a civil rights movement in the 1960s and 1970s (Fong, 2002).

The political power of Asian Americans today is also limited by their high percentage of foreign-born members and, for some groups, lack of English competency.

Rates of political participation (e.g., voting in presidential elections) are considerably lower than national norms. For example, as with Hispanic Americans, less than half (49%) of Asian Americans voted in the 2016 presidential election (vs. about 64% of non-Hispanic whites and blacks; U.S. Census Bureau, 2017g). Participation rates were similar for the 2008 and 2012 presidential elections, although slightly higher than in earlier presidential elections (File, 2013, pp. 3–5). Similar to Hispanic Americans, the group's impact on national politics will likely increase as more members Americanize, learn English, and become citizens.

There are signs of the group's growing power, especially in areas where they're most residentially concentrated. Asian Americans have been prominent in Hawaiian politics for decades, but they're increasingly involved in West Coast political life. In 2017, 15 Asian and Pacific Islanders served in the U.S. House of Representatives (about 2% of the membership) and three served in the Senate (Manning, 2017).

Jobs and Income

Similar to Hispanic Americans, Asian Americans' economic situation is mixed and complex. On some measures, Asian Americans, as a whole, exceed national norms, reflecting their high levels of academic achievement combined with the impressive educational credentials of many new immigrants. However, overall comparisons can mislead; we must also recognize the economic diversity within the group of Asian Americans.

Occupational profiles sustain the idea of success. Women and men are overrepresented in the highest occupational categories, reflecting the group's educational attainment. Asian American men are underrepresented among manual laborers, but, otherwise, the group's occupational profiles roughly approximate the wider society (U.S. Census Bureau, 2013).

Figure 8.13 shows median household incomes for Asian Americans and non-Hispanic whites since 1987 and reveals that Asian Americans have higher median household incomes, a picture of general affluence that dramatically contrasts with the other racial minority groups we've examined. The gap fluctuates, but Asian Americans' median household income is about 115% of whites.

This image of success, glittering at first, becomes more complicated and nuanced after examining different subgroups. Figure 8.14 displays median household incomes for all non-Hispanic whites, all Asian Americans, and the 10 largest groups. You can see, immediately, that economic success isn't universally shared: Of the 10 Asian American groups, two are notably below the average income for non-Hispanic whites and two others are essentially equal.

A more telling picture emerges when we consider income *per capita* (or per person) compared to median incomes for households. This is an important comparison because the apparent prosperity of many Asian American families is linked to their small business ownership within the enclave. These enterprises typically involve the entire family working many hours every day, with children adding their labor after school and on weekends. Other relatives (many of them new immigrants, a percentage of which are undocumented) also contribute. The household may post a high income because of these collective efforts, but, when spread across many family members, the glow of success is muted.

Figure 8.15 shows that, on per capita income, only one Asian American group notably exceeds non-Hispanic whites, while two others are roughly equal. The other groups

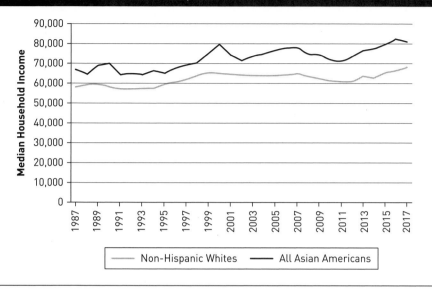

FIGURE 8.13 ■ Median Household Income for Non-Hispanic Whites and All Asian Americans, 1987–2017

Source: U.S. Bureau of the Census, 2018. Table H-5 Historical Income Tables.

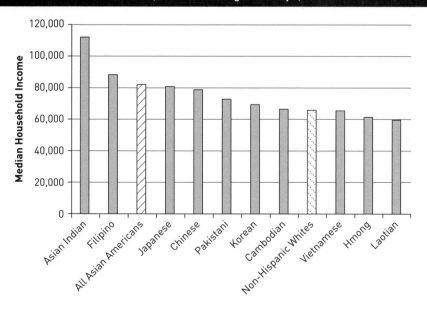

FIGURE 8.14 ■ Median Household Income for Non-Hispanic Whites, All Asian Americans, and the 10 Largest Groups, 2017

Source: U.S. Census Bureau. 2018. "American Community Survey, 2017, One-Year Estimates."

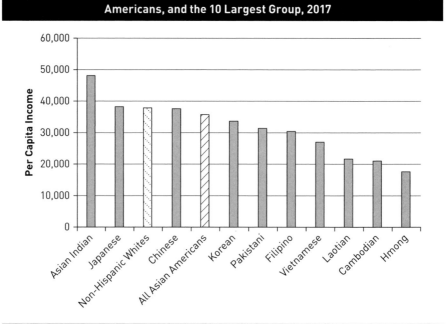

FIGURE 8.15 ■ Per Capita Income for Non-Hispanic Whites, All Asian Americans, and the 10 Largest Group, 2017

Source: U.S. Census Bureau. 2018. "American Community Survey, 2017, One-Year Estimates."

(including Korean Americans, one of the groups most dependent on small business ownership) have much lower levels of relative prosperity. In particular, the Southeast Asian groups with high percentages of refugees from the Vietnam War (especially the Hmong) are far below national norms on this measure.

Figure 8.16 provides additional evidence that the image of a so-called model minority—uniformly prosperous and successful—is greatly exaggerated. Asian Americans, unlike other racial minority groups, are overrepresented in the three highest income categories (32%) compared to non-Hispanic whites (24%). However, note that Asian Americans are also overrepresented in the lowest income category, reflecting the "bipolar" distribution of Chinese Americans and other groups.

Figures 8.17 and 8.18 complete our economic portrait of Asian Americans and reinforce our argument that this group is diverse and complex. While Asian Americans' poverty levels, as a group, are slightly below non-Hispanic whites, several groups have much higher rates of poverty, especially for children. As you've seen in other figures, Japanese Americans, Filipino Americans, and Asian Indian Americans are successful on this indicator, but other groups have poverty levels comparable to colonized racial minority groups.

Figure 8.18 examines the situation of several Asian American groups in terms of nativity. Again, you can see the great diversity across groups, with foreign-born Vietnamese Americans (largely refugees) and Korean Americans having the highest percentage of members earning less than $30,000. The U.S.–born for all six groups have much lower percentages of members with low incomes; in some cases (e.g., for Chinese Americans) the difference is quite dramatic.

FIGURE 8.16 ■ Distribution of Household Income for Non-Hispanic Whites and Asian Americans, 2017

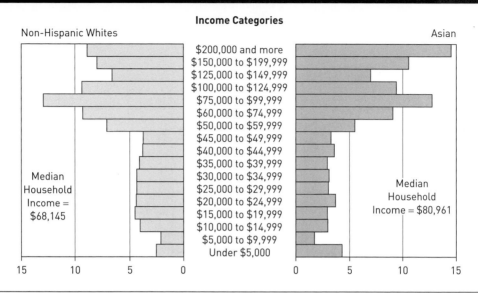

Source: U.S. Census Bureau (2017).

FIGURE 8.17 ■ Percentages of Families and Children in Poverty for Non-Hispanic Whites, All Asian Americans, and the 10 Largest Groups, 2017

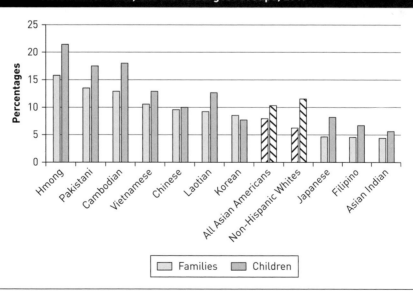

Source: U.S. Census Bureau (2018a). American Community Survey, 2017 One year estimates.

Note: Family poverty rates and child poverty rates use different units of analysis. Family rates represent the percentage of all families in the group below the poverty line. Children's rates are the percentage of all people in the group younger than 18 who live in poverty.

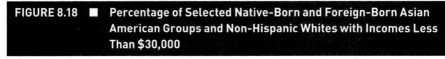

FIGURE 8.18 ■ Percentage of Selected Native-Born and Foreign-Born Asian American Groups and Non-Hispanic Whites with Incomes Less Than $30,000

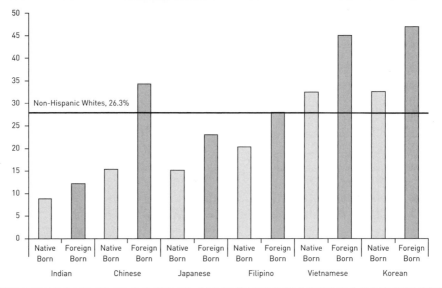

Source: Computed from Pew Research Center (2013).

These socioeconomic profiles reflect the diversity of Asian American groups. Some groups are prosperous and successful, and their financial wealth exceeds national norms, sometimes by a considerable margin. Others resemble other American racial minority groups. Japanese and Chinese Americans have the longest histories in the U. S. and generally rank at the top in measures of wealth and prosperity. Other groups—particularly those with large numbers of refugees from Southeast Asia—have not fared as well and have considerable poverty and economic distress. Some "bipolar" groups, such as Chinese Americans, fit in both categories. Additionally, the picture of economic distress for these groups would be much greater if we focused on undocumented immigrants, who are numerous in the community and concentrated in the informal, irregular economy.

Primary Structural Assimilation

Levels of integration at the primary level for Asian Americans are also highly variable across groups. Japanese Americans tend to be the most integrated on this dimension. One study found that of the six Asian American groups studied, Japanese Americans were the most likely to both have friends outside their group and to marry outside their group. The same study found that, as we'd expect, integration at the primary level was lower for the foreign-born and those with lower English fluency (Pew Research Center, 2013, pp. 32, 98).

Rates of primary integration tend to be higher than for other groups but are declining as the number of Asian Americans grows and the percentage of foreign-born Asians increases (Passel, Wang, & Taylor, 2010, p. 17). This pattern reflects the tendency of newcomers to marry within the group.

	Whites		Asian Americans			
			Men		Women	
Year	Men	Women	Foreign-Born	U.S.-Born	Foreign-Born	U.S.-Born
1980	96%	95%	58%	57%	45%	51%
2008	93%	92%	77%	53%	55%	52%

TABLE 8.2 ■ Percentage of Whites and Asian Americans Married to a Person of the Same Group, 1980 and 2008

Source: Qian and Lichter (2011, p. 1072). Copyright © 2011 National Council on Family Relations. Reprinted with permission.

Table 8.2 compares in-marriage trends of Asian Americans and whites in 1980 and 2008 following the format used in earlier chapters. Asian Americans have much lower rates of in-marriage than African Americans and Hispanic Americans, although they have somewhat higher rates than Native Americans. Again, this is partly a function of the relative sizes of these groups but also reflects the more favored position of Asian Americans in the dominant group's perceptions. However, when we turn to cohabitation, nearly half (46%) of Asian Americans who cohabit do so with someone outside of their racial/ethnic group. That's almost twice as much as Hispanic Americans (24%) and African Americans (20%), and three times the rate of whites (12%). This difference between marriage and cohabitation may be related to being native-born versus foreign-born, which reflects the Asian American group's degree of assimilation. Of those who cohabitate, a majority (59%) were born in the United States. As with other social trends, we see variation within the group. For example, people with more education are more likely to cohabit than those with less education (Livingston, 2017). Finally, note that the percentage of foreign-born Asian Americans marrying within the group increased for men and women. This is consistent with high rates of immigration in recent years and the idea that the first generation tends to socialize more with co-ethnics.

FOCUS ON CONTEMPORARY ISSUES
HOW SUCCESSFUL ARE ASIAN AMERICANS? AT WHAT PRICE?

By now, it should be clear that the idea of Asian Americans as model minorities is a stereotypical exaggeration. In addition to the material we've covered, let's consider a few other factors with regard to education and income.

First, researchers commonly find that Asian Americans—especially the foreign-born—earn less than whites of the same educational level (Kim & Sakamoto, 2010; Min, 2006). Additionally, the group is concentrated in cities, particularly

(Continued)

(Continued)

New York, Honolulu, Los Angeles, and San Francisco, which consistently rank as the most expensive places to live in America (Kiersz, 2018). Thus, the higher average incomes that Asian Americans earn buy less in the way of housing, food, and other necessities. This is magnified by the fact that Asian Americans' per capita income is lower than the national average. That is, their higher average incomes are shared across more people (see Figure 8.15).

Second, given their educational attainment, you'd expect Asian Americans to be well represented at the top of the employment ladder. Yet Asian American professionals are half as likely as comparable whites to get promoted to management. This holds true even in the technology industry, where Asian Americans are overrepresented (Gee & Peck, 2018). Asian Americans are also underrepresented on Fortune 500 boards, holding only 4.8% of board seats (Jones & Donnelly, 2017). The pattern is similar in government. In 2016, Asian Americans held almost 1 in 10 federal jobs but had only 4.4% of leadership positions. Given that Asian Americans are 12% of the professional workforce, we'd expect higher numbers (Gee & Peck, 2018).

Similar to other minority groups, Asian Americans face seemingly invisible barriers to workplace advancement. Hyun (2005) calls this the "bamboo ceiling"—similar to the "glass ceiling" that many women experience. Fisher (2005) describes it as "processes and barriers that exclude Asian Americans from executive positions on the basis of subjective factors such as 'lack of leadership potential' and 'lack of communication skills' that cannot be explained by job performance or qualifications."

Perceptions that Asian American employees are more competent but warm and quiet and likely to stay in their place (Berdahl & Min, 2012) contradict the image of *leader* (e.g., assertive, makes tough decisions, good at networking). These expectations may discourage managers from considering Asian Americans for some positions or including them in networking and mentoring opportunities that would help them, in part, advance to leadership (Hassan, 2018). Asian American women face additional challenges, since they must also contend with gender stereotypes.

Workplace advancement gives people the ability to develop and use their talents. Since people tend to earn more with each step up the "workplace ladder," the bamboo ceiling is another factor affecting some Asian Americans' income.

Yet, *not* fitting the model minority stereotype can have negative consequences. For example, Berdahl and Min (2012) created a scenario in which participants evaluated fictional workers and found that people disliked a "dominant East Asian" employee who went against expectations for meekness more than a "nondominant White coworker" who didn't fit expectations for whites (p. 141). Chou and Feagin (2008) point out the lose–lose dilemma facing many Asian Americans: If they live up to the model minority stereotype, people label them as "geeks" and "nerds." If they fail, they can be seen by themselves or others as inadequate, which, as we discussed earlier, can have serious psychological consequences.

The model minority stereotype distorts the realities of Asian American groups and can lead to oversimplified and negative views of other minority groups. For example, when modern racists attribute Asian American success to "Asian values" (e.g., strong work ethic, respect for education), it implies that other minority groups are less successful because they lack these values. This claim ignores the role structural barriers play in past-in-present discrimination. In the ever-evolving interplay of American group relations, the supposed success of Asian Americans can hurt other minority groups of color, particularly black Americans.

COMPARING MINORITY GROUPS: EXPLAINING ASIAN AMERICAN SUCCESS

To conclude, let's return to a question from the opening pages: How can we explain the apparent success of some Asian American groups? Relative affluence and high status aren't characteristics of most of the other minority groups we've examined. At first, there seems to be little in our theories and concepts to help us understand the situation of Asian Americans. As we've noted, it's important to recognize that the "success" label is simplistic and even incorrect for some groups, especially Southeast Asian groups, which have a high percentage of refugees and whose profiles resemble colonized racial minority groups. To focus this discussion, we'll concentrate on the groups with the longest histories in America: Chinese and Japanese Americans. We present different views on the types and causes of their success. Additionally, we compare Chinese and Japanese Americans with European immigrant groups and colonized minority groups. What crucial factors differentiate the groups' experiences? Can we understand these differences by using the Blauner and Noel hypotheses and other concepts?

Two different viewpoints offer explanations for Asian American success. One proposes a cultural explanation and accepts the evidence of Asian American success at face value. It attributes their success to "good Asian values," including respect for elders and authority figures, hard work, thriftiness, conformity, and politeness. These are highly compatible with U.S. middle-class Protestant values, which potentially helped Asian Americans gain acceptance and opportunities. The cultural explanation also is consistent with traditional assimilation theory and human capital theory. (See an example by Professor Harry Kitano in the Current Debates section online.)

The second view stresses how Chinese and Japanese Americans entered the U. S. and their reactions to the barriers of racism and exclusion. This is a "structural explanation," and it emphasizes contact situations, modes of incorporation, enclave economies, group cohesion, position in the labor market, and institutionalized discrimination, rather than cultural values.

The structural approach questions the notion that Asian Americans are successful and stresses the realities of Asian American poverty and the continuing patterns of racism and exclusion. Its approach is more compatible with the theories and concepts used throughout this book, and it identifies several important pieces needed to solve the puzzle of Asian success and put it in perspective. This isn't to suggest that the cultural approach is wrong or irrelevant. The issues we raise are complex and to fully understand them probably requires many perspectives.

Asian Americans and White Ethnics

Chinese and Japanese immigrants arrived in America around the same time as immigrants from Southern and Eastern Europe (Chapter 2). Both groups consisted mainly of young men, many of them sojourners, who were largely unskilled, from rural backgrounds, and not highly educated. European immigrants, similar to those from Asia, encountered massive discrimination and rejection and were also victims of restrictive legislation. Yet, the barriers to upward mobility for European immigrants (or at least for their descendants) fell away more rapidly than the barriers for Asian immigrants. Why?

Some important differences between the two immigrant experiences are clear, the most obvious being the greater racial visibility of Asian Americans. The cultural and linguistic markers that identified Eastern and Southern Europeans faded with each passing generation. However, Asian Americans aren't "pure immigrant" groups (see Blauner, 1972, p. 55). For most of the 20th century, Chinese and Japanese Americans remained in a less-favorable position than European immigrants and their descendants, excluded by their physical appearance from the mainstream economy until the decades following World War II.

Another important difference relates to position in the labor market. Immigrants from Southern and Eastern Europe entered the industrializing East Coast economy, where they took industrial and manufacturing jobs. Although such jobs were poorly paid and insecure, this location in the labor force gave European immigrants and their descendants the potential for upward mobility in the mainstream economy. At the very least, these urban industrial and manufacturing jobs put the children and grandchildren of European immigrants in positions from which skilled, well-paid, unionized jobs were reachable, as were managerial and professional careers.

In contrast, Chinese and Japanese immigrants on the West Coast were forced into ethnic enclaves and came to rely on jobs in the small business and service sector and, in the case of the Japanese, in the rural economy. These jobs didn't link Chinese and Japanese immigrants or their descendants to the industrial sector or to better-paid, more secure, unionized jobs. Furthermore, their exclusion from the mainstream economy was reinforced by overt, racially based discrimination from employers and labor unions (see Fong & Markham, 1991).

Asian Americans and Colonized Racial Minority Groups

Comparisons between Asian Americans and African Americans, Native Americans, and Hispanic Americans have generated a level of controversy and a degree of heat and passion that may be surprising at first. An examination of the issues and their implications, however, reveals that the debate involves some thinly disguised political and moral agendas and evokes sharply clashing views on the nature of American society. What seems on the surface to be merely an academic comparison of different minority groups turns out to be an argument about the quality of American justice and fairness—the very essence of American values.

What isn't in dispute is that some Asian groups (e.g., Japanese Americans) rank far above other racial minority groups on all the commonly used measures of secondary structural integration and equality. What people dispute is how to interpret these comparisons and assess their meanings. Of course, gross comparisons between entire groups can mislead. If we confine our attention to averages (e.g., mean levels of education or median income), we sustain the picture of Asian American success generally. However, if you observe the full range of differences within each group (e.g., the "bipolar" nature of occupations among Chinese Americans), you'll see that these images of success have been exaggerated and need to be placed in the proper context. (See an example by Pyong Gap Min in Current Debates section online.)

Even with these qualifications, however, discussion often slides into more ideological ground, and political and moral issues begin to cloud the debate. People take this general picture of Asian American success as proof that American society is truly the land of opportunity and that people who work hard and obey the rules will get ahead.

In Chapters 1 and 4, we discussed modern racism and noted that belief in the total openness and fairness of the U. S. places the responsibility for change on minority groups rather than on societal structures or past-in-present or institutionalized discrimination. People sometimes take Asian success as proof of this ideology's validity. The none-too-subtle implication is that other groups (African Americans, Hispanic Americans, and Native Americans) could achieve the same success as Asian Americans but choose not to. Thus, the relative success of Chinese and Japanese Americans becomes a device for criticizing other minority groups and delegitimizing their situations.

A structural approach to investigating Asian American success compares the history of the various racial minority groups and their modes of incorporation into the larger society. When Chinese and Japanese Americans built their enclave economies in the early 20th century, African Americans and Mexican Americans were concentrated in unskilled agricultural occupations. Native Americans were isolated on their reservations, and Puerto Ricans hadn't yet arrived on the mainland. It follows, then, that social class differences between these groups today flow from their respective situations in the past.

Many of the occupational and financial advances made by Chinese and Japanese Americans have been due to the high levels of education achieved by the second generations. Although Asian culture traditionally values education, the decision to invest limited resources in schooling is also quite consistent with the economic niche occupied by these immigrants. Education is one obvious, relatively low-cost strategy to upgrade the productivity and profit of a small-business economy and improve the group's overall economic status. Educated, English-speaking second-generation Chinese and Japanese Americans could act as intermediaries, bringing expertise and business acumen to the family enterprises and leading them to higher performance levels. Education might also be how the second generation could enter professional careers. This strategy may have been especially attractive to an immigrant generation that was relatively uneducated and barred from citizenship (Hirschman & Wong, 1986; see also Bonacich & Modell, 1980; Sanchirico, 1991).

The efforts to educate the next generation were largely successful. Chinese and Japanese Americans achieved educational parity with the larger society as early as the 1920s. One study found that for men and women born after 1915, the median years of schooling were actually higher for Chinese and Japanese Americans than they were for whites (Hirschman & Wong, 1986, p. 11).

Before World War II, both Asian groups were barred from the mainstream economy and from better jobs. When anti-Asian prejudice and discrimination declined in the 1950s, however, the Chinese and Japanese American second generations had the educational background necessary to take advantage of increased opportunities.

Thus, there was a crucial divergence in the development of Chinese and Japanese Americans compared to colonized minority groups. When native-born Chinese and Japanese Americans reached educational parity with whites, the vast majority of African Americans, Native Americans, and Mexican Americans were still victimized by Jim Crow laws and legalized segregation and excluded from opportunities for anything but rudimentary education. The Supreme Court decision in *Brown v. Board of Education of Topeka* (1954) was decades in the future, and most Native American schoolchildren were still being subjected to intense Americanization under the guise of a legitimate curriculum.

Today, these other racial minority groups have not completely escaped from the disadvantages imposed by centuries of institutionalized discrimination. African Americans have approached educational parity with white Americans only in recent years (Chapter 5), and the educational achievements of Native Americans and Mexican Americans remain far below national averages (Chapters 6 and 7, respectively).

The structural explanation argues that the recent upward mobility of Chinese and Japanese Americans is the result of how they incorporated themselves into American society, not so much their values and traditions. The logic of their enclave economy led the immigrant generation to invest in their children's education, making them better prepared to develop their businesses and seek opportunities in the larger society.

Finally, note that the structural explanation isn't consistent with traditional views of assimilation. The immigrant generation of Chinese and Japanese Americans responded to massive discrimination by withdrawing, developing ethnic enclaves, and becoming invisible to the larger society. Similar to Jewish Americans and Cuban Americans, Chinese and Japanese Americans used their traditional cultures and patterns of social life to create their own sub-communities, from which they launched the next generation. Contrary to traditional ideas about how assimilation is "supposed" to happen, we see, again, that integration can precede acculturation and that the smoothest route to integration may be the creation of a separate sub-society independent of the surrounding community.

Main Points

- Asian Americans and Pacific Islanders are diverse and have brought diverse cultural and linguistic traditions to the U. S. These groups are growing rapidly but are still only a tiny fraction of the total population. Similar to Hispanic Americans, Asian Americans have a high percentage of first-generation members who are growing more rapidly than the population as a whole.

- Chinese immigrants were victims of a massive campaign of discrimination and exclusion and responded by constructing enclaves. Chinatowns became highly organized communities, largely run by the local CCBAs and other associations. The second generation faced many barriers

to employment in the dominant society, although opportunities increased after World War II.

- Japanese immigration began in the 1890s and stimulated a campaign to oust the group from agriculture and curtail immigration from Japan. The Issei formed an enclave, but during World War II, Japanese Americans were forced into detention facilities, which devastated the group economically and psychologically.

- Recent Asian immigration is diverse in terms of national origin, contact situation, levels of human capital, and mode of incorporation in American society. Some immigrants are highly educated professionals, while others more closely resemble the peasant laborers from Mexico in recent decades and from Italy, Ireland, Poland, and many other nations in the past.

- Anti-Asian prejudice and discrimination, especially the overt kind, have declined in recent years but remain widespread. Research suggests that people perceive prejudice and discrimination as less of a problem for Asian Americans than for other racial minority groups. This might reflect positive stereotypes of Asian Americans and/ or the group's movement toward "honorary" whiteness.

- Levels of acculturation and secondary structural assimilation vary. Group members whose families have been in the U. S. longer tend to be highly acculturated and integrated. Recent immigrants from China, however, are "bipolar." Many are highly educated and skilled, but a sizable number are immigrant laborers with modest educational credentials and high levels of poverty.

- The notion that Asian Americans are a model minority is exaggerated, but comparisons with European immigrants and colonized minority groups suggest some reasons for their relative success.

Applying Concepts

The Japanese American Citizens League is one of the most significant Asian American civil rights organizations in the U. S. Part of its mission is to protect Asian Americans (and Pacific Islanders) from prejudice and discrimination. In 2009, it produced *Myths and Mirrors: Real Challenges Facing Asian American Students* to educate the non-Asian American population about cultural differences and similarities between the two groups. That publication inspired this Applying Concepts activity.

Below is a series of statements you might hear on a college campus. Although any of them might be spoken by a student of any background, which do you think are more likely to be said by an Asian American student? Which are more reflective of Anglo culture? Consider information about collectivist versus individualist cultures when answering.

Statement	Asian	Anglo
"I really love the social life on this campus—I really enjoy chatting with all different kinds of people about all sorts of everyday things. And I love to gossip."		
"It's really important to show respect to professors and college administrators."		
"I'm so proud to be recognized in front of the whole class for my research project."		

Statement	Asian	Anglo
"I don't like to talk in class, even when directly called on."		
"I don't think that people should bottle their emotions—say what you've gotta say!"		
"I wouldn't dream of moving away from my family right after graduation. I have family obligations to fulfill."		

See the next page to find our answers.

Review Questions

1. Describe the cultural characteristics of Asian American groups. How did these characteristics shape relationships with the larger society? How do they contribute to the perception of Asian American success?

2. Compare the contact situations for Chinese Americans, Japanese Americans, and Cuban Americans (Chapter 7). What common characteristics led each to create ethnic enclaves? How and why did these enclaves differ? How were they similar?

3. In what sense was the second generation of Chinese Americans delayed? How did this affect the group's relationship with the larger society?

4. Compare the campaigns to oppose Chinese and Japanese immigration. Does Noel's hypothesis adequately explain the differences? What similarities do you see with federal policies toward Mexican immigrants across the 20th century?

5. Compare Japanese detention centers with Indian reservations, especially regarding paternalism and coerced acculturation. How did Japanese American detentions affect the group economically? How were Japanese Americans compensated for their losses? Does this compensation set a precedent for similar payments to African Americans (reparations) for their losses under slavery? Why or why not?

6. How do the Barakumin illustrate "visibility" as a defining characteristic of minority group status? How is the minority status of this group maintained?

7. What gender differences characterize Asian American groups? How do women's and men's experiences vary?

8. Describe the situation of the Chinese and Japanese Americans in terms of prejudice and discrimination, acculturation, and integration. Are these groups truly "success stories"? How? What factors or experiences might account for their success? Describe the important group variations. Compare the integration and equality of Asian American groups with other American racial minorities. How do you explain the differences? How do the Noel and Blauner hypotheses help explain their differing situations?

Answers to Applying Concepts

Statement	Asian	Anglo
"I really love the social life on this campus—I really enjoy chatting with all different kinds of people about all sorts of everyday things. And I love to gossip."		X
"It's really important to show respect to professors and college administrators."	X	
"I'm so proud to be recognized in front of the whole class for my research project."		X
"I don't like to talk in class, even when directly called on."	X	
"I don't think that people should bottle their emotions—say what you've gotta say!"		X
"I wouldn't dream of moving away from my family right after graduation. I have family obligations to fulfill."	X	

Points to Consider

1. How might Asian Americans and Anglo American students behave differently because of their cultural backgrounds? How might they behave similarly? To what degree and in what kinds of situations?

2. How could the length of U.S. residency affect how people think, talk, and behave? For example, how would an Asian American from a family that's lived here since the 1800s differ from someone who came to the United States in 2019? How might age, gender, or social class affect people's values and norms?

3. More broadly, what kinds of issues might arise in situations where students make contact across ethnic or racial lines, face racism, or desire to date someone from another group? How? Realizing that your personal experiences aren't scientific, have you observed situations where cultural differences are problematic? Do those differences seem minimal or nonexistent? Explain.

Internet Learning Resources

SAGE edge™ offers teachers and students easy-to-use resources for review, study, and further exploration. See **http://edge.sagepub.com/diversity6e**

Note

1. Kiri Davis's 2007 updated version of the 1940s "doll test": https://www.youtube.com/watch?v=z0BxFRu_SOw

CHALLENGES FOR THE PRESENT AND THE FUTURE

Chapter 9   New Americans, Assimilation, and Old Challenges

Chapter 10   Minority Groups and U.S. Society: Themes, Patterns, and
             the Future

In Part 4, we analyze new immigrants, continuing our focus on issues of assimilation, inclusion, equality, racism, and xenophobia. Many of these issues relate to what it means to be an American; we've discussed and debated these issues throughout our nation's history. In the final chapter, we summarize the major themes of this book, bring our analysis to a close, and speculate about the future of race and ethnic relations in America.

NEW AMERICANS, ASSIMILATION, AND OLD CHALLENGES

Sade and four of his twenty-something friends are at a hookah cafe almost underneath the Verrazano-Narrows Bridge in Brooklyn. It's late, but the summer heat is strong and hangs in the air. They sit on the side-walk in a circle, water pipes bubbling between their white plastic chairs.

Sade is upset. He recently found out that his close friend of almost four years was an undercover police detective sent to spy on him, his friends, and his community. Even the guy's name . . . was fake, which particularly irked the twenty-four-year-old Palestinian American. . . .

"I was very hurt," he says. "Was it friendship, or was he doing his job?" He takes a puff from his water pipe. "I felt betrayed." The smoke comes out thick and smells like apples. . . . He shakes his head. . . .

Informants and spies are regular conversation topics [among Arab Americans] in the age of terror, a time when friendships are tested, trust disappears, and tragedy becomes comedy. If questioning friend-ship isn't enough, Sade has also had other problems to deal with. Sacked from his Wall Street job, he is convinced that the termination stemmed from his Jerusalem birthplace. Anti-Arab and anti-Muslim invectives were routinely slung at him there, and he's happier now in a technology firm owned and staffed by other hyphenated Americans. But the last several years have taken their toll. I ask him about life after September 11 for Arab Americans. "We're the new blacks," he says. "You know that, right?"

—Moustafa Bayoumi (2008, pp. 1–2)

Sade's comparison between Arab Americans and blacks may be overstated, but there's no question that America finds itself in a new era of group relations today. The traditional minority groups—black Americans, Mexican Americans, and others—have been joined by new groups from places that most Americans couldn't find on a map: Armenia, Zimbabwe, Bhutan, Guyana, and Indonesia, to name a few.

What do these newcomers contribute? What do they cost? How are they changing America? What will the country look like in 50 years? At the beginning of this book, we asked, "What does it mean to be an American?" How will that question be answered in the future?

———————————————

The world is on the move as never before, and migration connects even the most remote villages of every continent in a global network of population ebb and flow. As you've seen, people are moving everywhere, but the U. S. remains the single most popular destination. Migrants will pay huge amounts of money—thousands of dollars, veritable fortunes in economies where people survive on dollars a day—and undergo considerable hardship for the chance to reach America.

What motivates this population movement? How does it differ from migrations of the past? What impact will the newcomers have on America? Will they embrace American culture? What parts? How well will they integrate into American society, and in which parts of it?

We've been asking questions like these throughout this book. In this chapter, we focus specifically on current immigrants and the many issues raised by their presence. We mentioned some groups of new Americans in Chapters 7 and 8, but we'll elaborate in this chapter. We begin by addressing recent immigration generally. Then, we'll consider additional groups of new Americans, including Hispanic, Caribbean, and Asian groups; Arabs and Middle Easterners; and immigrants from sub-Saharan Africa. We hope this will help broaden your understanding of the wide variations in culture, motivations, and human capital of the current immigrant stream to America.

Next, we'll address the most important and controversial immigration issues facing America. We'll conclude with a brief return to the traditional minority groups: African Americans, Native Americans, and other people of color who still face issues of inequality and incomplete integration, and who must now pursue their long-standing grievances in an atmosphere where public attention and political energy are focused on new groups and issues.

CURRENT IMMIGRATION

As you know, the United States has experienced three different waves of mass immigration. In Chapter 2, we discussed the first two waves (see Figure 2.2). The first wave, from the 1820s to the 1880s, consisted of mostly Northern and Western European immigrants. The second, from the 1880s to the 1920s, brought primarily Southern and Eastern European immigrants. During these two periods, more than 37 million people immigrated to the U. S., an average rate of about 370,000 per year. These waves of newcomers transformed American society on every level: its neighborhoods, its cities, its cuisine, its accents and dialects, its religion, its popular culture, and so much more.

The third wave of mass immigration that we're experiencing promises to be equally transformative. This wave began after 1965 (when the U. S. changed immigration policy) and includes people from around the world. Since the mid-1960s, over 30 million newcomers have arrived (not counting undocumented immigrants). This rate of more than 670,000 people per year is much higher than the earlier period; however, the rate is lower as a percentage of the total population. Figure 9.1 shows that the number of legal immigrants per year has generally increased over this period, at least until the U.S. economy soured in more recent years.

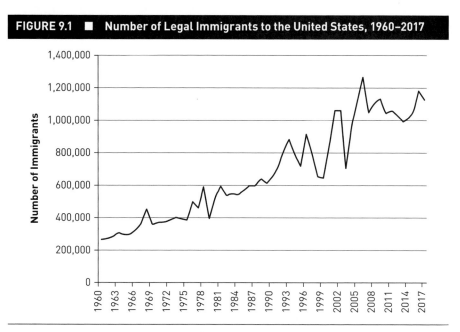

FIGURE 9.1 ■ Number of Legal Immigrants to the United States, 1960–2017

Source: U.S. Department of Homeland Security (2017a).

The official record for most immigrants in a year was set in 1907, when almost 1.3 million people arrived in America. That number was almost equaled in 2006 and, if undocumented immigrants had been included in the count, the 1907 record would have been eclipsed several times since the 1960s. (Again, though, remaining a smaller percentage of the population.)

The more recent wave of immigration is much more diverse than the first two. In 2017 alone, immigrants arrived from 199 separate nations—from Afghanistan and Albania to Zambia and Zimbabwe. Almost 40% were from Asia, about 15% were from Mexico alone, and approximately 8.6% of the newcomers were from Europe. Figure 9.2 lists the numbers for the top 25 sending nations for 2017. Note that the number of Mexican immigrants is more than double the number from China, the next-highest sending nation. Also, note the variety of nations and regions of origin. Immigration to the U. S. is truly a global phenomenon!

How will this new wave of immigration transform America? How will these new immigrants be transformed by living in America? What do they contribute? What do they cost? Will they adopt the ways of the dominant society? What are the implications if they don't?

We begin by reviewing several case studies of new Americans, focusing on information and statistics comparable to those in Chapters 5 through 8. Each group has had members in the U. S. for decades, some for more than a century. However, in all cases, the groups were quite small until the latter part of the 20th century. Although they're growing rapidly, all stay relatively small, and none makes up more than 1% of the

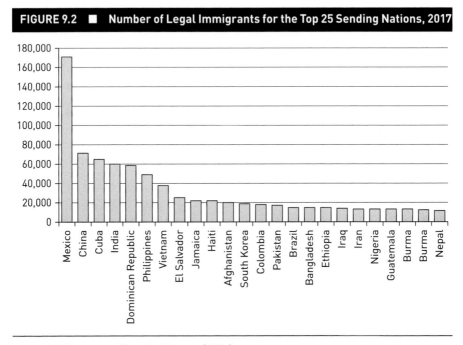

FIGURE 9.2 ■ Number of Legal Immigrants for the Top 25 Sending Nations, 2017

Source: U.S. Department of Homeland Security (2017a).

QUESTIONS FOR REFLECTION

1. What are some key differences between the first two waves of mass immigration from the 1820s to the 1920s and the current, post-1965 wave?

2. Why is the current wave of immigration so diverse? What are the possible outcomes, positive and negative, of this diversity for the future of American society?

population. Nonetheless, some will have a greater impact on American culture and society in the future, and some groups—Muslims and Arab and Middle Eastern Americans—have already become a focus of concern and controversy because of the events of September 11 and the ensuing war on terrorism.

NEW HISPANIC GROUPS: IMMIGRANTS FROM THE DOMINICAN REPUBLIC, EL SALVADOR, AND COLOMBIA

Immigration from Latin America, the Caribbean, and South America has been considerable, even when excluding Mexico. As with other sending nations, the volume of immigration from these regions increased after 1965 and has averaged about 200,000 per year. Generally, Latino immigrants—not counting those from Mexico—have composed about 25% of all immigrants since the 1960s (U.S. Department of Homeland Security, 2016).

The sending nations for these immigrants are economically less industrialized, and most have long-standing relations with the United States. In Chapter 7, we discussed the roles that Mexico and Puerto Rico have played as sources of cheap labor and the ties that led Cubans to immigrate to America. The other sending nations were similarly linked to the U. S., the dominant economic and political power in the region.

Although the majority of these immigrants bring modest educational and occupational qualifications by U.S. standards, they tend to be more educated, more urbanized, and more skilled than the average citizens of their home nations. Contrary to popular belief, they don't represent the poorest of the poor, the "wretched refuse" of their homelands. Similar to immigrants in the first two waves, they're generally ambitious, as evidenced by their willingness to attempt to succeed in a society that hasn't been notably hospitable to Latinos or people of color in the past (Florida, 2017). For example, in 2016, immigrants were twice as likely to be new entrepreneurs compared to U.S.–born entrepreneurs (Kauffman Index of Startup Activity, 2016). In 2014, immigrants generated more than $4,800,000,000 and employed about 19 million Americans (Kosten, 2018).

As you've read in Chapters 1, 7, and 8, most immigrants are fleeing extreme poverty or joblessness and they're also trying to seek opportunities for educational and professional advancement, for themselves or their children, generally not available in their home countries (Feliciano, 2006; Portes & Rumbaut, 1996). However, many leave for reasons such as violence and rampant crime and corruption (Hayes, 2018; Nuñez, Sepehr, & Sanchez, 2014).

This characterization applies to legal and undocumented immigrants alike. Moreover, the latter may illustrate the point more dramatically, because the cost of illegally entering the U. S. is considerable—much higher than legal entry. Forged papers and other costs of being smuggled into the country easily amount to many thousands of dollars, a considerable sum in nations where the usual wage is a tiny fraction of the U.S. average. Thus, the venture may require years of saving or the combined resources of a large kinship group. However, many people make that decision because chances of legal admission are slim (Levy, 2018). (For an example of someone's $12,630 journey from El Salvador that describes conditions in "stash houses," bribes to police, and kidnapping, see Kulish, 2018.)

Examining refugee applications for the most desperate of all migrants provides insights. After the Holocaust, 145 countries, including the U. S., signed the 1951 United Nations' Refugee Convention, vowing to protect anyone whose "life or freedom would be threatened" based on their race, religion, nationality, group membership, or political views (United Nations Refugee Agency, 1951, p. 3). Those protocols have changed occasionally, as has U.S. policy.

In fiscal year 2018, federal policy became stricter in two significant ways. First, it limited the number of refugees to 45,000. Of those, 22,491 were approved—almost four times less than in 2016—the lowest number since Congress created the Refugee Resettlement Program in 1980. Put another way, that's just 0.00087% of the world's 25.9 million refugees. In fiscal year 2019, the U. S. will decrease the cap to 30,000 refugees, even while 800,000 others have pending cases (Lopez & Bialik, 2017; Migration Policy Institute, n.d.; Pompeo, 2018; United Nations, 2017, p. 8).

Second, the government reversed position on the Convention guidelines, upheld in 2014 by the U.S. Board of Immigration Appeals, that domestic violence fell under the "group membership" designation for protection (based on gender) as did gang violence (because gangs often target specific groups). People seeking asylum from gang or domestic violence rarely get it and this change will make it harder. This decision will particularly affect people fleeing widespread violence in Central America, who already had rejection rates of 77%–90% for fiscal years 2011–2016 (Benner & Dickerson, 2018; Meyer & Pachico, 2018; TracImmigration, 2016).

Thus, many decide to attempt illegal entry. The passage can be extremely dangerous, particularly for Latin Americans (e.g., Hondurans, El Salvadorans) who may walk 1,000 miles or more in challenging terrain with limited necessities before reaching the U.S. southern border. For example, it would take 38 days to walk the 1,125 mile route from the Guatemalan–Mexican border to the border at McAllen, Texas—walking 10 hours a day at three miles per hour. It's more than double that to reach the California border (Giaritelli, 2018). That's before delays. This requires a level of courage (or desperation) that many Americans don't often associate with undocumented immigrants.

Rather than attempting to cover all South and Central American groups, we've selected three of the largest as case studies: the Dominican Republic, El Salvador, and Colombia. In recent years, these three groups have made up 7% to 8% of all immigrants and about 30% of the immigrants from Central and South America and the Caribbean. These groups had few members in the U. S. before the 1960s, and all have had high rates of immigration over the past four decades. However, the immigrants' motivation and experiences has varied across groups.

Three Case Studies

Table 9.1 presents some basic information about the groups. These data were mentioned in Chapter 7 but we repeat it here to provide a common frame of reference for the groups in this chapter. As you'll see, each of these groups has a high percentage of foreign-born members. As with other first-generation immigrants, proficiency in English is—predictably—an important issue. Although Colombian Americans approach national norms in education, the other two groups have relatively low levels of human capital (education). They're well below national norms for income and have higher rates of poverty.

Although these groups share commonalities, they have important differences. First, they differ in their "racial" makeup, with Dominicans seemingly more African, Colombians more European, and Salvadorans more Indigenous American—though there's variation within groups. In Chapter 7, we mentioned National Geographic's Genographic Project, which seeks to understand human migration over time (including the degree of mixing between groups) by looking at DNA samples. Their results show Colombians' DNA as primarily related to Southern Europeans (38%), Indigenous Americans (28%), and Western and Central Africans (17%), reflecting the original population, European colonizers, and enslaved people from Africa. Dominicans' backgrounds were primarily related to groups in Africa (49%) and Europe (about 40%; 29% Mediterranean, and 11% Northern European) though 4% was linked to indigenous groups (e.g., Taino people—see Puerto Ricans in Chapter 7) and was some related to Asia (National Geographic, 2017).

Second, the groups tend to settle in different places. Colombians are clustered in the South (49%), particularly in Florida (33%), and the Northeast (33%), mostly in New York and New Jersey (López, 2015a, p. 2). Dominicans are concentrated in the Northeast

TABLE 9.1 ■ Selected Characteristics of Three Hispanic American Groups and Non-Hispanic Whites, 2017

Group	Size	Percentage with Less Than a High School Diploma	Percentage with a College Degree or More	Percentage Foreign-Born	Percentage Who Speak English Less Than "Very Well"	Median Household Income	Percentage of Families in Poverty
Non-Hispanic whites	204,221,676	7.1	35.8	4.1	1.6	$65,696	6.2
Dominicans	2,081,419	27.7	18.3	53.8	41.7	$43,851	20.9
Salvadorans	2,310,784	45.0	10.2	57.1	47.9	$52,118	15.1
Colombians	1,222,960	12.2	33.4	61.6	37.7	$58,847	9.5

Source: U.S. Census Bureau (2018a). American Community Survey, 2017 1-year Estimates.

(79%), with 47% living in New York alone (López, 2015c, p. 3). In contrast, Salvadorans generally reside in the West (45%), mostly in California, and the South, mostly in Texas (Cohn, Passel, & Gonzalez-Barrera, 2017, p. 17).

Finally, groups' contact situations or entry conditions differ—a difference that you've learned is consequential. Salvadorans are more likely to be political refugees who fled a brutal civil war and political repression, while Dominicans and Colombians are more likely to be motivated by economics and the employment possibilities offered in America.

Dominicans

The Dominican Republic shares the Caribbean island of Hispaniola with Haiti. The island economy is still largely agricultural, although the tourist industry has grown in recent years. Unemployment and poverty are major problems, and Dominicans age 25 and over average about five years of education (World Bank, 2017). Dominican immigrants, similar to those from Mexico, are motivated largely by economics, and they compete for jobs with Puerto Ricans, other immigrant groups, and native-born workers with lower levels of education and job skills.

Although Dominicans are limited in their job options by the language barrier, they're somewhat advantaged by their willingness to work for lower wages. They're concentrated in the service sector as day laborers (men) or domestics (women). Dominican immigrants maintain strong ties with home and are a major source of income and support for the families left behind.

In terms of acculturation and integration, Dominicans are roughly similar to Mexican Americans and Puerto Ricans, although some studies suggest that they're possibly the most impoverished immigrant group (see Table 9.1 and Figures 7.15 and 7.17). A high percentage of Dominicans are undocumented, and many spend a great deal of money and take considerable risks to get to America. The portrait of poverty and low levels of education and job skills would probably be even more dramatic if these less-visible community members were included in the official, government-generated statistics (which we used to create the book's tables and figures).

Salvadorans

El Salvador, like the Dominican Republic, is a relatively poor nation, with a high percentage of the population relying on subsistence agriculture for survival. Approximately 35% of the population lives below the poverty level due to major problems with unemployment and underemployment. About 80% of the population is literate, and the population 25 years of age and older averages about six years of school (Central Intelligence Agency, 2017; World Bank, 2017).

El Salvador, similar to many other sending nations, has a difficult time providing sufficient employment opportunities for its population, and much of the pressure to migrate is economic. However, El Salvador also suffered through a brutal civil war in the 1980s, and many of the Salvadorans in the U. S. today are political refugees. The U. S., under President Ronald Reagan, refused to grant political refugee status to Salvadorans and returned many of them to El Salvador. This federal policy resulted in high numbers of undocumented immigrants and stimulated a sanctuary movement, led by American clergy, to help Salvadoran immigrants, both undocumented and legal, stay in the United States.

As with Dominicans, if the undocumented El Salvadoran immigrants were included in official government statistics, the picture of poverty would become more extreme.

Colombians

Colombia is somewhat more developed than most Central and South American nations but has suffered from more than 50 years of internal turmoil, civil war, and government corruption. It's a major center for the production and distribution of drugs to the world generally and the U. S. in particular, and the drug industry and profits are complexly intertwined with domestic strife.

Colombian Americans are closer to U. S. norms of education and income than are other Latino groups. For example, 33.4% have a college education, and the median household income is $58,847 (remember that *median* means half the household incomes are above and half are below). Median personal earnings are generally below $25,000 a year (López, 2015a; see Table 9.1, and Figures 7.15, and 7.17.) Recent immigrants are a mixture of less-skilled laborers and well-educated professionals seeking to further their careers. Of course, almost all Colombian Americans are law-abiding, but many must deal with the pervasive stereotype of Colombian drug smugglers or gangsters (not unlike the Mafia stereotype about Italian Americans).

NON-HISPANIC IMMIGRANTS FROM THE CARIBBEAN

Immigrants from the Western Hemisphere bring many traditions to the U. S. other than Hispanic ones. Two of the largest non-Latino groups come from Haiti and Jamaica in the Caribbean. Both nations are much less developed than the U. S., as suggested by immigrants' educational and occupational characteristics. Table 9.2 shows a statistical profile of both groups along with statistics for non-Hispanic whites for comparison.

TABLE 9.2 ■ Selected Characteristics of Two Non-Hispanic Caribbean Groups and Non-Hispanic Whites, 2017							
Group	Size	Percentage with Less Than a High School Diploma	Percentage with a College Degree or More	Percentage Foreign-Born	Percentage Who Speak English Less Than "Very Well"	Median Household Income	Percentage of Families in Poverty
Non-Hispanic whites	204,221,676	7.1	35.8	4.1	1.6	$65,696	6.2
Haitians	1,065,219	18.4	23.2	55.5	31.3	$50,935	13.5
Jamaicans	1,124,120	13.0	28.3	57.7	1.4	$55,631	9.9

Source: U.S. Census Bureau (2018a). American Community Survey, 2017 1-year Estimates.

Two Case Studies

Haitians

Haiti is the poorest country in the Western Hemisphere, and most people rely on small-scale subsistence agriculture to survive. Approximately 59% of the population lives below the poverty line, and the unemployment rate is about 40%. Haitians average less than three years of formal education, most of which is private and relatively unaffordable. About 40% of the population is illiterate (Central Intelligence Agency, 2017; World Bank, 2017).

Natural disasters and disease have exacerbated problems of poverty and political instability. In 2010, a massive 7.0 earthquake killed tens of thousands of people, possibly hundreds of thousands. (See the Puerto Rico section in Chapter 7 for why death rate discrepancies occur.) That year, Haiti also experienced a cholera outbreak—an illness that can kill within days. As of early 2019, it's infected 800,000 people and killed 9,000. The storm destroyed the homes of over 1.5 million people, and in 2014, more than a quarter million still lived in tent camps. Camp conditions such as overcrowding, lack of sanitation facilities, and malnourishment contributed to a near doubling of the tuberculosis rate. In 2016, Hurricane Matthew decimated the already-weak infrastructure (e.g., roads, communication) and 90% of the crops. More than a million people have been affected (Human Rights Watch, 2017; Koenig et al., 2015; Thorbecke, 2016; also see United Nations, n.d.).

Haitian migration was virtually nonexistent until the 1970s, when thousands began fleeing the brutal repression of the Duvalier dictatorship, which lasted for two generations (from 1957– 1986). In stark contrast to the U.S. treatment of Cuban immigrants around the same time (Chapter 7), the government began an intense campaign to keep Haitians out, first by defining them as economic refugees ineligible for asylum. Additionally, it actively intercepted boats in open water; but those who made it to land were incarcerated in large, newly established detention camps without parole, reversing a 1958 Supreme Court ruling that declared, "physical detention of aliens is now the exception, not the rule . . . which reflects the humane qualities of an enlightened civilization." The U.S. government returned thousands of people to Haiti, some to face political persecution, prison, and even death (Loyd & Mountz, 2018; Minian, 2018; Regan, 2016, p. xviii).

Stepick and colleagues (2001) argue that during this time, "no other immigrant group suffered more U.S. government prejudice and discrimination than Haitians" (p. 236) and that the harsh reception and disparate treatment reflected their "triple minority" status. First, they were immigrants with low levels of human capital and education, which created concerns about their ability to support themselves. (This also meant that they had relatively few resources with which to defend their self-interests.) Second, the majority spoke a language that was uncommon outside of Haiti (Haitian Creole), and a good number practiced a blend of voodoo and Christianity. Finally, they were black. As such, they were subject to centuries-old traditions of rejection, racism, and prejudice that were such an integral part of American culture.

Haitian Americans today are still mostly first-generation, recent immigrants. Overall, they're comparable to Hispanic Americans in terms of measures of equality such as income and poverty (see Figures 7.15 and 7.17). Yet, research shows that Haitians have continued to face the exclusion and discrimination based on their triple minority status. As a result, the second generation (the immigrants' children) have a relatively low level of academic achievement and a tendency to identify with the African American community. This suggests that some second-generation members are unlikely to move into the middle class and that their assimilation will be segmented (Stepick et al., 2001; Vanderkooy, 2011).

In 2017, the U.S. government rescinded Temporary Protected Status for nearly 60,000 Haitians who came to the U. S. after the 2010 earthquake. They're expected to leave by July 2019. This change will further impact the Haitian American community (Jordan, 2017).

Jamaicans

The Jamaican economy is more developed than Haiti's, and this is reflected in Jamaican immigrants' higher levels of education. On average, they possess significantly higher socioeconomic standing than Haitians (see Table 9.2). Jamaica's economy has been slow to develop and, similar to other economies throughout the less-industrialized world, it has faltered in recent decades, and the island nation has been unable to provide full employment for its citizens. The immigrant stream tends to be more skilled and educated, and as they leave to pursue opportunities, it creates a "brain drain" in their home country (as it does with other groups, including Asian Indians; Feliciano, 2006). This loss of the more-educated Jamaicans exacerbates Jamaica's development and growth problems.

Because the British colonized Jamaica, its citizens speak English—an advantage in assimilation. Yet, they're black and, similar to Haitians, they face the prejudice and discrimination and racism faced by other non-white groups in America. Poverty and institutionalized discrimination limit upward mobility for a segment of the group. Some, like other groups of color in the U. S., face the possibility of segmented assimilation and permanent exclusion from the economic mainstream. However, at least one study shows that many second-generation Jamaicans are moving into the mainstream economy and filling jobs comparable to those of others with their level of education, at least in New York City, where many of them live (Kasinitz, Mollenkopf, Waters, & Holdaway, 2008).

CONTEMPORARY IMMIGRATION FROM ASIA

Immigration from Asia has been considerable since the 1960s, averaging close to 300,000 people per year, or about 30% to 40% of all immigrants (U.S. Department of Homeland Security, 2016). Similar to Hispanic immigrants, the sending nations for Asians are considerably less economically developed than the U. S., and the primary motivation for most Asian immigrants is economic. As we noted in Chapter 8, however, the Asian immigrant stream is "bipolar" and includes many highly educated professionals along with the less skilled and less educated. Also, many Asian immigrants are refugees from the Vietnam War in Southeast Asia in the 1960s and 1970s; others are the spouses of U.S. military personnel who've been stationed throughout the region.

Again, rather than attempting to cover all Asian immigrant groups, we'll concentrate on four case studies: India, Korea, the Philippines, and Vietnam. Together, these groups make up about half of all Asian immigrants (U.S. Department of Homeland Security, 2016).

Four Case Studies

As you'll see in Table 9.3, these four groups are small and include a high percentage of foreign-born members. Their backgrounds, occupational profiles, levels of education, and incomes vary. In contrast to Hispanic immigrants, these groups generally have higher percentages of members who are fluent in English and have higher levels of education, making them relatively more prepared to compete for good jobs. We include non-Hispanic whites for comparison.

The four groups vary in their settlement patterns. Most are concentrated along the West Coast, but Asian Indians are roughly equally distributed on the East and West Coasts, and Vietnamese have a sizable presence in Texas, in part related to the fishing industry along the Gulf Coast.

Asian Indians

India, home to more than 1.3 billion people, is the second most populous nation in the world. India has many religions, ethnic groups, and languages (including 22 officially recognized ones). Overall, education levels are low; on average, people have less than five years of formal schooling (World Bank, 2017). About 71% of the population is literate (Central Intelligence Agency, 2017). However, about 35.6 million people are enrolled in some form of higher education ("All India Survey on Higher Education," 2018, p. iv). This means millions of educated Indians are looking for careers commensurate with their credentials. Because the Indian economy is relatively less developed, many college-educated Indians search for career opportunities abroad, and not only in America. One important legacy of India's long colonization by the British is that English is the language

TABLE 9.3 ■ Selected Characteristics of Four Asian American Groups and Non-Hispanic Whites, 2017							
Group	Size	Percentage with Less Than a High School Diploma	Percentage with a College Degree or More	Percentage Foreign-Born	Percentage Who Speak English Less Than "Very Well"	Median Household Income	Percentage of Families in Poverty
Non-Hispanic whites	204,221,676	7.1	35.8	4.1	1.6	$65,696	6.2
Asian Indians	4,402,362	7.8	73.7	68.5	18.2	$111,857	4.4
Koreans	1,887,914	7.0	54.7	56.8	32.4	$69,175	8.6
Filipinos	4,037,564	6.3	47.5	49.0	16.2	$88,231	4.5
Vietnamese	2,104,217	25.2	31.2	60.1	45.1	$65,643	10.6

Source: U.S. Census Bureau (2018a). American Community Survey, 2017 1-year Estimates.

of the educated. Thus, Indian immigrants to the U. S. tend to be not only well educated but English speaking (see Table 9.3).

In 1923, the Supreme Court ruled that Asian Indians weren't white; therefore, they couldn't become citizens. Immigration from India to the U. S. was low until the 1965 Immigration and Naturalization Act, and strict quotas were in place until 1970. The group's size was small at that time but increased to 200,600 by 1980. The group more than quintupled in size between 1990 and 2017 (see Table 8.1), and Indians are now the second-largest Asian American group (Chinese Americans are the largest group).

Indian immigrants tend to be a select, highly educated, and skilled group (see Table 9.3 and Figures 8.14 and 8.17). Indians are overrepresented in many prestigious occupations, including those in engineering, medicine, and computer programming and IT (Migration Policy Institute, 2014; U.S. Census Bureau, 2000b). Indian immigrants are part of a worldwide movement of educated peoples from less-industrialized countries to more-industrialized countries in search of better career opportunities, resources (e.g., technology), and compensation. One need not ponder the differences in career opportunities, technology, and compensation between the two nations for long to get some insight into the reasons for this movement. Other immigrants from India are more oriented to commerce and small business, and there's a sizable Indian ethnic enclave in many cities (Dingra, 2012; Kitano & Daniels, 1995; Sheth, 1995). In fiscal year 2016, they were 74% of immigrants who came to America on HB-1 work visas (temporary visas for skilled and specialized workers); compared to U.S.–born Americans, Indians are about twice as likely to be employed in business, science, and the arts (38% versus 73%; Zong & Batlova, 2017a).

Koreans

South Korean immigration to the U. S. began early in the 20th century, when laborers were recruited to help fill the void in the job market created by the 1882 Chinese Exclusion Act (see Chapter 8). This group was extremely small until the 1950s but grew after the Korean War. The group included refugees, "war brides" (women forced into sexual slavery as "comfort women" who later married U.S. military personnel), and children fathered by American soldiers (who were often abandoned and seen as highly unadoptable in Korea; National Association of Korean Americans, 2003; Yoon, 2017). As with other groups, immigration didn't become substantial until the 1965 Immigration and Naturalization Act. The number of Korean immigrants peaked in the late 1980s. The group's size in 2017 was about 2.4 times bigger than in 1990 (see Table 8.1). In 2017, Korean Americans made up about 4% of all immigrants and less than 1% of the U.S. population (Min, 2006; Pew Research Center, 2013).

Like Indian immigrants, South Korean immigrants include many middle-class, more-educated, professional people, many of whom were pushed from their homeland by a repressive military government. Korea transitioned to a more Western-style democracy in the late 1980s, and immigration declined as a result (see Figure 8.5).

Although differences in culture, language, and race make Koreans visible targets of discrimination, the high percentage of Christians among them (about 70%) may help them appear more acceptable to the dominant society. Churches play an important role for the Korean American community by offering assistance to newcomers and the less fortunate, serving as networks of mutual aid, and assisting with the numerous tasks that immigrants must do (e.g., government paperwork, registering to vote). They also help with childcare and business development (Bae-Hansard, 2015; see Kitano & Daniels, 2001).

Korean American immigrants created enclaves in many cities, and group members are heavily involved in small businesses and retail stores—particularly greengroceries with fruits and vegetables, though changes in the economy and Korean upward mobility have decreased these. Koreans have some of the highest rates of self-employment among immigrant groups (Min, 2006, 2008; also see Pew Research Center, 2013).

As with other groups, the enclave helps Korean Americans avoid discrimination and racism within the larger society and survive in an economic niche where lack of English fluency isn't a particular problem. In 2015, 64% of Korean Americans reported being fluent, although rates were lower for foreign-born individuals (47%; Pew Research Center, 2017a). However, the enclave has its perils and its costs. For one thing, the success of Korean enterprises depends heavily on the mutual assistance and financial support of other Koreans and the willingness of group members to work long hours for little or no pay. These resources would be weakened or destroyed by acculturation, integration, and the resultant decline in ethnic solidarity. Only by maintaining a distance from the dominant culture can the infrastructure survive.

The economic niches in which Korean-owned small businesses can survive are often in deteriorated neighborhoods populated largely by other minority groups, many of which see them as "profit-seeking, exploitative outsiders" (Marbella, 2015) and they've expressed hostility and resentment against Korean shop owners. For example, in the 1992 Los Angeles riots, Korean-owned businesses were some of the first to be looted and burned (Chapter 5). When asked why, one looter said simply, "Because we hate 'em. Everybody hates them" (Cho, 1993, p. 199). Pew Research Center (2013) data suggest that almost one quarter of Korean Americans (24%) report that "discrimination is a major problem." Thus, part of the price of survival for many Korean merchants is to place themselves in positions where antagonism and conflict with other minority groups is common (Kitano & Daniels, 1995; Light & Bonacich, 1988; Min, 2006; see also Hurh, 1998). That sometimes results in additional harms; for example, 26% of businesses damaged or looted from the 2015 Baltimore riots were Korean owned (Marbella, 2015).

Filipino Americans

The U. S. and the Philippines established ties in 1898, when Spain ceded the territory after its defeat in the Spanish–American War. The Philippines achieved independence following World War II, but the U. S. has maintained a strong military presence there for much of the past 70 years. American culture has heavily influenced the Philippines, and English remains one of two official languages. Thus, Filipino immigrants are often familiar with English, at least as a second language (see Table 9.3).

Today, Filipinos are the third-largest Asian American group, but their numbers became sizable only in the past few decades. In 1920, fewer than 1,000 Filipinos lived in the U.S.; by 1960, the group still numbered fewer than 200,000. Most of the recent growth has come from increased post-1965 immigration (see Figure 8.5). Many of the earliest immigrants were agricultural workers recruited for the sugar plantations of Hawaii and the fields of the West Coast. Because the Philippines were a U.S. territory, Filipinos could enter without regard to immigration quotas until 1935, when the nation became a self-governing commonwealth. Many recent immigrants have entered under the "family preference" provisions of the U.S. immigration policy.

Filipino immigrants are "bipolar" in their educational and occupational profiles. Some members work in the higher-wage primary labor market while others compete in the low-wage secondary sector (Agbayani-Siewert & Revilla, 1995; Espiritu, 1996; Kitano & Daniels, 1995; Min, 2006; Posadas, 1999). Since 1965, more than half of all Filipino immigrants were professionals in business and science, and many were working in the health and medical fields. For example, more than 20,000 immigrant medical graduate (IMG) physicians from the Philippines work in the U. S., the second largest of all immigrant groups. Many women immigrants were nurses actively recruited by U.S. hospitals to fill gaps in the labor force. In fact, nurses have become something of an export commodity in the Philippines. Thousands of trained nurses leave the Philippines every year to work around the world. About one third of immigrant nurses working in the U. S. came from the Philippines (Hohn, Lowry, Witte, & Fernández-Pena, 2016).

Vietnamese

A flow of refugees from Vietnam began in the 1960s due to the war in Southeast Asia. The war began in Vietnam but expanded when the U. S. attacked communist forces in Cambodia and Laos. In 1975, Saigon (the South Vietnamese capital) fell and the U.S. military left. About 3 million Southeast Asians were forced to leave their homelands and many, including those who had helped the U. S., fled in fear for their lives. About 1.6 million of these were Vietnamese, making them the largest group of Asian refugees.

Similar to Cuban refugees, the first wave of Vietnamese migrants to America (1975–1977) were middle- or upper-class and generally well educated. Second-wave migrants (1978–1997) were less educated and more impoverished. About 400,000 (of 700,000) were "boat people" who sailed to neighboring countries that grudgingly took them in. (Thousands more died at sea.) Many people waited in refugee camps for years, under severe deprivation, before being allowed to resettle in America. These later refugees typically arrived with few resources or social networks to ease transition (Kitano & Daniels, 1995; UNHCR, 2000).

Between 1980–2017, the group grew by a factor of nine, increasing from 231,000 people to more than 2.1 million (Alperin & Batalova, 2017). In 2017, they were about 4.7% of all immigrants and less than 1% of the U.S. population. Contrary to Asian American success stories and model minority myths, Vietnamese Americans have incomes and educational levels that are somewhat comparable to colonized minority groups (see Table 9.3 and Figures 8.14 and 8.17).

MIDDLE EASTERN AND ARAB AMERICANS

Immigration from the Middle East and the Arab world began in the 19th century but has never been particularly large. The earliest immigrants tended to be merchants, and the Middle Eastern community in the U. S. has been constructed around an ethnic small-business enclave. The number of Arab and Middle Eastern Americans has grown rapidly over the past several decades but remains a tiny percentage of the U.S. population. Table 9.4 displays some statistical information on the group, broken down by ancestry subgroups. The *Arab American* category is a general one and includes Lebanese, Egyptian, and Syrian Americans and many smaller groups.

These groups generally rank relatively high in income and education. All groups rank higher on college degree attainment than non-Hispanic whites—Egyptians and Iranians are even more educated. Thus, they fill jobs in the highest levels of the American job structure. Consistent with being an enclave minority, they are overrepresented in sales and underrepresented in occupations involving manual labor. Although poverty is a problem for the Arab American group, overall, most groups' median household income compares quite favorably to other U.S. residents.

Arab and Middle Eastern Americans are diverse and vary along many dimensions. For example, not all Middle Easterners are Arabic; Iranians, for example, are Persian. They bring different cultures, religions, family forms, and political views. Most are Muslim, but many are Christian. In 2017, Muslim Americans made up 1.1% of the U.S. population. Of the 3.45 million Muslim Americans, about three fourths (76%) are immigrants or children of immigrants. They come from many countries, with the highest rates coming from Pakistan (15%), Iran (11%), and India (7%; Pew Research Center, 2017b, pp. 31–32).

Similarly, Muslim American adults come from many racial and ethnic backgrounds. Nearly half (41%) of all Muslims living in the U. S. identify as *white*, a category that includes Middle Eastern, Arab, Persian, and other ethnic groups (Chapter 1). Nearly one third (28%) identify as *Asian* (including South Asia), and one fifth (20%) identify as *black*. Of U.S.–born Muslims, 35% identify as *white*, 32% as *black*, and 10% as *Asian* (Pew Research Center, 2017b, p. 35).

Almost one third (31%) of Muslims living in the U. S. have college or postgraduate degrees, which is comparable to educational attainment overall in America (Pew Research Center, 2017b, p. 23). However, Muslim immigrants have more education compared with U.S.–born Muslims. Specifically, 38% of foreign-born Muslims have a college degree or higher while only 21% of U.S.–born Muslims do (p. 41). The first national survey of Muslim Americans, which included the vast majority of Arab and Middle Eastern

TABLE 9.4 ■ Selected Characteristics of Arab Americans and Middle Eastern American and Non-Hispanic Whites, 2017							
Group	Size	Percentage with Less Than a High School Diploma	Percentage with a College Degree or More	Percentage Foreign-Born	Percentage Who Speak English Less Than "Very Well"	Median Household Income	Percentage of Families in Poverty
Non-Hispanic whites	204,221,676	7.1	35.8	4.1	1.6	$65,696	6.2
Arab Americans	2,005,223	9.9	48.5	46.0	22.3	$58,581	18.3
Lebanese	488,548	6.6	51.6	22.3	7.1	$76,805	8.3
Egyptians	259,548	3.6	67.9	58.5	24.0	$64,710	13.1
Syrians	177,171	10.2	45.8	37.7	19.9	$66,134	15.6
Iranians	476,967	4.8	64.3	64.7	25.1	$78,005	9.3
Turks	222,593	8.4	55.5	53.2	21.6	$73,566	10.3

Source: U.S. Census Bureau (2018a). American Community Survey, 2017 1-year Estimates.

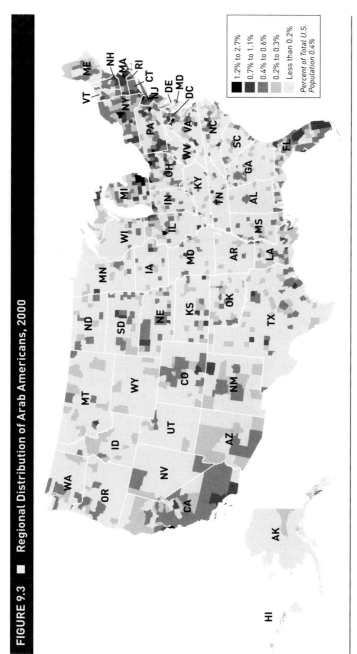

FIGURE 9.3 ■ Regional Distribution of Arab Americans, 2000

Percent of Total U.S.
Population 0.4%

Less than 0.2%
0.2% to 0.3%
0.4% to 0.6%
0.7% to 1.1%
1.2% to 2.7%

Source: De la Cruz and Brittingham (2003, p. 6).

Americans, found that they are largely assimilated; they have positive attitudes about America and they embrace American values (Pew Research Center, 2007). Research in 2017 produced similar findings: More than 90% of Muslim Americans agreed with the statements, "I am proud to be American" and "I have a lot in common with the average American" (Pew Research Center, 2017b, p. 51).

The vast majority of Arab and Middle Eastern Americans live in cities; most live in just five states (California, New Jersey, New York, Florida, and Michigan; see Figure 9.3). This settlement pattern reflects chains of migration set up decades ago and is similar to other recent immigrant groups, except for the heavy concentration in Michigan (especially in the Detroit area).

FOCUS ON CONTEMPORARY ISSUES

DETROIT'S ARAB AMERICAN COMMUNITY

Dr. Steven Gold

The greater Detroit area has long been a center of Arab American life. It continues to display vitality, with growing numbers of businesses, continued arrivals from the Middle East, and the creation of communal institutions such as the Arab American National Museum and the Islamic Center of America, the nation's largest Muslim house of worship. The population, which traces its local presence back more than 100 years, is large and growing. However, due to recent arrivals, difficulties in enumeration, and the effects of intermarriage, estimates of the population are subject to debate. While the 2010 U.S. census counted some 138,920 people of Arab and Middle Eastern origin in the tri-county Detroit area, the Zogby Worldwide polling firm pegs the community at more than 400,000.

Major nationality groups making up the Arab American population include Lebanese, Iraqi, Palestinian, and Yemeni. Additionally, these groups reflect considerable religious diversity associated with several traditions, including Chaldean, Melkite, Maronite, and Roman Catholics; Protestants and Orthodox Christians; and Sunni and Shi'a Muslims. Local enclaves based on nationality and religion are found throughout Metro Detroit's three counties,

revealing significant diversity in housing, class membership, and way of life.

Detroit's Arab Americans have created a broad array of organizations that address the population's social service, cultural, religious, health, educational, political, and economic needs. Among the most well-known is ACCESS (Arab Community Center for Economic and Social Services). Established in the early 1970s, ACCESS is the largest Arab American human services nonprofit in America. With 11 locations and more than 120 programs, it caters to a diverse population. Ismael Ahamed, the organization's founder, has gone on to serve as the director of the Michigan Department of Human Services—the state government's second-largest agency—and is currently associate provost of the University of Michigan–Dearborn. While inclusive and large-scale organizations such as ACCESS maintain a communitywide focus, others reflect particular concerns associated with the population's varied subgroups.

Arab Detroit is noted for its extensive self-employment. The population is estimated to own some 15,000 enterprises, with Chaldeans (Iraqi Catholics) and Lebanese having especially high rates of entrepreneurship. The growth of Arab American businesses is most evident in Dearborn, where thousands of Arabic signs advertise a whole range of goods and services to local customers. Simultaneously, Arab-owned shops, restaurants, car dealerships, gas stations, and professionals serve consumer needs throughout the region in neighborhoods ranging from the inner city to affluent suburbs.

Business success is enabled by a wide range of resources, including familial and communal ties and personal experience with self-employment. Additionally, the population's generally high levels of education and intact families are known to facilitate proprietorship. Indeed, Middle Eastern–origin groups have long revealed a propensity toward self-employment in the U. S. In 1911, the Dillingham Commission of the U.S. Congress found that more than 75% of Syrian immigrant men (who would now be classified as Lebanese) in New York were self-employed. Recent evidence suggests that the trend endures.

Finally, many ethnic organizations, including the Arab American Chamber of Commerce, Chaldean Federation of America, Arab American Women's Business Council, Chaldean American Chamber of Commerce, Chaldean American Bar Association, Chaldean American Association for Health Professionals, and Lebanese American Chamber of Commerce, provide services and contacts for Arab American entrepreneurs in southeast Michigan.

Despite the community's size, wealth, and influence, a number of activists and observers contend that the population suffers from significant hostility and discrimination. This includes racial profiling and surveillance by U.S. government agencies since September 11, 2001, and discrimination and violence by some Americans. The net impact of these trends causes Arab Americans to feel unsafe in their own homes, deprecated for their national and religious origins, pressured to apologize for acts they had nothing to do with, and compelled to cooperate with intrusive surveillance activities.

Based on decisions made by federal agencies, South Asians and Middle Easterners in the U. S. are treated as a special population. In the years following the September 11 attacks, more than 1,200 persons—who were neither named nor charged with crimes—were detained, with about half

being deported. Simultaneously, numerous ethnic and religious organizations representing the same nationalities have been accused of assisting terrorists—generally with little or no evidence—an action that permits the freezing of their assets and the criminalization of their members.

In addition to dealing with criminal justice and migration officials, Arab Americans also confront various forms of hostility, including insults, vandalism, and violence, as they go about their daily lives. This is evidenced by the cancellation of the Dearborn Arab International Festival in 2013, an event that for the previous 18 years brought together hundreds of thousands of people from throughout the U. S. and the world to enjoy Middle Eastern food and culture and family-friendly entertainment.

Fundamentalist Christian groups targeted the festival as a setting where they could confront Arabs and Muslims. Some, on record for publicly burning the Quran (the Muslim holy book)—brought a pig's head and other symbols insulting to Muslims to the festival. When the fundamentalist protestors won a 2010 lawsuit protecting their First Amendment rights, the city of Dearborn withdrew its support of the festival. Instead, officials encouraged the festival's organizers to hold it in a park, where public order could be more easily maintained.

Representatives of the Arab American community rejected this option because they favored the event's previous location, adjacent to numerous Arab businesses that were vital to improving the city's (and region's) economic and cultural vitality. With too little time to make alternative arrangements, the popular and highly successful event had to be cancelled.

In sum, Detroit's Arab community continues to grow and prosper, bringing vitality and development to a location more commonly associated with economic decline and population loss. Yet, even as its members seek to celebrate their successful participation in American life, the circumstances of their religion, heritage, and regional origins often result in their being denied access to opportunities that groups with different origins might take for granted.

Source: Gold (2002).

9/11 and Arab Americans

A faint strain of prejudice directed at Middle Easterners has always existed in American culture (e.g., see the low position of Turks in the 1926 social distance scales in Chapter 1). These feelings have intensified in recent decades as relations with various Middle Eastern nations and groups have worsened. For example, in 1979, the U.S. Embassy in Tehran, Iran, was attacked and occupied, and more than 50 Americans were held hostage for more than a year. The attack stimulated a massive reaction in the U. S., in which anti-Arab and anti-Muslim feelings figured prominently. Continuing anti-American activities across the Middle East in the 1980s and 1990s stimulated a backlash of resentment and growing intolerance in America.

These events pale in comparison to the events of September 11, 2001. Americans responded to the attacks on the World Trade Center and the Pentagon by Arab terrorists with an array of emotions that included bewilderment, shock, anger, patriotism, and deep sorrow for the victims, their families, and the nation. Though the 19 attackers were from Saudi Arabia, the United Arab Emirates, Egypt, and Lebanon, research shows increased prejudicial rejection of Middle Easterners, Arabs, Muslims, and any group even vaguely associated with the perpetrators of attacks. In the nine weeks following September 11, more than 700 violent attacks were reported to the Arab American Anti-Discrimination Committee, followed by another 165 violent incidents in the first nine months of 2002 (Arab American Anti-Discrimination Committee, 2002). In this same period, there were more than 80 incidents in which Arab Americans were removed from airplanes because of their ethnicity, more than 800 cases of employment discrimination, and "numerous instances of denial of service, discriminatory service, and housing discrimination" (Ibish, 2003, p. 7). In 2017, anti-Muslim assaults surpassed 2001 levels (see Figure 9.4; Kishi,

---

FIGURE 9.4   ■   Anti-Muslim Assaults from 2000 to 2016

Anti-Muslim assaults exceed 2001 total
Anti-Muslim assaults in U.S. reported to the FBI

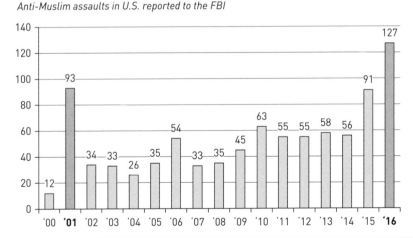

Source: Kishi (2017). "Anti-Muslim assaults surpass 2001 level."

2017). Anti-Muslim hate crimes are up, too. Although most religion-based hate crimes are against Jews (Chapter 4), it's notable that hate crimes against Muslims are 10 times higher in 2017 compared to 1997 (Federal Bureau of Investigation [FBI], 1997, 2017).

Thus, although the Arab and Middle Eastern American communities are small in size, they've assumed a prominent place in the nation's attention. The majority denounce and reject terrorism and violence, but many Americans hold strong stereotypes about them that, like other stereotypes, are often applied uncritically. A 2017 Pew Research Center survey asked participants to apply a "feeling thermometer" toward nine religious groups, including Jews, Buddhists, Mormons, Hindus, and Catholics. The lower the score, the more negative the rating. Muslims had an average of 48 degrees, up from 40 in 2014. However, people still ranked them lower than any other group, including atheists (who averaged 50 degrees in 2017, up from 41 in 2014; Pew Research Center, 2017b). This evaluation of Islam as less desirable than other religions is reflected in Figure 9.5. As you'll see, a majority of Muslim Americans (62%) feel that Islam isn't accepted as "mainstream."

Muslim Americans are very concerned about becoming scapegoats in the war on terror. As Figure 9.5 shows, half (50%) say that it's recently become more difficult to be a Muslim in America (Pew Research Center, 2017b) compared with 53% responding that way after 9/11 (Pew Research Center, 2007). Furthermore, almost three fourths of American Muslims (71%) are "at least somewhat concerned about extremism in the name of Islam occurring in the U. S." (Abdo, 2017). Three quarters of American Muslims said there's "a lot of discrimination" against their group members. Being perceived as Arab or Muslim—for example, based on appearance (e.g., wearing a hijab), name (e.g., Ahmad), or language or accent—may lead to individual discrimination such as interpersonal microaggressions (Chapter 8). Or it may include verbal threats and physical violence (of the kind documented by the FBI). At the macrolevel of society, customs and laws may be discriminatory, even if they're not intended as such. For example, the USA Patriot Act, passed in 2001, allows for long-term detention of suspects and a wider scope for searches and surveillance, including profiling at airport security checks. Similarly, it led to greater restrictions on entering the country, as did the 2017 Executive Order 13769, "Protecting the Nation from Foreign Terrorist Entry into the U. S.," also called the "Muslim Ban." These and other policies have caused concern for many Americans about violations of due process and suspension of basic civil liberties for Arab Americans and/or Muslim Americans.

Relations between Arab Americans and the larger society are certainly among the most tense and problematic for any minority group. Given the U.S. invasions of Iraq and Afghanistan following 9/11 and the continuing threat of further terrorist attacks, it's unlikely that tensions will ease any time soon.

FIGURE 9.5 ■ U.S. Muslims' Concerns

Half say it is getting tougher to be Muslim in the U.S.

% of U.S. Muslims who say it has become _____ to be Muslim in the U.S. in recent years

	%
More difficult	50
Hasn't changed much	44
Easier (VOL.)	3
DK/ref.	3
	100

Source: Survey conducted Jan. 23-May 2, 2017

"U.S. Muslims Concerned About Their Place in Society, but Continue to Believe in the American Dream"

PEW RESEARCH CENTER

Source: Pew Research Center (2017b). http://www.pew forum.org/2017/07/26/findings-from-pew-research-centers-2017-survey-of-us-muslims/.

IMMIGRANTS FROM AFRICA

African immigrants are the final group of new Americans we'll discuss. African immigration was quite low until the usual increase after the 1965 Immigration and Naturalization Act. In 1960, Africans were about 5% of all immigrants and have been about 10% since 2000. The number of Africans in the U. S. has more than doubled since 1990. This rapid growth suggests that these groups may have a greater impact on America in the future.

Table 9.5 shows the total number of sub-Saharan Africans in the U. S. in 2015, along with the two largest national groups. The category *sub-Saharan Africans* was an attempt to improve on 1950s labels with a decidedly racial framework (e.g., *black Africa*). While that's an improvement, *sub-Saharan* still has problems. First and foremost, it can't possibly encompass the diversity of the 46 countries within it (some include 48). It doesn't even make complete geographic sense, since several countries categorized as *sub-Saharan* are *on* the Sahara (Haldevang, 2016). Nevertheless, that label is used most often. Since we can't possibly address all the countries in this very broad category, we'll focus on the two with the most immigrants: Nigerians and Ethiopians.

Although their numbers are growing, Nigerians and Ethiopians are tiny minorities, only about 0.2% of the U.S. population. They're recent immigrants and have a lot of first-generation members. Nigerian and Ethiopian immigrants tend to be highly skilled and educated, and both compare favorably to national norms for education. Similar to other groups, many are motivated by employment opportunities in the U.S. job structure. However, this creates "brain drain" for their home countries (Migration Policy Institute, 2015).

TABLE 9.5 ■ Selected Characteristics of Sub-Saharan African Groups and Non-Hispanic Whites, 2017							
Group	Size	Percentage with Less Than a High School Diploma	Percentage with a College Degree or More	Percentage Foreign-Born	Percentage Who Speak English Less Than "Very Well"	Median Household Income	Percentage of Families in Poverty
Non-Hispanic whites	204,221,676	7.1	35.8	4.1	1.6	$65,696	6.2
All sub-Saharan Africans	3,893,865	11.5	34.5	42.2	14.0	$47,958	17.5
Ethiopians	312,444	12.6	29.8	69.0	32.5	$49,067	16.1
Nigerians	426,158	3.1	62.8	59.6	9.6	$65,940	11.6

Source: U.S. Census Bureau (2018a).

Nigeria is a former British colony, so the relatively high level of English fluency among its immigrants isn't surprising. Table 9.5 shows that, on average, group members have translated their relatively high levels of human capital, including English fluency, into a favorable economic position. They compare quite favorably with national norms in their income levels.

You'll see in Table 9.5 that, compared with Nigerians, Ethiopians rank lower on English fluency and their backgrounds vary more. This group includes the poorest refugees who fled domestic unrest along with the educated elite in search of employment opportunities. Although Ethiopians' educational levels compare favorably with national norms, they have much lower levels of income and, therefore, much higher rates of poverty. These contrasts suggest that Ethiopians are less able to translate their educational credentials into higher-ranked occupations.

MODES OF INCORPORATION

As the case studies included in this chapter (and in Chapters 7 and 8) demonstrate, recent immigrant groups occupy a wide array of different positions in America. To understand this diversity, it's helpful to examine the contact situation, group characteristics (e.g., race, religion, human capital on arrival), and the reaction of the larger society. American immigrants have followed three main modes of incorporation: entrance through the primary labor market, the secondary labor markets (Chapter 4), or the ethnic enclave. We'll consider each pathway separately and relate them to the groups in this chapter.

Immigrants and the Primary Labor Market

The primary labor market consists of desirable jobs with greater security, higher pay, and more benefits. The immigrants entering this sector tend to be highly educated, skilled professionals who are generally fluent in English; many were educated at American universities. They're highly integrated into the global urban–industrial economy and, in many cases, they're employees of multinational corporations and are transferred here by their companies. These immigrants are affluent, urbane, and dramatically different from the laborers so common in the past (e.g., from Ireland and Italy) and in the present (e.g., from the Dominican Republic and Mexico). India, Egypt, Iran, and Nigeria have high percentages of members entering the primary labor market.

Because they tend to be affluent, immigrants with professional backgrounds have somewhat greater protection from racist reactions than their more unskilled counterparts. This may partly be due to a greater sense of competition among people with low income levels. Although they come closer to Blauner's pure immigrant group than most minority groups we've considered, racism still complicates their lives. Additionally, Islamic group members must confront discrimination and prejudice based on their religious affiliation.

Immigrants and the Secondary Labor Market

This mode of incorporation is more typical for immigrants with less education and fewer job skills. These jobs aren't as desirable because they offer lower pay, little security, and few benefits and are often seasonal or in the underground, informal economy. Some examples include domestic work, construction jobs where workers are paid "off the books" and working conditions are unregulated by government authorities or labor unions, and some illegal activities (e.g., drug sales, sex work). Employers who control these jobs often prefer hiring undocumented immigrants because they're easier to control since their precarious legal and economic status makes them less likely to complain about working conditions (e.g., long hours, being paid less than minimum wage) or to report abuses to the authorities. The groups with high percentages of members in the secondary labor market include Dominicans, Haitians, and the less-skilled and less-educated kinfolk of higher-status immigrants.

Immigrants and Ethnic Enclaves

As you've seen, some immigrant groups—especially those that bring financial capital and business experience—have established ethnic enclaves. Some enter the country as entrepreneurs and become owners of small businesses (e.g., shops); their less-skilled and less-educated co-ethnics serve as a source of cheap labor for these enterprises. The enclave provides contacts, financial and other services, and social support for the new immigrants of all social classes. Historically, Korean Americans, Cubans, and some Arab American groups were particularly likely to follow this path.

Summary

These modes of incorporation suggest the different relationships possible between new Americans and the larger society. The contemporary stream of immigrants entering the U. S. is extremely diverse and includes people from the most sophisticated and urbane to the most desperate and despairing. This variety can be seen in a list of occupations in which recent immigrants are overrepresented. In 2017, men were overrepresented in STEM jobs (science, technology, engineering, and math) such as biologists, construction and maintenance workers, taxi drivers, farm laborers, and waiters. For women, they were overrepresented in STEM jobs such as chemists, nurses, statisticians, produce packers, manicurists, laundry workers, sewing machine operators, and domestics (Bureau of Labor Statistics, 2018; Desilver, 2017; Enchautegui, 2015; Thomas & Logan, 2012).

QUESTIONS FOR REFLECTION

3. Describe the characteristics of the largest groups of immigrants from Central America, the Caribbean, Asia, the Middle East, and Africa. What are their main commonalities and differences?

4. Which groups are most likely to assimilate into the primary labor market, the secondary labor market, and the enclave? Explain each of your answers.

COMPARATIVE FOCUS

THE ROMA: EUROPE'S "TRUE MINORITY"

Dr. Andria D. Timmer

Professor Andria D. Timmer studies the Roma of Europe. She lived and worked in Hungarian Roma communities for several years while conducting research.

The Roma (often called *Gypsies*) live throughout the world but primarily in Europe. Figure 9.6 shows their geographic distribution; note that they live in every European country. The Roma have been part of Central and Eastern European societies since at least the 14th century, when they arrived in several migratory waves from India. Although they've lived in Europe for more than half a millennium, they're still treated as recent immigrants in many respects. Thus, the Roma illustrate Gordon's and others' point that length of residence in a

country isn't necessarily related to a group's ability to assimilate and gain acceptance (Chapter 2).

The Roma aren't a singular group; they comprise several different ethnic enclaves. In most cases, different groups have little in common and are often more similar to the majority members of the country where they reside than to one another. However, from a pan-European perspective, they're often considered a single group. To understand how these different peoples get grouped together, it's necessary to review the definition of *minority group* (Chapter 1). We'll use the first two elements of the definition to examine the situation of the Roma in Europe.

The first and most important defining characteristic of a minority group is disadvantage or

FIGURE 9.6 ■ Roma Population in Europe, 2009

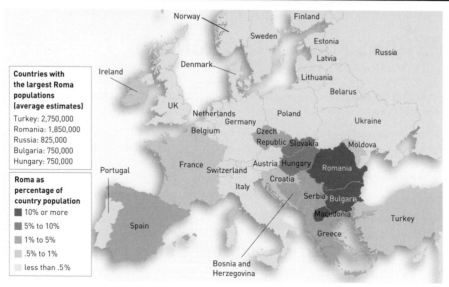

Countries with the largest Roma populations (average estimates)

Turkey: 2,750,000
Romania: 1,850,000
Russia: 825,000
Bulgaria: 750,000
Hungary: 750,000

Roma as percentage of country population

■ 10% or more
■ 5% to 10%
■ 1% to 5%
▪ .5% to 1%
  less than .5%

Source: SAGE.

(Continued)

(Continued)

inequality; this is something that all Roma groups share. Violence and intolerance toward Roma are an ever-present reality. Roma neighborhoods often lack necessities, such as running water and regular trash collection. As an egregious form of discrimination, Roma youth are frequently educated apart from their majority group peers; they receive a lower-quality education that leaves them unable to compete for jobs. Unemployment rates for the Roma stand somewhere between 70% and 95%, depending on region.

The second defining characteristic of a minority group is a visible trait or characteristic. Linguistic, genetic, and ethnographic evidence shows that the Roma ancestors migrated from northern India sometime between the 7th and 10th centuries. Therefore, contemporary populations share physical features with Indian populations, especially skin color. The Roma have few cultural ties with India; and, as mentioned previously, few cultural characteristics connect all Roma groups together. Very few—apart from English and Irish Traveler groups, who aren't Indian descendants—still practice the stereotypical nomadic lifestyle. Many have lost the use of their native tongue or use it only in their homes.

The deep divide between Roma and non-Roma in Europe largely results from a long history of isolation and segregated living. Government and civil-sector programs have done little to address segregation but have, generally, endeavored to improve living conditions in Roma settlements. They've helped build new houses and sponsored environmental clean-up projects, but few programs try to integrate Roma families into the larger national communities where they reside. As long as residential segregation, prejudice, and discrimination persist, the Roma will remain isolated and segregated, with the consequences that brings.

QUESTIONS FOR REFLECTION

5. Are the Roma a typical minority group? How do they compare to African Americans or Native Americans? What important differences and similarities can you identify?

6. What stereotypes do Americans believe about the Roma ("Gypsies")? Where do these ideas come from? In Chapter 1, we noted that stereotypes tend to fall into two categories: one for groups that occupy a low status and the other for groups that are "too" successful. Into which category do American stereotypes of the Roma fall? Why?

IMMIGRATION: ISSUES AND CONTROVERSIES

The Attitudes of Americans

One crucial factor affecting the fate of immigrant groups is the larger society's attitude, particularly of the groups with the most influence on governmental policymakers.

Overall, American public opinion is split on the issue of immigration. Today, the majority of Americans regard immigration as a positive force, and this percentage has increased in the past few years (see Figure 7.5). In 2017, a national survey found that more than half (59%) of Americans said immigrants strengthened the country, while 33% described them as a burden. In 1994, public opinion was nearly the opposite: 63% of Americans viewed immigrants as a burden and 31% thought they strengthened the country (Jones, 2016). That said, many Americans are still vehemently opposed to immigration and immigrants.

Our nation's history is replete with anti-immigrant and nativist groups and activities, including those that opposed the immigration from Europe (Chapter 2), Mexico (Chapter 7), and China and Japan (Chapter 8). The present is no exception: As immigration has increased over the past several decades, so has the number and visibility of anti-immigrant groups, particularly in the states along the Mexican border.

Contemporary anti-immigrant movements have generated a number of state laws. One of the most controversial and widely publicized is Arizona's State Bill 1070, which was signed into law in 2010. Among other provisions, the law required law enforcement officers to check the immigration status of anyone they stopped, detained, or arrested if they had a "reasonable" suspicion that the person might be here illegally. Supporters of the legislation argued that it would help control unauthorized immigration. Opponents raised fears of racial profiling and legalized anti-Hispanic discrimination and expressed considerable concern that the legislation would deter Hispanic Americans from reporting crimes they'd witnessed or experienced (e.g., assault).

In 2012, the Supreme Court invalidated most of the provisions in Arizona's State Bill 1070, though several states had passed similar bills by then. In 2011, Alabama's House passed Bill 56, considered by some as particularly punitive. Among other provisions, it required schools to verify the immigration status of students in Grades K–12, banned undocumented immigrants from soliciting work, and made it illegal to give rides or rent apartments to the undocumented. However, most of that law's provisions were repealed in 2013 (Vock, 2013).

Demonstrating the idea that Americans are ambivalent about immigration, other states passed legislation favorable to immigrants during the same period. Some states (e.g., Colorado, Oregon) extended in-state tuition to undocumented immigrants who graduated from their high school system, and others (e.g., Georgia, Illinois) allowed them to get driver's licenses (Wogan, 2013).

Researchers have identified several important reasons for people's views on immigration, many consistent with the ideas we've examined. For example, competition between groups for scarce resources (e.g., jobs, political power, neighborhood control) and a sense of threat generate prejudice and racism. Guided by the Noel hypothesis (Chapter 3) and the Robber's Cave experiment (Chapter 1), we'd expect negative feelings toward immigrants to be strongest among those who feel most threatened by the increased immigration over the past several decades, such as the most economically vulnerable Americans (e.g., see Wallace & Figueroa, 2012) or the 65% of Americans who, in 2016, reported anxiety about personal or familial unemployment (Cooper, Cox, Dionne, Lienesch, Jones, & Galston, 2016).

Yet, some research (Hainmueller & Hiscox, 2010; Reyna, Dobria, & Wetherell, 2013) found little correlation between anti-immigrant feelings and one's personal economic situation. Rather, they found that both high- and low-status respondents were less concerned with their own pocketbooks and more focused on the potential costs of low-skill immigrants—for schooling, health care, and other services—and their impact on the U.S. economy generally. For example, in 2016, 54% of Americans surveyed in a national poll said that undocumented immigrants drive down overall wages by working for less (Cooper et al., 2016). So, while the issue of resources still plays a role in one's attitudes, the concern is at a broader level, not a personal one.

Yet, competition is more than fights over jobs and votes. Many opponents to immigration in the U. S. seem motivated by a collective sense of threat that newcomers will compromise the way of life and the cultural integrity of the host nation. For example, in 2016, national polls found that the majority of Americans (57%) feel Islamic values conflict with American values (Cooper et. al, 2016) and a majority (55%) worry about "foreign influence" on the American way of life, a rate that's even higher among working-class people. Likewise, Cox, Lienesch, and Jones (2017) report that many Americans feel that rapid social change has them "often feeling like a stranger in [their] own country." These defensive forms of prejudice stimulate powerful emotions, as you've seen repeatedly throughout this book.

Finally, you've seen that prejudice and negative feelings toward other groups is motivated by many factors, not only competition. Anti-immigrant attitudes are highly correlated with other forms of prejudice and are caused by the same processes we examined in earlier chapters—for example, exposure to racist cultural norms and values during childhood and low levels of education (Pettigrew, Wagner, & Christ, 2007).

Is everyone who has reservations and questions about immigration a racist? Absolutely not. While anti-immigrant feelings, prejudice, and a sense of threat seem linked, this doesn't mean that everyone who opposes immigration are bigots or that all proposals to decrease the flow of immigrants are racist. These are serious and complex issues, and it isn't helpful simply to label people as bigots or dismiss their concerns as prejudiced.

However, we need to clearly recognize that anti-immigrant feelings—particularly the most extreme—are linked to some of the worst parts of traditional American culture: the same racist and prejudicial views that justified slavery and the near-genocide of Native Americans. We've seen those feelings in polling data that shows that the majority of Americans didn't support refugees resettling here at other points in our history—from Germany during/after WWII, Hungary (1950s), Vietnam/Laos/Cambodia (1970s), Cuba and Haiti (1980s), Iraq/Afghanistan (2000s), and Syria (2015; DeSilver, 2015).

In popular culture (Twitter, YouTube, talk radio and cable TV news shows, letters to the editor, etc.), people regularly use these views to demonize immigrants, blame them for social problems, and stoke irrational fears and rumors (e.g., Mexican immigrants want to return parts of the Southwest to Mexico). At any rate, when American traditions of prejudice and racism are linked to feelings of group threat and individual insecurity, the possibilities for extreme reactions, hate crimes, and poorly designed policies and laws become formidable.

The Immigrants

A 2009 national survey of immigrants, which also included interviews with participants, found that their attitudes and views on several topics differed from those of native-born Americans. For example, immigrant respondents were more likely to see immigration as a positive force and more likely to say that immigrants work hard and pay their fair share of taxes. In comparison to their home countries, an overwhelming majority (88%) felt that America offered better opportunities to make a living. Beyond economics, they said that America had a trustworthy legal system (70%), better health care (67%), better education (62%), and more independent media and free speech (55%) and was a better place to raise their families (55%). Two thirds (63%) believed that hard work leads to success, even without networks of support (Bittle & Rochkind, 2010).

More recently, Taylor and colleagues (2013) also documented immigrants' willingness to take advantage of opportunities through their commitment to hard work. Large majorities of Hispanic (78%) and Asian (68%) immigrants supported the idea that hard work results in success, an endorsement of the Protestant ethic that exceeds that of the general public (58%) (p. 85). However, the survey also showed that some immigrants feel ambivalent about American culture. For example, only 32% of Hispanic immigrants and 14% of Asian immigrants believed that the family is stronger in the U. S. than in their homelands, and less than half (44% of Hispanic and 36% of Asian immigrants) said that moral values are better in America (p. 77).

Another helpful report (López, Bialik, & Radford, 2018) used census data to compile a statistical portrait of the 43.7 million Americans—about 13.5% of the population are foreign-born or first-generation immigrants. As you'd expect, Mexicans are the single largest segment of this group (27%), with South and East Asian immigrants matching that (27%). However, Asian immigration began outpacing Mexican immigration in early 2009. About 32% of the foreign-born immigrated before 1980 (including surviving members of the last great wave of European immigrants), but an almost equal percentage (29%) are newcomers who arrived after 2000. A slim majority (51%) of immigrants speak English "very well," a key factor for assimilation. Overall, 30% have college degrees. That's comparable to 31.6% of the U.S.–born group and a significant increase from 1960, when only 5.1% of immigrants had a college education. Education, occupation, income, and poverty vary significantly across groups.

By synthesizing information throughout this book, we can say that the immigrant stream is highly diversified; therefore, the U. S. is growing more diverse. Most immigrants, from all nations, are motivated primarily by economics and the absence of viable opportunities at home. Those from less-industrialized nations bring little human capital, education, or job skills, but others bring glowing educational and professional credentials.

As in the past, the first generation are often more oriented to their homes than to America. Many, especially the low-skilled immigrants, don't have the time, energy, or opportunity to absorb much of Anglo culture or the English language, while others—the more skilled and educated—move easily between their home and American cultures. Similar to past waves of immigrants, the least skilled and educated are determined to find a better way of life for themselves and their children, even if the cost of doing so is living on the margins of society.

QUESTIONS FOR REFLECTION

7. How does the societal response to immigrants vary across time and across groups (for example, European or Chinese immigrants in the 1800s, groups that came in 1965–2000, and the most recent newcomers who arrived after 2000)?

8. Is it fair to label Americans as prejudiced against immigrants? Or are Americans largely welcoming? What are some causes of anti-immigrant and pro-immigrant attitudes?

9. What characteristics do immigrants bring? What are their motivations for immigrating?

Costs and Benefits

Many Americans believe that immigration is a huge drain on the nation's economic resources, that immigrants take jobs from native-born workers; strain schools, housing markets, and medical facilities; and don't pay taxes. For example, Saad (2010) found that 61% of respondents had these concerns. These issues are complex and hotly debated—so much so that the passion and intensity of feeling on all sides often compromises the objective analysis of data.

The debate is further complicated because conclusions vary, depending on which immigrants are being discussed and the level of analysis being used. For example, conclusions depend on whether we focus on less-skilled/undocumented immigrants or on highly educated professional immigrants entering the primary job market. Immigrants in their 20s and 30s are more likely to make a net contribution (especially if they have no children) than those who are over 65 and out of the workforce. Also, the conclusions from national studies may differ from studies of local communities, because the former spreads the costs over the entire population while the latter concentrates costs in a specific locality.

Finally, costs and benefits are distributed differently. Working-class Americans will feel the costs of immigration more sharply, since they are more likely to compete with less-educated immigrants for jobs. However, they're also less likely to purchase goods and services made more affordable by immigrant labor (e.g., childcare, housekeepers, lawn care).

Employment

Research on job loss shows that undocumented immigrants are concentrated in physically demanding jobs or other jobs where few Americans work (e.g., meat processing, agriculture, cleaning). According to a national survey by the Pew Research Center (2018), a majority (71%) of Americans concurred, saying that immigrants "fill jobs citizens do not want." Other immigrants work in enclave economies that wouldn't exist without their co-ethnics' economic activity. Thus, immigrants, especially the undocumented, tend to not have a negative effect on native-born workers' employment overall (Bean & Stevens, 2003; Kochhar, 2006; Meissner, 2010; National Academies of Sciences, Engineering, and Medicine [NASEM], 2017).

Wages

A comprehensive 550-page report by NASEM (2017) argued that any impact on employment and wages is slight and felt mostly by prior immigrants and native-born high school dropouts who compete with immigrants for low-wage work (p. 266). In some higher-paying fields (e.g., technology), U.S.–born workers could experience decreased wages if a significant number of immigrants were available and if companies chose to replace U.S.–born employees with lower-cost immigrants (e.g., immigrants with H1-B visas; Borjas, 2016).

Use of Public Services

Contrary to widespread belief, research, especially at the national level, finds that immigrants aren't a particular burden on public services (NASEM, 2017). First, the majority of immigrants aren't eligible for most publicly funded services (e.g., Medicaid, food stamps), and undocumented immigrants are ineligible for virtually all services. The exceptions are immigrant children who can benefit from programs for children and schools (West, 2011). (Schools must educate all children, regardless of status, a right upheld by the Supreme Court in *Plyler v. Doe* [1982], which found that the benefits to society would outweigh economic costs.)

Cost of Public Services

Another concern about immigrants is the strain they place on government services. Again, these issues are complex and far from settled, but generally, the use of public services by immigrants is lower than their proportional contributions, especially for undocumented immigrants, whose vulnerable legal status sharply limits their use of services (Bean & Stevens, 2003; Marcelli & Heer, 1998; Simon, 1989). For example, the conservative Cato Institute found that U.S.–born Americans use 39% more welfare benefits than immigrants. This contradicts their earlier findings and those of others (e.g., Camarota, 2015). Why? Because they changed their unit of analysis from *household* to *individual* (Nowrasteh & Orr, 2018). Since households may contain many people, that measure falsely "inflate[s] immigrant welfare use." NASEM (2017) found that immigrant-related costs and contributions change over time. The first generation uses about $57 billion a year. The second generation has more education, better jobs, and higher wages and therefore pays more taxes. They add about $30 billion a year. The third generation has even more human capital and contributes about $223 billion per year.

As a side note, data on welfare use depends on how people define *welfare*. Typically, benefits to middle- and upper-class individuals aren't called *public assistance*. For example, the government/taxpayers fund public universities; yet this "welfare" program disproportionately helps the middle- and upper-class. Likewise, homeowners get a tax break. Many Americans, especially racial/ethnic minorities, don't get this government subsidy. Finally, many workers—primarily those with college degrees in professional jobs—can buy into their company's private health care plans. Those costs tend to be offset by the government (e.g., through tax credits; Rosenbaum, 2018). So, who decides what qualifies as "welfare"? This issue is relevant for many Americans, such as those who demonize the poor for using public services or those who don't realize they themselves use "welfare." However, it's especially relevant to immigrants as the government considers policy changes that would deny entry or permanent green-card status for anyone seen as a potential "public charge" likely to use public assistance programs.

Taxes

Some employers are likely to pay undocumented immigrants "off the books," therefore allowing immigrants to receive their wages tax-free. However, the vast majority of immigrants (50% to 75%, depending on the study) pay local, state, and federal taxes and make proportional contributions to Social Security and Medicare automatically through payroll deduction (White House, 2005). Gee, Gardner, and Wiehe (2016) found that undocumented immigrants pay a substantial amount in local and state taxes (e.g. sale, income, property), totaling over 11 billion dollars a year. Additionally, they pay a disproportionate amount—8% of their income compared to the richest 1% of Americans, whose tax rate is only 5.4% (p. 1). Finally, all immigrants pay sales taxes and consumption taxes (e.g., on gas, cigarettes, and alcohol). (See the Current Debates section in our online resources.)

Some evidence suggests that immigrants play a crucial role in keeping the Social Security system solvent. On-the-books-workers contribute to this system via payroll taxes (e.g., Federal Insurance Contributions Act [FICA]). After retirement, they can withdraw those funds. This source of retirement income is being severely strained by the "baby boomers"—the large number of Americans born between 1945 and 1960 who are now retiring—because they live longer than previous generations and need more money as a result. Additionally, since the U.S. birth rate has stayed low over the past four decades, fewer U.S.–born workers exist to replace the funds that boomers withdraw as Social Security and Medicare benefits. Undocumented immigrants in particular pay into the system but (probably) will never draw money out because of their unauthorized status. They thus provide a tidy surplus—$7 billion a year or more—to subsidize boomers' retirements and keep the system alive for GenXers, millennials, and other generations of Americans (Porter, 2005; see also Dewan, 2013).

Other Economic Benefits

Immigrants boost the economy in other ways, too. First, they have spending power and put money back into the economy. Second, as noted earlier, they run thousands of businesses that hire millions of U.S.–born Americans and contribute billions to the economy. Third, by working at lower wages, immigrants reduce the cost of consumer goods for everyone virtually every time they go shopping; eat at a restaurant; pay for home construction, repairs, or maintenance; or place a loved one in a nursing home (for an overview, see Griswold, 2012). Finally, higher-educated immigrants spur technological development that has widespread benefits (NASEM, 2017).

Conclusions about the impact of immigration may change with new research. Concerns about the economic impact of immigrants aren't unfounded and we acknowledge that the six states and many localities with the largest immigrant populations (e.g., Texas, California, New York) will feel the impact more than others as they grapple with an influx of newcomers in their housing markets, schools, health care facilities, and elsewhere. However, a lack of awareness about immigration (e.g., declining immigrant population, immigrants' economic contributions) and immigrants exacerbates fears. Prejudice and racism, particularly in a climate of "us versus them" also plays a role. Current opposition to immigration may be a reaction to *who* as much as to *how many* or *how expensive*.

Undocumented Immigrants

A national survey in 2018 found that 69% of Americans felt sympathy toward undocumented immigrants, while 31% didn't. Those differing views consistently appeared in polling data for 2006 (63%/37%), 2010 (64%/36%), and 2014 (66%/34%; Pew Research Center, 2018). (See Chapter 5 about surveys and prejudice for what else could be going on with this data.) Yet, even if Americans feel sympathy, many are still concerned about illegal immigration.

The high level of concern is understandable because the volume of illegal immigration has been significant for a few decades, increasing almost 2.5 times between 1990 and 2000. Figure 9.7 shows that the estimated number of undocumented immigrants increased more than 40% between 2000 (8.6 million) and 2007 (12.2 million), though it's tended to decline since 2008. By 2017, the population was about 10.7 million—less

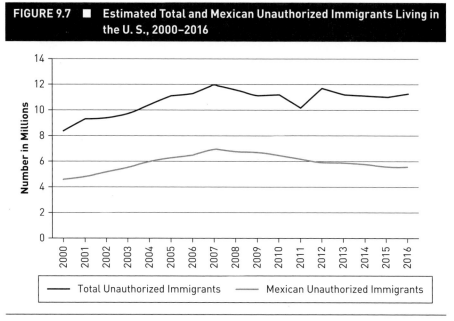

FIGURE 9.7 ■ Estimated Total and Mexican Unauthorized Immigrants Living in the U. S., 2000–2016

Source: Passel and Cohn (2017). "As Mexican Share Declined, U.S. Unauthorized Immigrant Population Fell in 2015 Below Recession Level" Pew Research Center.

than in 2005. About 55% of all current unauthorized immigrants are from Mexico (Passel & Cohn, 2017). In fiscal year 2017, the Department of Homeland Security processed 77.6 million people here on tourist, temporary worker, student, or diplomatic visas. About 700,000 of them stayed when their visas expired, making them another (but tiny) source of undocumented immigrants in comparison to illegal border crossings (Navarro, 2018; Passel & Cohn, 2018, p. 8).

One of the reasons the supply of unauthorized immigrants is so high is the continuing demand for cheap labor. As we've noted on several occasions, the Global South—and Mexico in particular—has functioned as a reserve labor force for the U.S. economy for decades. Even in 2010, after several years of economic recession, undocumented immigrants provided a sizable percentage of the workforce in many states and as much as 10% of the workers in several others (see Figure 9.8).

The demand for cheap (undocumented) labor varies by industry. In 2016, "farming, fishing and forestry" was the industry with the biggest proportion of undocumented workers. Most of the jobs in that industry were agricultural. In 2016, 23.6% of farming

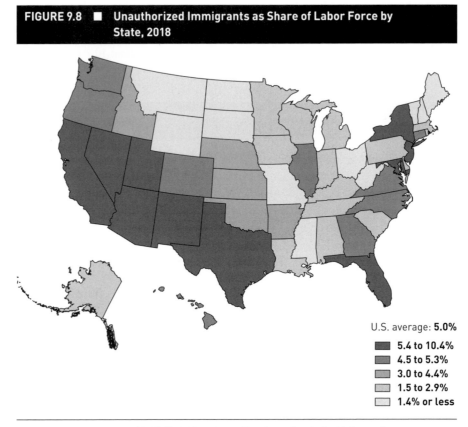

FIGURE 9.8 ■ Unauthorized Immigrants as Share of Labor Force by State, 2018

U.S. average: **5.0%**

- 5.4 to 10.4%
- 4.5 to 5.3%
- 3.0 to 4.4%
- 1.5 to 2.9%
- 1.4% or less

Source: Pew Research Center (2018). "U.S. Unauthorized Immigrant Population Estimates."

jobs were done by undocumented workers—a disproportionate rate, given that they're only 5% of the total workforce. Rates in construction were similar—13% was done by undocumented workers. Specific jobs had even higher rates of undocumented workers, such as roofers (31%) and drywall installers (30%; Passel & Cohn, 2018, p. 29). Some people argue that the U.S. agriculture and the food supply industries would collapse without the contributions of undocumented workers.

Many efforts are still being made to curtail and control the flow of unauthorized immigrants. Various states have attempted to lower the appeal of the U. S. by limiting benefits and opportunities. Other than the aforementioned State Bill 1070 in Arizona, one of the best known of these attempts occurred in 1994, when California voters passed Proposition 187, which would have denied educational, health care, and other services to undocumented immigrants. The policy was declared unconstitutional, however, and was never implemented.

Other efforts to decrease the flow of undocumented immigration have included proposals to limit welfare benefits for immigrants, denial of in-state college tuition to the children of undocumented immigrants, increases in the size of the Border Patrol, and, most prominently in recent years, the construction of a taller and wider wall along the border with Mexico. Over the past decade, many proposals to reform the national immigration policy—similar to the 1965 Immigration and Naturalization Act—have been hotly debated at the highest levels of government, but none have passed. Although Americans will still be concerned about this problem, many people wonder what can be done (within the framework of a democratic, humane society) to curtail the flow of people. The social networks that deliver immigrants—documented and undocumented—are too well established, and the demand for cheap labor in the U. S. is simply insatiable. In fact, denying services, as envisioned in Proposition 187, may make undocumented immigrants *more* attractive as a source of labor by reducing their ability to resist exploitation. For example, if the children of undocumented immigrants weren't permitted to attend school, they'd become more likely to join the army of cheap labor on which some employers depend. Who would benefit from barring access to public schools or denying in-state college tuition for the children of undocumented immigrants?

DREAMers

In 2001, the U.S. Senate considered the Development, Relief, and Education for Alien Minors (DREAM) Act. This act, like so many attempts to address immigration issues, stalled and was never passed, but it did give a name to a population that's increased in size since that time and remains a continuing concern: the children of undocumented immigrants who were brought to America as young children ("DREAMers").

DREAMers are in the United States illegally but not by personal choice. They aren't citizens of the United States (unlike the children born in America to undocumented immigrants who have birthright citizenship). In many ways, they're not citizens of their "native" land either. Many have never visited their "homeland" and are unfamiliar with its customs or even its language. The DREAM Act offered people meeting specific criteria (e.g., graduated from high school or has a GED) to pursue permanent residency (i.e., a "green card"). During the conditional status period, recipients must fulfill additional criteria (e.g., more education, military service). Eventually, they could apply for citizenship.

This part of the population is caught in the middle—residents of the U. S. but not citizens, strangers to their parent's homelands. They live in fear of deportation, and their undocumented status can prevent them from competing for jobs in the primary labor market, getting a driver's license, attending college, or receiving unemployment benefits or food stamps. Where do the roughly two million DREAMers (most of them Mexican) belong?

Attempts to revive the 2001 bill have failed, as did various alternative measures. Because of the political gridlock at the highest levels of government, many group members feared that their situation would never be reasonably addressed, let alone resolved.

In June 2012, the Obama administration enacted a program under which the children of undocumented immigrants could apply to stay in the U. S. without threat of deportation: Deferred Action for Childhood Arrivals (DACA). Those who met the conditions of the program (e.g., they must be high school graduates with no significant criminal violations) can get driver's licenses and work permits and can attend college. More than 500,000 people applied to and were approved for the program.

The program grants a two-year, renewable reprieve from deportation for the DREAMers (but not for their parents and other relatives). It doesn't offer permanent legal status or a pathway to citizenship. Despite its limited scope, the program is controversial. President Trump promised to end it during his campaign for the presidency (because it was created by the executive order of one president, it can be rescinded by the executive order of succeeding presidents). And, in the fall of 2017, he acted to do so. He has since signaled a possible willingness to compromise on this issue, and the fate of the DREAMers remains uncertain (Stolberg & Alcindor, 2017). A majority of Americans (72%) support DREAMers earning legal resident status if they join the military or go to college, up from 57% in 2011 (Vandermaas-Peeler, Cox, Fisch-Friedman, & Jones, 2017).

QUESTIONS FOR REFLECTION

10. Do immigrants cost more than they contribute? Use information from this and other chapters to support your answer. What noneconomic costs/contributions should we consider and why?

11. What societal factors affect the size of the undocumented population? How do these factors compare with those shaping overall immigration to the U. S.?

12. What should be done to resolve the situation for DREAMers (if anything)? If you were a DREAMer, what would you want people to consider?

13. What should be done to resolve the situation for the millions of the world's refugees (if anything)?

FOCUS ON CONTEMPORARY ISSUES
BIRTHRIGHT CITIZENSHIP

In the debate about birthright citizenship, some people will note that the U. S. and Canada are the only two advanced industrial nations in the Western Hemisphere to automatically confer citizenship on any baby born within their borders. Yet, it's not that simple. Culliton (2012) argues that approximately 30 countries around the world (mostly in Latin America) have birthright citizenship policies, though some have restrictions such as a minimal amount of time someone needs to be in the country. Birthright citizenship is grounded in *Jus soli* or the "right of the soil." In many countries, it's common law created through customary practice. Therefore, the focus on the U. S. as only one of "two advanced industrialized nations" isn't quite accurate.

The policy of birthright citizenship emerged from the Fourteenth Amendment to the U.S. Constitution, after the Civil War, to guarantee the citizenship rights of formerly enslaved people. It says that "all persons born or naturalized in the United States . . . are citizens." Since then, the courts have interpreted it as a guarantee for citizenship to anyone born on American soil. For example, in 1895, Wong Kim Ark visited China. When he tried to reenter, customs refused his claim of citizenship. Though he was born in San Francisco, they thought "his race, language, color and dress" was that of a Chinese person. Because of the Chinese Exclusion Acts, he wasn't allowed to go home but was held in detention. Eventually, the Supreme Court ruled that he was an American citizen because he was born in America (*United States v. Wong Kim Ark* [1897/1989]).

With that context, let's establish some facts. In 2016, four million babies were born in America, including 250,000 to undocumented immigrants. That's down by 36% since 2007. Another 5 million children lived with at least one unauthorized immigrant parent, up from around 4.5 million in 2007 (Passel, Cohn, & Gramlich, 2018).

The main argument against birthright citizenship is cost (see Federation for American Immigration Reform, 2010). Undocumented immigrants tend to be poor. The costs of delivery and care for newborns is millions of dollars per year—costs passed on to taxpayers that strain local, state, and national treasuries. A related concern is that when these children reach 21, they could sponsor their parents to become permanent legal residents, which adds to financial and cultural concerns.

Others say that ending birthright citizenship would reduce the incentive to enter America illegally. This argument seems logical; yet, research on immigrant parents who had a baby in 2009 showed that 61% had been in the U.S. for approximately five years and 31% had been here for at least two years (Passel & Cohn, 2011, p. 12). In other words, they weren't having babies soon after crossing the border, which suggests their primary motivation for migrating is something else—probably employment, as we've discussed. Thus, ending birthright citizenship would have little impact on population flows because getting citizenship for their children isn't the driving force. Alternatively, consider European nations: They may not grant birthright citizenship, yet they have a sizeable—and growing—population of unauthorized immigrants.

Ending birthright citizenship could have other costs. If citizenship were granted at birth only to children of U.S. citizens, the government would have to establish some procedure to check parental status. This would involve research, administrators, and any other expenses related to federal programs. For those who want greater limits on government, this additional governmental reach is troubling.

(Continued)

(Continued)

Furthermore, some research argues that the repeal of birthright citizenship would increase the size of the unauthorized immigrant population and create a large, permanent class of marginalized people, alien to America and to their home countries. Essentially, this group would be stateless, without full citizenship rights anywhere, making them easily exploited. This is the case for the Dominican Republic's "ghost citizens" who became stateless after a 2013 court ruling "stripped nationality from anyone born to undocumented foreign parents or grandparents since 1929." Without official documents, ghost citizens' lives are strictly limited—for example, they can be refused medical treatment and educational opportunities. They can't work in the formal economy, which puts them at risk for exploitation within the underground economy. They can't earn government benefits (e.g., pensions) or file formal complaints if they are victimized. If they travel and are stopped at security checkpoints, they can be detained or forced to leave the country.

Finally, they can't legally get married or have their children's births officially documented, which means their children will also become ghost citizens (Amnesty International, 2015; Fix, 2015; Van Hook, 2010).

These points barely scratch the surface of a complex legal, political, economic, and social issue. Birthright citizenship will probably be a prominent issue in American politics for some time. As you consider evidence and opinions, remember to exercise your critical faculties: Are claims supported by evidence from verifiable sources? Do the arguments come from advocacy or special interest groups that are known to favor or oppose immigration reform? Is the issue being used to frighten voters or demonize immigrants? Is the language needlessly inflammatory or vague? It is easy to get swept up in the emotions of the moment, but remember that this issue affects the lives of literally millions of people and that there's a lot at stake here for both the migrants and for America.

IS CONTEMPORARY ASSIMILATION SEGMENTED?

In Chapter 2, we reviewed the patterns of acculturation and integration that typified the adjustment of Europeans who immigrated to the U. S. before the 1930s. Although their process of adjustment wasn't smooth or simple, these groups eventually acculturated and achieved levels of education and affluence comparable to national norms.

Will contemporary immigrants experience similar success? Will their children and grandchildren rise in the occupational structure to positions similar to those of the dominant group? Will their cultures and languages fade and disappear?

Final answers to these questions must await future developments. In the meantime, there's considerable debate on these issues. Some analysts argue that the success story of the white ethnic groups won't be repeated and that assimilation for contemporary immigrants will be segmented: Some will enjoy success and rise to middle-class prosperity, but others will become mired in the urban underclass, beset by crime, drugs, school failure, and marginal, low-paid, menial jobs (Haller, Portes, & Lynch, 2011, p. 737).

Other analysts find that the traditional perspective on assimilation—particularly Gordon's model of assimilation—continues to provide a useful framework for describing the experience of contemporary immigrants. They argue that these groups will be successful, as earlier immigrants were. Next, we'll review the most important and influential arguments from each side of this debate. Finally, we'll attempt to reach some conclusions about the future of assimilation.

The Case for Segmented Assimilation

This thesis has many advocates, including some of the most important researchers in this area of the social sciences. Here, we'll focus on two of the most important works. The first presents an overview and the second is based on an important, continuing research project on the second generation, the children of contemporary immigrants.

Assimilation Now versus Then

Sociologist Douglas Massey (1995) argued that there are three crucial differences between past (before the 1930s) and contemporary (after the mid-1960s) assimilation experiences. Each calls the traditional perspective into question.

First, the flow of European immigrants to America slowed to a mere trickle after the 1920s because of restrictive legislation, the worldwide depression of the 1930s, and World War II (see Figure 2.2). Immigration in the 1930s, for example, was less than 10% of the flow in the early 1920s. Thus, as the children and grandchildren of the European immigrants Americanized and grew to adulthood in the 1930s and 1940s, few new immigrants fresh from the old country replaced them in the ethnic neighborhoods. European cultural traditions and languages weakened rapidly with the passing of the first generation and the Americanization of their descendants.

It is unlikely, argues Massey, that a similar hiatus will interrupt contemporary immigration. For example, as Figure 9.7 shows, the number of undocumented immigrants remained high even after the economic recession that began in 2007. Massey argues that immigration has become continuous, and as some immigrants (or their descendants) Americanize and rise to success and affluence, new immigrants will replace them and keep the ethnic cultures and languages vital and whole.

Second, the speed and ease of modern transportation and communication will maintain cultural and linguistic diversity. A century ago, European immigrants could maintain contact with the old country only by mail, and many had no realistic expectation of ever returning. Modern immigrants, in contrast, can return to their homes in a day or less and use telephones, e-mail, and the Internet to stay in intimate contact with the family and friends they left behind. Thus, the cultures of modern immigrants can be kept vital and whole in ways that weren't available (or even imagined) 100 years ago.

Third, and perhaps most important, contemporary immigrants face an economy and a labor market that are vastly different from those faced by European immigrants of the 19th and early 20th centuries. The latter group generally rose in the class system as the economy shifted from manufacturing to service (see Figure 4.3). Today, rates of upward mobility have decreased, and the children of contemporary immigrants—especially those whose parents are undocumented—face myriad challenges in securing access to a quality education (Massey, 1995).

For the European immigrants a century ago, assimilation meant a gradual rise to middle-class status and suburban comfort, a process often accomplished in three generations. Massey fears that assimilation today is segmented and that a large percentage of the descendants of contemporary immigrants—especially many of the "peasant immigrants," such as some Hispanic groups, Haitians, and other people of color—face permanent membership in a growing underclass population and continuing marginalization and powerlessness.

The Second Generation

An analysis of the second generation of recent immigrant groups (Haller et al., 2011) also found support for the segmented assimilation model. The researchers interviewed the children of immigrants in the Miami and San Diego areas at three different times—in the early 1990s (when they were at an average age of 14), three years later, and 10 years later, when the respondents were at an average age of 24. The sample was large (more than 5,000 respondents at the beginning) and representative of the second generation in the two metropolitan areas where the study was conducted. This is an important study because its longitudinal design permits the researchers to track these children of immigrants in precise detail.

FIGURE 9.9 ■ Paths of Immigrant Mobility across Generations

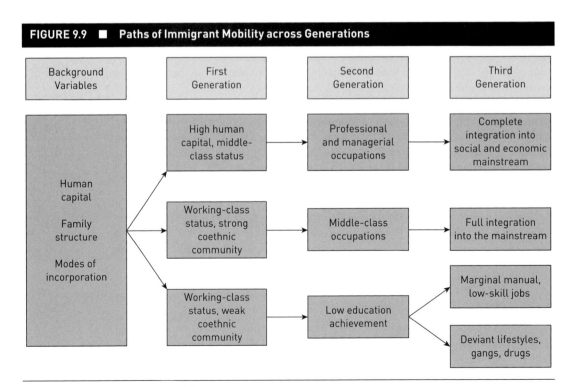

Source: Based on Haller et al. (2011, p. 738).

Haller and colleagues (2011) argue, consistent with Massey (1995) and with many of the points made previously in this book, that contemporary immigrants face a number of barriers to successful adaptation, including racial prejudice (because the huge majority of the population is nonwhite), a labor market sharply split between a primary sector that requires high levels of education and a secondary sector that is low paid and insecure, and a widespread criminal subculture (based on gangs and drug sales) that provides a sometimes-attractive alternative to the conventional pursuit of success through education.

Whether immigrants and their descendants can overcome these obstacles depends decisively on three factors (listed at the far left of Figure 9.9). Figure 9.9 also depicts several different projected pathways of mobility across the generations. Immigrants who arrive with high levels of human capital enter the primary labor market, and their descendants generally have entered the economic and social mainstream by the third generation (see the top row of Figure 9.9). The descendants of immigrants with lower levels of human capital can succeed if they benefit from strong families and strong co-ethnic communities that reinforce parental discipline. This pathway,

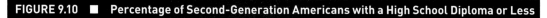

FIGURE 9.10 ■ Percentage of Second-Generation Americans with a High School Diploma or Less

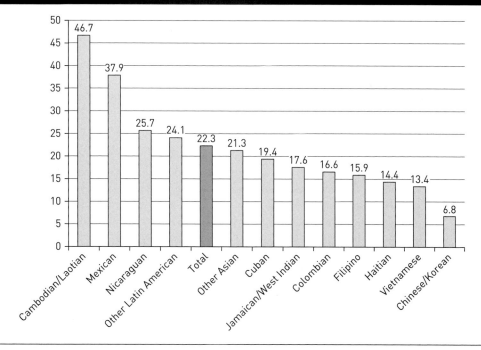

Source: Based on Haller et al. (2011, p. 742).

Notes: Chinese and Korean Americans were combined, as were Cambodian and Laotian Americans, because of similar patterns and to create groups large enough for statistical analysis.

Other Latin American consists mostly of Salvadoran and Guatemalan Americans.

Other Asian is a diverse group that includes many nationalities.

FIGURE 9.11   ■   **Percentage of Second-Generation Men Incarcerated**

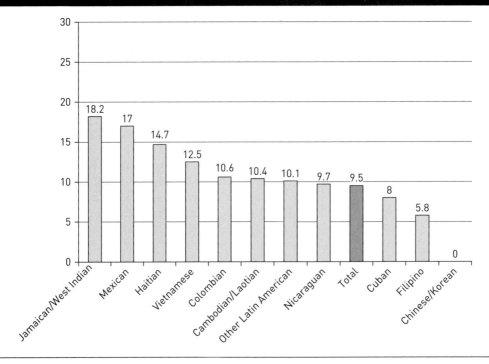

Source: Based on Haller et al. (2011, p. 742).

Notes: Chinese and Korean Americans were combined, as were Cambodian and Laotian Americans, because of similar patterns and to create groups large enough for statistical analysis.

Other Latin American consists mostly of Salvadoran and Guatemalan Americans.

depicted in the middle row of Figure 9.9, also results in full acculturation and integration in the economic mainstream by the third generation. The bottom row of the figure outlines a very different pathway for a large percentage of some contemporary immigrant groups. The mode of incorporation for these immigrants doesn't place them in a strong co-ethnic community. Further, they may experience weaker family structures, sometimes because of their undocumented status or because the family is split between the U. S. and their home country. The result is lower educational achievement and economic marginalization and, potentially, assimilation into gangs, drug subcultures, and similar groups.

The researchers present a variety of evidence to support segmented assimilation theory. For example, the second generations of different groups have different experiences in school, different income levels, and different interactions with the criminal justice system. Figure 9.10 shows some of these differences and illustrates the large variations in the percentage of second generation individuals (by ethnic group) who don't pursue education beyond high school. Figure 9.11 shows patterns of incarceration by group.

These patterns aren't random. Rather, they reflect large differences in the human capital of the immigrant generation and variations in modes of incorporation (especially in terms of legal status and racial prejudice). They show that large percentages of the second (and third and later) generations of some groups are likely to assimilate into low-status, marginalized, or deviant sectors of American society in direct contradiction to the patterns predicted by some versions of traditional assimilation theory.

Another important recent study reinforces some of these points. Sociologists Telles and Ortiz (2008) studied a sample of Mexican Americans who were interviewed in 1965 and again in 2000. They found evidence of strong movements toward acculturation and integration on some dimensions (e.g., language) but not on others. Even fourth-generation members of their sample continued to live in "the barrio" and marry within the group and didn't reach economic parity with Anglos. The authors single out institutional discrimination (e.g., underfunding of public schools that serve Mexican American neighborhoods) as a primary cause of the continuing separation, a point consistent with Massey's (1995) conclusion regarding the decreasing rates of upward mobility in American society.

The Case for Traditional Assimilation Theory

Other recent studies come to a very different conclusion regarding the second generation: They are generally rising relative to their parents. This contradicts the segmented assimilation thesis and supports traditional assimilation theories. These studies (e.g., Alba & Nee, 2003; Bean & Stevens, 2003; Kasinitz et al., 2008; White & Glick, 2009) argue that contemporary assimilation will ultimately follow the same course that it followed for European immigrant groups 100 years ago, as described in Gordon's theory (Chapter 2).

For example, two studies (Alba & Nee, 2003; Bean & Stevens, 2003) find that most contemporary immigrant groups are acculturating and integrating at the usual three-generation pace. Those groups that appear to be lagging behind this pace (notably Mexicans) may take as many as four to five generations, but their descendants will eventually find their way into the primary job market and the cultural mainstream.

Studies of acculturation show that immigrants' values become Americanized and that English language proficiency grows with time of residence and generation (Bean & Stevens, 2003, p. 168). We discussed some of these patterns in Chapter 7 (see Figure 7.8 and Table 7.4).

In terms of structural integration, contemporary immigrant groups may be narrowing the income gap over time, although many groups (e.g., Dominicans, Mexicans, Haitians, and Vietnamese) are disadvantaged by low levels of human capital at the start (Bean & Stevens, 2003, p. 142). Figures 9.12 and 9.13 illustrate this process with respect to wage differentials between Mexican and white non-Hispanic men and women of various generations and levels of education. (As you look at these figures, remember that complete income equality with non-Hispanic whites would be indicated if the bar touched the 100% line at the top of the graph.)

Looking first at all men workers (the leftmost bars in Figure 9.12), it is evident that recent Mexican immigrants earned a little less than half of what white men earned.

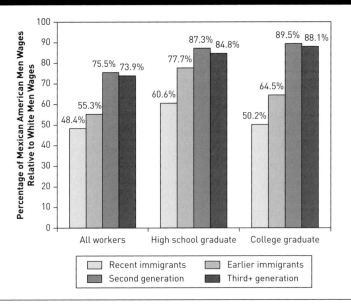

FIGURE 9.12 ■ Wage Differential of Mexican American Workers Relative to Whites (Men)

Source: Bean and Stevens (2003, p. 139).

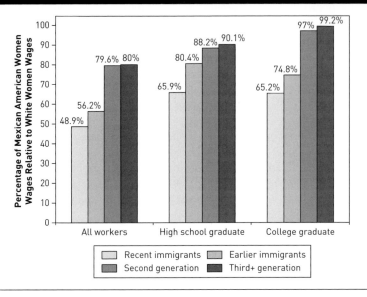

FIGURE 9.13 ■ Wage Differentials of Mexican American Workers Relative to Whites (Women)

Source: Bean and Stevens (2003, p. 139).

The difference in income is smaller for earlier immigrants and even smaller for second and third generations of Mexicans. Separating out men with high school diplomas (the middle bars) and college degrees (the rightmost bars), the wage differential is generally lower for the more-educated members of each generation. That is, income equality tends to increase over the generations and as education increases.

However, note that third-generation men don't rise relative to their parents' generation. This contradicts the view that assimilation will proceed in a linear, stepwise fashion across the generations and is reminiscent of the findings of Telles and Ortiz (2008) noted earlier. For women (Figure 9.13), the wage differential also shrinks as the generations pass and the level of education increases. Note that for third-generation, college-educated women, the wage differential shrinks virtually to zero, indicating integration on this variable (at least compared with dominant group women).

Another study (Taylor et al., 2013) used census data to compare immigrants and their children and generally found that the latter rose in the society relative to the former. The second generation had higher incomes and levels of education and lower levels of poverty. For example, for Hispanics, median household income rose from $34,600 for the immigrant generation to $48,400 for the second generation. Levels of education showed a similar upgrade: Almost half the immigrant generation had less than a high school education compared with only 17% of the second generation. The study found similar but less dramatic improvements for Asians, largely because of the high levels of human capital brought by the immigrant generation (e.g., 50% had college degrees).

These patterns generally support the traditional perspective on assimilation. Income and education generally improve by generation, although the pattern isn't linear or complete. The second and third generations, on average, are moving toward the economic mainstream, although they don't close the gap completely. Bean and Stevens (2003) conclude that the patterns in Figures 9.12 and 9.13 are substantially consistent with the three-generation model. The assimilation trajectory of Mexican Americans and other recent immigrant groups isn't toward the urban poor, the underclass, or the disenfranchised, disconnected, and marginalized. Assimilation isn't segmented but is substantially repeating the experiences of the European groups on which Gordon (1964) based his theory.

Summary

How can we reconcile the directly contradictory conclusions supported by the segmented and traditional perspectives on assimilation? In large part, this debate concerns the type of evidence and judgments about how much weight to give various facts and trends. On one hand, Massey's (1995) points about the importance of the postindustrial economy, declining opportunities for less-educated workers, and the neglect that's typical of inner-city schools are well taken. Other studies provide evidence to support the segmented assimilation thesis.

Yet, even the least-educated immigrant groups have found economic niches where they and their families manage long enough for their children and grandchildren to rise in the social structure, a pattern that's been at the core of the American immigrant experience for almost two centuries.

This debate will continue, and new evidence and interpretations will appear. Ultimately, however, these disputes may continue until immigration stops (which is very

QUESTIONS FOR REFLECTION

14. What are the arguments and evidence for the segmented assimilation model and for the traditional assimilation theory?

15. Which of these perspectives is more convincing? Why?

unlikely to happen, as Massey points out) and the fate of the descendants of the last immigrant groups is measured.

RECENT IMMIGRATION IN HISTORICAL AND GLOBAL CONTEXT

The current wave of immigration to the U. S. is part of a centuries-old process that spans the world. Underlying this immense and complex population movement are the powerful forces of continuing industrialization, economic development, and globalization. The United States and other advanced industrial nations are the centers of growth in the global economy, and immigrants flow to the areas of greater opportunity. In the 19th century, the population moved largely from Europe to the Western Hemisphere. Over the past 50 years, the movement has been from the Global South to the Global North. This pattern reflects the simple geography of industrialization and opportunity and the fact that the more-industrialized nations are in the Northern Hemisphere.

The U. S. has been the world's dominant economic, political, and cultural power for much of the past 100 years, and the preferred destination of most immigrants. Newcomers from around the world continue the collective, social nature of past population movements (Chapter 2). The direction of their travels reflects contemporary global inequalities: Labor continues to flow from the less-industrialized nations to the more-industrialized nations. The direction of this flow isn't accidental or coincidental. It is determined by the differential rates of industrialization and modernization across the world. Immigration contributes to the wealth and affluence of the more-industrialized societies and particularly to the dominant groups and elite classes of those societies.

The immigrant flow is also a response to the dynamics of globalization, particularly since the 1980s (Sen & Mamdouh, 2008). The current era of globalization has been guided by the doctrine of *neoliberalism*, or free trade, which urges nations to eliminate barriers to the movement of goods and capital. The North American Free Trade Agreement (NAFTA), mentioned on several occasions in this book, is an example of a neoliberal policy. These policies open less-industrialized nations such as Mexico to consumer goods manufactured and controlled by large transnational corporations. These corporations frequently undersell goods made in those countries, which often drives small-scale local farmers and manufacturers out of business.

Additionally, international agencies (such as the International Monetary Fund [IMF]) that regulate the global economy put pressure on nations to reduce the size of their governmental sector. This often means that a country's budget for health and education is slashed and that services once controlled and subsidized by the government (e.g., water, electricity) are sold to private businesses, which then raise prices beyond what many people can afford. The combined result of these global forces is an increasingly vulnerable population in less-industrialized nations, unable to provide for themselves, educate their children, or afford the simplest of daily necessities.

Americans generally see immigrants as individuals acting on their own free will and, often, illegally. ("They chose to come to America and break the law.") However, that picture changes when we see immigration as the result of these powerful global economic and political forces. While domestic economies and social systems crumble, the victims of neoliberal globalization are left with few choices: They cross borders into the U. S. and to other advanced industrial nations. They do so illegally, if they have to, because "it is the best choice to achieve a dignified life—if not for themselves, then for their children" (Sen & Mamdouh, 2008, p. 7).

When viewed through the lens of globalization, it is clear that this population movement will continue because immigrants simply have no choice. It is unlikely that they can be stopped by further militarization of the border or by building bigger and taller walls. Historically, immigrants come to the U. S. in such numbers because the alternatives in their home countries are unacceptable or nonexistent.

This perspective suggests that the tendency to reject, demonize, and criminalize immigrants is self-defeating. Punitive, militaristic policies won't stem the flow of people from the Global South to the Global North. Globalization, in its neoliberal form, is incomplete: It allows for the free movement of goods and capital but not of people. It benefits transnational corporations and the mega-businesses that produce consumer goods but victimizes the vulnerable citizens of the less-industrialized nations. As long as these forms of globalization hold, the population pressure from south to north will continue.

NEW IMMIGRANTS AND OLD ISSUES

In this chapter, we focused on some issues raised by high levels of immigration since the 1960s. As we discuss, debate, and consider these issues, we need to remember a fundamental fact about modern American society: The issues of the traditional minority groups—African Americans and Native Americans, for example—haven't been resolved. As we saw in earlier chapters, these groups have been a part of American society from the beginning, but they remain, in many ways, distant from achieving complete equality and integration.

Many of the current issues facing these groups relate to class and race. The urban underclass is disproportionately made up of people of color and continues to have marginal access to education and job opportunities, decent housing, and good health care when compared with the dominant Anglo society. While it is probably true that America is more open and tolerant than ever before, we must not mistake a decline in blatant racism or a reduction in overt discrimination with its demise. As you've seen, abundant evidence shows that racism and discrimination haven't declined but have merely changed form and that the patterns of exclusion and deprivation sustained in the past continue today.

Similarly, gender issues and sexism remain on the national agenda. Blatant sexism and overt discrimination against women are probably at historic lows, but, again, we cannot mistake change for disappearance. Most important, minority women remain the victims of a double jeopardy and are among the most vulnerable and exploited segments of society. Many women in the new immigrant groups are in similarly vulnerable positions.

Some societal trends exacerbate these problems of exclusion and continuing prejudice and sexism. For example, the continuing shift in subsistence technology from manufacturing to the service sector privileges groups that, in the past and today, have had access to education. The urban underclass consists disproportionately of groups that were excluded from education in the past and have unequal access in the present.

New immigrant groups have abundant problems and need to find ways to pursue their self-interests in their new society. Some segments of these groups—the well-educated professionals seeking to advance their careers in the world's most advanced economy—will be much more likely to find ways to avoid the harshest forms of American rejection and exclusion. Similarly, the members of the traditional minority groups that have gained access to education and middle-class status will enjoy more opportunities than previous generations could have imagined. (As you've seen, however, their middle-class position will be more precarious than their dominant-group counterparts.)

Will we become a society in which ethnic and racial groups are permanently segmented by class, with the more favored members enjoying a higher (if partial) level of acceptance while other group members languish in permanent exclusion and segmentation? What does it mean to be an American? What *should* it mean?

Main Points

- Since the mid-1960s, immigrants have been coming to America at nearly record rates. Most of these immigrant groups have co-ethnics who were in the U. S. for years, but others are new Americans.

- Recent immigrant groups include Hispanics, non-Hispanic Caribbeans, Asians, Arabs and Middle Easterners, and Africans. Some are driven by economic needs, others are political refugees, and some are highly educated. All of these groups face multiple issues, including racism, institutionalized discrimination, and a changing U.S. economy. Arab Americans remain a special target for hate crimes and for security concerns.

- Contemporary immigrants experience three different modes of incorporation: the primary labor market, the secondary labor market, and the enclave. The pathway of each group is strongly influenced by the amount of human capital they bring, their race, the attitude of the larger society, and many other factors.

- Relations between immigrants and the larger society are animated by a number of issues, including the relative costs and benefits of immigration, concerns about undocumented immigrants, and the speed of assimilation. One important issue currently being debated by social scientists is whether assimilation for new Americans will be segmented or whether it will ultimately follow the pathway established by immigrant groups from Europe in the 19th and 20th centuries.

- Segmented assimilation theory, in contrast to traditional assimilation theory, predicts that not all immigrants will rise to the middle class and that some will become part of a permanent, marginalized underclass. At present, evidence supports both theories.

- Prominent immigration issues include relative costs and benefits of immigration, the fate of undocumented immigrants, and the situation of DREAMers. Immigration is thought to be a generally positive force in the economy. DREAMers are undocumented immigrants who were brought to the U. S. as children. An executive order in 2012 allows DREAMers who meet certain criteria to stay in the U. S. for a renewable two-year term without fear of deportation. In 2017, the Trump administration ended it.

Applying Concepts

Listed below are five nations, the number of immigrants each sent to the U. S. in 2012, and the level of literacy for each. How familiar are you with these new Americans? Can you identify the geographical region from which each group comes and the most common religious affiliation in its homeland? Also, what's your best guess as to whether immigrants from each group are above or below national averages for education, income, and poverty levels?

Nation of Origin	Number of Immigrants, 2012	Percentage Literate, Home Nation	Region of the World	Most Common Religion	Percentage with a College Degree or More	Median Household Income	Percentage of Families in Poverty
Nepal	10,198	57			__ Above __ Below	__ Above __ Below	__ Above __ Below
Ghana	10,592	72			__ Above __ Below	__ Above __ Below	__ Above __ Below
Guyana	5,683	92			__ Above __ Below	__ Above __ Below	__ Above __ Below
Peru	12,609	90			__ Above __ Below	__ Above __ Below	__ Above __ Below
Ukraine	7,642	100			__ Above __ Below	__ Above __ Below	__ Above __ Below

See the end of this section for the answers.

Review Questions

1. What differences exist among these new Americans in terms of their motivations for coming to America? What are the implications of these various factors for their reception and adjustment to the United States?

2. Compare the Hispanic and Asian immigrant groups discussed in this chapter. What important differences and similarities can you identify in terms of modes of incorporation and human capital? What are the implications of these differences for the experiences of these groups?

3. Compare Arab and Middle Eastern immigrant groups with those from the Caribbean. Which group is more diverse? What differences exist in their patterns of adjustment and assimilation? Why do these patterns exist?

4. Compare African immigrants with immigrants from other groups. How do they differ? What are the implications of these differences for their adjustment to the larger society?

5. What, in your opinion, are the most important issues facing the U. S. in terms of immigration and assimilation? How are these issues playing out in your community? What are the implications of these issues for the future of America?

6. Will assimilation for contemporary immigrants be segmented? After examining the evidence and arguments presented by different sides, and using information from this and previous chapters, which side of the debate seems more credible? Why? What are the implications of this debate? What will the U. S. look like in the future if assimilation is segmented? How will the future change if assimilation follows the traditional pathway? Which of these scenarios is more desirable for immigrant groups? For society as a whole? For various segments of U.S. society (e.g., employers, labor unions, African Americans, consumers, the college educated, the urban underclass)?

Answers to Applying Concepts

Nation of Origin	Number of Immigrants, 2012	Percentage Literate, Home Nation	Region of the World	Most Common Religion	Percentage with a College Degree or More	Median Household Income	Percentage of Families in Poverty
Nepal	10,198	57	South Asia	Hindu (81%)	X Above Below	Above X Below	X Above Below
Ghana	10,592	72	Western Africa	Christian (71%)	X Above Below	Above X Below*	X Above Below
Guyana	5,683	92	Northern South America	Christian (56%), Hindu (28%)	Above X Below	X Above Below	Equal

Nation of Origin	Number of Immigrants, 2012	Percentage Literate, Home Nation	Region of the World	Most Common Religion	Percentage with a College Degree or More	Median Household Income	Percentage of Families in Poverty
Peru	12,609	90	Western South America	Catholic (81%)	Above X Below**	Above X Below	X Above Below
Ukraine	7,642	100	Eastern Europe	Eastern Orthodox (77%)	X Above Below	X Above Below	Above X Below

Sources: Number of immigrants (U.S. Department of Homeland Security, 2012); percentage literate and dominant religion (Central Intelligence Agency, 2013); education, income, and poverty (U.S. Census Bureau, 2013).

*The Ghanaian median household income is only $40 less than the national average.

**The difference is less than 1%.

Internet Learning Resources

SAGE edge™ offers teachers and students easy-to-use resources for review, study, and further exploration. See **http://edge.sagepub.com/diversity6e**

10

MINORITY GROUPS AND U.S. SOCIETY

Themes, Patterns, and the Future

Throughout the last nine chapters, we've analyzed ideas and theories about dominant–minority relations, examined the historical and contemporary situations of U.S. minority groups, and surveyed different dominant–minority situations around the world. Now it's time to reexamine our major themes and concepts and determine what conclusions we can derive from our analysis.

However, our understandings are limited by who we are, where we come from, and what we've experienced. Our ability to imagine the realities faced by others is never perfect, and how we see the world depends very much on where we are situated in the social structure.

If we hope to understand the forces that have created dominant–minority relationships in the U. S. and around the world, we must find ways to surpass the limitations of our individual experiences. This will require us to face the ugly realities of the past and present. We believe that the information and ideas developed in this book can help liberate our sociological imaginations from the narrow confines of our own experiences and perspectives.

As we look backward to the past and forward to the future, it seems appropriate to paraphrase historian Oscar Handlin (1951): "Once I thought to write a history of the minority groups in America. Then, I discovered that the minority groups were American history" (p. 3).

THE IMPORTANCE OF SUBSISTENCE TECHNOLOGY

One of the most important sociological ideas we've developed is that large social, political, and economic forces shape dominant–minority relations, and they change as these broad characteristics change. To understand the evolution of America's minority groups is to understand the history of the United States, from the earliest colonial settlement to the modern megalopolis. As you've seen throughout the book, these same broad forces have left their imprint on many societies around the world.

Subsistence technology is the most basic force shaping a society and the relationships between dominant and minority groups in that society. In the colonial United States, minority relations were bent to the demands of a land-hungry, labor-intensive agrarian technology, and the early relationships between Africans, Europeans, and Native Americans flowed from the colonists' desire to control land and labor. By the mid-1800s, two centuries after Jamestown was founded, the same dynamics that had enslaved African Americans and nearly annihilated Native Americans made a minority group out of Mexican Americans.

The agrarian era ended in the 19th century as the new technologies of the industrial revolution increased the productivity of the economy and eventually changed every aspect of life in the U. S. The paternalistic, oppressive systems used to control the labor of minority groups in the agrarian era gave way to competitive systems of group relations. These newer systems evolved from more rigid forms to more fluid forms as industrialization and urbanization progressed.

As the United States developed, new minority groups were created, and old minority groups, including women and LGBTQIA[1] people, were transformed. Rapid industrialization, combined with the opportunities available on the frontier, made the U. S. an attractive destination for immigrants from Europe, Asia, Latin America, and other parts of the world. Immigrants helped farm the Great Plains, mine the riches of the West, and, above all, supply the armies of labor needed by industrialization.

The descendants of European immigrants benefited from the continuing industrialization of the economy, rising slowly in the social class structure as the economy grew and matured. Immigrants from Asia and Latin America were not so fortunate. Chinese and Japanese Americans survived in ethnic enclaves on the fringes of the mainstream society, and Mexican Americans and Puerto Ricans supplied low-paid manual labor for the rural and the urban economies. For much of the 20th century, Asian and Hispanic Americans were barred from higher-paid jobs and widespread access to dominant group institutions.

The racial minority groups, particularly African Americans, Mexican Americans, and Puerto Ricans, entered the urban working class after European American ethnic groups began to move up in the occupational structure, at a time when the supply of manual, unskilled jobs was dwindling. Thus, the processes that allowed upward mobility for European Americans failed to work for other racial minority groups, who confronted urban poverty and bankrupt cities in addition to the continuing barriers of racial prejudice and institutional discrimination.

Immigration to the U. S. has been quite high for the past several decades. It has supplied our nation with highly educated professionals to help staff the postindustrial economy as well as undocumented immigrants who work in the secondary labor market, the enclaves, and the irregular economy. This stream of people has evoked the usual American nativism and racism, along with intense debates—in the social sciences and in the general public—about the cost and benefits of the immigrants and their ultimate place in American society.

We can only speculate about what the future holds, but the emerging information-based, high-tech society is unlikely to offer many opportunities to people with lower levels of education and few occupational skills. It seems highly likely that, at least for the near future, a substantial percentage of racial and colonized minority groups and some recent immigrant groups will be participating in the mainstream economy at lower levels than will the dominant group, the descendants of the European immigrants, and the more advantaged recent immigrant groups. This outcome would be consistent with the segmented assimilation thesis discussed in Chapter 9. Upgraded urban educational systems, job training programs, and other community development programs might alter the grim scenario of continuing exclusion, but current public opinion on matters of race and discrimination makes creation of such programs unlikely.

The perpetuation of the status quo will bar a significant percentage of the population from participating fully in the mainstream economy. Those segments of the African, Hispanic, and Asian American communities currently mired in the urban underclass will continue to compete with some of the newer immigrants for jobs in the low-wage, secondary labor market or in alternative opportunity structures, including crime.

Shifts in subsistence technology also helped transform gender relations and women's lives in particular. In the postindustrial era, women are heavily involved in the paid labor force and, because of the concerted, long-term efforts of the feminist movements, enjoy more opportunities and choices than ever before. However, as we've documented, women still face gender gaps in wages, "glass ceilings," sexual harassment, and other gender-related challenges and limitations. Women today are less constrained by institutional barriers, stereotypes, and presumptions of inferiority compared with the past. However, men (as a group) still reap "invisible privileges," from intimate family relations to corporate boardrooms. Globally, women's status continues to depend heavily on subsistence technology, and women in more agrarian societies face especially formidable barriers to gender equality.

As with other minority groups, non-heterosexuals have benefited from the greater acceptance and inclusion associated with more educated, more advanced industrial societies. The relative anonymity of urban spaces provided opportunities for LGBTQIA people to find one another, develop a sense of community, and form organizations to fight discrimination based on sexual orientation. In recent decades, after considerable struggle, hard work, and activism, LGBTQIA Americans experienced several triumphs, including the legalization of same-gender marriage and the ability to openly serve in the military. However, new political leadership, especially at the state and federal levels, has overturned prior laws and policies that gave LGBTQIA people greater equality as well as protection under the law. Much work remains to be done for LGBTQIA people to achieve full equality, especially in the areas of civil rights and discrimination.

THE IMPORTANCE OF THE CONTACT SITUATION, GROUP COMPETITION, AND POWER

Throughout this book, we've stressed the importance of the contact situation—the conditions under which the minority group and dominant group first come into contact with each other. Blauner's distinction between immigrant and colonized minority groups is fundamental, a distinction so basic that it helps clarify minority group situations centuries after the initial contact period. In Part 3, we used Blauner's distinction as an organizing principle and covered American minority groups in approximate order from "colonized" to "immigrant." The groups covered first (African Americans and Native Americans) are clearly at a greater disadvantage in contemporary society than are the groups covered last (especially Asian immigrants with their high levels of human capital) and the white ethnic groups (covered in Chapter 2).

For example, prejudice, racism, and discrimination against African Americans remain formidable forces in contemporary America, even though they may have softened into more subtle forms. In contrast, prejudice and discrimination against European American groups such as Irish, Italian, and Polish Americans have nearly disappeared today (with the exception of anti-Semitism), even though they were quite formidable just a few generations ago.

In the same way, contemporary immigrant groups that are nonwhite and bring few resources and low levels of human capital (e.g., Haitians) may experience segmented assimilation and find themselves in situations resembling those of colonized minority groups. Contemporary immigrant groups that are at the opposite end of the continuum (e.g., Asian Indians) are more likely to approximate the experiences of white ethnics and find themselves in some version of middle-class suburbia.

Noel's hypothesis states that if three conditions—ethnocentrism, competition, and a differential in power—are present in the contact situation, ethnic or racial stratification will result. The relevance of ethnocentrism is largely limited to the actual contact situation, but the other two concepts help clarify the changes occurring after initial contact.

We've examined many instances in which group competition—or even the threat of competition—increased prejudice and led to greater discrimination and more repression. Recall, for example, the opposition of the labor movement (dominated by European American ethnic groups) to Chinese immigrants. The anti-Chinese campaign led to the Chinese Exclusion Act of 1882, the first significant restriction on immigration to the United States. There are parallels between campaigns for exclusion in the past and current ideas about ending or curtailing immigration. Clearly, some part of the current opposition to immigration is motivated by a sense of threat and the fear that immigrants are a danger not only to jobs and the economy but also to the cultural integrity of American society.

Noel's third variable—differential in power—determines the outcome of the initial contact situation and which group becomes dominant and which becomes minority. Following the first contact, the superior power of the dominant group helps it sustain the minority group's inferior position.

Minority groups, by definition, have fewer power resources, but they characteristically use what they have to improve their situations. Improvements in the situations of American minority groups since the middle of the 20th century have been due in large part to the fact that they finally acquired some power resources of their own (especially African Americans, who typically led the way in protest and demands for change). For example, one important source of power for the civil rights movement in the South during the 1950s and 1960s was the growth of African American voting strength in the North. After World War II, the African American electorate became too sizable to ignore, and its political power helped pressure the federal government to act and pass the legislation that ended the Jim Crow era.

Minority status being what it is, however, each of the groups we've discussed (except for the white ethnic groups) still controls relatively few resources and is limited in its ability to pursue its self-interests. Many of these limitations are economic and related to social class; many minority groups simply lack the resources to finance political campaigns for reform or to exert significant political pressure. Other limitations include small group size (e.g., Asian American groups), language barriers (e.g., many Hispanic American groups), and divided loyalties within the group (e.g., Native Americans separated by tribal allegiances).

At any rate, the relative powerlessness of minority groups today is a legacy of the contact situations that created these groups in the first place. Generally, colonized groups are at a greater power disadvantage than immigrant groups. Contact situations set agendas for group relations that continue to exert influence centuries after the initial meeting.

Given everything that we've examined in this book, it's obvious that competition and differences in power resources will continue to shape intergroup relations (including relations between minority groups themselves) well into the future. Because they are so basic and consequential, jobs will continue to be primary objects of competition, but plenty of other issues will divide the nation. Included on this divisive list will be debates about crime and the criminal justice system, welfare reform, national health care policy, school integration, bilingual education, immigration policy, and multicultural school curricula.

These and other public issues will continue to separate us along ethnic and racial lines because those lines have become so deeply embedded in the economy, in politics, in our schools and neighborhoods, and in virtually every nook and cranny of American society. These deep divisions reflect fundamental realities about who gets what in the United States, and they will continue to reflect the distribution of power and stimulate competition along group lines for generations to come.

Of course, some of our most important concepts do not fit all dominant–minority group situations. For example, there is no contact situation for women and men (or other gender-identified people)—there's no time in history when they didn't exist together. Similarly, it's impossible to identify a contact situation between people of different sexual orientations. However, researchers have documented persistent patterns of inequality, marginalization, and denigration and both women and LGBTQIA people seem to fit Blauner's category of colonized minority groups.

For women, highly visible physical markers of group membership help maintain the system of oppression, similar to that of racial minority groups. For LGBTQIA people, the dynamics of social visibility are subtler and more varied. However, as anyone who has "come out" can attest, visibility can bring fundamental changes in personal relationships, occupational opportunities, and other areas of life.

Blauner's hypothesis may not be literally applicable to women and LGBTQIA people, but Noel's concepts of power and competition are central to both group situations. Both have had to organize, acquire resources, and confront the bastions of privilege in the streets and in the courtrooms to gain greater equality. Resistance to their efforts has been constant and formidable, even though the long-term trend has been toward inclusion (even with recent setbacks).

For women, American society made a formal (and, many would argue, partial and unfulfilled) commitment to equality many decades ago. The struggle for acceptance and an end to stigma and marginalization continues for people who are LGBTQIA.

The U. S. is currently embroiled in a deeply felt controversy over whether that commitment to equality should be extended to them, a struggle that reminds us that competition can be symbolic and cultural and independent from the distribution of resources, such as jobs, income, and political representation.

THE IMPORTANCE OF INTERSECTIONALITY

All too often, and this book is probably no exception, dominant and minority groups are seen as somewhat undifferentiated. Although overgeneralizations are sometimes difficult to avoid, we want to stress again the diversity within each of the groups we've examined. Minority group members vary from one another by age, gender, region of residence, level of education, urban versus rural residence, political ideology, religion, and in other ways. The experience of one segment of the group (e.g., college-educated, fourth-generation, native-born Chinese American women) may bear little resemblance to the experience of another (e.g., undocumented Chinese immigrant men with less than a high school education). The problems of some members may not be the problems of others.

One way we've tried to highlight the importance of this diversity is by stressing gender differentiation within each minority group. Studies of minority groups by U.S. social scientists have focused predominantly on men (e.g., black men, Asian men); they've studied minority women's experiences much less often. The groups we've examined have strong patriarchal traditions. As a result, women, regardless of race or ethnicity, have had much less access to leadership roles and higher-status positions compared to men. Thus, women generally have subordinate status, even within their racial and ethnic groups. Researchers are only beginning to fully explore the ways that minority group women's experiences are different from and similar to those of minority group men and dominant group women.

Generalizations about all women or all men seldom conform to reality. Feminist organizations working for gender equality have needed to adopt an intersectional approach and consider variations in girls' and women's experiences as they relate to race, ethnicity, class, sexual orientation, age, religion, disability, and other social factors. Although mainstream feminists increasingly frame issues in more inclusive terms, not everyone who might benefit from feminist activism feels that the movement represents them or their concerns. Because gender inequality, including inequality for people who identify outside the gender binary (e.g., transgender, gender fluid) remains a persistent problem worldwide, the extent to which feminist efforts incorporate an intersectional approach will undoubtedly shape the relative success of the movement domestically and globally.

Likewise, LGBTQIA individuals vary considerably by race, ethnicity, social class, gender, age, religion, and other factors. Compared with straight, white couples who are both employed, partnered white men tend to have higher household incomes because men, on average, earn more than women for the same job. Conversely, the household income for two men of minority racial backgrounds tends to be lower because people of color tend to earn less, on average, than whites. Two women of any background will tend to mirror the patterns of inequality discussed in earlier chapters. Moreover, gay liberation movements have faced challenges not unlike those of feminist groups, in that their efforts to alter public policy often privilege white, middle-class concerns over other issues.

Gender, class, race, ethnicity, and sexual orientation can intersect to create especially heavy burdens for some people. As we have seen, women of every minority group have had to take the least-desirable, lowest-status positions available in the economy, often while raising children and attending to other family needs. They have been expected to support other members of their families, kinship groups, and communities, often sacrificing their own self-interests for the welfare of others. At the other end of the continuum, affluent, white, Anglo, heterosexual, Protestant men have enjoyed—and continue to enjoy—a system of privilege and advantage so pervasive that it's often invisible, especially to its beneficiaries. Likewise, a working-class man of color and an upper-class Anglo man may have similarities based on their gender, but class and race shape their experiences differently. Similar comparisons can be made for almost any pair of Americans, which highlights the need to recognize the differences in our society as well as people's diverse realities.

ASSIMILATION AND PLURALISM

It's fair to conclude that some of the traditional or "melting pot" views of assimilation do not adequately explain the diversity and complexity of minority group experiences in the U. S. For example, there is little evidence to support the idea that assimilation is a linear, inevitable process. European immigrants fit that model better than other groups, but as the ethnic revival of the 1960s demonstrated, assimilation and ethnic identity can take surprising turns.

Also without support is the belief that a simple, ordered relationship exists between the various stages of assimilation: acculturation, integration into public institutions, integration into the private sector, and so forth. We've seen that some groups integrated before they acculturated, others have become more committed to their ethnic or racial identity over time, and still others have been acculturated for generations but aren't any closer to full integration. New expressions of ethnicity come and go, and minority groups emerge, combine, and recombine in unexpected and seemingly unpredictable ways. The 1960s saw a reassertion of ethnicity and loyalty to old identities among some groups, even as other groups developed new coalitions and invented new ethnic identities (e.g., pan-tribalism among Native Americans). No simple or linear view of assimilation can begin to make sense of the array of minority group experiences.

Indeed, the very desirability of assimilation has been subject to debate. Since the 1960s, many people in minority groups have questioned the wisdom of becoming a part of a sociocultural structure built by the systematic exploitation of minority groups. Pluralistic themes increased in prominence as the commitment of the larger society to racial equality faltered. Virtually every minority group, including women and LGBTQIAs, proclaimed the authenticity of its own experiences, its own culture, and its own version of history, separate from but as valid as those of the dominant groups. From what might have seemed like a nation on the verge of integration in the 1950s (at least for white ethnic groups), America evolved into what, in the 1960s, might have seemed like a Tower of Babel for some people—especially white Americans. That time in history shattered the consensus that assimilation was the best solution and the most sensible goal for all of America's groups (if such a consensus ever really existed).

Let's review the state of acculturation and integration in the U. S. on a group-by-group basis:

- African Americans are highly acculturated. Despite the many unique cultural traits forged in America and those that survive from Africa, black Americans share language, values and beliefs, and most other aspects of culture with white Americans. In terms of integration, in contrast, African Americans present a mixed picture. For middle-class, more-educated members of the group, American society offers more opportunities for upward mobility and success than ever before. Without denying the prejudice, discrimination, and racism that remain, this segment of the group is in a favorable position to achieve higher levels of affluence and power for their children and grandchildren. At the same time, a large percentage of African Americans remain mired in poverty, and for them, affluence, security, and power are as distant as they were a generation ago (perhaps even more so). As a group, African Americans experience high levels of residential and school segregation, and unemployment and poverty remain serious problems, perhaps even more serious than a generation ago.

- Native Americans are less acculturated than African Americans, and some tribes and organizations are trying to preserve Native American cultures and languages. Overall, however, the strength and vitality of these traditions is probably decreasing. Some measures of integration show improvement, but many Native Americans are among the most isolated and impoverished minority group members in the U. S. One possible bright spot for some Native communities lies in the further development of the gambling industry, which could allow for the development of tribal infrastructure such as schools, health clinics, job training centers, and so forth.

- Members of the largest Hispanic American groups are also generally less acculturated than African Americans. Hispanic traditions and the Spanish language have been sustained by the exclusion and isolation of these groups within the U. S. and have been continually renewed and revitalized by immigration. Cubans have moved closer to equality than have Mexican Americans and Puerto Ricans, but they did so by resisting assimilation and building an ethnic enclave economy. Mexican Americans and Puerto Ricans share many of the problems of poverty that confront African Americans, and they are below national norms on measures of equality and integration.

- The smaller Hispanic groups consist mostly of new immigrants who are just beginning the assimilation process. Many members of these groups, along with Mexican Americans and Puerto Ricans, are less educated and have few occupational skills, and they face the dangers of becoming part of a permanent underclass. Nonetheless, some evidence suggests that these groups (or, more accurately, their descendants) may eventually find their way into the American mainstream.

- As with Hispanic Americans, the extent of assimilation among Asian Americans is highly variable. Some groups (e.g., third- and fourth-generation Japanese and Chinese Americans) have virtually completed the assimilation process and compare favorably to national norms in terms of integration and equality (at least in terms of group averages). Some Asian American groups (the more elite immigrants from India and the Philippines) seem to be finding a place in the American mainstream. Other groups consist largely of newer immigrants with occupational and educational profiles that often resemble those of colonized minority groups, and these groups face the same dangers of permanent marginalization and exclusion. Still other Asian American groups (e.g., Korean Americans) have constructed ethnic enclaves and pursue economic equality by resisting acculturation.

- Only European American ethnic groups (covered in Chapter 2) seem to approximate the traditional models of assimilation. The development of even these groups, however, has taken unexpected twists and turns, and the pluralism of the 1960s and 1970s suggests that ethnic traditions and ethnic identity, in some form, may withstand the pressures of assimilation for generations to come. Culturally and racially, these groups are the closest to the dominant group. If they still retain a sense of ethnicity after generations of acculturation and integration (even if it is merely symbolic), what is the likelihood that the sense of group membership will fade in the racially stigmatized minority groups?

- Different normative expectations continue to shape the experiences of boys/men and girls/women throughout their lives. In that sense, acculturation has not been reached. Women are equal to men on some measures of equality (e.g., education), but large gaps in other areas (e.g., income) persist. These gaps vary by race, ethnicity, sexual orientation, and other factors. Generally, however, we can say that women are disproportionately concentrated in less-well-paid occupations and they continue to confront glass ceilings and other limits to their social mobility.

For racial and ethnic minority groups, assimilation is far from accomplished. The group divisions that remain are real and consequential; they cannot be willed away by pretending we are all "just American." Group membership continues to be important because it continues to be linked to fundamental patterns of exclusion and inequality. The realities of pluralism, inequality, and ethnic and racial identity persist to the extent that the American promise of a truly open opportunity structure continues to fail. The group divisions forged in the past and perpetuated over the decades by racism and discrimination will remain to the extent that racial and ethnic group membership continues to be correlated with inequality and position in the social class structure.

Along with economic and political pressures, other forces help sustain the pluralistic group divisions. Despite evidence to the contrary, some people argue that ethnicity is rooted in biology and can never be fully eradicated (e.g., see van den Berghe, 1981). Although this may be an extreme and increasingly rare position, there is little doubt that many people find their own ancestries to be a matter of great interest. Some (perhaps most) of the impetus behind the preservation of ethnic and racial identity may result from vicious and destructive intergroup competition. In other ways, though, ethnicity can be a positive force that helps people locate themselves in time and space and understand their position in the contemporary world. Ethnicity remains an important aspect of self-identity and pride for many Americans from every group and tradition. It seems unlikely that this sense of a personal link to particular groups and heritages within U.S. society will soon fade.

Can we survive as a pluralistic, culturally and linguistically fragmented, racially and ethnically unequal society? What will save us from balkanization and fractionalization? Given our history of colonization and racism, can the U. S. move closer to the relatively harmonious models of race relations found elsewhere?

As we deal with these questions, we need to remember that in and of itself, diversity is no more *bad* than unity is *good*. Our society has grown to a position of global preeminence despite, or perhaps because of, our diversity. In fact, many people have argued that our diversity is a fundamental and essential characteristic of U.S. society and a great strength to be cherished and encouraged. Sociologist Ronald Takaki (1993) offers this eloquent endorsement:

> As Americans, we originally came from many different shores and our diversity has been at the center of the making of America. While our stories contain the memories of different communities, together they inscribe a larger narrative. Filled with what Walt Whitman celebrated as the "varied carols" of America, our history generously gives all of us our "mystic chords of memory."

> Throughout our past of oppressions and struggles for equality, Americans of different races and ethnicities have been "singing with open mouths their strong melodious songs" in the textile mills of Lowell, the cotton fields of Mississippi, on the Indian reservations of South Dakota, the railroad tracks high in the Sierras of California, in the garment factories of the Lower East Side, the cane fields of Hawaii, and a thousand other places across the country. Our denied history "bursts with telling." As we hear America singing, we find ourselves invited to bring our cultural diversity [into the open], to accept ourselves. (p. 428)

To this heady mix of diversity in race, ethnicity, language, and culture, we must add the dimensions of gender and sexual orientation and their infinite intersections and combinations with group membership. As poet Walt Whitman suggested, the "varied carols" of American life are voiced by a complex, diversified chorus: The tune won't be the same for heterosexual, middle-class African Americans as for lesbian, Hispanic immigrants with low levels of human capital. How can we sort out this complexity? How can we answer the question we raised at the beginning of this book: What does it mean to be an American?

The question for our future might not be so much "Which is better: unity or diversity?" as "What blend of pluralism and assimilation will serve us best in the 21st century?" How can our society prosper without suppressing its rich diversity? How can we increase the degree of openness, fairness, and justice without individuals and groups feeling threatened? The one-way, Anglo-conformity mode of assimilation of the past is too narrow and destructive to be a blueprint for our future, but extreme forms of minority group pluralism and separatism might be equally harmful.

How much unity do we need? How much diversity is most beneficial for society? These are questions you must answer for yourself, and they are questions you'll face in numerous ways over the course of your life. We do not pretend that the ideas we've presented can fully resolve every present issue or others that will arise in the future. As long as immigrants and minority groups are a part of the United States, as long as prejudice and discrimination and inequality persist, the debates will continue, and new issues will arise as old ones are resolved.

As U.S. society attempts to deal with new immigrants, varieties of gender expression, and unresolved minority grievances, we should recognize that it's not diversity per se that threatens stability but rather the realities of exclusion and marginalization, split labor markets, racial and ethnic stratification, poverty, and institutionalized discrimination. We need to focus on the issues that confront us with an honest recognition of the past and the economic, political, and social forces that have shaped us. As the United States continues to remake itself, an informed sense of where we've been will help us decide where we should go next and, perhaps, how best to get there.

MINORITY GROUP PROGRESS AND THE IDEOLOGY OF AMERICAN INDIVIDUALISM

There is so much sadness, misery, and unfairness in the history of minority groups that evidence of progress sometimes goes unnoticed. Lest we be guilty of ignoring the good news in favor of the bad, let us note some of the ways in which the situations of American minority groups have improved. Evidence of progress is easy to find for some groups; we need look only to the relative economic, educational, and income equality of European American ethnic groups and some Asian American groups. Minority group members can be found at the highest levels of success, affluence, and prestige, suggesting that the U. S. has become more tolerant and open. For example, women (in large numbers) have entered occupations historically filled only by men. The election of Barack Obama, our first African American president, represents progress (though it does not mean our society is post-racial). Likewise, the 2018 midterm elections saw record numbers of women and sexual, religious, and racial and ethnic minorities elected to Congress.

Although prejudice in all its forms unquestionably exists, research documents a general decline in traditional (overt) racism and prejudice, sexism, and homophobia (though, since 2016, we've seen an increase). The strong racial and ethnic sentiments and stereotypes of the past are no longer the primary vocabulary for discussing race relations among dominant group members, at least not in public. (Similar shifts have occurred in attitudes toward women and LGBTQIA people.)

The decrease in blatant bigotry is, without a doubt, a positive change. However, in many ways, negative intergroup feelings and stereotypes have not disappeared; they've simply changed form. Many people now express the same racist and sexist feelings in subtler ways—called *modern* or *symbolic* racism and sexism. Key to modern racism and sexism is the belief that routes of upward mobility in American society are equally open to all. (However, as you've learned, it's also clear that the blatant bigotry of the past has not disappeared: Hate groups and racist epithets have reappeared in the everyday language of our society.)

The individualistic view of social mobility is consistent with the human capital perspective and the traditional melting-pot view of assimilation. Taken together, these ideologies present a powerful and widely shared perspective on the nature of minority group problems in modern American society. Proponents of these views tend to be unsympathetic to the plight of minorities and to programs intended to ameliorate these problems, such as affirmative action. The overt bigotry of the past has typically been replaced by blandness and an indifference more difficult to define and harder to measure than "old-fashioned" racism. Nevertheless, it is still resistant and unsympathetic to change.

We've argued that the most serious problems facing contemporary minority groups, however, are structural and institutional, not individual or personal. For example, the scarcity of jobs and high rates of unemployment in the inner cities are the result of economic and political forces beyond the control not only of the minority communities but also of local and state governments. The marginalization of the minority group labor force reflects the essence of modern American capitalism. The mainstream, higher-paying, blue-collar jobs available to people with modest educational credentials are controlled by national and multinational corporations, which maximize profits by automating their production processes and moving the jobs that remain to areas outside the U. S., where cheap labor is abundant.

Additionally, you've learned that some of the more effective strategies for pursuing equality require strong in-group cohesion and networks of cooperation, not heroic individual effort. Immigration to this country is (and always has been) a group process that involves extensive, long-lasting networks of communication and chains of population movement, usually built around family ties and larger kinship groups. Group networks continue to operate in America and assist individual immigrants with early adjustments and later opportunities for jobs and upward mobility. A variation on this theme is the ethnic enclave found among many different groups.

Survival and success in America for all minority groups has had more to do with group processes than with individual will or motivation. The concerted, coordinated actions of the minority community provided support during hard times and, when possible, provided the means to climb higher in the social structure during good times. Far from being a hymn to individualism, the story of U.S. minority groups—whether based on race, ethnicity, gender, or sexual orientation—is profoundly sociological.

A FINAL WORD

U.S. society and its minority groups are linked in fractious unity. They are part of the same structures but are separated by lines of color and culture and by long histories (and clear memories) of exploitation and unfairness. This society owes its prosperity and position of prominence in the world no less to the labor of minority groups than to that of the dominant group. By harnessing the labor and energy of these minority groups, the U. S. has grown prosperous and powerful, but the benefits have flowed disproportionately to members of the dominant group.

Since the middle of the 20th century, minority groups have demanded greater openness, fairness, equality, justice, and respect. Some of these demands have been met, at least verbally, and society as a whole has rejected the overt, oppressive racism of the past.

Yet, minority group progress has stalled well short of equality, and the patterns of poverty, discrimination, marginality, and despair continue to negatively influence millions of people.

As we face the 21st century, the dilemmas of America's minority groups remain the primary unresolved domestic issue facing the nation. The answers of the past—faith in assimilation and the belief that success in America is open to all who simply try hard enough—have proved inadequate, even destructive and dangerous, because they help sustain the belief that the barriers to equality no longer exist and that any remaining inequalities are the problem of the minority groups, not the larger society.

These issues of equality and access won't solve themselves or simply fade away. They will continue to manifest themselves in myriad ways—through protest activities, rancorous debates, diffused rage, and pervasive violence. The solutions and policies that will carry us through these coming travails are not clear. Only by asking the proper questions, realistically and honestly, can we hope to find the answers that will help our society fulfill its promises to the millions who are currently excluded from achieving the American Dream.

The U. S. is one of many ethnically and racially diverse nations in the world. As world communication networks, immigration, trade, and transportation increasingly connect people globally, diversity-related challenges (and opportunities) will become more international in their scope and implications. For example, agreements between the U. S. and Latin American nations will directly affect immigration patterns, and organizations representing women and sexual-orientation minorities will develop more international ties. In many ways, the patterns of dominant–minority relations discussed in this book have already been reproduced in other parts of the world. The mostly Anglo industrialized nations of the Northern Hemisphere have continuously exploited the labor and resources of the mostly nonwhite, undeveloped nations of the Southern Hemisphere. Thus, the tensions and resentments we've observed in the U. S. are being reproduced globally.

The United States is neither the most nor the least diverse country in the world. Likewise, it is not the most or the least successful in confronting the problems of prejudice, discrimination, and racism. However, the multigroup nature of our society, along with the present influx of immigrants from around the world, presents an opportunity to improve on our record. A society that finds a way to deal fairly and humanely with issues of diversity and difference, prejudice and inequality, exclusion and marginalization, and racism and discrimination can provide a sorely needed model for other nations and, indeed, for the world.

SUMMARY

- Subsistence technology is the most basic force shaping society and group relationships. Agrarian technology created competition for land and labor, resulting in the subjugation of some groups and the near-extermination of others. The evolution of subsistence technology through the industrial and postindustrial stages continued to shape the situation of minority groups—including women and LGBTQIA—and the nature of dominant–minority conflict.

- The contact situation creates dynamics that affect dominant–minority relations for centuries (or longer). We've analyzed these dynamics using Blauner's distinction between immigrant and colonized minority groups and Noel's concepts of ethnocentrism, competition, and power. We've seen many ways that different contact situations continue to affect minority groups.

- Intersectionality reminds us that we are each privileged and disadvantaged in many ways according to our social statuses (e.g., race, gender, class) and how social forces shape our lives. We need to continually recognize the diversity within groups.

- The extent of acculturation and integration is highly variable from group to group. Of the racial and ethnic minority groups, only the descendants of the European immigrant groups have approached full assimilation. Each of the other groups we've considered ranks below white ethnics in terms of acculturation and integration. Some of these groups (Hispanic and Asian American groups in particular) have been affected by high rates of immigration in recent decades. Gender retains significant strength in American culture. Women rank below men on many measures of integration and equality. Generally, LGBTQIA minorities are gaining more acceptance but continue to face significant issues of inequality and marginalization.

- The sociological perspective locates the source of minority problems in the structure and everyday functioning of the larger society. It rejects the assumption that mobility and opportunity are equally open to all and thereby counters the individualistic view held by many Americans. Sociology takes account of the history of dominant–minority relations, the evolving subsistence technology, globalization, and the changing political, cultural, and economic processes that structure modern societies. It offers a broad view of groups and social structures, grounded in research and guided by critical thinking and thoughtful reflection.

Note

1. LGBTQIA stands for lesbian, gay, bisexual, transgender, queer/questioning, intersex, and asexual/ally.

REFERENCES

Abdo, G. (2017). Like most Americans, U.S. Muslims concerned about extremism in the name of Islam. *Pew Research Center*. Retrieved August 30, 2017, from http://www.pewresearch.org/fact-tank/2017/08/14/like-most-americans-u-s-muslims-concerned-about-extremism-in-the-name-of-islam/

Abrahamson, H. (1980). Assimilation and pluralism. In S. Thernstrom, A. Orlov, & O. Handlin (Eds.), *Harvard encyclopedia of American ethnic groups* (pp. 150–160). Cambridge, MA: Harvard University Press.

Ackerman, H. (n.d.). *The Cuban rafter phenomenon.* Retrieved from http://balseros.miami.edu

Acuña, R. (1988). *Occupied America* (3rd ed.). New York, NY: Harper & Row.

Acuña, R. (1999). *Occupied America* (4th ed.). New York, NY: Harper & Row.

Adarand Constructors Inc. v. Pena, 515 U.S. 200 (1995)

Affirming a Divide. (2012). *The Economist*. Retrieved January 8, 2019, from http://www.economist.com/node/21543494

Agbayani-Siewert, P., & Revilla, L. (1995). Filipino Americans. In P. G. Min (Ed.), *Asian Americans: Contemporary issues and trends* (pp. 143–168). Thousand Oaks, CA: SAGE.

Agiesta, J. (2015, July 2). Poll: Majority sees Confederate flag as southern pride symbol, not racist. *CNN*. Retrieved from https://www.cnn.com/2015/07/02/politics/confederate-flag-poll-racism-southern-pride/index.html

Aizer, A., & Doyle, J. J. (2015). Juvenile incarceration, human capital and future crime: Evidence from randomly-assigned judges. *Quarterly Journal of Economics*, 130(2), 759–803.

Alba, R. (1985). *Italian Americans: Into the twilight of ethnicity.* Englewood Cliffs, NJ: Prentice Hall.

Alba, R. (1990). *Ethnic identity: The transformation of white America.* New Haven, CT: Yale University Press.

Alba, R. (1995). Assimilation's quiet tide. *The Public Interest*, 119, 9–19.

Alba, R., & Nee, V. (1997). Rethinking assimilation theory for a new era of immigration. *International Migration Review*, 31, 826–875.

Alba, R., & Nee, V. (2003). *Remaking the American mainstream: Assimilation and contemporary immigration.* Cambridge, MA: Harvard University Press.

Aleiss, A. (2005). *Making the white man's Indian: Native Americans and Hollywood movies.* Westport, CT: Praeger.

Alexander, M. (2012). *The new Jim Crow: Mass incarceration in the age of colorblindness.* New York, NY: New Press.

All India survey on higher education. (2018, January 5). *Ministry of resource development.* Retrieved from http://mhrd.gov.in/sites/upload_files/mhrd/files/New%20AISHE%202017-18%20Launch_Final.pdf

Allen, P. G. (1992). *The sacred hoop: Recovering the feminine in American Indian traditions.* New York, NY: Open Road Integrated Media.

Almasy, S., & Yan, H. (2014a). London is latest city to see protests as Ferguson dismay spreads. *CNN*. Retrieved November 26, 2014, from http://edition.cnn.com/2014/11/26/us/national-ferguson-demonstrations/index.html

Almasy, S., & Yan, H. (2014b). Protesters fill streets across country as Ferguson protests spread coast to coast. *CNN*. Retrieved August 10, 2017, from http://www.cnn.com/2014/11/25/us/national-ferguson-protests/

Almquist, E. M. (1979). Black women and the pursuit of equality. In Jo Freeman (Ed.), *Women: A feminist perspective* (pp. 430–450). Palo Alto, CA: Mayfield.

Alonso, A. A. (1998). *Rebuilding Los Angeles: A lesson of community reconstruction*. Retrieved from http://www.streetgangs.com/academic/1998.Alonso-RLAreport-final-001.pdf

Alperin, E., & Batalov, J. (2017, February 8). Korean immigrants in the United States. *Migration Policy Institute*. Retrieved from https://www.migrationpolicy.org/article/korean-immigrants-united-states

Alvarez, L. (2017, November 17). A great migration from Puerto Rico is set to transform Orlando. *New York Times*. Retrieved from https://www.nytimes.com/2017/11/17/us/puerto-ricans-orlando.html

Alvarez, R. (1973). The psychohistorical and socioeconomic development of the Chicano community in the United States. *Social Science Quarterly*, 53, 920–942.

Amazon Watch. (2017, February 3). Over 700,000 people demand banks stop financing the Dakota Access Pipeline. Retrieved August 18, 2017, from http://amazonwatch.org/news/2017/0203-over-700000-people-demand-banks-stop-financing-the-dakota-access-pipeline

American Civil Liberties Union. (2013). *The war on marijuana in black and white*. Retrieved from https://www.aclu.org/billions-dollars-wasted-racially-biased-arrests

American Sociological Association. (2003). *The importance of collecting data and doing scientific research on race*. Washington, DC: Author. http://www.asanet.org/sites/default/files/savvy/images/press/docs/pdf/asa_race_statement.pdf

Amistad Research Center. (n.d.). *Fannie Lou Hamer: Papers of a civil rights activist, political activist, and woman*. Retrieved from https://www.gale.com/binaries/content/assets/gale-us-en/primary-sources/archives-unbound/primary-sources_-archives-unbound_fannie-lou-hamer_papers-of-a-civil-rights-activitist-political-activist-and-woman.pdf

Amnesty International. (2015, November 19). *Dominican Republic: "Without paper, I am no one": Stateless people in the Dominican Republic*. Retrieved April 11, 2019, from https://www.amnesty.org/en/documents/amr27/2755/2015/en/

Amott, T., & Matthaei, J. (1991). *Race, gender, and work: A multicultural history of women in the United States*. Boston, MA: South End.

Andersen, M. L. (1993). *Thinking about women: Sociological perspectives on sex and gender* (3rd ed.). New York, NY: Macmillan.

Anderson, B. (2000). *Doing the dirty work? The global politics of domestic labour*. New York, NY: Zed Books.

Anderson, C. (2016). *White rage: The unspoken truth of our racial divide*. New York, NY: Bloomsbury Publishing USA.

Anderson, E. (2015). The white space. In *Sociology of race and ethnicity* (Vol. 1; pp. 10–21). doi: 10.1177/2332649214561306

Anderson, K. (2016). *A recognition of being: Reconstructing native womanhood* (2nd ed.). Toronto, Canada: Women's Press.

Anderson, S. (2018, May 17). New research shows immigrants may boost employment of natives. *Forbes*. Retrieved from https://www.forbes.com/sites/stuartanderson/2018/05/17/new-research-shows-immigrants-may-boost-employment-of-natives/#39999a861600

Anonymous. (1924, October). The Jew and the club. *The Atlantic*. Retrieved August 3, 2017, from https://www.theatlantic.com/magazine/archive/1924/10/the-jew-and-the-club/306258/

Anti-Defamation League (ADL). (2017a). *The ADL global 100: An index of anti-Semitism*. Retrieved from http://global100.adl.org/

Anti-Defamation League (ADL). (2017b). Audit of anti-Semitic incidents year in review. *ADL*. Available at https://www.adl.org/resources/reports/2017-audit-of-anti-semitic-incidents

Anti-Defamation League (ADL). (2017c). In first, new ADL poll finds majority of Americans concerned about violence against Jews and other minorities, want administration to act. *ADL*. Retrieved from https://www.adl.org/news/press-releases/in-first-new-adl-poll-finds-majority-of-americans-concerned-about-violence

Arab American Anti-Discrimination Committee. (2002). *ADC fact sheet: The condition of Arab Americans post 9/11*. Retrieved from http://www.adc.org/terror_attack/9-11aftermath.pdf

Arciniega, G. M., Anderson, T. C., Tovar-Blank, Z. G., & Tracey, T. J. G. (2008). Toward a fuller conception of machismo: Development of a traditional machismo and caballerismo scale. *Journal of Counseling Psychology*, 55(1), 19–33.

Asahina, R. J. (2007). *Just Americans: How Japanese Americans won a war at home and abroad*. New York, NY: Gotham Books.

Ashkenas, J., Park, H., & Pearce, A. (2017, August 24). Even with affirmative action, blacks and Hispanics are more underrepresented at top colleges than 35 years ago. *New York Times*. Retrieved from https://www.nytimes.com/interactive/2017/08/24/us/affirmative-action.html

Ashmore, R., & DelBoca, F. (1976). Psychological approaches to understanding group conflict. In P. Katz (Ed.), *Towards the elimination of racism* (pp. 73–123). New York, NY: Pergamon.

Associated Press. (2005, November 13). Asian youth persistently harassed by U.S. peers. *USA Today*. Retrieved from http://usatoday30.usatoday.com/news/nation/2005-11-13-asian-teens-bullied_x.htm

Associated Press. (2015, November 1). U.S. Episcopal Church installs first black leader. *NBC*. Retrieved August 8, 2017, from http://www.nbcnews.com/news/us-news/u-s-episcopal-church-installs-first-black-leader-n455381

Austin, A. (2010). *Different race, different recession: American Indian unemployment in 2010* (Issue Brief 289). Washington, DC: Economic Policy Institute. Retrieved from http://epi.3cdn.net/94a339472e6481485e_hgm6bxpz4.pdf

Austin, B. (2018). 1619: Virginia's first Africans. *Hampton History Museum*. Retrieved from http://www.HamptonHistoryMuseum.org/1619

Australian Bureau of Statistics. (2016). *National Aboriginal and Torres Strait Islander Social Survey, 2014–15*. Retrieved April 28, from http://www.abs.gov.au/ausstats/abs@.nsf/mf/4714.0

Australian Government. (2015). *The dreaming*. Retrieved August 18, 2017, from http://www.australia.gov.au/about-australia/australian-story/dreaming

Axtell, J., & Sturtevant, W. C. (1980, July). The unkindest cut, or who invented scalping. *The William and Mary Quarterly*, 37(3), 451–472. Retrieved April 10, 2019, from http://www.jstor.org/stable/1923812

Baca Zinn, M., & Eitzen, D. S. (1990). *Diversity in families*. New York, NY: HarperCollins.

Baca Zinn, M., & Thornton Dill, B. (Eds.). (1994). *Women of color in U.S. society*. Philadelphia, PA: Temple University Press.

Badger, E., & Bui, Q. (2018, October 1). Detailed maps show how neighborhoods shape children for life. *New York Times*. Retrieved from https://www.nytimes.com/2018/10/01/upshot/maps-neighborhoods-shape-child-poverty.html

Bae-Hansard, S. (2015). *Korean ethnic churches' benefits to Korean immigrant entrepreneurs and their families* (master's thesis). Vanderbilt University, Nashville, Tennessee. Retrieved from https://etd.library.vanderbilt.edu/available/etd-03232015-113841/.../Bae-Hansard.pdf

Bailey, I. G. (n.d.). *Sharecropper contract, 1867*. Retrieved from https://www.gilderlehrman.org/content/sharecropper-contract-1867

Ball, R. (2009). Social distance in Japan: An exploratory study. *Michigan Sociological Review*, 23, 105–113.

Banner, S. (2005). *How the Indians lost their land: Law and power on the frontier*. Cambridge, MA: Harvard University Press.

Barringer, H., Takeuchi, D., & Levin, M. (1995). *Asians and Pacific Islanders in the United States*. New York, NY: Russell Sage Foundation.

Bauer, M. (2008). *Close to slavery. Guest worker programs in the United States. A report of the southern poverty law center*. Retrieved from https://www.splcenter.org/20130218/close-slavery-guestworker-programs-united-states

Bayoumi, M. (2008). *How does it feel to be a problem?* New York, NY: Penguin Books.

Beagle, C. (2016). *Siente lenguas: The rhetorical history of Dolores Huerta and the rise of Chicana rhetoric* (PhD dissertation). University of New Mexico. Retrieved from http://dspace.unm.edu/bitstream/handle/1928/31702/Garcia_Diss_LoboVault.pdf?sequence=1&isAllowed=y

Bean, F., & Stevens, G. (2003). *America's newcomers and the dynamics of diversity*. New York, NY: Russell Sage Foundation.

Becerra, R. (1988). The Mexican American family. In C. H. Mindel, R. W. Habenstein, & R. Wright Jr. (Eds.), *Ethnic families in America: Patterns and variations* (3rd ed., pp. 141–172). New York, NY: Elsevier.

Bell, D. (1973). *The coming of post-industrial society*. New York, NY: Basic Books.

Bell, D. (1992). *Race, racism, and American law* (3rd ed.). Boston, MA: Little, Brown.

Benedict, R. (1946). *The chrysanthemum and the sword: Patterns of Japanese culture*. Boston, MA: Houghton Mifflin.

Benjamin, L. (2005). *The black elite*. Lanham, MD: Rowman & Littlefield.

Benner, K., & Dickerson, C. (2018, June 11). *New York Times*. Retrieved from https://www.nytimes .com/2018/06/11/us/politics/sessions-domestic-vio lence-asylum.html

Benowitz, J. M. (2017). *Encyclopedia of American women and religion* (2nd ed.). Santa Barbara, CA: ABC-CLIO.

Berdahl, J. L., & Min, J-A. (2012). Prescriptive stereotypes and workplace consequences for East Asians in North America. *Cultural Diversity and Ethnic Minority Psychology*, 18(2), 141–145. doi: 10.1037/a0027692.

Berger, M. S. (2010). The centrality of the Talmud. In J. R. Baskin & K. Seeskin (Eds.), *The Cambridge guide to Jewish history, religion, and culture* (pp. 311–336). Cambridge: Cambridge University Press.

Berndt, R. M., & Berndt, C. H. (1987). *End of an era: Aboriginal labour in the Northern Territory*. Canberra: Australian Institute of Aboriginal Studies.

Bernheimer, C. S. (1908, November 12). Prejudice against the Jews in the United States. *The Independent*, 65.

Berry, J. W. (1980). Acculturation as varieties of adaptation. In A. M. Padilla (Ed.), *Acculturation: Theory, models, and some new findings* (pp. 9–25). Boulder, CO: Westview.

Bertrand, M., & Mullainathan, S. (2004). Are Emily and Greg more employable than Lakisha and Jamal? A field experiment on labor market discrimination. *American Economic Review*, 94, 991–1013.

Billings, D. (2017). *Deep denial: The persistence of white supremacy in the United States history and life*. Roselle, NJ: Crandall, Dostie & Douglass Books, Inc.

Bird, E. (1999). Gendered construction of the American Indian in popular media. *Journal of Communication*, 49, 60–83.

Biskupic, J. (1989, October 28). House approves entitlement for Japanese-Americans. *Congressional Quarterly Weekly Report*, p. 2879.

Black Lives Matter Global Network. (n.d.). What we believe. *Black Lives Matter*. Retrieved from https:// blacklivesmatter.com/about/what-we-believe/

Black-Gutman, D., & Hickson, F. (1996). The relationship between racial attitudes and social-cognitive development in children: An Australian study. *Developmental Psychology*, 32, 448–457.

Blackmon, D. A. (2009). *Slavery by another name: The re-enslavement of black Americans from the Civil War to World War II*. New York, NY: Knopf Doubleday Publishing Group.

Blank, R. M., Dabady, M., & Citro, C. F. (Eds.). (2004). *Measuring racial discrimination: Panel on methods for assessing discrimination*. *The National Academies Press*. Retrieved August 30, 2017, from https://www .nap.edu/read/10887/chapter/1

Blassingame, J. W. (1972). *The slave community: Plantation life in the Antebellum South*. New York, NY: Oxford University Press.

Blau, P. M., & Duncan, O. D. (1967). *The American occupational structure*. New York, NY: Wiley.

Blauner, R. (1972). *Racial oppression in America*. New York, NY: Harper & Row.

Blessing, P. (1980). Irish. In S. Thernstrom, A. Orlov, & O. Handlin (Eds.), *Harvard encyclopedia of American ethnic groups* (pp. 524–545). Cambridge, MA: Harvard University Press.

Bloome, D., & Muller, C. (2015). Tenancy and African American marriage in the postbellum south. *Demography*, 52(5), 1409–1430.

Blumer, H. (1965). Industrialization and race relations. In G. Hunter (Ed.), Industrialization and race relations: A symposium (pp. 200–253). London, UK: Oxford University Press.

Bobo, L. (1988). Group conflict, prejudice, and the paradox of contemporary racial attitudes. In P. Katz & D. Taylor (Eds.), *Eliminating racism: Profiles in controversy* (pp. 85–114). New York, NY: Plenum.

Bobo, L. (2001). Racial attitudes and relations at the close of the twentieth century. In N. Smelser, W. Wilson, & F. Mitchell (Eds.), *America becoming: Racial trends and their consequences* (Vol. 1, pp. 264–301). Washington, DC: National Academy Press.

Bobo, L. D., Charles, C. Z., Krysan, M., & Simmons, A. D. (2012). The real record on racial attitudes. In P. Marsden (Ed.), *Social trends in American life: Findings from the general social survey since 1973* (pp. 38–83). Princeton, NJ: Princeton University Press.

Bodley, J. H. (2013). *The small nation solution: How the world's smallest nations can solve the world's biggest problems.* Lanham: MD. AltaMira Press.

Bodnar, J. (1985). *The transplanted.* Bloomington: Indiana University Press.

Bogardus, E. (1933). A social distance scale. *Sociology and Social Research*, 17, 265–271.

Bolter, J. (2017, February 1). The evolving and diversifying nature of migration to the U.S.–Mexico border. *Migration Policy Institute.* Retrieved from http://www .migrationpolicy.org/article/evolving-and-diversify ing-nature-migration-us-mexico-border

Bonacich, E., & Modell, J. (1980). *The economic basis of ethnic solidarity: Small business in the Japanese American community.* Berkeley: University of California Press.

Bonilla-Silva, E. (2001). *White supremacy and racism in the post–civil rights era.* Boulder, CO: Lynne Rienner.

Bonilla-Silva, E. (2003). "New racism," color-blind racism, and the future of whiteness in America. In A. Doane & E. Bonilla-Silva (Eds.), *White out: The continuing significance of racism* (pp. 271–284). New York, NY: Routledge.

Bonilla-Silva, E. (2006). *Racism without racists* (2nd ed.). Lanham, MD: Rowman & Littlefield.

Bonilla-Silva, E. (2017). *Racism without racists: Color-blind racism and the persistence of racial inequality in America* (5th ed.). Lanham, MD: Rowman & Littlefield.

Boo, K. (2001a, April 9). After welfare. *New Yorker.* Retrieved from https://www.newyorker.com/magazine/ 2001/04/09/after-welfare

Boo, K. (2001b, August 18). The marriage cure. *New Yorker.* Retrieved from https://www.newyorker.com/ magazine/2003/08/18/the-marriage-cure

Booth, A., Granger, D., Mazur, A., & Kivligham, K. (2006). Testosterone and social behavior. *Social Forces*, 86, 167–191.

Bordewich, F. (1996). *Killing the white man's Indian.* New York, NY: Doubleday.

Borjas, G. J. (2016, September/October). Yes, immigration hurts American workers. *Politico.* Retrieved from https://www.politico.com/magazine/story/2016/09/ trump-clinton-immigration-economy-unemploy ment-jobs-214216

Bornstein, M. H. (2017). The specificity principle in acculturation science. *Perspectives on Psychological Science*, 12(1), 3–45. Available at https://www.ncbi .nlm.nih.gov/pubmed/28073331

Borstelmann, T. (2009). *The Cold War and the color line.* Cambridge, MA: Harvard University Press.

Boschma, J., & Brownstein, R. (2016, February 29). The concentration of poverty in American schools. *The Atlantic.* Available at https://www.theatlantic .com/education/archive/2016/02/concentration-poverty-american-schools/471414/

Bossen, L., & Gates, H. (2017). *Bound feet, young hands: Tracking the demise of footbinding in village China.* Redwood City, CA: Stanford University Press.

Boswell, T. (1986). A split labor market analysis of discrimination against Chinese immigrants, 1850–1882. *American Sociological Review*, 51, 352–371.

Bourcier, N. (2012, October 23). Brazil comes to terms with its slave trading past. *The Guardian.* Retrieved July 20, 2017, from https://www.theguardian.com/world/ 2012/oct/23/brazil-struggle-ethnic-racial-identity

Bouvier, L. F., & Gardner, R. W. (1986, November). Immigration to the U.S.: The unfinished story. *Population Bulletin*, 41, 1–50.

Boyer, P. S., Clark, C. E., Hawley, S., Kett, J. F., & Rieser, A. (2008). *The enduring vision: A history of the American people, concise*. Boston, MA: Cengage Learning.

Brennan Center for Justice. (2013). *Voting laws roundup 2013*. Retrieved from http://www.brennancenter.org/analysis/election-2013-voting-laws-roundup

Brennan Center for Justice. (2018). *New voting restrictions in America*. Retrieved from https://www.brennancenter.org/sites/default/files/analysis/New%20Voting%20Restrictions.pdf

Brilliant, M. (2010). *The color of America has changed: How racial diversity shaped civil rights reform in California, 1941–1978*. Oxford, UK: Oxford University Press.

Brody, D. (1980). Labor. In S. Thernstrom, A. Orlov, & O. Handlin (Eds.), *Harvard encyclopedia of American ethnic groups* (pp. 609–618). Cambridge, MA: Harvard University Press.

Bronson, P., & Merryman, A. (2009, September 14). Even babies discriminate: A nurtureshock excerpt. *Newsweek*. http://www.newsweek.com/even-babies-discriminate-nurtureshock-excerpt-79233

Brown v. Board of Education of Topeka, 247 U.S. 483 (1954).

Brown, A. (2014). U.S. Hispanic and Asian populations growing, but for different reasons. *Pew Research Center*. Retrieved August 26, 2017, from http://www.pewresearch.org/fact-tank/2014/06/26/u-s-hispanic-and-asian-populations-growing-but-for-different-reasons/

Brown, A., & Atske, S. (2019, January 18). Blacks have made gains in U.S. political leadership, but gaps remain. *Pew Research Center*. Retrieved from http://www.pewresearch.org/fact-tank/2019/01/18/blacks-have-made-gains-in-u-s-political-leadership-but-gaps-remain/

Brown, A., & Patten, E. (2013). Statistical profile: Hispanics of Puerto Rican origin in the United States, 2011. *Pew Hispanic Center*. Washington, DC: Pew Hispanic Center. Retrieved from http://www.pewhispanic.org/2013/06/19/hispanics-of-puerto-rican-origin-in-the-united-states-2011/

Brown, N. D. (2015). *The brotherhood of sleeping car porters: The civil rights movement* (thesis). The University of Toledo, OH. https://etd.ohiolink.edu/!etd.send_file?accession=toledo1430166476&disposition=attachment

Brown, R. (1995). *Prejudice: Its social psychology*. Cambridge, MA: Blackwell.

Bruzgulis, A. (2015, June 22). Confederate flag wasn't flown at South Carolina Statehouse until 1961, pundit claims. *PunditFact*. Retrieved from https://www.politifact.com/punditfact/statements/2015/jun/22/eugene-robinson/confederate-flag-wasnt-flown-south-carolina-state-/

Bucciferro, J. R. (2015). Racial inequality in Brazil from independence to the present. In L. Bértola & J. Williamson (Eds.), *Has Latin American inequality changed direction* (pp. 171–194). New York, NY: Springer.

Buchanan, B. (2005). The empire of political thought: Civilization, savagery and perceptions of indigenous government. *History of the Human Sciences*, 18(2), 1–22.

Budech, K. A. (2014). *Missing voices, hidden fields: The gendered struggles of female farmworkers* (thesis). Pitzer College, Claremont, CA. Retrieved from http://scholarship.claremont.edu/cgi/viewcontent.cgi?article=1056&context=pitzer_these

Bulwa, D. (2010, July 9). Mehserle convicted of involuntary manslaughter. *San Francisco Chronicle*. Retrieved from http://www.sfgate.com/bayarea/article/Mehserle-convicted-of-involuntary-manslaughter-3181861.php

Buraku Liberation and Human Rights Research Institute. (2005). *Thirty years after the emergence of the Buraku lists scandal*. Retrieved from http://www.blhrri.org/old/blhrri_e/news/new137/new137-2.htm05

Bureau of Labor Statistics. (2018, May 17). Foreign-born workers: Labor force characteristics—2017. *U.S. Department of Labor*. Retrieved from https://www.bls.gov/news.release/pdf/forbrn.pdf

Buriel, R. (1993). Acculturation, respect for cultural differences, and biculturalism among three generations of Mexican American and Euro-American school children. *Journal of Genetic Psychology*, 154, 531–544.

Butler, P. (2018). *Chokehold: Policing black men*. New York, NY: The New Press.

Caldwell, K. L. (2008). "Look at her hair": The body politics of black womanhood in Brazil. *Transforming*

Anthropology, 11(2), 18–29. doi: 10.1525/tran.2003. 11.2.18.

Camarillo, A., & Bonilla, F. (2001). Hispanics in a multicultural society: A new American dilemma? In N. Smelser, W. Wilson, & F. Mitchell (Eds.), *America becoming: Racial trends and their consequences* (Vol. 2, pp. 103–134). Washington, DC: National Academy Press.

Camarota, S. (2015, September 10). Welfare use by immigrant and native households: An analysis of Medicaid, cash, food, and housing programs. *Center for Immigration Studies*. Retrieved from https://cis.org/Report/Welfare-Use-Immigrant-and-Native-Households

Cardona, N. (2015, September 22). 50 years before Rosa Parks, a bold Nashville streetcar protest defied segregation. [Podcast]. *NPR*. Retrieved from http://nashvillepublicradio.org/post/50-years-rosa-parks-bold-nashville-streetcar-protest-defied-segregation#stream/0

Carpenter, R. (1998). *Father Charles E. Coughlin: Surrogate spokesman for the disaffected*. Westpoint, CT: Greenwood.

Carruthers, C. K., & Wanamaker, M. H. (2016). *Separate and unequal in the labor market: Human capital and the Jim Crow wage gap*. NBER Working Paper No. 21947. Retrieved from https://www.nber.org/papers/w21947

Castleman, B. L., & Page, L. C. (2014). *Summer melt supporting low-income students through the transition to college*. Boston, MA: Harvard Education Press.

Catalyst. (2018, October 31). *Quick take: Women in the workforce—global*. Retrieved from https://www.catalyst.org/research/women-in-the-workforce-global/#footnote3_tm9qrf4

Central Intelligence Agency. (2013). *The world factbook, 2013–14*. Washington, DC: Author. Retrieved from https://www.cia.gov/library/publications/the-world-factbook/geos/xx.html

Central Intelligence Agency. (2017). *The world factbook*. Retrieved April 17, 2017, from https://www.cia.gov/library/publications/the-world-factbook/geos/sf.html

Central Intelligence Agency. (2018). *The world factbook 2018*. Washington DC. Retrieved from https://www.cia.gov/library/publications/the-world-factbook/

Central Statistics Office [Ireland]. (2017). *Table 1 Components of Population Change, 1987–2017*. Retrieved from https://www.cso.ie/en/releasesandpublications/er/pme/populationandmigrationestimatesapril2017/

Chan, S. (1990). European and Asian immigrants into the United States in comparative perspective, 1820s to 1920s. In V. Yans-McLaughlin (Ed.), *Immigration reconsidered: History, sociology, and politics* (pp. 37–75). New York, NY: Oxford University Press.

Chapman, G. (2004). Geographical distribution of environmental factors influencing human skin coloration. *American Journal of Physical Anthropology*, 125(3), 292–302.

Chavez-Dueñas, N. Y., Adames, H. Y., & Organista, K. C. (2013). Skin-color prejudice and within-group racial discrimination. *Hispanic Journal of Behavioral Sciences*, 36(1), 3–26. doi: 10.1177/073998 6313511306.

Chetty, R., Friedman, J. N., Hendren, N., Jones, M. R., & Porter, S. R. (2018). *The opportunity atlas: Mapping the childhood roots of social mobility. Harvard University and NBER*. CES Paper #18-42. September. Retrieved from https://www.census.gov/ces/pdf/opportunity_atlas_paper.pdf

Children's Defense Fund. (2017). *The state of America's children*. Retrieved from https://www.childrensdefense.org/wp-content/uploads/2018/06/2017-soac.pdf

Chirot, D. (1994). *How societies change*. Thousand Oaks, CA: SAGE.

Cho, S. (1993). Korean Americans vs. African Americans: Conflict and construction. In R. Gooding-Williams (Ed.), *Reading Rodney King, reading urban uprising* (pp. 196–211). New York, NY: Routledge & Kegan Paul.

Choo, C. (2016). The health of Aboriginal children in Western Australia 1829–1960. In J. Boulton (Ed.), *Aboriginal children history and health: Beyond social determinants*. New York, NY: Routledge.

Chou, R., & Feagin, J. (2008). *The myth of the model minority: Asian Americans facing racism*. Boulder, CO: Paradigm.

Chowkwanyun, M., & Segall, J. (2012, August 24). The rise of the majority-Asian suburb. *CityLab*. Retrieved from http://www.citylab.com/politics/2012/08/rise-majority-asian-suburb/3044/

Chung, M. (2015, December 22). Breaking barriers: African-American firsts in 2015. *NBC News*. Retrieved August 8, 2017, from http://www.nbcnews.com/news/nbcblk/breaking-barriers-african-american-firsts-2015-n478556

Churchill, W. (1985, December). Resisting relocation: Dine and Hopis fight to keep their land. *Dollars and Sense*, 112–115.

Churchill, W. (1997). *A little matter of genocide: Holocaust and denial in the Americas, 1492 to the present*. San Francisco, CA: City Light Books.

Clark, K. B., & Clark, M. K. (1940). Skin color as a factor in racial identification of negro preschool children. *The Journal of Social Psychology*, 11, 159–169.

Clark, K. B., & Clark, M. K. (1950). Emotional factors in racial identification of negro preschool children. *Journal of Negro Education*, 19, 341–350.

Clark's Sector Model, US (n.d.). In *Wikipedia*. Retrieved April 13, 2019, from https://en.wikipedia.org/wiki/Post-industrial_society#/media/File:Clark%27s_Sector_model.png

Clements, N. (2014). *Black war: Fear, sex and resistance in Tasmania*. Brisbane, Australia: University of Queensland Press.

CNN Library. (2017, May 16). Mexico drug war fast facts. *CNN*. Retrieved from http://www.cnn.com/2013/09/02/world/americas/mexico-drug-war-fast-facts/index.html

Coates, T-N. (2010, August 9). Small truth papering over a big lie. *The Atlantic*. Retrieved May 5, 2017, from https://www.theatlantic.com/national/archive/2010/08/small-truth-papering-over-a-big-lie/61136/

Coates, T-N. (2014, June 24). The case for reparations. *The Atlantic*. Retrieved August 10, 2017, from https://www.theatlantic.com/projects/reparations

Coates, T-N. (2015). *Between the world and me*. New York, NY: Spiegel & Grau.

Cohen, A., & Taylor, E. (2000). *American pharaoh, Mayor Richard J. Daley: His battle for Chicago and the nation*. New York, NY: Little, Brown.

Cohen, F. S. (1945). *Handbook of federal Indian law: With reference tables and index* (4th ed.). Washington, DC: U.S. Government Printing Office.

Cohen, J. (1982). *The friars and the Jews: The evolution of medieval anti-Judaism*. Ithaca, NY: Cornell University Press.

Cohen, S. M. (1985). *The 1984 national survey of American Jews: Political and social outlooks*. New York, NY: American Jewish Committee.

Cohn, D. (2010, March 3). Census history: Counting Hispanics. *Pew Research Center*. Retrieved from http://www.pewsocialtrends.org/2010/03/03/census-history-counting-hispanics-2/

Cohn, D., Passel, J., & Gonzalez-Barrera, A. (2017, December 7). Rise in U.S. immigrants from El Salvador, Guatemala and Honduras outpaces growth from elsewhere. *Pew Research Center*. Washington, DC: Pew Research Center. Retrieved from http://www.pewhispanic.org/wp-content/uploads/sites/5/2017/12/Pew-Research-Center_Central_American-migration-to-U.S._12.7.17.pdf

Colby, S. L., & Ortman, J. M. (2015). Projections of the size and composition of the U.S. population, 2014 to 2060. *Current Population Reports*. Retrieved April 11, 2017, from https://www.census.gov/content/dam/Census/library/publications/2015/demo/p25-1143.pdf

Collins, P. H. (2000). *Black feminist thought: Knowledge, consciousness, and the politics of empowerment* (2nd ed.). New York, NY: Routledge.

Commonwealth of Australia. (1997). *Bringing them home. Report of the national inquiry into the separation of Aboriginal and Torres Strait Islander children from their families*. Retrieved August 18, 2017, from http://www.humanrights.gov.au/sites/default/files/content/pdf/social_justice/bringing_them_home_report.pdf

Congressional Record. (2007, February 12). *House of Representatives*, 153(3), 3721.

Connor, P., & Krogstad, J. M. (2016, October 5). Key facts about the world's refugees. *Pew Research Center*. Retrieved from http://www.pewresearch.org/fact-tank/2016/10/05/key-facts-about-the-worlds-refugees/

Conot, R. (1967). *Rivers of blood, years of darkness*. New York, NY: Bantam.

Constitutional Rights Foundation. (n.d.). *Race and voting in the segregated South*. Retrieved August 10, 2017, from http://www.crf-usa.org/black-history-month/race-and-voting-in-the-segregated-south

Conzen, K. N. (1980). Germans. In S. Thernstrom, A. Orlov, & O. Handlin (Eds.), *Harvard encyclopedia of American ethnic groups* (pp. 405–425). Cambridge, MA: Harvard University Press.

Cooper, B., Cox, D., Dionne Jr., E. J., Lienesch, R., Jones, R. P., & Galston, W. A. (2016, June 24). How immigration and concerns about cultural change are shaping the 2016 election. *PRRI*. Retrieved from https://www.prri.org/research/prri-brookings-poll-immigration-economy-trade-terrorism-presidential-race/

Cooper, H. L. F. (2015). War on drugs policing and police brutality. *Substance Use and Misuse*, 50(8/9), 1188–94. doi: 10.3109/10826084.2015.1007669.

Cornell, S. (1987). American Indians, American dreams, and the meaning of success. *American Indian Culture and Research Journal*, 11, 59–71.

Cornell, S. (1988). *The return of the Native: American Indian political resurgence*. New York, NY: Oxford University Press.

Cornell, S. (1990). Land, labor, and group formation: Blacks and Indians in the United States. *Ethnic and Racial Studies*, 13, 368–388.

Cornell, S. (2006). *What makes first nations enterprises successful? Lessons from the Harvard project*. Tucson, AZ: Native Nations Institute for Leadership, Management, and Policy.

Cornell, S., & Kalt, J. (1998). *Sovereignty and nation-building: The development challenge in Indian country today*. Cambridge, MA: Harvard Project on American Indian Economic Development.

Cornell, S., Kalt, J., Krepps, M., & Taylor, J. (1998). *American Indian gaming policy and its socioeconomic effects: A report to the National Impact Gambling Study Commission*. Cambridge, MA: Economics Resource Group.

Corral, O., Negrete, T. F., Nesmith, S. A., & Anasagasti, S. (2016, November 26). The day Fidel Castro ceded power to his brother. *Miami Herald*. Retrieved from https://www.miamiherald.com/news/nation-world/world/americas/fidel-castro-en/article117213333.html

Cortes, C. (1980). Mexicans. In S. Thernstrom, A. Orlov, & O. Handlin (Eds.), *Harvard encyclopedia of American ethnic groups* (pp. 697–719). Cambridge, MA: Harvard University Press.

Cose, E. (1993). *The rage of a privileged class*. New York, NY: HarperCollins.

Coski, J. M. (2009). *The Confederate battle flag*. Boston, MA: Harvard University Press.

Costner, K. (Director). (1990). *Dances with Wolves*. [Motion Picture]. United states: TIG Productions, Inc.

Council of Energy Resource Tribes. (n.d.). *About CERT*. Retrieved October 11, 2015, http://74.63.154.129/aboutus-philosophyHistory.html

Cox, D., Lienesch, R., & Jones, R. P. (2017, May 9). Beyond economics: Fears of cultural displacement pushed the white working class to Trump. *PRRI/The Atlantic Report*. Retrieved from https://www.prri.org/research/white-working-class-attitudes-economy-trade-immigration-election-donald-trump/

Cox, D., Navarro-Rivera, J., & Jones, R. P. (2016, March 8). Race, religion, and political affiliation of Americans' core social network. *Public Religion Research Institute*. Retrieved July 20, 2017, https://www.prri.org/research/poll-race-religion-politics-americans-social-networks/

Craven, W. F. (1970). *The southern colonies in the seventeenth century, 1607–1689: A history of the south* (Vol. 1). Baton Rouge, LA: Louisiana State University Press.

Cristol, D., & Gimbert, B. (2008). Racial perceptions of young children: A review of literature post-1999. *Early Childhood Education*, 36, 201–207.

Cuddy, A. J. C., Fiske, S. T., & Glick, P. (2008). Warmth and competence as universal dimensions of social perception: the stereotype content model and the BIAS map. In M. P. Zanna (Ed.), *Advances in experimental psychology*, 40, 61–149. San Diego, CA: Elsevier Academic Press.

Culliton, K. (2012). Born in the Americas: Birthright citizenship and human rights. *Harvard Human Rights Law Journal*, 25(1).

Curtin, P. (1990). *The rise and fall of the plantation complex*. New York, NY: Cambridge University Press.

D'Alessio, S., Stolzenberg, L., & Eitle, D. (2002). The effect of racial threat on interracial and intraracial crimes. *Social Science Research*, 31, 392–408.

D'Angelo, R. (2001). *The American civil rights movement: Readings and interpretations*. New York, NY: McGraw-Hill.

D'Orso, M. (1996). *Like Judgment Day: The ruin and redemption of a town called Rosewood*. New York, NY: Putnam.

Dakota Access, LLC. (n.d.). *About the Dakota Access Pipeline*. Retrieved August 18, 2017, from https://daplpipelinefacts.com/about-the-dakota-access-pipeline/

Davidson, J. M. (2004). Rituals captured in context and time: Charm use in North Dallas freedman's town (1869–1907), Dallas, Texas. *Historical Archaeology*, 38(2), 22–54.

Davis, B. J. (2008). *The national grape boycott: A victory for farmworkers*. Minneapolis, MN: Compass Point Books.

Davis, M. E., Vakalahi, H. F. O., & Scales, R. (2015). Women of color in the academy: From trauma to transformation. In K. De Welde & A. Stepnick (Eds.), *Disrupting the culture of silence: Confronting gender inequality and making change in higher education* (pp. 265–277). Arlington, VA: Stylus Publishing.

Dawson, M. C., & Bobo, L. D. (2009). One year later and the myth of a post-racial society. *Du Bois Review: Social Science Research on Race*, 6(2), 247–249.

De la Cruz, P., & Brittingham, A. (2003). *The Arab population: 2000*. Retrieved from http://www.census.gov/prod/2003pubs/c2kbr-23.pdf

Debo, A. (1970). *A history of the Indians of the United States*. Norman: University of Oklahoma Press.

DeSilver, D. (2015, November 19). U.S. public seldom has welcomed refugees into country. *Pew Research Center*. Retrieved from http://www.pewresearch.org/fact-tank/2015/11/19/u-s-public-seldom-has-welcomed-refugees-into-country/

Dewan, S. (2013, July 2). Immigration and social security. *New York Times*. Retrieved from http://economix.blogs.nytimes.com/2013/07/02/immigration-and-social-security/?_r=0

Dhingra, P. (2012). *Life behind the lobby*. Redwood City, CA: Stanford University Press.

Diamond, J. (1998). *Guns, germs, and steel: The fates of human societies*. New York, NY: W. W. Norton & Company.

Dickerson, C. (2017a, November 13). After hurricane, signs of a mental health crisis haunt Puerto Rico. *New York Times*. Retrieved from https://www.nytimes.com/2017/11/13/us/puerto-rico-hurricane-maria-mental-health.html

Dickerson, C. (2017b, May 17). Immigration arrests rise sharply as a Trump mandate is carried out. *New York Times*. Retrieved from https://www.nytimes.com/2017/05/17/us/igration-enforcement-ice-arrests.html

Digital Public Library of America. (n.d.). *Prisoners at home: Everyday life in Japanese internment camps*. Retrieved from https://dp.la/exhibitions/japanese-internment/employment

Dinnerstein, L. (1977). The East European Jewish immigration. In L. Dinnerstein & F. C. Jaher (Eds.), *Uncertain Americans* (pp. 216–231). New York, NY: Oxford University Press.

DiTomaso, N. (2013). *The American non-dilemma: Racial inequality without racism*. New York, NY: Russell Sage Foundation.

Dolan, J. P. (2010). *The Irish Americans: A history*. New York, NY: Bloomsbury.

Dollard, J. (1937). *Caste and class in a southern town*. New Haven, CT: Yale.

Dollinger, M. A. (2005). African American–Jewish relations. In R. S. Levy, D. P. Bell, & W. C. Donahue (Eds.), *Antisemitism: A historical encyclopedia of prejudice and persecution* (Vol. 1, pp. 4–5). Santa Barbara, CA: ABC-CLIO.

Dovere, E-I. (2018, November 10). The midterms swept in a new class of black politicians. *The Atlantic*. Retrieved from https://www.theatlantic.com/politics/archive/2018/11/black-candidates-who-clinched-house-and-state-races/575491/

Doyle, A. B., & Aboud, F. E. (1995). A longitudinal study of white children's racial prejudice as a socio-cognitive development. *Merrill-Palmer Quarterly*, 41, 209–228.

Drake, S. G. (1845). *The book of the Indians, or, biography and history of the Indians of North America, from its first discovery to the year 1841* (9th ed.). Boston, MA: Benjamin B. Mussey.

Du Bois, W. E. B. (1961). *The souls of black folk*. Greenwich, CT: Fawcett.

Dubrulle, H. (2016). *Lies, damn lies, and statistics: Slavery and the 1.6%*. Retrieved April 30, 2017, from https://saintanselmhistory.wordpress.com/2016/02/05/lies-damn-lies-and-statistics-slavery-and-the-1-6/

Duleep, H. O. (1988). *Economic status of Americans of Asian descent*. Washington, DC: U.S. Commission on Civil Rights.

Dumont, J. C., & LeMaitre, G. (2011). *Counting immigrants and ex-patriots in OECD countries: A new perspective*. OECD Working Paper. Retrieved from http://www.oecd.org/dataoecd/27/5/33868740.pdf

Dwyer, R. E. (2010). Poverty, prosperity, and place: The shape of class segregation in the age of extremes. *Social Problems*, 57, 114–137.

Dyble, M., Salali, G. D., Chaudhary, N., Page, A., Smith, D., & Thompson, J. (2015). Sex equality can explain the unique social structure of hunter-gatherer bands. *Science*, 348(6236), 796–798.

Dyke & Sparhawk. (1865). *constitution or form of government for the people of Florida, as revised, amended and agreed upon, at a convention of the people, begun and holden at the city of Tallahassee, on the 25th day of October, A.D. 1865, together with the ordinances adopted by said convention*. Tallahassee, FL: Dyke & Sparhawk.

Eckholm, E. (2010, July 28). Congress moves to narrow cocaine sentencing disparity. *New York Times*. Retrieved from http://www.nytimes.com/2010/07/29/us/politics/29crack.html?adxnnl=1&pagewanted=print&adxnnlx=1382103459-x0tOpZ4wq4lKuhvMAc5weg

Edin, K., & Kefalas, M. H. (2005). *Promises I can keep: Why poor women put motherhood before marriage*. Berkeley: University of California Press.

Egelko, B. (2009, January 15). BART shooting draws Rodney King case parallels. *San Francisco Chronicle*. Retrieved from http://www.sfgate.com/bayarea/article/BART-shooting-draws-Rodney-King-case-parallels-3176756.php

Elkins, S. (1959/2013). *Slavery: A problem in American institutional and intellectual life*. Chicago, IL: University of Chicago Press.

Ellsworth, S. (1982). *Death in a promised land: The Tulsa race riot of 1921*. Baton Rouge: Louisiana State University Press.

Emory University. (2013). Trans-Atlantic slave database voyages: African names. *Slave Voyages*. Retrieved August 4, 2017, http://www.slavevoyages.org/resources/names-database

Enchautegui, M. E. (2015, October 13). Immigrant and native workers compete for different low-skilled jobs. *Urban Institute*. Retrieved from https://www.urban.org/urban-wire/immigrant-and-native-workerscompete-different-low-skilled-jobs

Ennis, S., Rios-Vargas, M., & Albert, N. (2011). *The Hispanic population: 2010*. Washington, DC: U.S. Census Bureau. Retrieved from http://www.census.gov/prod/cen2010/briefs/c2010br-04.pdf

Equal Justice Initiative. (2017). *Lynching in America: Confronting the legacy of racial terror* (3rd ed.). New York, NY: New American Library. Retrieved August 10, 2017, from https://lynchinginamerica.eji.org/report/

Equity and Excellence Commission. (2013). *For each and every child*. Retrieved from https://www2.ed.gov/about/bdscomm/list/eec/equity-excellence-commission-report.pdf

Erie, S. P., & Kogan, V. (2016). Machine bosses, reformers, and the politics of ethnic and minority incorporation. In R. H. Bayor (Ed.), *Handbook of American immigration and ethnicity* (pp. 302–318). New York, NY: Oxford University Press.

Espinosa, K., & Massey, D. (1997). Determinants of English proficiency among Mexican migrants to the United States. *International Migration Review*, 31, 28–51.

Espiritu, Y. (1996). Colonial oppression, labour importation, and group formation: Filipinos in the United States. *Ethnic and Racial Studies*, 19, 29–48.

Essien-Udom, E. U. (1962). *Black nationalism.* Chicago, IL: University of Chicago Press.

Estrada, G. S. (2011). Two spirits, Nádleeh, and LGBTQ2 Navajo gaze. *American Indian Culture and Research Journal,* 35(4), 167–190.

Evans, S. M. (1979). *Personal politics.* New York, NY: Knopf.

Evans, S. M. (1980). *Personal politics: The roots of women's liberation in the civil rights movement and the new left.* New York, NY: Vintage Books.

Evans, S. M. (1989). *Born for liberty: A history of women in America.* New York, NY: Free Press.

Ezard, J. (2001, February 16). Germans knew of Holocaust horror about death camps: Details of deaths of Jews and other groups in concentration camps were well publicized. *The Guardian.* Available at https://www.theguardian.com/uk/2001/feb/17/johnezard

Fadiman, A. (1998). *The spirit catches you and you fall down.* New York, NY: Farrar, Straus, & Giroux.

Falicov, C. J. (2010). Changing constructions of machismo for Latino men in therapy: The devil never sleeps. *Family Process,* 49(3), 309–329. doi: 10.1111/j.1545-5300.2010.01325.x.

Farivar, M. (2017, May 2). U.S. Justice Department defends record against hate crimes. *VOA News.* Retrieved August 9, 2017, from https://www.voanews.com/a/justice-department-defends-record-against-hate-crime/3835580.html

Farley, J. (2000). *Majority–minority relations* (4th ed.). Englewood Cliffs, NJ: Prentice Hall.

Farley, R. (1996). *The new American reality.* New York, NY: Russell Sage Foundation.

Fausto-Sterling, A. (1993, March/April). The five sexes: Why male and female are not enough. *The Sciences,* 20–24.

Faux, J. (2004, February 2). NAFTA at 10: Where do we go from here? *Nation,* 11–14.

Feagin, J. R. (2001). *Racist America: Roots, current realities, and future reparations.* New York, NY: Routledge.

Feagin, J. R., & Feagin, C. B. (1986). *Discrimination American style: Institutional racism and sexism.* Malabar, FL: Robert E. Krieger.

Feagin, J. R., & O'Brien, E. (2004). *White men on Race: Power, privilege, and the shaping of cultural consciousness.* Boston, MA: Beacon Press.

Fears, D. (2007, November 20). Hate crime reporting uneven. *Washington Post,* p. A3.

Federal Bureau of Investigation (FBI). (1997). *Hate crime statistics 1997.* Retrieved from https://ucr.fbi.gov/hate-crime/1997

Federal Bureau of Investigation (FBI). (2015). Table 1. Incidents, offenses, victims, and known offenders by bias motivation, 2015. *2015 hate crime statistics.* Retrieved August 9, 2017, from https://ucr.fbi.gov/hate-crime/2015/tables-and-data-declarations/1tabledatadecpdf

Federal Bureau of Investigation (FBI). (2017). Table 1. Incidents, offenses, victims, and known offenders by bias motivation, 2017. *2017 hate crime statistics.* Table 1 Retrieved from https://ucr.fbi.gov/hate-crime/2017/tables/table-1.xls

Federation for American Immigration Reform. (2010). *Birthright citizenship.* Retrieved from http://www.fairus.org/issue/birthright-citizenship?A=SearchResult&SearchID=2723806&ObjectID=5123842&ObjectType=35

Feliciano, C. (2006). *Another way to assess the second generation: Look at the parents.* Washington, DC: Migration Policy Institute. Retrieved from http://www.migrationinformation.org/USfocus/display.cfm?ID=396

Fennell, C. C. (2013). Group identity, individual creativity, and symbolic generation in a BaKongo diaspora. *International Journal of Historical Archaeology,* 7(1), 1–31.

File, T. (2013). *The diversifying electorate: Voting rates by race and Hispanic origin in 2012 (and other recent elections).* Washington, DC: U.S. Census Bureau. Retrieved from http://www.census.gov/prod/2013pubs/p20-568.pdf

Firefighters Local Union No. 1784 v. Stotts, 467 U.S. 561 (1984)

Fisher v. University of Texas at Austin, 570 U.S. 11–345 (2013)

Fisher, A. (2005, August 8). Piercing the "bamboo ceiling." *CNN*. Retrieved from https://money.cnn.com/2005/08/08/news/economy/annie/fortune_annie080805/index.htm

Fisher, M. (2008). Does campus diversity promote friendship diversity? A look at interracial friendships in college. *Social Science Quarterly*, 89, 623–655.

Fitzpatrick, J. P. (1976). The Puerto Rican family. In C. H. Mindel & R. W. Habenstein (Eds.), *Ethnic families in America* (pp. 173–195). New York, NY: Elsevier.

Fitzpatrick, J. P. (1980). Puerto Ricans. In S. Thernstrom, A. Orlov, & O Handlin (Eds.), *Harvard encyclopedia of American ethnic groups* (pp. 858–867). Cambridge, MA: Harvard University Press.

Fitzpatrick, J. P. (1987). *Puerto Rican Americans: The meaning of migration to the mainland* (2nd ed.). Englewood Cliffs, NJ: Prentice Hall.

Fix, M. (2015). Repealing birthright citizenship: The unintended consequences. *Migration Policy Institute*. Retrieved from https://www.migrationpolicy.org/news/repealing-birthright-citizenship-unintended-consequences

Flanagan, M. S. (2015). Irish women's immigration to the United States after the potato famine, 1860–1900. *Dominican University of California*. Reviewed from https://scholar.dominican.edu/cgi/viewcontent.cgi?article=1051&context=senior-theses

Flavia, C. P., Amado, R. C., Lambertucci, J. R., Rocha, J., Antunes, C. M., & Pena, S. D. J. (2003). Color and genomic ancestry in Brazilians. *Proceedings of the National Academy of Sciences of the United States of America*, 100(1), 177–182. doi: 10.1073/pnas.0126614100.

Florida, R. (2012, January 11). The geography of women's economic opportunities. *CityLab*. Retrieved February 24, 2019, from https://www.citylab.com/life/2012/01/how-economic-development-helps-worlds-women/907/

Florida, R. (2017, June 27). Immigrants boost wages for everyone. *CityLab*. Retrieved January 25, 2019, from https://www.citylab.com/equity/2017/06/immigration-wages-economics/530301/

Foner, E. (2011). *Reconstruction: America's unfinished revolution, 1863–1877*. New York, NY: Harper Collins.

Fong, E., & Markham, W. (1991). Immigration, ethnicity, and conflict: The California Chinese, 1849–1882. *Sociological Inquiry*, 61, 471–490.

Fong, T. (2002). *The contemporary Asian American experience* (2nd ed.). Upper Saddle River, NJ: Prentice Hall.

Foraker Act. (1900). Retrieved from http://college.cengage.com/history/world/keen/latin_america/8e/assets/students/sources/pdfs/167_foraker_act_of_1900.pdf

Foreman, A. (2015, February). Why footbinding persisted in China for a millennium. *Smithsonian*. Retrieved from https://www.smithsonianmag.com/history/why-footbinding-persisted-china-millennium-180953971/

Forner, P. S. (1980). *Women and the American labor movement: From World War I to the present*. New York, NY: Free Press.

Forstall, R. L. (1996). *Population of states and counties of the United States: 1790 to 1990*. Washington, DC: Department of Commerce, U.S. Bureau of the Census Population Division.

Fox, M. (2012, September 14). Lia Lee dies; life went on around her, redefining care. *New York Times*. Retrieved from https://www.nytimes.com/2012/09/15/us/life-went-on-around-her-redefining-care-by-bridging-a-divide.html

Franco, M. (2008). *Parallel empires: The Vatican and the United States—two centuries of alliance and conflict*. New York, NY: Double Day.

Frankel, J. (1997). *The fate of the European Jews, 1939–1945: Continuity or contingency?* New York, NY: Oxford University Press.

Franklin, J. H. (1967). *From slavery to freedom* (3rd ed.). New York, NY: Knopf.

Franklin, J. H., & Moss, A. (1994). *From slavery to freedom* (7th ed.). New York, NY: McGraw-Hill.

Frazier, E. F. (1957). *Black bourgeoisie: The rise of a new middle class*. New York, NY: Free Press.

Fresh, A. (2018). The effect of the Voting Rights Act on enfranchisement: Evidence from North Carolina. *The Journal of Politics*. doi:10.1086/697592.

Freyre, G. (1946). *The masters and the slaves: A study in the development of Brazilian civilization.* New York, NY: Knopf.

Friedman, M. (n.d.). *Inflation calculator.* Retrieved 2017 from https://westegg.com/inflation/infl.cgi

Fry, R. (2007). *The changing racial and ethnic composition of U.S. public schools.* Washington, DC: Pew Hispanic Center. Retrieved from http://pewhispanic.org/files/reports/79.pdf

Fryer, R. G., Jr. (2018). *Reconciling results on racial differences in police shootings.* Retrieved from https://scholar.harvard.edu/files/fryer/files/fryer_police_aer.pdf

Gabaccia, D. (1991). Immigrant women: Nowhere at home? *Journal of American Ethnic History, 10*(4), 61–87.

Gallagher, C. (2001, April). *Playing the ethnic card: How ethnic narratives maintain racial privilege.* Paper presented at the Annual Meetings of the Southern Sociological Society, Atlanta, GA.

Gallup. (2012). *Presidential job approval.* Retrieved from http://www.gallup.com/poll/124922/presidentialapproval-center.aspx

Gallup. (2017a). *Gallup race relations fact sheet.* Retrieved August 5, 2017, from http://www.gallup.com/poll/1687/race-relations.aspx

Gallup. (2017b, January 23). *Obama weekly job approval.* Retrieved from http://www.gallup.com/poll/121199/Obama-Weekly-Job-Approval-Demographic-Groups.aspx

Gannon, M. (2016). Race is a social construct, scientists argue. *Scientific American.* Retrieved April 15, 2017, from https://www.scientificamerican.com/article/race-is-a-social-construct-scientists-argue/

Gans, H. (1979). Symbolic ethnicity: The future of ethnic groups and cultures in America. *Ethnic and Racial Studies, 2,* 1–20.

Gans, H. (1997). Toward a reconciliation of "assimilation" and "pluralism": The interplay of acculturation and ethnic retention." *International Migration Review, 31*(4), 875–892.

Garcia-Navarro, L. (2015, August 12). Dark-skinned or black? How Afro-Brazilians are forging a collective identity. *NPR.* Retrieved from http://www.npr.org/sections/codeswitch/2015/08/12/431244962/dark-skinned-or-black-how-afro-brazilians-are-forging-a-collective-identity

Garvey, M. (1969). *Philosophy and opinions of Marcus Garvey* (Vols. 1–2). Edited by A. Jacques Garvey. New York, NY: Atheneum.

Garvey, M. (1977). *Philosophy and opinions of Marcus Garvey* (Vol. 3; A. Jacques Garvey & E.U. Essien-Udom, Eds.). London, UK: Frank Cass.

Gee, B., & Peck, D. (2018, May 31). Asian Americans are the least likely group in the U.S. to be promoted to management. *Harvard Business Review.* Retrieved from https://hbr.org/2018/05/asian-americans-are-the-least-likely-group-in-the-u-s-to-be-promoted-to-management

Gee, L. C., Gardner, M., & Wiehe, M. (2016). Undocumented immigrant's state and local tax contributions. *Institute on Taxation and Economic Policy.* Retrieved from https://itep.org/undocumented-immigrants-state-local-tax-contributions-1/

Gellately, R. (2002). *Backing Hitler: Consent and coercion in Nazi Germany.* Oxford, UK: OUP.

Genovese, E. D. (1974). *Roll, Jordan, roll: The world the slaves made.* New York, NY: Pantheon.

George-Kanentiio, D. M. (2000). *Iroquois culture & commentary.* Santa Fe, NM: Clear Light Publishers.

George-Kanentiio, D. M. (2006). *Iroquois on fire: A voice from the Mohawk nation.* Westport, CT: Greenwood Publishing Group.

Gerstenfeld, P. (2004). *Hate crime: Causes, controls, and controversies.* Thousand Oaks, CA: SAGE.

Gerstenfeld, P. B., Grant, D. R., & Chiang, C. P. (2003). Hate online: A content analysis of extremist Internet sites. *Analyses of Social Issues and Public Policy, 3*(1), 29–44.

Gerth, H., & Mills, C. W. (Eds.). (1946). *From Max Weber: Essays in sociology.* New York, NY: Oxford University Press.

Geschwender, J. A. (1978). *Racial stratification in America.* Dubuque, IA: William C. Brown.

Giaritelli, A. (2018, October 23). Here's how long it takes to walk from Mexico's southern border to the US. *Washington Examiner*. Retrieved January 25, 2019, https://www.washingtonexaminer.com/news/heres-how-long-it-takes-to-walk-from-mexicos-southern-border-to-the-us

Ginsberg, R. B. (2013). Dissent in *Shelby County v. Holder* 570 U.S. 529.

Glaeser, E., & Vigdor, J. (2012). *The end of the segregated century: Racial separation in America's neighborhoods, 1890–2010*. New York, NY: Manhattan Institute, Center for State and Local Leadership. Retrieved from http://www.manhattan-institute.org/html/cr_66.htm

Glazer, N., & Moynihan, D. (1970). *Beyond the melting pot* (2nd ed.). Cambridge, MA: MIT Press.

Gleason, P. (1980). American identity and Americanization. In S. Thernstrom, A. Orlov, & O. Handlin (Eds.), *Harvard encyclopedia of American ethnic groups* (pp. 31–57). Cambridge, MA: Harvard University Press.

Goff, P. A., Jackson, M. C., Allison, B., Di Leone, L., Culotta, C., M., & DiTomasso, N. A. (2014). The essence of innocence: Consequences of dehumanizing black children. *Journal of Personality and Social Psychology*, 106(4), 526–545. doi: 10.1037/a003566.

Goldfield, D., Abbott, C., Anderson, V. D., Argersinger, J. A. E., Argersinger, P. H., & Barney, W. M. (2002). *The American journey: A history of the United States*. Upper Saddle River, NJ: Prentice Hall.

Goldstein, A., & Suro, R. (2000, January 16). A journey on stages: Assimilation's pull is still strong but its pace varies. *Washington Post*, p. A1.

Goldstein, J. (2013, August 12). Judge rejects New York's stop-and-frisk policy. *New York Times*. Retrieved from http://www.nytimes.com/2013/08/13/nyregion/stop-and-frisk-practice-violated-rights-judge-rules.html

Golway, T. (2014). *Machine made: Tammany Hall and the creation of modern American politics*. New York, NY: W. W. Norton & Company.

Gomez, L. (2008). *Manifest destinies: The making of the Mexican American race*. New York: NYU Press.

Gonzalez, J. (2011). *Harvest of empire: A History of Latinos in America*. New York, NY: Penguin Books.

Gonzalez, L. (2001, October). Viva Spanglish! *Texas Monthly*. October. Retrieved from https://www.texasmonthly.com/articles/viva-spanglish/

Gonzalez-Barrera, A. (2015, November 19). More Mexicans leaving than coming to the U.S. *Pew Research Center*. Retrieved from http://www.pewhispanic.org/2015/11/19/more-mexicans-leaving-than-coming-to-the-u-s/

Gonzalez-Barrera, A., & Lopez, M. H. (2013, May 1). A demographic portrait of Mexican-origin Hispanics in the United States. *Pew Research Center*. Retrieved from http://www.pewhispanic.org/2013/05/01/a-demographic-portrait-of-mexican-origin-hispanics-in-the-united-states/

Gordon, M. M. (1964). *Assimilation in American life: the role of race, religion, and national origins*. New York, NY: Oxford University Press.

Goren, A. (1980). Jews. In S. Thernstrom, A. Orlov, & O. Handlin (Eds.), *Harvard encyclopedia of American ethnic groups* (pp. 571–598). Cambridge, MA: Harvard University Press.

Goudreau, I. (2000). La semantica fugitiva: "Raza," color y vida cotidiana en Puerto Rico. *Revista de Ciencias Sociales (Nueva Epoca)*, 9, 52–71.

Gourevitch, P. (1999). *We wish to inform you that tomorrow we will be killed with our families: Stories from Rwanda*. New York, NY: Picador.

Gradín, C. (2007). *Why is poverty so high among Afro-Brazilians? A decomposition analysis of the racial poverty gap* (Discussion Paper Series). Retrieved July 20, 2017, from http://ftp.iza.org/dp2809.pdf

Gramlich, J. (2018, January 12). The gap between the number of blacks and whites in prison is shrinking. *Pew Research Center*. Retrieved from http://www.pewresearch.org/fact-tank/2018/01/12/shrinking-gap-between-number-of-blacks-and-whites-in-prison/

Grant-Thomas, A., & Orfield, G. (Eds.). (2008). *Twenty-first century color lines: Multiracial change in contemporary America*. Philadelphia, PA: Temple University Press.

Gratz v. Bollinger, 539 U.S. 244 (2003)

Grebler, L., Moore, J. W., & Guzman, R. C. (1970). *The Mexican American people*. New York, NY: Free Press.

Greeley, A. M. (1974). *Ethnicity in the United States: A preliminary reconnaissance*. New York, NY: Wiley.

Green, D. (1999). Native Americans. In A. Dworkin & R. Dworkin (Eds.), *The minority report* (pp. 255–277). Orlando, FL: Harcourt-Brace.

Greenberg, J. (2015, February 17). Sonia Sotomayor's family is from Puerto Rico, not "immigrant family." *PolitiFact*. Retrieved from http://www.politifact.com/punditfact/statements/2015/feb/17/laura-ingraham/ingraham-says-sotomayor-comes-immigrant-family/

Greene, D., & Newport, F. (2018, April 23). American public opinion and the Holocaust. *Gallup*. Available at https://news.gallup.com/opinion/polling-matters/232949/american-public-opinion-holocaust.aspx

Grey, G. (1841). *Journals of two expeditions of discovery in Northwest and Western Australia: during the years 1837, 38, and 39, under the authority of Her Majesty's government. Describing many newly discovered, important, and fertile districts, with observations on the moral and physical condition of the Aboriginal inhabitants* (Vol. 1). London, UK: T. and W. Boone. Retrieved August 18, 2017, from https://books.google.com/books?id=jfsoAAAAYAAJ

Griswold, D. T. (2012). Immigration and the welfare state. *Cato Journal*, 32, 159–174.

Gross, S. R., Possley, M., & Stephens, K. (2017). *Race and wrongful convictions in the United States*. Irvine: National Registry of Exonerations, Newkirk Center for Science and Society, University of California Irvine. Retrieved from http://www.law.umich.edu/special/exoneration/Documents/Race_and_Wrongful_Convictions.pdf

Grutter v. Bollinger, 539 U.S. 306 (2003)

Guedel, W. G. (2014). Sovereignty, economic development, and human security in Native American nations. *American Indian Law Journal*, 3, 17–39.

Gugliotta, G. (2008, July). The great human migration. *Smithsonian*. Retrieved April 15, 2017, http://www.smithsonianmag.com/history/the-great-human-migration-13561/

Gullah Geechee Cultural Heritage Corridor. (n.d.). *Roots*. Retrieved August 5, 2017, from https://www.gullahgeecheecorridor.org

Gutiérrez, D. G. (n.d.). *A historic overview of Latino immigration and the demographic transformation of the United States*. Retrieved from https://www.nps.gov/heritageinitiatives/latino/latinothemestudy/immigration.htm#_edn1

Gutman, H. (1976). *The black family in slavery and freedom, 1750–1925*. New York, NY: Vintage.

Haan, A., & Thorat, S. (2012). Addressing group inequalities: Social policies in emerging economies' great transformation. *European Journal of Development Research*, 24, 105–124.

Hacker, A. (1992). *Two nations: Black and white, separate, hostile, unequal*. New York, NY: Scribner's.

Hagler, J. (2015). It is time to update the Voting Rights Act. *Center for American Progress*. Retrieved November 28, 2016, from https://www.americanprogress.org/issues/race/news/2015/08/06/118888/it-is-time-to-update-the-voting-rights-act/

Hainmueller, J., & Hiscox, M. (2010). Attitudes toward highly skilled and low-skilled immigration: Evidence from a survey experiment. *American Political Science Review*, 104, 61–84.

Hakimzadeh, S., & Cohn, D. (2007). *English language usage among Hispanics in the United States*. Washington, DC: Pew Hispanic Center.

Halberstam, D. (1998). *The children*. New York, NY: Fawcett Books.

Haldevang, M. (2016, September 1). Why do we still use the term "sub-Saharan Africa"? *QuartzAfrica*. Retrieved from https://qz.com/africa/770350/why-do-we-still-say-subsaharan-africa/

Haley, A. (1976). *Roots: The saga of an American family*. New York, NY: Doubleday.

Hall, A. (2011, April 28). Ninety-eight percent of Texas confederate soldiers never owned a slave. *Dead Confederates: A Civil War era blog*. Retrieved from https://deadconfederates.com/2011/04/28/ninetyeight-percent-of-texas-confederate-soldiers-never-owned-a-slave/

Hall, A. V., Hall, E. V., & Perry, J. L. (2016). Shooting black and blue: Exploring racial bias and law enforcement in the killings of unarmed black male civilians. *American Psychologist*, 71(3), 175–186. Retrieved January 25, 2019 from http://scholarship.sha.cornell.edu/articles/887

Hall, G. M. (2009). *Slavery and African ethnicities in the Americas: Restoring the links*. Chapel Hill: University of North Carolina Press.

Hall, M., & Renee, S. (2016, December 30). Breaking barriers in 2016: A year of firsts among African Americans. *NBC News*. Retrieved August 8, 2017, http://www.nbcnews.com/news/nbcblk/breaking-barriers-2016-year-firsts-among-african-americans-n701291

Haller, W., Portes, A., & Lynch, S. (2011). Dreams fulfilled, dreams shattered: Determinants of segmented assimilation in the second generation. *Social Forces*, 89, 733–762.

Hämäläinen, P. (2008). *The Comanche empire*. New Haven, CT: Yale University Press.

Hamer, F. L. (1967). *To praise our bridges: An autobiography of Fannie Lou Hamer*. Jackson, MS: KIPCO.

Hand, M. (2017, November 6). Ohio sues developer behind Dakota Access Pipeline over pollution issues. *ThinkProgress*. Retrieved from https://thinkprogress.org/ohio-sues-rover-pipeline-438c4b6b9516/

Handlin, O. (1951). *The uprooted*. New York, NY: Grosset & Dunlap.

Handlin, O. (2002). *The uprooted: The epic story of the great migrations that made the American people*. Philadelphia, PA: University of Pennsylvania Press.

Hansen, M. L. (1952). The third generation in America. *Commentary*, 14, 493–500.

Hanskins, J. D. (2014). *Working skin: Making leather, making a multicultural Japan*. Berkeley: University of California Press.

Hanson, J. R., & Rouse, L. P. (1987). Dimensions of Native American stereotyping. *American Indian Culture and Research Journal*, 11, 33–58.

Harjo, S. (1996). Now and then: Native peoples in the United States. *Dissent*, 43, 58–60.

Harris, A. P. (2008). From color line to color chart: Racism and colorism in the new century. *Berkeley Journal of African-American Law & Policy*, 10, 52–69. doi: 10.15779/Z380C9X.

Hartman, H. (n.d.). *Gender roles in colonial America*. Retrieved August 18, 2017, from http://www.wou.edu/history/files/2015/08/Holly-Hartman-HST-499.pdf

Hartmann, M. (2014, August 14). In a stunning reversal, police join peaceful protest in Ferguson. *New York*. Retrieved from http://nymag.com/daily/intelligencer/2014/08/ferguson-protest-thursday.html

Hartocollis, A. (2018a, October 19). Harvard rated Asian-American applicants lower on personality traits, suit says. *New York Times*. Retrieved from https://www.nytimes.com/2018/06/15/us/harvard-asian-enrollment-applicants.html

Hartocollis, A. (2018b, October 19). Harvard's admissions process, once secret, is unveiled in affirmative action trial. *New York Times*. Retrieved from https://www.nytimes.com/2018/10/19/us/harvard-admissions-affirmative-action.html

Hassan, A. (2018, June 23). Confronting Asian-American stereotypes. *New York Times*. Retrieved from https://www.nytimes.com/2018/06/23/us/confronting-asian-american-stereotypes.html

Havekes, E., Bader, M., & Kryson, M. (2016). Realizing racial and ethnic neighborhood preferences? Exploring the mismatches between what people want, where they search, and where they live. *Population Research and Policy Review*, 35, 101–126.

Hawkins, H. (1962). *Booker T. Washington and his critics: The problem of negro leadership*. Boston, MA: D. C. Heath.

Hayes, C. (2018, June 25). Thousands of immigrants pass through the southern border. Why are they fleeing their home countries? *USA Today*. Retrieved from https://www.usatoday.com/story/news/2018/06/25/immigrant-family-separation-why-flee-home-countries/729013002/

Healy, J. (2016a, September 11). From 280 Tribes, a protest on the plains. *New York Times*. Retrieved August 18, 2017, https://www.nytimes.com/interactive/2016/09/12/us/12tribes.html

Healy, J. (2016b, August 26). North Dakota oil pipeline battle: Who's fighting and why. *New York Times*. Retrieved August 18, 2017, from https://www.nytimes.com/2016/11/02/us/north-dakota-oil-pipeline-battle-whos-fighting-and-why.html?smid=pl-share

Herberg, W. (1960). *Protestant–Catholic–Jew: An essay in American religious sociology*. New York, NY: Anchor.

Hernandez, T. K. (2007). Latino inter-ethnic employment discrimination and the diversity defense. *FLASH: The Fordham Law Archive of Scholarship and History*, 42, 259–316. Retrieved August 10, 2017, from http://ir.lawnet.fordham.edu/faculty_scholarship/13

Hetey R. C., Monin, B., Maitreyi, A., & Eberhardt, J. L. (2016). Data for change: A statistical analysis of police stops, searches, handcuffings, and arrests in Oakland, Calif., 2013–2014. *Stanford SPARQ*. Retrieved from http://www2.oaklandnet.com/oakca1/groups/police/documents/webcontent/oak059291.pdf

Higham, J. (1963). *Strangers in the land: Patterns of American nativism, 1860–1925*. New York, NY: Atheneum.

Hill, J. (1995). Mock Spanish: A site for the indexical reproduction of racism in American English. *Language and Culture: Symposium, 2*. Retrieved from http://language-culture.binghamton.edu/symposia/2/part1/

Hinton, E. (2016). *The war on poverty to the war on crime*. Cambridge, MA: Harvard University Press.

Hirschman, C. (1983). America's melting pot reconsidered. *Annual Review of Sociology*, 9, 397–423.

Hirschman, C., & Wong, M. (1984). Socioeconomic gains of Asian Americans, blacks, and Hispanics: 1960–1976. *American Journal of Sociology*, 90, 584–607.

Hirschman, C., & Wong, M. (1986). The extraordinary educational attainment of Asian-Americans: A search for historical evidence and explanations. *Social Forces*, 65, 1–27.

Hirst, K. K. (2017, June 26). Out of Africa hypothesis—did all humans evolve in Africa? *ThoughtCo*. Retrieved April 15, 2017, https://www.thoughtco.com/out-of-africa-hypothesis-172030

His Horse Is Thunder, D., Anderson, N., & Miller, D. G. (2013). *Building the foundation for success: Case studies of breaking through tribal colleges and universities*. Boston, MA: Jobs for the Future. Retrieved from http://www.jff.org/sites/default/files/publications/BuildingFoundationSuccess_ExSumm_040813.pdf

Historic Jamestown. (2018). The first Africans. *Jamestown rediscovery*. Available at https://historicjamestowne.org/history/the-first-africans/

History, Art, & Archives, U.S. House of Representatives, Office of the Historian. (2008). *Black-American Representatives and Senators by Congress, 1870–2007*. Washington, DC: U.S Government Printing Office. Retrieved April 10, 2019, from https://history.house.gov/Exhibitions-and-Publications/BAIC/Historical-Data/Black-American-Representatives-and-Senators-by-Congress/

Hochschild, A. (1979). Emotion work, feeling rules, and social structure. *American Journal of Sociology*, 85, 551–575.

Hoeffel, E., Rastogi, S., Kim, M. O., & Shahid, H. (2012). *The Asian population: 2010*. Washington, DC: U.S. Census Bureau. Retrieved from http://www.census.gov/prod/cen2010/briefs/c2010br-11.pdf

Hohn, M. D., Lowry, J. P., Witte, J. C., & Fernández-Pena, J. R. (2016). *Immigrants in health care: Keeping Americans healthy through care and innovation*. Retrieved August 30, 2017, from http://s3.amazonaws.com/chssweb/documents/22231/original/health_care_report_FINAL_20160629.pdf?1467209316

Hollinger, D. A. (2003). Amalgamation and hypodescent: The question of ethnoracial mixture in the history of the United States. *The American Historical Review*, 108(5), 1363–1390.

Holmes, R. C. (2017). It's been 10 weeks since Hurricane Maria hit Puerto Rico. Here's where recovery stands. *PBS News*. Retrieved from https://www.pbs.org/newshour/nation/its-been-10-weeks-since-hurricane-maria-hit-puerto-rico-heres-where-recovery-stands

Hönke, J. (2013). *Transnational companies and security governance: Hybrid practices in a postcolonial world*. London, UK: Routledge.

Hopcroft, R. (2009). Gender inequality in interaction: A evolutionary account. *Social Forces*, 87, 1845–1872.

Hostetler, J. (1980). *Amish society*. Baltimore, MD: Johns Hopkins University Press.

How to tell your friends from the Japs. (1941, October–December). *Time*, p. 33.

Hoxie, F. (1984). *A final promise: The campaign to assimilate the Indian, 1880–1920*. Lincoln: University of Nebraska Press.

Hraba, J. (1994). *American ethnicity* (2nd ed.). Itasca, IL: F. E. Peacock.

Huber, J. (2007). *On the origins of gender inequality*. Colorado Springs, CO: Paradigm.

Hughes, M., & Thomas, M. (1998). The continuing significance of race revisited: A study of race, class, and quality of life in America, 1972 to 1996. *American Sociological Review*, 63, 785–803.

Hult, J. (2017). Dakota Access sued over farmland damage in South Dakota. *Argus Leader*. Retrieved from http://www.argusleader.com/story/news/2017/11/01/dakota-access-sued-over-farmland-damage-south-dakota/822273001/

Human Rights Watch. (2017). *Haiti: Events of 2017*. Retrieved from https://www.hrw.org/world-report/2018/country-chapters/haiti

Humane Borders. (2018). *Deaths on the border, 1999–2018*. Retrieved from http://www.humaneborders.info/app/map.asp

Huntington, S. (2004). *Who are we? The challenges to America's national identity*. New York, NY: Simon & Schuster.

Hurh, W. M. (1998). *The Korean Americans*. Westport, CT: Greenwood.

Hyun, J. (2005). *Breaking the bamboo ceiling: Career strategies for Asians*. New York, NY: Harper Collins.

Ibish, H. (Ed.). (2003). *Report on hate crimes and discrimination against Arab Americans: The post–September 11 Backlash*. Washington, DC: American-Arab Anti-Discrimination Committee. Retrieved from http://www.adc.org/hatecrimes/pdf/2003_report_web.pdf

Iceland, J., Weinberg, D., & Steinmetz, E. (2002). *Racial and ethnic residential segregation in the United States: 1980–2000* (U.S. Census Bureau, Series CENSR-3). Washington, DC: U.S. Government Printing Office. Retrieved from http://www.census.gov/prod/2002pubs/censr-3.pdf

Ifill, G. (2009). *The breakthrough: Politics and race in the age of Obama*. New York, NY: Doubleday.

The Impact of Immigrant Women on America's Labor Force. (2017, March 8). *American Immigration Council*. Retrieved from https://www.americanimmigrationcouncil.org/research/impact-immigrant-women-americas-labor-force

Inglis, T. (2007). Catholic identity in contemporary Ireland: Belief and belonging to tradition. *Journal of Contemporary Religion*, 22(2), 205–220.

International Labour Organization. (2017). *Global estimates of modern slavery: Forced labour and forced marriage*. Retrieved January 8, 2019, from https://www.ilo.org/global/publications/books/WCMS_575479/lang--en/index.htm

International Organization for Migration. (2014). *Fatal journeys: Tracking lives lost during migration* (T. Brian & F. Lascko, Eds.). Geneva, Switzerland: Author. Retrieved from http://www.iom.int/files/live/sites/iom/files/pbn/docs/Fatal-Journeys-Tracking-Lives-Lost-during-Migration-2014.pdf

Jablonski, N. G., & Chaplin, G. (2010). Human skin pigmentation as an adaptation to UV radiation. *PNAS*, 107(Supplement 2), 8962–8968. Retrieved August 3, 2017, from http://www.pnas.org/content/107/Supplement_2/8962.full

Jackson, B. (2000). *Splendid slippers: A thousand years of an erotic tradition*. Berkeley, CA: Ten Speed Press.

Jackson, P. (1984). Women in 19th century Irish emigration. *International Migration Review*, 18(4), 1004–1020.

Jacobs, D., & Wood, K. (1999). Interracial conflict and interracial homicide: Do political and economic rivalries explain white killings of blacks or black killings of whites? *American Journal of Sociology*, 105, 157–180.

Jacobs, M. D. (2009). *White mother to a dark race: Settler colonialism, maternalism, and the removal of indigenous children in the American west and Australia, 1880–1940*. Lincoln: University of Nebraska Press.

Jacobson, M. F. (1999). *Whiteness of a different color*. Cambridge, MA: Harvard University Press.

Jaher, F. C. (1996). *A scapegoat in the new wilderness: The origins and rise of anti-Semitism in America*. Cambridge, MA: Harvard University Press.

Jargowsky, P. (2015). The architecture of segregation: Civil unrest, the concentration of poverty, and public policy. *The Century Foundation*. Retrieved July 20, 2017, from https://tcf.org/content/report/architecture-of-segregation/

Jibou, R. M. (1988). Ethnic hegemony and the Japanese of California. *American Sociological Review*, 53, 353–367.

Joe, J., & Miller, D. (1994). Cultural survival and contemporary American Indian women in the city. In M. Zinn & B. T. Dill (Eds.), *Women of color in U.S. society* (pp. 185–202). Philadelphia, PA: Temple University Press.

Johnson, J. (2014, October 9). "Border security in the 21st century": Remarks by Secretary of Homeland Security Jeh Johnson: As delivered. *Homeland Security*. Retrieved from https://www.dhs.gov/news/2014/10/09/remarks-secretary-homeland-security-jeh-johnson-border-security-21st-century

Johnson, J. (2016). United States Border Patrol southwest family unit subject and unaccompanied alien children apprehensions fiscal year 2016. Statement by Secretary Johnson on southwest border security. *U.S. Customs and Border Protection*. Retrieved from https://www.cbp.gov/newsroom/stats/southwest-border-unaccompanied-children/fy-2016

Johnson, T. (2011, February 1). Free trade: As U.S. corn flows south, Mexicans stop farming. *McClatchy Dc Bureau*. Retrieved from http://www.mcclatchydc.com/news/nation-world/world/article24609829.html

Jones, B. (2016). Americans' views of immigrants marked by widening partisan, generational divides. *Pew Research Center*. Retrieved August 30, 2017, from http://www.pewresearch.org/fact-tank/2016/04/15/americans-views-of-immigrants-marked-by-widening-partisan-generational-divides/

Jones, C. (1949). An end to the neglect of the problems of the negro woman! *Political Affairs*. Retrieved from https://palmm.digital.flvc.org/islandora/object/ucf%3A4865

Jones, J. (1985). *Labor of love, labor of sorrow: Black women, work, and the family from slavery to the present*. New York, NY: Basic Books.

Jones, J., & Schmitt, J. (2014). A college degree is no guarantee. *Center for Economic and Policy Research*. Retrieved from http://cepr.net/documents/black-coll-grads-2014-05.pdf

Jones, J. M. (2013, August 9). Most in U.S. say it's essential that immigrants learn English. *Gallup*. Retrieved April 21, 2017, http://www.gallup.com/poll/163895/say-essential-immigrants-learn-english.aspx?version=print

Jones, J. M. (2016). Americans' optimism about blacks' opportunities wanes. *Gallup*. Retrieved August 3, 2017, http://www.gallup.com/poll/193697/americans-optimism-blacks-opportunities-wanes.aspx

Jones, N., & Bullock., J. (2012). *The two or more races population: 2010*. Washington, DC: U.S. Census Bureau. http://www.census.gov/prod/cen2010/briefs/c2010br-13.pdf

Jones, S., & Donnelly, G. (2017, June 20). Only 1 In 5 new board appointees at Fortune 500 companies are not white. *Fortune*. Retrieved from http://fortune.com/2017/06/19/one-in-5-fortune-500-board-appointees-last-year-was-from-an-underrepresented-group/

Jordan, M. (2017, November 20). Trump administration ends temporary protection for Haitians. *New York Times*. Retrieved from https://www.nytimes.com/2017/11/20/us/haitians-temporary-status.html

Jordan, W. (1968). *White over black: American attitudes towards the negro: 1550–1812*. Chapel Hill: University of North Carolina Press.

Josephy, A. M. (1968). *The Indian heritage of America*. New York, NY: Knopf.

Kahn, C. (2017, June 19). Cuba's small businesses brace for new U.S. trade, travel restrictions. *NPR*. Retrieved from http://www.npr.org/2017/06/19/533481614/cubas-small-businesses-brace-for-new-u-s-trade-travel-restrictions

Kallen, H. M. (1915a). Democracy versus the melting pot I. *Nation*, 100(2590), 190–194.

Kallen, H. M. (1915b). Democracy versus the melting pot II. *Nation*, 100(2591), 217–222.

Kasarda, J. D. (1989). Urban industrial transition and the underclass. *Annals of the American Academy of Political Science*, 501, 26–47.

Kasindorf, M. (2012, March 6). Racial tensions are simmering in Hawaii's melting pot. *USA Today*. Retrieved from http://usatoday30.usatoday.com/news/nation/2007-03-06-hawaii-cover_N.htm

Kasinitz, P., Mollenkopf, J. H., Waters, M. C., & Holdaway, J. (2008). *Inheriting the city: The children of immigrants come of age*. New York, NY: Russell Sage Foundation.

Katz, M. B., & Stern, M. J. (2008). *One nation divisible: What America was and what it is becoming*. New York, NY: Russell Sage Foundation.

Katz, P. (1976). The acquisition of racial attitudes in children. In P. Katz (Ed.), *Towards the Elimination of Racism* (pp. 125–154). New York, NY: Pergamon.

Katz, P. (2003). Racists or tolerant multiculturalists? How do they begin? *American Psychologist*, 58, 897–909.

Katznelson, I. (2005). *When affirmative action was white: An untold history of racial inequality in twentieth-century America*. New York, NY: Norton.

Kauffman Index of Startup Activity. (2016). *Entrepreneurial demographics, national*. Retrieved January 25, 2019, from https://www.kauffman.org/microsites/kauffman-index/profiles/entrepreneurial-demographics/national?Demographic=Nativity&Report=StartupActivity

Kaw, E. (1993). Medicalization of racial features: Asian American women and cosmetic surgery. *Medical Anthropology Quarterly*, 7(1), 74–89.

Kearney, D., & Knight, H. L. (1978, February 28). Appeal from California. The Chinese Invasion. Workingmen's Address. *Indianapolis Times*. Retrieved from http://historymatters.gmu.edu/d/5046/

Keels, M., & Harris, K. (2014). Intercultural dating at predominantly white universities: The maintenance and crossing of group borders. *Societies*, 4, 363–379.

Kennedy, R. (2001). Racial trends in the administration of criminal justice. In N. Smelser, W. Wilson, & F. Mitchell (Eds.), *America becoming: Racial trends and their consequences* (Vol. 2, pp. 1–20). Washington, DC: National Academy Press.

Kennedy, R. C. (2001). On this day. *New York Times*. Retrieved August 3, 2017, from http://www.nytimes.com/learning/general/onthisday/harp/0728.html

Kennedy, R. E. (1973). *The Irish: Emigration, marriage, and fertility*. Berkeley: University of California Press.

Kennedy, R. J. (1944). Single or triple melting pot? Intermarriage trends in New Haven, 1870–1940. *American Journal of Sociology*, 49, 331–339.

Kennedy, R. J. (1952). Single or triple melting pot? Intermarriage trends in New Haven, 1870–1950. *American Journal of Sociology*, 58, 56–59.

Kephart, W., & Zellner, W. (1994). *Extraordinary groups*. New York, NY: St. Martin's Press.

Kessler, J. (2017). *Yes, Virginia (Dare), there is such a thing as white genocide*. Retrieved August 12, 2017, from http://www.vdare.com/articles/yes-virginia-dare-there-is-such-a-thing-as-white-genocide

Kheel Center, Cornell University. (2017). *The 1911 Triangle Factory Fire*. Retrieved December 10, 2017, from http://www.ilr.cornell.edu/index.html

Kiersz, A. (2018, September 5). The most and least expensive places to live in America. *Business Insider*. Retrieved from https://www.businessinsider.com/america-most-expensive-places-to-live-2018-5

Killian, L. (1975). *The impossible revolution, Phase 2: Black power and the American dream*. New York, NY: Random House.

Kim, C., & Sakamoto, A. (2010). Have Asian American men achieved labor market parity with white men? *American Sociological Review*, 75(6), 934–957. https://doi.org/10.1177/0003122410388501

Kim, K. C., & Kim, S. (1999). The multiracial nature of Los Angeles unrest in 1992. In K. Chung Kim (Ed.), *Koreans in the hood: Conflict with African Americans* (pp. 17–38). Baltimore, MD: Johns Hopkins University Press.

Kinder, D. R., & Sears, D. O. (1981). Prejudice and politics: Symbolic racism versus racial threats to the good life. *Journal of Personality and Social Psychology*, 40, 414–431.

Kindy, K., Fisher, M., Tate, J., & Jenkins, J. (2015, December 26). A year of reckoning: Police fatally shoot nearly 1,000. *Washington Post*. Retrieved from http://www.washingtonpost.com/sf/investiga

tive/2015/12/26/a-year-of-reckoning-police-fatally-shoot-nearly-1000/

King., M. L., Jr. (1958). *Stride toward freedom: The Montgomery story.* New York, NY: Harper & Row.

King, M. L., Jr. (1963). *Why we can't wait.* New York, NY: Mentor.

King, M. L., Jr. (1968). *Where do we go from here: Chaos or community?* New York, NY: Harper & Row.

Kinosian S., & Holpuch, A. (2018, December 18). Fleeing home alone: The migrant children blocked at Mexican border. *The Guardian.* Retrieved from https://www.theguardian.com/world/2018/dec/18/unaccompanied-children-tijuana-us-immigration

Kishi, K. (2017, November 15). Assaults against Muslims in U.S. surpass 2001 level. *Pew Research Center.* Retrieved from http://www.pewresearch.org/fact-tank/2017/11/15/assaults-against-muslims-in-u-s-surpass-2001-level/

Kitano, H. H. L. (1980). Japanese. In S. Thernstrom, A. Orlov, & O. Handlin (Eds.), *Harvard encyclopedia of American ethnic groups* (pp. 561–571). Cambridge, MA: Harvard University Press.

Kitano, H., & Daniels, R. (1988). *Asian Americans: Emerging minorities.* Englewood Cliffs, NJ: Prentice Hall.

Kitano, H., & Daniels, R. (1995). *Asian Americans: Emerging minorities* (2nd ed.). Englewood Cliffs, NJ: Prentice Hall.

Kitano, H., & Daniels, R. (2001). *Asian Americans: Emerging minorities* (3rd ed.). Upper Saddle River, NJ: Prentice Hall.

Kluegel, J. R., & Smith, E. R. (1982). Whites' beliefs about blacks' opportunities. *American Sociological Review, 47,* 518–532.

Kochhar, R. (2004). *The wealth of Hispanic households: 1996 to 2002.* Washington, DC: Pew Hispanic Center. Retrieved from http://pewhispanic.org/files/reports/34.pdf

Kochhar, R. (2006). *Growth in the foreign-born workforce and employment of the native born.* Washington, DC: Pew Hispanic Center. Retrieved from http://pewhispanic.org/files/reports/69.pdf

Kochhar, R., & Cilluffo, A. (2017, November 1). How wealth inequality has changed in the U.S. since the Great Recession, by race, ethnicity and income. *Pew Research Center.* Retrieved from http://www.pewresearch.org/fact-tank/2017/11/01/how-wealth-inequality-has-changed-in-the-u-s-since-the-great-recession-by-race-ethnicity-and-income/

Kochhar, R., Fry, R., & Taylor, P. (2011). *Wealth gap rises to record highs between whites, blacks, and Hispanics.* Washington, DC: Pew Research Center. Retrieved from http://www.pewsocialtrends.org/files/2011/07/SDT-Wealth-Report_7-26-11_FINAL.pdf

Koenig, S. P., Rouzier, V., Vilbruna, S. C., Morose, W., Collins, S. E., Joseph, P., Decome, D., . . . & Pape, J. W. (2015). Tuberculosis in the aftermath of the 2010 earthquake in Haiti. *World Health Organization.* Retrieved from https://www.who.int/bulletin/volumes/93/7/14-145649/en/

Kolchin, P. (1993). *American slavery 1619–1877.* New York, NY: Hill and Wang.

Kosten, D. (2018, July 11). Immigrants as economic contributors: Immigrant entrepreneurs. *National Immigration Forum.* Retrieved January 25, 2019, from https://immigrationforum.org/article/immigrants-as-economic-contributors-immigrant-entrepreneurs/

Kovaleski, S. F., Turkewitz, J., Goldstein, J., & Barry, D. (2016, December 10). An alt-right makeover shrouds the swastikas. *New York Times.* Retrieved August 13, 2017, from https://www.nytimes.com/2016/12/10/us/alt-right-national-socialist-movement-white-supremacy.html

Krauss, M. (1996). Status of Native American language endangerment. In G. Canoni (Ed.), *Stabilizing indigenous languages.* Flagstaff: Center for Excellence in Education, Northern Arizona University.

Kraybill, D. B., & Bowman, C. F. (2001). *On the backroad to heaven: Old order Hutterites, Mennonites, Amish, and Brethren.* Baltimore, MD: Johns Hopkins University Press.

Kristofic, J. (2011). *Navajos wear Nikes: A reservation life.* Albuquerque: University of New Mexico Press.

Krogstad, J. (2017). Key facts about the Latino vote in 2016. *Pew Research Center.* Retrieved from https://

www.pewresearch.org/fact-tank/2016/10/14/key-facts-about-the-latino-vote-in-2016/

Krogstad, J. M., & Gonzalez-Barrera, A. (2015). A majority of English-speaking Hispanics in the U.S. are bilingual. *Pew Research Center*. Retrieved from http://www.pewresearch.org/fact-tank/2015/03/24/a-majority-of-english-speaking-hispanics-in-the-u-s-are-bilingual/

Krogstad, J. M., & Lopez, M. H. (2016, November 29). Hillary Clinton won Latino vote but fell below 2012 support for Obama. *Pew Research Center*. Retrieved from http://www.pewresearch.org/fact-tank/2016/11/29/hillary-clinton-wins-latino-vote-but-falls-below-2012-support-for-obama/

Krogstad, J. M., & Lopez, M. H. (2017, May 12). Black voter turnout fell in 2016, even as a record number of Americans cast ballots. *Pew Research Center*. Retrieved July 20, 2017, from http://www.pewresearch.org/fact-tank/2017/05/12/black-voter-turnout-fell-in-2016-even-as-a-record-number-of-americans-cast-ballots/#

Krogstad, J. M., Starr, K. J., & Sandstrom, A. (2017, March 29). Key findings about Puerto Rico. *Pew Research Center*. Retrieved from http://www.pewresearch.org/fact-tank/2017/03/29/key-findings-about-puerto-rico/

Krysan, M., & Farley, R. (2002). The residential preferences of blacks: Do they explain persistent segregation? *Social Forces*, 80, 937–981.

Kulish, N. (2018, June 30). What it costs to be smuggled across the U.S. border. *New York Times*. Retrieved from https://www.nytimes.com/interactive/2018/06/30/world/smuggling-illegal-immigration-costs.html

Lacy, D. (1972). *The white use of blacks in America*. New York, NY: McGraw-Hill.

Lai, H. M. (1980). Chinese. In S. Thernstrom, A. Orlov, & O. Handlin (Eds.), *Harvard encyclopedia of American ethnic groups* (pp. 217–234). Cambridge, MA: Harvard University Press.

Lamont-Brown, R. (1993). The Burakumin: Japan's underclass. *Contemporary Review*, 263, 136–140.

Landale, N., & Oropesa, R. S. (2002). White, black, or Puerto Rican? Racial self-identification among mainland and island Puerto Ricans. *Social Forces*, 81, 231–254.

Landrieu, M. (2017, May 23). Mitch Landrieu's speech on the removal of Confederate monuments in New Orleans. *New York Times*. Retrieved August 12, 2017, from https://www.nytimes.com/2017/05/23/opinion/mitch-landrieus-speech-transcript.html

Lane, B. (2016, June 29). Bancorpsouth fined $10.6 million for discriminatory lending, redlining. *Housingwire*. Retrieved from https://www.housingwire.com/articles/37405

Lang, S. (2010). *Men as women, women as men: Changing gender in Native American cultures*. Austin, TX: University of Texas Press.

Lansford, T. (2007). Banking. In J. Patrick (Ed.), *Renaissance and reformation* (Vol. 1; pp. 84–91). New York, NY: Marshall Cavendish.

Law, V. (2017). The alt-right holds MASSIVE rally to defend white heritage in Charlottesville. *AltRight.com*. Retrieved August 12, 2017, from https://altright.com/2017/05/15/alt-right-rallies-to-defend-white-heritage-in-charlottesville/

Lawson, S. F. (2009). African American voting rights, part one, 1865–1900. In *Civil rights in America: Racial voting rights*. Washington, DC: A National Historic Landmarks Theme Study. Susan Cianci Salvatore, Project Manager. Retrieved August 10, 2017, from https://www.nps.gov/nhl/learn/themes/CivilRights_VotingRights.pdf

Lee, C. (2009). Sociological theories of immigration: Pathways to integration for U.S. immigrants. *Journal of Human Behavior in the Social Environment*, 19(6), 730–744.

Lee, J., & Bean, F. D. (2007). Reinventing the color line: Immigration and America's new racial/ethnic divide. *Social Forces*, 86(2), 561–586.

Lee, S. (1998). Asian Americans: Diverse and growing. *Population Bulletin*, 53(2), 1–40.

Lee, S. J., Park, E., & Wong, J-H. S. (2017). Racialization, schooling, and becoming American: Asian American experiences. *Educational Studies*, 53, 492–510. doi:10.1080/00131946.2016.1258360

Lee, S. S-H. (2015). *Asian Americans and the 1992 Los Angeles riots/uprising*. doi: 10.1093/acrefore/978019932 9175.013.15.

Lenski, G. (1984). *Power and privilege: A theory of social stratification*. Chapel Hill: University of North Carolina Press.

Lenski, G., Nolan, P., & Lenski, J. (1995). *Human societies: An introduction to macrosociology* (7th ed.). New York, NY: McGraw-Hill.

Leonard, D. J., & Lugo-Lugo, C. R. (2015). *Latino history and culture: An encyclopedia*. New York, NY: Routledge.

Leslie, N. S. (2016, March 8). There's a difference: Code switching, Spanglish and bilingual advertising. *Linked In*. Retrieved from https://www.linkedin.com/pulse/theres-difference-code-switching-spanglish-bilingual-leslie-ph-d-

Levin, J., & McDevitt, J. (1993). *Hate crimes: The rising tide of bigotry and bloodshed*. New York, NY: Plenum.

Levine, L. (1977). *Black culture and black consciousness*. New York, NY: Oxford University Press.

Levy, G. (2018). Five things to know about immigration and asylum in the U.S. *U.S. News*. Retrieved from https://www.usnews.com/news/national-news/articles/2018-06-25/five-things-to-know-about-immigration-and-asylum-in-the-us

Lewin, T. (2012, March 6). Black students face more discipline, data suggests. *New York Times*. Retrieved August 8, 2017, from http://www.nytimes.com/2012/03/06/education/black-students-face-more-harsh-discipline-data-shows.html

Lewis, J., & D'Orso, M. (1999). *Walking with the wind: A memoir of the movement*. New York, NY: Harvest Books.

Lewis, O. (1959). *Five families: Mexican case studies in the culture of poverty*. New York, NY: Basic Books.

Lewis, O. (1965). *La vida: A Puerto Rican family in the culture of poverty*. New York, NY: Random House.

Lewis, O. (1966, October). The culture of poverty. *Scientific American*, 19–25.

Lewis, V., Emerson, M., & Klineberg, S. (2011). Who we'll live with: Neighborhood composition preferences of whites, blacks, and Latinos. *Social Forces*, 89, 1385–1408.

Lewy, G. (2004). Were American Indians the victims of genocide? *Commentary*, 118, 55–63.

Library of Congress. (1865). *13th Amendment to the U.S. Constitution*. Retrieved August 10, 2017, from http://www.loc.gov/rr/program/bib/ourdocs/13thamendment.html

Lichtblau, E. (2013, March 1). The Holocaust just got more shocking. *New York Times*. Retrieved from https://www.nytimes.com/2013/03/03/sunday-review/the-holocaust-just-got-more-shocking.html#story-continues-2

Lieberman, R. C. (1998). *Shifting the color line: Race and the American welfare system*. Cambridge, MA: Harvard University Press.

Lieberson, S. (1980). *A piece of the pie: Blacks and white immigrants since 1880*. Berkeley: University of California Press.

Lieberson, S., & Waters, M. C. (1988). *From many strands*. New York, NY: Russell Sage Foundation.

Light, I., & Bonacich, E. (1988). *Immigrant entrepreneurs: Koreans in Los Angeles, 1965–1982*. Berkeley: University of California Press.

Lincoln, C. E. (1961). *The black Muslims in America*. Boston, MA: Beacon.

Ling, H. (2000). Family and marriage of late-nineteenth and early-twentieth century Chinese immigrant women. *Journal of American Ethnic History*, 9, 43–65.

Liptak, A. (2009, June 29). Supreme Court finds bias against white firefighters. New York Times. Retrieved from https://www.nytimes.com/2009/06/30/us/30scotus.html

Liptak, A. (2013, June 25). Supreme Court invalidates key part of the Voting Rights Act. *New York Times*. Retrieved from http://www.nytimes.com/2013/06/26/us/supreme-court-ruling.html

Liptak, A. (2016, June 23). Supreme Court upholds affirmative action program at University of Texas. *New York Times*. Retrieved from https://www.nytimes.com/2016/06/24/us/politics/supreme-court-affirmative-action-university-of-texas.html

Liptak., A., & Shear, M. (2018, June 26). Trump's travel ban is upheld by Supreme Court. *New York Times*.

Retrieved from https://www.nytimes.com/2018/06/26/us/politics/supreme-court-trump-travel-ban.html

Liptak, A., & Wines, M. (2017, May 15). Strict North Carolina voter ID law thwarted after Supreme Court rejects case. *New York Times*. Retrieved July 20, 2017, https://www.nytimes.com/2017/05/15/us/politics/voter-id-laws-supreme-court-north-carolina.html

Livingston, G. (2017, June 8). Among U.S. cohabiters, 18% have a partner of a different race or ethnicity. *Pew Research Center*. Retrieved August 26, 2017, from http://www.pewresearch.org/fact-tank/2017/06/08/among-u-s-cohabiters-18-have-a-partner-of-a-different-race-or-ethnicity/

Livingston, G., & Brown, A. (2017). Intermarriage in the U.S. 50 years after *Loving v. Virginia*. *Pew Research Center*. Washington, DC: Pew Research Center. Retrieved August 9, 2017, from http://www.pewsocialtrends.org/2017/05/18/intermarriage-in-the-u-s-50-years-after-loving-v-virginia/

Lockhart, P. R. (2018a, December 31). 911 calls on black people were one of 2018's biggest stories about race. *Vox*. Retrieved from https://www.vox.com/identities/2018/12/31/18159465/living-while-black-racial-profiling-911-police-racism

Lockhart, P. R. (2018b, August 1). Living while black and the criminalization of blackness. *Vox*. Retrieved from https://www.vox.com/explainers/2018/8/1/17616528/racial-profiling-police-911-living-while-black

Loewen, J. (2005). *Sundown towns: A hidden dimension of American racism*. New York, NY: Simon & Schuster.

Logan, J., Alba, R., & McNulty, T. (1994). Ethnic economies in metropolitan regions: Miami and beyond. *Social Forces*, 72, 691–724.

Logan, J., & Stults, B. (2011). *The persistence of segregation in the metropolis: New findings from the 2010 census*. Retrieved from http://www.s4.brown.edu/us2010/Data/Report/report2.pdf

Logan, T. D. (2015). *A time (not) apart: A lesson in economic history from cotton picking books*. Retrieved from https://www.asc.ohio-state.edu/logan.155/pdf/Pres_Address_09-02-15.pdf

Logsdon, J. R. (n.d.). *Power, ignorance, and anti-Semitism: Henry Ford and his war on Jews*. Retrieved from https://history.hanover.edu/hhr/99/hhr99_2.html

Longerich, P. (2010). *Holocaust: The Nazi persecution and murder of the Jews*. New York, NY: Oxford University Press.

Lopata, H. Z. (1976). *Polish Americans*. Englewood Cliffs, NJ: Prentice Hall.

López, G. (2015a, September 15). Hispanics of Colombian origin in the United States, 2013. *Pew Research Center*. Washington, DC: Pew Research Center. Retrieved from http://www.pewresearch.org/wp-content/uploads/sites/5/2015/09/2015-09-15_colombia-fact-sheet.pdf

López, G. (2015b, September 15). Hispanics of Cuban origin in the United States, 2013. *Pew Research Center*. Retrieved from http://assets.pewresearch.org/wp-content/uploads/sites/7/2015/09/2015-09-15_cuba-fact-sheet.pdf

López, G. (2015c, September 15). Hispanics of Dominican origin in the United States, 2013. *Pew Research Center*. Washington, DC: Pew Research Center. Retrieved from http://www.pewresearch.org/wp-content/uploads/sites/5/2015/09/2015-09-15_dominican-republic-fact-sheet.pdf

López, G. (2015d, September 15). Hispanics of Mexican origin in the United States, 2013. *Pew Research Center*. Retrieved from http://www.pewhispanic.org/2015/09/15/hispanics-of-mexican-origin-in-the-united-states-2013/

López, G., & Bialik, K. (2017, May 3). Key findings about U.S. immigrants. *Pew Research Center*. Retrieved from http://www.pewresearch.org/fact-tank/2017/05/03/key-findings-about-u-s-immigrants/

López, G., Bialik, K., & Radford, J. (2018, November 30). Key findings about U.S. immigrants. *Pew Research Center*. Retrieved from http://www.pewresearch.org/fact-tank/2018/11/30/key-findings-about-u-s-immigrants/

Los Angeles Times Editorial Board. (2015, April 17). Cuba off the U.S. terrorism list: Goodbye to a Cold War relic. *Los Angeles Times*. Retrieved from http://www.latimes.com/opinion/editorials/la-ed-cuba-20150417-story.html

Los Angeles Times Graphics Staff. (2017, April 26). L.A. riots by the numbers. *Los Angeles Times*. Retrieved from https://www.latimes.com/local/1992riots/la-me-riots-25-years-20170420-htmlstory.html

Loving v. Virginia, 388 U.S. 1 (1967)

Lowcountry Digital History Initiative at the College of Charleston. (n.d.). *New World labor systems: American Indians*. Retrieved from http://ldhi.library.cofc.edu/exhibits/show/africanpassageslowcountryadapt/introductionatlanticworld/new_world_labor_systems

Lowenthall, T. A. (2014). *Race and ethnicity in the 2020 census: Improving data to capture a multiethnic America*. Leadership Conference Education Fund. http://civilrightsdocs.info/pdf/reports/Census-Report-2014-WEB.pdf

Lowery, W., Leonnig, C. D., & Berman, M. (2014, August 13). Even before Michael Brown's slaying in Ferguson, racial questions hung over police. *Washington Post*. Retrieved from https://www.washingtonpost.com/politics/even-before-teen-michael-browns-slaying-in-mo-racial-questions-have-hung-over-police/2014/08/13/78b3c5c6-2307-11e4-86ca-6f03cbd15c1a_story.html

Loyd, J. M., & Mountz, A. (2018). *Boats, borders, and bases: Race, the Cold War, and the rise of migration detention in the United States*. Berkeley: University of California Press.

Lurie, J. (2014, August 27). 10 hours in Ferguson: A visual timeline of Michael Brown's death and its aftermath. *Mother Jones*. Retrieved August 10, 2017, from http://www.motherjones.com/politics/2014/08/timeline-michael-brown-shooting-ferguson/

Lurie, N. O. (1982). The American Indian: Historical background. In N. Yetman & C. Hoy Steele (Eds.), *Majority and minority* (3rd ed., pp. 131–144). Boston, MA: Allyn & Bacon.

Lyman, S. (1974). *Chinese Americans*. New York, NY: Random House.

Madley, B. (2016). *An American genocide: The United States and the California Indian catastrophe, 1846–1873*. New Haven, CT: Yale University Press.

Main, J. L. (2012). *Only Shinran will not betray us: Takeuchi Ryō'on (1891–1967), the Ōtani-ha administration, and Burakumin* (PhD thesis). McGill University,

Montreal. Retrieved from http://digitool.library.mcgill.ca/webclient/StreamGate?folder_id=0&dvs=1554846583194~796

Mak, S. (2017). Japanese Latin Americans. *Densho Encyclopedia*. Retrieved August 26, 2017, from http://encyclopedia.densho.org/Japanese_Latin_Americans/

Malcolm X. (1964). *The autobiography of Malcolm X*. New York, NY: Grove.

Mann, B. A. (2008). Women in native woodland societies. In B. E. Johansen & B. M. Pritzker (Eds.), *Encyclopedia of American Indian history* (Vol. 1, pp. 190–196). Santa Barbara, CA: ABC-CLIO.

Mann, C. (2011). *1491: New revelations of the Americas before Columbus*. New York, NY: Vintage Books.

Mann, S. A. (1989, Summer). Slavery, sharecropping, and sexual inequality. *Signs*, 14(4), 774–798. Retrieved from https://www.jstor.org/stable/3174684

Manning, J. (2017). Membership of the 115th congress: A profile. *Congressional Research Service, 7*. Retrieved from https://fas.org/sgp/crs/misc/R44762.pdf

Mannix, D. P. (1962). *Black cargoes: A history of the Atlantic slave trade*. New York, NY: Viking.

Manyika, J., Lund, S., Chui, M., Bughin, J., Woetzel, J., Batra, P., Ko, R., & Sanghvi, S. (2017). *Jobs lost, jobs gained: What the future of work will mean for jobs, skills, and wages*. Retrieved from https://www.mckinsey.com/featured-insights/future-of-work/jobs-lost-jobs-gained-what-the-future-of-work-will-mean-for-jobs-skills-and-wages

Marable, M. (2011). *Malcolm X: A life of reinvention*. New York, NY: Penguin.

Marbella, J. (2015, June 13). Korean-American merchants face hurdles in rebuilding after Baltimore riot. *Baltimore Sun*. Retrieved from https://www.baltimoresun.com/business/bs-md-korean-stores-freddie-gray-20150613-story.html

Marcelli, E., & Heer, D. (1998). The unauthorized Mexican immigrant population and welfare in Los Angeles County: A comparative statistical analysis. *Sociological Perspectives*, 41, 279–303.

Marcuse, H. (2018). *Historical dollar-to-marks currency conversion page*. Retrieved from http://www.history.ucsb.edu/faculty/marcuse/projects/currency.htm

Marteleto, L. (2012). Educational inequality by race in Brazil, 1982–2007: Structural changes and shifts in racial classification. *Demography*, 49, 337–358.

Martin, P., & Midgley, E. (1999). Immigration to the United States. *Population Bulletin*, 54(2), 1–44.

Marx, K., & Engels, F. (1967). *The communist manifesto*. Baltimore, MD: Penguin. (Original work published 1848.)

Masci, D. (2016). How income varies among U.S. religious groups. *Pew Research Center*. Washington DC: Pew Research Center. Retrieved April 16, 2017, from http://www.pewresearch.org/fact-tank/2016/10/11/how-income-varies-among-u-s-religious-groups/

Massarik, F., & Chenkin, A. (1973). United States national Jewish population study: A first report. In *American Jewish year book, 1973* (Vol. 74; pp. 264–306). New York, NY: American Jewish Committee.

Massey, D. (1995). The new immigration and ethnicity in the United States. *Population and Development Review*, 21, 631–652.

Massey, D. (2000). Housing discrimination 101. *Population Today*, 28(1), 4.

Massey, D. (2007). *Categorically unequal: The American stratification system*. New York, NY: Russell Sage Foundation.

Massey, D., & Denton, N. (1993). *American apartheid*. Cambridge, MA: Harvard University Press.

Mastro, D., Behm-Morawitz, E., & Ortiz, M. (2007). The cultivation of social perceptions of Latinos: A mental models approach. *Media Psychology*, 9(2), 347–365. doi:10.1080/15213260 701286106.

Masuda, A., Anderson, P. L., Twohig, M. P., Feinstein, A. B., Chou, Y. Y., Wendell, J. W., & Stormo, A. R. (2009). Help-seeking experiences and attitudes among African American, Asian American, and European American college students. *International Journal for the Advancement of Counselling*, 31(3), 168–180.

Matas, C. (2016, September 13). *Federal government halts pipeline construction on American Indian sacred grounds*. Retrieved August 18, 2017, from https://rlp.hds.harvard.edu/news/federal-government-halts-pipeline-construction-american-indian-sacred-grounds

Matiash, C., & Rothman, L. (2016, March 3). The beating that changed America: What happened to Rodney King 25 years ago. *Time*. Retrieved from http://time.com/4245175/rodney-king-la-riots-anniversary/

Maurer, E. L. (2017, March 14). Raising a glass to Irish American women. *National Women's History Museum*. Retrieved from https://www.womenshistory.org/articles/raising-glass-irish-american-women

McCabe, K., & Roundtree, D. J. (2009). *Justice older than the law: The life of Dovey Johnson Roundtree*. Jackson, MS: University Press of Mississippi.

McConahy, J. B. (1986). Modern racism, ambivalence, and the modern racism scale. In J. R. Dovidio & S. Gartner (Eds.), *Prejudice, discrimination, and racism* (pp. 91–125). Orlando, FL: Academic Press.

McCook, B. (2011). *The borders of integration: Polish migrants in Germany and the United States, 1870–1924*. Athens, OH: Ohio University Press.

McCown, B. A. (2018, June 4). What ever happened to the Dakota Access Pipeline? *Forbes*. Retrieved from https://www.forbes.com/sites/brighammccown/2018/06/04/what-ever-happened-to-the-dakota-access-pipeline/

McDevitt, J., Levin, J., & Bennett, S. (2002). Hate crime offenders: An expanded typology (abstract). *Journal of Social Issues*, 58(2), 303–317.

McDuffie, E. S. (2018, May 22). Black women, the Nation of Islam, and the pursuit of freedom. *Black Perspectives*. Retrieved from https://www.aaihs.org/black-women-the-nation-of-islam-and-the-pursuit-of-freedom/

McKibben, B. (2016, September 6). A pipeline fight and America's dark past. *New Yorker*. Retrieved August 18, 2017, from http://www.newyorker.com/news/daily-comment/a-pipeline-fight-and-americas-dark-past

McKinley, J. (2009, January 8). In California, protests after man dies at hands of transit police. *New York Times*. Retrieved from https://www.nytimes.com/2009/01/09/us/09oakland.html

McKinley, J. (2010, July 9). Officer guilty in killing that inflamed Oakland. *New York Times*. Retrieved August 10, 2017, from http://www.nytimes.com/2010/07/09/us/09verdict.html

McLemore, S. D. (1973). The origins of Mexican American subordination in Texas. *Social Science Quarterly*, 53, 656–679.

McNickle, D. 1(973). *Native American tribalism: Indian survivals and renewals*. New York, NY: Oxford University Press.

McPherson, M., Smith-Lovin, L., & Brashears, M. (2006). Social isolation in America: Changes in core discussion networks over two decades. *Social Forces*, 71, 353–375.

McWilliams, C. (1961). *North from Mexico: The Spanish-speaking people of the United States*. New York, NY: Monthly Review.

Medoff, M. (1999). Allocation of time and hateful behavior: A theoretical and positive analysis of hate and hate crimes. *American Journal of Economics and Sociology*, 58, 959–973.

Meek, B. (2006). And the Indian goes "How!": Representations of American Indian English in white public space. *Language in Society*, 35, 93–128.

Meenes, M. (1941). American Jews and anti-Semitism. *The Journal of Negro Education*, 10, 557–566.

Megargee, G. P. (Ed.). (2009). *The United States Holocaust memorial museum encyclopedia of camps and ghettos, 1933–1945*. Bloomington, IN: Indiana University Press. Retrieved from https://www.ushmm.org/online/camps-ghettos-download/EncyclopediaVol-I_PartA.pdf

Meissner, D. (2010, May 2). 5 myths about immigration. *Washington Post*, p. B2.

Menes, R. (2001). *Corruption in cities: Graft and politics in American cities at the turn of the twentieth century*. Fairfax, VA: George Mason University.

Meyer, M., & Isacson, A. (n.d.). *On the front lines: Border security, migration, and humanitarian concerns in south Texas*. Retrieved from https://www.wola.org/files/1502_stx/index.html

Meyer, M., & Pachico, E. (2018, February 1). Fact sheet: U.S. immigration and Central American asylum seekers. *The Washington Office on Latin America*. Retrieved January 25, 2019, from https://www.wola.org/analysis/fact-sheet-united-states-immigration-central-american-asylum-seekers/

Meyer, R. (2017a, June 14). The Standing Rock Sioux claim "victory and vindication" in court. *The Atlantic*. Retrieved August 18, 2017, from https://www.theatlantic.com/science/archive/2017/06/dakota-access-standing-rock-sioux-victory-court/530427/

Meyer, R. (2017b, October 4). What's happening with the relief effort in Puerto Rico? *The Atlantic*. Retrieved from https://www.theatlantic.com/science/archive/2017/10/what-happened-in-puerto-rico-a-timeline-of-hurricane-maria/541956/

Migration Policy Institute. (n.d.). *U.S. annual refugee resettlement ceilings and number of refugees admitted, 1980–present*. Retrieved from https://www.migrationpolicy.org/programs/data-hub/charts/us-annual-refugee-resettlement-ceilings-and-number-refugees-admitted-united

Migration Policy Institute. (2014). *The Indian Diaspora in the United States*. Retrieved from https://www.migrationpolicy.org/sites/default/files/publications/RAD-IndiaII-FINAL.pdf

Migration Policy Institute. (2015, June). *The Nigerian Diaspora in the United States* (MPI). Prepared for the Rockefeller Foundation-Aspen Institute Diaspora Program (RAD). Retrieved from https://www.migrationpolicy.org/sites/default/files/publications/RAD-Nigeria.pdf

Min, P. G. (Ed.). (1995). *Asian Americans: Contemporary trends and issues*. Thousand Oaks, CA: SAGE.

Min, P. G. (2006). *Asian Americans: Contemporary trends and issues* (2nd ed.). Thousand Oaks, CA: SAGE.

Min, P. G. (2008). *Ethnic solidarity for economic survival: Korean greengrocers in New York City*. New York, NY: Russell Sage Foundation.

Minian, A. R. (2018, December 1). America didn't always lock up immigrants. *New York Times*. Retrieved from https://www.nytimes.com/2018/12/01/opinion/.../border-detention-tear-gas-migrants.htm

Minnesota Population Center. (2016). National Historical Geographic Information System: Version 11.0 [Database]. Minneapolis: University of Minnesota. http://doi.org/10.18128/D050.V11.0

Mirandé, A. (1985). *The Chicano experience: An alternative perspective*. Notre Dame, IN: University of Notre Dame Press.

Mirandé, A. (2017). *Behind the mask: Gender hybridity in a Zapotec community*. Tucson: University of Arizona Press.

Mississippi Band of Choctaw Indians. (2017). *Tribal profile*. Retrieved from http://www.choctaw.org/img/tribalprofile.pdf

Misty Copeland, Top 100. (2016). *The root*. Retrieved August 8, 2017, from http://onehundred.theroot.com/facewall/the-root-100-2016/#misty-copeland

Montes-Alcalá, C. (2000). Attitudes towards oral and written code-switching in Spanish-English bilingual youths. In A. Roca (Ed.), *Research on Spanish in the United States* (pp. 218–227). Somerville, MA: Cascadilla Press.

Moore, J. W. (1970). *Mexican Americans*. Englewood Cliffs, NJ: Prentice Hall.

Moore, J. W., & Pachon, H. (1985). *Hispanics in the United States*. Englewood Cliffs, NJ: Prentice Hall.

Moore, J. W., & Pinderhughes, R. (1993). *In the barrios: Latinos and the underclass debate*. New York, NY: Russell Sage Foundation.

Moquin, W., & Van Doren, C. (Eds.). (1971). *A documentary history of Mexican Americans*. New York, NY: Bantam.

Morales, L. (2010). Amid immigration debate, Americans' views ease slightly. *Gallup Politics*. Retrieved from http://www.gallup.com/poll/141560/Amid-Immigration-Debate-Americans-Views-Ease-Slightly.aspx

Morawska, E. (1990). The sociology and historiography of immigration. In V. Yans-McLaughlin (Ed.), *Immigration reconsidered: History, sociology, and politics* (pp. 187–238). New York, NY: Oxford University Press.

More Perfect. (2018, February 23). The gun show. *Radiolab*. Retrieved from https://www.wnycstudios.org/story/radiolab-presents-more-perfect-gun-show

Morgan v. Virginia, 328 U.S. 373. (1946)

Morgan, E. (1975). *American slavery, American freedom*. New York, NY: Norton.

Morin, R., Parker, K., Stepler, R., & Mercer, A. (2017). What police think about their jobs. *Pew Research Center*. Washington, DC: Pew Research Center. Retrieved August 10, 2017, from http://www.pewsocialtrends.org/2017/01/11/behind-the-badge/

Morlin, B. (2017). Extremists' "Unite the Right" rally: A possible historic alt-right showcase? *Southern Poverty Law Center*. Retrieved August 13, 2017, from https://www.splcenter.org/hatewatch/2017/08/07/extremists-unite-right-rally-possible-historic-alt-right-showcase

Morris, A. D. (1984). *The origins of the civil rights movement*. New York, NY: Free Press.

Morris, A. D. (2015). *The scholar denied: W. E. B. Du Bois and the birth of modern sociology*. Oakland, CA: University of California Press.

Moynihan, D. (1965). *The negro family: The case for national action*. Washington, DC: U.S. Department of Labor.

Mozingo, J., & Jennings, A. (2015, August 13). 50 years after Watts: "There is still a crisis in the black community." *Los Angeles Times*. Retrieved August 9, 2017, from http://www.latimes.com/local/wattsriots/la-me-watts-african-americans-20150813-story.html

Mufson, S. (2016, October 28). Why Hollywood, environmentalists and Native Americans have converged on North Dakota. *Washington Post*. Retrieved August 18, 2017, from https://www.washingtonpost.com/business/economy/why-hollywood-environmentalists-and-native-americans-have-converged-on-north-dakota/2016/10/28/007620c8-9c8f-11e6-9980-50913d68eacb_story.html

Muller, J. Z. (2010). *Capitalism and the Jews*. Princeton, NJ: Princeton University Press.

Murguia, E., & Foreman, T. (2003). Shades of whiteness: The Mexican American experience in relation to Anglos and blacks. In A. Donane & E. Bonilla-Silva (Eds.), *White out: The continuing significance of racism* (pp. 63–72). New York, NY: Routledge.

Myrdal, G. (1962). *An American dilemma: The negro problem and modern democracy*. New York, NY: Harper & Row. (Original work published 1944.)

Nabakov, P. (Ed.). (1999). *Native American testimony* (Rev. ed.). New York, NY: Penguin.

Nash, A. N., & Strobel, C. (2006). *Daily life of Native Americans from post-Columbian through nineteenth-century America*. Westport, CT: Greenwood Publishing Group.

Nash, N. (2018, October 22). To the next "BBQ Becky": Don't call 911. Call 1-844-WYT-FEAR. *New York Times*. Retrieved from https://www.nytimes.com/2018/10/22/opinion/calling-police-racism-wyt-fear.html

National Academies of Sciences, Engineering, and Medicine (NASEM). (2017). *The economic and fiscal consequences of immigration*. Washington, DC: The National Academies Press. Retrieved from https://doi.org/10.17226/23550

National Advisory Commission. (1968). *Report of the National Advisory Commission on civil disorders*. New York, NY: Bantam Books.

National Association of Korean Americans. (2003). *A brief history of Korean Americans*. (J. H. Kim, J-Y Yuh, E. H. Kim, & E-Y Yu, Eds.). Retrieved August 30, 2017, from http://www.naka.org/resources/history.asp

National Center for Juvenile Justice. (2018). *Juvenile arrest rates by offense, sex, and race*. Retrieved from https://www.ojjdp.gov/ojstatbb/crime/JAR_Display.asp?ID=qa05274

National Congress of American Indians. (n.d.). *An introduction to Indian Nations in the United States*. Retrieved August 18, 2017, from http://www.ncai.org/about-tribes/indians_101.pdf

National Fair Housing Alliance. (2018). *2017 fair housing trends report*. Retrieved from https://nationalfairhousing.org/wp-content/uploads/2017/07/TRENDS-REPORT-2017-FINAL.pdf

National Geographic Society. (2017). *Reference populations—Geno 2.0 next generation*. Retrieved from https://genographic.nationalgeographic.com/reference-populations-next-gen/

National Indian Gaming Commission. (2011). *NIGC Tribal Gaming Revenues*. Retrieved from http://www.nigc.gov/LinkClick.aspx?fileticket=1k4B6r6dr-U%3d&tabid=67

National Indian Gaming Commission. (2018a). *FY13–FY17 gaming revenues by range*. Retrieved from https://www.nigc.gov/images/uploads/reports/Chart2017GamingRevenuesbyRange.pdf

National Indian Gaming Commission. (2018b). *GGR trending*. Retrieved from https://www.nigc.gov/images/uploads/reports/Graph2017GrossGamingRevenueTrends.pdf

National Institute of Justice. (2008). *What motivates hate offenders?* Retrieved from https://www.nij.gov/topics/crime/hate-crime/pages/motivation.aspx

National Opinion Research Council. (1972–2016). *General Social Survey*. Chicago, IL: Author. Retrieved from http://www.norc.org/Research/Projects/Pages/general-social-survey.aspx

National Park Service. (n.d.). *Operating the underground railroad*. Retrieved August 4, 2017, from https://www.nps.gov/nr/travel/underground/opugrr.htm

National Park Service. (2015a). *Japanese Americans at Manzanar*. Retrieved August 26, 2017, from https://www.nps.gov/manz/learn/historyculture/japanese-americans-at-manzanar.htm

National Park Service. (2015b). *Veto of the Freedmen's Bureau bill*. Retrieved August 10, 2017, from https://www.nps.gov/anjo/learn/historyculture/freedmens-bureau.htm

National Women's Law Center. (2017). *National snapshot: Poverty among women & families, 2016*. Retrieved from https://nwlc.org/wp-content/uploads/2017/09/Poverty-Snapshot-Factsheet-2017.pdf

The National WWII Museum. (n.d.). *How did Hitler happen?* https://www.nationalww2museum.org/war/articles/how-did-hitler-happen

Navarro, W. (2018). Nonimmigrant admissions to the United States: Fiscal year 2017. *Annual Flow Report, Office of Statistics*. Retrieved from https://www.dhs.gov/sites/default/files/publications/Nonimmigrant_Admissions_2017.pdf

Neal, D., & Armin, R. (2014). *The prison boom and the lack of black progress after Smith and Welch* (NBER

Working Paper No. 20283]. National Bureau of Economic Research website: http://www.nber.org/papers/w20283

Neal, S. (2017). Views of racism as a major problem increase sharply, especially among democrats. *Pew Research Center*. Retrieved from https://www.pewresearch.org/fact-tank/2017/08/29/views-of-racism-as-a-major-problem-increase-sharply-especially-among-democrats/

Neary, I. (2003). Burakumin at the end of history. *Social Research*, 70, 269–294.

Nelli, H. S. (1980). Italians. In S. Thernstrom, A. Orlov, & O. Handlin (Eds.), *Harvard encyclopedia of American ethnic groups* (pp. 545–560). Cambridge, MA: Harvard University Press.

Nellis, A. (2016). The color of justice: Racial and ethnic disparity in state prisons. *The Sentencing Project*. Retrieved from https://www.sentencingproject.org/wp-content/uploads/2016/06/The-Color-of-Justice-Racial-and-Ethnic-Disparity-in-State-Prisons.pdf

Nelson, L. A. (2008). Native American agriculture. In M. Walker & J. Cobb (Eds.), *The new encyclopedia of southern culture* (Vol. 11, pp. 88–92). Chapel Hill: University of North Carolina Press. Retrieved August 18, 2017, from http://www.jstor.org/stable/10.5149/9781469616681_walker.20

Newport, F. (2013). In U.S., 24% of young black men say police dealings unfair. *Gallup*. Retrieved from http://www.gallup.com/poll/163523/one-four-young-black-men-say-police-dealings-unfair.aspx?version=print

Newport, F. (2016). Public opinion context: Americans, race, and police. *Gallup*. Retrieved July 20, 2017, from http://www.gallup.com/opinion/polling-matters/193586/public-opinion-context-americans-race-police.aspx?g_source=attitudes+police+race&g_medium=search&g_campaign=tiles

Ngo, V. H. (2008). A critical examination of acculturation theories. *Critical Social Work*, 9(1). Retrieved August 5, 2017, from http://www1.uwindsor.ca/criticalsocialwork/a-critical-examination-of-acculturation-theories

Nichols, R. L. (1986). Indians in nineteenth century America: A unique minority. In R. L. Nichols (Ed.), *The American Indian: Past and present* (3rd ed., pp. 127–136). New York, NY: Newbury Award Records.

Nirenberg, D. (2014). *Anti-Judaism: The western tradition*. New York, NY: W. W. Norton & Company.

Nishi, S. (1995). Japanese Americans. In P. G. Min (Ed.), *Asian Americans: Contemporary trends and issues* (pp. 95–133). Thousand Oaks, CA: SAGE.

Nixon, R. (2018, April 26). Federal agencies lost track of nearly 1,500 migrant children placed with sponsors. *New York Times*. Retrieved from https://www.nytimes.com/2018/04/26/us/politics/migrant-children-missing.html?module=inline

Noel, D. (1968). A theory of the origin of ethnic stratification. *Social Problems*, 16, 157–172.

Nolan, P., & Lenski, G. (2004). *Human societies*. Boulder, CO: Paradigm.

Norris, T., Vines, P., & Hoeffel, E. (2012). The American Indian and Alaska Native population: 2010. *2010 Census Briefs*. Washington, DC: U.S. Census Bureau. Retrieved from http://www.census.gov/prod/cen2010/briefs/c2010br-10.pdf

Norwood, S. H. (2013). *Antisemitism and the American far left*. Cambridge, UK: Cambridge University Press.

Novak, M. (1973). *The rise of the unmeltable ethnics: Politics and culture in the 1970s*. New York, NY: Collier.

Nowrasteh, A., & Orr, R. (2018, May 10). Immigration and the welfare state: Immigrant and native use rates and benefit levels for means-tested welfare and entitlement programs. *Cato Institute*. Retrieved from https://www.cato.org/publications/immigration-research-policy-brief/immigration-welfare-state-immigrant-native-use-rates#full

NPR, Robert Wood Johnson Foundation, & Harvard T. H. Chan School of Public Health. (2017a, October). *Discrimination in America: Experiences and views of African Americans*. Retrieved April 10, 2019, from https://www.rwjf.org/content/dam/farm/reports/reports/2017/rwjf441128

NPR, Robert Wood Johnson Foundation, & Harvard T. H. Chan School of Public Health. (2017b, November). *Discrimination in America: Experiences and views of Asian Americans*. Retrieved April 10, 2019, from https://www.rwjf.org/content/dam/farm/reports/reports/2017/rwjf441128

NPR, Robert Wood Johnson Foundation, & Harvard T. H. Chan School of Public Health. (2017c, November). *Discrimination in America: Experiences and views of white Americans.* Retrieved April 10, 2019, from https://www.rwjf.org/content/dam/farm/reports/surveys_and_polls/2017/rwjf441554

NPR, Robert Wood Johnson Foundation, & Harvard T. H. Chan School of Public Health. (2018, January). *Discrimination in America: Final summary.* Retrieved April 10, 2019, from https://www.rwjf.org/content/dam/farm/reports/surveys_and_polls/2018/rwjf443620

Nuñez, C., Sepehr, J., & Sanchez, E. (2014). Why people migrate: 11 surprising reasons. *Global Citizen.* Retrieved from https://www.globalcitizen.org/en/content/why-people-migrate-11-surprising-reasons/

Obama, B. (2008, March 18). Barack Obama's speech on race. *New York Times.* Retrieved from http://www.nytimes.com/2008/03/18/us/politics/18text-obama.html?pagewanted=all

O'Connell, P. (2016). *International migration in Ireland, 2016.* Retrieved from http://www.ucd.ie/geary/static/publications/workingpapers/gearywp201707.pdf

O'Dell, R., González, D., & Castellano, J. (2017). "Mass disaster" grows at the U.S.–Mexico border, but Washington doesn't seem to care. *Desert Sun.* Retrieved from https://www.azcentral.com/story/news/politics/border-issues/2017/12/14/investigation-border-patrol-undercounts-deaths-border-crossing-migrants/933689001/

Odo, F. (2002). Contact and conflict: Asia and the Pacific: Through 1900. In F. Odo (Ed.), *The Columbia documentary history of the Asian American experience* (pp. 9–126). New York, NY: Columbia University Press.

Ogunwole, S. (2006). *We the people: American Indians and Alaska Natives in the United States.* Washington, DC: U.S. Census Bureau. Retrieved from http://www.census.gov/prod/2006pubs/censr-28.pdf

Oklahoma Commission to Study the Tulsa Race Riot of 1921. (2001). *A report by the Oklahoma Commission to Study the Tulsa Race Riot of 1921.* Retrieved from https://www.okhistory.org/research/forms/freport.pdf

Oliver, M., & Shapiro, T. (2006). *Black wealth, white wealth* (2nd ed.). New York, NY: Taylor and Francis.

Oliver, M., & Shapiro, T. (2008, October). Sub-prime as a black catastrophe. *American Prospect,* A9–A11.

Olivo, A., & Eldeib, D. (2013, March 17). Catholic church works to keep up with growing Latino membership. *Chicago Tribune.* Retrieved from http://articles.chicagotribune.com/2013-03-17/news/ct-met-chicago-latino-catholics-20130317_1_latino-appointments-latino-candidates-priests

Olson, J. S., & Wilson, R. (1984). *Native Americans in the twentieth century.* Provo, UT: Brigham Young University Press.

Omi, M., & Winant, H. (1986). *Racial formation in the United States from the 1960s to the 1980s.* New York, NY: Routledge & Kegan Paul.

Orfield, G., Ee, J., Frankenberg, E., & Siegel-Hawley, G. (2016, May 16). Brown at 62: School segregation, by race, poverty, and state. *Civil Rights Project, UCLA.* Retrieved July 20, 2017, from https://www.civilrightsproject.ucla.edu/research/k-12-education/integration-and-diversity/brown-at-62-school-segregation-by-race-poverty-and-state

Orfield, G., & Lee, C. (2007). *Historic reversals, accelerating resegregation, and the need for new integration strategies.* Los Angeles, CA: Civil Rights Project, UCLA. Retrieved from http://www.eric.ed.gov/PDFS/ED500611.pdf

Orser, C. E. (1994). The archaeology of African-American slave religion in the antebellum South. *Cambridge Archaeological Journal,* 4(1), 33–45. doi:10.1017/S0959774300000950.

Osaki, T. (2016, December 19). New law to fight bias against "Baraku" seen falling short. *Japan Times.* Retrieved January 25, 2019, from https://www.japantimes.co.jp/news/2016/12/19/reference/new-toothless-law-fight-bias-burakumin-seen-falling-short/

Oswalt, W., & Neely, S. (1996). *This land was theirs.* Mountain View, CA: Mayfield.

Pager, D., & Shepherd, H. (2008). The sociology of discrimination: Racial discrimination in employment, housing, credit, and consumer markets. *Annual Review of Sociology*, 34, 181–209.

Parish, P. J. (1989). *Slavery: History and historians*. New York, NY: Harper & Row.

Park, H., & Mykhyalyshyn, I. (2016, June 16). L.G.B.T. people are more likely to be targets of hate crimes than any other minority group. *New York Times*. Retrieved August 9, 2017, from https://www.nytimes.com/inter active/2016/06/16/us/hate-crimes-against-lgbt.html

Park, R. E., & Burgess, E. W. (1924). *Introduction to the science of society*. Chicago, IL: University of Chicago Press.

Park, S., Hongub, N., & Daily, J. W. (2016). Native American foods: History, culture, and influence on modern diets. *Journal of Ethnic Foods*, 3(3), 171–177. doi: 10.1016/j.jef.2016.08.001.

Parker, K., Horowitz, J. M., Morin, R., & Lopez, M. H. (2015). Chapter 7: The many dimensions of Hispanic racial identity. *Pew Research Center*. Retrieved April 10, 2019, from https://www.pewsocial trends.org/2015/06/11/chapter-7-the-many-dimen sions-of-hispanic-racial-identity/

Parrillo, V., & Donoghue, C. (2013). The national social distance study: Ten years later. *Sociological Forum*, 28, 597–614.

Passel, J., & Cohn, D. (2011). Unauthorized immi-grant population: National and state trends, 2010. *Pew Research Center*. Washington, DC: Pew Hispanic Center. Retrieved from http://pewhispanic.org/files/reports/133.pdf

Passel, J., & Cohn, D. (2017). As Mexican share declined, U.S. unauthorized immigrant popula-tion fell in 2015 below recession level. *Pew Research Center*. Retrieved from http://www.pewresearch .org/fact-tank/2017/04/25/as-mexican-share-de clined-u-s-unauthorized-immigrant-popula tion-fell-in-2015-below-recession-level/

Passel, J., & Cohn, D. (2018). Unauthorized immigrant total dips to lowest level in a decade. *Pew Research Center*. Washington, DC: Pew Hispanic Center. Retrieved from https://www.pewhispanic.org/2018/11/27/u-s-unauthorized-immigrant-total-dips-to-lowest-level-in-a-decade/

Passel, J., Cohn, D., & Gonzalez-Barrera, A. (2012). Net migration from Mexico falls to zero—and perhaps less. *Pew Research Center*. Washington, DC: Pew Hispanic Center. Retrieved from https://www.pewhispanic .org/2012/04/23/net-migration-from-mexico-falls-to-zero-and-perhaps-less/

Passel, J., Cohn, D., & Gonzalez-Barrera, A. (2013). Population decline of unauthorized immigrants stalls, may have reversed. *Pew Research Center*. Washington, DC: Pew Research Center. Retrieved from http://www .pewhispanic.org/2013/09/23/population-decline-of-un authorized-immigrants-stalls-may-have-reversed

Passel, J., Cohn, D., & Gramlich, J. (2018, November 1). Number of U.S.–born babies with unauthorized immigrant parents has fallen since 2007. *Pew Research Center*. Retrieved from http://www.pewresearch.org/fact-tank/2018/11/01/the-number-of-u-s-born-ba bies-with-unauthorized-immigrant-parents-has-fall en-since-2007/

Passel, J., Wang, W., & Taylor, P. (2010). Marrying out: One-in-seven new U.S. marriages is interracial or interethnic. *Pew Research Center*. Washington, DC: Pew Research Center. Retrieved from http://www.pewso cialtrends.org/2010/06/04/marrying-out/

Patton, S., & Farley, A. P. (2018, May 16). There's no cost to white people who call 911 about black people. There should be. *Washington Post*. Retrieved from https://www.washingtonpost.com/news/posteverything/wp/2018/05/16/theres-no-cost-to-white-people-who-call-911-about-black-people-there-should-be/

PBS. (n.d.). Sharecropping and changes in the south-ern economy. *American Experience*. Retrieved from https://www.pbs.org/wgbh/americanexperience/features/reconstruction-sharecropping-and-chang es-southern-economy

PBS. (1998a). *Africans in America: Conditions of antebel-lum slavery 1830–1860*. Retrieved August 4, 2017, from https://www.pbs.org/wgbh/aia/part4/4p2956.html

PBS. (1998b). *Africans in America: From indentured ser-vitude to racial slavery*. Retrieved August 4, 2017, http://www.pbs.org/wgbh/aia/part1/1narr3.html

PBS. (1998c). *Africans in America: Harriet Tubman*. Retrieved from https://www.pbs.org/wgbh/aia/part4/4p1535.html

PBS. (1998d). *Indentured servants in the U. S.* Retrieved April 29, 2017, from http://www.pbs.org/opb/history detectives/feature/indentured-servants-in-the-us/

Pedraza, S. (1998). Cuba's revolution and exodus. *The Journal of International Institute*, 5(2). Retrieved from http://hdl.handle.net/2027/spo.4750978.0005.204

Peer, B. (2012, October 10). The girl who wanted to go to school. *New Yorker*. Retrieved from https://www.newyorker.com/news/news-desk/the-girl-who-wanted-to-go-to-school

Pego, D. (1998). To educate a nation: Native American tribe hopes to bring higher education to an Arizona reservation. *Black Issues in Higher Education*, 15, 60–63.

Percy, L. (1922, July). The modern Ku Klux Klan. *Atlantic Monthly*, 130, 122–128.

Perez, L. (1980). Cubans. In S. Thernstrom, A. Orlov, & O. Handlin (Eds.), *Harvard encyclopedia of American ethnic groups* (pp. 256–261). Cambridge, MA: Harvard University Press.

Perrow, C. (1986). *Complex organizations* (3rd ed.). New York, NY: Random House.

Petersen, W. (1971). *Japanese Americans*. New York, NY: Random House.

Peterson, M. (1995). Leading Cuban-American entrepreneurs: The process of developing motives, abilities, and resources. *Human Relations*, 48, 1193–1216.

Peterson, N. (2005). What can the pre-colonial and frontier economies tell us about engagement with the real economy: Indigenous life projects and the conditions for development. In D. J. Austin-Broos & G. Macdonald (Eds.), *Culture, economy and governance in Aboriginal Australia: Proceedings of a workshop held at the University of Sydney, 30 November–1 December 2004*. Sydney, Australia: Sydney University Press.

Pettigrew, T. (1958). Personality and sociocultural factors in intergroup attitudes: A cross-national comparison. *Journal of Conflict Resolution*, 2, 29–42.

Pettigrew, T. (1971). *Racially separate or together?* New York, NY: McGraw-Hill.

Pettigrew, T., Wagner, U., & Christ, O. (2007). Who opposes immigration? Comparing German and North American findings. *Du Bois Review*, 4, 19–39.

Pettit, B., & Sykes, B. (2017). Incarceration. *Pathways*, 24–26. Retrieved from https://inequality.stanford.edu/sites/default/files/Pathways_SOTU_2017.pdf

Pettit, B., & Western, B. (2004). Mass imprisonment and the life course: Race and class inequality in U.S. incarceration. *American Sociological Review*, 69, 151–169.

Pettit, E. J. (2015). Aborigines' dreaming or Britain's terra nullius: Perceptions of land use in colonial Australia. *The Iowa Historical Review*, 5(1), 23–60. Retrieved August 18, 2017, from http://ir.uiowa.edu/cgi/viewcontent.cgi?article=1030&context=iowa-historical-review

Pew Hispanic Center. (2004). *Survey brief: Assimilation and language*. Washington, DC: Author. Retrieved from https://www.pewhispanic.org/2004/03/19/assimilation-and-language/

Pew Hispanic Center. (2005). *Hispanics: A people in motion*. Washington, DC: Author. Retrieved from http://pewhispanic.org/files/reports/40.pdf

Pew Research Center. (2007). Muslim Americans: Middle class and mostly mainstream. *Pew Research Center*. Washington, DC: Author. Retrieved from http://pewresearch.org/assets/pdf/muslim-americans.pdf

Pew Research Center. (2013). *The rise of Asian Americans*. Washington, DC: Author. Retrieved April 6, 2019, from http://www.pewsocialtrends.org/2012/06/19/the-rise-of-asian-americans/

Pew Research Center. (2014a). The party of nonvoters. *Pew Research Center*. Washington, DC: Author. Retrieved August 9, 2017. Retrieved from http://www.people-press.org/2014/10/31/the-party-of-nonvoters-2/

Pew Research Center. (2014b). The shifting religious identity of Latinos in the United States. *Pew Research Center*. Washington, DC: Author. Retrieved from http://www.pewforum.org/2014/05/07/the-shifting-religious-identity-of-latinos-in-the-united-states/

Pew Research Center. (2015, June 11). *The many dimensions of Hispanic racial identity*. Washington, DC: Author, June 11. Retrieved from http://www.pewsocialtrends.org/2015/06/11/chapter-7-the-many-dimensions-of-hispanic-racial-identity/#fn-20523-48

Pew Research Center. (2016). On views of race and inequality, blacks and whites are worlds apart.

Pew Research Center. Retrieved July 20, 2017 http://www.pewsocialtrends.org/2016/06/27/1-demographic-trends-and-economic-well-being/

Pew Research Center. (2017a, September 8). Koreans in the U.S. fact sheet. *Pew Research Center*. Retrieved from https://www.pewsocialtrends.org/fact-sheet/asian-americans-koreans-in-the-u-s/

Pew Research Center. (2017b, July 26). U.S. Muslims concerned about their place in society, but continue to believe in the American dream. *Pew Research Center*. Washington, DC: Author. Retrieved August 30, 2017, from http://assets.pewresearch.org/wp-content/uploads/sites/11/2017/07/25171611/u.s.-muslims-full-report.pdf

Pew Research Center. (2018, June 28). Shifting public views on legal immigration into the U.S. *Pew Research Center*. Retrieved from http://www.people-press.org/2018/06/28/shifting-public-views-on-legal-immigration-into-the-u-s/

Pezzella, F. S. (2016). *Hate crime statutes: A public policy and law enforcement dilemma*. New York, NY: Springer.

Phillips, P. (2016). *Blood at the root: A racial cleansing in America*. New York, NY: W. W. Norton & Company.

Phillips, U. (1918). *American negro slavery: A survey of the supply, employment, and control of negro labor as determined by the plantation regime*. New York, NY: Appleton.

Pilgrim, D. (2007). *Irene Morgan v. Commonwealth of Virginia*. Retrieved August 9, 2017, from http://www.ferris.edu/jimcrow/question/dec07/index.htm

Pippert, W. (1983, June 15). Detainment cost Japanese-Americans up to $6.2 billion. *UPI*. Retrieved August 26, 2017, from http://www.upi.com/Archives/1983/06/15/Detainment-cost-Japanese-Americans-up-to-62-billion/7203424497600/

Pitt, L. (1970). *The decline of the Californios: A social history of the Spanish-speaking Californians, 1846–1890*. Berkeley: University of California Press.

Plessy v. Ferguson, 163 U.S. 537 (1896)

Plyler v. Doe, 457 U.S. 202 (1982)

Pollard, K., & O'Hare, W. (1999). America's racial and ethnic minorities. *Population Bulletin*, 54(3), 29–39.

Pompeo, M. R. (2018, September 17). *Remarks to the media*. Retrieved from https://www.state.gov/secretary/remarks/2018/09/285960.htm

Population Reference Bureau. (2014). *2014 world population data sheet*. Washington, DC: Author. Retrieved from http://www.prb.org/Publications/Datasheets/2014/2014-world-population-data-sheet/data-sheet.aspx

Porter, E. (2005, April 5). Illegal immigrants are bolstering Social Security with billions. *New York Times*, p. A1.

Portes, A. (1990). From south of the border: Hispanic minorities in the United States. In V. Yans-McLaughlin (Ed.), *Immigration reconsidered* (pp. 160–184). New York, NY: Oxford University Press.

Portes, A., & Bach, R. L. (1985). *Latin journey: Cuban and Mexican immigrants in the United States*. Berkeley: University of California Press.

Portes, A., & Manning, R. (1986). The immigrant enclave: Theory and empirical examples. In S. Olzak & J. Nagel (Eds.), *Competitive Ethnic Relations* (pp. 47–68). New York, NY: Academic Press.

Portes, A., & Rumbaut, R. (1996). *Immigrant America: A portrait* (2nd ed.). Berkeley: University of California Press.

Portes, A., & Rumbaut, R. (2001). *Legacies: The story of the immigrant second generation*. New York, NY: Russell Sage Foundation.

Portes, A., & Shafer, S. (2006). *Revisiting the enclave hypothesis: Miami twenty-five years* later (Working Paper No. 06-10). Princeton, NJ: Center for Migration and Development, Princeton University. Retrieved from https://www.princeton.edu/cmd/working-papers/papers/wp0610.pdf

Posadas, B. (1999). *The Filipino Americans*. Westport, CT: Greenwood.

Potok, M. (2013). The year in hate and extremism. *Southern Poverty Law Center*. Retrieved from http://www.splcenter.org/home/2013/spring/the-year-in-hate-and-extremism

Potter, G. (1973). *To the golden door: The story of the Irish in Ireland and America*. Westport, CT: Greenwood.

Poushter, J. (2016, September 16). European opinions of the refugee crisis in 5 charts. *Pew Research Center*. Retrieved from http://www.pewresearch.org/fact-tank/2016/09/16/european-opinions-of-the-refugee-crisis-in-5-charts/

Powlishta, K., Serbin, L., Doyle, A., & White, D. (1994). Gender, ethnic, and body-type biases: The generality of prejudice in childhood. *Developmental Psychology*, 30, 526–537.

Price, T. (2010). What is Spanglish? The phenomenon of code-switching and its impact amongst US Latinos. *Début: The Undergraduate Journal of Languages, Linguistics and Area Studies*, 1(1). Retrieved from www.llas.ac.uk/debut

Qian, Z., & Lichter, D. (2011). Changing patterns of interracial marriage in a multiracial society. *Journal of Marriage and Family*, 75, 1065–1084.

Qin, D. B., Way, N., & Rana, M. (2008). The "model minority" and their discontent: Examining peer discrimination and harassment of Chinese American immigrant youth. In H. Yoshikawa & N. Way (Eds.), *Beyond the family: Contexts of immigrant children's development* (pp. 27–42).

Quillian, L. (2006). New approaches to understanding racial prejudice and discrimination. *Annual Review of Sociology*, 32, 299–328.

Quillian, L., & Campbell, M. (2003). Beyond black and white: The present and future of multiracial friendship segregation. *American Sociological Review*, 68, 540–567.

Quiros, L. (2009). *The social construction of racial and ethnic identity among women of color from mixed ancestry: Psychological freedoms and sociological constraints* (PhD dissertation). City University of New York, New York. Retrieved from http://academicworks.cuny.edu/cgi/viewcontent.cgi?article=2996&context=gc_etds

Qureshi, B. (2013, August 9). From wrong to right: A U.S. apology for Japanese internment. *National Public Radio*. Retrieved from https://www.npr.org/sections/codeswitch/2013/08/09/210138278/japanese-internment-redress

Rader, B. G. (1983). *American sports: From the age of folk games to the age of spectators*. Englewood Cliffs, NJ: Prentice Hall.

Rall, R. M. (2016). Forgotten students in a transitional summer: Low-income racial/ethnic minority students experience the summer melt. *The Journal of Negro Education*, 85(4), 462–479.

Raymer, P. (1974, August). Wisconsin's Menominees: Indians on a seesaw. *National Geographic*, 228–251.

Reardon, S. F., Robinson-Cimpian, J. P., & Weathers, E. S. (2014). Patterns and trends in racial/ethnic and socioeconomic academic achievement gaps. In H. A. Ladd & E. B. Fiske (Eds.), *Handbook of research in education finance and policy* (2nd ed.). New York, NY: Routledge.

Reagan, T. (2018). *Non-Western educational traditions: Local approaches to thought and practice* (4th ed.). New York, NY: Taylor and Francis.

Regan, M. (2016). *Detained and deported: Stories of immigrant families under fire*. Boston, MA: Beacon Press.

Reber, E. A. S. (1998). *Buraku Mondai in Japan: Historical and modern perspectives and directions for the future from the perspective of an American researcher*. Retrieved from https://core.ac.uk/download/pdf/35272710.pdf

Reid, M. (2014). *Brazil: The troubled rise of a global power*. New Haven, CT: Yale University Press.

Reséndez, A. (2016). *The other slavery: The uncovered story of Indian enslavement in America*. Boston, MA: Houghton Mifflin Harcourt.

Reyna, C., Dobria, O., & Wetherell, G. (2013). The complexity and ambivalence of immigration attitudes: Ambivalent stereotypes predict conflicting attitudes toward immigration policies. *Cultural Diversity and Ethnic Minority Psychology*, 19, 342–356.

Reynolds, H. (2006). *The other side of the frontier: Aboriginal resistance to the European invasion of Australia*. Sydney, Australia: University New South Wales Press.

Ricci v. DeStefano, 557 U.S. (2009)

Richardson, C. M., & Luker, R. E. (2014). *Historical dictionary of the civil rights movement*. Lanham, MD: Rowman & Littlefield.

Ridgeway, C. (2011). *Framed by gender: How gender inequality persists in the modern world*. New York, NY: Oxford University Press.

Risério, A. (2007). *The Brazilian utopia and the black movements*. San Paolo, Brazil.

Rivera, L. A. (2015). *Pedigree: How elite students get elite jobs*. Princeton, NJ: Princeton University Press.

Roberts, J. (2013). Opinion in *Shelby County v. Holder* 570 U.S. 529.

Robertson, C. (1996). Africa and the Americas? Slavery and women, the family, and the gender division of labor. In D. Gaspar & D. Hine (Eds.), *More than chattel: Black women and slavery in the Americas* (pp. 4–40). Bloomington: Indiana University Press.

Robinson, G. (2012). *After camp: Portraits in midcentury Japanese American life and politics*. Berkeley: University of California Press.

Robles, F. (2017, June 11). 23% of Puerto Ricans vote in referendum, 97% of them for statehood. *New York Times*. Retrieved from https://www.nytimes.com/2017/06/11/us/puerto-ricans-vote-on-the-question-of-statehood.html?r=0

Rockquemore, K. A., & Brunsma, D. (2008). *Beyond black: Biracial identity in America* (2nd ed.). Lanham, MD: Rowman & Littlefield.

Rodriguez, C. (1989). *Puerto Ricans: Born in the USA*. Boston, MA: Unwin-Hyman.

Rodriguez, C., & Cordero-Guzman, H. (1992). Placing race in context. *Ethnic and Racial Studies*, 15, 523–542.

Rodriguez, J. P. (1997). *The historical encyclopedia of world slavery* (Vol. 1.). Santa Barbara, CA: ABC-CLIO.

Rojas, L. B. (2011, April 1). The forgotten history of the Filipino laborers who worked with Cesar Chavez. *Southern California Public Radio (SCPR)*. Retrieved from http://www.scpr.org/blogs/multiamerican/2011/04/01/7203/the-asian-american-farm-worker-legacy/

Roscoe, W. (1991). *The Zuni man–woman*. Albuquerque, NM: University of New Mexico Press.

Rosenbaum, S. (2018, October 16). A new "public charge" rule affecting immigrants has major implications for Medicaid. *The Commonwealth Fund*. Retrieved from https://www.commonwealthfund.org/blog/2018/new-public-charge-rule-affecting-immigrants-has-major-implications-medicaid

Rosenblatt, K., & Siemaszko, C. (2017, July 10). Confederate flag raised at South Carolina statehouse in protest by secessionist party. *NBC*. Retrieved August 12, 2017, from http://www.nbcnews.com/news/us-news/confederate-flag-rises-south-carolina-statehouse-protest-secessionist-party-n781331

Rosenblum, K. E., & Travis, T-M. C. (2002). *The meaning of difference: American constructions of race, sex and social class, and sexual orientation* (3rd ed.). New York, NY: McGraw-Hill.

Rosenfield, M. (2002). Measures of assimilation in the marriage market: Mexican Americans 1970–1990. *Journal of Marriage and the Family*, 64, 152–163.

Rosich, K. (2007). *Race, ethnicity, and the criminal justice system*. Washington, DC: American Sociological Association. Retrieved from http://www.asanet.org/images/press/docs/pdf/ASARaceCrime.pdf

Ross, J. (2014, May 27). African-Americans with college degrees are twice as likely to be unemployed as other graduates. *The Atlantic*. Retrieved from https://www.theatlantic.com/politics/archive/2014/05/african-americans-with-college-degrees-are-twice-as-likely-to-be-unemployed-as-other-graduates/430971/

Rothman, J. (2016, December 4). When bigotry paraded through the streets. *The Atlantic*. Retrieved from https://www.theatlantic.com/politics/archive/2016/12/second-klan/509468/

Rothstein, R. (2014, March 6). Modern segregation. *Economic Policy Institute*. Retrieved June 7, 2017, from http://www.epi.org/publication/modern-segregation/

Rothstein, R. (2017). *The color of law: A forgotten history of how our government segregated America*. New York, NY: Liveright Publishing Corporation.

Rouse, L., & Hanson, J. (1991). American Indian stereotyping, resource competition, and status-based prejudice. *American Indian Culture and Research Journal*, 15, 1–17.

Royster, D. (2003). *Race and the invisible hand: How white networks exclude black men from blue-collar jobs*. Berkeley: University of California Press.

Rozenblit, M. L. (2010). European Jewry: 1800–1933. In J. R. Baskin & K. Seeskin (Eds.), *The Cambridge guide to Jewish history, religion, and culture* (pp. 169–207). Cambridge, UK: Cambridge University Press.

Rumbaut, R. (1991). Passage to America: Perspectives on the new immigration. In A. Wolfe (Ed.), *America at century's end* (pp. 208–244). Berkeley: University of California Press.

Rushforth, B. (2012). *Bonds of alliance: Indigenous and Atlantic slaveries in New France.* Chapel Hill: University of North Carolina Press.

Rusin, S., Zong, J., & Batalova, J. (2015, April 7). Cuban immigrants in the United States. *Migration Policy Institute.* Retrieved January 12, 2017, from http://www.migrationpolicy.org/article/cuban immigrants-united-states

Russell, J. W. (1994). *After the fifth sun: Class and race in North America.* Englewood Cliffs, NJ: Prentice Hall. Retrieved January 12, 2017, from http://www.migrationpolicy.org/article/cuban-immigrants-united-states

Saad, L. (2010). Americans value both aspects of immigration reform. *Gallup Politics.* Retrieved from http://www.gallup.com/poll/127649/Americans-Value-Aspects-Immigration-Reform.aspx

Saenz, R. (2005). *The social and economic isolation of urban African Americans.* Washington, DC: Population Reference Bureau.

Salhani, J. (2015, September 6). Why people are calling out cops for being racist in Brazil. *ThinkProgress.* Retrieved July 20, 2017, from https://thinkprogress.org/why-people-are-calling-out-cops-for-being-racist-in-brazil-d26b4dc2076d

Sammon, A. (2016, September 9). A history of Native Americans protesting the Dakota Access Pipeline. *Mother Jones.* Retrieved August 18, 2017, from http://www.motherjones.com/environment/2016/09/dakota-access-pipeline-protest-timeline-sioux-standing-rock-jill-stein/

Sanchirico, A. (1991). The importance of small business ownership in Chinese American educational achievement. *Sociology of Education,* 64, 293–304.

Santiago, C. R. V. (2001). Space, and the Puerto Rican citizenship. *Denver University Law Review.*

Retrieved from http://academic.udayton.edu/race/02rights/PRico02.htm

Santiago, E. (1993). *When I was Puerto Rican.* Cambridge, MA: De Capo Press.

Sarah Keys v. Carolina Coach Company, 64 MCC 769. (1955)

Sastry, A., & Bates, K. G. (2017, April 26). When LA erupted in anger: A look back at the Rodney King riots. *NPR.* Retrieved from https://www.npr.org/2017/04/26/524744989/when-la-erupted-in-anger-a-look-back-at-the-rodney-king-riots

Satter, B. (2009). *Family properties: Race, real estate, and the exploitation of black urban America.* New York, NY: Henry Holt.

Savage, C. (2017, August 1). Justice department to take on affirmative action in college admissions. *New York Times.* Retrieved August 10, 2017, from https://www.nytimes.com/2017/08/01/us/politics/trump-affirmative-action-universities.html

Sawyer, N. (2017, November 6). Activists paint Anti-DAPL mural outside Wells Fargo. *SFWeekly.* Retrieved from http://www.sfweekly.com/news/activists-paint-anti-dapl-mural-outside-wells-fargo/

Sayers, D. O., Burke, P. B., & Henry, A. M. (2007). The political economy of exile in the Great Dismal Swamp. *International Journal of Historical Archaeology,* 11(1), 60–97.

Schachter, A. (2016). From "different" to "similar": An experimental approach to understanding assimilation. *American Sociological Review,* 81(5), 98–1013.

Schafer, J., & Navarro, J. (2004). The seven-stage hate model: The psychopathology of hate groups. *The FBI Law Enforcement Bulletin,* 72, 1–9.

Schlesinger, A. M., Jr. (1992). *The disuniting of America: Reflections on a multicultural society.* New York, NY: Norton.

Schmid, C. (2001). *The politics of language: Conflict, identity, and cultural pluralism in comparative perspective.* New York, NY: Oxford University Press.

Schoen Consulting. (2018). *The Holocaust knowledge and awareness study.* http://cc-69bd.kxcdn.com/

wp-content/uploads/2018/04/Holocaust-Knowledge-Awareness-Study_Executive-Summary-2018.pdf

Schoener, A. (1967). *Portal to America: The lower east side, 1870–1925*. New York, NY: Holt, Rinehart, & Winston.

Schorr, D. (2008). A new, "post-racial" political era in America. *NPR*. Retrieved August 1, 2017, from http://www.npr.org/templates/story/story.php?storyId=184894

Schuette v. BAMN, 572 U.S. 12–682 (2014)

Schurz, C. (1865). *Report on the condition of the South*. Available from http://wps.pearsoncustom.com/wps/media/objects/2429/2487430/pdfs/schurz.pdf

Sears, D. (1988). Symbolic racism. In P. Katz & D. Taylor (Eds.), *Eliminating racism: Profiles in controversy* (pp. 53–84). New York, NY: Plenum.

Sears, D., & Henry, P. J. (2003). The origins of modern racism. *Journal of Personality and Social Psychology*, 85, 259–275.

Seattle Civil Rights and Labor History Project. (n.d.). *Racially restrictive covenants*. Retrieved August 26, 2017, from http://depts.washington.edu/civilr/covenants_database.htm

See, K. O., & Wilson, W. J. (1988). Race and ethnicity. In N. J. Smelser (Ed.), *Handbook of Sociology* (pp. 223–242). Newbury Park, CA: SAGE.

Selzer, M. (1972). *Kike: Anti-Semitism in America*. New York, NY: Meridian.

Sen, R., & Mamdouh, F. (2008). *The accidental American: Immigration and citizenship in the age of globalization*. San Francisco, CA: Berrett-Koehler.

The Sentencing Project. (2015). *The changing racial dynamics of women's incarceration*. Retrieved from https://www.sentencingproject.org/wp-content/uploads/2015/12/The-Changing-Racial-Dynamics-of-Womens-Incarceration.pdf

Shannon, W. V. (1964). *The American Irish*. New York, NY: Macmillan.

Shapiro, T., Meschede, T., & Osoro, S. (2013). *The roots of the widening racial wealth gap: Explaining the black–white economic divide*. Waltham, MA: Institute on Assets and Social Policy, Brandeis University. Retrieved from http://iasp.brandeis.edu/pdfs/Author/shapiro-thomas-m/racialwealthgapbrief.pdf

Sheet Metal Workers v. EEOC. (1986)

Shelby County v. Holder, 570 U.S. 529. (2013)

Sherif, M., Harvey, O. J., White, B. J., Hood, W. R., & Sherif, C. W. (1961). *The robber's cave experiment: Intergroup conflict and cooperation*. Norman, OK: University Book Exchange.

Sheth, M. (1995). Asian Indian Americans. In P. G. Min (Ed.), *Asian American: Contemporary issues and trends* (pp. 168–198). Thousand Oaks, CA: SAGE.

Shevitz, A. H. (2005). Restricted public accommodations. In R. S. Levy, D. P. Bell, & W. C. Donahue (Eds.), *Antisemitism: A historical encyclopedia of prejudice and persecution* (Vol. 1 A–K, p. 597). Santa Barbara, CA: ABC-CLIO.

Simmons, G. Z. (2011). *Oral history interview conducted by Joseph Mosnier*. Gainesville, FL. Retrieved August 9, 2017, from https://www.loc.gov/item/afc2010039_crhp0049/

Simon, J. (1989). *The economic consequences of immigration*. Cambridge, MA: Blackwell.

Simpson, G., & Yinger, M. (1985). *Racial and cultural minorities: An analysis of prejudice and discrimination*. New York, NY: Plenum.

Simpson, K. (2012, February 15). The great migration: Creating a new black identity in Los Angeles. *KCET*. Retrieved from https://www.kcet.org/history-society/the-great-migration-creating-a-new-black-identity-in-los-angeles

Singhvi, A., & Parlapiano, A. (2017, February 3). Trump's immigration ban: Who is barred and who is not. *New York Times*. Retrieved from https://www.nytimes.com/interactive/2017/01/31/us/politics/trump-immigration-ban-groups.html?mcubz=0

Skinner, B. (2008). A world enslaved. *Foreign Policy*, 165, 62–68.

Sklare, M. (1971). *America's Jews*. New York, NY: Random House.

Small, M. L., Harding, D. J., & Lamont, M. (2010). Reconsidering culture and poverty. *Annals of the American Academy of Political and Social Science*, 629, 6. Retrieved from http://ann.sagepub.com/content/629/1/6

Smedley, A. (2007). *Race in North America: Origin and evolution of a worldview* (3rd ed.). Boulder, CO: Westview.

Smith, A. (2014, January 6). African Americans and technology use. *Pew Research Center.* Retrieved from http://www.pewinternet.org/2014/01/06/african-americans-and-technology-use/

Smith, A. F. (2013). *Food and drink in American History: A "full course" encyclopedia.* Santa Barbara, CA: ABC-CLIO.

Smith, T., & Dempsey, G. (1983). The polls: Ethnic social distance and prejudice. *Public Opinion Quarterly*, 47, 584–600.

Smithers, G. D. (2008). *Science, sexuality, and race in the United States and Australia, 1780–1940.* Lincoln: University of Nebraska Press.

Smithsonian National Museum of American History. (n.d.-a). *The promise of freedom.* Retrieved August 10, 2017, from http://americanhistory.si.edu/brown/history/1-segregated/promise-of-freedom.html

Smithsonian National Museum of American History. (n.d.-b). *Separate is not equal.* Retrieved from http://americanhistory.si.edu/brown/history/1-segregated/jim-crow.html

Snipp, C. M. (1989). *American Indians: The first of this land.* New York, NY: Russell Sage Foundation.

Snipp, C. M. (1992). Sociological perspectives on American Indians. *Annual Review of Sociology*, 18, 351–371.

Snipp, C. M. (1996). The first Americans: American Indians. In S. Pedraza & R. G. Rumbaut (Eds.), *Origins and destinies: Immigration, race, and ethnicity in America* (pp. 390–403). Belmont, CA: Wadsworth.

Snyder, C. (2010). *Slavery in Indian country: The changing face of captivity in early America.* Cambridge, MA: Harvard University Press.

Social Science Data Analysis Network. (n.d.). Segregation: Dissimilarity indices. *CensusScope.* Retrieved from http://www.censusscope.org/us/s40/p75000/chart_dissimilarity.html

Soennichsen, J. (2011). *The Chinese Exclusion Act of 1882.* Santa Barbara, CA: Greenwood Publishing Group.

Sopel, J. (2015, August 15). US flag raised over reopened Cuba embassy in Havana. *BBC.* Retrieved from http://www.bbc.com/news/world-latin-america-33919484

Southern Poverty Law Center (SPLC). (n.d.). *Nation of Islam.* Retrieved from https://www.splcenter.org/fighting-hate/extremist-files/group/nation-islam

Southern Poverty Law Center (SPLC). (2017, February 15). *Hate groups increase for second consecutive year as Trump electrifies radical right.* Retrieved August 30, 2017, from https://www.splcenter.org/news/2017/02/15/hate-groups-increase-second-consecutive-year-trump-electrifies-radical-right

Southern Poverty Law Center (SPLC). (2018). *Hate groups, 1999–2017.* Retrieved from https://www.splcenter.org/hate-map

Spicer, E. H. (1980). American Indians. In S. Thernstrom, A. Orlov, & O Handlin (Eds.), *Harvard encyclopedia of American ethnic groups* (pp. 58–122). Cambridge, MA: Harvard University Press.

Spickard, P. (1996). *Japanese Americans: The formation and transformations of an ethnic group.* New York, NY: Twayne.

Spilde, K. (2001). The economic development journey of Indian nations. *Indian Gaming.* Retrieved from http://www.indiangaming.org/library/articles/the-economic-development-journey.shtml

Spilde, K., & Taylor, J. B. (2013). Economic evidence on the effects of the Indian Gaming Regulatory Act on Indians and non-Indians. *UNLV Gaming Research & Review Journal*, 17(1), 13–30.

Stack, C. B. (1974). *All our kin: Strategies for survival in a black community.* New York, NY: Basic Books.

Stainback, K., & Tomaskovic-Devey, D. (2012). *Documenting desegregation: Racial and gender segregation in private-sector employment since the civil rights act.* New York, NY: Russell Sage.

Stallard, K., Ehrenreich, B., & Sklar, H. (1983). *Poverty in the American dream: Women & children first*. New York, NY: South End Press.

Stampp, K. (1956). *The peculiar institution: Slavery in the Antebellum South*. New York, NY: Random House.

Stanford University. (n.d.). Bayard Rustin. *King encyclopedia*. https://kinginstitute.stanford.edu/ency clopedia/rustin-bayard

Stannard, D. E. (1992). *American Holocaust*. New York, NY: Oxford University Press.

Staples, R. (1988). The black American family. In C. Mindel, R. Habenstein, & R. Wright (Eds.), *Ethnic Families in America* (3rd ed.; pp. 303–324). New York, NY: Elsevier.

Steinberg, S. (1981). *The ethnic myth: Race, ethnicity, and class in America*. New York, NY: Atheneum.

Steinberg, S. (2011, January 13). Poor reason: Culture still doesn't explain poverty. *Boston Review*. Retrieved from http://www.bostonreview.net/steinberg.php

Stephens, A. H. (1861). "'Corner stone' speech." Presented on March 21, Savannah, GA. Retrieved April 29, 2017, http://teachingamericanhistory.org/library/document/cornerstone-speech/

Stepler, R., & Lopez, M. H. (2016). U.S. Latino population growth and dispersion has slowed since onset of the Great Recession. *Pew Research Center*. Retrieved from https://www.pewhispanic.org/wp-content/uploads/sites/5/2016/09/PH_2016.09.08_Geography.pdf

Stevenson, M., & Mayson, S. G. (2018). The scale of misdemeanor justice. 98 B.U. L. Rev. 98. *Boston University Law Review*, 731.

Stoddard, E. (1973). *Mexican Americans*. New York, NY: Random House.

Stokes, B. (2016, June 7). Euroskepticism beyond Brexit. *Pew Research Center*. Retrieved from http://www.pewglobal.org/2016/06/07/euroskep ticism-beyond-brexit/#eurefugees

Stolberg, S. G., & Alcindor, Y. (2017, September 14). Trump's support for law to protect "Dreamers" lifts its chances. *New York Times*. Retrieved from https://www.nytimes.com/2017/09/14/us/politics/trump-da-ca-dreamers.html

Stolberg, S. G., & Rosenthal, B. M. (2017, August 12). Man charged after white nationalist rally in Charlottesville ends in deadly violence. *New York Times*. Retrieved from https://www.nytimes.com/2017/08/12/us/char lottesville-protest-white-nationalist.html

Stoll, M. (2004). *African Americans and the color line*. New York, NY: Russell Sage Foundation.

Strother, L., Ogorzalek, T., & Piston, S. (2017a, June 12). The Confederate flag largely disappeared after the Civil War. The fight against civil rights brought it back. *Washington Post*. Retrieved August 12, 2017, from https://www.washingtonpost.com/news/monkey-cage/wp/2017/06/12/confederate-symbols-largely-dis appeared-after-the-civil-war-the-fight-against-civ il-rights-brought-them-back/?hpid=hp_hp-cards_hp-card-politics%3Ahomepage%2Fcard

Strother, L., Ogorzalek, T., & Piston, S. (2017b). Pride or prejudice? Racial prejudice, southern heritage, and white support for the confederate battle flag. *Du Bois Review*, 14(1), 295–323.

Stuckey, S. (1987). *Slave culture: Nationalist theory and the foundations of black America*. New York, NY: Harper & Row.

Stuyvesant, P. (1995). Petition to expel the Jews from New Amsterdam. In P. R. Mendes-Flohr & J. Reinharz (Eds.), *The Jew in the modern world: A documentary history* (p. 452). Oxford University Press, 1995.

Sue, D. W., Bucceri, J., Lin, A. I., Nadal, K. L., & Torino, G. C. (2007). Racial microaggressions and the Asian American experience. *Cultural Diversity and Ethnic Minority Psychology*, 13, 72–81.

Sumner, W. G. (1906). *Folkways: A study of the sociological importance of usages, manners, customs, mores, and morals*. Boston, MA: Ginn and Company.

Sunda, M. (2015, October 23). Japan's hidden caste of untouchables. *BBC News*. Retrieved from https://www.bbc.com/news/world-asia-34615972

Swain, J., Laughland, O., Lartey, J., & McCarthy, C. (2015, December 31). Young black men killed by US police at highest rate in year of 1,134 deaths. *The Guardian*. Retrieved from https://www.theguardian.com/us-news/2015/dec/31/the-counted-police-killings-2015-young-black-men

Swaney, K. R. (2004). An ideological war of "blood and soil" and its effect on the agricultural propaganda and policy of the Nazi party, 1929–1939. *The Gettysburg Historical Journal*, 3(6).

Taíno Museum. (2017). *Taino*. Retrieved fromhttp://tainomuseum.org/taino/

Takaki, R. (1993). *A different mirror: A history of multicultural America*. Boston, MA: Little, Brown.

Takao Ozawa v. United States, 260 U.S. 178 (1922)

Taylor, A. (2014, November 12). 20 years after the 1994 Cuban raft exodus. *The Atlantic*. Retrieved from https://www.theatlantic.com/photo/2014/11/20-years-after-the-1994-cuban-raft-exodus/100852/

Taylor, J., & Kalt, J. (2005). *American Indians on reservations: A databook of socioeconomic change between the 1990 and 2000 censuses*. Cambridge, MA: The Harvard Project on American Indian Economic Development. Retrieved from https://hpaied.org/sites/default/files/publications/American IndiansonReservationsADatabookofSocioeconomic Change.pdf

Taylor, P., Cohn, D., Livingston, G., Funk, C., & Morin, R. (2013). *Second generation Americans: A portrait of adult children of immigrants*. Washington, DC: Pew Research Center. Retrieved from http://www.pewsocialtrends.org/files/2013/02/FINAL_immigrant_generations_report_2-7-13.pdf

Taylor, P., Lopez, M., Martinez, J., & Velasco, G. (2012). When labels don't fit: Hispanics and their views of identity. *Pew Research Center*. Washington, DC: Pew Hispanic Center. Retrieved from http://www.pewhispanic.org/2012/04/04/when-labels-dont-fit-hispanics-and-their-views-of-identity/

Taylor, U. Y. (2017). *The promise of patriarchy: Women and the Nation of Islam*. Chapel Hill: University of North Carolina Press.

Telles, E. (2004). *Race in another America: The significance of skin color in Brazil*. Princeton, NJ: Princeton University Press.

Telles, E., & Ortiz, V. (2008). *Generations of exclusion: Mexican Americans, assimilation, and race*. New York, NY: Russell Sage Foundation.

Theoharis, J. (2006). *The black power movement: Rethinking the civil rights–black power era*. New York, NY: Routledge.

Theoharis, J. (2013). *The rebellious life of Mrs. Rosa Parks*. Boston, MA: Beacon Press.

Thernstrom, S. (2004). Rediscovering the melting pot—still going strong. In T. Jacoby (Ed.), *Reinventing the melting pot: The new immigrants and what it means to be American* (pp. 47–59). New York: NY Basic Books.

Thomas, K. J., & Logan, I. (2012). African female immigration to the United States and its policy implications. *Canadian Journal of African Studies*, 46(1), 87–107.

Thomas, W. (1997). Navajo cultural constructions of gender and sexuality. In S-E. Jacobs, W. Thomas, & S. Lang (Eds.), *Two-spirit people: Native American gender identity, sexuality, and spirituality* (pp. 156–173). Champaign, IL: University of Illinois Press.

Thorbecke, C. (2016, October 10). Haiti in desperate need of a "massive humanitarian response," aid groups say. *ABCNews*. Retrieved from https://abcnews.go.com/International/haiti-desperate-massive-humanitarian-response-aid-groups/story?id=42700881

Thornton, R. (2001). Trends among American Indians in the United States. In N. Smelser, W. Wilson, & F. Mitchell (Eds.), *America becoming: Racial trends and their consequences* (Vol. 1, pp. 135–169). Washington, DC: National Academy Press.

Tilly, C. (1990). Transplanted networks. In V. Yans-McLaughlin (Ed.), *Immigration reconsidered: History, sociology, and politics* (pp. 79–95). New York, NY: Oxford University Press.

TracImmigration. (2016, December 13). *Continued rise in asylum denial rates: Impact of representation and nationality*. Retrieved January 5, 2019, from http://trac.syr.edu/immigration/reports/448/

Treuer, A. (2012). *Everything you wanted to know about Indians but were afraid to ask*. St. Paul, MN: Borealis Books.

Treuer, D. (2012). *Rez life: An Indian's journey through reservation life*. New York, NY: Atlantic Monthly Press.

Treuer, D. (2019). *The heartbeat of Wounded Knee*. New York, NY: Riverhead Books.

Tribune Wire Reports. (2014, October 11). Riot erupts near St. Louis over police shooting of teen. *Chicago Tribune*. Retrieved August 10, 2017, from http://www.chicagotribune.com/news/nationworld/chi-missouri-police-shooting-20140810-story.html

Troost, W. (n.d.). The Freedmen's Bureau. Retrieved March 29, 2019, from https://eh.net/encyclopedia/the-freedmens-bureau/

Tsai, S-S. H. (1986). *The Chinese experience in America*. Bloomington: Indiana University Press.

U.S. Bureau of Labor Statistics. (2013). *1972–2013: Labor force characteristics by race and ethnicity*. Retrieved from https://www.bls.gov/opub/reports/race-and-ethnicity/archive/race_ethnicity_2013.pdf

U.S. Bureau of Labor Statistics. (2016). *Employment status of civilian noninstitutionalized population by sex, age, and race*. Retrieved from https://www.bls.gov/cps/cpsaat05.pdf

U.S. Bureau of Labor Statistics. (2017a). *Employment by major industry sector (2006, 2016, and projected 2026)*. Retrieved October 24, 2018, from https://www.bls.gov/emp/tables/employment-by-major-industry-sector.htm#2

U.S. Bureau of Labor Statistics. (2017b). *Employment status of population by sex, marital status and presence of children*. Retrieved from https://www.bls.gov/news.release/famee.t05.htm

U.S. Bureau of Labor Statistics. (2018). *Unemployment rates by sex, age, race, and Latino or Hispanic ethnicity*. Retrieved from https://www.bls.gov/web/empsit/cpsee_e16.htm

U.S. Bureau of the Census. (2018a). *Historical Poverty Tables, Tables 3 and 4*. https://www.census.gov/data/tables/time-series/demo/income-poverty/historical-poverty-people.html

U.S. Bureau of the Census. (2018b). *Table A-2: Percentage of people age 25 and older who have completed high school or college by race, Hispanic origin and sex, 1940–2017*. Retrieved from https://www.census.gov/data/tables/time-series/demo/educational-attainment/cps-historical-time-series.html

U.S. Bureau of the Census. (2018c). *Table H-5 historical income tables*. Retrieved from https://www.census.gov/data/tables/time-series/demo/income-poverty/historical-income-households.html

U.S. Bureau of the Census. (2018d). *Table HINC-02 age of householder-households, by total money income type of household, race and Hispanic origin of householder*. Retrieved from https://www.census.gov/data/tables/2017/demo/cps/hinc-02.html

U.S. Census Bureau. (1978). *Statistical abstract of the United States, 1977*. Washington, DC: Author.

U.S. Census Bureau. (1990). Summary File 3. Retrieved from http://factfinder2.census.gov/faces/nav/jsf/pages/index.xhtml

U.S. Census Bureau. (1993). *Statistical abstract of the United States, 1992*. Washington, DC: Government Printing Office.

U.S. Census Bureau. (2000a). Summary file 1. *Census 2000*. Retrieved from https://www.census.gov/census2000/sumfile1.html

U.S. Census Bureau. (2000b). Summary file 4. *Census 2000*. Retrieved from https://www.census.gov/census2000/SF4.html

U.S. Census Bureau. (2002). *Statistical abstract of the United States, 2001*. Washington, DC: Author.

U.S. Census Bureau. (2004). Ancestry. In *Census atlas of the United States* (pp. 138–155). Retrieved from http://www.census.gov/population/www/cen2000/censusatlas/pdf/9_Ancestry.pdf

U.S. Census Bureau. (2005). *Statistical abstract of the United States, 2005*. Washington, DC: Author.

U.S. Census Bureau. (2007). *Statistical abstract of the United States, 2007*. Washington, DC: Author. Available at http://www.census.gov/compendia/statab/past_years.html

U.S. Census Bureau. (2008). 1990 summary tape file 3. *American fact finder*. Retrieved from http://factfinder.census.gov/servlet/DatasetMainPageServlet?_program=DEC&_tabId=DEC2&_submenuId=datasets_1&_lang=en&_ts=222966 429406

U.S. Census Bureau. (2010). *Statistical abstract of the United States: 2010*. Washington, DC: Author. Retrieved from http://www.census.gov/compendia/statab/2010/2010edition.html

U.S. Census Bureau. (2011). *Statistical abstract of the United States, 2011*. Washington, DC: Author.

U.S. Census Bureau. (2012a). *2010 census American Indian and Native Alaska summary file*. Retrieved from http://factfinder2.census.gov/faces/nav/jsf/pages/index.xhtml

U.S. Census Bureau. (2012b). Most children younger than age 1 are minorities, Census Bureau reports. *Newsroom Archive*. News release. http://www.census.gov/newsroom/releases/archives/population/cb12-90.html

U.S. Census Bureau. (2012c). *Statistical abstract of the United States, 2012*. Washington, DC: Government. U.S. Census Bureau. (2013a). *American community survey 3-year estimates, 2010–2012*. Retrieved from http://factfinder2.census.gov/faces/tableservices/jsf/pages/productview.xhtml?pid=ACS_sumfile_2010_2012&prodType=document

U.S. Census Bureau. (2013). Selected characteristics of people 15 years and over, by total money income in 2012, work experience in 2012, race, Hispanic origin, and sex (Table PINC-01). *Current Population Survey*. Retrieved from http://www.census.gov/hhes/www/cpstables/032013/perinc/pinc01_000.htm

U.S. Census Bureau. (2015a). *2014 national population projections*. Retrieved August 3, 2017, from http://www.census.gov/population/projections/data/national/2014/summarytables.html

U.S. Census Bureau. (2015b). American community survey, 2015. *Comparative demographic estimates*. Retrieved April 15, 2017, from https://factfinder.census.gov/faces/tableservices/jsf/pages/productview.xhtml?pid=ACS_15_5YR_CP05&prodType=table

U.S. Census Bureau. (2015c). Languages spoken at home. *American Community Survey, 2009–2013*. Retrieved from https://www.census.gov/data/tables/2013/demo/2009-2013-lang-tables.html

U.S. Census Bureau. (2015d). *Most comprehensive language data ever released from the Census Bureau*.
Retrieved from https://www.census.gov/newsroom/press-releases/2015/cb15-185html

U.S. Census Bureau. (2016a). American Community Survey, 2016, 5-year estimates. *Fact Finder*. Retrieved from https://factfinder.census.gov/faces/tableservices/jsf/pages/productview.xhtml?pid=ACS_16_5YR_B04006&prodType=table

U.S. Census Bureau. (2016b). American Indian and Alaska Natives alone for selected tribal groupings. *American fact finder*. Retrieved from https://factfinder.census.gov/faces/tableservices/jsf/pages/productview.xhtml?pid=ACS_16_5YR_B02014&prodType=table

U.S. Census Bureau. (2016c). *Data: PINC-01. Selected characteristics of people 15 years and over, by total money income, work experience, race, Hispanic origin, and sex*. Retrieved from https://www.census.gov/data/tables/time-series/demo/income-poverty/cps-pinc/pinc-01.html#par_textimage_14

U.S. Census Bureau. (2016d). *Table H1: Households by type and tenure of householder for selected characteristics, 2016*. Retrieved July 14, 2017, from https://www.census.gov/data/tables/2016/demo/families/cps-2016.html

U.S. Census Bureau. (2017a). 2016 American community survey, 1-year estimates. *Fact Finder*. Retrieved from https://factfinder.census.gov/faces/tableservices/jsf/pages/productview.xhtml?pid=ACS_16_1YR_S0201&prodType=table U.S. Census Bureau. (2017b). *2017 national population projections tables*. Available at https://www.census.gov/data/tables/2017/demo/popproj/2017-summary-tables.html

U.S. Census Bureau. (2017b). *American community survey, 2015, one-year estimates*. Retrieved from https://factfinder.census.gov/faces/tableservices/jsf/pages/productview.xhtml?src=bkmk

U.S. Census Bureau. (2017c). Selected characteristics of the native and foreign born population. *2012–2016 American Community Survey, 5-year estimates*. Retrieved from https://factfinder.census.gov/faces/tableservices/jsf/pages/productview.xhtml?pid=ACS_16_5YR_S0501&prodType=table

U.S. Census Bureau. (2017d). *Table H-1. Households by type and tenure of householder for selected characteristics, 2017*. Retrieved from https://www.census.gov/data/tables/2017/demo/families/cps-2017.html

U.S. Census Bureau. (2017e). *Table P-36 historical income tables: People full-time year-round workers by median income and sex.* Retrieved from https://www.census.gov/data/tables/time-series/demo/income-poverty/historical-income-people.html

U.S. Census Bureau. (2017f). *Table PINC-03 educational attainment of people 25 years old and over, by total money earnings, work experience, age, race, Hispanic origin, and sex.* Retrieved from https://www.census.gov/data/tables/time-series/demo/income-poverty/cps-pinc/pinc-03.html

U.S. Census Bureau. (2017g). *Voting and registration in the election of November 2016. Table 4.* Retrieved from https://census.gov/data/tables/time-series/demo/voting-and-registration/p20-580.html

U.S. Census Bureau. (2018a). American community survey, 2017. 1-year estimates. *Fact Finder.* Retrieved from https://factfinder.census.gov/faces/tableservices/jsf/pages/productview.xhtml?pid=ACS_17_1YR_S0201&prodType=table

U.S. Census Bureau. (2018b). Historical income tables. *Table P-36.* Retrieved from https://www.census.gov/data/tables/time-series/demo/income-poverty/historical-income-people.html

U.S. Commission on Civil Rights. (1976). *Puerto Ricans in the continental United States: An uncertain future.* Washington, DC: Government Printing Office.

U.S. Commission on Civil Rights. (1992). *Civil rights issues facing Asian Americans in the 1990s.* Washington, DC: Government Printing Office.

U.S. Department of Education. (2018, May). Public school teacher spending on classroom supplies. *NCES 2018-097.* Retrieved from https://nces.ed.gov/pubs2018/2018097.pdf

U.S. Department of Education Office for Civil Rights. (2014). *Civil rights data collection: Data Snapshot: School Discipline.* Retrieved August 8, 2017, from https://ocrdata.ed.gov/Downloads/CRDC-School-Discipline-Snapshot.pdf

U.S. Department of Homeland Security. (2012). *Yearbook of immigration statistics, 2012.* Retrieved from http://www.dhs.gov/yearbook-immigration-statistics-2012-legal-permanent-residents

U.S. Department of Homeland Security. (2016). *Yearbook of immigration statistics, 2015.* Retrieved April 15, 2017, from https://www.dhs.gov/sites/default/files/publications/Yearbook_Immigration_Statistics_2015.pdf

U.S. Department of Homeland Security. (2017). *Yearbook of immigration statistics 2016.* Retrieved from https://www.dhs.gov/immigration-statistics/yearbook/2016

U.S. Department of Homeland Security. (2018a). *Table 1. Persons obtaining lawful permanent resident status by region and country of birth: Fiscal years 1820–2017.* Retrieved from https://www.dhs.gov/immigration-statistics/yearbook/2017/table1

U.S. Department of Homeland Security. (2018b). *Table 3. Persons obtaining lawful permanent resident status by region and country of birth: Fiscal years 2015–2017.* Retrieved from https://www.dhs.gov/immigration-statistics/yearbook/2017/table3

U.S. Department of Justice Civil Rights Division. (2015). *Investigation of the Ferguson police department.* Retrieved August 10, 2017, from https://www.courts.mo.gov/file.jsp?id=95274

U.S. Government Accountability Office. (2016). *K–12 education: Better use of information could help agencies identify disparities and address racial discrimination.* Retrieved July 20, 2017, from http://www.gao.gov/assets/680/676745.pdf

U.S. Immigration and Naturalization Service. (1993). *Statistical yearbook of the immigration and naturalization service, 1992.* Washington, DC: Government Printing Office.

U.S. Parks Service. (n.d.). *Indian reservations in the continental United States.* Retrieved January 15, 2017, from https://www.nps.gov/nagpra/DOCUMENTS/ResMAP.HTM

U.S. Sentencing Commission. (2017, November 14). *Demographic differences in sentencing: An update to the 2012 Booker Report.* Washington, DC. Retrieved from https://www.ussc.gov/sites/default/files/pdf/research-and-publications/research-publications/2017/20171114_Demographics.pdf

Udry, R. (2000). Biological limits of gender construction. *American Sociological Review, 65,* 443–457.

UNHCR. (2000). Flight from Indochina. *The State of The World's Refugees 2000*. Retrieved from https://www.unhcr.org/3ebf9bad0.pdf

United Nations. (n.d.). *New UN system approach on cholera in Haiti*. Retrieved from http://www.un.org/News/dh/infocus/haiti/Haiti_UN_System_Cholera.pdf

United Nations. (1948). *Convention on the prevention and punishment of the crime of genocide*. New York, NY: United Nations. Retrieved from http://www.hrweb.org/legal/genocide.html

United Nations. (2017). *The international migration report highlights*. Retrieved from https://www.un.org/development/desa/publications/international-migration-report-2017.html

United Nations Department of Economic and Social Affairs. (2018). *The international migration report 2017*. https://www.un.org/development/desa/publications/international-migration-report-2017.html

United Nations Department of Economic and Social Affairs, Population Division. (2013). *Population facts* (No. 2013/2). Retrieved from http://esa.un.org/unmigration/documents/The_number_of_international_migrants.pdf

United Nations Development Programme Human Development Reports. (2016). *Human Development Indicators*. Retrieved from http://hdr.undp.org/en/countries/profiles/MEX

United Nations Refugee Agency. (1951). *Convention relating to the status of refugees*. Retrieved from https://www.unhcr.org/3b66c2aa10

United Press International (UPI). (1986, December 25). Marquette Frye dead; "man who began riot." *New York Times*. Retrieved from https://www.nytimes.com/1986/12/25/obituaries/marquette-frye-dead-man-who-began-riot.html

United States Border Patrol. (n.d.). *Total illegal alien apprehensions by fiscal year*. Retrieved from https://catalog.data.gov/dataset/u-s-border-patrol-fiscal-year-apprehension-statistics-nationwide-fy-2017

United States Border Patrol. (2017). *Apprehensions/seizure statistics*. Retrieved from https://defenseoversight.wola.org/primarydocs/1712_bp_stats_sm.pdf

United States Holocaust Memorial Museum. (n.d.). Pogroms. *Holocaust encyclopedia*. https://encyclopedia.ushmm.org/content/en/article/pogroms

United States v. Wong Kim Ark, 169 U.S. 649 (1987/1989)

United Steelworkers of America, AFL-CIO-CLC v. Weber, 443 U.S. 193 (1979)

Valentine, S., & Mosley, G. (2000). Acculturation and sex-role attitudes among Mexican Americans: A longitudinal analysis. *Hispanic Journal of Behavioral Sciences*, 22, 104–204.

Van Ausdale, D., & Feagin, J. (2001). *The first R: How children learn race and racism*. Lanham, MD: Rowman & Littlefield.

van den Berghe, P. L. (1967). *Race and racism: A comparative perspective*. New York, NY: Wiley.

van den Berghe, P. L. (1981). *The ethnic phenomenon*. New York, NY: Elsevier.

Van Hook, J. (2010). *The demographic impacts of repealing birthright citizenship*. Retrieved from http://www.migrationpolicy.org/pubs/BirthrightInsight-2010.pdf

Vanderkooy, P. N. (2011). *Life pathways of Haitian-American young adults in South Florida*. FIU Electronic Theses and Dissertations. Digitalcommons.fiu.edu/etd/411

Vandermaas-Peeler, A., Cox, D., Fisch-Friedman, M., & Jones, R. P. (2017, December 5). One nation, divided, under Trump: Findings from the 2017 American values survey. *Public Religion Research Institute*. Retrieved from https://www.prri.org/research/american-values-survey-2017/#

Vargas-Ramos, C. (2005). Black, trigueño, white . . . ? Shifting racial identification among Puerto Ricans. *Du Bois Review*, 2, 267–285.

Vasquez, J. M. (2014). The whitening hypothesis challenged: Biculturalism in Latino and non-Hispanic white intermarriage. *Sociological Forum*, 29(2), 386–407. doi:10.1111/socf.12089.

Veterans Stand For Standing Rock. (n.d.). [Facebook Group]. Retrieved from https://www.facebook.com/events/1136540643060285/

Vicens, A. J. (2016, August 3). Here's what's happening in the battle for voting rights. *Mother Jones*. Retrieved June 12, 2017, from http://www.motherjones.com/politics/2016/08/voting-rights-decisions-across-country-update/

Vincent, T. G. (1976). *Black power and the Garvey movement*. San Francisco, CA: Ramparts.

Vinje, D. (1996). Native American economic development on selected reservations: A comparative analysis. *American Journal of Economics and Sociology*, 55, 427–442.

Vock, D. (2013, October 30). With little choice, Alabama backs down on immigration law. *Stateline*. Retrieved from http://www.pewstates.org/projects/stateline/headlines/with-little-choice-alabama-backs-down-on-immigration-law-85899516441

Von Drehle, D. (2004). *Triangle: The fire that changed America*. New York, NY: Grove Press.

Wade, P. (1997). *Race and ethnicity in Latin America*. London, UK: Pluto Press.

Wagley, C., & Harris, M. (1958). *Minorities in the new world: Six case studies*. New York, NY: Columbia University Press.

Walker, A. (1983). *In search of our mothers' gardens*. San Diego, CA: Harcourt Brace, Jovanovich.

Wallace, M., & Figueroa, R. (2012). Determinants of perceived immigrant job threat in the American states. *Sociological Perspectives*, 55, 583–612.

Wang, W. (2012). The rise of intermarriage: Rates, characteristics vary by race and gender. *Pew Research Center*. Washington, DC: Pew Research Center. Retrieved from http://www.pewsocialtrends.org/2012/02/16/therise-of-intermarriage

Warren, K. F. (Ed.). (2008). *Encyclopedia of U.S. campaigns, elections, and electoral behavior*. Thousand Oaks, CA: SAGE.

Washington University Milken Institute School of Public Health. (2018). *Ascertainment of the estimated excess mortality from Hurricane Maria in Puerto Rico*. Retrieved from http://tinyurl.com/y44aqafc

Washington, B. T. (1965). *Up from slavery*. New York, NY: Dell.

Washington, R. (2005). Sealing the sacred bonds of holy matrimony. *Genealogy Notes*, 37(1). Retrieved from https://www.archives.gov/publications/prologue/2005/spring/freedman-marriage-recs.html

Waters, M. 1990. *Ethnic options*. Berkeley: University of California Press.

Wax, M. (1971). *Indian Americans: Unity and diversity*. Englewood Cliffs, NJ: Prentice-Hall.

Weeks, P. (1988). *The American Indian experience*. Arlington Heights, IL: Forum.

Weinberg, S. S., Gabaccia, D., Diner, H. R., & Seller, M. S. (1992). The treatment of women in immigration history: A call for change [with comments and response]. *Journal of American Ethnic History*, 11(4), 25–69.

Wellner, A. (2007). *U.S. attitudes toward interracial dating are liberalizing*. Washington, DC: Population Reference Bureau. Retrieved from http://www.prb.org/Publications/Articles/2005/USAttitudesTowardInterracialDatingAreLiberalizing.aspx

Welter, B. (1966). The cult of true womanhood: 1820–1860. *American Quarterly*, 18(2), 151–174.

Wessell, T. R. (1986). Agriculture, Indians, and American history. In R. L. Nichols (Ed.), *The American Indian: Past and present* (3rd ed., pp. 1–9). New York, NY: Newbury Award Records.

West, D. (2011). The costs and benefits of immigration. *Political Science Quarterly*, 126, 427–443.

White House. (2005). *Economic report of the president*. Washington, DC: Government Printing Office. Retrieved from http://www.gpoaccess.gov/eop/2005/2005_erp.pdf

White, D. G. (1985). *Ar'n't I a woman? Female slaves in the plantation South*. New York, NY: Norton.

Whiting, R. (1990). *You gotta have Wa*. New York, NY: Macmillan.

Wilensky-Lanford, B. (2015, September 22). Coming to America: A brief history of U. S.—Papal diplomacy. *New Republic*. Available at https://newrepublic.com/article/122890/brief-history-us-papal-relations

Wilkens, R. (1992, May 3). L.A.: Images in the flames; looking back in anger: 27 years after Watts, our nation remains divided by racism. *Washington Post*, p. C1.

Wilkerson, I. (2011). *The warmth of other suns: The epic story of America's great migration*. New York, NY: Penguin Random House.

William, J., & Adler, J. R. (2015). A proposed typology of online hate crime. *Open Access Journal of Forensic Psychology*, 7, 64–89. Retrieved from https://www.researchgate.net/publication/296431755_A_Proposed_Typology_of_Online_Hate_Crime

Williams, G. (1995). *Life on the color line*. New York, NY: Dutton.

Wilson, J. (2000). *The earth shall weep: A history of Native America*. New York, NY: Grove Press.

Wilson, J. P., Hugenberg, K., & Rule, N. O. (2017). Racial bias in judgments of physical size and formidability: From size to threat. *Journal of Personality and Social Psychology*, 113(1), 59–80. doi: 10.1037/pspi00.

Wilson, W. J. (1973). *Power, racism, and privilege: Race relations in theoretical and sociohistorical perspectives*. New York, NY: Free Press.

Wilson, W. J. (1987). *The truly disadvantaged: The inner city, the underclass, and public policy*. Chicago, IL: University of Chicago Press.

Wilson, W. J. (1996). *When work disappears*. New York, NY: Knopf.

Wilson, W. J. (2009). *More than just race*. New York, NY: W. W. Norton.

Wingfield, A., & Feagin, J. (2010). *Yes we can? White racial framing and the 2008 presidential campaign*. New York, NY: Routledge.

Wirth, L. (1945). The problem of minority groups. In R. Linton (Ed.), *The science of man in the world* (pp. 347–372). New York, NY: Columbia University Press.

Wogan, J. B. (2013, November 13). Alabama's anti-immigration law gutted. *Governing*. Retrieved from http://www.governing.com/news/headlines/gov-alabamas-anti-immigration-law-dies-amid-hunger-for-reform.html

Washington Office on Latin America (WOLA). (2017, July 17). *House releases Department of Homeland Security appropriations bill*. Retrieved from https://www.wola.org/2017/07/house-releases-department-homeland-security-appropriations-bill/

Woldoff, R. A. (2011). *White flight/black flight: The dynamics of racial change in an American neighborhood*. Ithaca, NY: Cornell University Press.

Wolfe, B., & McCartney, M. (Eds.). (2015). Indentured servants in colonial Virginia. *Encyclopedia Virginia*. Charlottesville, VA: Virginia Foundation for the Humanities. Retrieved August 4, 2017, from http://www.EncyclopediaVirginia.org/Indentured_Servants_in_Colonial_Virginia

Wolfenstein, E. V. (1993). *The victims of democracy: Malcolm X*. New York, NY: Guilford Press.

Wong, M. (1995). Chinese Americans. In P. G. Min (Ed.), *Asian Americans: Contemporary trends and issues* (pp. 58–94). Thousand Oaks, CA: SAGE.

Woodward, C. V. (1974). *The strange career of Jim Crow* (3rd ed.). New York, NY: Oxford University Press.

World Bank. (2013). *Data: Mexico*. Retrieved from http://data.worldbank.org/country/mexico

World Bank. (2017). *Education statistics*. Retrieved August 30, 2017, from http://databank.worldbank.org/data/reports.aspx?source=Education-Statistics:-Education-Attainment

World Economic Forum. (2017). *The global gender gap report, 2016*. Retrieved from http://reports.weforum.org/global-gender-gap-report-2016/?doing_wp_cron=1533911248.6298370361328125000000

Wormser, R. (n.d.-a). Morgan v. Virginia (1946). *PBS*. Retrieved from https://www.thirteen.org/wnet/jimcrow/stories_events_morgan.html

Wormser, R. (n.d.-b). The rise and fall of Jim Crow. *PBS*. Retrieved August 10, 2017, http://www.pbs.org/wnet/jimcrow/stories_events_freed.html

Worsnop, R. (1992, May 8). Native Americans. *CQ Researcher*, 387–407.

Wright, R. (1940). *Native son*. New York, NY: Harper & Brothers.

Wright, R. (1945). *Black boy: A record of childhood and youth*. New York, NY: Harper & Brothers.

Wu, E. D. (2015). The color of success: Asian Americans and the origins of the model minority. *Journal of Transnational American Studies*, 6(1).

Wyman, M. (1993). *Round trip to America*. Ithaca, NY: Cornell University Press.

Yamato, A. (1994). Racial antagonism and the formation of segmented labor markets: Japanese Americans and their exclusion from the workforce. *Humboldt Journal of Social Relations*, 20, 31–63.

Yancey, G. (2003). *Who is white? Latinos, Asians, and the new black/non-black divide*. Boulder, CO: Lynne Rienner.

Yinger, J. M. (1985). Ethnicity. *Annual Review of Sociology*, 11, 151–180.

Yoon, J. (2017). *The Korean comfort women commemorative campaign: Role of intersectionality, symbolic space, transnational circulation in politics of memory and human rights* (PhD dissertation). University of Tennessee, Knoxville, Tennessee. Retrieved from https://trace .tennessee.edu/utk_graddiss/45122017

Yudell, M., Roberts, D., DeSalle, R., & Tishkoff, S. (2016). Taking race out of human genetics. *Science*, 351(6273), 564–565. doi: 10.1126/science.aac4951

Zhang, Q. (2010). Asian Americans beyond the model minority stereotype: The nerdy and the left. *Journal of International and Intercultural Communication*, 3, 20–27. doi: 10.1080/17513050903428109

Zecker, R. M. (2011). *Race and America's immigrant press: How the Slovaks were taught to think like white people*. New York, NY: Bloomsbury Publishing USA.

Zentella, A. C. (2003). "José can You See": Latin@ responses to racist discourse. In D. Sommer (Ed.), *Bilingual games* (pp. 51–68). New York, NY: Palgrave Press.

Zerflin. (2019). *Client highlight: How white supremacy attempts to make slavery and segregation, "soooo long ago."* Retrieved from http://zerflin.com/2016/04/06/ client-highlight-how-white-supharemacy-attempts- to-make-slavery-and-segregation-soooo-long-ago/

Zhou, M. (1992). *Chinatown*. Philadelphia, PA: Temple University Press.

Zhou, M., & Logan, J. R. (1989). Returns on human capital in ethnic enclaves: New York City's Chinatown. *American Sociological Review*, 54, 809–820.

Zong, J., & Batalov, J. (2017a, August 31). Indian Immigrants in the United States. *Migration Policy Institute*. Retrieved from https://www.migrationpolicy .org/article/indian-immigrants-united-states

Zong, J., & Batalov, J. (2017b, February 8). Korean immigrants in the United States. *Migration Policy Institute*. Retrieved from https://www.migrationpolicy .org/article/korean-immigrants-united-states

GLOSSARY

abolitionism: The movement to abolish slavery.

acculturation: The process by which one group (generally a minority or immigrant group) learns the culture of another group (generally the dominant group); also called **cultural assimilation.**

affective prejudice: The emotional or feeling dimension of individual prejudice. The prejudiced individual attaches negative emotions to members of other groups.

affirmative action: Programs designed to reduce the effects of past institutional discrimination or increase diversity in workplaces and schools.

Alien Land Act: A bill passed by the California legislature in 1913 declaring that aliens who were ineligible for citizenship (effectively meaning only immigrants from Asia) were also ineligible to own land.

Americanization: The model of assimilation in which groups are pressured to conform to Anglo American culture (also called **Anglo conformity**).

Anglo conformity: The model of assimilation in which groups are pressured to conform to Anglo American culture (also called **Americanization**).

anti-Semitism: Prejudice or ideological racism directed specifically toward Jews.

apartheid: The policy of extreme racial segregation formerly followed in South Africa.

ascribed status: A position in society that is assigned to the individual, usually at birth. Examples of ascribed status include positions based on ethnicity, race, and gender.

assimilation: The process by which formerly distinct and separate groups come to share a common culture and merge together socially.

Black Power movement: A coalition of African American groups that rose to prominence in the 1960s. Some central themes of the movement were black nationalism, autonomy for African American communities, and pride in race and African heritage.

Blauner hypothesis: A hypothesis that states that minority groups created by colonization will experience more intense prejudice, racism, and discrimination than those created by immigration. The disadvantaged status of colonized groups will persist longer and be more difficult to overcome than the disadvantaged status faced by groups created by immigration.

bourgeoisie: The elite or ruling class in an industrial society that owns or controls the means of production.

Bracero: A Mexican laborer in the United States, especially in relation to the Bracero Program.

Bureau of Indian Affairs: The agency of the U.S. government that has primary responsibility for the administration of American Indian reservations.

bureaucracies: Large-scale, impersonal, formal organizations that govern by detailed rules and regulations (i.e., "red tape") that generally apply to everyone.

capital-intensive (technology): Capital-intensive technology replaces hand labor with machine labor. Large amounts of capital are required to develop, purchase, and maintain the machines.

caste system: A closed system of stratification with no mobility between positions. A person's class at birth is permanent and unchangeable.

chattel: An item of personal property. In a system of chattel slavery, slaves were defined by law not as persons but as the personal property of their owners.

Chicanismo: A militant ideology of the Mexican American protest movement that appeared in the

1960s. The ideology took a critical view of U.S. society, made strong demands for justice and an end to racism, expressed a positive image for the group, and incorporated other pluralistic themes.

Chicano/a: A group name for Mexican Americans associated with the ideology of **Chicanismo**, which emerged in the 1960s.

Chinese Exclusion Act: Passed in 1882 by the U.S. Congress, it banned virtually all immigration from China.

civil rights movement: The effort of African Americans and their allies in the 1950s and 1960s to end de jure segregation in the South.

cognitive prejudice: The thinking dimension of individual prejudice. The prejudiced individual thinks about members of other groups in terms of stereotypes.

colonized minority groups: Groups whose initial contact with the dominant group was through conquest or colonization.

competition: A situation in which two or more parties struggle for control of some scarce resource.

cultural assimilation: See **acculturation.**

cultural pluralism: A situation in which groups have not acculturated or integrated; each maintains a distinct identity.

culture: All aspects of the way of life associated with a group of people. Culture includes language, beliefs, norms, values, customs, technology, and many other components.

culture of poverty: A belief asserting that poverty causes certain personality traits—such as the need for instant gratification—which, in turn, perpetuate poverty.

Dawes Allotment Act of 1887: A key piece of U.S. government policy that divided Native American land into smaller units for individual ownership and moved indigenous people away from their tribal communities.

de facto segregation: A system of racial separation and inequality that appears to result from voluntary choices about where to live, work, and so forth. Often, this form of segregation is really de jure segregation in thin disguise.

de jure segregation: Racial segregation that is institutionalized in local and state law.

deindustrialization: The shift from a manufacturing economy to a service-oriented, information-processing economy.

detention centers: Camps that held Japanese Americans during World War II; also called **relocation camps**.

differential in power: Any difference between two or more groups in their ability to achieve their goals.

discrimination: The unequal or unfair treatment of a person or persons based on their group membership.

dissimilarity index: A measure of residential segregation. The higher the score, the greater the segregation, and scores above 60 are considered to indicate extreme segregation.

dominant group: The group that benefits from and typically tries to sustain minority group subordination.

enclave minority group: A group that establishes its own neighborhood and relies on a set of interconnected businesses, each of which is usually small in scope, for its economic survival.

ethclass: The group formed by the intersection of social class and racial or ethnic groups.

ethnic minority groups: Minority groups identified primarily by cultural characteristics, such as language or religion.

ethnic revival: The movement toward increased salience for ethnic identity, which began for European Americans in the 1960s.

ethnic succession: The process by which white ethnic groups affected one another's positions in the social class structure.

ethnocentrism: Judging other groups, societies, or cultures by the standards of one's own.

extractive (or primary) occupations: Those that produce raw materials, such as food and agricultural products, minerals, and lumber; these often involve unskilled manual labor, require little formal education, and are generally low paying

fatalism: The view that one's fate is beyond one's control.

fluid competitive systems: Systems of group relations in which minority group members are freer to compete for jobs and other scarce resources; this is associated with advanced industrialization.

gender: Social characteristics typically associated with women or men. Gender is a social status or position in the social structure. People typically assume a gender identity that is normative and congruent with their biology (e.g., one born male typically identifies with being a boy or man).

gender norms: Societal expectations for behavior based on one's gender status (e.g., girl, boy).

genocide: The deliberate attempt to exterminate an entire group.

hate crime: A criminal offense against a person or property motivated in whole or in part by the offender's bias against a race, religion, disability, sexual orientation, ethnicity, gender, or gender identity.

*huiguan***:** Associations in Chinese American society based on the region of China from which an individual or his or her family came. The *huiguan* performed a number of social and welfare functions.

human capital theory: Consistent with the traditional view of assimilation, this theory considers success to be a direct result of individual efforts, personal values and skills, and education.

ideological racism: A belief system asserting that a particular group is inferior. Although individuals may subscribe to racist beliefs, the ideology itself is incorporated into the culture of the society and passed on from generation to generation.

immigrant minority groups: Groups whose initial contact with the dominant group was through immigration.

indentured servants: Contract laborers who are obligated to serve a particular master for a specified length of time.

Indian Reorganization Act (IRA): Federal legislation passed in 1934 that was intended to give Native American tribes more autonomy.

industrial revolution: The shift in subsistence technology from **labor-intensive** agriculture to **capital-intensive** manufacturing.

institutional discrimination: A pattern of unequal treatment based on group membership that is built into the daily operations of society.

integration: The process by which a minority group enters the social structure of the dominant society; also called **structural assimilation.**

intermarriage: Marriage between members of different groups; also called **marital assimilation.**

intersectionality: A theoretical perspective in sociology that stresses the crosscutting, linked nature of inequality and the multiplicity of statuses that all people occupy.

Issei: First-generation immigrants from Japan.

Jim Crow system: The system of rigid competitive race relations that followed Reconstruction in the South. The system lasted from the 1880s until the 1960s and was characterized by laws mandating racial separation and inequality.

labor-intensive (technology): A form of production in which the bulk of the effort is provided by human beings working by hand. Machines and other labor-saving devices are rare or absent.

level of development: The stage of societal evolution. The stages discussed in this book are agrarian, industrial, and postindustrial.

life chances: Opportunities and access to resources such as nutritious food, health care, education, and a job that provides a good income.

*machismo***:** A cultural value system stressing men's dominance, virility, and honor.

manufacturing (or secondary) occupations: Occupations involving the transformation of raw materials into finished products ready for the marketplace. An example is an assembly line worker in an automobile plant.

*marielitos***:** Refugees from Cuba who arrived in the United States in 1980.

marital assimilation: See **intermarriage.**

means of production: The materials, resources, and social relations by which a society produces and distributes goods and services.

melting-pot (assimilation): A type of assimilation in which all groups contribute in roughly equal amounts to the creation of a new culture and society.

middleman minority groups: Groups that rely on interconnected businesses, dispersed throughout a community, for economic survival.

minority group: A group that experiences a pattern of disadvantage or inequality, has a visible identifying trait, and is a self-conscious social unit. Membership is usually determined at birth, and group members tend to form intimate relations within the group.

miscegenation: Marriage or sexual relations between members of different racial groups.

modern institutional discrimination: A more subtle and covert form of institutional discrimination that is often unintentional and unconscious.

modern racism: A subtle and indirect form of prejudice that incorporates negative feelings about minority groups but not the traditional stereotypes. Also known as *color-blind racism* and *symbolic racism.*

multiculturalism: A general term for some versions of pluralism in the United States. Generally, multiculturalism stresses mutual respect for all groups and celebrates the multiplicity of heritages that have contributed to the development of the United States.

New Immigration: Immigration from Southern and Eastern Europe to the United States between the 1880s and the 1920s.

Nisei: Second-generation Japanese Americans.

Noel hypothesis: A theory about the creation of minority groups that asserts that if two or more groups come together in a contact situation characterized by ethnocentrism, competition, and a differential in power, some form of racial or ethnic stratification will result.

nonviolent direct action: The central tactic used during the civil rights movement in the South to defeat de jure segregation.

Old Immigration: Immigration from Northern and Western Europe to the United States between the 1820s and the 1880s.

Operation Wetback: A government program developed in the 1950s to deport illegal immigrants from Mexico.

past-in-present institutional discrimination: Patterns of inequality or unequal treatment in the present that are caused by some pattern of discrimination in the past.

paternalism: A form of dominant–minority relations often associated with plantation-based, labor-intensive agrarian technology. In paternalistic relations, minority groups are extremely unequal and highly controlled. Rates of overt conflict are low.

patriarchy: Systems of dominance by men. In a patriarchal society, men tend to monopolize power and decision making.

plantation system: A labor-intensive form of agriculture that required large tracts of land and a large, cheap labor force. This was the dominant form of agricultural production in the American South before the Civil War.

pluralism: A situation in which groups maintain separate identities, cultures, and organizational structures.

postindustrial society: A society dominated by service work, information processing, and high technology.

power: The ability to affect the decision-making process of a social system.

prejudice: The tendency of individuals to think and feel negatively toward others.

prestige: The amount of honor or respect accorded a particular person or group.

primary labor market: The segment of the labor market that encompasses better-paying, higher-status, more-secure jobs, usually in large bureaucracies.

primary sector: Relationships and groups that are intimate and personal. Groups in the primary sector are small.

principle of third-generation interest: The notion that the grandchildren of immigrants will stress their ethnicity much more than the second generation will.

proletariat: The workers in an industrial society.

Protestant ethic: Stresses hard work, success, and individualism and was analyzed by Max Weber in his sociological classic, *The Protestant Ethic and the Spirit of Capitalism.*

race relations cycle: A concept associated with Robert Park, who believed that relations between different groups would go through predictable cycles from conflict to eventual assimilation.

racial minority groups: Minority groups identified primarily by physical characteristics such as skin color (e.g., Asian Americans).

Reconstruction: The period of Southern race relations following the Civil War. Reconstruction lasted from 1865 until the 1880s and saw many racial reforms, all of which were reversed during de jure segregation or the Jim Crow era.

relocation camps: See **detention centers.**

repatriation: A government campaign begun during the Great Depression of the 1930s to deport illegal immigrants back to Mexico. The campaign also caused some legal immigrants and native-born Mexican Americans to leave the United States.

revolution: A minority group goal. A revolutionary group wishes to change places with the dominant group or create a new social order, perhaps in alliance with other groups.

rigid competitive group system: A system of group relations in which the dominant group seeks to exclude minority groups or limit their ability to compete for scarce resources such as jobs.

Sansei: Third-generation Japanese Americans.

secondary labor market: The segment of the labor market that includes low-paying, low-skilled, insecure jobs.

secondary sector: Relationships and organizations that are public, task oriented, and impersonal. Organizations in the secondary sector can be large.

segmented assimilation: The idea that assimilation can have a number of outcomes, in addition to eventual entry into mainstream society. Some groups may enter the middle class, but others may be permanently excluded, marginalized, and impoverished.

selective perception: The tendency to see only what one expects to see; associated with stereotyping in individual prejudice.

separatism: A minority group goal. A separatist group wishes to sever all ties with the dominant group.

service (or tertiary) occupations: Jobs that involve providing services. Examples include retail clerk, janitor, and schoolteacher.

sexism: Belief systems that label women as inferior to men and rationalize their lower social status.

sharecropping: A system of farming often used in the South during de jure segregation. The sharecropper (often black) or tenant worked the land, which was actually owned by someone else (usually white), in return for a share of the profits at harvest time. The landowner supplied a place to live and credit for food and clothing.

social classes: Groups of people who command similar amounts of valued goods and services, such as income, property, and education.

social constructions: Perceptions and ideas shared by a group. These perceptions become real to the people who share them.

social distance: The degree of intimacy a person is willing to accept with members of other groups.

social mobility: Movement up and down the stratification system.

social structure: The networks of social relationships, groups, organizations, communities, and institutions that organize the work of a society and connect individuals to one another and to the larger society.

socialization: The process of physical, psychological, and social development by which a person learns his or her culture.

sojourners: Immigrants who intend to return to their countries of origin.

stereotypes: Overgeneralizations that are thought to apply to all members of a group.

stratification: The unequal distribution of valued goods and services (e.g., income, job opportunities, prestige and fame, education, health care) in society; the social class system.

structural assimilation: See **integration.**

structural mobility: Rising occupational and social class standing that is the result of changes in the overall structure of the economy and labor market, as opposed to individual efforts.

structural pluralism: A situation in which a group has acculturated but is not integrated.

subsistence technology: The means by which a society satisfies basic needs. An agrarian society relies on labor-intensive agriculture, whereas an industrial society relies on machines and inanimate fuel supplies.

symbolic ethnicity: A sense of ethnicity that is superficial, voluntary, and changeable.

termination: A policy by which all special relationships between the federal government and Native Americans would be abolished.

tongs: Secret societies in Chinatowns that sometimes fought with each other and with other organizations over control of resources.

triple melting pot: The idea that structural assimilation for white ethnic immigrants took place within the context of the three major American religions.

two-spirit: Within indigenous cultures, people who identify as both genders or identify outside of the Western gender binary of girl/woman or boy/man.

urban underclass: The urban lower classes, consisting largely of African Americans and other minority groups of color, which have been more or less permanently barred from the mainstream economy and the primary labor market.

vicious cycle (of prejudice): A process in which a condition (e.g., minority group inferiority) is assumed to be true, and forces are then set in motion to create and perpetuate that condition.

Yonsei: Fourth-generation Japanese Americans.

INDEX

Page numbers followed by f and t indicate figures and tables.

Abolitionism, 114, 115–116
Aboud, F. E., 34
Abrams, Stacey, 188
ACCESS (Arab Community Center for Economic and
    Social Services), 416
Acculturation
    African Americans and, 227, 458
    Asian Americans and, 373–375, 458–459
    European American ethnic groups and, 459
    gender and, 459
    Hispanic Americans and, 315, 327–328, 327f, 458
    industrialization era and, 153
    integration without, 58–59
    Native Americans and, 258–259, 279–281, 458
    slavery and, 117–118
    without integration, 133
    women and, 459
    See also Assimilation; Education; Language
Acculturation stage, 53
Affective prejudice, 31
Affirmative action, 170–173, 226f
African Americans
    acculturation and, 227, 458
    arrest rates, 209–211, 210f
    black protest movement, 152–153
    civil rights movement, 189–194
    community resources, pooling of, 193–194
    comparison with other minority groups, 132–133,
        281, 287–288, 300, 319, 399–400
    competition with white ethnic groups, 150–151
    criminal justice system and, 201–212
    culture of, 114
    de facto segregation, 193–194
    education and, 209
    employment rights for, 189
    family institution and culture of poverty theory,
        213f, 218–221, 219f, 221f
    fear of, 204
    geographic distribution of, 89, 89f, 228–231, 229f
    Great Migration and life in the North, 149f, 150, 151f
    growth trends in U.S. population, 6, 7f
    hate crimes against, 175
    high school and college graduation rates,
        231–232, 233f
    housing discrimination and homeownership rates,
        168–170, 169f, 218
    institutional discrimination and, 40
    Jim Crow system (de jure segregation) and, 140,
        144–148
    job integration and income equality, 235–238,
        236–237f
    political power since WWII, 232–235
    poverty rates, 237–238, 238f
    Reconstruction and, 143–144
    separatism and, 61
    social distance and, 38
    unemployment rates, 216–218, 217f
    urban poverty and underclass, 214–215
    urban unrest, 195–196, 204–205
    voting and, 143–144, 146–147, 154, 189, 234–235
    See also Black-white relations, contemporary;
        Slavery
African immigrants, recent, 420t
Afrofuturism, 227
Agrarian society. See preindustrial agrarian society
Alabama House bill 56, 425
Alaska Natives, 252t, 254, 275f, 285, 286f, 287f
Alba, Richard, 94
Alcatraz occupation, 264
Alexander, M., 211
Alianza de Mercedes (Alliance of Land Grants), 313
Alien Land Act (1913, CA), 359
Alt-Right, 207–208
American Indian Movement (AIM), 264
American Indians. See Native Americans
American South
    Brown vs. Board, response to, 190
    Confederate-related objects in, 206–208
    institutional discrimination and, 40
    modernization of agriculture in, 188–189

racist ideology and, 40
rigid competitive system and, 143
See also Slavery
Americanization as type of assimilation, 51–52. *See also* Assimilation
Anderson, Kim, 256
Anglo-conformity, 51–52. *See also* Assimilation
Anti-Coolie Act (Chinese Police Act) of 1862, 353
Anti-Semitism, 73–75
Apartheid, 11
Arab Americans, 177, 399–400, 413–419, 414t, 415f
Arizona State Bill 1070, 326, 425, 433
Arrest rates for African Americans, 209–211, 210f. *See also* Incarceration rates
Ascribed status, 13
Ashley, Maurice, 188
Asian Americans
    acculturation, 373–375, 458–459
    comparison with other minority groups, 366, 389–392
    contact situation and development, Chinese American, 353–358
    contact situation and development, Japanese American, 358–366
    cultures, 351–352
    education, 357–358, 379–381, 379–381f, 439f
    growth trends in U.S. population, 6, 7f
    on hard work, 427
    in Hawaii, 128
    immigration, contemporary, 367–368f, 367–369, 409–413
    jobs, income, and poverty, 382–386, 383–386f
    marriage and primary structural assimilation, 386–387
    model minority stereotype, 358, 364, 372–373, 384, 387–388
    political power, 381–382
    prejudice and discrimination against, 370–373
    residential patterns, 375–379, 376–378f
    self-description by, 351
    size and growth of, 340–341, 349t, 350f
    See also Specific groups
Asian Indians
    acculturation and, 373
    immigration case study, 410–411, 410t
    income levels, 386f
    percentage foreign-born population, 350f
    size and growth, 349t, 350f, 368f
    Vietnamese compared to, 369

Assimilation
    African Americans and, 227–240
    Asian Americans and, 373–378
    Black Power movement and, 197–198
    civil rights movement and, 193
    complexity of, 457
    current status of, 457–461
    defined, 50
    degree of similarity and preference hierarchy, 84
    desirability or undesirability of, 457
    ethnic succession and pathways of integration, 79–82
    gender and, 86–87
    generational pattern of, 76–79, 438f
    Hispanic Americans and, 52, 324, 341
    human capital theory, 56, 71–72
    Irish and Southern and Eastern European laborers and, 69–70
    Jewish immigrants and, 71
    labor unions and immigrant women, 80–81
    language and, 49–50, 52, 59–61
    melting pot view of, 51, 85, 133, 457
    Native Americans and, 50, 279–286, 289
    past vs. contemporary experiences of, 437–438
    pluralism and, 58–59
    Protestant Northern and Western Europeans and, 67–68
    recent immigrants and, 95
    religion and, 84–85
    second generation of recent immigrant groups and, 438–441
    segmented-assimilation hypothesis, 95, 437–441
    slavery and, 116–118
    social class and, 85–86
    sojourners, 88
    structural mobility and, 83
    traditional perspective on, 52–56, 54t, 94–95, 441–443
    types of, 50–51
    See also Acculturation; Immigration, migration, and immigrants
Australian Aborigines, 271–272
Awareness in minority groups, 12–13
Aztecs, 133

Bayoumi, Moustafa, 400
Bean, Frank, 443
Beauty standards, 374–375
Berry, Halle, 222
Biles, Simone, 188

Biology and race, 23

Biracial people, 222

Birthright citizenship, 435–436

Bisexual Americans. *See* LGBTQIA Americans

Black Codes, 145

Black Lives Matter (BLM) Global Network, 206

Black middle class, 212–214, 213f

Black Muslims, 197–198

Black Muslims. *See* Nation of Islam (NOI)

Black Panther Party, 197

Black Power movement, 196–198, 227

Blacks. *See* African Americans

Black-white relations, contemporary
    acculturation and, 227
    Black Power movement and black protest,
        196–198
    Brazil, comparison to, 201–202
    civil rights movement and end of de jure
        segregation, 188–194
    class inequality, increasing, 212–215, 213f
    criminal justice system and, 201–212
    current status, 187–188, 242–243, 242f
    de facto segregation, 193–194
    family institution and culture of poverty theory,
        213f, 218–221, 219f, 221f
    fear and, 185–187, 203–204
    mixed-race and new racial identities, 201–202,
        221–223
    modern institutional discrimination, 215–218
    prejudice vs. modern racism, 223–227, 224f
    primary structural assimilation, 238–240
    secondary structural assimilation, 228–238
    separation, continuing, 203–208
    separatism and, 203–208
    urban unrest and riots, 195–196, 204–205
    See also African Americans

Blassingame, John, 119

Blau, Peter M., 56

Blauner, Robert, 109–111, 117–118, 126

Blauner hypothesis
    African American acculturation and, 227
    Asian Americans and, 369
    colonized vs. immigrant minority groups, 109–111,
        453–454
    fluid competitive systems and, 161
    Hispanic Americans and, 130–131, 298, 300
    Native Americans and, 126, 250–251, 258, 289
    racial inequality and, 116, 144
    women, LGBT people, and, 455
    See also Colonized minority groups

Bogardus, Emory, 35

Bonilla-Silva, Eduardo, 38, 343

Border identities, 222

Border Patrol, U.S., 303, 307, 308t

Bourgeoisie, 15

Boycotts, 191, 314

Bracero Program, 304

Brazil, 201–202

Brotherhood of Sleeping Car Porters, 189

Brown, Linda, 190

Brown, Michael, 205

Brown v. Board of Education of Topeka, 190, 231

Browning thesis, 342–343

Brunsma, David, 222

Burakumin of Japan, 364–365

Bureau of Indian Affairs (BIA), 258

Bureaucracy, 156

Bus boycotts, 191

Butler, Paul, 186

California Proposition 187, 433

Californios, 129–130

Cambodian Americans
    acculturation and, 373
    education, 379f, 380f, 439f
    English proficiency, 374f
    incarceration rates, 440f
    income levels, 383–384f
    percentage foreign-born population, 350f
    poverty levels, 385f
    size and growth, 349t, 350f, 367–368
    urbanization of, 378f
    See also Asian Americans

Canada, French colonization of, 134

Capital-intensive production, 65

Carey, Mariah, 222

Casinos, American Indian, 275–277, 276f, 276t

Caste system, slavery and, 113

Castro, Fidel, 320

Catholicism, 73, 81–82, 84, 318

Census Bureau categories, 23–24

Chattel, 112–114

Chávez, César, 314

Cherokee nation, 127, 252t, 260

Chicanismo, 312–313, 314–315

Childbearing and gender, 28

Children, development of prejudice in, 34

Chile, 166f

Chin, Vincent, 177

Chinatowns, 355–356

Chinese Americans
as both colonized and immigrant minority group, 110–111
comparison with other minority groups, 366, 389–392
culture and, 351–352
early immigration and anti-Chinese campaign, 354–355, 370
education, 380–381, 380–381f, 439f
ethnic enclave and, 355–356
expulsion of immigrants, 61
incarceration rates, 440f
language and, 373, 374f
population trends and delayed second generation, 354–355, 355f
residential patterns, 375, 378f
second generation, 357–358
size and growth of group, 349t, 350f
survival and development, 356–357
See also Asian Americans
Chinese Consolidated Benevolent Associations (CCBAs), 356
Chinese Exclusion Act (1882), 61, 354, 370
Chinese Massacre of 1871, 354
Chinese Police Act (Anti-Coolie Act) of 1862, 353
Chivington, John, 266
Choctaw Nation, 252t, 255, 274, 275f
Chou, Rosalind, 388
Cicano/Chicana, self-description as, 313
Citizenship, birthright, 435–436
Civil Rights Act (1964), 192
Civil rights movement, 189–194, 454
Civil War monuments, 206–208
Clark, Kenneth, 374
Clark, Mamie, 374
Class. *See* social class
Classification and labels, 7–9
Coates, Ta-Nehisi., 119
Code-switching, 343
Cognitive prejudice, 31
Collier, John, 259
Collins, Patricia Hill, 15, 17–18
Colombian Americans
case study, 405t, 407
education, 334, 334f, 405, 439f
incarceration rates, 440f
income and poverty levels, 337–338f, 338
population, size, and growth, 297–298f, 299t
residential patterns, 405
in urbanized areas, 331f
See also Hispanic Americans

Colonized minority groups
Asian Americans compared to, 390–392
Hispanic groups and, 298–299
immigrant minority groups vs., 109–111
LGBTQIA people, 455
Mexican Americans as, 130–131, 309–310
Native Americans as, 126, 255
women, 455–456
See also Blauner hypothesis
Color-blind racism. *See* modern racism
Colorism, 25
Competition
between African Americans and white ethnic groups, 150–151, 204
Asian Americans and, 353–354, 370–371
disagreement over prejudice and, 426
Mexican Americans and, 131, 310
Native Americans and, 126
in Noel hypothesis, 107–108, 109t, 111, 116f, 454
prejudice and, 31–32
rigid competitive group relations, 142
slavery and, 112t
Confederate-related objects, 206–208
Confucianism, 351, 352
Congress of Racial Equality, 191
Contact situation
African Americans compared to Native Americans and, 287–288
Blauner hypothesis, 109–111
Chinese American, 353
Hawaii, 128
Hispanic Americans and, 129, 316, 406
importance of, 454
Japanese Americans, 358–359
minority group status creation and, 104
modes of incorporation for recent immigrants, 421–422
Native Americans and, 123, 250
Noel hypothesis, 107–109, 109t, 111, 112t
situations not fitting, 455
Spanish, French, and English colonization, compared, 133–134
Copeland, Misty, 188
Council of Energy Resource Tribes, 270
Crime
arrest rates for African Americans, 209–211, 210f
hate crimes and hate groups, 173–177, 174f, 176f
incarceration rates, 440f
Prohibition, immigrants, and, 82

Criminal justice system and African Americans, 201–212

Crusade for Justice, 313

Cuban Americans
assimilation and, 324, 341
comparison to other minority groups, 323, 325
contact period, 320
education, 334, 334f, 439f
ethnic enclave and income levels, 322–325, 324f
immigration and marielitos, 320–321
incarceration rates, 440f
income and poverty levels, 337f, 338, 338f
population, size, and growth, 297–298f, 299t
regional concentrations, 321–322
socioeconomic characteristics, 322–325
stereotypes of, 325–326
in urbanized areas, 331f
See also Hispanic Americans

Cultural assimilation stage, 53. *See also*
Acculturation

Cultural pluralism, 58

Culture
African American, 114
American Indian, 253–256, 258–259, 279–281
Asian, 351–352
defined, 53
prejudice and, 33
Puerto Rican, 318
slaves maintaining, 117
social distance and, 35–38
women as keepers of, 87
See also Acculturation

Culture of poverty theory, 219–220, 301

Curry, Michael, 188

DACA (Deferred Action for Childhood Arrivals), 434

DAPL oil pipeline project, 267–268

Dating, interracial, 238–239

Davis, Kiri, 374

Dawes Allotment Act (1887), 258

De facto segregation, 193–194

De jure segregation, 144–148, 188–194. *See also* Jim
Crow system

Dearborn Arab International Festival, 417

Debt bondage, 122

Deferred Action for Childhood Arrivals (DACA), 434

Deindustrialization, 141–142, 157. *See also*
Postindustrial society

Detention centers, 360–362

Detroit, Arab American community in, 416–417

Development, Relief, and Education for Alien Minors
(DREAM) Act, 433–434

DeVernay, Ava, 187–188

Differentials in power. *See* power differentials

Discrimination
Asian Americans and, 354, 358–359, 370–373
defined, 39
dominant-minority relations and, 39
in employment, 170
Hispanic Americans and, 325–326
immigration and, 72–76
institutional, 40–41
Jim Crow system, 140, 144–148
Native Americans and, 278
past-in-present institutional discrimination,
167–170, 213–214
residential discrimination, racial, 168–170, 169f
See also Institutional discrimination

Disparate impact doctrine, 171

Dissimilarity index, 228, 230f

Diversity vs. unity, 459–461. *See also* Assimilation;
Dominant-minority relations; Pluralism

Doll studies, 374

Dominant groups, defined, 11

Dominant-minority relations
degree of similarity and, 84
discrimination and, 39
European immigrants, structural mobility, and, 83
globalization and, 159–160
ideological racism and, 39–40
individual vs. societal and thinking/feeling vs.
doing, 29, 30t
industrialization and, 155–160
institutional discrimination and, 40–41
power, distribution of resources, and, 95–97
prejudice and, 31–41
societal development and, 95–97
society characteristics and, 104
subsistence technology transformations and,
140–141
See also Industrialization and industrial society

Dominican Americans
case study, 405t, 406
education, 334f, 405
income and poverty levels, 337–338f, 338
population, size, and growth, 297–298f, 299t
residential patterns, 405–406
in urbanized areas, 331f
See also Hispanic Americans

Doyle, A. B., 34

DREAMers, 433–434
Drugs, war on, 209–211
Du Bois, W. E. B., 152
Dual labor market, 159
Duncan, Otis Dudley, 56

Ecuadorian Americans
    education, 334f
    income and poverty levels, 337–338f
    population, size, and growth, 297–298f, 299t
    in urbanized areas, 331f
    See also Hispanic Americans
Education
    affirmative action in higher education, 171–172
    African Americans and, 209, 231–232, 233f
    Asian Americans and, 357–358, 379–381, 379–381f
    Asian Indians and, 410–411
    enclaves and, 71
    Hispanic Americans and, 331, 332f, 334–335,
        334f, 405
    industrialization and, 158–159
    interracial friendships on college campuses, 239
    Native Americans and, 258–259, 273, 274, 274f,
        282–283, 283f
    Nigerian and Ethiopian immigrants and, 420
    school desegregation and integration, 190,
        231–232
    second-generation immigrants and, 439–440
    structural mobility and, 83
El Salvador, 406–407. *See also* Salvadoran
    Americans
Elkins, Stanley, 117
Enclave minority groups and enclave economies
    Chinese Americans, 355–356
    Cuban Americans, 322–325
    generational pattern and, 77
    integration and, 58–59
    Japanese Americans, 359–360, 363–364
    Jewish Americans, 70–71
    Korean Americans, 412
    Middle Eastern Americans, 413–414
    as mode of incorporation for recent immigrants, 422
    modern slavery and, 123
English language. *See* language
Equal opportunity, beliefs in, 12–13, 13f
Equality and inequality. *See* inequality
Ethclasses, 85–86
Ethiopian immigrants, 420–421, 420t
Ethnic enclaves. *See* enclave minority groups and
    enclave economies

Ethnic minority groups, defined, 12
Ethnic revival, 91–92
Ethnic succession, 79–82, 319
Ethnocentrism
    Asian Americans and, 354
    browning thesis and, 342–343
    European immigrants and, 67
    Mexican Americans and, 130–131
    in Noel hypothesis, 107–108, 109t, 111, 116f, 454
    slavery and, 112t
European American identity, new, 93
European immigrants
    acculturation and, 459
    chain immigration and, 71–72
    by decade and origin, 66f
    evolution of white ethnicity and, 91–92
    geographic distribution of descendants, 88–90, 89f
    industrialization and, 64–65
    integration and equality, 90–91, 90t
    Irish and Southern and Eastern European
        immigrant laborers, 69–70
    Jewish, from Eastern Europe, 70–71
    language and, 60
    massive migration (1820s to 1920s), 50, 63–64
    Northern and Western European Protestants,
        66–67
    numbers of emigrants by country, 63f
    See also Assimilation; White ethnics and white
        ethnicity
Evans, Sara M., 87
Evolution, human, 19–21, 20f
Executive Order No. 8802, 189
Executive Order No. 9066, 362
Executive Order No. 13769, 419
Extractive (primary) occupations, 157, 158f

Fadiman, Anne, 369
Fair Employment Practices Commission, 189
Fair Housing Act (1968), 169
Family institution, 218–221, 219f
Fatalism, 219
Feagin, Joe, 343, 388
Fear, 185–187, 203–204
Federal Housing Administration (FHA), 168
Ferguson shooting, 205–206
Fifteenth Amendment to the U.S. Constitution,
    143–144, 154
Filipino Americans
    acculturation and, 373
    education, 379f, 380f, 439f

English proficiency, 374f
immigration case study, 410t, 412–413
incarceration rates, 440f
income levels, 383–384f, 386f
percentage foreign-born population, 350f
poverty levels, 385f
residency patterns, 375
size and growth, 349t, 350f, 368f
urbanization of, 378f
See also Asian Americans
Fisher, Amy, 172
Fisher v. University of Texas at Austin, 172
Fish-in protest, 264
Fluid competitive systems, 160–161, 161t
Foot binding, 352
Ford, Henry, 74–75
Foreman, Tyrone, 342
Fourteenth Amendment to the U.S. Constitution, 435
Foxwoods Casino, Conn., 275–276
Free trade, 444. *See also* North American Free Trade
     Agreement (NAFTA)
Freedmen's Bureau, 143, 144
French colonization in Canada, 134
Friendships, interracial, 238–239
Frye, Marquette, 195–196

Gadsden Purchase (1853), 129
Gallagher, Charles, 93
Gandhi, Mohandas, 314
Garvey, Marcus, 152, 197
Gay Americans. *See* LGBTQIA Americans
Gellately, R., 62
Gender
     acculturation and, 459
     assimilation patterns and, 86–87
     black protest and, 199–200
     Chicano protest movement and, 314–315
     childbearing and, 28
     deindustrialization, globalization, and, 162–163
     diversity and, 460
     Hispanic Americans and, 339
     industrialization and, 153–154
     intersectionality and, 27, 28, 456
     jobs and income, postindustrial, 162–164, 163–165f
     Mexican Americans and, 131–132
     Native Americans and, 126–127
     patriarchy and, 25
     persistent issues and sexism, 446
     sexism, 27, 446
     slavery and, 119–121

social construction of, 27–29
     as source of differentiation, 25
     worldwide gender inequality, 26f
     See also Women
Gender Gap Index, 25–27, 26f
Gender norms, 25, 28
Gender roles, 28, 87, 453
Generational pattern of assimilation, 76–79, 91
Genetic variation, 23
Genocide, 11
Genocides, 61–62, 265–267
German Americans
     economic and educational characteristics, 90t
     geographic distribution of, 89, 89f
     immigration, 68
     preference hierarchy and, 84
Germany, immigration to, 333
Gilbert-Kahn model of class, 15f
Ginsberg, Ruth Bader, 193
Global perspective, immigration and globalization,
     41–43, 42f
Globalization, 159–160, 305–306, 444–445
Gonzales, Sylvia, 314
Gonzalez, Rodolfo, 313
Gordon, Milton, 53–56, 54t, 85, 132–133
Grandfather clauses, 147
Grant, Oscar, 205
Great Migration, 149f, 150, 151f, 196
Great Sioux Nation, 267
Guatemalan Americans
     education, 334, 334f
     income and poverty levels, 337–338f
     population, size, and growth, 297–298f, 299t
     in urbanized areas, 331f
     See also Hispanic Americans
Guilt, 102
Gutiérrez, José Angel, 313
Gypsies, 423–424

Haitian Americans, 407–409, 407t, 439–440f
Haley, Alex, 117
Hamer, Fannie Lou, 200
Handlin, Oscar, 451
Hansen, Marcus, 91, 93
Harris, Marvin, 11
Hate crimes and hate groups, 173–177, 174f, 176f.
     See also Ku Klux Klan (KKK)
Hawaii, 128
Herberg, Will, 85
Hill, Jane, 344–345

Hispanic Americans
    acculturation, 327–328, 327f, 458
    assimilation and, 52, 341
    Colombian case study, 405t, 407
    as colonized and immigrant groups, 298–299
    Cuban Americans, 320–325
    Dominican case study, 405t, 406
    education, 331, 332f, 334–335, 334f, 405, 439f
    evolution of American racial order and, 341–343
    gender and inequality, 339
    growth trends in U.S. population, 6, 7f
    on hard work, 427
    hate crimes against, 175
    housing discrimination and, 169f
    intermarriage and primary structural
        assimilation, 340, 340f
    jobs, income, and poverty, 335–339, 337–338f
    labels, group names, and self-identification, 300
    political power, 335
    population, size, and growth of, 297–298f, 299t
    prejudice and discrimination, 325–326
    Puerto Ricans, 316–320
    as racial minority and ethnic minority, 299–300
    recent immigration patterns, 403–405
    residential patterns, 328–331, 329–331f
    Salvadoran case study, 405t, 406–407
    same-sex marriage attitudes of, 328, 328t
    See also Specific groups
Hmong Americans
    acculturation and, 373
    education, 379f, 380f
    English proficiency, 374f
    income levels, 383–384f, 383f
    percentage foreign-born population, 350f
    poverty levels, 385f
    residency patterns, 375
    size and growth, 349t, 350f, 369
    urbanization of, 378f
    See also Asian Americans
Holocaust, 61–62, 74, 265
Homeownership rates, 168–170, 213–214, 218
Honduran Americans
    education, 334, 334f
    income and poverty levels, 337–338f
    population, size, and growth, 297–298f, 299t
    in urbanized areas, 331f
    See also Hispanic Americans
Hopi, 260
Housing discrimination. *See* residential patterns,
    discrimination, and segregation

Huerta, Dolores, 315
Huiguan, 356
Human capital theory, 56, 71–72
Huntington, Samuel, 342

Ideological racism, 29, 39–41
Ideology, 21
Illegal immigrants. *See* undocumented immigrants
Immigrant minority groups, in Blauner hypothesis,
    109–111, 298. *See also* Blauner hypothesis
Immigrant tales, 93
Immigration, migration, and immigrants
    African immigrants, recent, 420t
    Asian American, 353–354, 358–359, 367–368f,
        367–369, 409–413, 410t
    attitudes of immigrants on, 427
    birthright citizenship issue, 435–436
    chain immigration, 71–72
    colonization, intergroup competition, and, 309–310
    costs and benefits of, 428–433
    Cuban American, 320–321
    debate over immigration policy in U.S., 306–309
    Dominican, Salvadoran, and Guatemalan,
        403–407, 405t
    DREAMers, 433–434
    to Europe compared to U.S., 332–333
    expulsion policies, 61
    geographic distribution of descendants, 88–90, 89f
    globalization and, 41–43, 42f
    Haitian and Jamaican, 407–409, 407t
    Hispanic population growth and, 296
    immigrant deaths on southern U.S. border, 44f
    industrialization and, 64–65
    Ireland and, 96f, 97
    mass immigrations, first and second wave of,
        50–51, 60, 401
    mass immigrations, third wave of, 394–395f,
        401–403
    Mexican American, 301–310, 302f, 303t, 309f
    Mexican conditions and immigration policy,
        302–305
    Middle Eastern and Arab, 413–419, 414t, 415f
    modes of incorporation for recent immigrants,
        421–422
    NAFTA and, 43, 305–306, 444
    National Origins Act (1924) and quota system, 76
    Old Immigration vs. New Immigration, 65, 84
    prejudice, racism, and discrimination against,
        72–76
    public opinion on, 308–309, 309f, 425–426

Puerto Ricans and, 316–318
push and pull, 301–302, 316–318, 320–321
race and migration, 19–21, 20f
recent, 95
repatriation campaign, 304
statistical portrait of foreign-born or first-generation immigrants, 427
unaccompanied children, 307, 307f
women immigrants, 86–87
See also Assimilation; European immigrants; Undocumented immigrants
Immigration Reform and Control Act (1986), 305, 308
Incarceration rates, 440f
Indentured servants, 105, 111, 112t, 122–123
India, 410–411. *See also* Asian Indians
Indian Claims Commission, 264
Indian Removal Act (1830), 126
Indian Reorganization Act (IRA), 259–260
Indian Self-Determination and Education Assistance Act (1975), 263, 270
Indians, American. *See* Native Americans
Individualism, 462
Industrial Revolution, 64–65, 66f, 141–142
Industrialization and industrial society
acculturation and integration during era of, 153
African Americans, impact on, 143–153
bureaucracy and rationality, 156
dual labor market, 159
education and, 158–159
gender, race, and, 153–154
globalization and, 159–160
growth of, 158f
occupational specialization, 155–156
rigid competitive group relations, 142, 161t
shift from paternalistic to rigid competitive group relations, 141–142
subsistence technology trends and characteristics, 141t
urbanization, 155
white-collar jobs and service sector, growth of, 156–157
Inequality
African Americans and, 144–145, 153, 188–189, 201–202, 212–215, 224–226, 235–238, 236–237f, 243
Black Power movement and, 198–199
Blauner hypothesis and, 144
contact situation and, 116, 116f
de facto segregation and, 193–194
as defining characteristic of minority groups, 11

dominant-minority relations and, 95–97, 115–121
gender inequality, 25–29, 26f, 119–121, 162–166, 165f, 456
global, 444
Hispanic Americans and, 313, 319–320
intersectionality, multiple roles, and, 457
LGBTQIA people and, 456
modern institutional discrimination and, 167, 215–218
modern racism and, 38–39
Native Americans and, 284f, 285–286
Noel hypothesis and, 107–109
paternalism and, 112–113
pluralism and, 459
Reconstruction and, 143–144
Roma and, 423–424
slavery and, 115–121, 152
stratification and social classes, 14
theoretical perspectives on, 14–18
See also Discrimination; Poverty; Social class; Stratification
Institutional discrimination
defined, 29
dominant-minority relations and, 40–41
modern, 167–173, 216–217
past-in-present, 167–170, 213–214
slavery and, 115–121
Integration stage, 53–54
Integration without acculturation, 58–59. *See also* Secondary structural assimilation
Intermarriage. *See* marriage and intermarriage
International Monetary Fund (IMF), 445
Intersectionality, 17–18, 27, 456–457
Intersex Americans. *See* LGBTQIA Americans
Intimate relationships within minority groups, 13
Ireland, immigration into and out of, 96f, 97
Iriquois, 254, 255
Irish Americans
boxing and, 82
Catholicism and, 81
economic and educational characteristics, 90t
generational patterns, 78–79
geographic distribution of, 89, 89f
as immigrants laborers, 69–70
labor unions and, 80
political machines and, 79–80
preference hierarchy and, 84
prejudice and discrimination against, 72
women immigrants, 86
Iroquois federation, 127, 252t

Issei, 359–360, 363
Italian Americans
    criminal organizations and, 82
    economic and educational characteristics, 90t
    gender and work, 87
    geographic distribution of, 89, 89f
    prejudice and discrimination against, 73
    sports and, 82
    structural assimilation compared to WASPs, 78, 78t

Jamaican Americans, 407t, 409, 439f, 440f
Jamestown colony, 104–105, 125
Japan, Burakumin of, 364–365
Japanese American Citizens League, 360
Japanese Americans
    anti-Japanese campaign, 358–359
    comparison with other minority groups, 366, 389–392
    culture and, 351
    education and, 380f
    ethnic enclave and, 359–360
    geographic distribution of, 89f
    in Hawaii, 128
    immigration, 358–359
    integration and, 386
    language and, 374f
    post-WWII generations, 363–364
    residential patterns, 375, 378f
    second generation (Nisei), 360
    size and growth of group, 349t, 350f
    social distance and, 36
    WWII detention centers, 360–362
    See also Asian Americans
Jeter, Derek, 222
Jewish Americans
    Americanization, commitment to, 88
    anti-Semitism against, 73–75
    enclave economy and, 70–71
    Holocaust, 61–62, 74, 265
    immigrant women and work, 87
    immigration from Eastern Europe, 70–71
    social distance and, 38
Jim Crow system, 140, 144–148
Johnson, Andrew, 144
Johnson, Lyndon B., 192
Jones, William, 185
Jones-Shafroth Act (1915), 316
"Journey of Reconciliation," 191

Kallen, Horace, 57
Kaw, Eugenia, 374–375

Kearney, Denis, 354
Kennedy, Ruby Jo, 85
Keys, Alicia, 222
Keys, Sarah Louise, 191
King, Martin Luther, Jr., 148, 190, 192
King, Rodney, 204–205, 412
Klamath tribe, 260–261
Korean Americans
    education, 379f, 380f, 439f
    English proficiency, 374f
    immigration case study, 410t, 411–412
    incarceration rates, 440f
    income levels, 383–384f, 384, 386f
    percentage foreign-born population, 350f
    poverty levels, 385f
    size and growth, 349t, 350f, 368f
    urbanization of, 378f
    See also Asian Americans
Korean War, 411
Kristofic, Jim, 250
Ku Klux Klan (KKK), 74, 75, 147, 174, 190, 192

Labor
    African American job integration and income
        equality, 235–238, 236–237f
    African American women and, 153–154, 235
    Asian Americans and, 354, 358, 359
    closed employment networks and racial
        exclusion, 216–217
    Hispanic Americans and, 309–310, 317, 335–336
    Irish and Southern and Eastern European
        immigrant laborers, 69–70
    Jim Crow system and control of black labor,
        145–146
    need for and slavery, 105
    occupational specialization, 155–156
    plantation system and labor supply problem, 107
    primary, secondary, and tertiary occupations,
        157, 158f
    primary and secondary labor markets, 159,
        421–422
    Protestant work ethic, 67, 93, 216–218, 224, 427
    racial discrimination in the job market, 170
    self-employment, 323, 324f, 416–417
    seniority-based personnel policies, 168
    sharecropping, 145–146
    split labor market theory, 310, 312, 336–338, 354
    white-collar jobs and service sector, growth of,
        156–157
    working immigrant women, 86–87

Labor unions, 80–81, 189, 314
Labor-intensive production, 65
Landrieu, M., 206
Language
  acculturation and, 60
  American Indian languages, 279–280, 280f
  Asian Americans and, 373, 374f
  assimilation and, 49–50, 52, 59–61
  English Only laws, 59–61
  Haitians and, 408
  Hispanic Americans and, 327–328, 327f
  Nigerian and Ethiopian immigrants and, 421
  slaves and, 118
Laotian Americans
  acculturation and, 373
  education, 379f, 439f
  English proficiency, 374f
  incarceration rates, 440f
  income levels, 383–384f
  percentage foreign-born population, 350f
  poverty levels, 385f
  size and growth, 349t, 350f, 367–368
  urbanization of, 378f
  See also Asian Americans
Latin American racial sensibilities, 201–202
Latinos. *See* Hispanic Americans
League of United Latin American Citizens (LULAC), 312
Lenski, Gerhard, 15, 16–17, 104, 254
Lesbian Americans. *See* LGBTQIA Americans
Level of analysis, 29, 30t
Level of development, Lenski on, 16–17
Lewis, O., 301
LGBTQIA Americans
  diversity and, 460
  hate crimes against, 175
  intersectionality and, 456
  subsistence-technology shifts and, 452, 453
Life chances, 18
"Living While Black" (LWB), 203–204
Lopez De La Cruz, Jessie, 314
López Tijerina, Reies, 313
LULAC (League of United Latin American Citizens), 312
Lynch, Loretta, 188

Machismo, 301
Majority-minority schools, 231–232
Malcolm X, 197–198
Mali, 166, 166f
Mandela, Nelson, 148
Manufacturing (secondary) occupations, 157, 158f

Maquiladoras, 305
Marielitos, 321
Marital assimilation, 54
Marriage and intermarriage
  African Americans and, 238–240, 240t
  Asian Americans and, 386–387, 387f
  Burakumin of Japan and, 365
  Hispanic Americans and, 340, 340f
  interracial and interethnic, 8–9, 9f
  miscegenation laws, 13
  Native Americans and, 285, 287f
  religion, ethnicity, and, 85
  stages of assimilation and, 54
Marshall, Thurgood, 190
Martin, Trayvon, 187
Marx, Karl, 15–16, 19
Marxism, 15
Massacre at Sand Creek, 266
Massey, Douglas, 437, 439, 443–444
Matrix of domination, 18
Means of production, 15
Medicare benefits, 430
Mehserle, Johannes, 205
Melanin, 19–21
Melting pot, 51, 85, 133, 457. *See also* Assimilation
Menominee tribe, 260–261
Mexican Americans
  in Arizona and New Mexico, 130
  assimilation and, 341
  in California, 129–130
  Chicanismo, 312–313, 314–315
  colonization, continuing, 310–312
  comparison with other minority groups, 132–133,
    300, 315, 319, 323
  contact situation, 129
  culture, 300–301, 315
  education, 334, 334f, 439f
  gender and the Chicano protest movement,
    314–315
  gender relations among, 131–132
  geographic distribution of, 89, 89f
  immigrant deaths on the border, 44f
  immigration, 301–310, 302f, 303t, 309f
  incarceration rates, 440f
  income levels, 337–338f, 338, 441–443, 442f
  NAFTA and, 43
  Noel and Blauner hypotheses and, 130–131, 300
  organizations and labor leaders, 313–314
  population, size, and growth, 297–298, 297–298f, 299t
  protest and resistance, 312

stereotypes of, 130, 325
in Texas, 129
in urbanized areas, 331f
whitening thesis and, 341–342
See also Hispanic Americans
Mexico, 133–134, 302, 305–306
Middle Eastern Americans, 413–419, 414t
Middleman minority group, 58–59
Migration. *See* immigration, migration, and
immigrants
Minority groups
definition and characteristics of, 10–14
ethnic vs. racial, 12
increasing diversity and, 6–7, 7f
labels and classification issues, 7–9
progress and, 461–462
social change, activism, and, 178
stratification and minority group status, 18–19
See also Specific groups
Miscegenation laws, 13
Mixed-race people, 201–202, 221–223, 318–319
Mobility. *See* social mobility; structural mobility
Model minority stereotype, 358, 364, 372–373, 384,
387–388
Modern institutional discrimination, 167–173,
216–217
Modern racism, 38–39, 62, 223–227, 224f, 461
Modern sexism, 461
Morgan, Irene, 191
Morgan v. Virginia, 191
Mother Jones, 80
El Movimiento, 312–315
Moynihan, Daniel, 218–219
Muhammad, Elijah, 198
Multiculturalism, 57–58
Murguia, Edward, 343
Muslim Americans. *See* Arab Americans
Muslim Ban, 419
Myrdal, Gunnar, 33

NAACP (National Association for the Advancement
of Colored People), 152, 190, 191
NAFTA (North American Free Trade Agreement), 43,
305–306, 444
Nation of Islam (NOI), 197–198, 199
National Congress of American Indians (NCAI),
263–264
National Day of Remembrance, 362
National Origins Act (1924), 76, 142–143, 304
Native American Church, 280

Native Americans
acculturation and, 258–259, 279–281, 458
African American slavery and, 111, 112t
assimilation, pluralism, and, 50, 279–286, 289
Blauner and Noel hypotheses and, 125–126,
250–251, 258, 289
broken treaties and compensation suits, 275
casinos and other development, 275–277, 276f, 276t
comparison with other minority groups, 132–133,
271–272, 281, 287–288
contact period, 123–125, 250
cultures, 253–256, 258–259, 279–281
Daws Allotment Act and, 258
diversity among, 123–124
education and schools, 258–259, 273, 274, 274f,
282–283, 283f
federal government policies and relations,
256–263, 268–269, 269t
forced expulsion and emigration of, 61, 126
gender relations among, 126–127, 255–256
genocide question, 265–267
geographic distribution of, 89
growth trends in U.S. population, 6, 7f
Indian Reorganization Act and, 259–260
industry and job creation on reservations, 270–271
jobs, income, and poverty rates, 273–275, 275f,
284–285, 285–286f
language and, 49, 279–280, 280f
marriage among and outside, 285, 287t
natural resources issues, 270
numbers and population trends, 251–253, 252t, 253f
paternalism, BIA, and, 258
plantation labor supply problem and, 107
political power, 256–257, 283
population losses, 125, 265–267
progress and challenges, 288–289
protest movements and resistance, 263–269, 269t
reservations, 257–259, 257f, 270–271
residential patterns, 281–282, 282f
Self-Determination Act and, 263
separatism and, 61
social distance and, 38
stereotyping, prejudice, and discrimination
against, 277–278
termination of tribes, 260–261
urbanization of, 261–262, 261f
Native Hawaiians, 128
Navajo, 127, 250, 256, 271, 273, 275f
Nazi Holocaust, 61–62, 74, 265
Neoliberalism, 444

Neo-slavery, 145
New Deal, 168
New Immigration, 65
The New Jim Crow (Alexander), 211
New York Shirtwaist Strike of 1909, 81
Nicaraguan Americans
    education, 334f, 439f
    incarceration rates, 440f
    income and poverty levels, 337–338f
    population, size, and growth, 297–298f, 299t
    in urbanized areas, 331f
    See also Hispanic Americans
Nigerian immigrants, 420–421, 420t
Nisei, 360, 363
Nixon, Edgar, 199
Nixon, Richard M., 198, 263
Noel hypothesis
    Asian Americans and, 353
    features of the contact situation, 107–109, 109t
    fluid competitive systems and, 161
    importance of, 454
    Jim Crow system and, 145
    LGBTQIA people and, 455
    Mexican Americans and, 130–131, 300
    Native Americans and, 125–126, 289
    public opinion and, 425
    slavery and, 111, 112t
NOI (Nation of Islam), 197–198, 199
Nonviolent direct action, 190–192
North American Free Trade Agreement (NAFTA), 43,
        305–306, 444
Norwegian Americans, 66–67, 89, 90t

Obama, Barack, 5, 187, 201, 203, 222, 234, 240–241, 461
O'Brien, E., 343
Occupational specialization, 155–156
Old Immigration, 65
Operation Wetback, 304
Organized crime, 82
Ortiz, Vilma, 441

Pacific Islanders as percentage of U.S. population, 6,
        7f. *See also* Asian Americans; Hawaii
Pakistani Americans
    education, 379f, 380f
    English proficiency, 374f
    income levels, 383–384f
    percentage foreign-born population, 350f
    poverty levels, 385f
    size and growth, 349t, 350f

    urbanization of, 378f
    See also Asian Americans
Parish, Peter, 113
Park, Robert, 52–53, 57, 95
Parks, Rosa, 190–191, 199
Passamaquoddy tribe, 275
Past-in-present institutional discrimination,
        167–170, 213–214
Paternalism
    characteristics of, 161t
    industrialization and, 142
    Mexican Americans and, 309–310
    Native Americans and, 258
    slavery and, 112–114
Patriarchy, 27, 352. *See also* Gender
Pearl Harbor, 360–361
Penobscot tribe, 275
Pequot tribe, 275–276
Philippines, 352, 368, 373, 412–413. *See also* Filipino
        Americans
Plantation system and labor supply, 107
Plessy v. Ferguson, 147, 190
Pluralism
    assimilation and, 58–59
    current status of, 459–461
    defined, 50
    ethnic revival and, 92
    interest in, 57–58
    Kallen and, 57
    middleman minority group, 58–59
    multiculturalism and, 57–58
    Native Americans and, 281
    structural, 58, 133, 153
    types of, 58–59
Polish Americans, 81, 90t
Politics and political power
    African Americans and, 146–147, 232–235
    Asian Americans and, 381–382
    ethnic succession and political machines, 79–80
    Hispanic Americans and, 335
    Native Americans and, 256, 283
    See also Power differentials
Populism, 146–147
Portes, Alejandro, 323
Postindustrial society
    fluid competitive systems and, 160–161, 161t
    gender inequality and, 162–166
    hate crimes and hate groups, 173–177, 174f, 176f
    Lenski on, 17
    modern institutional discrimination, 167–173

subsistence technology and, 141–142, 141t
white-collar and service jobs and, 157
Poverty
African American rates of, 237–238, 238f
in African American, woman-headed families,
220–221, 221f
Asian Americans and, 384, 385f
Hispanic Americans and, 305–306, 336, 338, 338f
Native Americans and, 273–275, 275f, 285, 286f
urban, 214–215
Powderly, Terence, 80
Powell, Colin, 234
Power differentials
African Americans and, 211–212
civil rights movement and, 454
contact situation and, 454
Hispanic Americans and, 300
Jim Crow system, Apartheid, and, 147–148
Mexican Americans and, 131
in Noel hypothesis, 108, 109t, 111, 116f
paternalism and, 112–113
perspective taken and, 17
slavery and, 112t, 114, 115–121, 119, 122–123
war on drugs and, 211–212
Preindustrial agrarian society
acculturation in context of, 132–133
gender and relations in, 28–29, 119–121
in Hawaii, 128
Jamestown colony and, 104–105
level of development and, 17
Mexican Americans in, 129–132
Native Americans in, 125–126
paternalistic relations in, 112–114, 142, 161t
peasant origins of immigrant laborers, 69
plantation system and labor supply problem, 107
subsistence technology trends and
characteristics, 141t
See also Slavery
Prejudice
Arab Americans and, 418–419, 418–419f
Asian Americans and, 370–373
children and development of, 34
cognitive vs. affective prejudice and stereotypes, 31
competition between groups and origins of,
31–32
cultural, socialization, and persistence of, 33
decline of, 461
defined, 31
Hispanic Americans and, 325–326
immigration and, 72–76

Jim Crow system and, 148
modern racism and, 38–39, 223–227, 224f
Native Americans and, 277–278
public opinion and, 425–426
slavery and, 115–116, 116f
social distance rankings and, 35–38
sociology of individual prejudice, 39
Prestige, Weber on, 16
Primary (extractive) occupations, 157, 158f
Primary labor market, 159, 421
Primary sector, 53
Primary structural assimilation
African Americans and, 238–240
Asian Americans and, 386–387
in Hawaii, 128
Hispanic Americans and, 339–340
Native Americans and, 285, 287f
See also Marriage and intermarriage
Principle of third-generation interest, 91
Prohibition, 82
Proletariat, 15
Proposition 14, 196
Protean identity, 223
Protest movements and resistance
African American, 152–153, 196–198, 227
American Indian, 263–269, 269t
Mexican American, 312–313, 314–315
See also Civil rights movement
Protestant work ethic, 67, 93, 216–218, 224, 427
Pseudotolerance, 113
Public assistance, 429–430
Puerto Ricans
assimilation and, 341
comparison to other minority groups, 319–320
cultural transitions, 318–319
education, 334, 334f
hurricane impacts, 317–318
income levels, 337f, 338, 338f
migration and employment, 316–318
population, size, and growth, 297f, 299t
race and, 299–300
stereotypes of, 325–326
in urbanized areas, 331f
See also Hispanic Americans

Queer Americans. *See* LGBTQIA Americans

Race
biology and, 23
biracial people, 222

browning thesis, 342–343
Burakumin of Japan and, 364–365
dichotomy, racial, 201
Dominicans and, 405
evolution of American racial order, 341–343
gender and, 27
genetic variation between and within races, 23
Hispanic Americans and, 299–300
human evolution, migration, and, 19–21, 20f
in Latin America, 201–202
mixed-race and new racial identities, 201–202,
    221–223, 318–319
Puerto Ricans and, 318–319
racial etiquette system, 147
rationality and, 156
slavery and, 113
social construction of, 23–25
trichotomy thesis, 343
Western traditions and, 21–23
whitening thesis, 341–342
Race relations cycle, 52–53
Racial minority groups, defined, 12
Racial profiling, 211–212
Racism
    ideological, 39–41
    immigration and, 72–76
    Jim Crow system and, 148
    modern, 38–39, 61, 223–227, 224f, 461
    slavery and, 115–116, 116f
    See also Discrimination; Prejudice
Randolph, A. Philip, 189
Rationality, 156
Raza Unida, La (The United People), 313
Reconstruction, 143–144
Red Power movement, 264–268
Refugees, limits on, 404
Religion
    Catholicism and anti-Catholicism, 73, 81–82,
        84–85, 318
    ethnicity and, 85
    immigrants and, 81–82, 84–85
    Korean immigrants and, 411–412
    Middle Eastern immigrants and, 414
    Native American Church, 280
    Protestant work ethic, 67, 93, 216–218,
        224, 427
    Puerto Ricans and, 318
    slaves and, 117
    WASPs (white Anglo-Saxon Protestants), 78, 78t
Repatriation, 304

Residential patterns, discrimination, and
    segregation
    African Americans and, 196, 228–231, 229f
    Asian Americans and, 375–379, 376–378f
    Hispanic Americans, 405–406
    Hispanic Americans and, 328–331, 329–331f
    Native Americans and, 281–282, 282f
    past-in-present discrimination and,
        168–170, 169f
Revolutionary minority groups, 61
Ricci v. DeStefano, 171
Rice, Condoleezza, 234
Richards, Doyin, 185
Rigid competitive group relations, 142, 161t
Riots, 195–196, 204–205, 412
Robber's Cave experiment, 32
Robert, John, 192–193
Rock, Chris, 374
Rockquemore, Kerry Ann, 222
Roma, 423–424, 423f
Roof, Dylann, 207
Roosevelt, Franklin D., 168, 189, 259, 360–361
Roosevelt, Theodore, 49, 52, 303
Rumford Fair Housing Act (1963), 196
Russian Americans, 90t
Rustin, Bayard, 191
Rwanda, 265–266

Saenz, Rogelio, 214
Salvadoran Americans
    case study, 405t, 406–407
    education, 334, 334f, 405
    income and poverty levels, 337–338f
    population, size, and growth, 297–298f, 299t
    residential patterns, 406
    in urbanized areas, 331f
    See also Hispanic Americans
Sand Creek Massacre, 266
Sansei, 364, 366
Santiago, Esmerelda, 396
Sarah Keys v. Caroline Coach Company, 191
Saunders, Ben, 186
Scapegoating, 177
School desegregation and integration, 190,
    231–232, 331
Schooling. *See* education
Schuette v. BAMN, 172
Secondary (manufacturing) occupations, 157, 158f
Secondary labor market, 159, 421–422
Secondary sector, 53

Secondary structural assimilation
African Americans and, 228–238
Asian Americans and, 375–379
Hispanic Americans and, 328–339
Native Americans and, 281–285
See also Education; Residential patterns,
discrimination, and segregation
Segmented-assimilation hypothesis, 95, 437–441
Segregation
African American acculturation and, 458
Asian Americans and, 356–357, 360, 361, 378–379
de facto (African Americans), 193–194
de jure (African Americans), 144–148, 188–194, 288
enclave economy vs. ghettos and, 323
Hispanic Americans and, 311–312, 328–331,
334–335
Native Americans and, 281–282, 283
Roma and, 424
separatism and, 194
See also Black-white relations, contemporary;
Enclave minority groups and enclave
economies; School desegregation and
integration
Selective perception, 39
Self-determination of American Indians, 262–263, 270
Self-employment, 323, 324f, 416–417
Seniority-based personnel policies, 168
Separatism, 61, 194
September 11, 2001, attacks, 417, 418–419
Service sector, 156–157, 158f
Sex trafficking, 122–123
Sexism, 27, 446, 461. *See also* Gender
Sexual orientation. *See* LGBTQIA Americans
Shafer, Steven, 323
Sharecropping, 145–146
Sherif, Muzafer, 32
Similarity, degree of, 84
Simmons, Gwendolyn Zoharah, 199
Singular identity, 222
Skin color, 22f
Skin color and melanin, 19–21
Skinner, Benjamin, 122
Slavery
abolitionism, 114, 115–116
African American culture and, 114
assimilation and, 116–118
in Brazil, 202
caste system and, 113
chattel, 112–114
contact situation and, 107–112

gender and, 27, 119–121
ideological racism and, 40
labor supply problem in plantation system and, 107
in Mexico and Canada, 134
modern, 122–123
neo-slavery, 145
origins of, 105–112, 112t
paternalistic relations and, 112–114
population of in south, 118, 121–122t
power, inequality, institutional discrimination,
and, 115–121
powerlessness and resistance of slaves, 114
prejudice, racism, and, 115–116, 116f
pseudotolerance and, 113
regional variations, 118–119
routes of the slave trade, 106f
social construction of race and, 25
Zong slave ship and the slave trade, 103
Slovak Americans, 90t
Social class
black middle class, 212–214, 213f
Cuban Americans and, 324
Gilbert-Kahn model of, 15f
hate crimes and, 175–177
immigrants and ethclasses, 85–86
minority group status vs., 18–19
race and, 21–23
urban poverty and underclass, African American,
214–215, 445
in U.S. society, 14, 15f
Weber on, 16
See also Inequality; Stratification
Social construction
of categories and groups, 7–9
of gender, 27–29
of race, 23
Social distance, 35–38, 39t, 370, 418
Social mobility
African Americans and, 458
Asian Americans and, 340, 364, 390
caste systems and, 113
decreasing rates of, 437–438, 439–440
education and, 278, 281–282
ethnic succession and pathways of, 79–82
European Americans and, 390, 452
fluid competitive systems and, 160–161
gender and, 459
generational paths of, 438f
Hispanic Americans and, 315, 319–320, 322
human capital theory and, 56

individualistic view of, 462
second generation and, 77
stratification and, 18–19
See also Structural mobility
Social Security benefits, 430
Social structure
 assimilation and, 53
 in Chinatowns, 356
 cultural survival and, 281, 288
 European colonization and, 133–134
 primary and secondary sectors, 53
 structural assimilation, 53–54, 78, 78t
 structural pluralism, 58, 133, 153
 See also Industrialization and industrial society;
  Institutional discrimination; Social class
Socialization and prejudice, 33
Sojourners, 88
The South. *See* American South
South African Apartheid, 147–148
South Korea, 411. *See also* Korean Americans
Southern Poverty Law Center (SPLC), 175
Southern Pride, 206
Sovereignty, 126
Spanish colonization, 133–134
Spanish explorers, 104–105
Split labor market theory, 310, 312, 336–338, 354
Sports and ethnic succession, 82
Stack, C. B., 220
Standing Rock Sioux (SRS), 267–268
Status attainment, 56
Steinberg, Stephen, 87
Stereotypes
 of African Americans, 198, 204, 225, 287
 anti-Semitism and, 73–74
 of Arab Americans, 419
 of Asian Americans, 340, 356, 358, 360, 364,
  370–373, 375, 384, 387–388
 of Catholics, 73
 in cultural heritage, 33
 decline of, 461
 development of, in children, 34
 gender and, 18, 87, 453
 of Hispanic Americans, 313, 325–326, 344–345, 407
 of Mexican Americans, 130, 325
 modern racism and, 224
 of Native Americans, 277–278, 287
 prejudice and, 31
 President Obama and, 241
Stevens, Gillian, 443
Stewart, Vincent R., 188

Stratification
 minority group status and, 18–19
 racist ideologies, institutional discrimination, and,
  40–41
 social classes in U.S. society, 14
 theoretical perspectives on, 14–18
 See also Inequality; Social class
Structural assimilation, 53–54, 78, 78t, 85–86. *See
 also* Primary structural assimilation; Secondary
 structural assimilation; Social structure
Structural mobility, 83
Structural pluralism, 58, 133, 153
Student Nonviolent Coordinating Committee, 199
Subordinate groups, 11. *See also* Minority groups
Subprime home loans, 218
Sub-Saharan African immigrants, 420t
Subsistence technology
 civil rights movement and, 193
 importance of, 451–453
 Lenski on, 16–17
 transformations in, 140–141, 141t
 See also Preindustrial agrarian society
Summer melt, 159
Swedish Americans, 90t
Symbolic ethnicity, 92–93
Symbolic racism. *See* modern racism

Takaki, Ronald, 347, 460
Takao Ozawa v. United States, 348
Taxes, undocumented immigrants paying, 430
Tecumseh, 254
Tejanos, 129
Telles, Edward, 441
Termination policy, 260–261
Tertiary (service) occupations, 157, 158f
Thamer, H-U., 62
Thirteenth Amendment, 145
Timmer, Andria D., 423
Tongs, 356
Trail of Broken Treaties march, 264–265
Transcendent identity, 222
Transgender Americans. *See* LGBTQIA Americans
Treaty of Guadalupe Hidalgo (1848), 129
Treuer, David, 49
Triangle Shirtwaist Company, 81
Trichotomy thesis, 343
Triple melting pot, 85
Truman, Harry, 189
Trump, Donald, 5, 43, 173, 326, 404, 434
Tubman, Harriet, 114

Turner, Nat, 114
Two-spirit people, 255

Ukrainian Americans, 90t
Underground Railroad, 114
Undocumented immigrants
  Asian, 368, 373, 386
  attitudes toward, 424–426, 431–433, 435–436
  birthright citizenship and, 435–436
  deportation of, 305, 308–309
  Dominican, 406
  DREAMers, 433–434
  economic impacts of, 428–433
  informal economy and, 339, 421–422
  labor movement and, 314
  legislative measures against, 326, 425, 433
  number of, 305, 431f, 432f
  reasons for, 404
  Salvadoran, 407
  second-generation assimilation issues, 437
Unemployment rates
  African Americans and, 154, 216–218, 217f
  Asian Americans and, 360
  Australian Aborigines and, 272
  hate crimes and, 175–177
  Hispanic Americans and, 336
  in inner cities, 462
  Native Americans and, 262, 276t, 284
  Roma and, 424
"Unite the Right," 207–208
United Farm Workers, 314
United Nations Refugee Convention, 404
United States
  as nation of immigrants, 4–6
  population percentage by race and ethnicity, 6, 7f
  race in Brazil compared to, 201–202
  See also Specific groups and topics
United States-Mexico-Canada Agreement (USMCA), 306
Universal Negro Improvement Association, 152
Uprising of 20,000, 81
Upward mobility. See social mobility; structural mobility
Urban underclass, 215
Urban unrest, 195–196, 204–205
Urbanization
  African Americans and the Great Migration, 149f, 150, 151f
  Asian American groups and, 378f

industrialization and, 155
  Native Americans and, 261–262, 261f
U.S. Border Patrol, 303, 307, 308t
U.S. Immigration Service, 303
USA Patriot Act, 419
USMCA (United States-Mexico-Canada Agreement), 306

Vicious cycle of prejudice, 33, 33f
Vietnamese Americans
  acculturation and, 373
  education, 379f, 380f, 439f
  English proficiency, 374f
  immigration case study, 410t, 413
  incarceration rates, 440f
  income levels, 383–384f, 384, 386f
  percentage foreign-born population, 350f
  poverty levels, 385f
  religion and, 352
  residency patterns, 375
  size and growth, 349t, 350f, 367–369, 368f
  urbanization of, 378f
  See also Asian Americans
Virginia General Assembly declaration on slavery, 105
Visibility
  Burakumin of Japan and, 364–365
  as characteristic of minority groups, 12
  gender, 25–27
  LGBTQIA people and, 455–456
  race, 19–21
Voting and African Americans, 143–144, 146–147, 154, 189, 234–235
Voting Rights Act (1965), 192–193, 234

Wagley, Charles, 11
Washington, Booker T., 152
WASPs (white Anglo-Saxon Protestants) and structural assimilation, 78, 78t
Watts riots, 195–196, 204–205
Weber, Max, 15, 16
Welfare benefits, 429–430
White, D. G., 119
White ethnics and white ethnicity
  Asian Americans compared to, 389–390
  European American identity, new, 93–94
  evolution of white ethnicity and ethnic revival, 91–92
  integration, equality, and, 90–91, 90t
  as percentage of U.S. population, 6, 7f

stable location of, 90
symbolic ethnicity and decline of white ethnicity, 92–93
WASPs and structural assimilation, 78, 78t
See also European immigrants
White flight, 196
White Mountain Apaches, 270
White-collar jobs, 156–157, 158f
Whitening thesis, 341–342
Whitman, Walt, 460
Wilder, Douglas, 234
Williams, Gregory (Billy), 221
Women
  acculturation and, 459
  African American, 153–154, 235
  American Indian, 126–127, 255, 259–260, 262
  Black Protest and, 199–200
  Chicano protest movement and, 314–315
  Chinese American, 352, 357
  Filipina, 413
  foot binding, 352
  foreign-born, 311, 311f
  Hispanic, 339
  Japanese American, 361–362
  jobs and income, postindustrial, 162–164, 163–165f
  as keepers of culture, 87

Mexican American, 131–132, 309–310
  as minority group, 13
  poverty in woman-headed African American families, 220–221, 221f
  slavery and, 119–121
  status in global perspective, 165–166, 166f
  subsistence-technology shifts and, 453
  wage differential by immigration generation, 441–443, 442f
  working immigrant women, 86–87
  See also Gender
Women as minority group. *See* gender
Woods, Tiger, 222
Work. *See* labor
Workingman's Party (WP), 354
World War II, 189, 357, 360–362
Wounded Knee, South Dakota, 264
Wright, Jeremiah, 241
Wright, Richard, 140

Yance, George, 342
Yonsei, 364, 366
Yousafzai, Malala, 165–166

Zimmerman, George, 187
Zong (slave ship), 103

ABOUT THE AUTHORS

Joseph F. Healey is professor emeritus of sociology at Christopher Newport University in Virginia. He received his PhD in sociology and anthropology from the University of Virginia. An innovative and experienced teacher of numerous race and ethnicity courses, he has written articles on minority groups, the sociology of sport, social movements, and violence, and he is also the author of *Statistics: A Tool for Social Research* (11th ed., Cengage, 2017).

Andi Stepnick is a professor of sociology at Belmont University in Tennessee. Her scholarship includes *Disrupting the Culture of Silence: Confronting Gender Inequality and Making Change in Higher Education* (with K. De Welde, Stylus Publishing, 2014). The book blends research with action steps and resources to help universities create greater gender equality on their campuses. CHOICE named it a 2015 Outstanding Academic Title. Her work appears in *Teaching Sociology, Teaching Social Problems, Sex Roles*, and other publications. She teaches a variety of courses, including the Sociology of Gender, Visual Sociology, Medical Sociology, Family Problems, and Men, Masculinities, and Media. She received Belmont's Presidential Faculty Achievement Award (2004–2005) for exceptional dedication to students. She earned her PhD from Florida State University.